Thomas Bros. Maps
CALIFORNIA ROAD ATLAS AND TRAVEL GUIDE

NEW REVISED

TABLE OF CONTENTS

INDEX OF DETAIL MAPS

INDEX OF COUNTIES

CALIFORNIA

THE FOLLOWING CRITERIA WERE USED IN CHOOSING DETAIL COVERAGE: MAJOR COLLEGES, CONVENTION CENTERS AND AREAS, COMMERCIAL TRUCKING AND TRANSPORTATION ROUTES, COUNTY GOVERNMENT CENTERS, AIRPORTS, COMMERCIAL HARBORS, TOURIST ENTERTAINMENT, MAJOR MILITARY AREAS AND MAJOR HISTORICAL POINTS AND SITES.

COPYRIGHT, © 1983 BY Thomas Bros. Maps
17731 COWAN, IRVINE, CALIFORNIA 92714, (714) 863-1984
550 JACKSON ST., SAN FRANCISCO, CALIFORNIA 94133, (415) 981-7520

P9-BIW-483

B How To Use Your Road Atlas

This Atlas is divided into three types of maps....HIGHWAY, ARTERIAL and DETAIL maps.

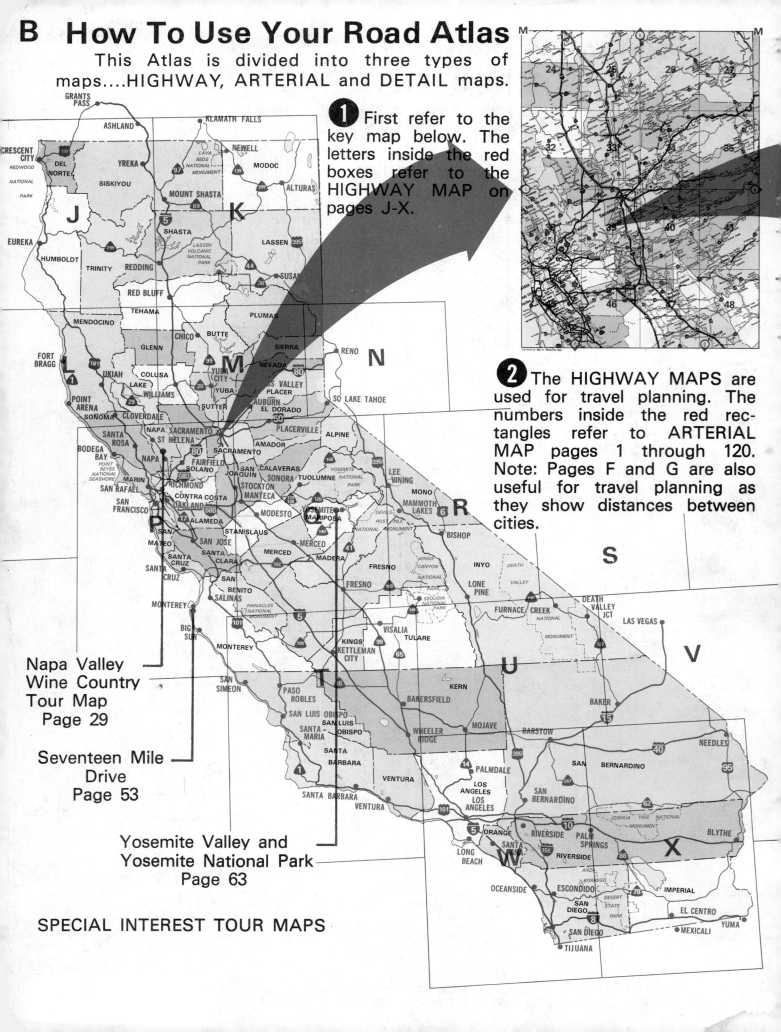

1 First refer to the key map below. The letters inside the red boxes refer to the HIGHWAY MAP on pages J-X.

2 The HIGHWAY MAPS are used for travel planning. The numbers inside the red rectangles refer to ARTERIAL MAP pages 1 through 120. Note: Pages F and G are also useful for travel planning as they show distances between cities.

Napa Valley
Wine Country
Tour Map
Page 29

Seventeen Mile
Drive
Page 53

Yosemite Valley and
Yosemite National Park
Page 63

SPECIAL INTEREST TOUR MAPS

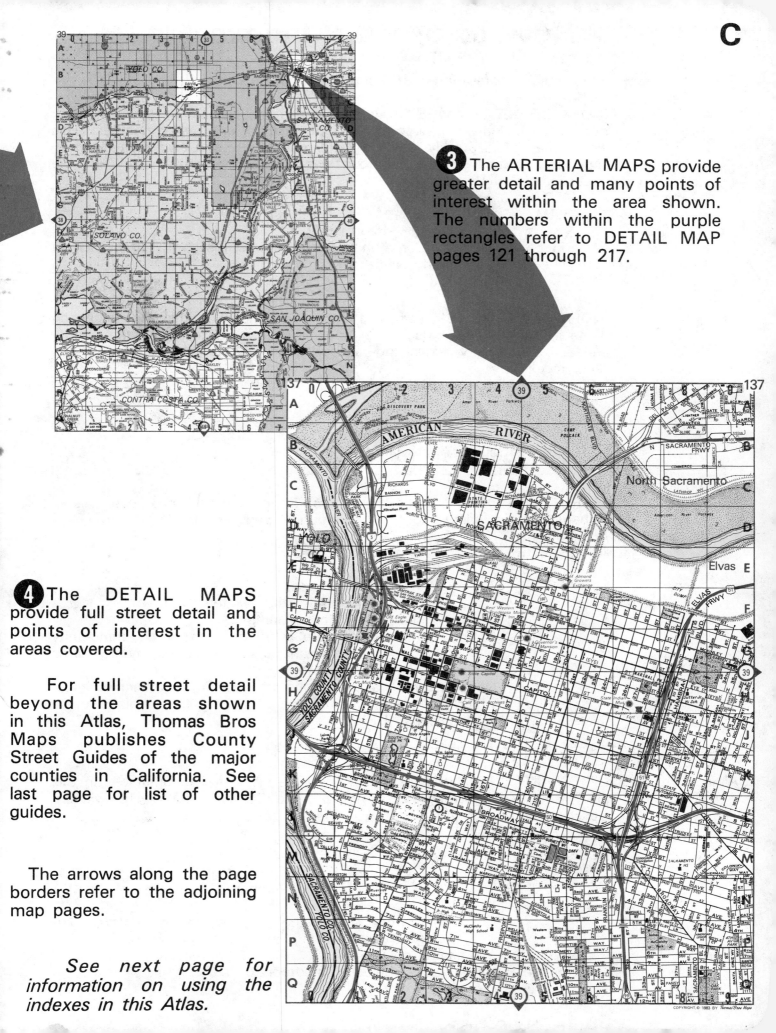

3 The ARTERIAL MAPS provide greater detail and many points of interest within the area shown. The numbers within the purple rectangles refer to DETAIL MAP pages 121 through 217.

4 The DETAIL MAPS provide full street detail and points of interest in the areas covered.

For full street detail beyond the areas shown in this Atlas, Thomas Bros Maps publishes County Street Guides of the major counties in California. See last page for list of other guides.

The arrows along the page borders refer to the adjoining map pages.

See next page for information on using the indexes in this Atlas.

D How to use the Indexes

This book contains six separate indexes. Samples are shown below.

Page A...............''INDEX OF DETAIL MAPS''...lists all the communities having detail maps in this atlas. Includes the community abbreviation and page number. This index is useful to quickly locate a major community and also as a directory explaining some of the abbreviations of communities used in the street index.

Example...... ALAMEDA........A.............159
ANAHEIM.........ANA.......193
└── Page Number
└── Community Abbreviation (used in street index)
└── Community Name

Page A...............''INDEX OF COUNTIES''...lists all the counties shown in this atlas including those in surrounding states. This index is used both to locate the county and as a directory explaining abbreviations of communities in all the other indexes.

Example....ALA.........ALAMEDA.........46
ALP.........ALPINE.............42
└── Page Number
└── County Name
└── County Abbreviation

Page 300............''STREET INDEX''...all MAJOR streets in the state have been listed alphabetically including county or community, page and grid.

Example...... A ST W   H   146   G3
ABBOTT DR   KER   80   G3
└── Grid on Atlas Page
└── Page Number
└── City - Community Abbreviation (see page A for meaning)
└── Street Name ...streets are listed once for each community they are in so it is important to check the community name when the name is repeated.

Note: Common abbreviations are used in street names all of which are shown on the top of page 300, in this example ''DR'' means ''DRIVE''.

Page 318............''CITIES AND COMMUNITIES INDEX''...all the cities and communities in this atlas are listed alphabetically along with the COUNTY name abbreviation, zip code, page and grid.

Example.....*ALBANY   ALA   94706   38   Q5
ALBERHILL   RCO   92303   99   L1
└── Grid on Page
└── Page Number
└── Zip Code
└── County Abbreviation (see page A for expanded name - Riverside County in this example).
└── Community Name

Note: An asterisk means this is an incorporated city.

How to use the Indexes

Page 322............"HIGHWAY INDEX"...all highways in the state are listed by route number once in each county. The index is divided into the three types of highways (Federal, Interstate, State).

Example...... 5....YOL....33....L1
└─ Grid on Page
└─ Page Number
└─ County Abbreviation (see page A for expanded name which is Yolo County in this example).
└─ Interstate Highway 5 (because it is on the interstate list).

Page 322............"POINTS OF INTEREST INDEX"...all major points of interest throughout the atlas are categorized and listed alphabetically with the page and grid location. These points are all shown on the map pages by a symbol for their type. This index can be used two ways: first to give descriptive information about a point of interest already located on a map page; second to find a point of interest of the type you want from the index.

Examples:

✈ AIRPORTS......Major airports having regularly scheduled commercial flights.
✈ Minor airports are shown on the map pages but not listed.

⚱ AMUSEMENT PARKS......Major "Theme" parks with rides and/or shows.

⌣ BEACHES.......County and State Beaches with facilities.

🎓 COLLEGES..... Colleges and Universities with addresses.

⛳ GOLF COURSES......Courses where PGA and LPGA tournaments are played.

⚓ HARBORS......Deep water shipping harbors.

🛒 HISTORICAL SITES.....Major features and maintained historical sites with descriptions.

🅗 HOTELS..........Many hotels listed have been selected from the AAA approved listing.

⛪ MISSIONS......All of the old Spanish missions with their current claim to fame.

🌲 PARKS AND NATIONAL FORESTS......State Parks, Federal Parks and National Forests with descriptive information.

✳ POINTS OF INTEREST.....Prominent features that may or may not fall into other categories. Well worth reviewing for any area through which you plan to travel.

⛵ RECREATION LAKES, RIVERS & MARINAS.....Includes boating and camping facilities available.

⛷ SKI AREAS....Major runs or areas only.

🎭 THEATERS..... Drama, opera, live stage.

🍇 WINERIES...... All wineries having tours or tasting rooms.

F

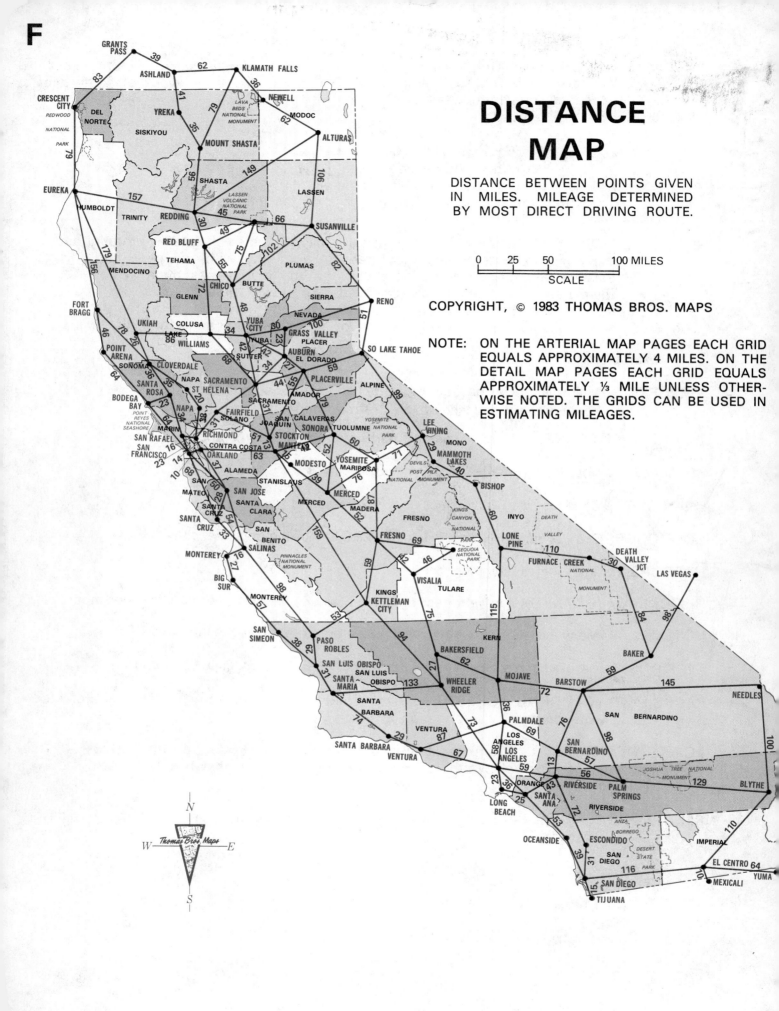

DISTANCE MAP

DISTANCE BETWEEN POINTS GIVEN IN MILES. MILEAGE DETERMINED BY MOST DIRECT DRIVING ROUTE.

0 25 50 100 MILES
SCALE

NOTE: ON THE ARTERIAL MAP PAGES EACH GRID EQUALS APPROXIMATELY 4 MILES. ON THE DETAIL MAP PAGES EACH GRID EQUALS APPROXIMATELY ⅓ MILE UNLESS OTHERWISE NOTED. THE GRIDS CAN BE USED IN ESTIMATING MILEAGES.

MILEAGE CHART

MILEAGE DETERMINED BY MOST DIRECT DRIVING ROUTE.

	BAKERSFIELD	CHICO	EUREKA	FRESNO	LAS VEGAS	LONG BEACH	LOS ANGELES	MERCED	MODESTO	OAKLAND	PALM SPRINGS	REDDING	RIVERSIDE	SACRAMENTO	SALINAS	SAN DIEGO	SAN FRANCISCO	SAN JOSE	SAN LUIS OBISPO	SANTA ANA	SANTA BARBARA	SANTA ROSA	SOUTH LAKE TAHOE	STOCKTON	VENTURA
ALTURAS	577	207	292	470	624	705	650	415	374	379	720	142	645	297	471	741	360	392	577	683	737	367	241	342	692
ANAHEIM	138	505	718	245	274	24	30	302	341	443	100	577	42	415	346	86	449	403	235	4	128	485	490	370	102
AUBURN	306	90	321	199	601	441	420	143	106	115	518	175	473	34	207	539	121	151	339	452	444	131	86	70	421
BAKERSFIELD		362	555	107	284	132	113	163	200	285	209	433	177	272	206	232	283	241	114	143	146	340	398	227	115
BARSTOW	129	491	684	236	155	123	131	292	330	414	123	559	78	401	335	180	412	385	264	116	205	469	395	356	174
BENICIA	292	144	287	177	578	429	396	123	84	37	510	187	466	58	106	513	43	49	236	456	341	61	164	74	374
BISHOP	222	360	553	235	284	308	277	223	252	314	308	396	177	265	347	360	335	321	357	301	327	382	176	240	296
BLYTHE	339	705	918	446	208	228	230	501	521	622	129	775	171	616	530	222	619	575	433	202	314	676	686	568	287
BODEGA BAY	404	189	266	249	632	491	451	194	156	74	568	246	527	141	165	594	64	109	294	516	400	23	256	152	431
BURBANK	104	465	659	210	294	31	9	266	304	383	111	536	67	376	304	127	377	334	200	45	93	421	446	330	64
CHICO	362		218	254	620	498	475	198	160	172	575	73	543	89	264	638	180	212	389	509	490	166	170	134	477
CLAREMONT	135	497	691	308	246	47	26	298	336	415	79	568	23	408	336	107	409	366	226	23	118	453	469	360	88
DAVIS	287	83	282	180	582	422	399	134	87	66	499	155	454	15	158	520	74	102	320	433	425	83	127	60	402
DEATH VALLEY	238	530	703	395	213	229	206	393	422	484	306	566	262	435	475	407	505	491	352	324	366	552	346	410	336
EL CENTRO	322	706	872	427	303	219	213	482	520	615	110	775	110	618	536	110	601	561	413	201	308	660	596	554	279
EUREKA	555	218		446	797	683	669	390	353	288	788	149	743	287	381	776	269	323	508	722	614	219	338	332	643
FAIRFIELD	278	132	276	171	561	412	391	118	79	45	489	173	457	43	132	554	55	78	260	423	362	57	150	51	389
FORT BRAGG	460	199	156	353	730	597	551	292	255	180	674	288	629	217	280	669	176	216	401	608	507	119	319	233	534
FRESNO	107	254	446		284	239	220	56	93	178	316	325	272	165	134	339	185	151	140	250	245	233	251	120	222
GRASS VALLEY	329	78	320	222	624	464	443	166	129	138	541	163	496	57	230	562	144	174	362	475	467	154	115	93	444
LAGUNA BEACH	162	528	741	269	288	34	55	324	363	465	115	598	62	437	368	75	471	425	257	19	150	507	511	391	123
LA JOLLA	219	625	763	326	319	90	103	382	419	507	122	667	79	492	428	13	517	449	309	79	203	536	529	450	172
LASSEN NATIONAL PARK	437	102	202	329	695	573	550	273	235	247	650	45	618	164	339	713	255	287	459	584	562	241	199	209	552
LAS VEGAS	284	620	797	284		276	286	446	484	567	276	640	231	567	488	332	568	524	414	269	354	610	466	510	323
LONE PINE	159	420	593	285	224	232	209	283	312	374	277	456	233	325	365	337	395	381	273	245	285	442	236	300	254
LONG BEACH	132	498	683	239	276		24	294	333	417	118	568	60	407	338	103	427	383	218	25	120	477	479	361	93
LOS ANGELES	113	475	669	220	286	23		276	314	393	103	546	59	386	314	119	387	344	204	36	96	431	456	340	66
MAMMOTH LAKES	262	320	513	195	324	348	317	283	212	274	348	356	217	225	307	400	295	281	397	341	367	342	130	200	336
MANTECA	215	147	345	108	499	348	329	54	15	63	425	219	380	44	99	447	73	65	248	382	354	123	144	13	330
MARTINEZ	288	146	290	172	571	424	391	118	79	28	507	191	460	61	101	509	38	47	233	453	338	64	168	70	369
MERCED	163	198	390	56	446	324	314		37	123	368	269	339	109	105	395	130	115	195	305	300	172	194	64	278
MODESTO	200	160	353	93	484	333	314	37		84	410	232	365	72	104	432	92	77	233	344	339	135	156	27	315
MOJAVE	62	424	617	169	229	117	94	225	262	347	162	495	118	334	268	213	345	303	190	130	116	402	351	289	87
MONTEREY	216	278	399	149	504	356	334	115	138	111	433	350	388	190	18	442	122	75	145	367	250	170	272	141	273
NAPA	331	150	255	224	613	463	439	169	130	46	540	191	495	61	145	566	56	88	270	492	363	36	168	69	390
NEEDLES	281	638	821	383	108	269	279	439	476	560	190	729	224	548	481	311	561	517	416	262	352	603	552	508	316
NEVADA CITY	334	83	325	227	629	469	448	171	134	143	546	168	501	62	235	567	149	179	367	480	472	159	110	98	449
NEWPORT BEACH	155	519	735	262	279	21	43	317	366	458	108	592	55	430	361	81	465	418	230	12	141	498	502	382	114
OAKLAND	285	172	288	178	567	417	393	123	84		494	218	449	81	99	520	10	42	224	446	317	60	195	73	344
ONTARIO	141	493	696	247	222	44	37	303	341	420	77	573	21	413	341	125	414	371	232	33	123	458	483	367	103
OXNARD	122	485	650	229	316	85	59	271	322	351	165	555	117	395	252	178	379	329	142	97	38	421	478	349	7
PALMDALE	98	460	653	205	244	81	58	261	298	383	126	531	82	370	304	182	381	339	221	94	116	438	387	325	87
PALM SPRINGS	209	575	788	316	276	118	103	368	410	494		658	56	484	415	135	504	460	306	96	199	554	435	438	172
PALO ALTO	261	213	302	171	544	403	364	135	97	43	480	251	433	120	74	482	33	20	205	426	311	89	223	92	342
PASADENA	109	475	688	216	259	31	7	271	310	394	104	554	52	384	315	134	404	360	210	42	95	454	463	338	68
PLACERVILLE	282	133	331	175	525	416	395	122	83	125	493	205	461	44	177	548	131	127	309	427	429	141	59	55	397
REDDING	433	73	149	325	640	568	546	269	232	218	658		600	161	334	680	218	246	431	579	537	223	249	206	548
RENO	[illegible]	194	342	297	[illegible]	[illegible]	[illegible]	[illegible]	[illegible]	216	[illegible]	[illegible]	[illegible]	132	308	[illegible]	[illegible]	249	434	503	507	229	61	177	496
RICHMOND	299	163	276	192	581	431	407	137	98	14	508	204	462	74	113	534	24	56	238	460	331	50	181	82	358
RIVERSIDE	177	543	743	272	231	60	56	326	365	449	56	600		439	367	92	463	413	259	43	147	509	379	406	125
SACRAMENTO	272	89	287	165	567	407	386	109	72	81	484	161	439		173	505	87	117	305	418	410	97	107	45	387
SALINAS	206	264	381	134	488	338	314	105	104	99	415	334	367	173		441	101	57	125	349	218	160	251	122	245
SAN BERNARDINO	167	534	714	269	228	63	59	325	362	439	57	595	13	436	360	104	444	401	260	48	154	486	436	389	123
SAN DIEGO	232	638	776	339	332	103	119	395	432	520	135	680	92	505	441		530	462	322	92	216	549	542	493	185
SAN FRANCISCO	283	180	269	185	568	427	387	130	92	10	504	218	463	87	101	530		45	230	452	336	56	192	88	367
SAN JOSE	241	212	323	151	524	383	344	115	77	37	460	246	413	117	54	462	45		185	406	291	96	197	72	322
SAN JUAN CAPISTRANO	163	529	742	270	289	40	55	325	364	466	116	599	63	438	369	66	472	426	258	20	151	508	512	114	124
SAN LUIS OBISPO	114	384	508	140	414	218	204	195	233	224	306	431	259	305	125	322	230	185		238	106	281	382	254	137
SAN MATEO	313	199	288	181	554	413	374	125	86	29	490	237	443	106	84	492	19	30	215	436	321	75	209	78	352
SAN PEDRO	134	496	690	242	285	9	22	298	336	415	126	568	68	408	336	118	409	366	213	37	108	454	478	362	75
SAN RAFAEL	306	167	260	199	588	438	414	144	105	21	515	243	470	83	121	559	18	64	246	470	339	39	181	94	366
SANTA ANA	143	509	722	250	269	25	35	305	344	446	96	579	43	418	349	84	452	406	238		131	488	492	372	104
SANTA BARBARA	146	490	614	245	354	120	96	300	339	317	199	537	147	410	218	216	336	291	106	131		387	490	374	31
SANTA CRUZ	239	230	354	150	524	379	344	116	109	75	456	275	411	146	33	462	74	29	162	390	268	129	229	101	300
SANTA MARIA	145	415	539	171	428	194	170	226	264	255	273	462	221	336	156	290	261	216	31	205	74	312	413	285	103
SANTA ROSA	340	166	219	233	610	477	431	172	135	60	554	223	509	97	160	549	56	96	281	488	387		199	113	414
SAUSALITO	298	183	276	200	583	442	402	145	107	25	519	259	478	99	116	545	15	60	245	467	351	55	207	103	382
SEQUOIA NATIONAL PK	129	343	556	84	408	258	234	139	178	335	235	385	303	252	209	361	272	228	178	269	276	329	335	206	262
SONOMA	331	163	239	224	613	468	439	170	130	46	540	204	495	75	146	584	43	89	271	495	364	20	181	82	391
SONORA	215	189	387	108	498	380	366	52	42	105	420	261	391	86	157	447	115	107	247	357	352	165	139	55	330
SOUTH LAKE TAHOE	398	170	388	251	465	479	456	194	156	195	435	249	379	107	251	542	192	197	382	492	490	199		131	471
STOCKTON	227	134	332	120	510	361	340	64	27	73	438	206	406	45	122	493	88	72	254	372	374	113	131		342
SUSANVILLE	465	105	257	356	599	600	577	299	262	275	677	110	645	191	369	714	252	280	465	613	571	257	133	240	582
UKIAH	402	147	179	295	672	539	493	234	197	135	616	184	571	159	222	611	118	158	343	550	449	62	253	175	476
VALLEJO	310	147	265	203	592	442	418	131	92	25	519	186	474	57	124	545	35	67	249	471	342	46	266	65	370
VENTURA	115	477	643	222	323	93	66	278	315	344	172	548	125	387	245	185	367	322	137	104	31	414	471	342	
YOSEMITE NATIONAL PK	199	263	476	92	435	331	307	83	122	174	408	333	364	172	188	434	184	178	236	342	329	234	133	129	330
YREKA	531	171	205	427	698	657	638	372	335	307	747	98	689	263	423	756	317	346	534	668	630	325	315	297	645
YUBA CITY	313	48	290	206	608	448	427	150	113	122	525	133	480	41	214	546	128	158	346	459	451	201	145	86	428
YUMA	379	742	922	491	299	278	271	545	584	674	169	816	221	655	595	173	655	614	473	260	368	702	646	603	337

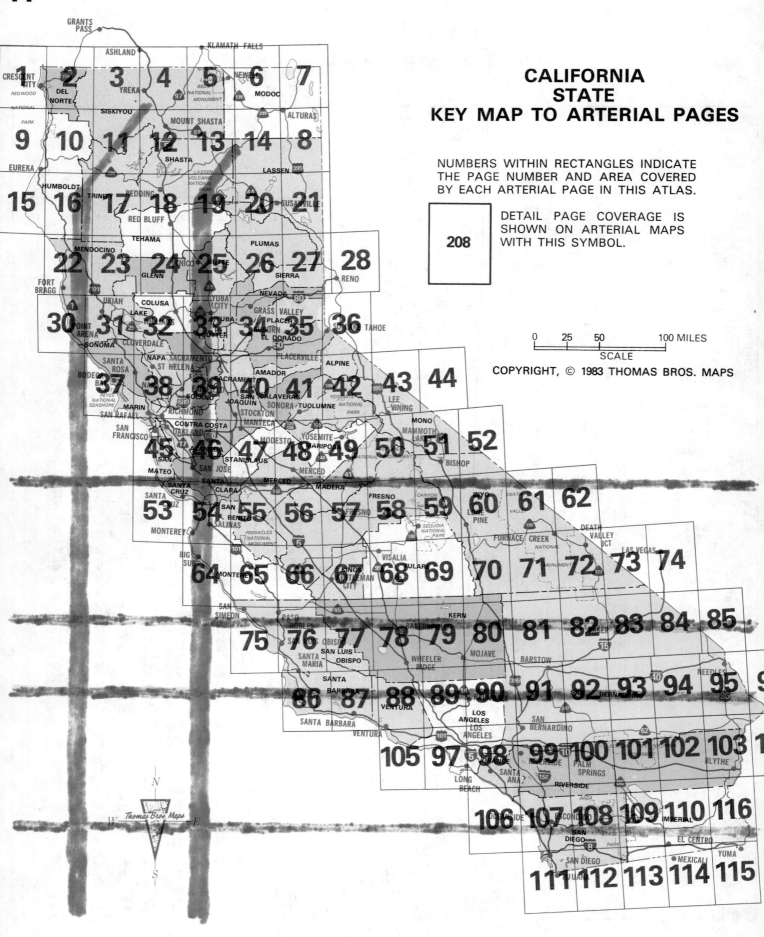

H

CALIFORNIA
STATE
KEY MAP TO ARTERIAL PAGES

NUMBERS WITHIN RECTANGLES INDICATE
THE PAGE NUMBER AND AREA COVERED
BY EACH ARTERIAL PAGE IN THIS ATLAS.

208 DETAIL PAGE COVERAGE IS
SHOWN ON ARTERIAL MAPS
WITH THIS SYMBOL.

0   25   50   100 MILES
SCALE

COPYRIGHT, © 1983 THOMAS BROS. MAPS

LEGEND

DETAIL PAGES

EXPLANATION OF MAP SYMBOLS

ARTERIAL PAGES

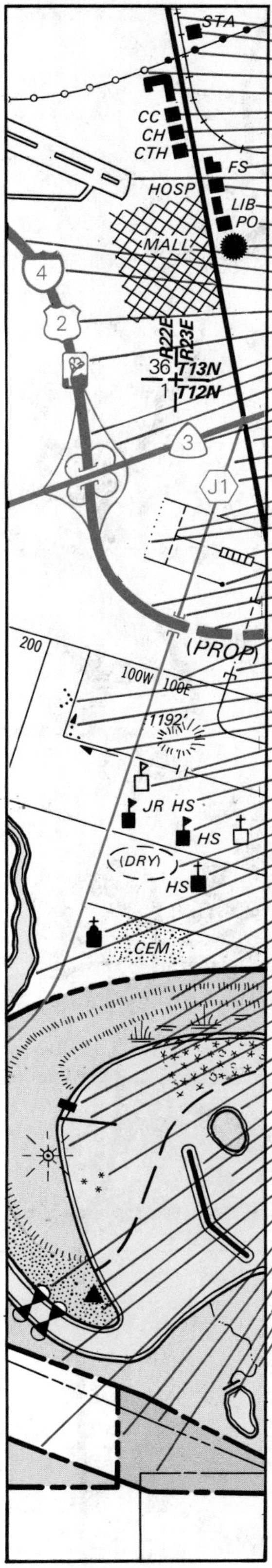

RAILROAD
STATION (TRAIN, BUS, RANGER)
RAPID TRANSIT SYSTEM
UNDERGROUND RAPID TRANSIT SYSTEM
BUILDINGS
CHAMBER OF COMMERCE
CITY HALL
COURT HOUSE
FIRE STATION
MAJOR AIRPORT
HOSPITAL
LIBRARY
POST OFFICE
COMMUNITY SHOPPING CENTER
REGIONAL SHOPPING CENTER
FREEWAY
INTERSTATE HIGHWAY NUMBER
U S HIGHWAY NUMBER
STATE SCENIC ROUTE
TOWNSHIP & RANGE TICK
FREEWAY RAMP NUMBER
FREEWAY INTERCHANGE
HIGHWAY
STATE HIGHWAY NUMBER
PRIMARY ROAD
SECONDARY ROAD
COUNTY ROUTE NUMBER
MINOR ROAD
PRIVATE, DIRT OR PROPOSED ROAD
UNDEVELOPED-CONST. NOT PROP.
STAIRWAY
STREET TERMINATION
FREEWAY UNDER CONSTRUCTION
BRIDGE
FREEWAY PROPOSED
BLOCK NUMBERS IN HUNDREDS
100 E (ONE HUNDRED EAST)
TUNNEL
TERMINATION OF STREET NAME
EXTENSION OF STREET NAME
MOUNTAIN PEAK & ELEVATION
ONE WAY STREET
GATE
PUBLIC ELEMENTARY SCHOOL
PUBLIC JUNIOR HIGH SCHOOL
PUBLIC HIGH SCHOOL
PAROCHIAL ELEMENTARY SCHOOL
DRY LAKE
PAROCHIAL HIGH SCHOOL
MISSION
RIVER
CEMETERY
INTERNATIONAL BOUNDARY
LEVEE
SWAMP, MARSH
SHORE
UNDERWATER PARK
BOAT LAUNCH
PIER
LIGHTHOUSE
FERRY
ROCK, BARE OR AWASH
ISLAND
BREAKWATER
LOCKS
WATER
CAMPGROUND
PARK, GOLF COURSE
STATE BOUNDARY
COUNTY BOUNDARY
CITY BOUNDARY
RANCHO BOUNDARY
POINT OF INTEREST BOUNDARY
DAM
LAKE
CREEK, CANAL

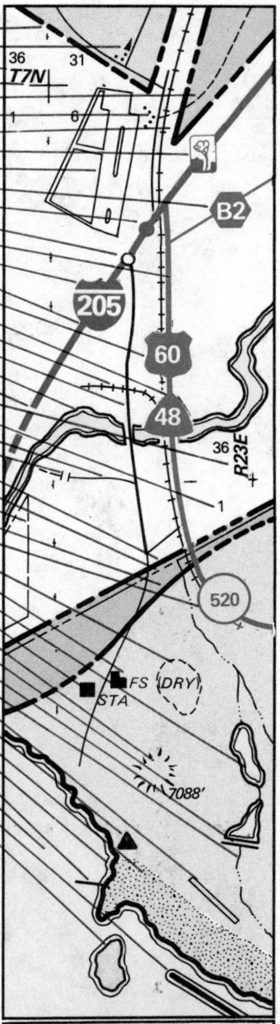

COUNTY BOUNDARY
EXTENSION OF STREET NAME
TOWNSHIP NUMBER
TOWNSHIP AND RANGE TICKS
PRIVATE DIRT OR PROPOSED ROAD
TERMINATION OF STREET NAME
CITY BOUNDARY
STATE SCENIC ROUTE
MAJOR AIRPORT
COUNTY ROUTE NUMBER
CITY
COMMUNITY
HIGHWAY
INTERSTATE HIGHWAY NUMBER
FREEWAY
U S HIGHWAY NUMBER
STATE HIGHWAY NUMBER
RAILROAD
PRIMARY ROAD
RIVER
FREEWAY UNDER CONSTRUCTION
RANGE NUMBER
SECTION NUMBER (1 SECTION = 1 SQ. MILE)
SECONDARY ROAD, MINOR ROAD
GATE
STATE BOUNDARY
RANCHO BOUNDARY
POINT OF INTEREST BOUNDARY
INTERNATIONAL BOUNDARY
FOREIGN HIGHWAY NUMBER
DRY LAKE
FIRE STATION
LAKE
RANGER STATION
MOUNTAIN
PEAK ELEVATION
DAM
CREEK
AIRPORT, AIRSTRIP
CAMPGROUND
PARK
SHORE
PIER
WATER
BREAKWATER
ISLAND

MAJOR DEPARTMENT STORES

B	BROADWAY
BF	BUFFUMS
BK	BULLOCKS
C	CAPWELLS
E	EMPORIUM
LH	LIBERTY HOUSE
MA	MACY'S
M	MAY CO
MW	MONTGOMERY WARD
NM	NEIMAN-MARCUS
N	NORDSTROM
O	OHRBACHS
P	J C PENNEY
R	ROBINSONS
S	SEARS
SF	SAKS FIFTH AV

POINTS OF INTEREST

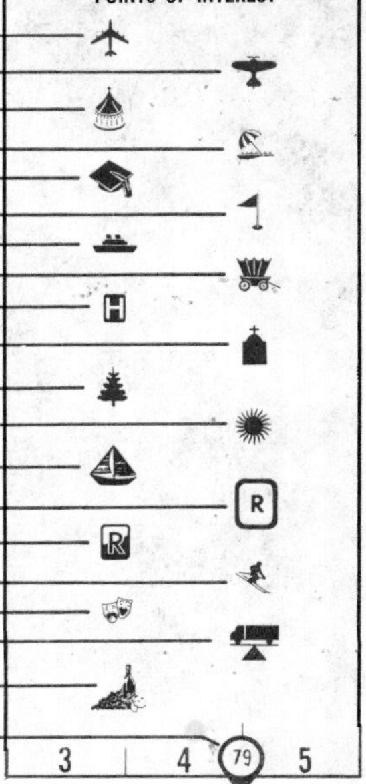

AIRPORTS (MAJOR)
AIRPORTS (MINOR)
AMUSEMENT PARKS
BEACHES
COLLEGES AND UNIVERSITIES (MAJOR)
GOLF COURSES
HARBORS
HISTORICAL SITES
HOTELS
MISSIONS
STATE & FEDERAL PARKS & NATIONAL FORESTS
POINTS OF INTEREST (MISCELLANEOUS)
RECREATION LAKES, RIVERS & MARINAS
REST STOPS
REST STOPS (CLOSED IN WINTER)
SKI AREAS
THEATERS
TRUCK SCALES
WINERIES
PAGE NUMBER OF
ADJOINING MAP

SCALE OF DETAIL MAPS
1 INCH TO 2200 FEET *

MILES   0   ¼   ½   1
KILOMETERS   0   .25   .5   1

SCALE OF ARTERIAL MAPS
1 INCH TO 5 MILES *

MILES   0   2.5   5   10
KILOMETERS   0   2.5   5   10

*UNLESS OTHERWISE NOTED

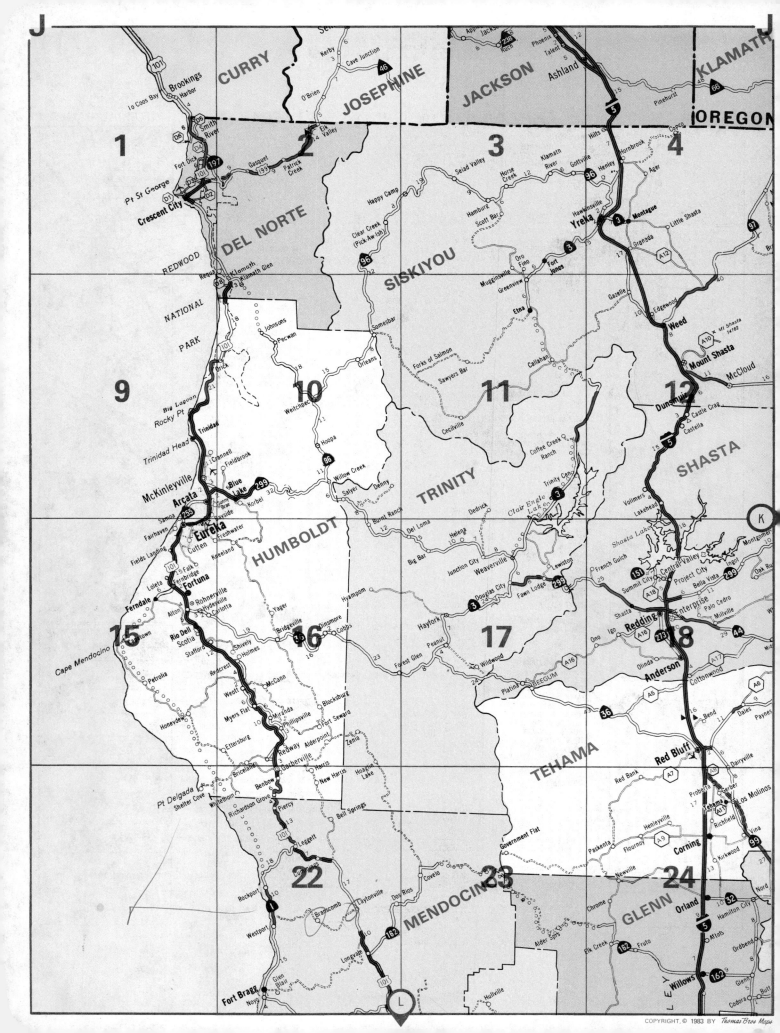

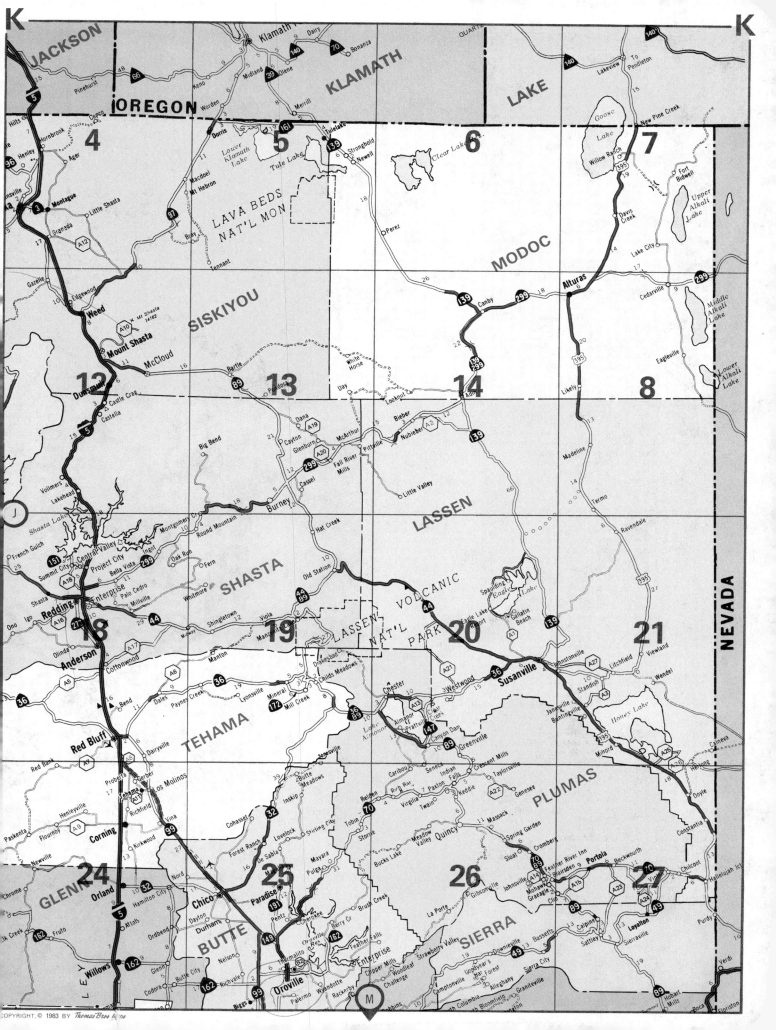

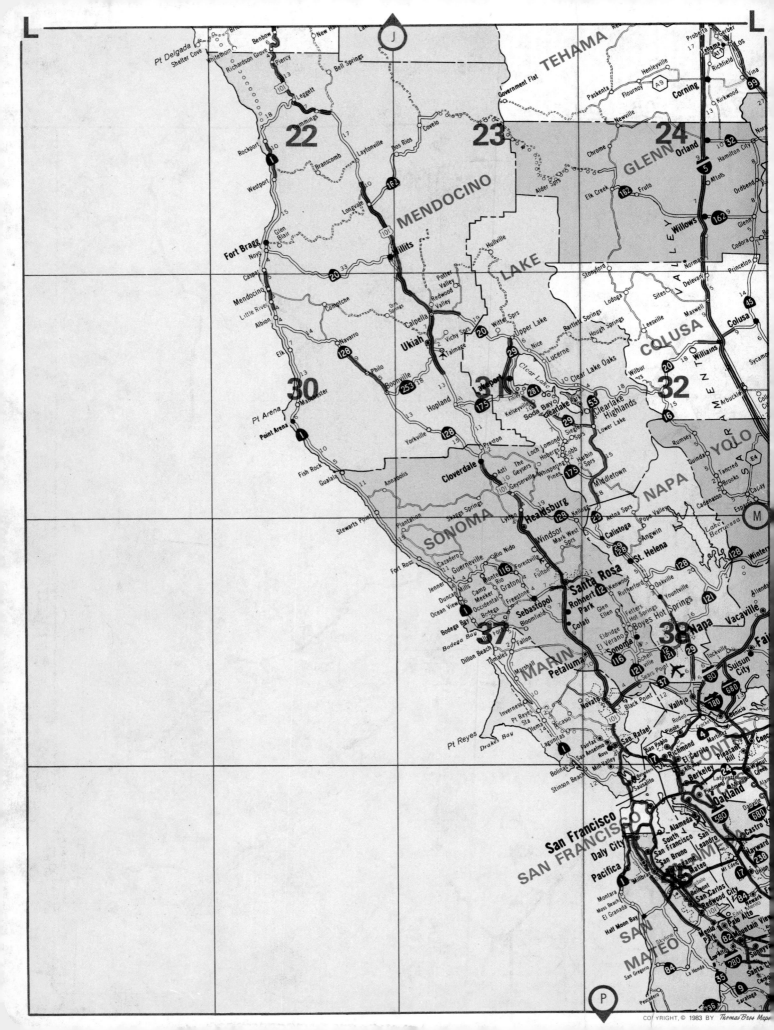

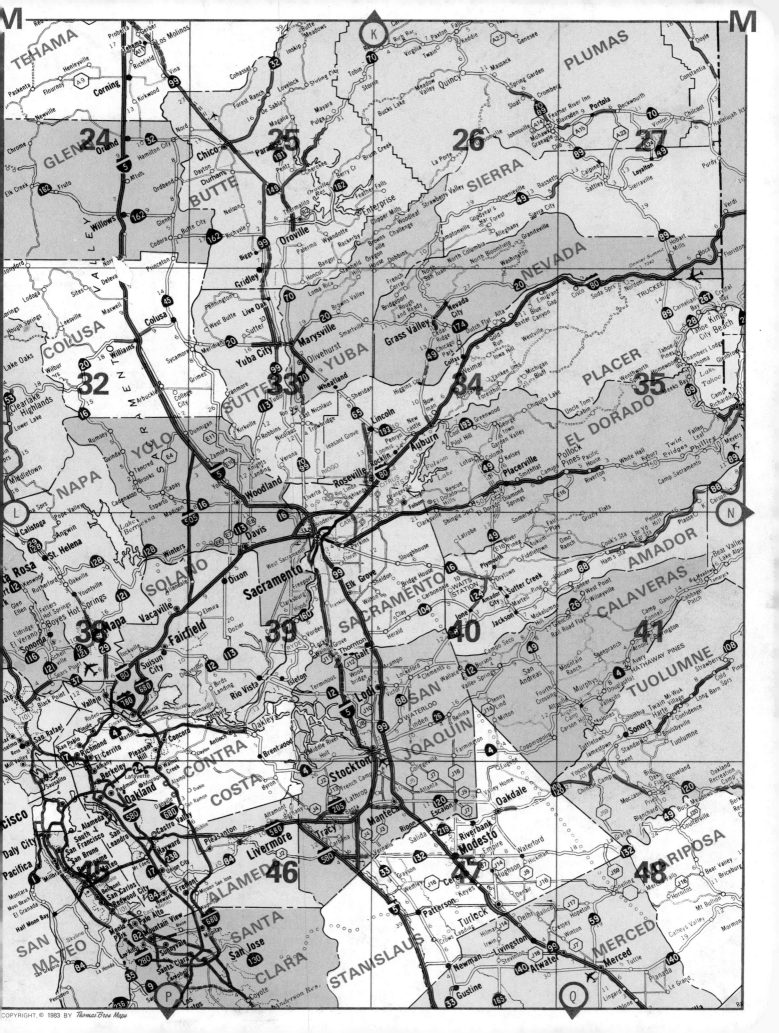

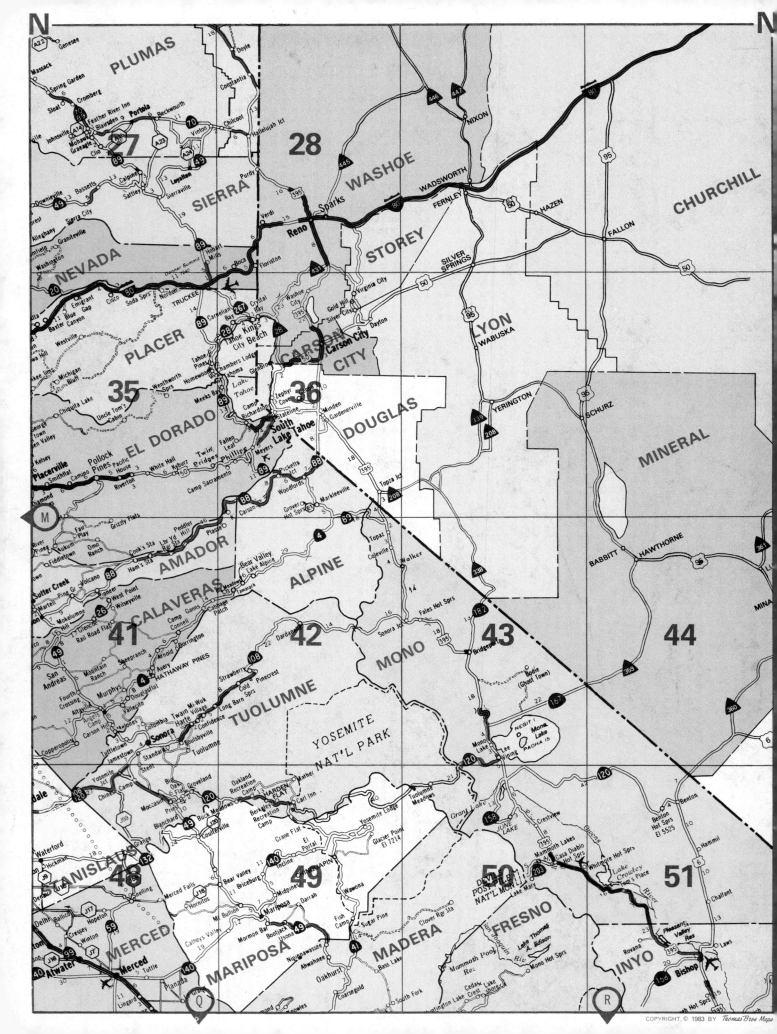

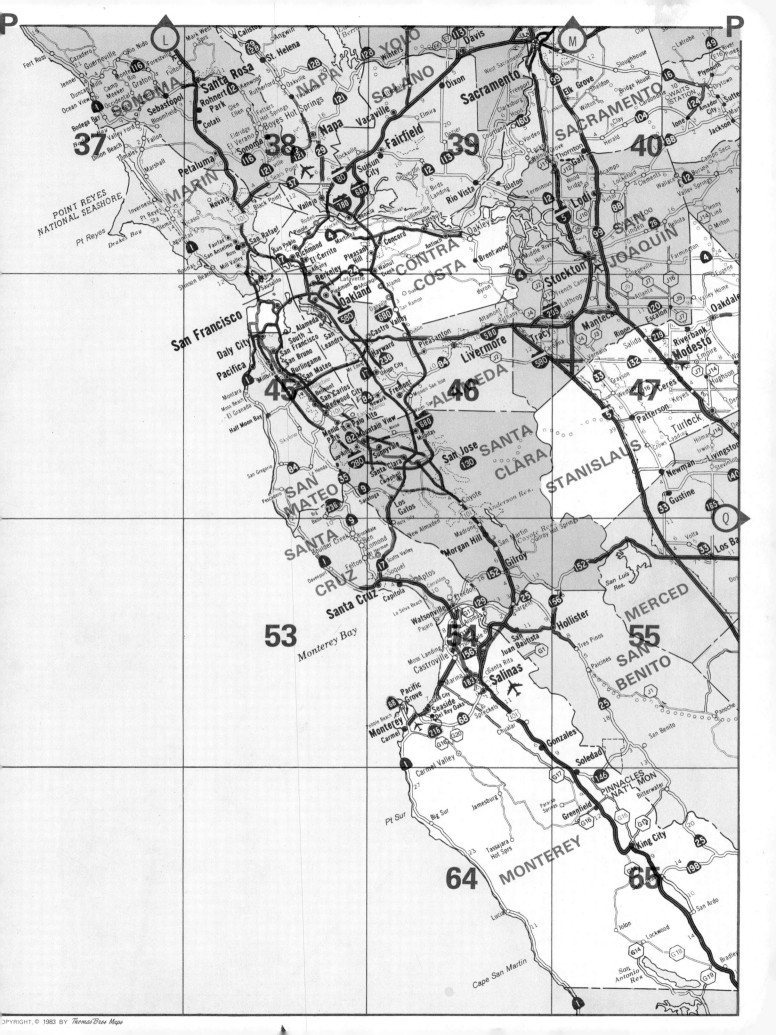

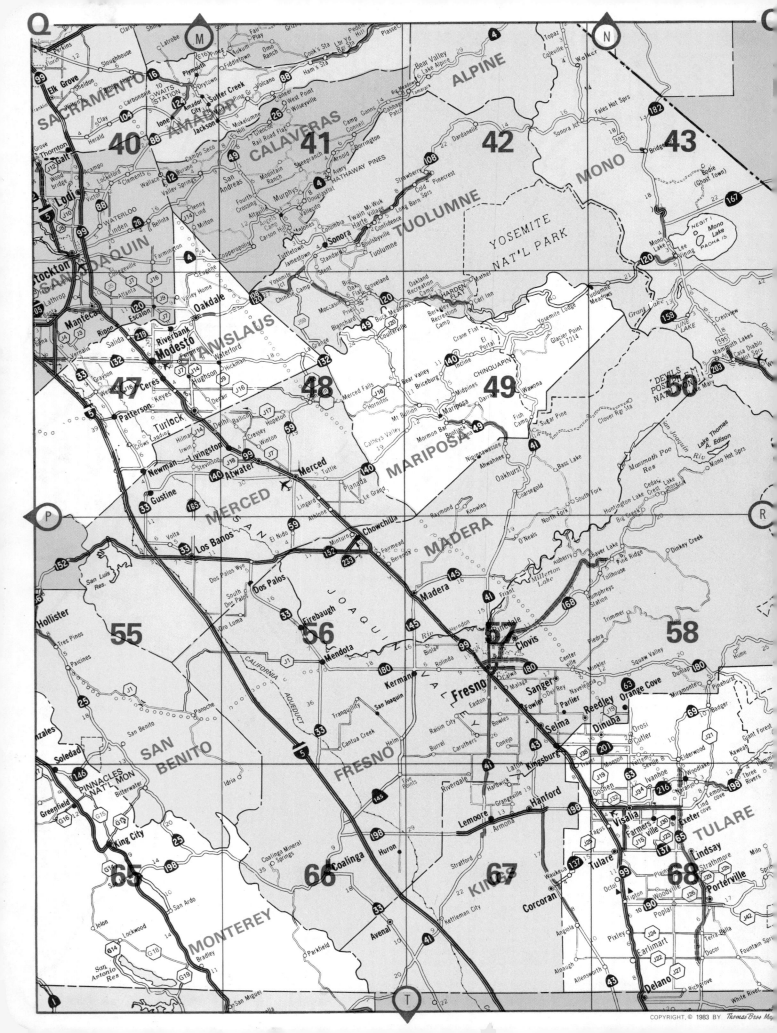

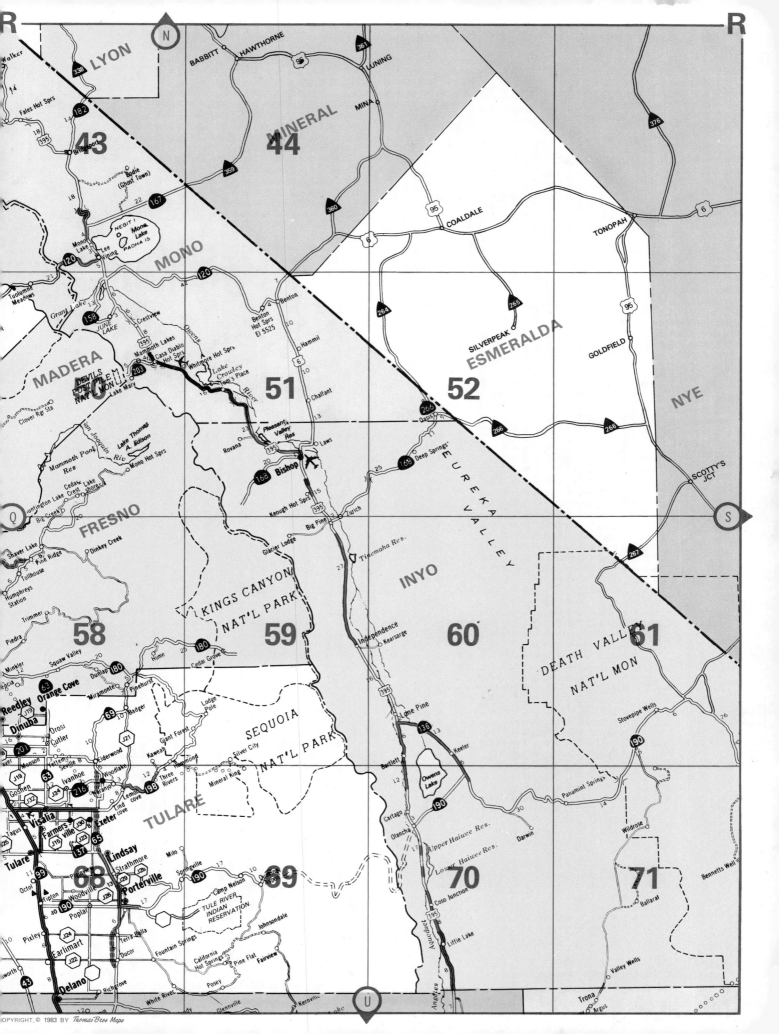

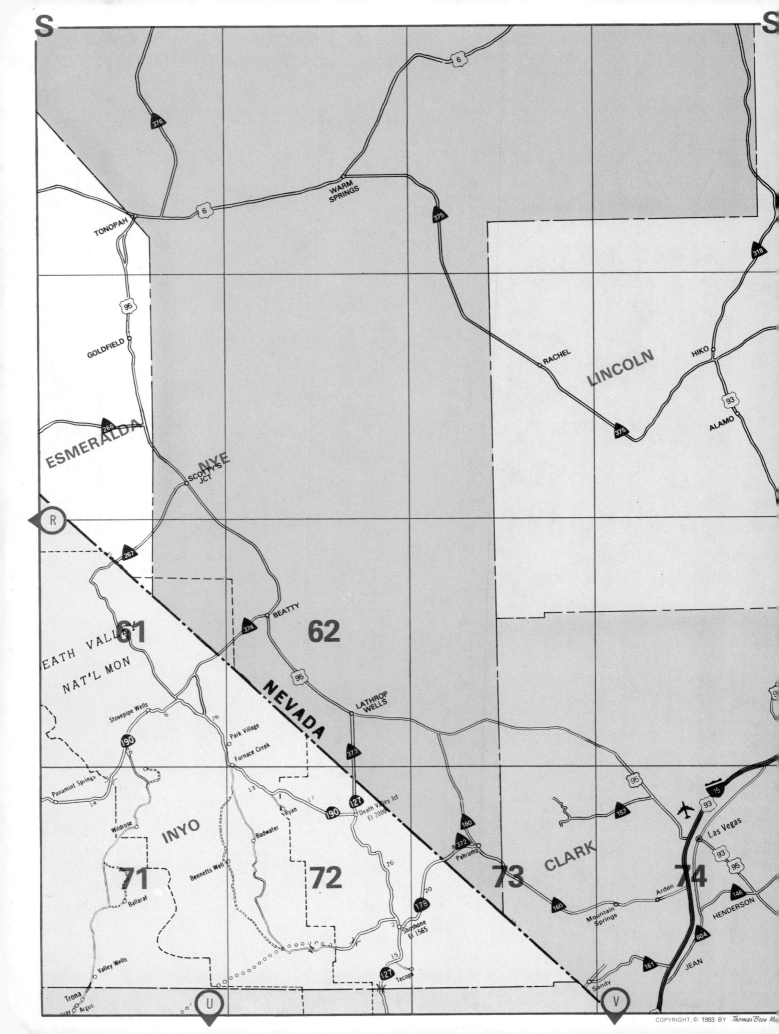

S   S

376

6

WARM
SPRINGS

375

318

TONOPAH

95

RACHEL   LINCOLN   HIKO

GOLDFIELD

93

ESMERALDA   266   375   ALAMO

NYE

SCOTTY'S
JCT

R

267

61   374   BEATTY   62

EATH VALLEY   95

NAT'L MON   NEVADA

Stovepipe Wells   LATHROP
WELLS

190   Park Village   373

Furnace Creek

Panamint Springs   95

14   Ryan   127   Death Valley Jct   15
190   El 2000   157

INYO   Badwater   160

372   CLARK   93

71   Bennetts Well   72   Pahrump   73   74

Las Vegas

93
95

160   Arden   146

178   Mountain   HENDERSON
Springs

Shoshone   604
El 1565

Valley Wells   127   JEAN

161

Trona   Tecopa   Sandy
Argus

U   V

COPYRIGHT, © 1983 BY ThomasBros Ma

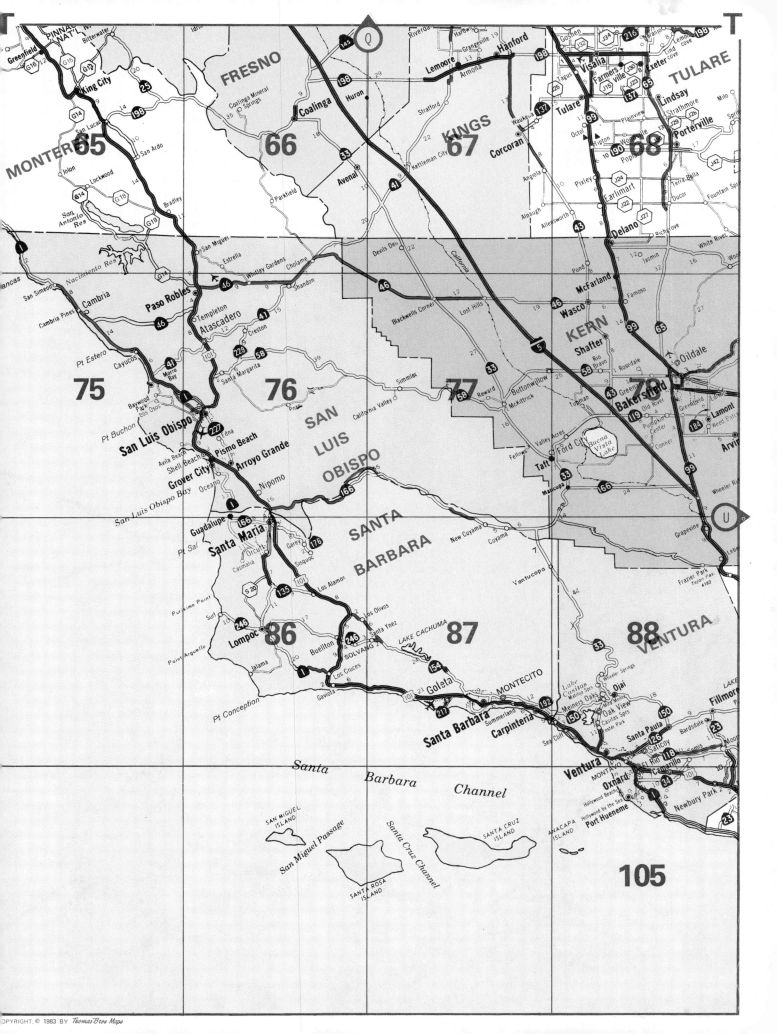

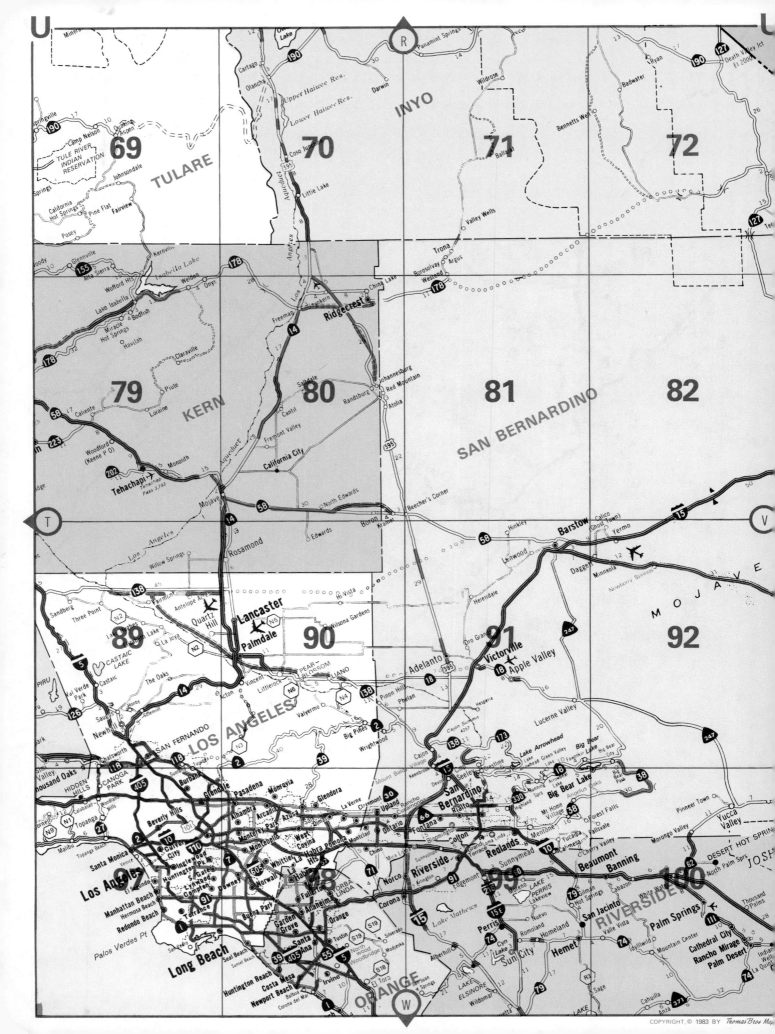

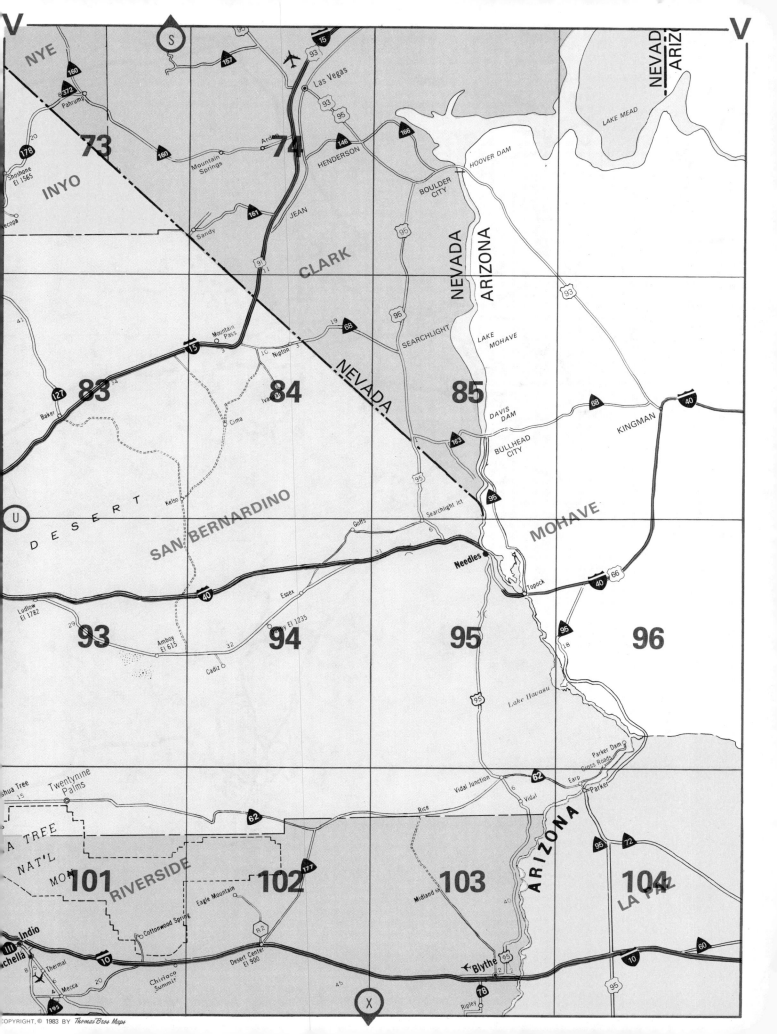

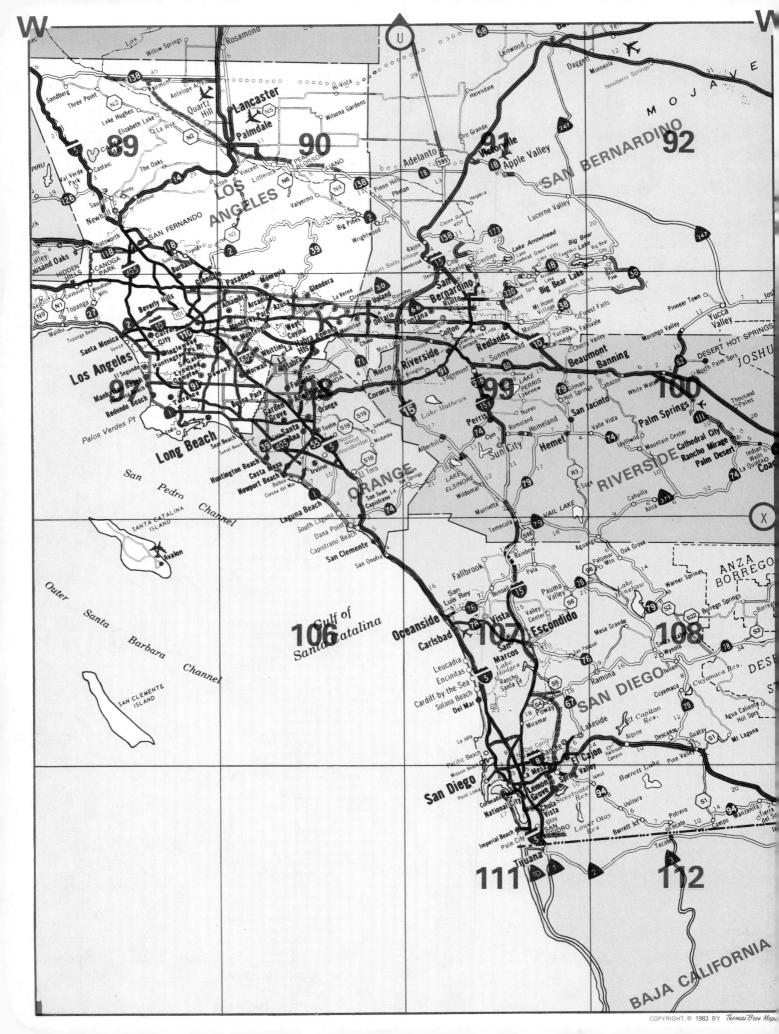

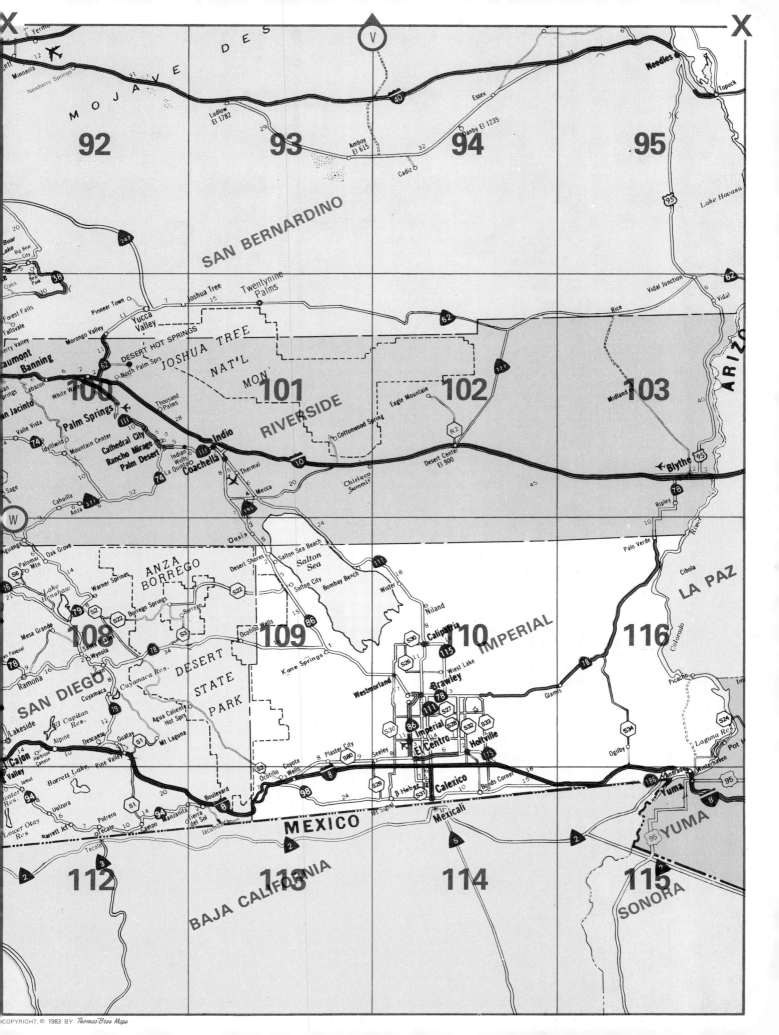

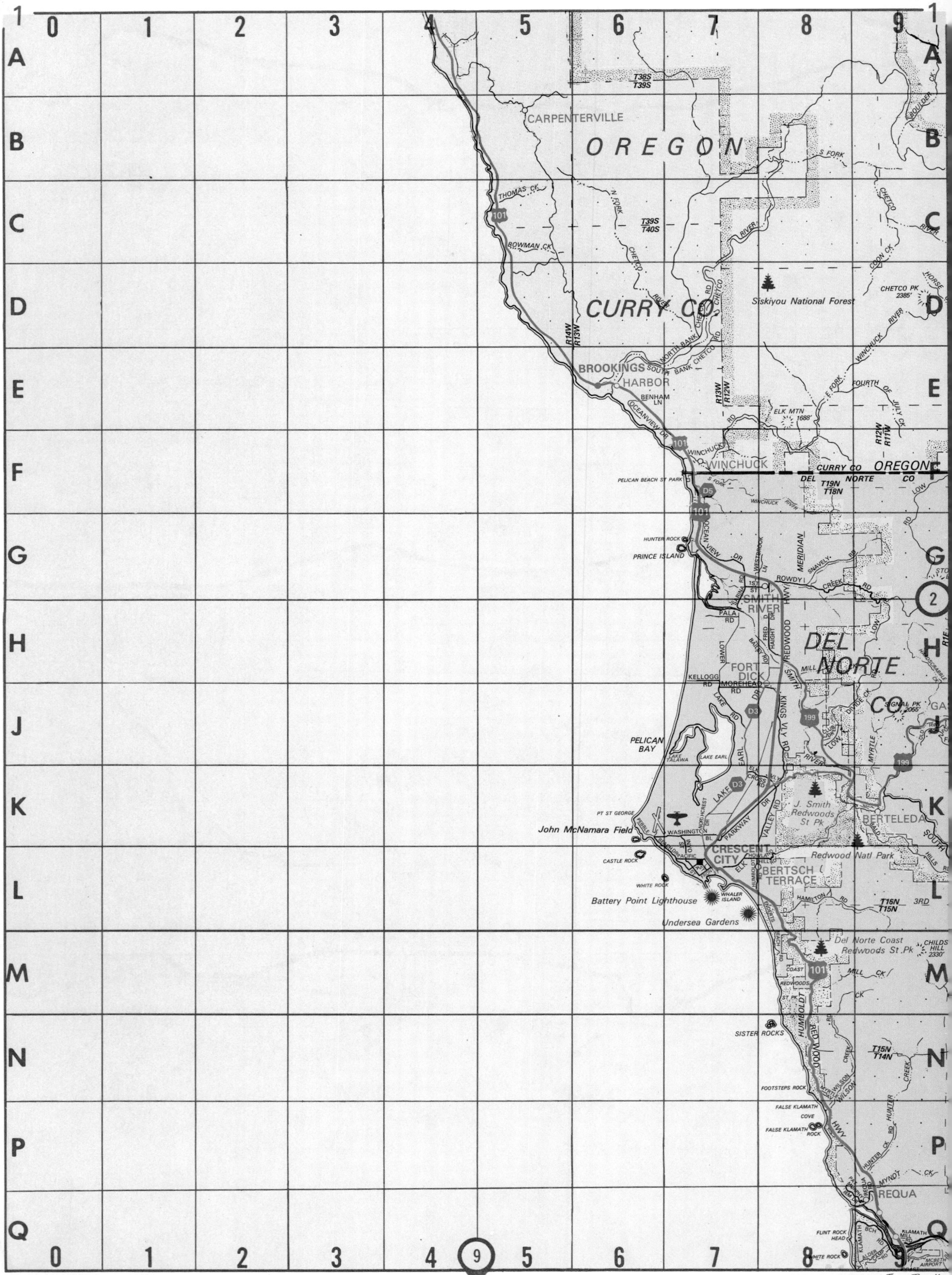

A

CARPENTERVILLE

B

O R E G O N

T38S
T39S

C

THOMAS CK

101

BOWMAN CK

N FORK

T39S
T40S

CHETCO RIVER

D

CURRY CO

Siskiyou National Forest

CHETCO PK
2385'

CHETCO RIVER

COON CK

HORSE CK

R14W
R13W

NORTH BANK CHETCO RD

BULL

WINCHUCK RIVER

E

BROOKINGS
HARBOR

SOUTH BANK CHETCO RD

BENHAM LN

OCEANVIEW DR

101

R13W
R12W

ELK MTN
1688'

E FORK

FOURTH OF JULY CK

R12W
R11W

F

WINCHUCK

101

PELICAN BEACH ST PARK

D5

S FORK

WINCHUCK RIVER

CURRY CO OREGON
DEL NORTE CO

T19N
T18N

LOW

G

HUNTER ROCK
PRINCE ISLAND

OCEAN VIEW DR

WESTBROOK LN

MERIDIAN

SNAVELY

ROWDY

1ST ST

SMITH
RIVER

CREEK RD

STO

2

H

PALA RD

FRED HAIGHT DR

BARRY

LEWIS

REDWOOD

SMITH

MILL

**DEL
NORTE**

ROSSCHOBERGE

HZ

J

KELLOGG RD

FORT
DICK

MOREHEAD RD

LAKE RD

D3

LAKE EARL

EARL

SANDS WY RD

RIVER

199

DIVIDE CK

LOW

MYRTLE

SIGNAL PK
2055'

199

GA

CO

K

PT ST GEORGE

John McNamara Field

PELICAN
BAY

LAKE TALAWA

LAKE EARL

HILLCREST

D3

ELK VALLEY CROSS RD

NORTHCREST DR

PARKWAY

LAKF

VALLEY DR

J. Smith
Redwoods
St Pk

BERTELEDA

SOUTH HILLS

L

CASTLE ROCK

WHITE ROCK

Battery Point Lighthouse

Undersea Gardens

WASHINGTON BL

PEBBLE

WHALER ISLAND

**CRESCENT
CITY**

PACIFIC

ELK

HOWLAND

HAMILTON

BERTSCH
TERRACE

Redwood Natl Park

HAMILTON RD

T16N
T15N

3RD

M

COAST

REDWOODS ST PK

COAST REDWOODS

Del Norte Coast
Redwoods St.Pk

101

MILL CK

CHILDS
HILL
2330'

CK

N

SISTER ROCKS

HUMBOLDT

REDWOOD

CREEK

WILSON

WILSON

HWY

T15N
T14N

CREEK

HUNTER

N

P

FOOTSTEPS ROCK

FALSE KLAMATH
COVE

FALSE KLAMATH
ROCK

HUNTER CK RD

MYNOT CK

P

Q

REQUA

FLINT ROCK
HEAD

KLAMATH BCH

PETE ROCK

KLAMATH

MYRTLE

MCBETH
AIRPORT

KLAMATH MILL

Q

9

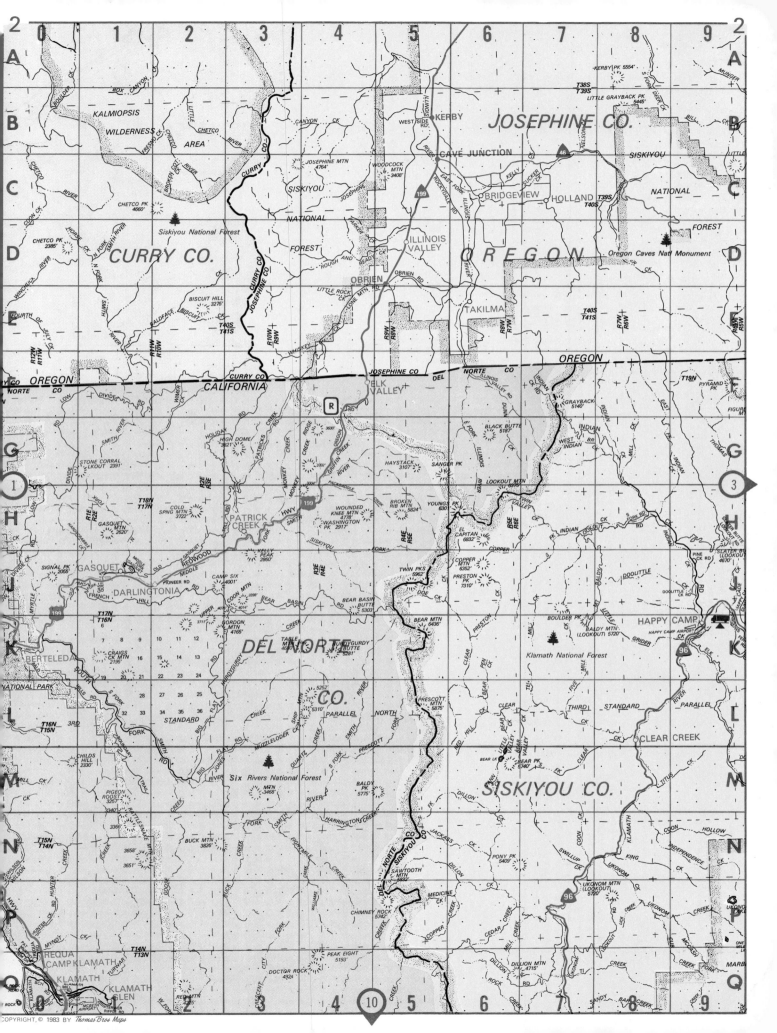

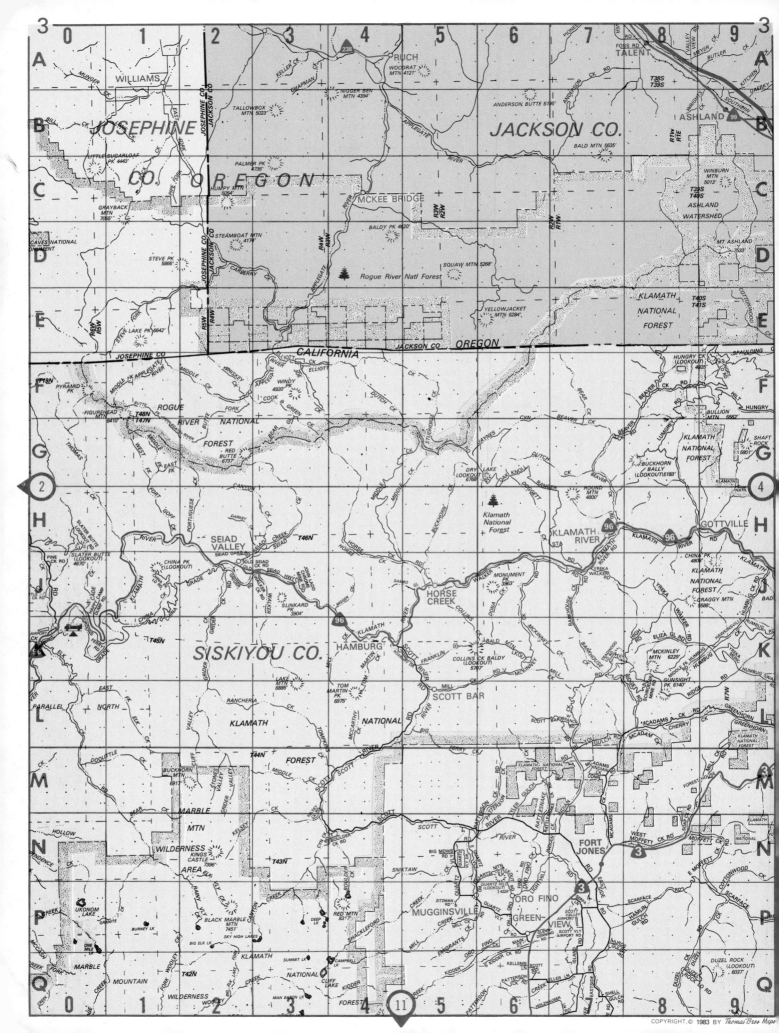

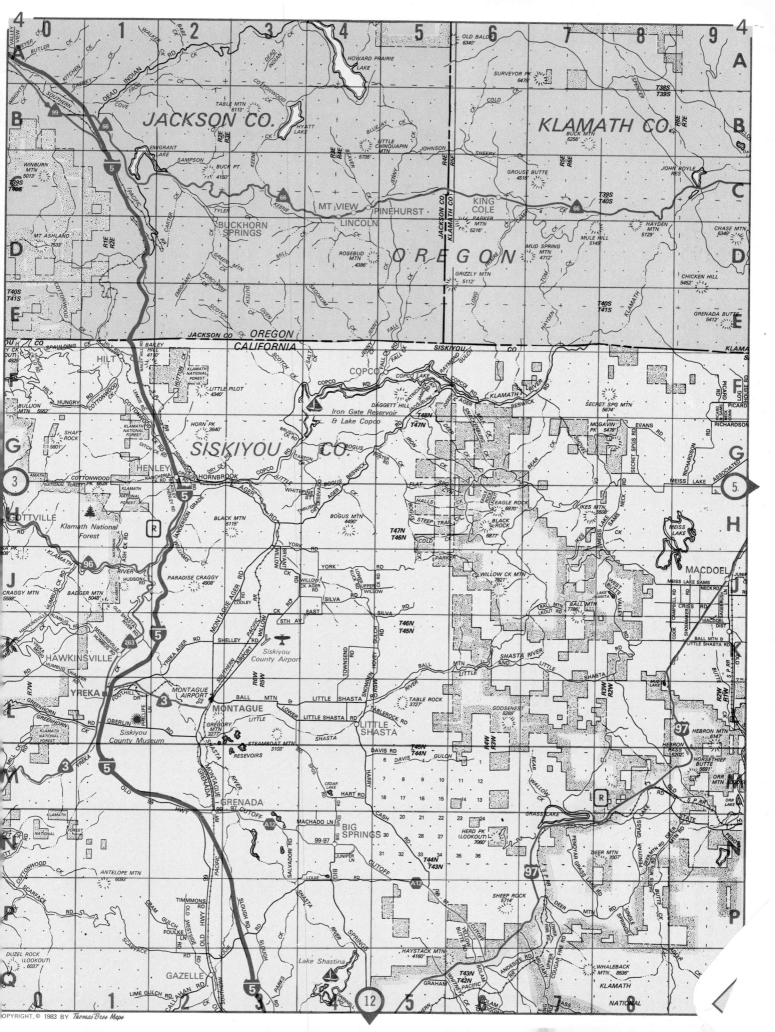

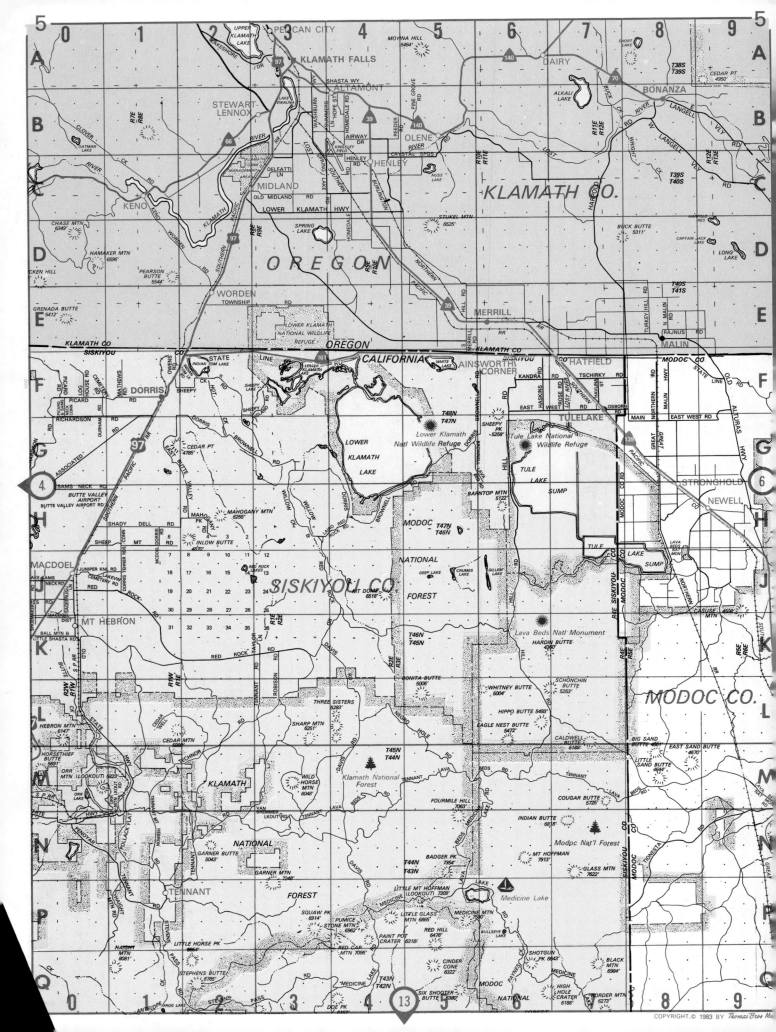

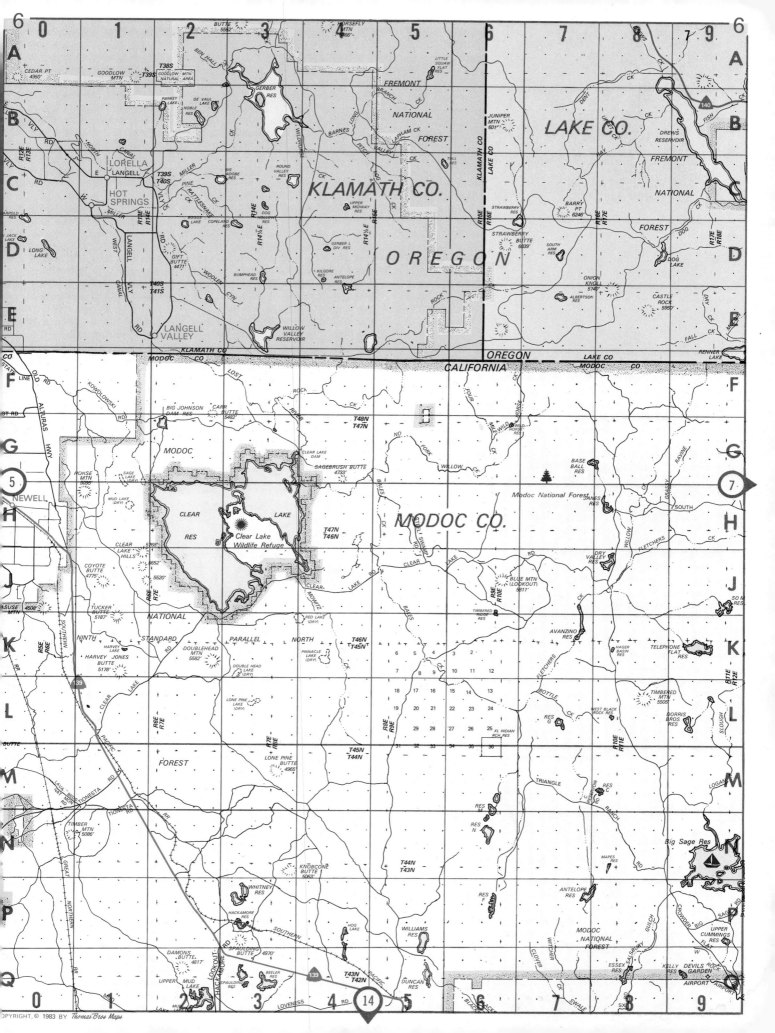

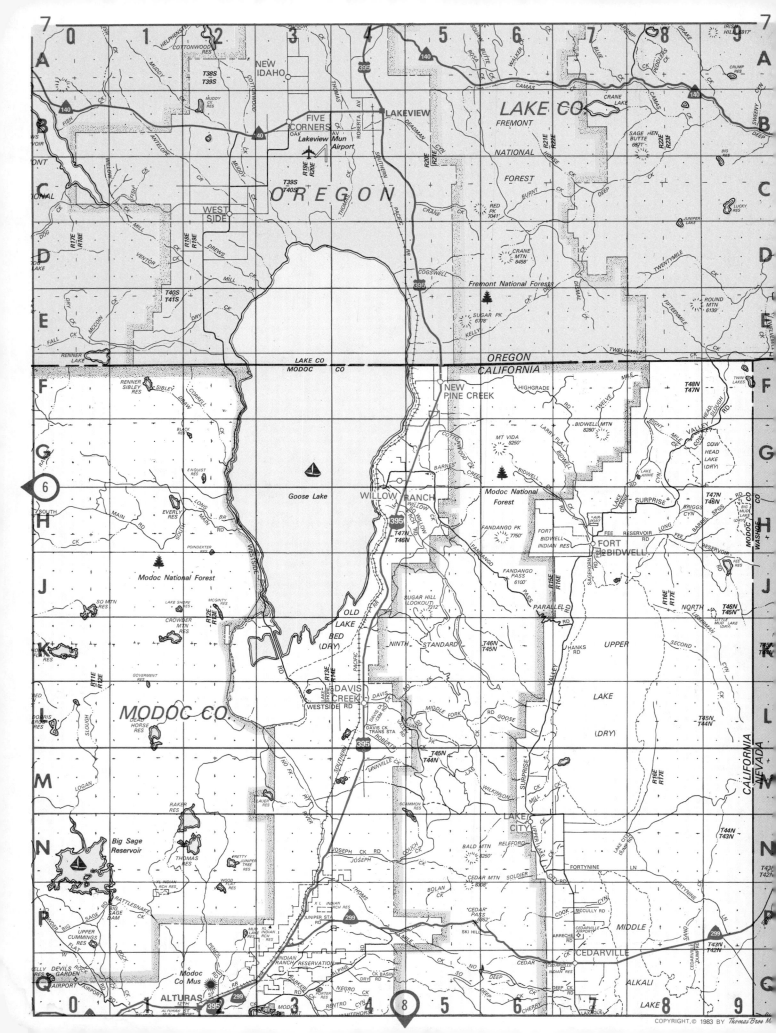

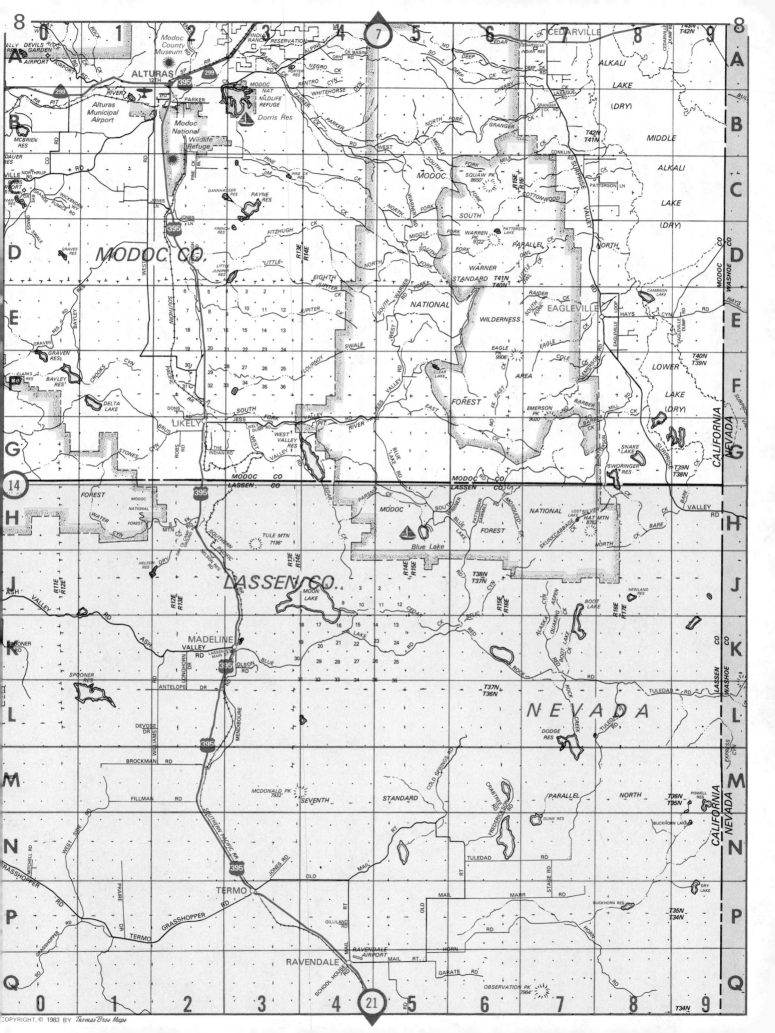

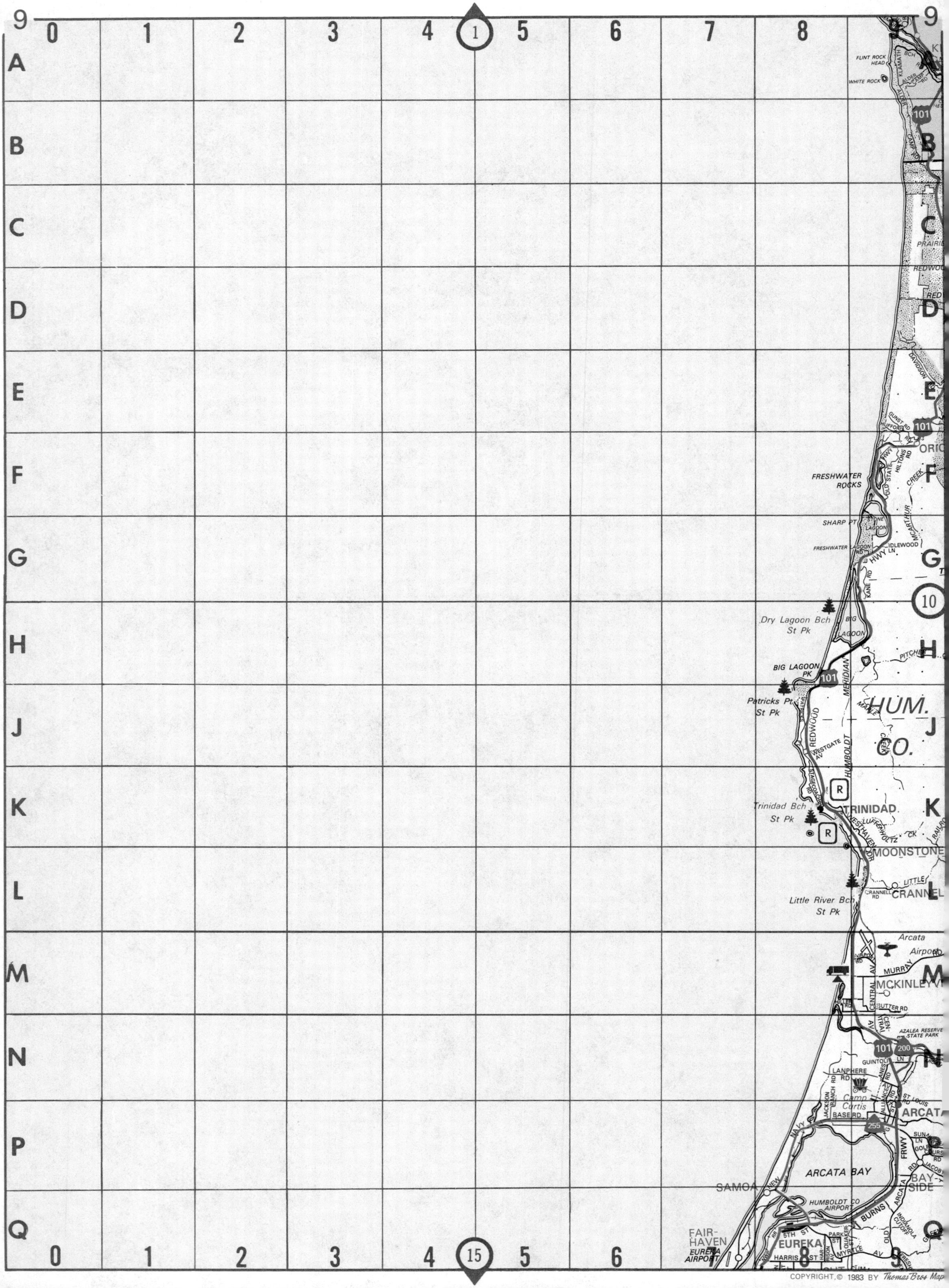

| | 0 | 1 | 2 | 3 | 4 ① 5 | 6 | 7 | 8 | 9 |

A

B

C

D

E

F

FRESHWATER ROCKS

G

H

Dry Lagoon Bch St Pk

BIG LAGOON PK

Patricks Pt St Pk

J

HUM. CO.

K

Trinidad Bch St Pk

TRINIDAD

MOONSTONE

L

Little River Bch St Pk

CRANNEL

M

Arcata Airport

MCKINLEY

N

AZALEA RESERVE STATE PARK

LANPHERE RD

Camp Curtis BASE RD

ARCAT

P

ARCATA BAY

BAY-SIDE

SAMOA

HUMBOLDT CO AIRPORT

BURNS

Q

FAIR-HAVEN

EUREKA

EUREKA AIRPORT

| | 0 | 1 | 2 | 3 | 4 ⑮ 5 | 6 | 7 | 8 | 9 |

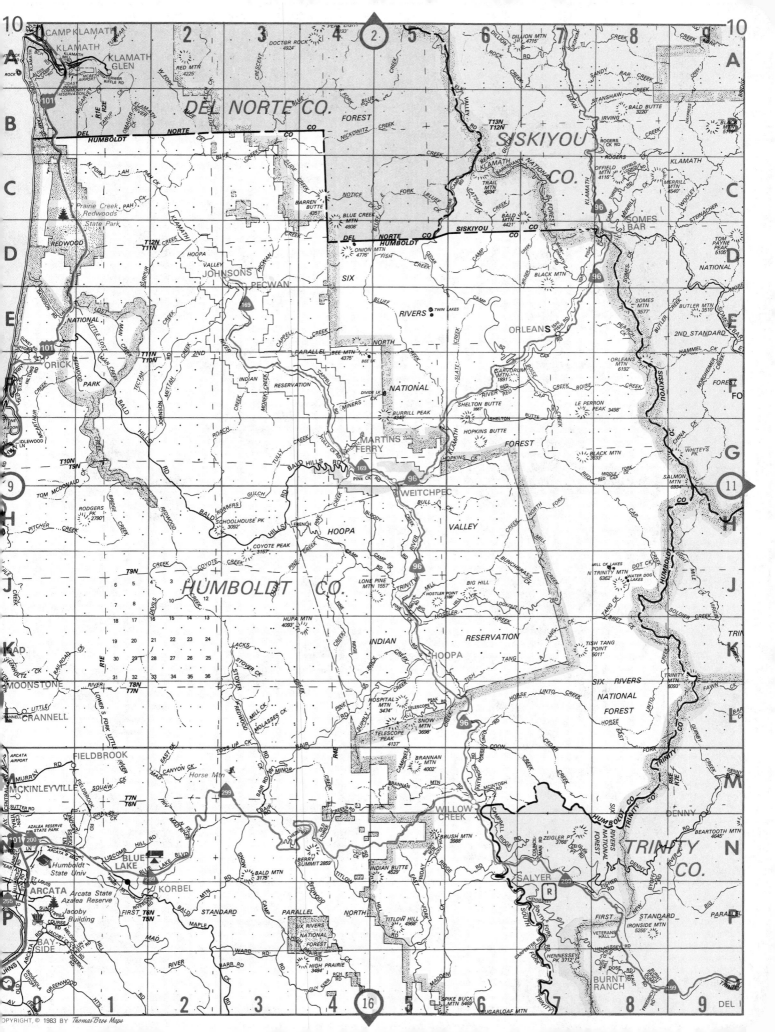

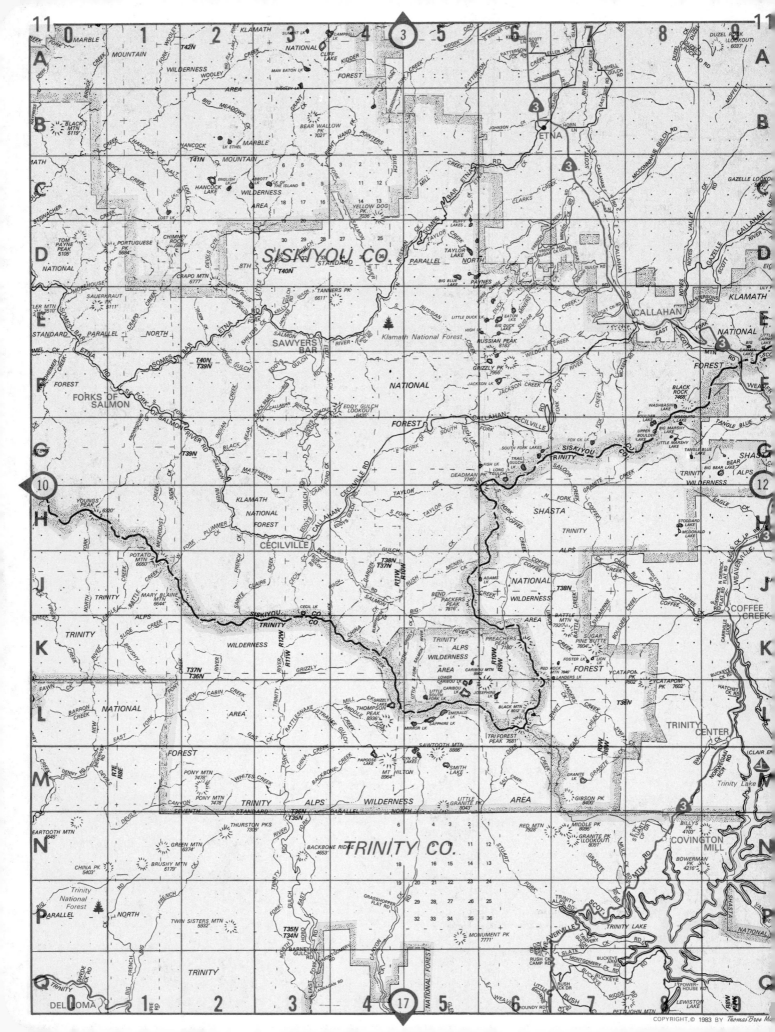

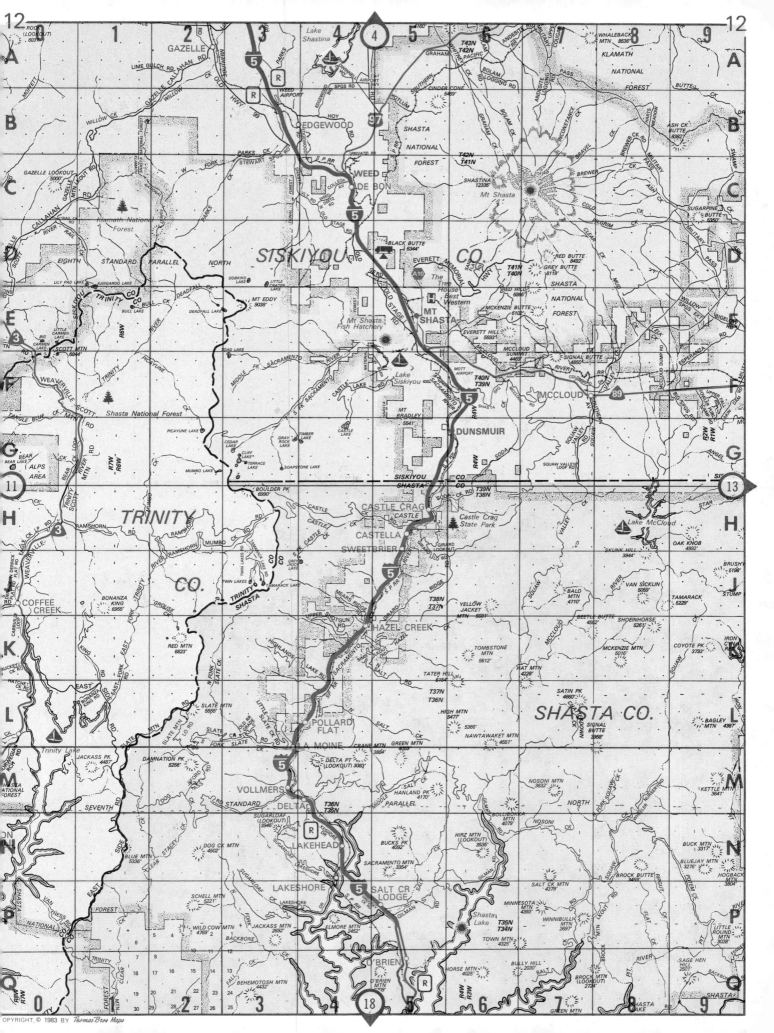

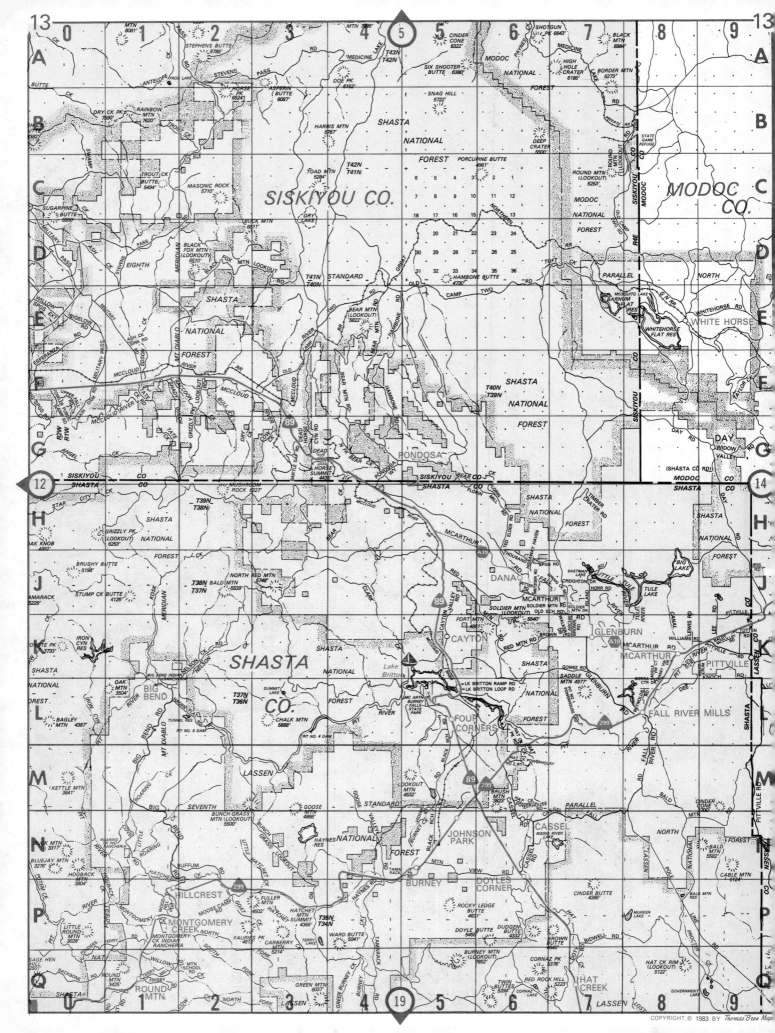

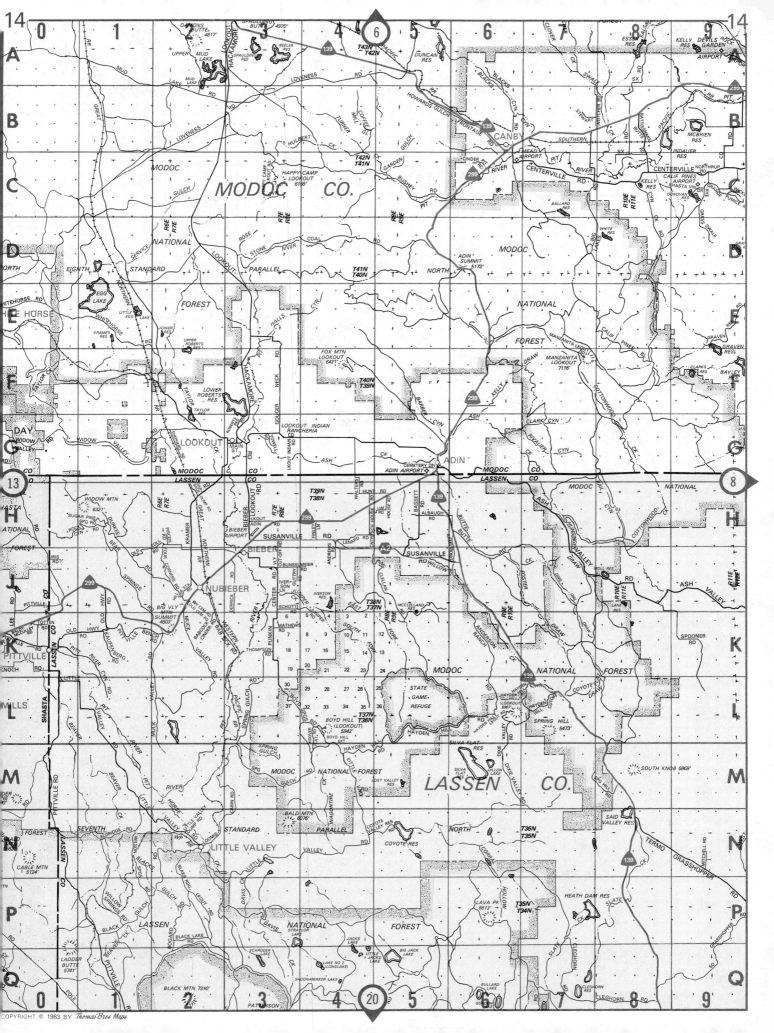

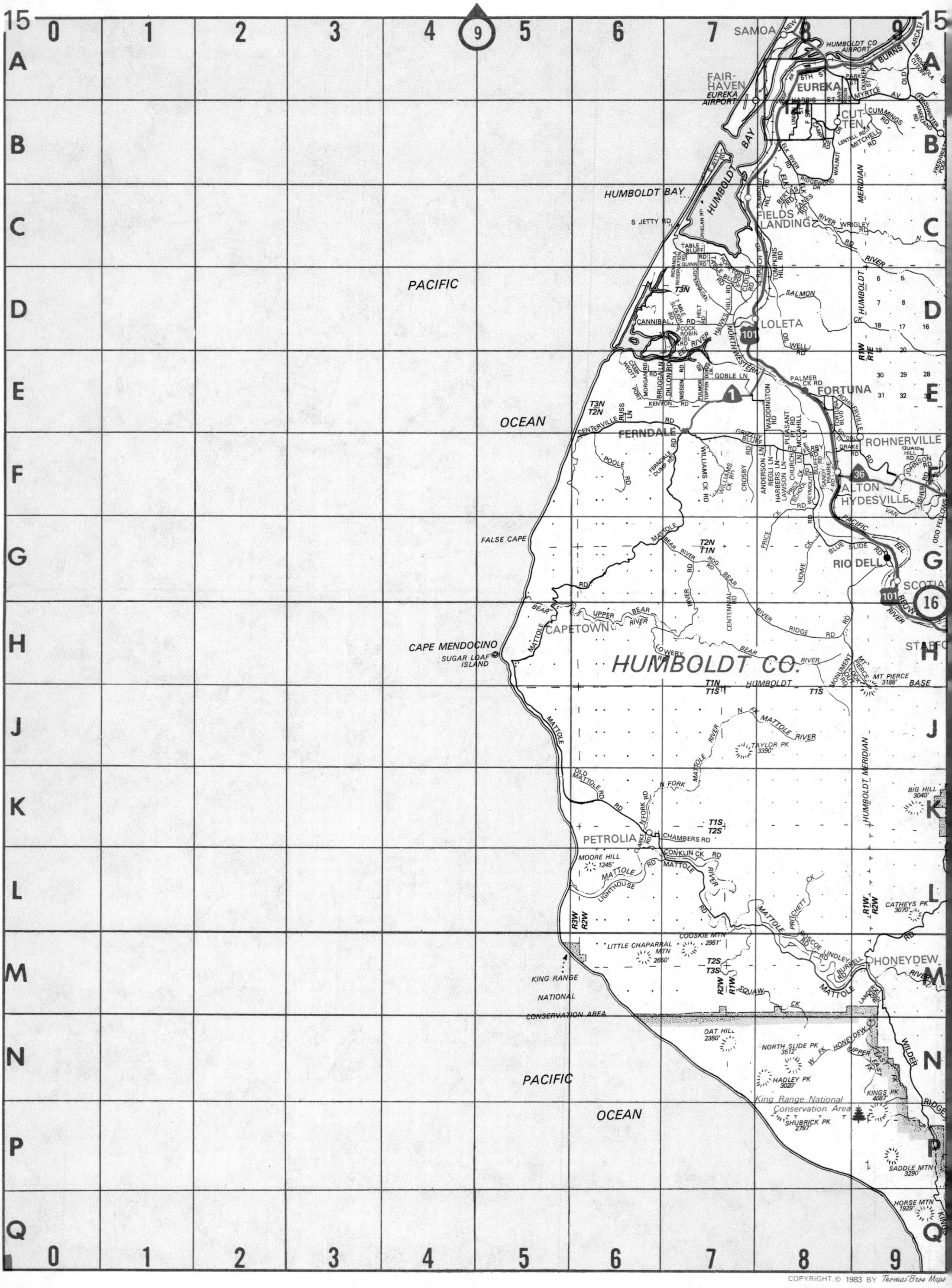

PACIFIC

OCEAN

SAMOA
HUMBOLDT CO. AIRPORT
BURNS
FAIR-HAVEN
EUREKA
EUREKA AIRPORT
CUT-TEN
CUMMINGS

HUMBOLDT BAY
S JETTY RD
FIELDS LANDING
RIVER WRIGLEY
MERIDIAN

TABLE BLUFF
CANNIBAL
LOLETA
101

FORTUNA
ROHNERVILLE
PALMER CK RD
WADDINGTON

FERNDALE
T3N T2N
RUSS LN
CENTERVILLE RD
DILLON RD
GRIFFITH BLUFF
ALTON
HYDESVILLE
36

POOLE RD
FERNDALE DUMP RD
WILLIAMS CK RD
CROSBY
PRICE

FALSE CAPE
MATTOLE
T2N T1N
BEAR RIVER
RIDGE RD
BEAR RIVER
HOWE
BLUE SLIDE RD
RIO DELL
SCOTIA
101
16

BEAR RIVER
UPPER BEAR RIVER
CENTENNIAL RIDGE RD
BEAR RIVER
STAFFORD

CAPETOWN
CAPE MENDOCINO
SUGAR LOAF ISLAND
MATTOLE
LOWERY RD

HUMBOLDT CO.
T1N T1S
HUMBOLDT
T1S
MT PIERCE 3188
BASE

N FK MATTOLE RIVER
MATTOLE RIVER
TAYLOR PK 3350
HUMBOLDT MERIDIAN

OLD MATTOLE RD
N FORK
MATTOLE
BIG HILL 3040

PETROLIA
MOORE HILL 1245'
T1S T2S
CHAMBERS RD

CONKLIN CK RD
MATTOLE
MATTOLE LIGHTHOUSE
PRITCHETT
CATHEYS PK 3070
R1W R2W

R2W R3W
LITTLE CHAPARRAL MTN 2660'
COOSKIE MTN 2951'
T2S T3S
BURRELL RD
HONEYDEW
MATTOLE RIVER

KING RANGE
NATIONAL
CONSERVATION AREA
OAT HILL 2350
NORTH SLIDE PK 3612
HONEYDEW
WILDER RIDGE

PACIFIC

OCEAN

HADLEY PK 3020
King Range National Conservation Area
SHUBRICK PK 2797
KINGS PK 4087
KINGS PEAK RIDGE

SADDLE MTN 3290

HORSE MTN 1929

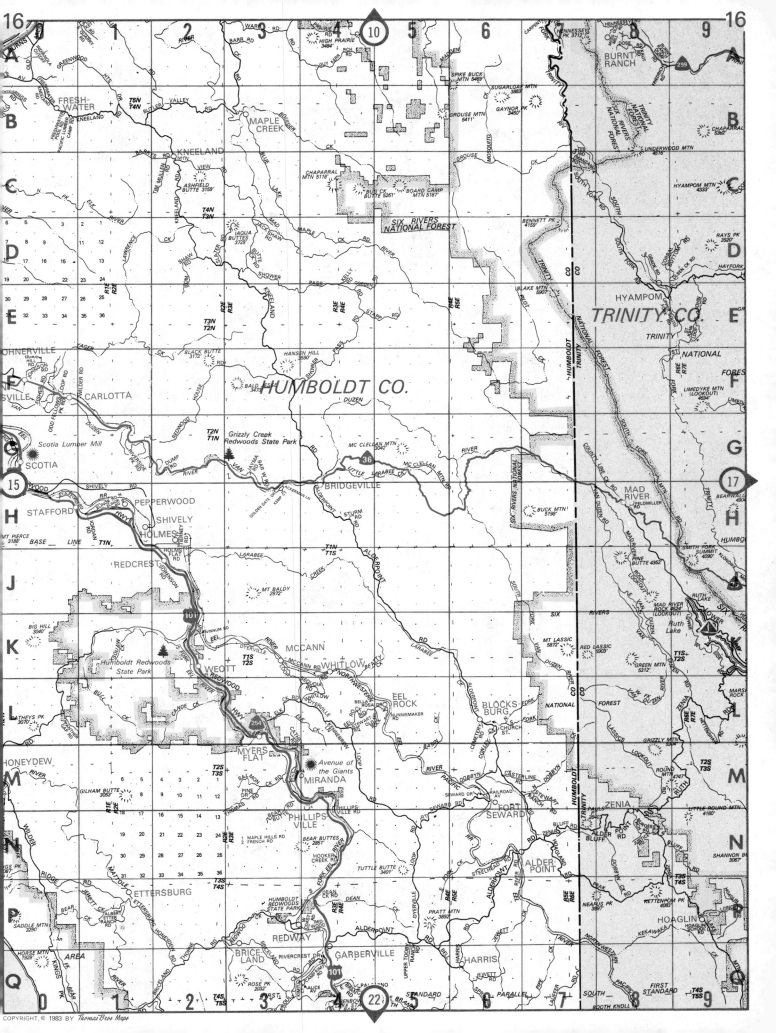

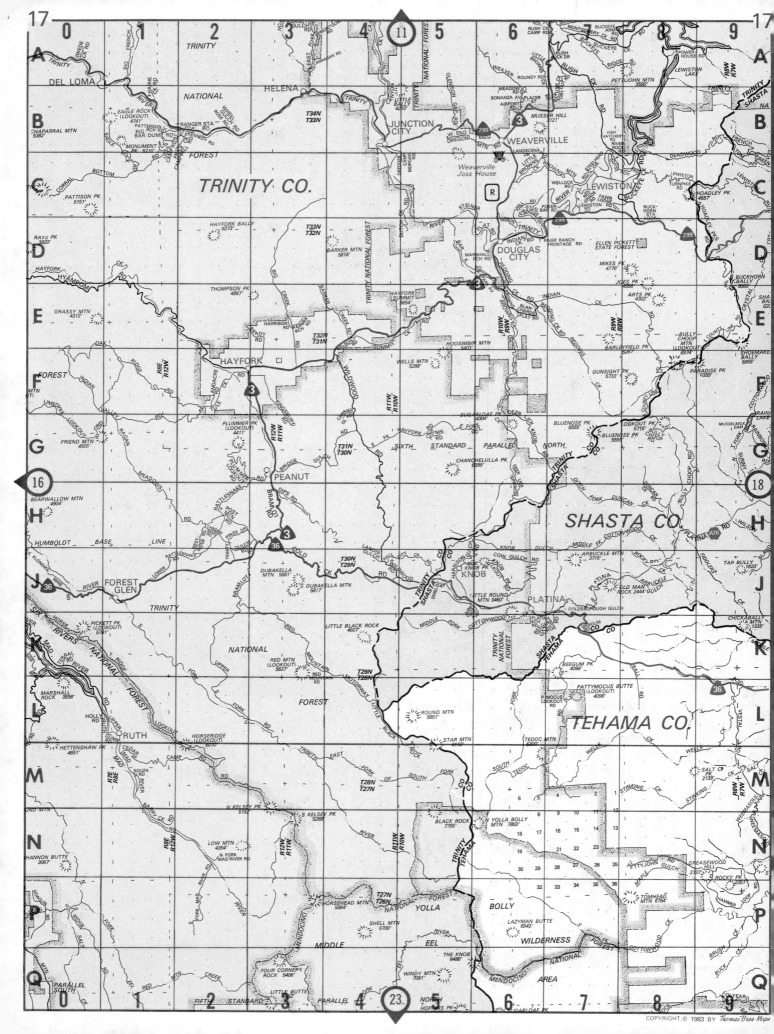

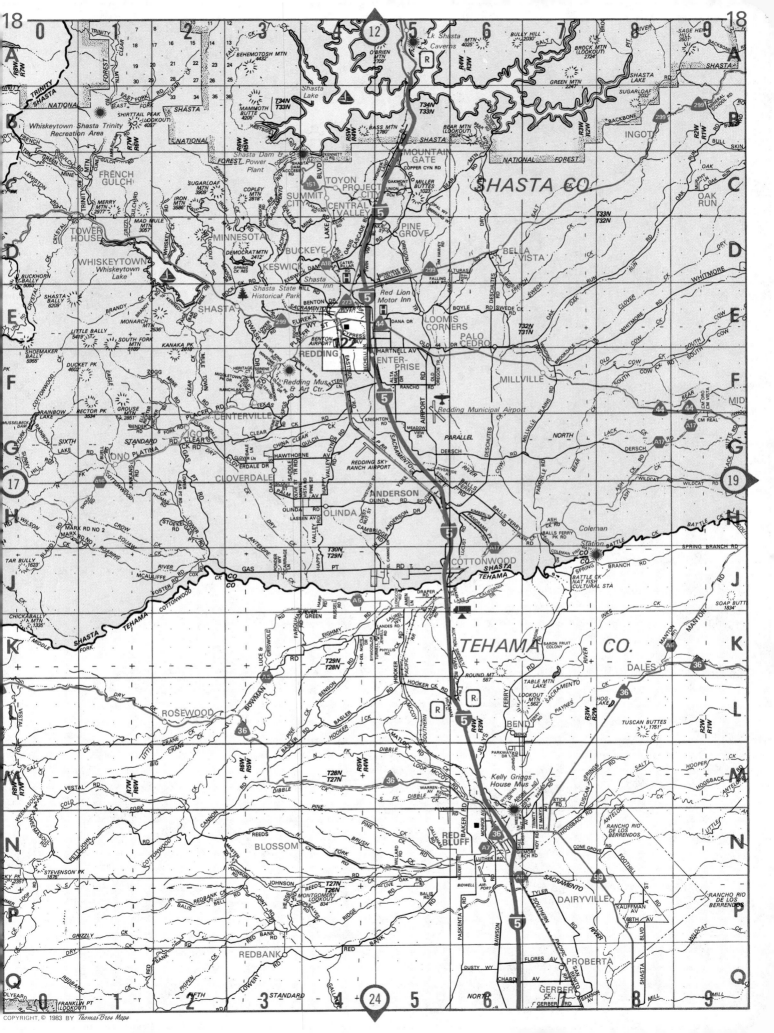

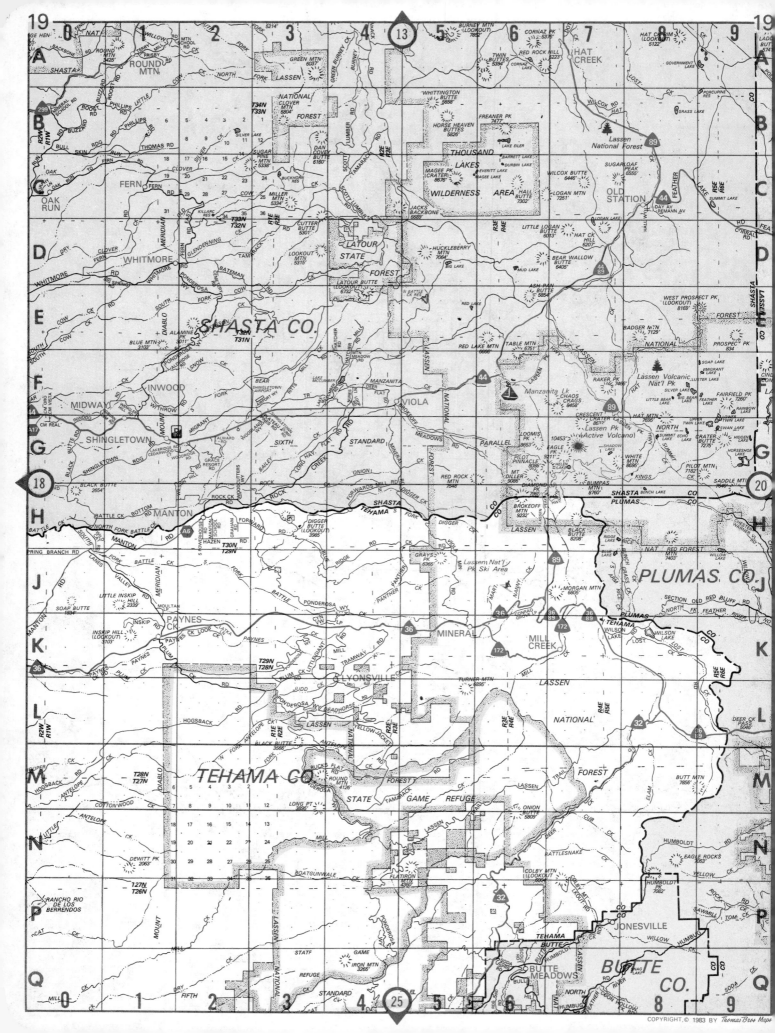

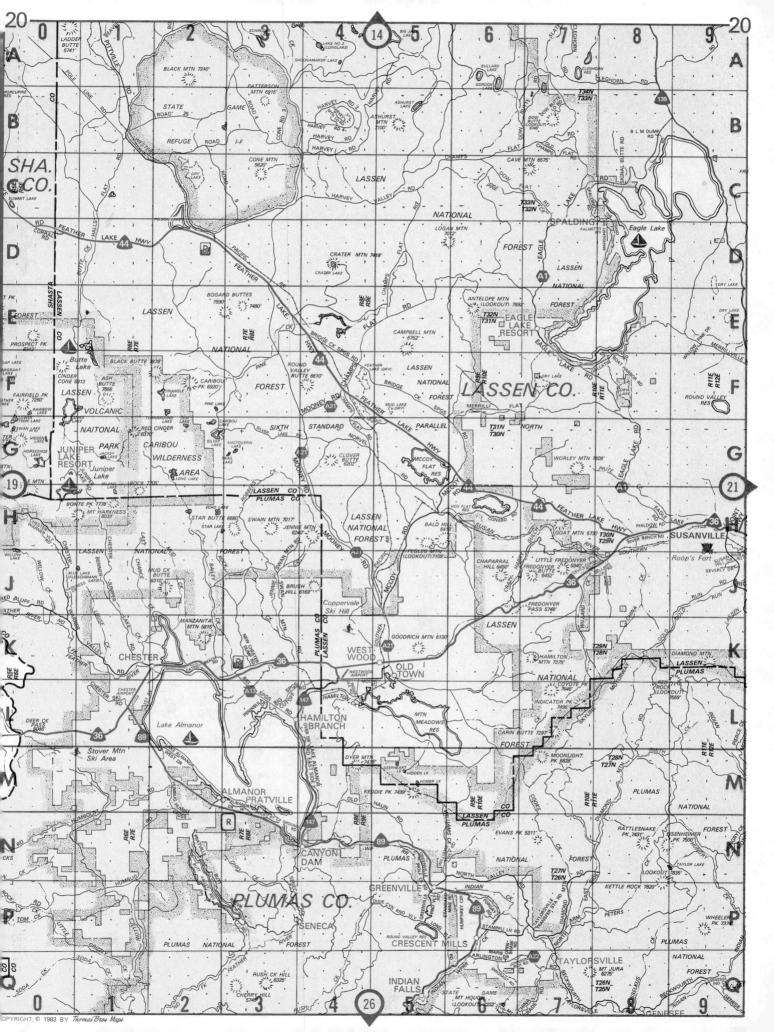

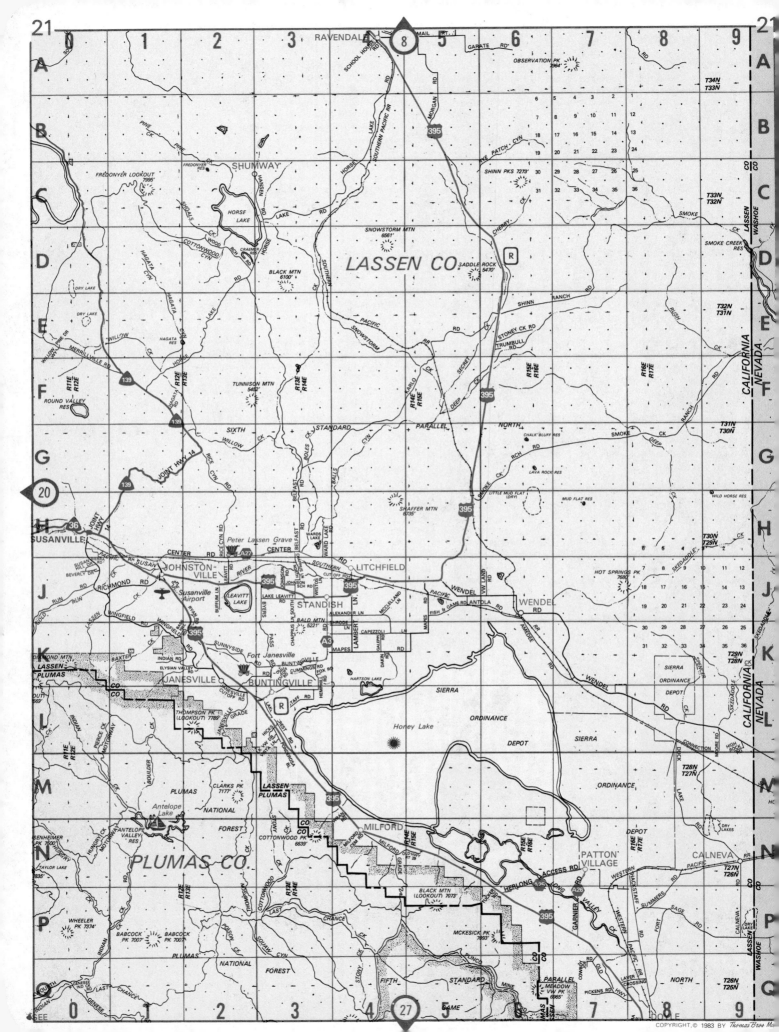

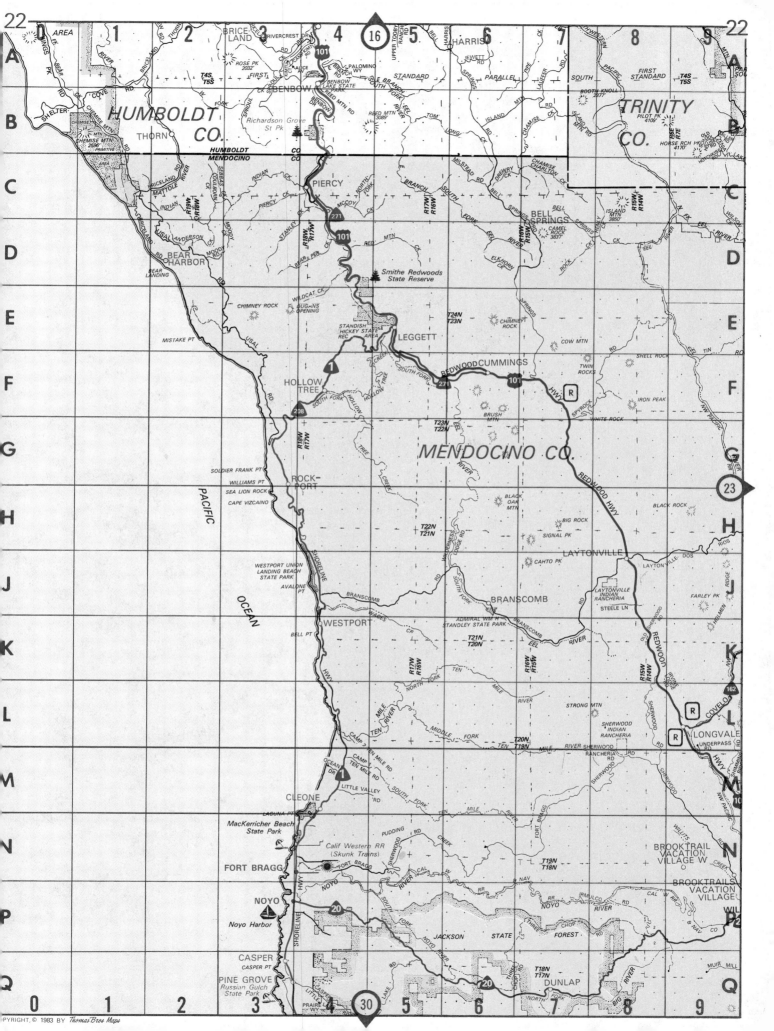

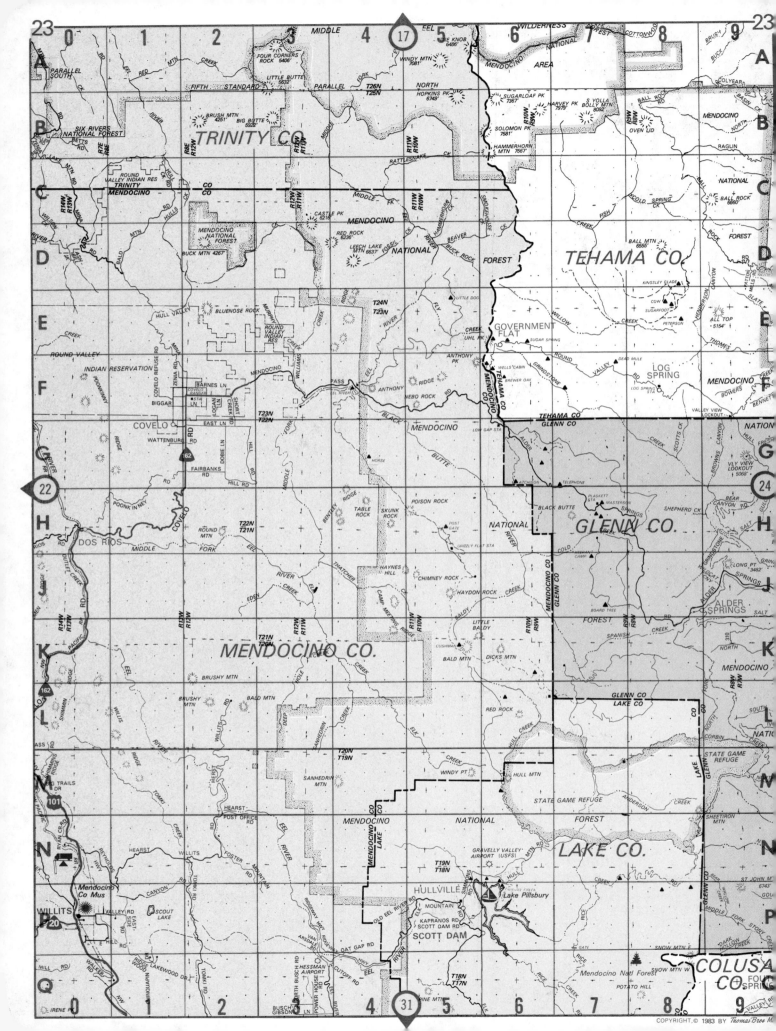

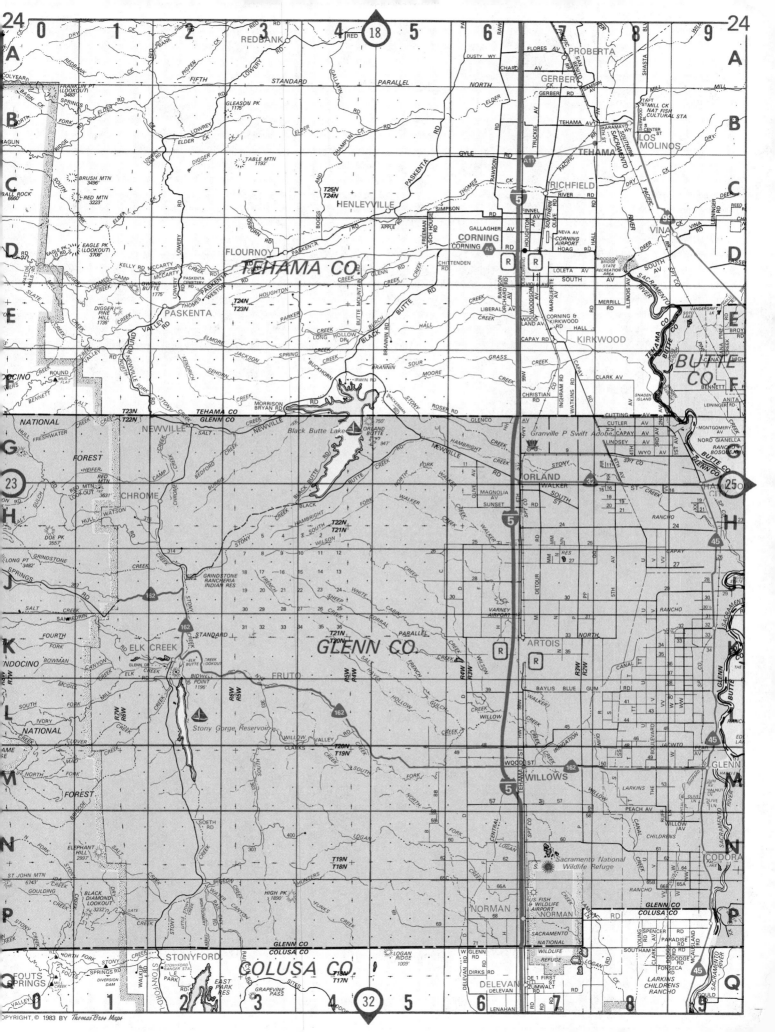

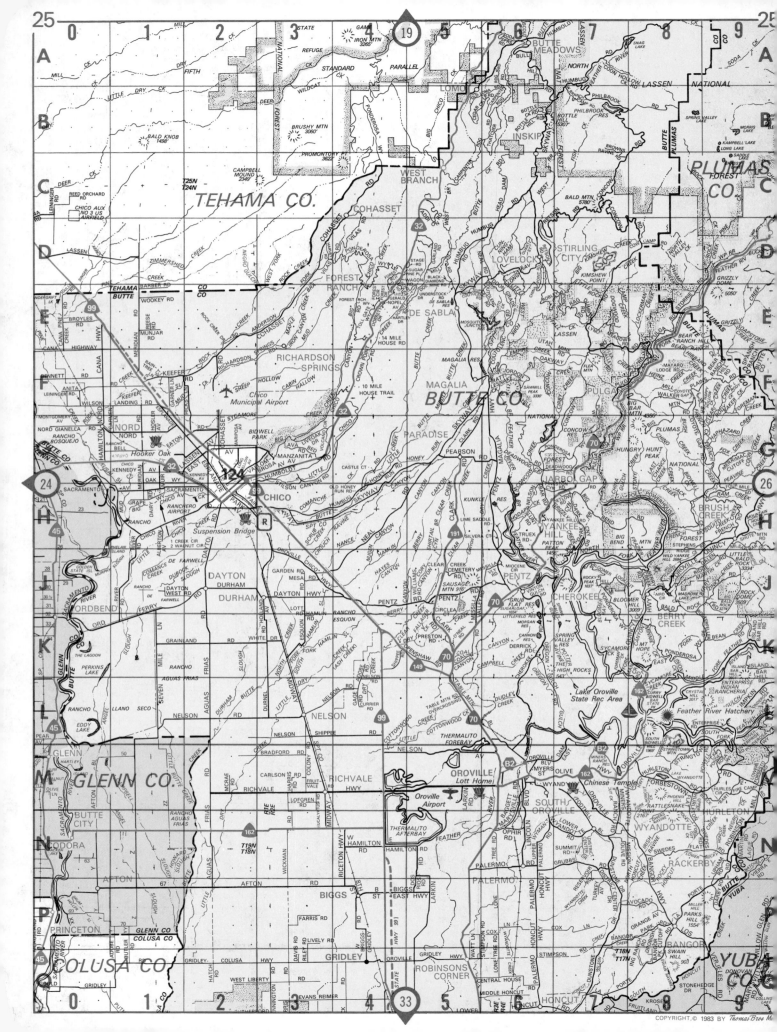

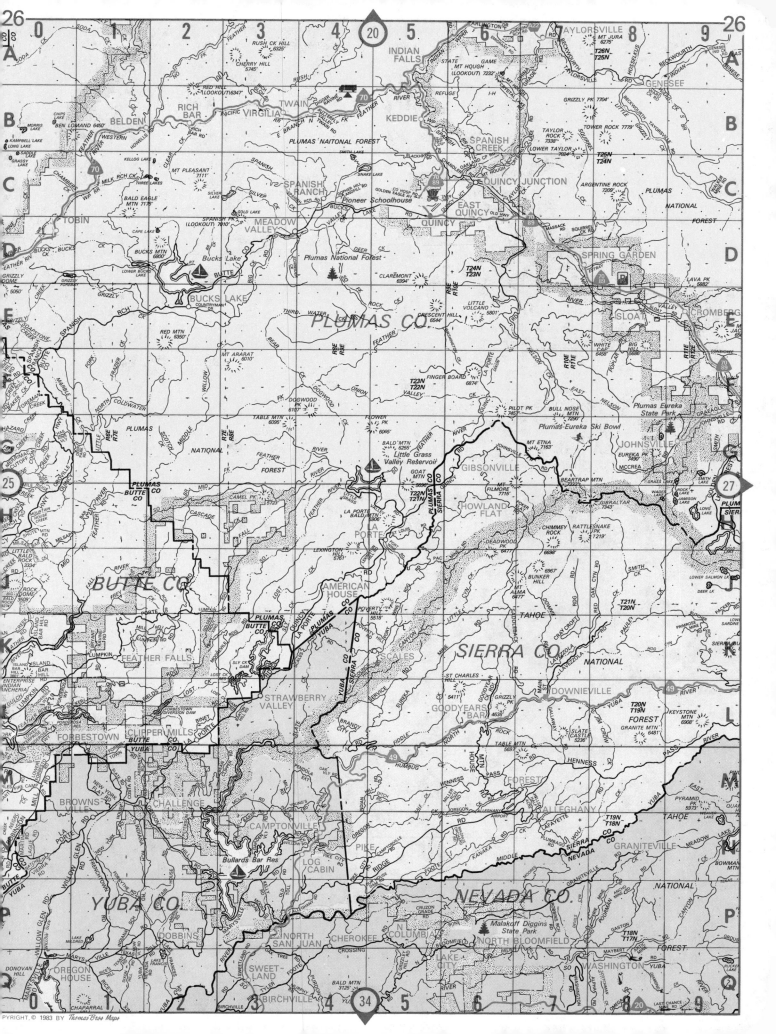

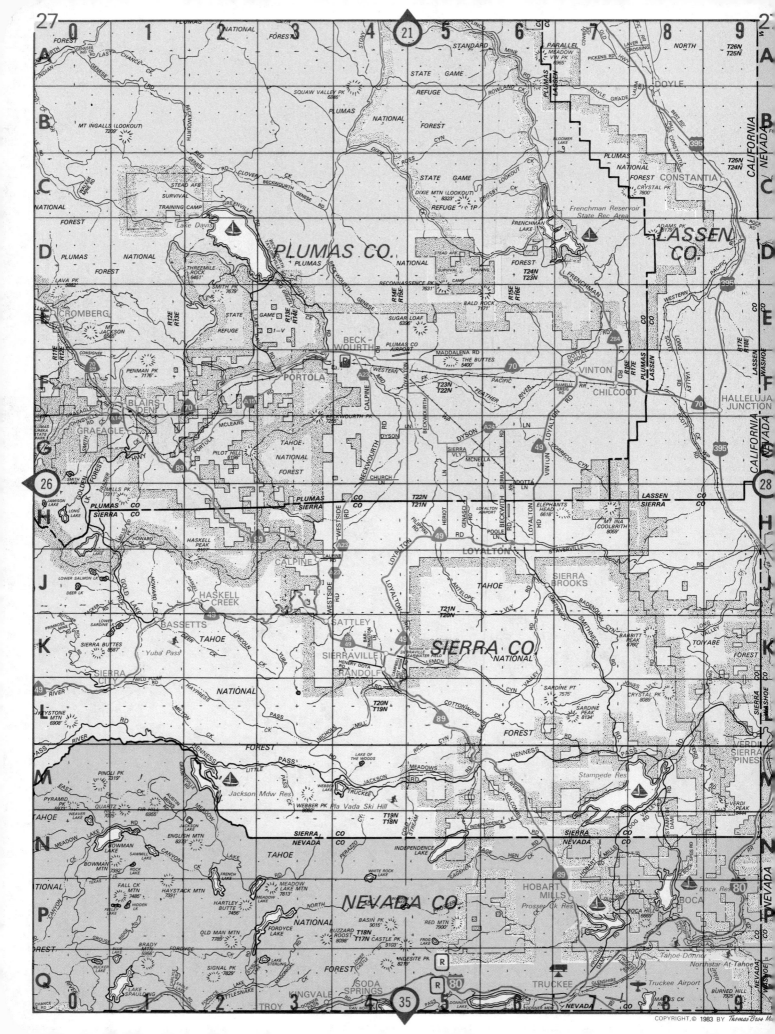

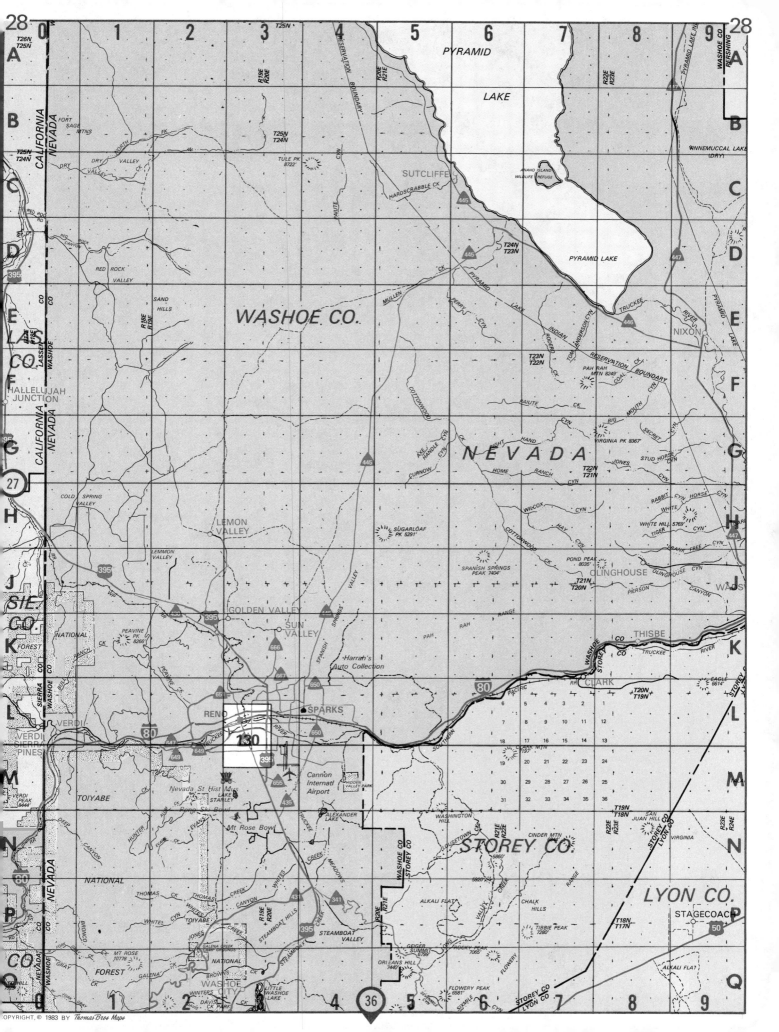

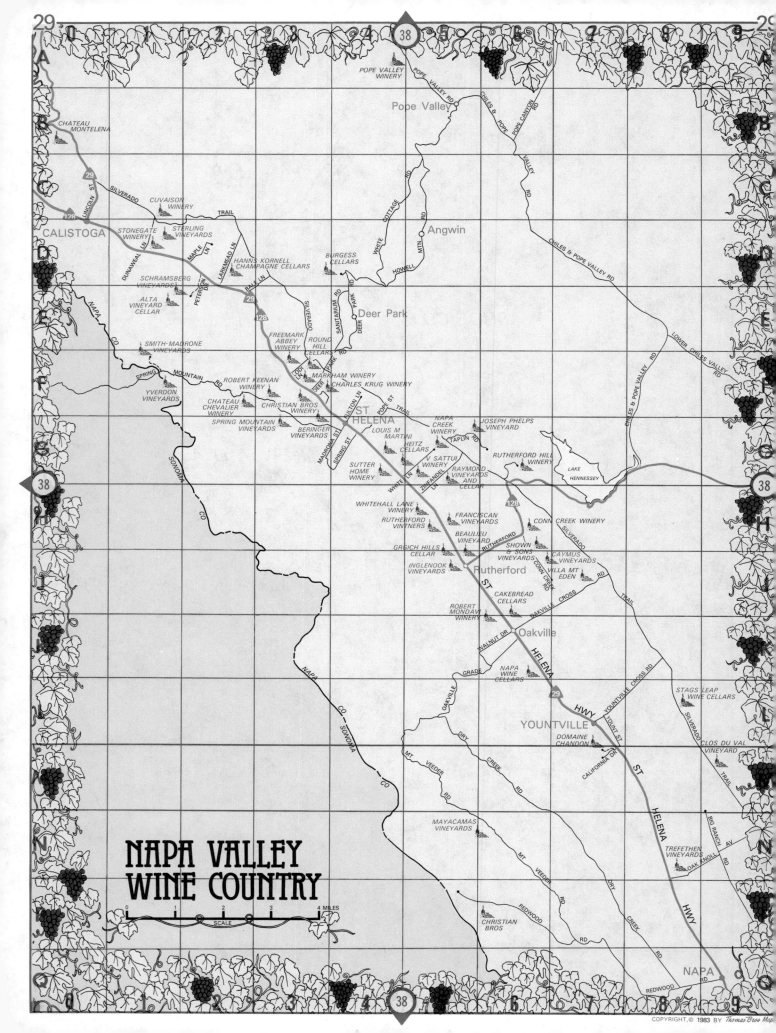

NAPA VALLEY WINE COUNTRY

SCALE 0 1 2 3 4 MILES

COPYRIGHT © 1983 BY Thomas Bros Maps

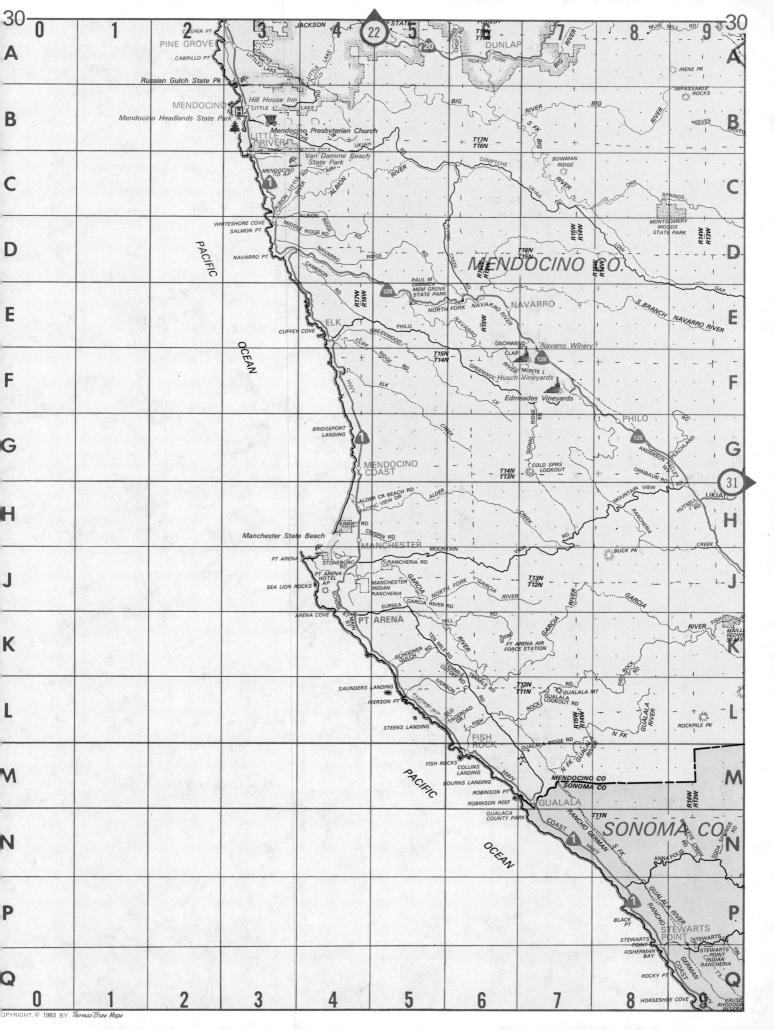

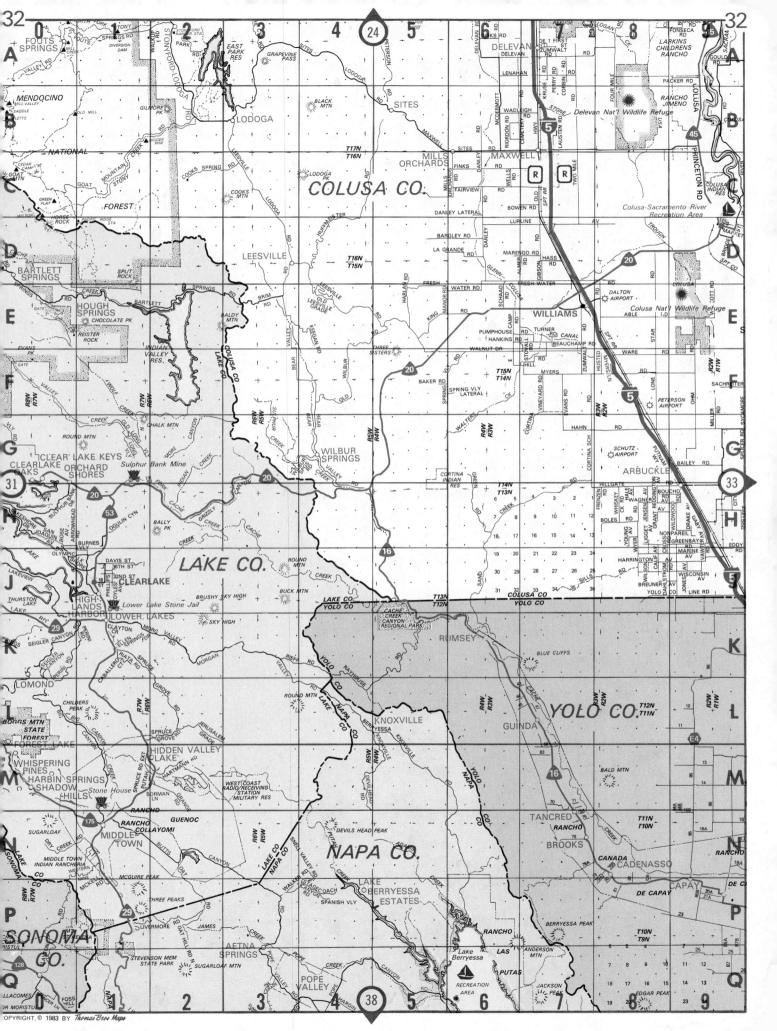

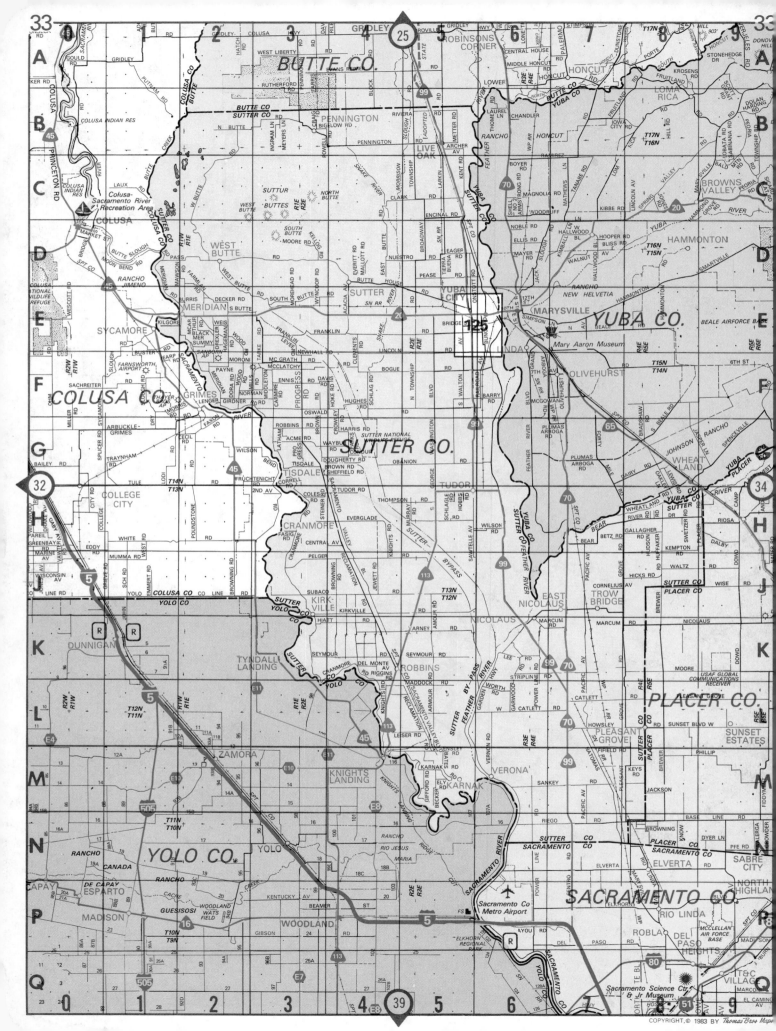

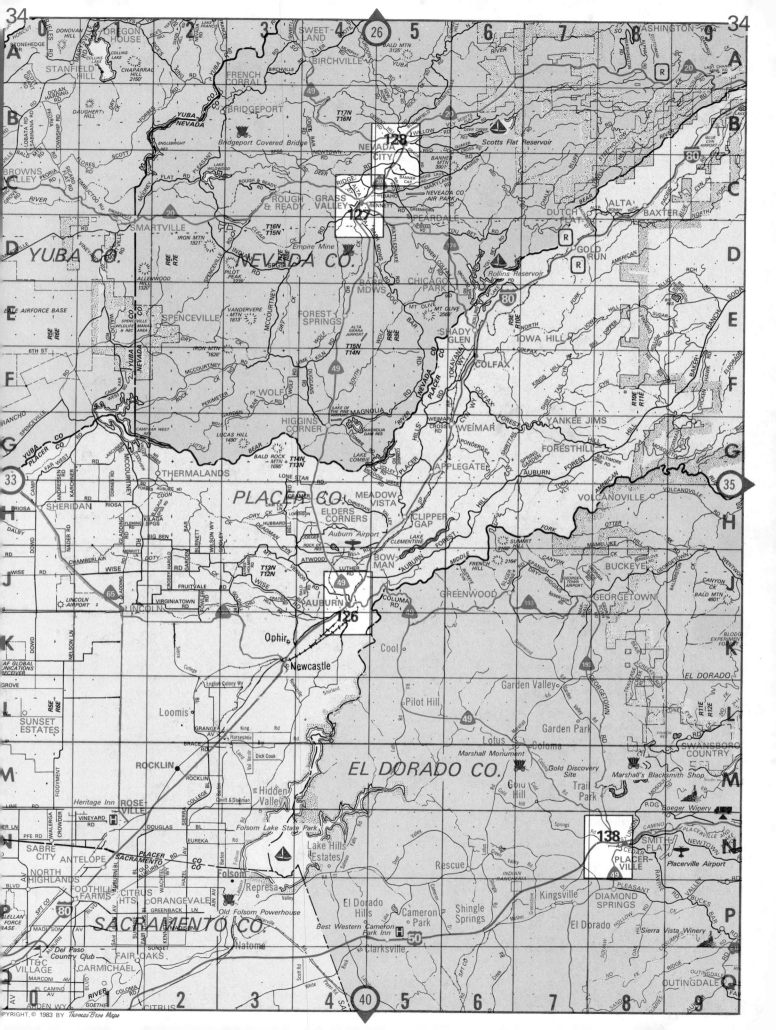

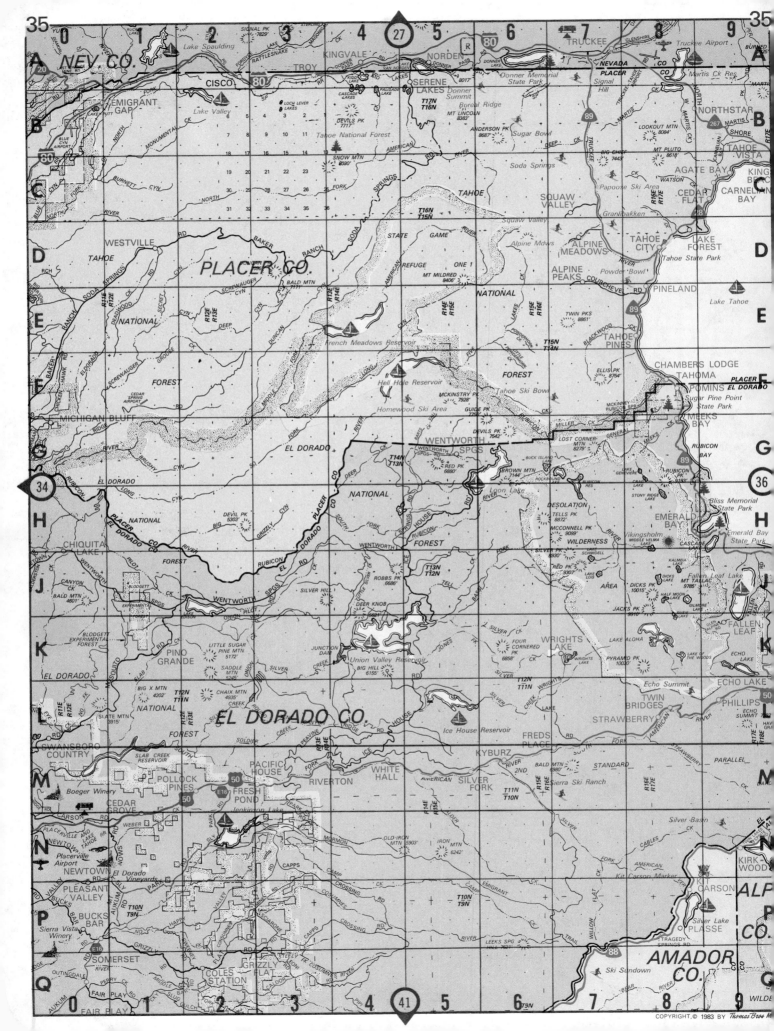

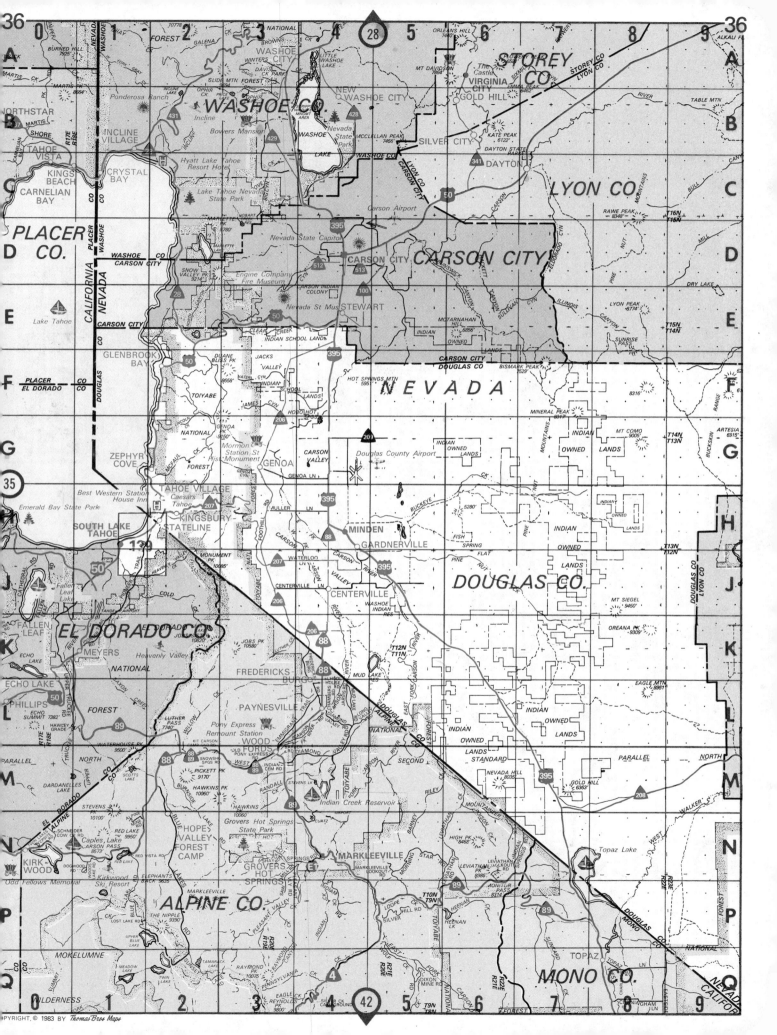

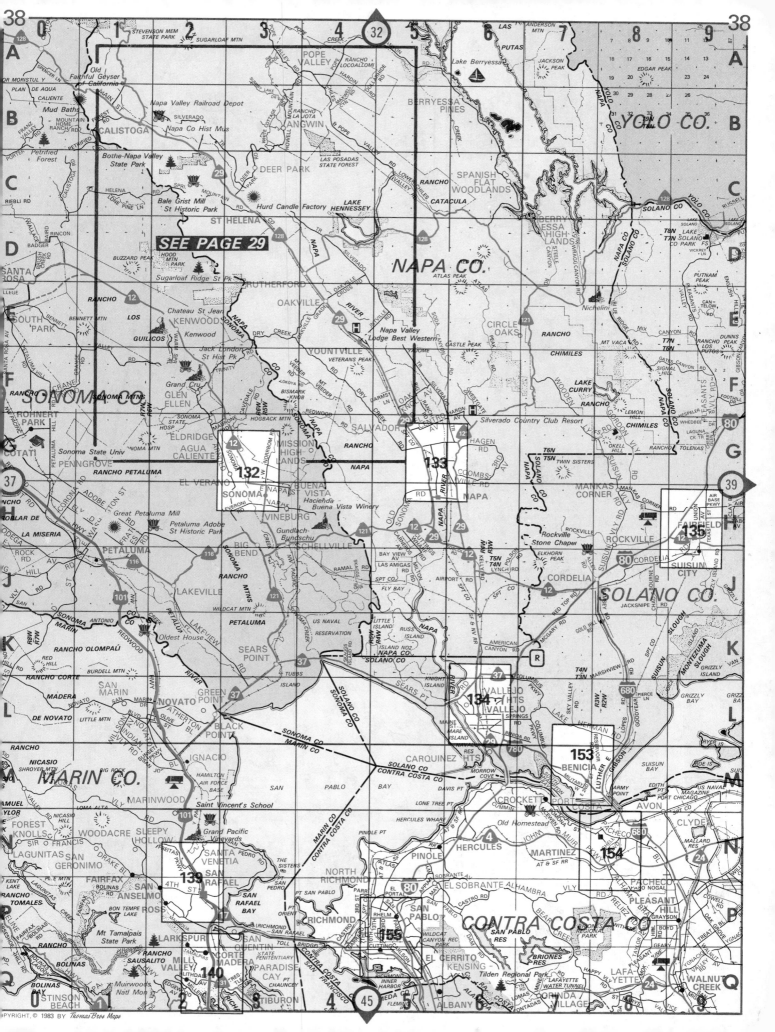

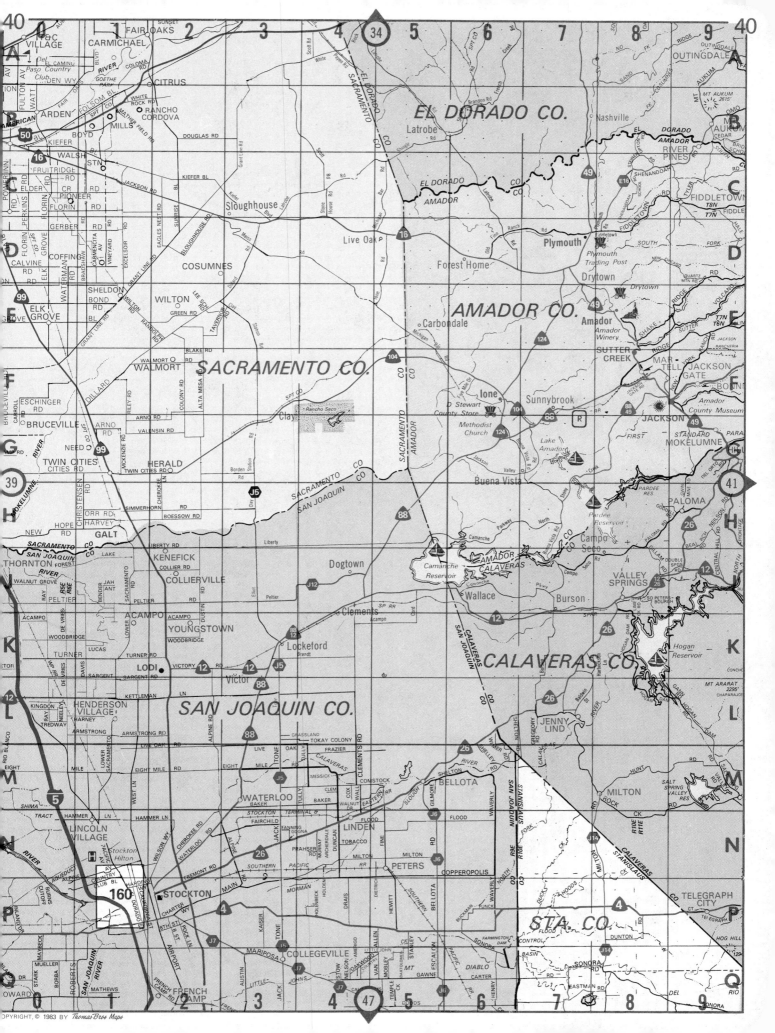

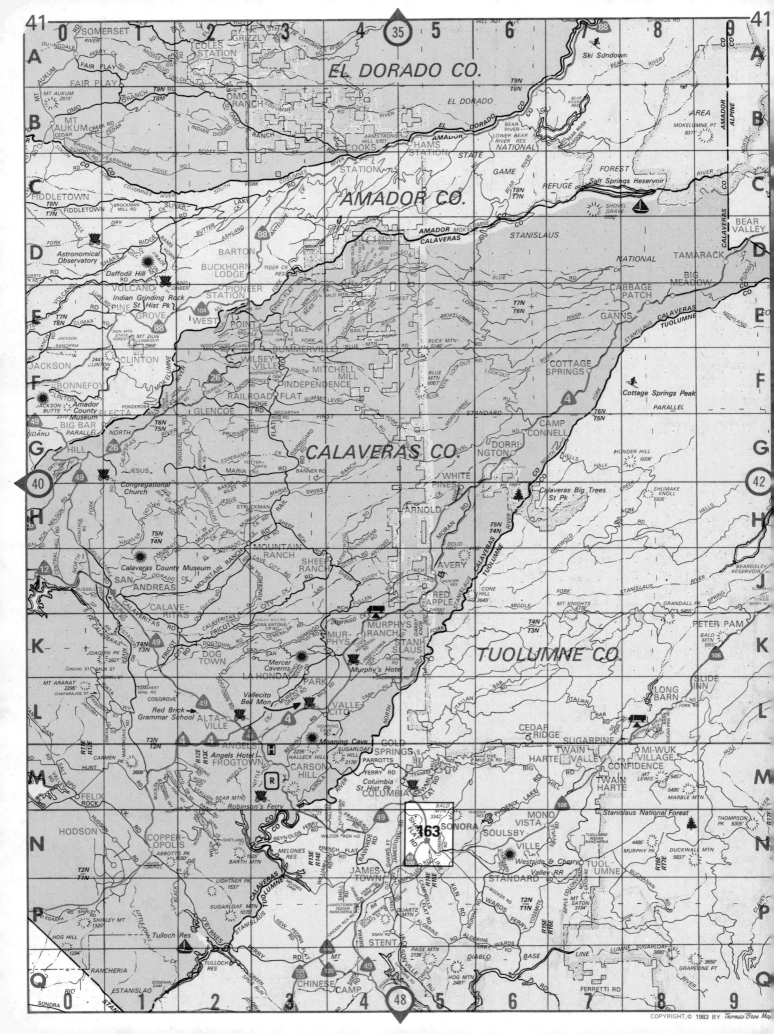

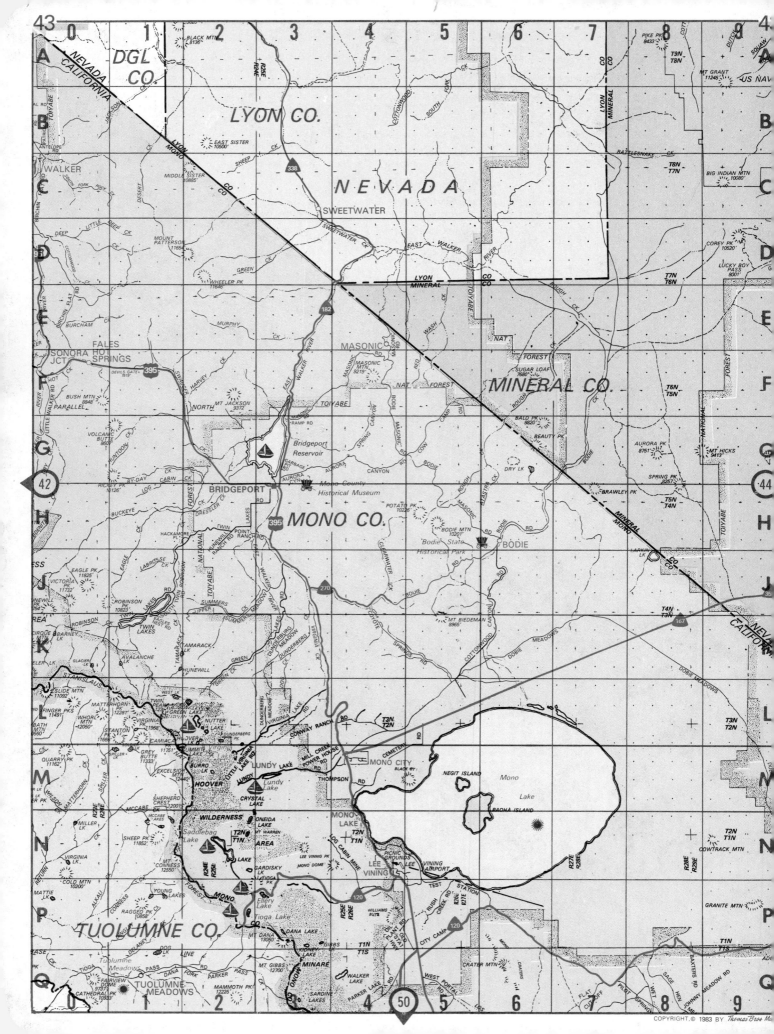

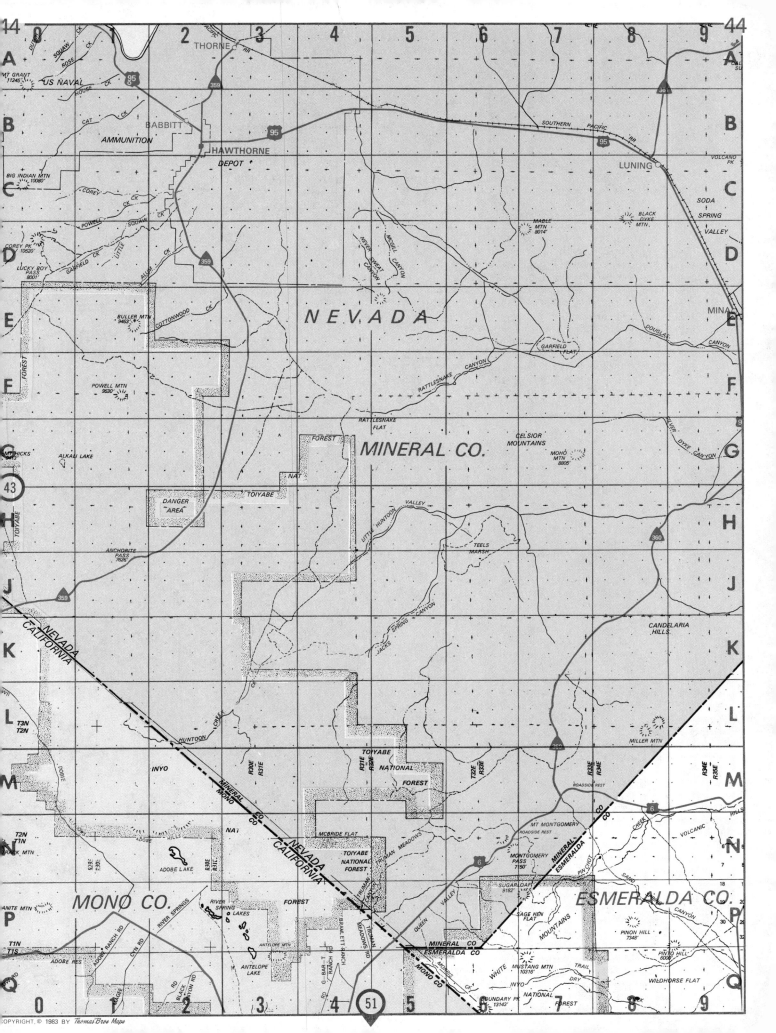

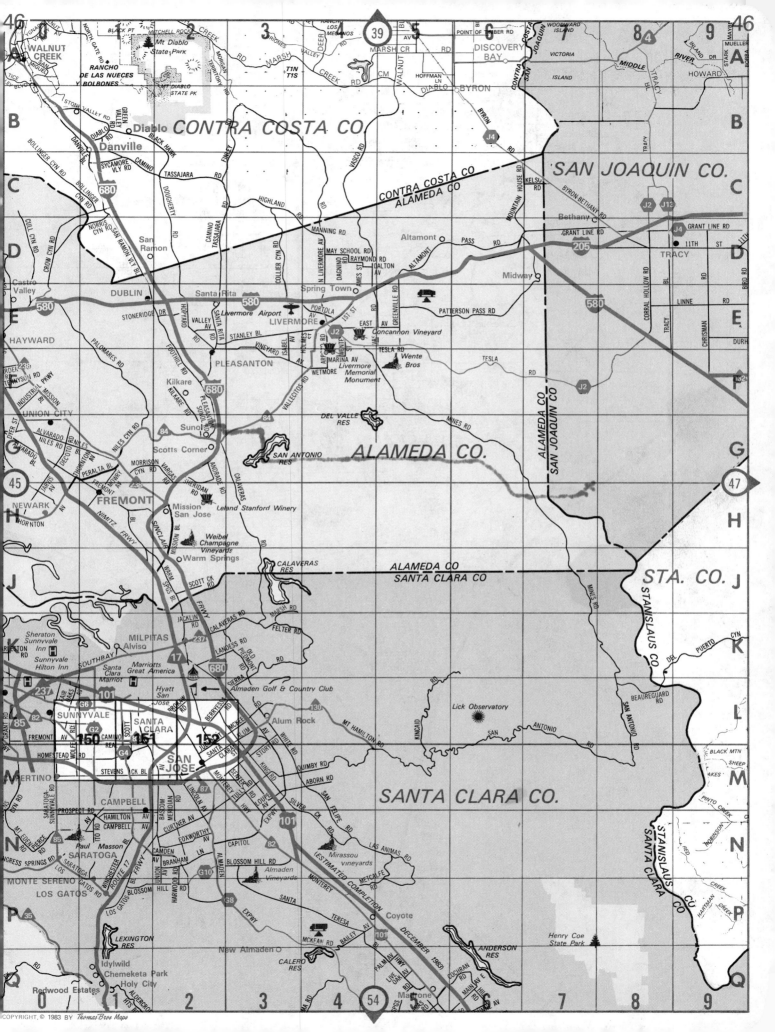

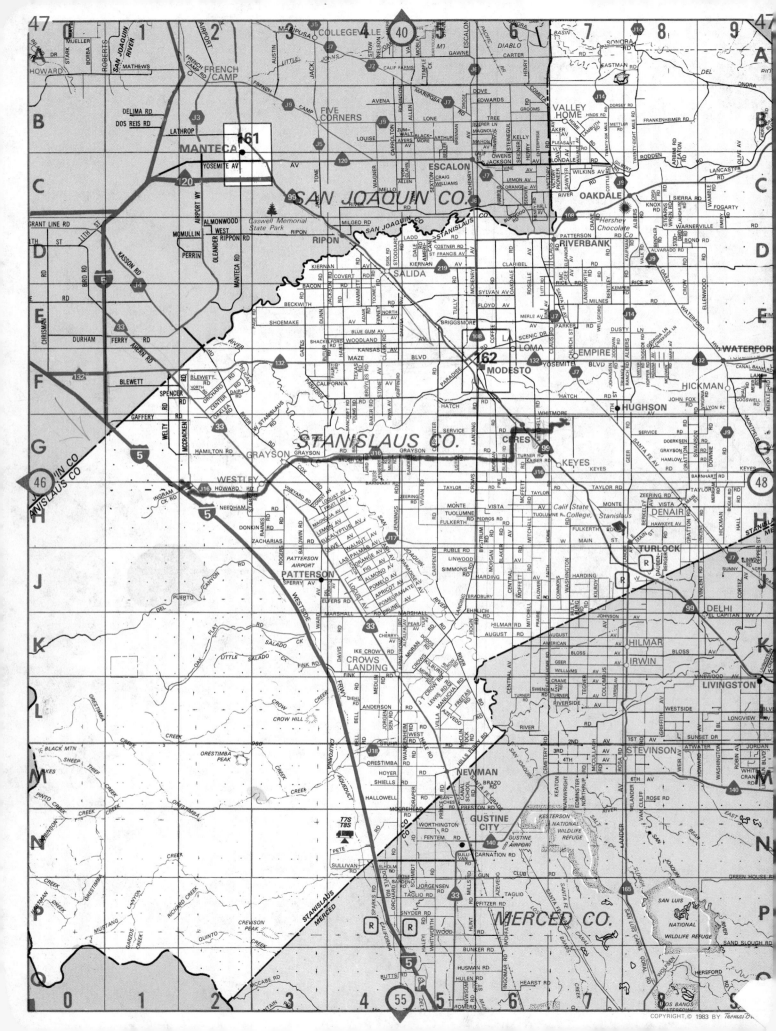

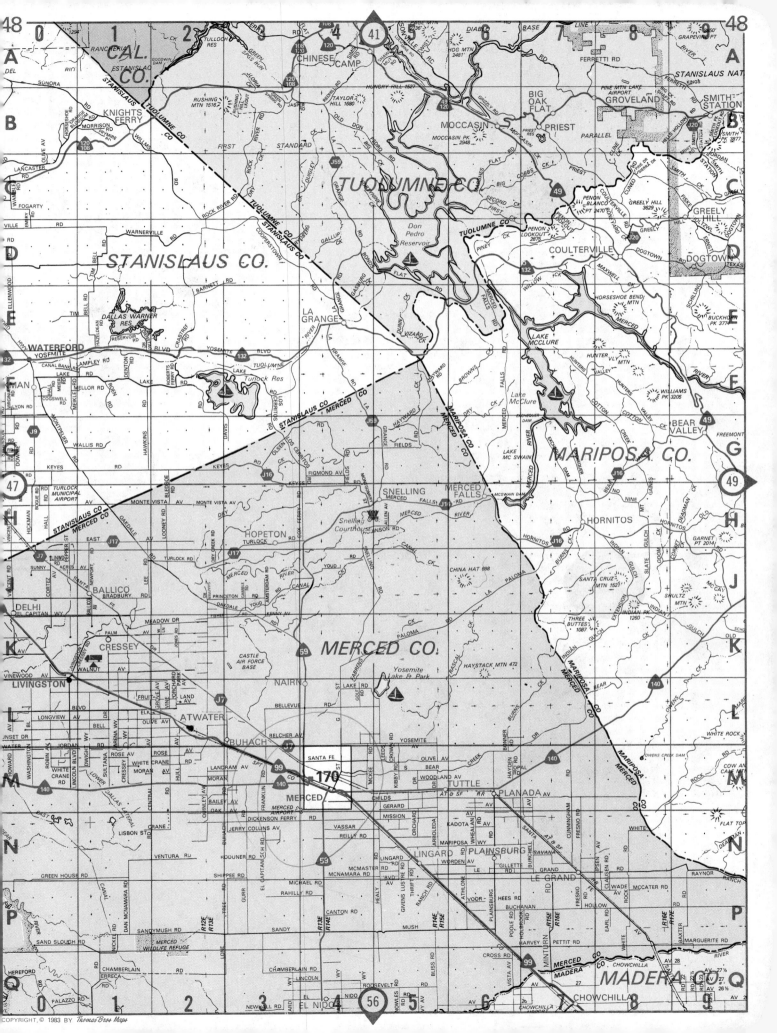

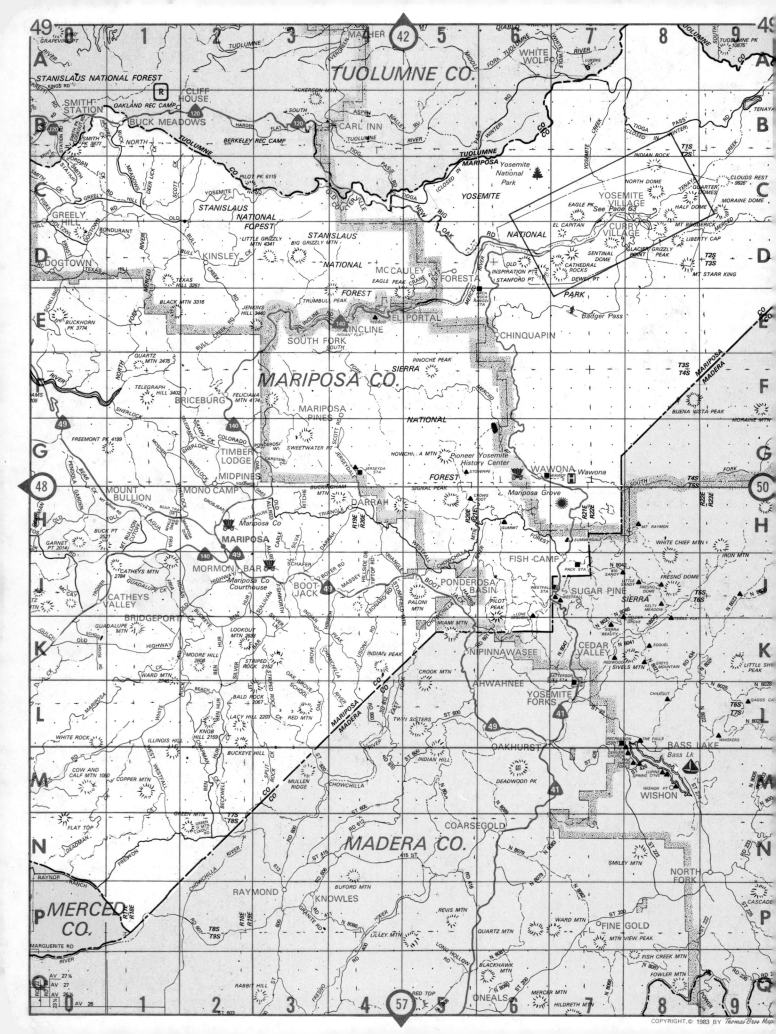

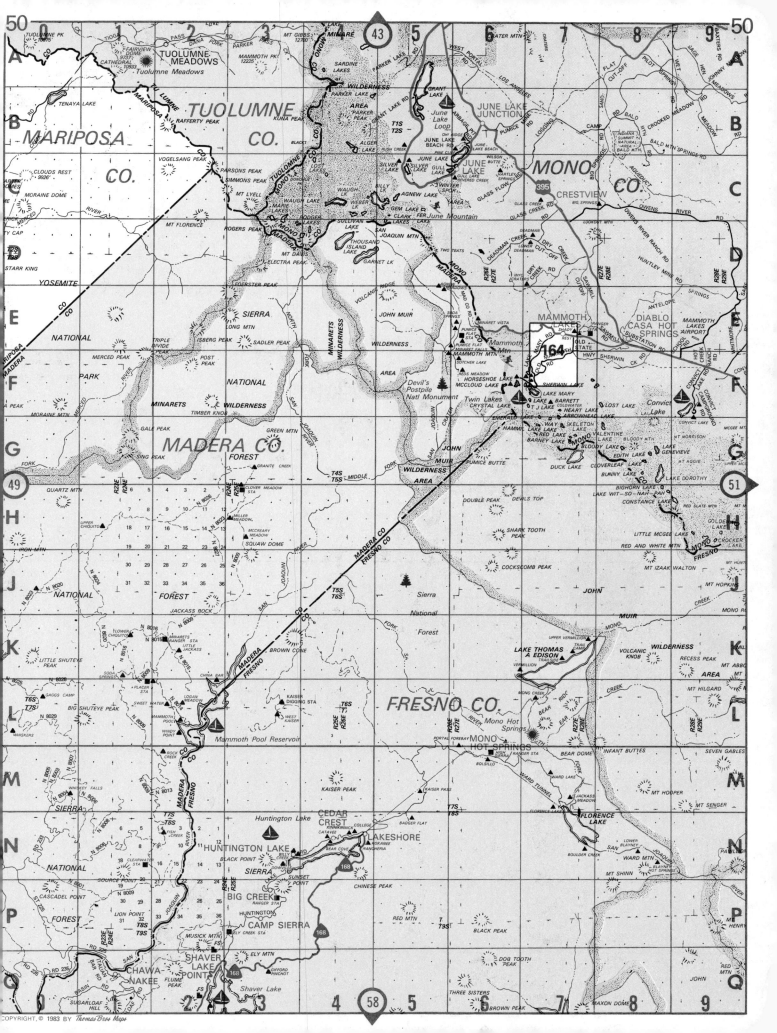

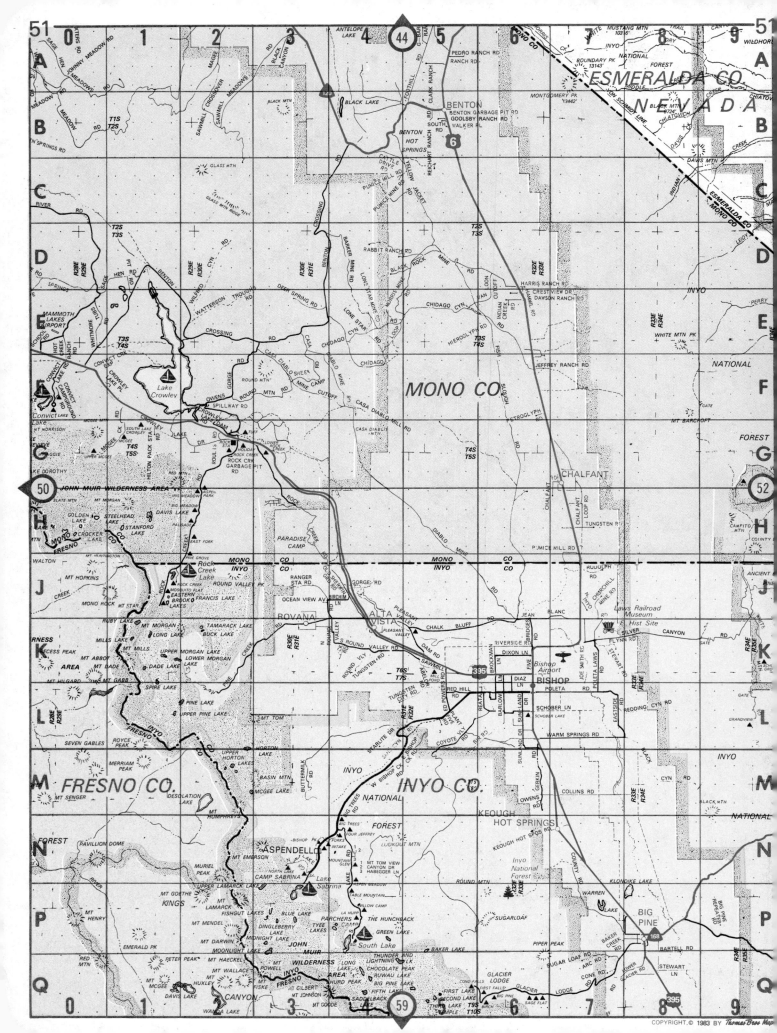

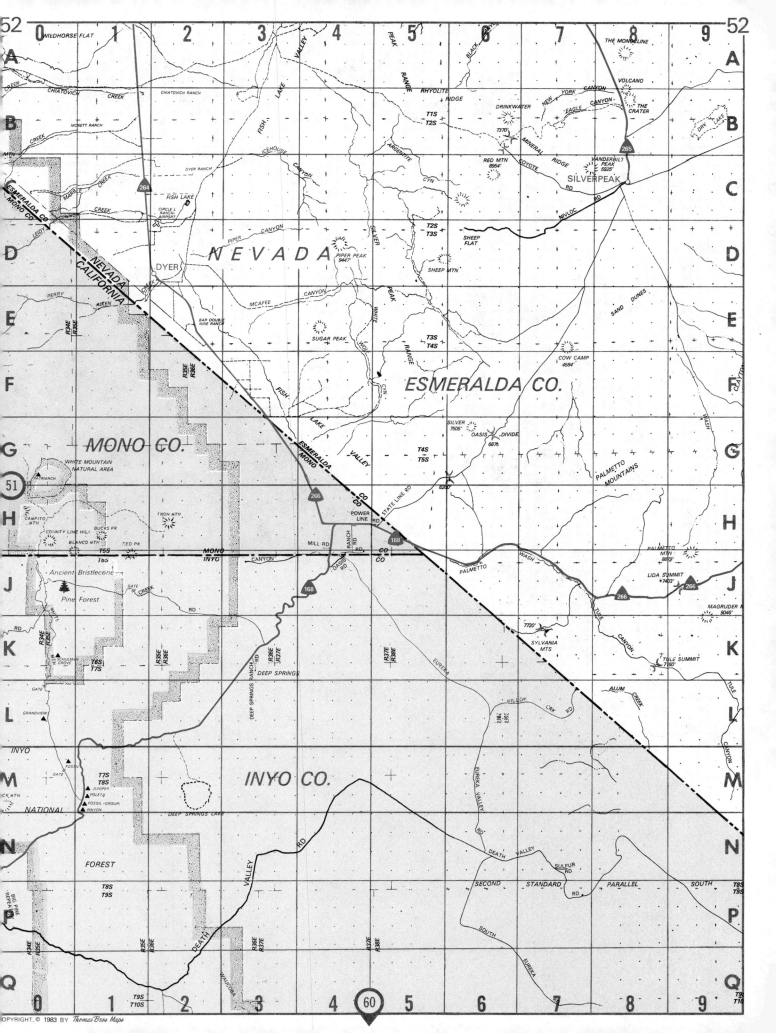

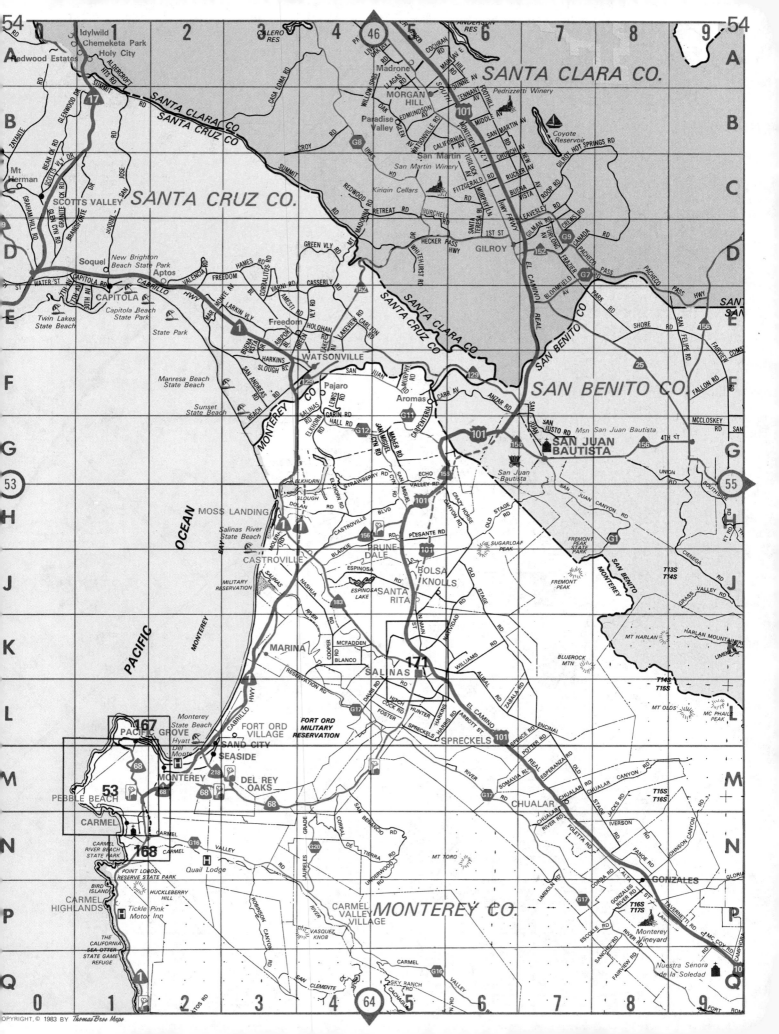

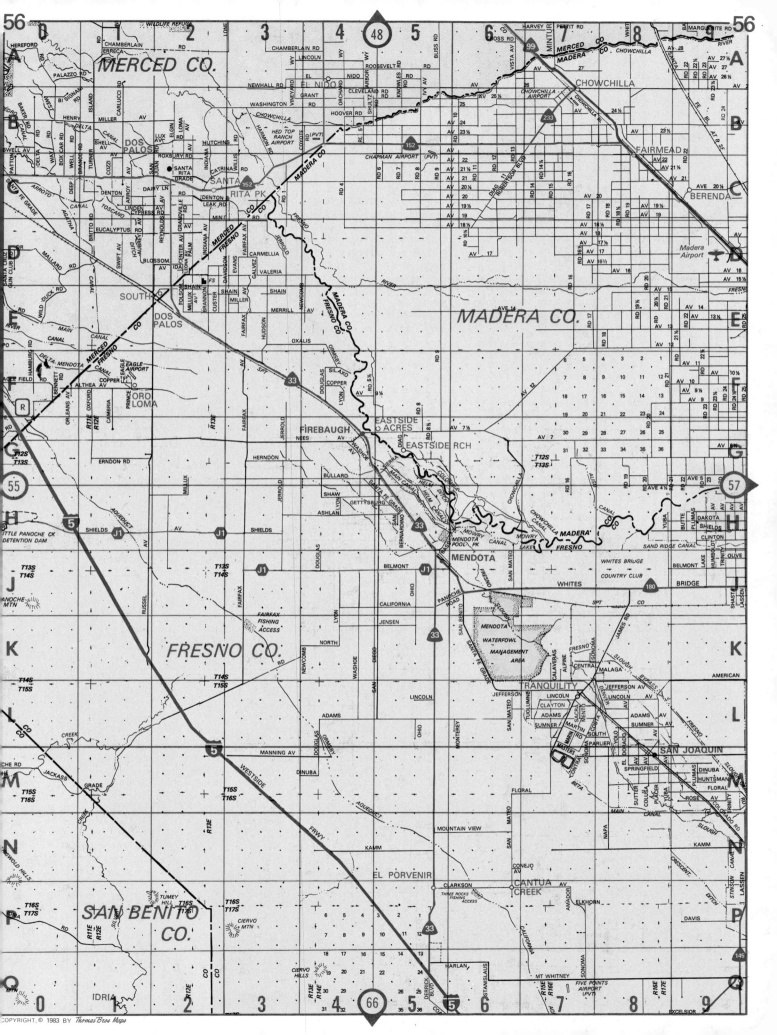

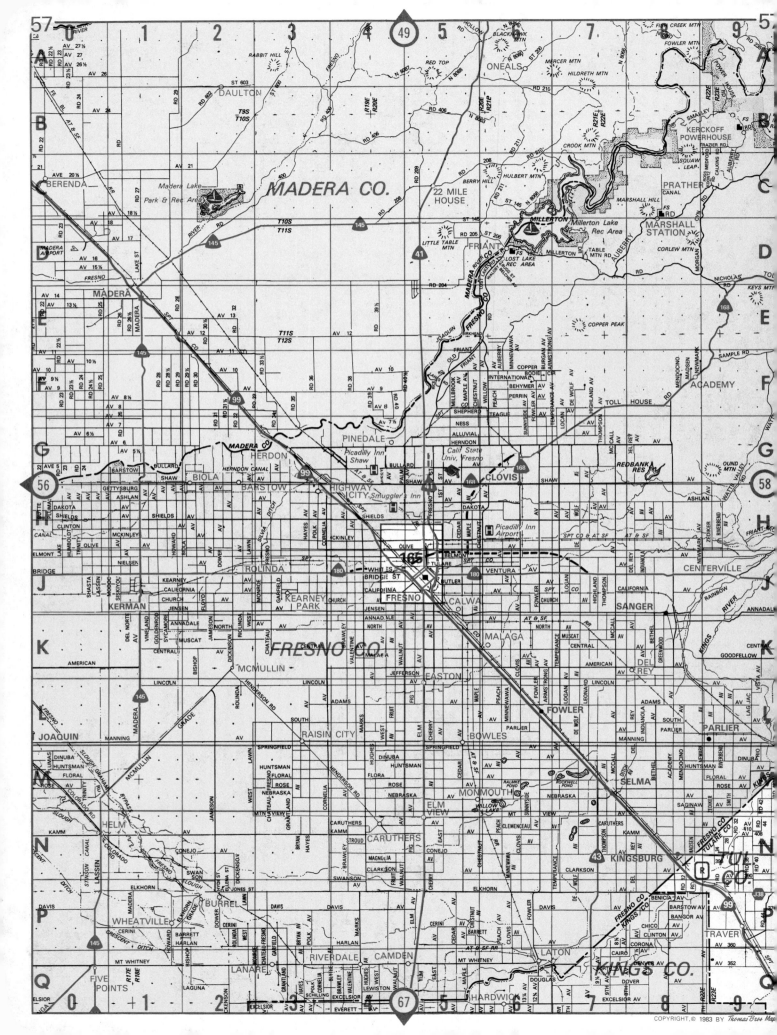

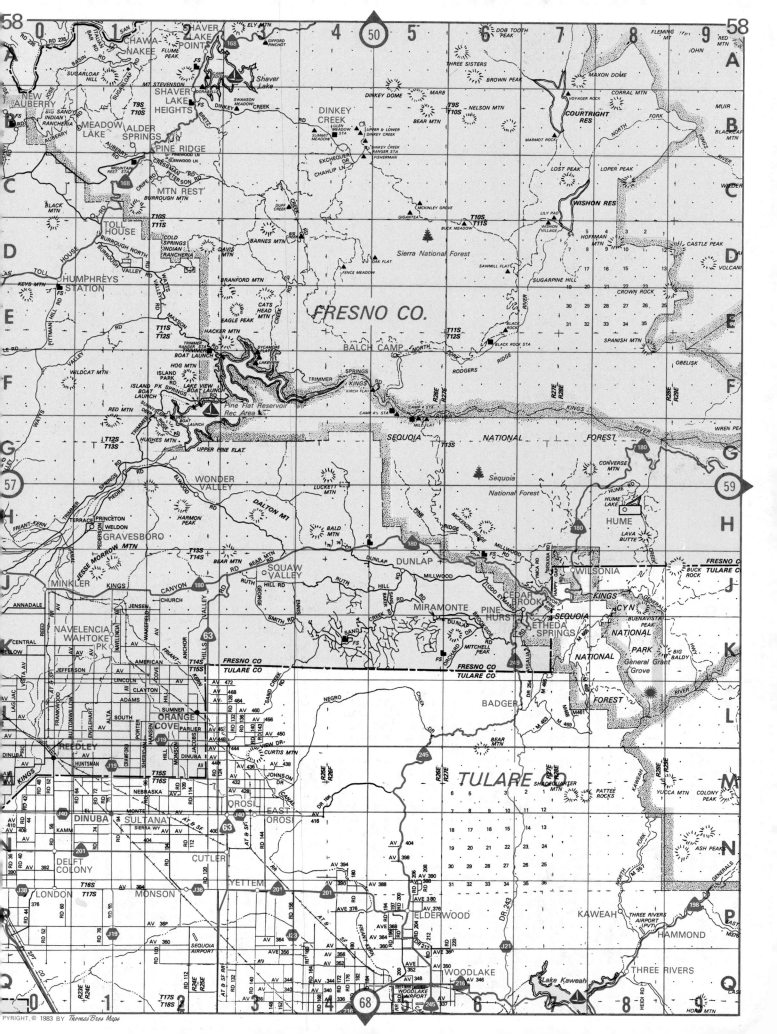

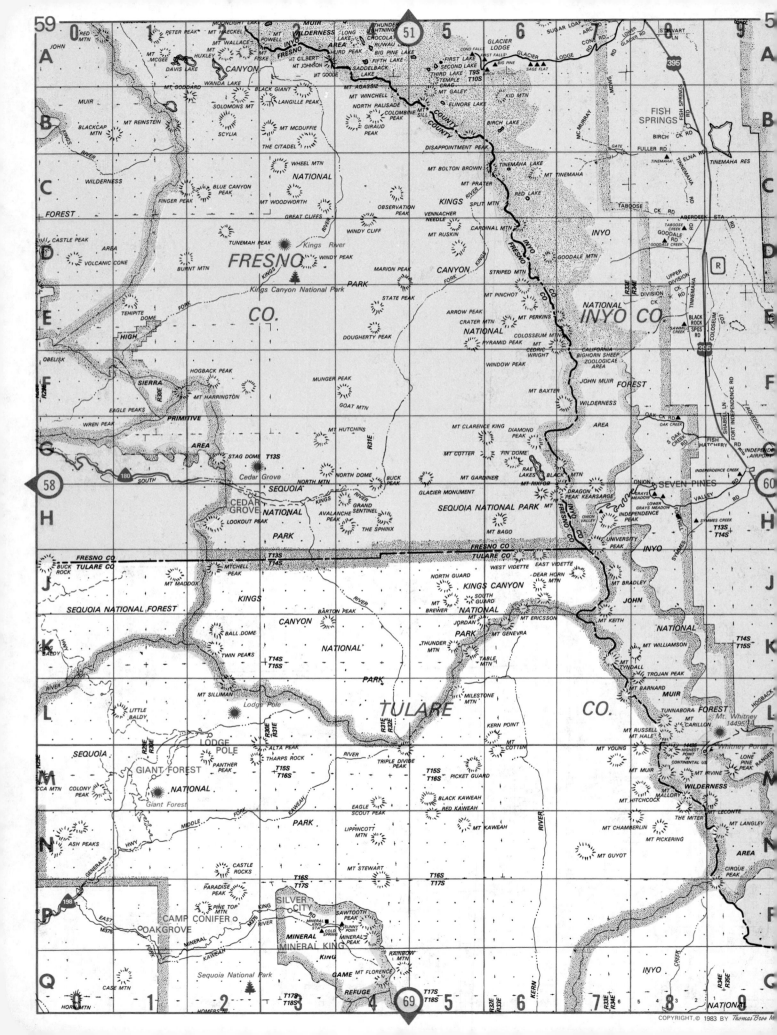

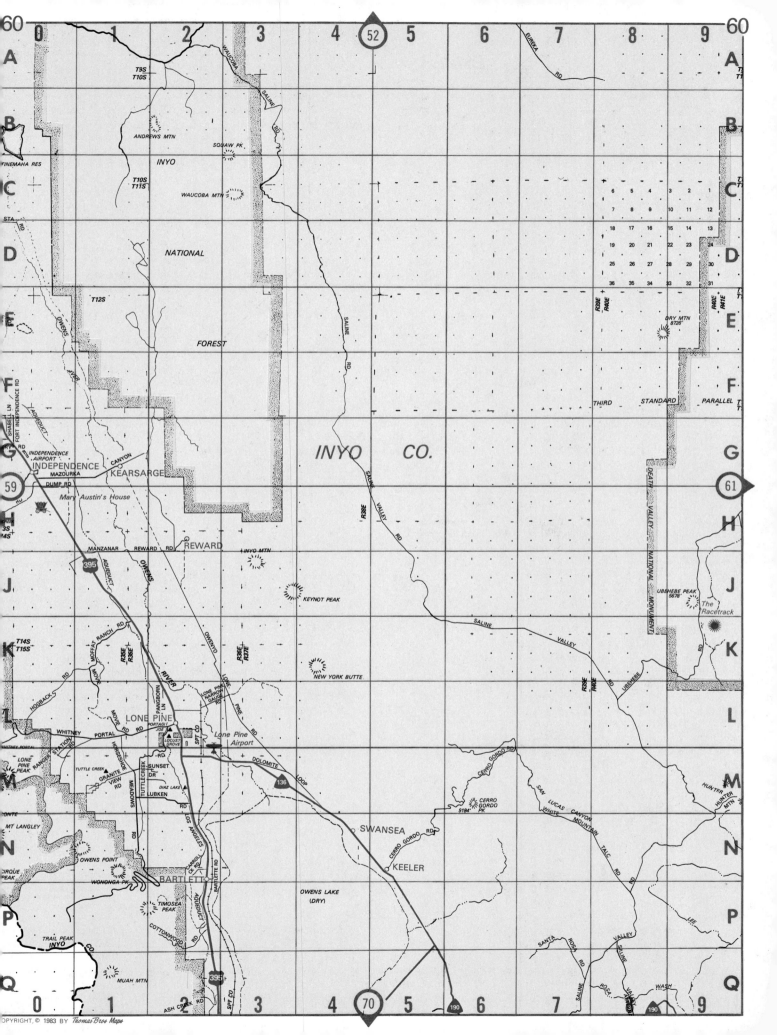

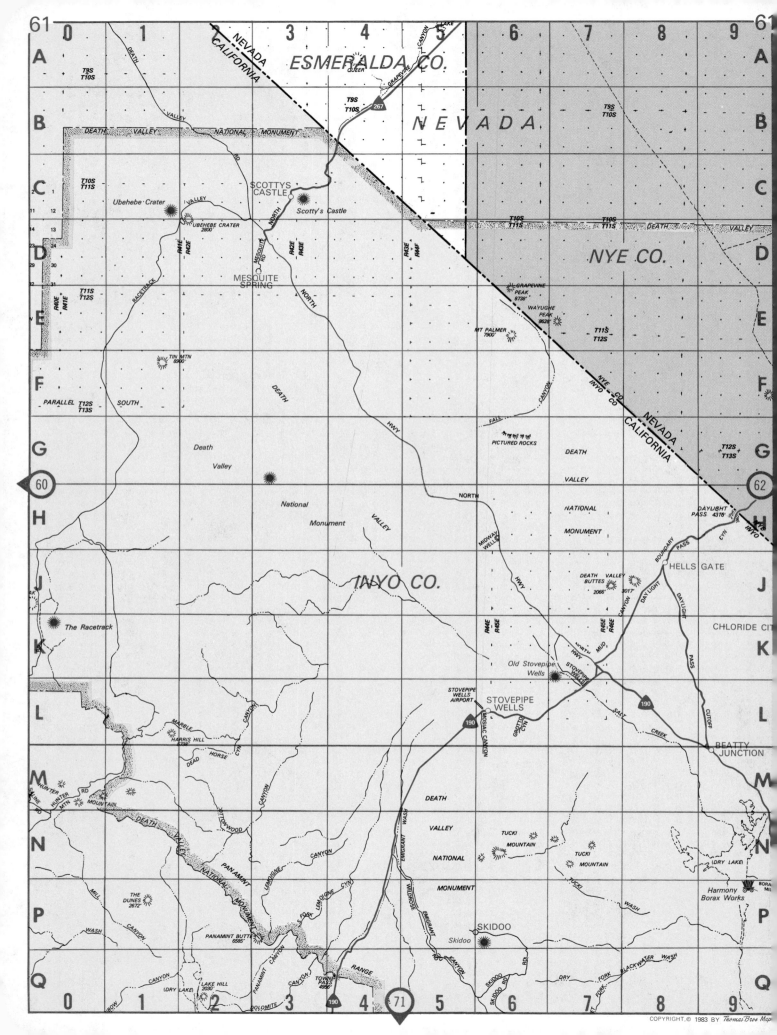

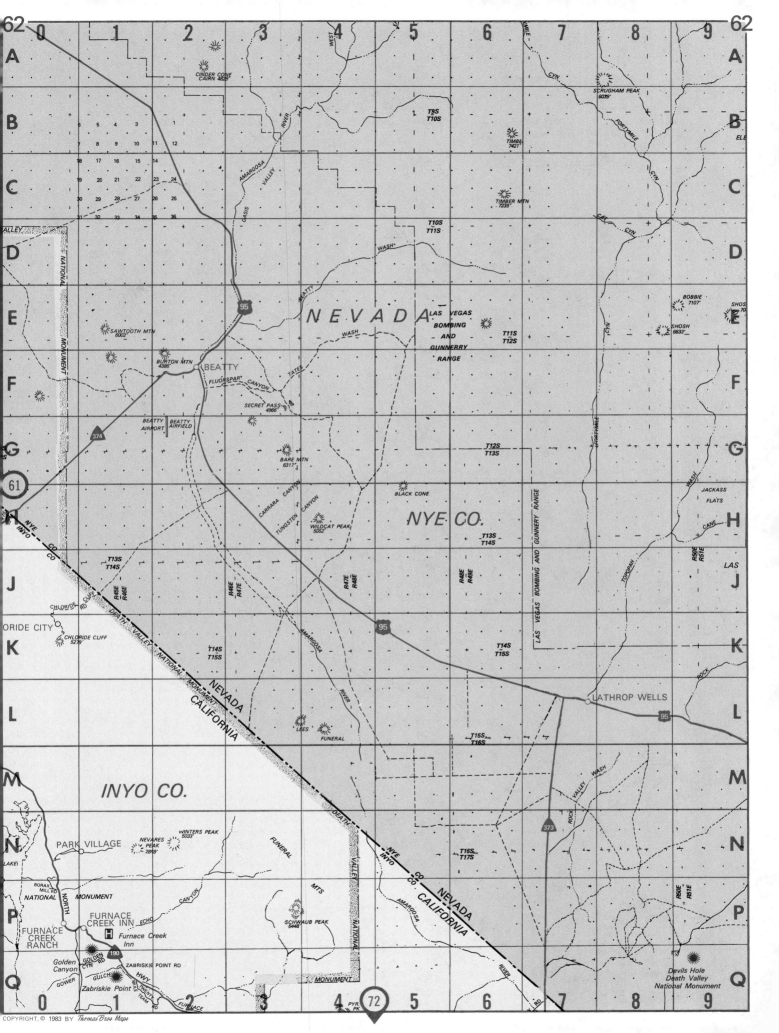

0 1 2 3 4 5 6 7 8 9

A **CINDER CONE CAIRN 4829'**

SCRUGHAM PEAK 6039'

B T9S T10S

TIMBE 7421'

FORTYMILE ELE

C TIMBER MTN 7239'

CYN

T10S T11S

WASH

D

E 95 N E V A D A LAS VEGAS BOMBING AND GUNNERRY RANGE

BOBBIE 7107' SHOS 70

SHOSH 6633'

SAWTOOTH MTN 6002'

T11S T12S

WASH

F BURTON MTN 4388'

BEATTY

FLUORSPAR CANYON TATE

SECRET PASS 4966'

G 374 BEATTY AIRPORT BEATTY AIRFIELD

BARE MTN 6317'

T12S T13S

JACKASS FLATS

61 CARRARA CANYON TUNGSTEN CANYON

BLACK CONE

CANE

H NYE CO.

WILDCAT PEAK 5052'

T13S T14S

NYE CO INYO CO

R50E R51E

LAS

T13S T14S

R45E R46E R46E R47E R47E R48E R48E R49E

J CHLORIDE RD 95

CHLORIDE CLIFF DEATH VALLEY NATIONAL MONUMENT

95 TOPOPAH

ORIDE CITY CHLORIDE CLIFF 5279'

K NEVADA CALIFORNIA

AMARGOSA

T14S T15S T14S T15S

ROCK

LATHROP WELLS 95

L RIVER

LEES FUNERAL

T15S T16S

ROCK VALLEY WASH

M INYO CO.

373

T16S T17S

R50E R51E

N PARK VILLAGE

NEVARES PEAK 2869' WINTERS PEAK 5033'

FUNERAL

DEATH VALLEY NATIONAL

NYE INYO CO CO NEVADA CALIFORNIA

AMARGOSA

BORAX MILL RD NATIONAL MONUMENT NORTH

MTS

P LAKE

FURNACE CREEK INN

ECHO CANYON

SCHWAUB PEAK 6448'

AMARGOSA

DEVILS HOLE

FURNACE CREEK RANCH

H FURNACE CREEK Inn

190

RIVER

Devils Hole Death Valley National Monument

Q Golden Canyon GOLDEN CYN RD 190 ZABRISKIE POINT RD

GOWER GULCH

Zabriskie Point TWENTY TEAM RD FURNACE

MONUMENT

72

0 1 2 3 4 PYR PK 5 6 7 8 9

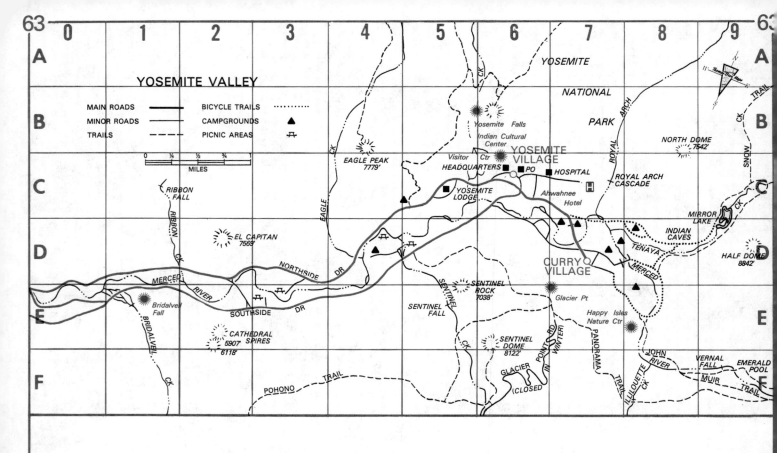

YOSEMITE VALLEY

MAIN ROADS
MINOR ROADS
TRAILS

BICYCLE TRAILS
CAMPGROUNDS
PICNIC AREAS

MILES

YOSEMITE NATIONAL PARK

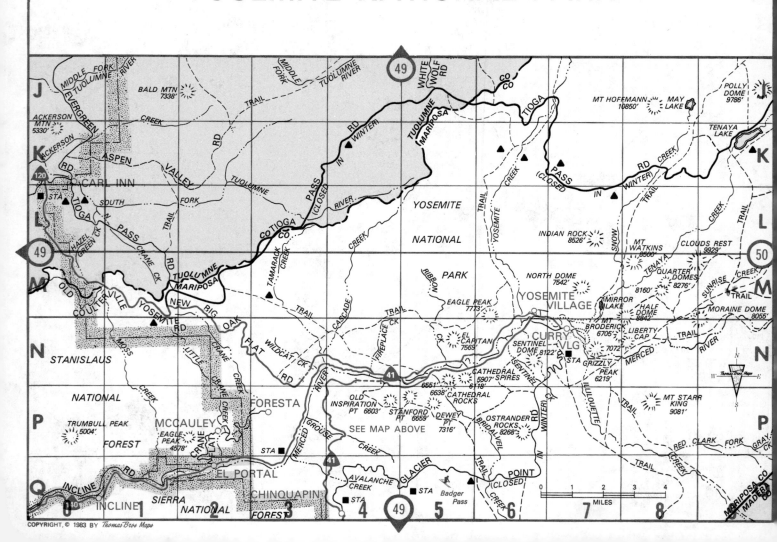

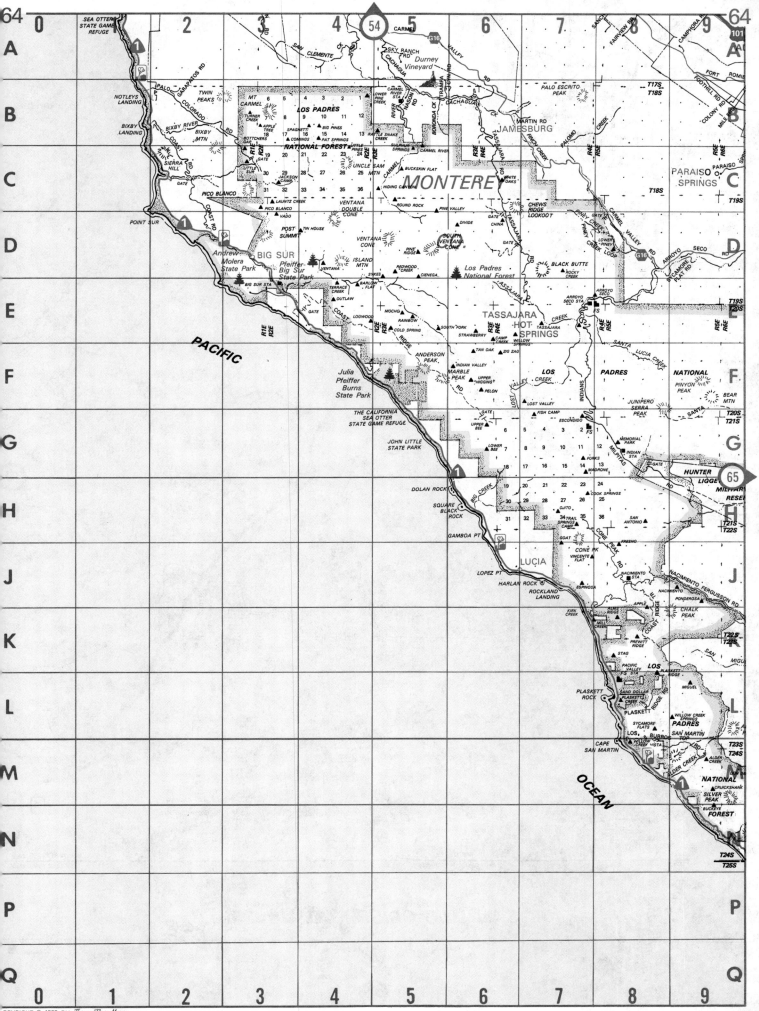

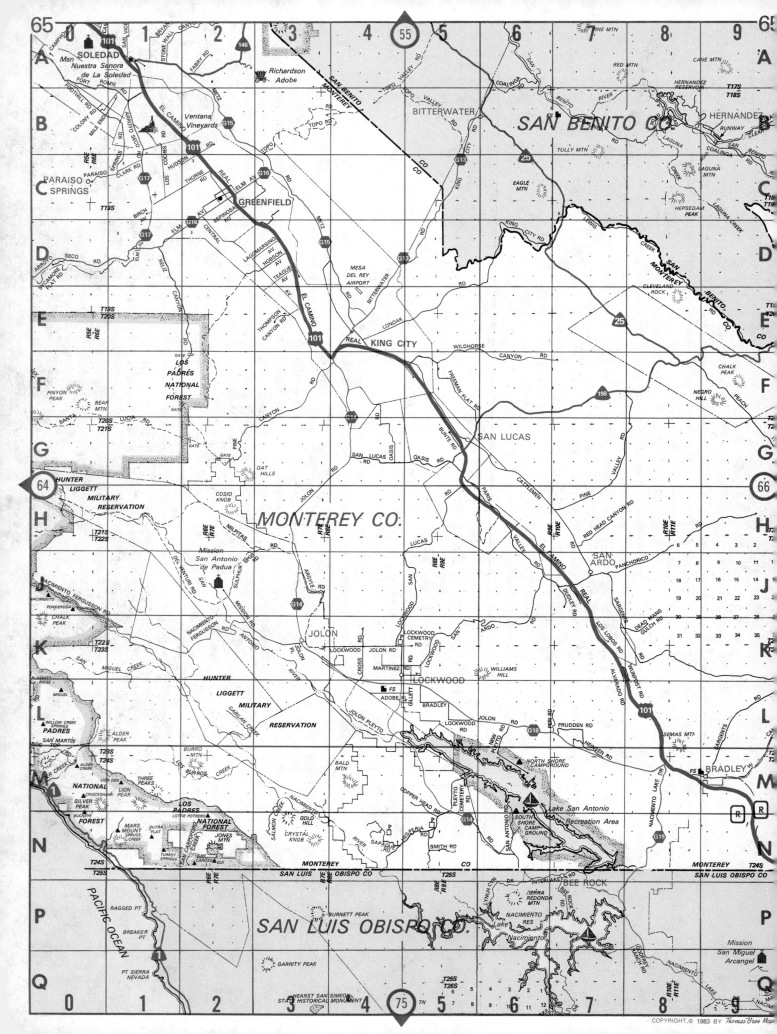

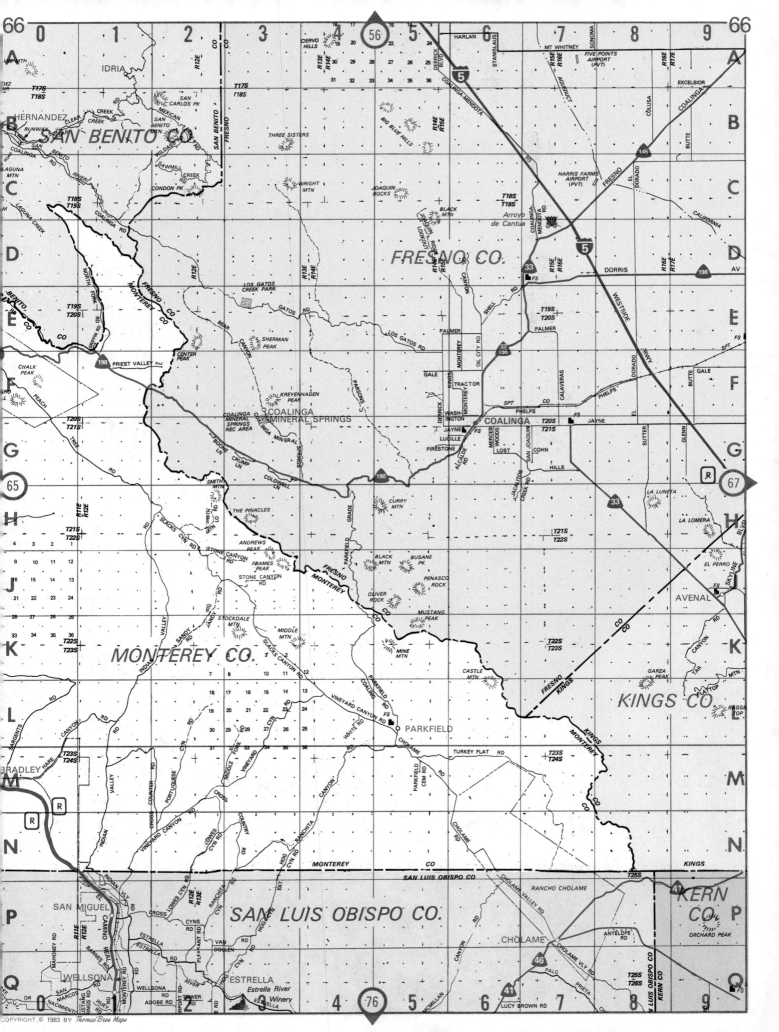

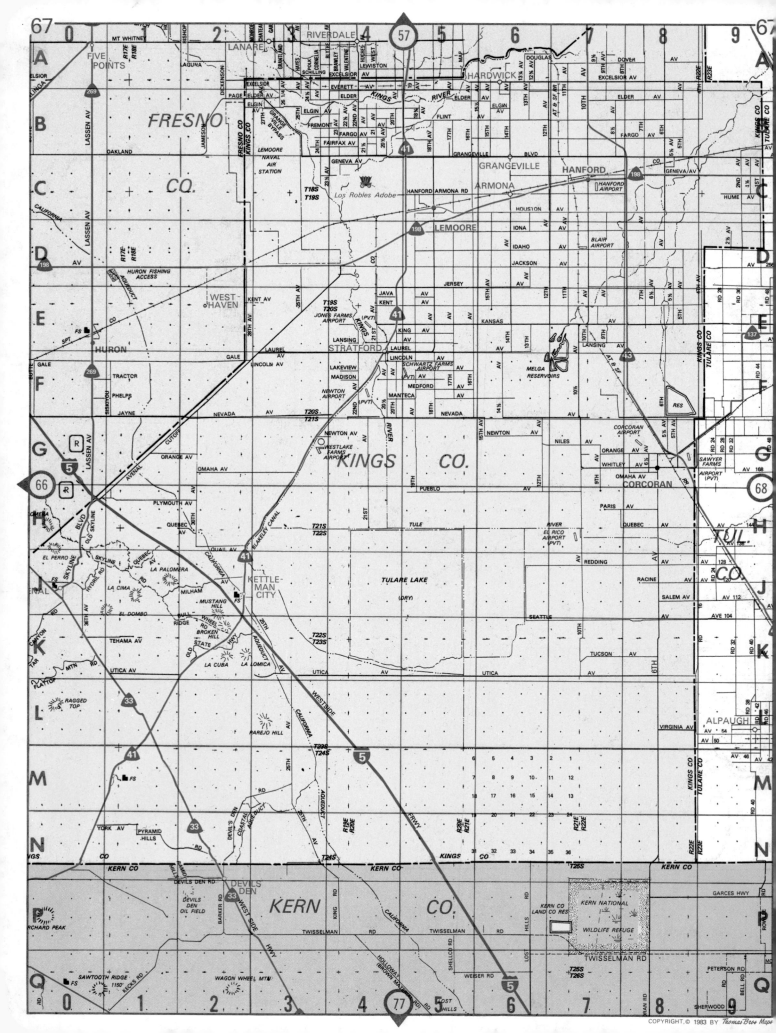

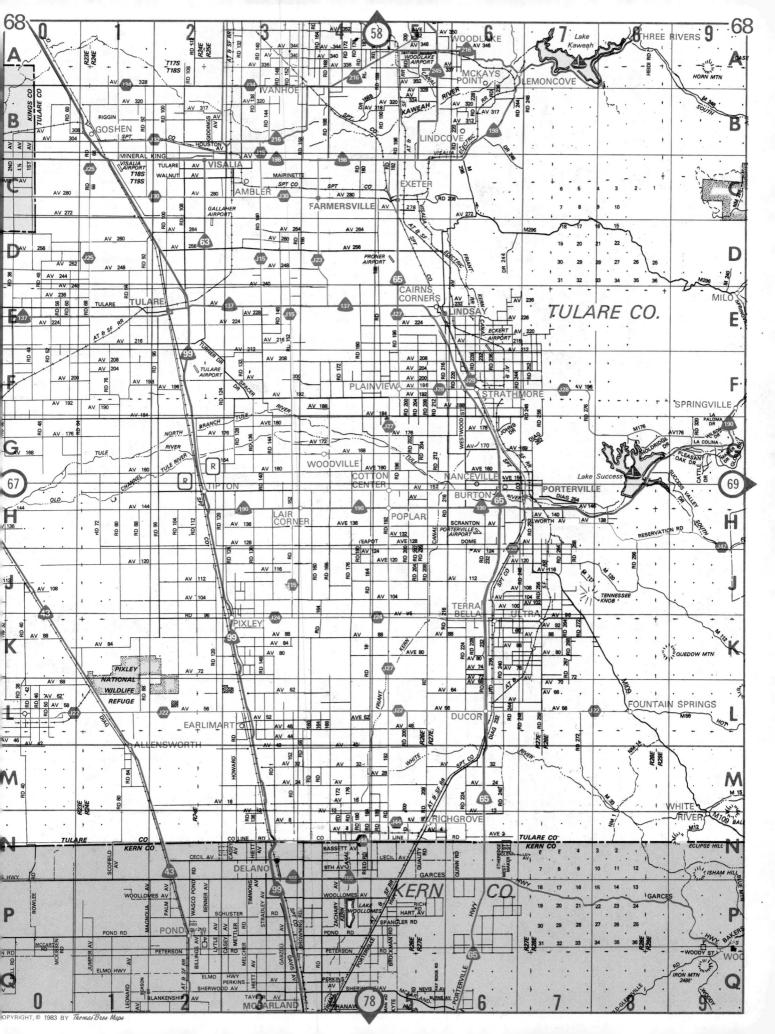

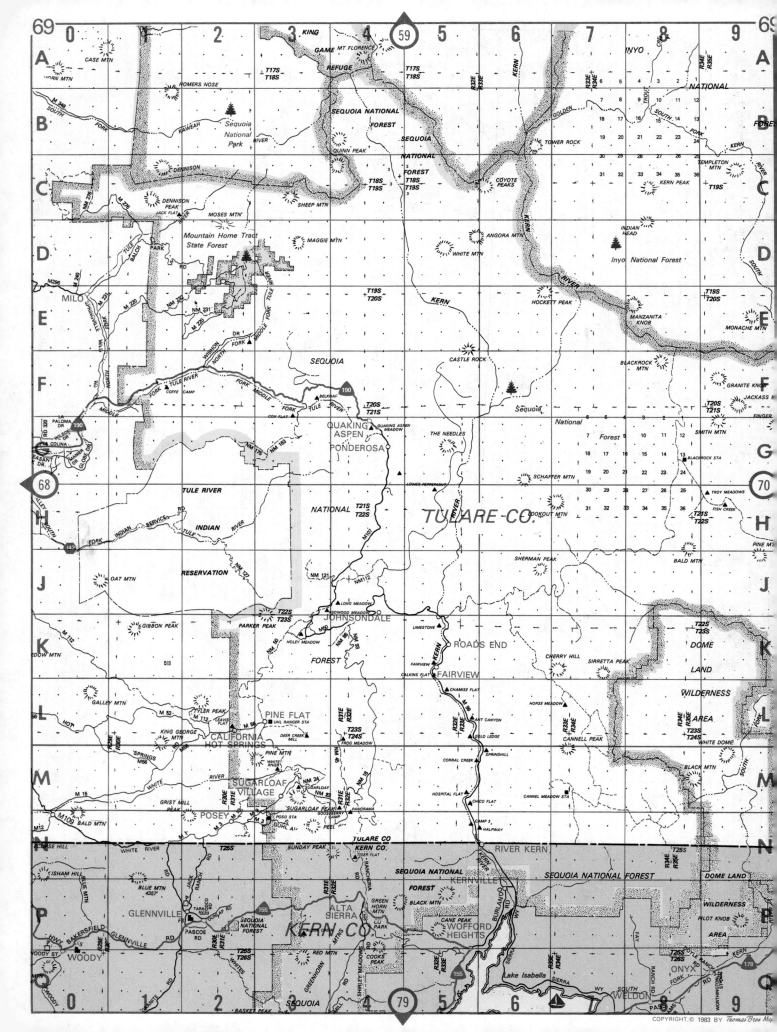

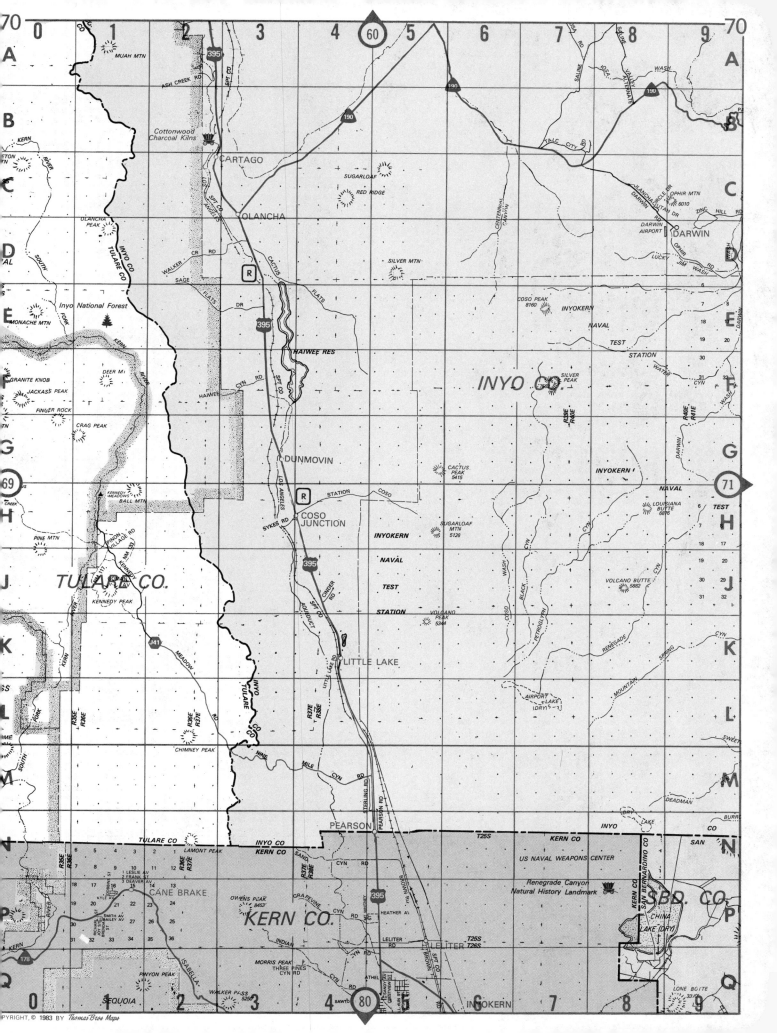

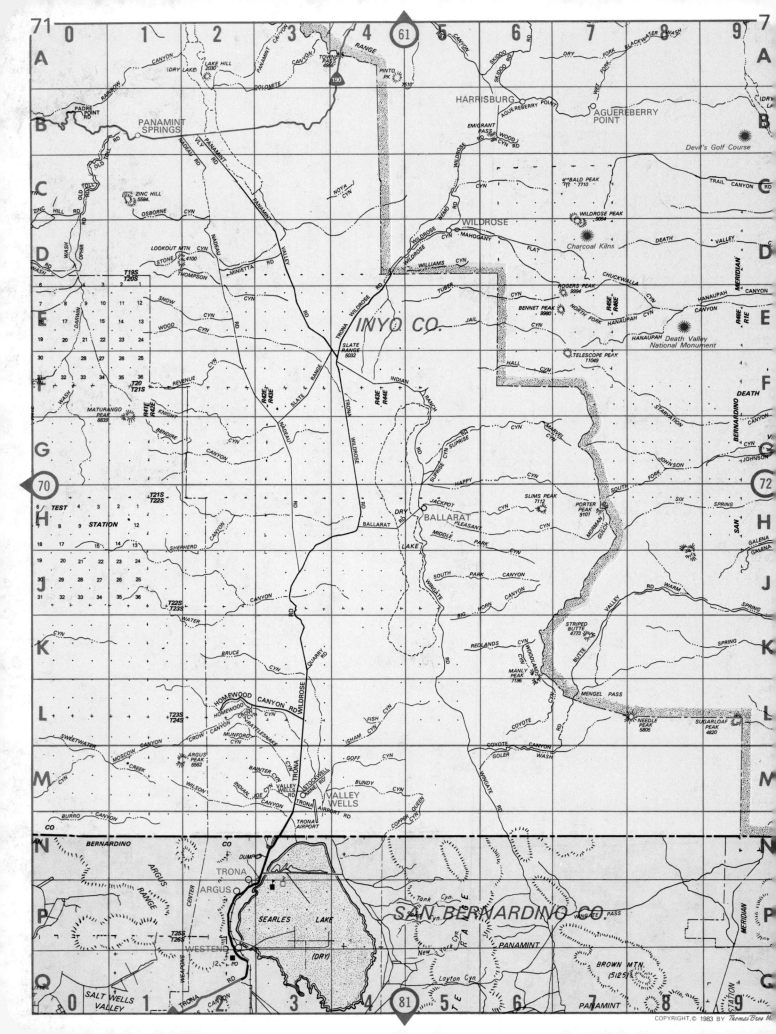

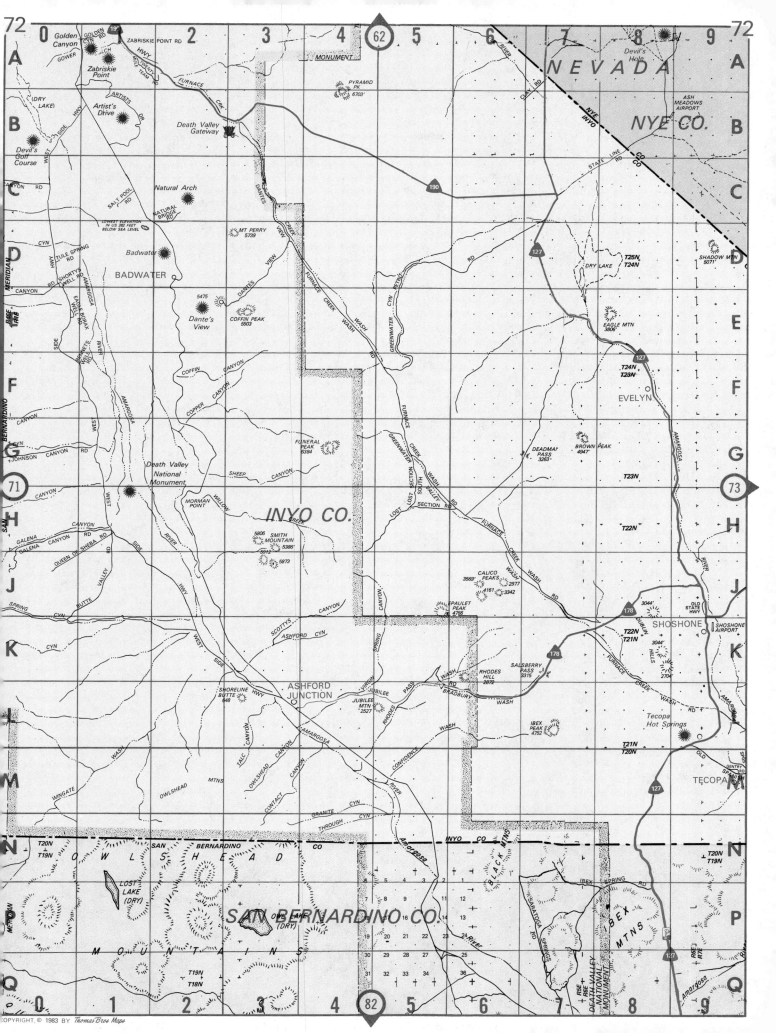

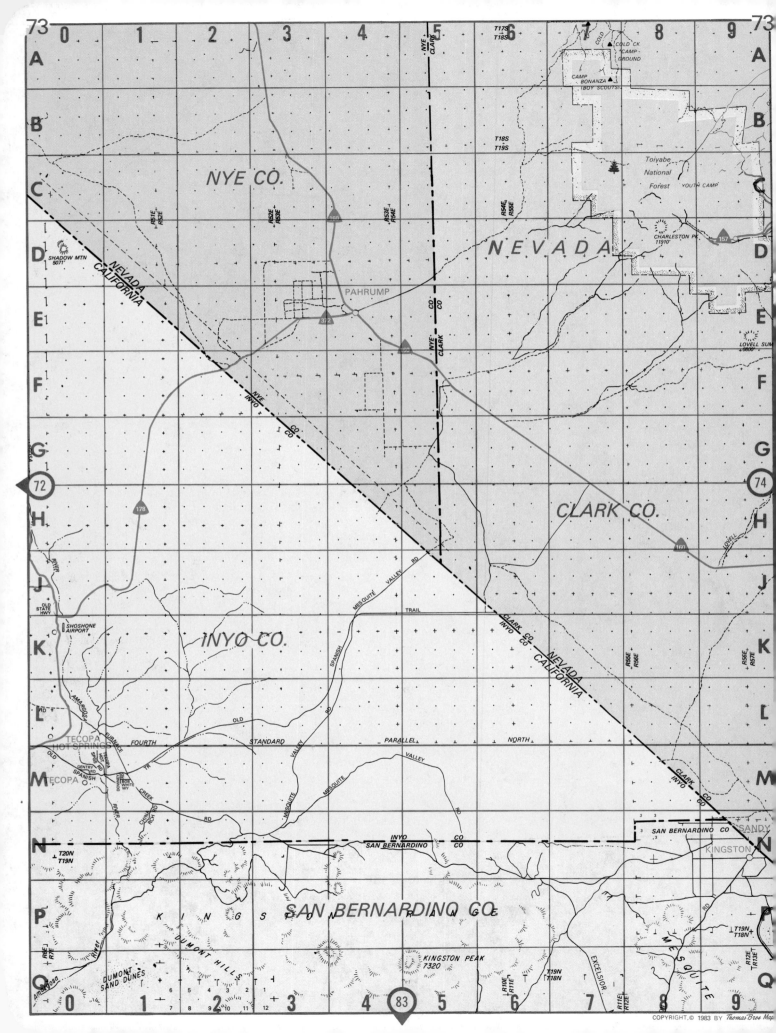

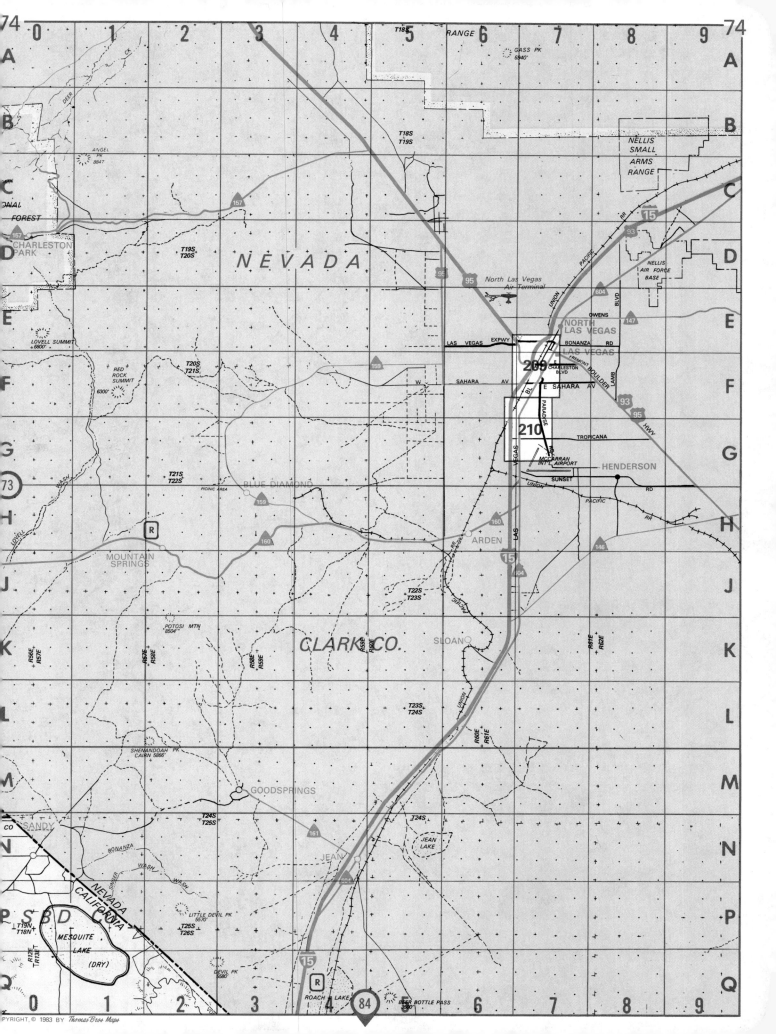

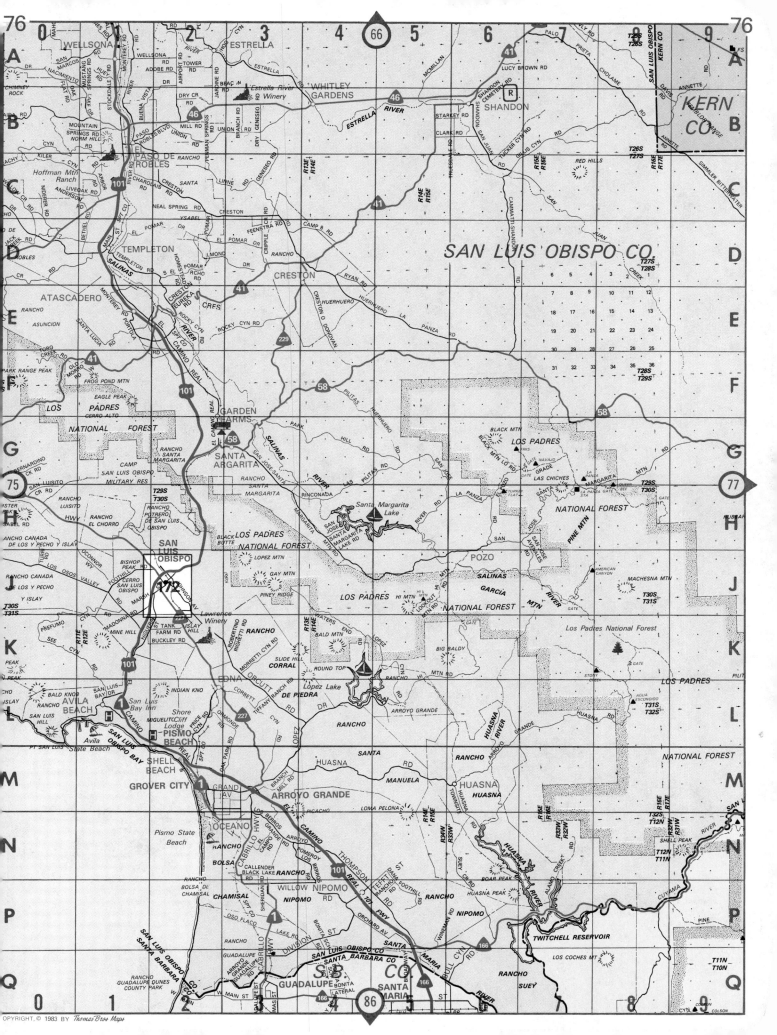

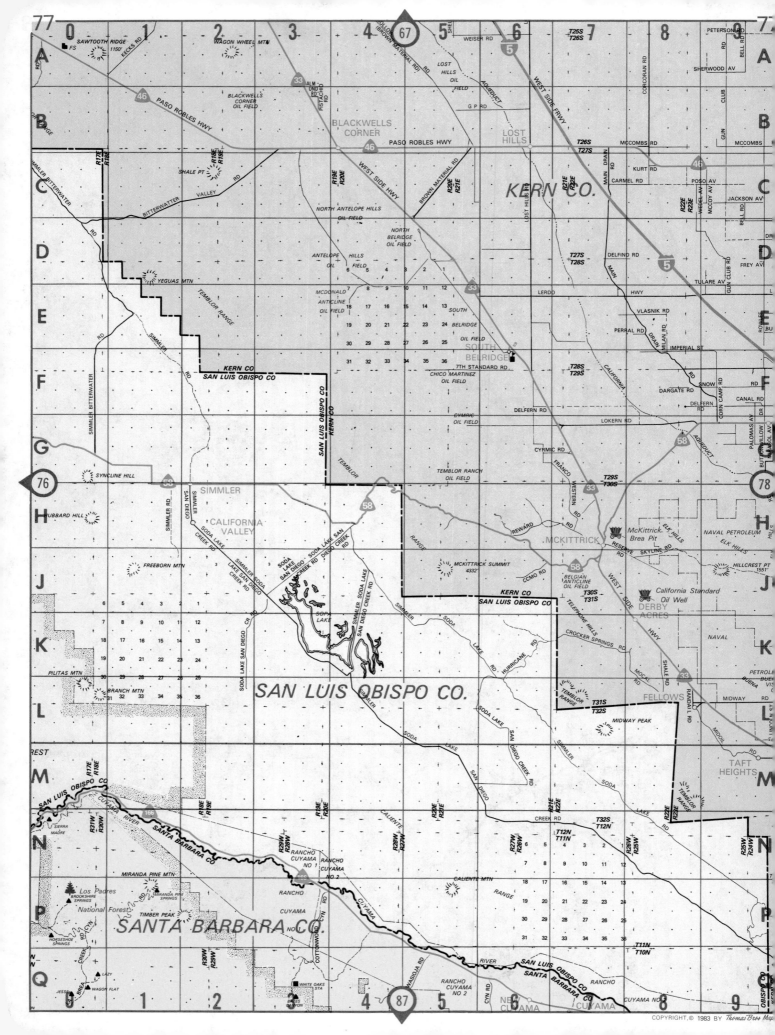

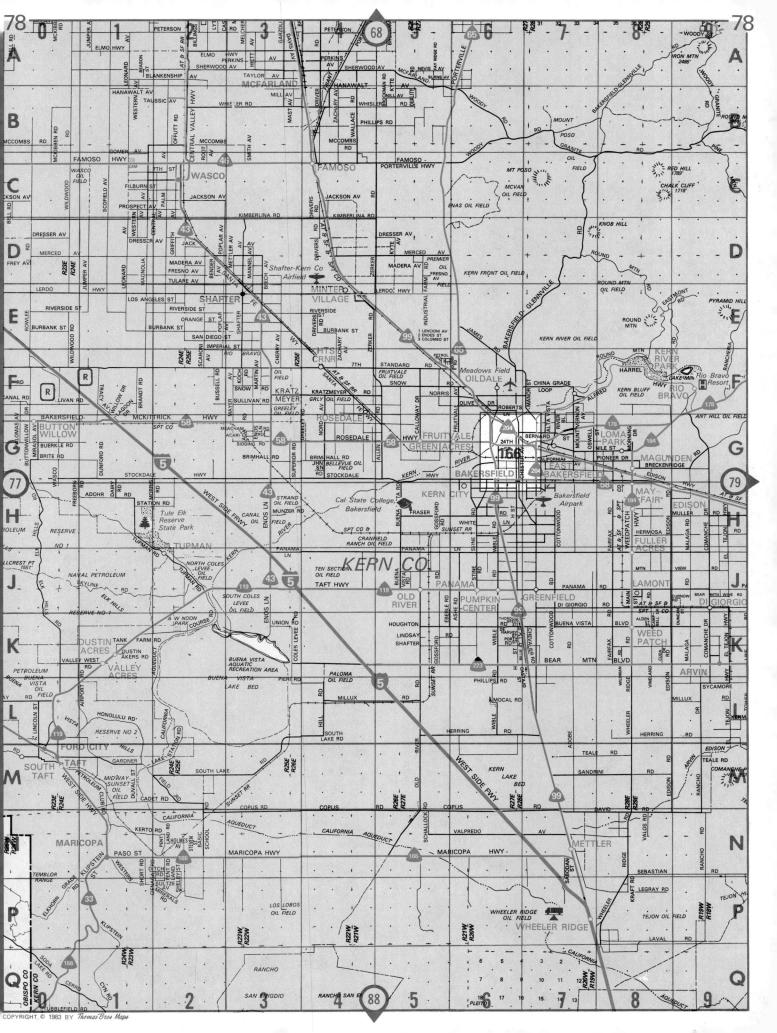

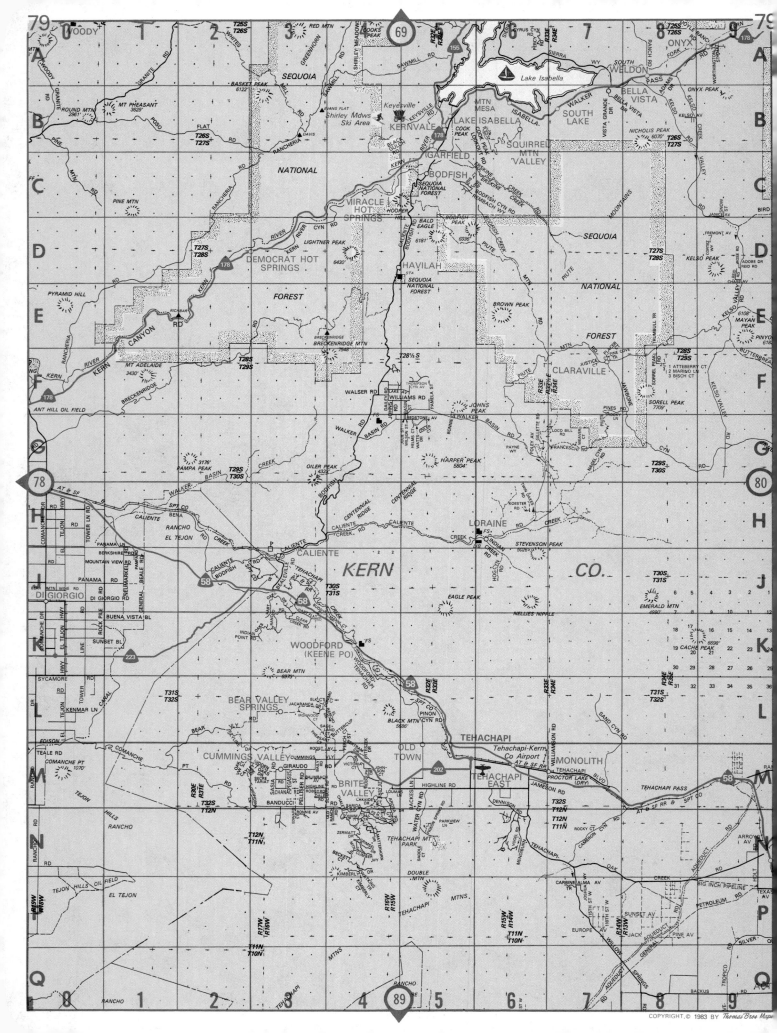

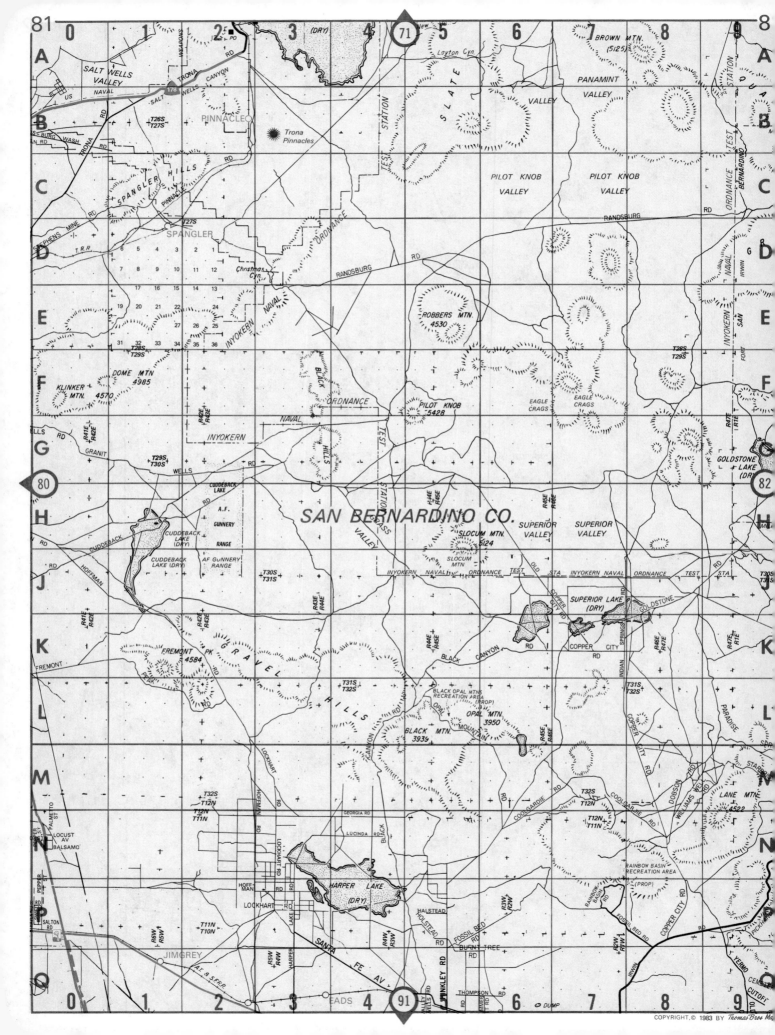

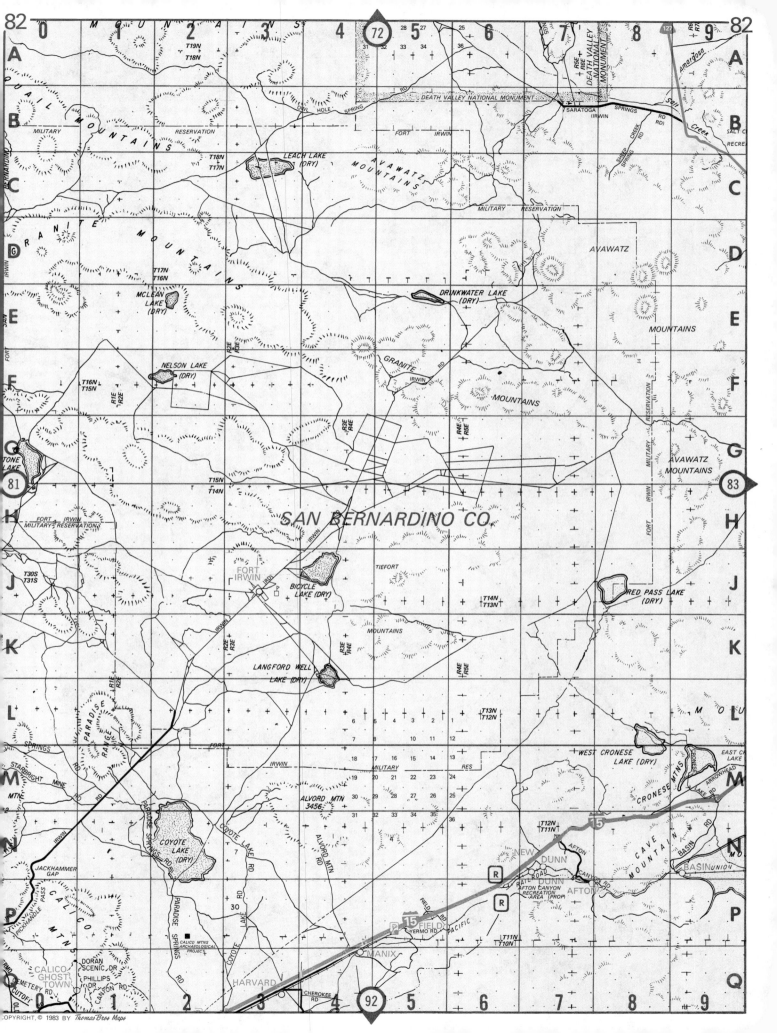

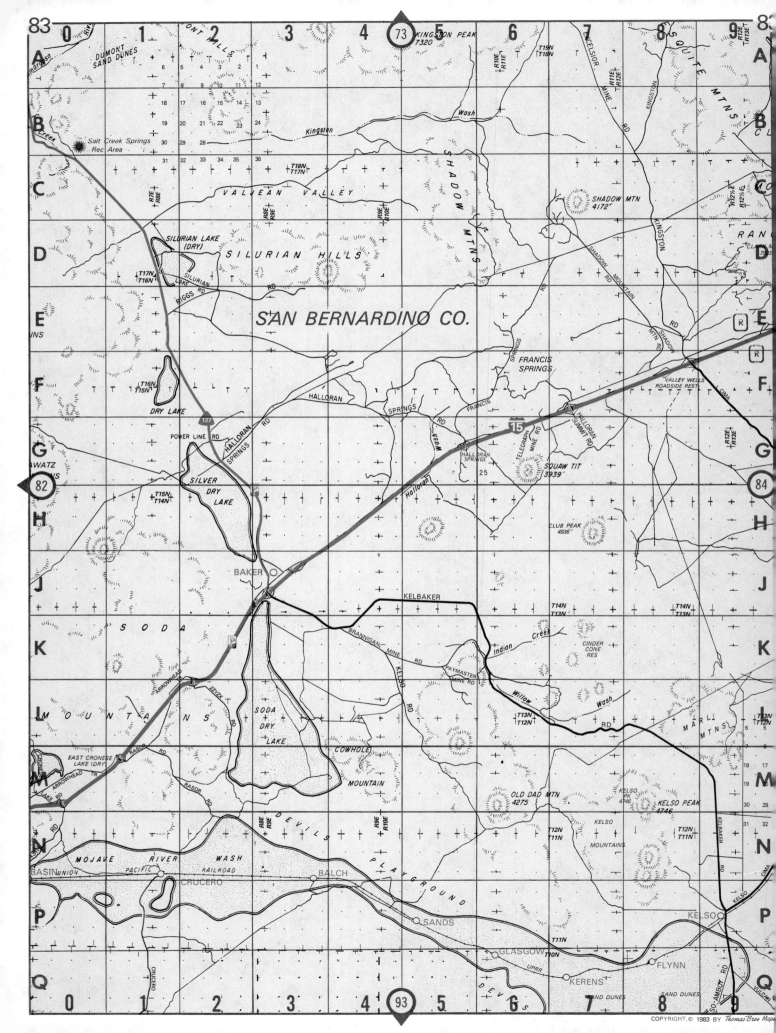

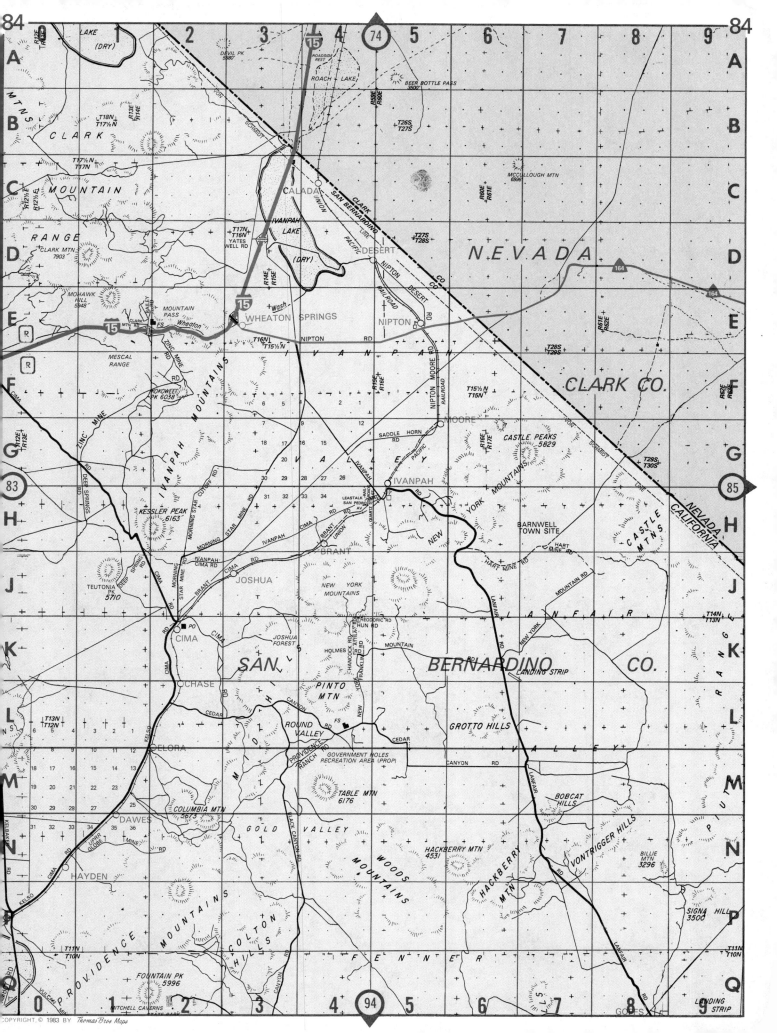

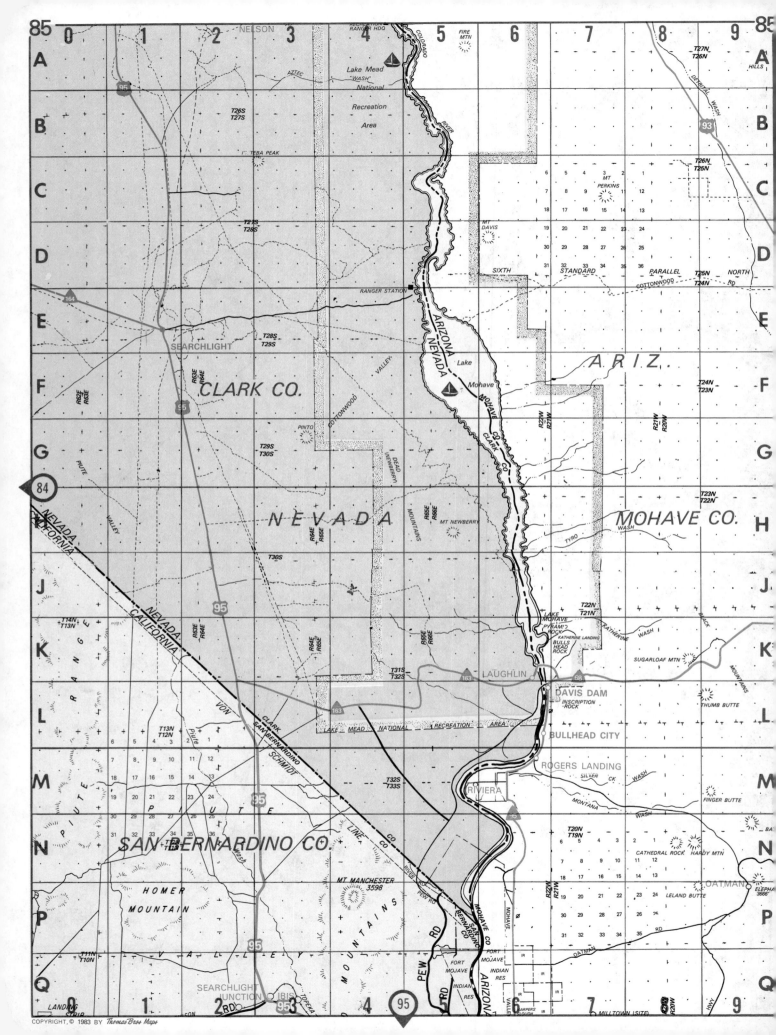

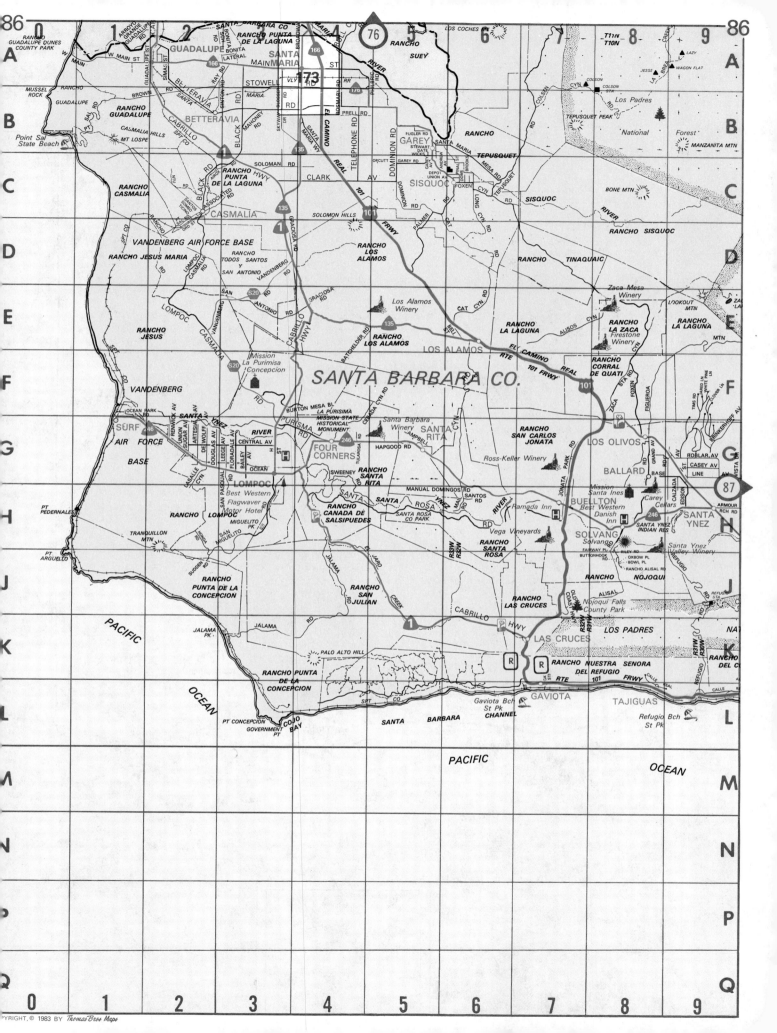

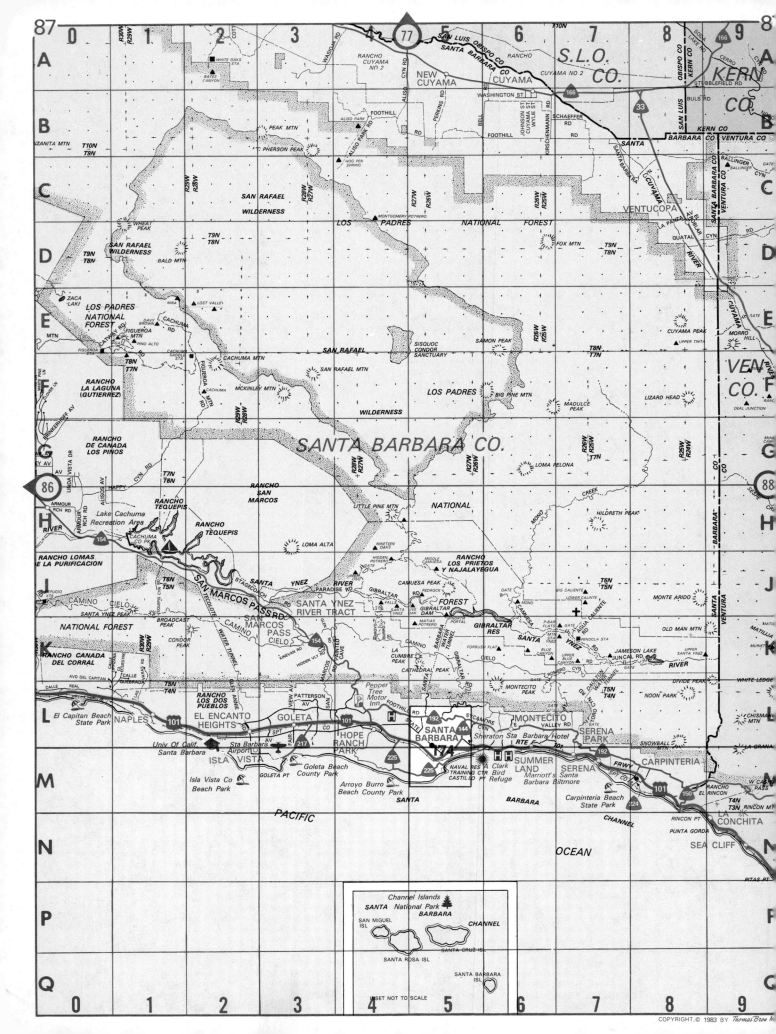

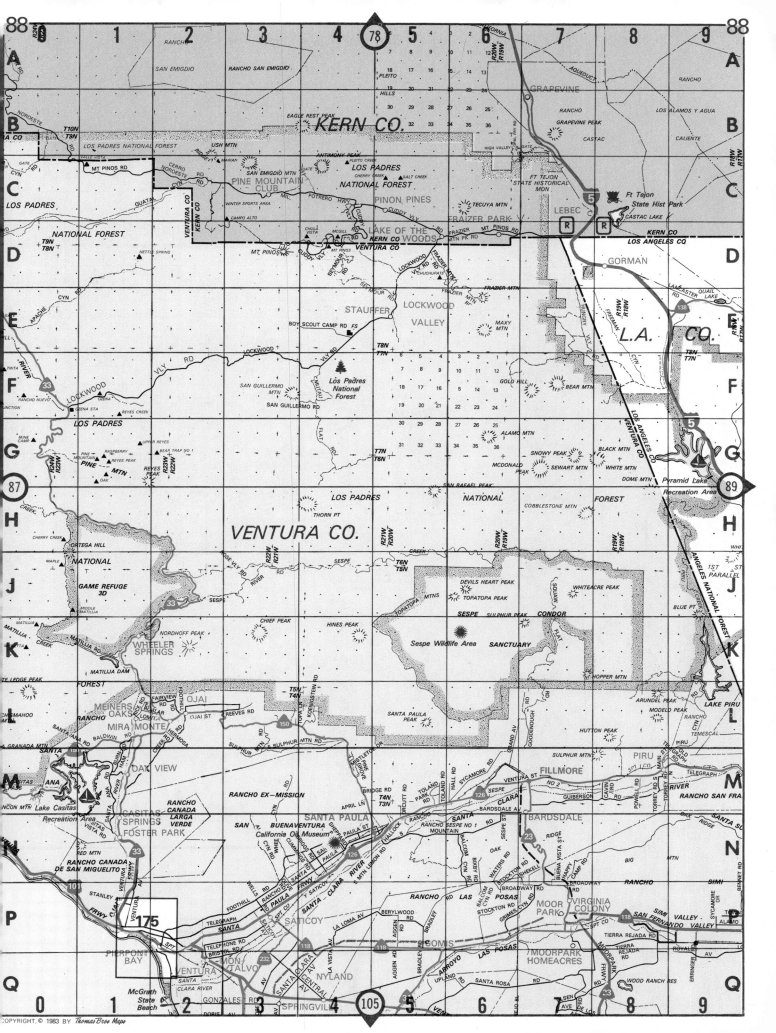

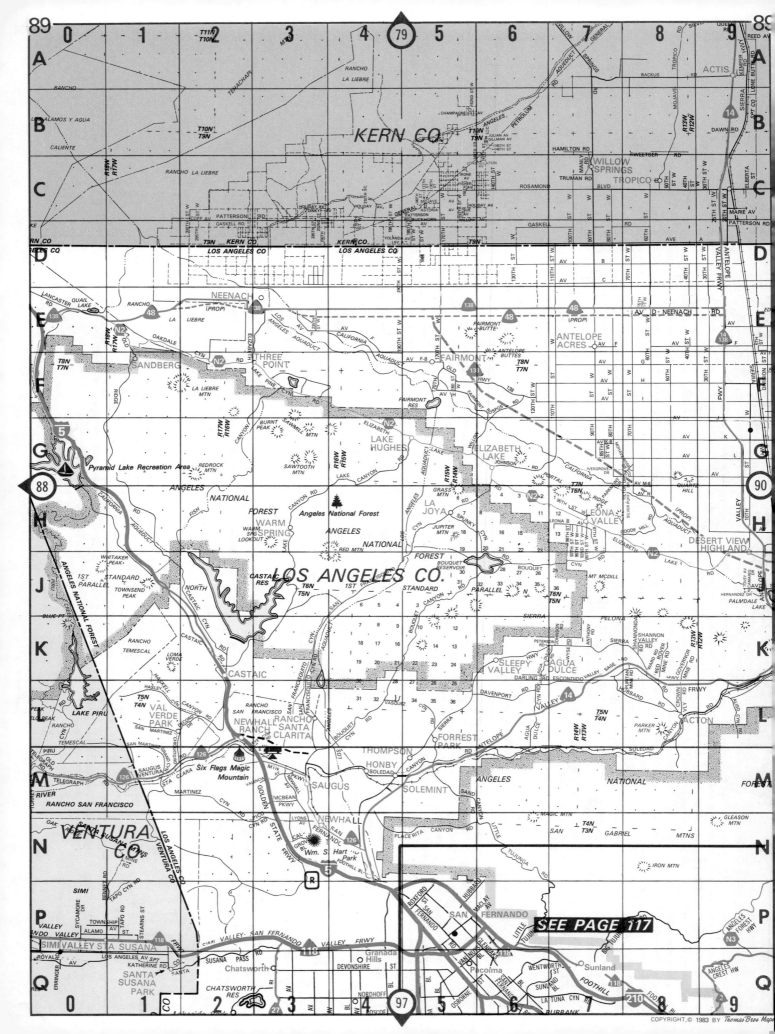

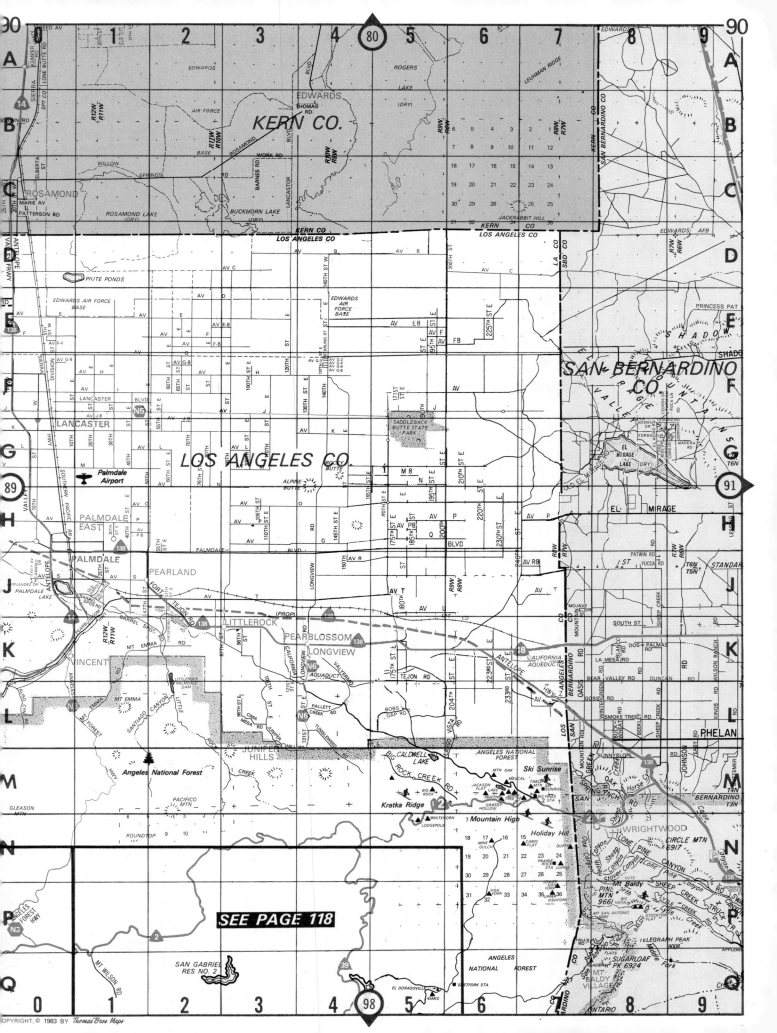

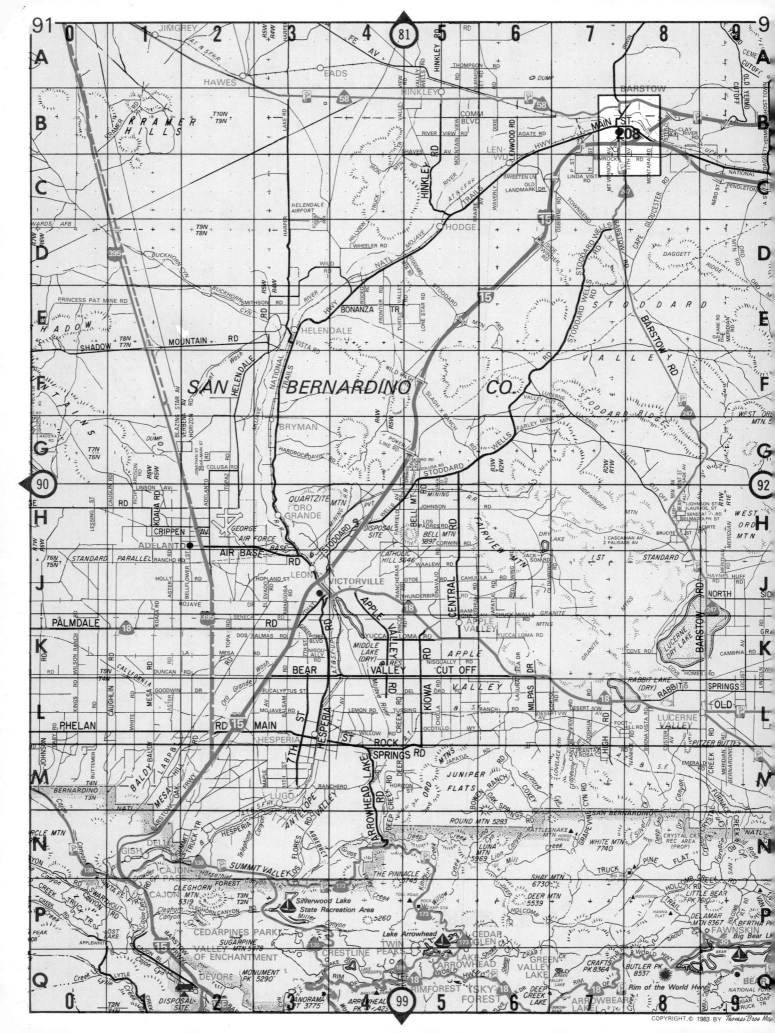

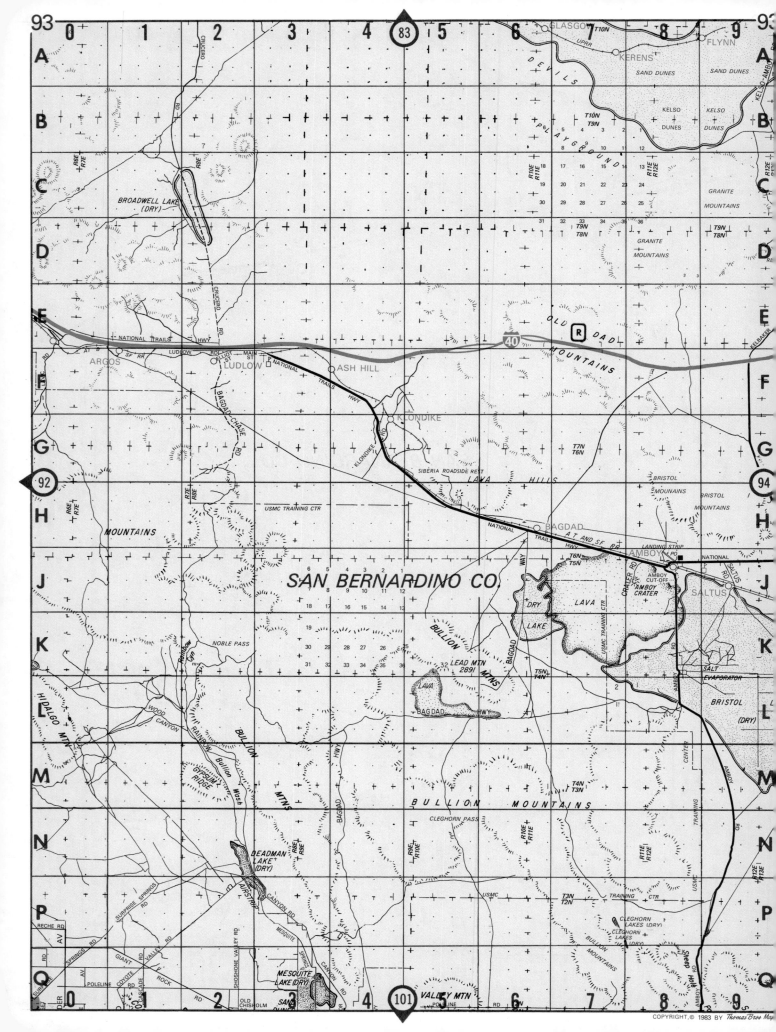

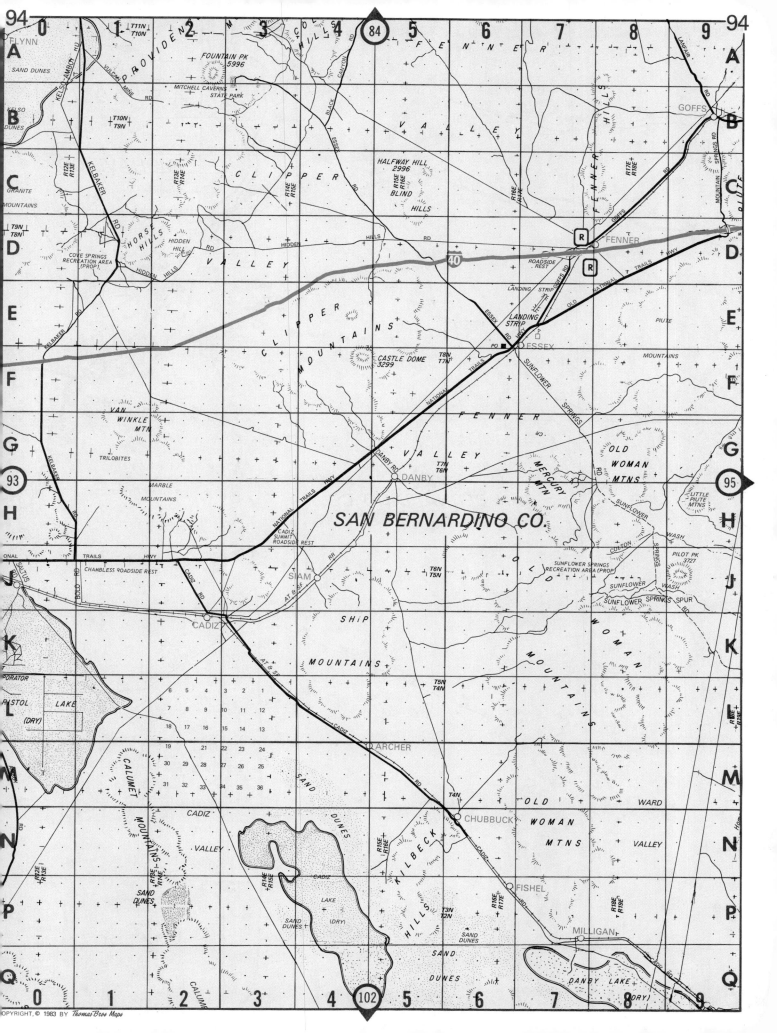

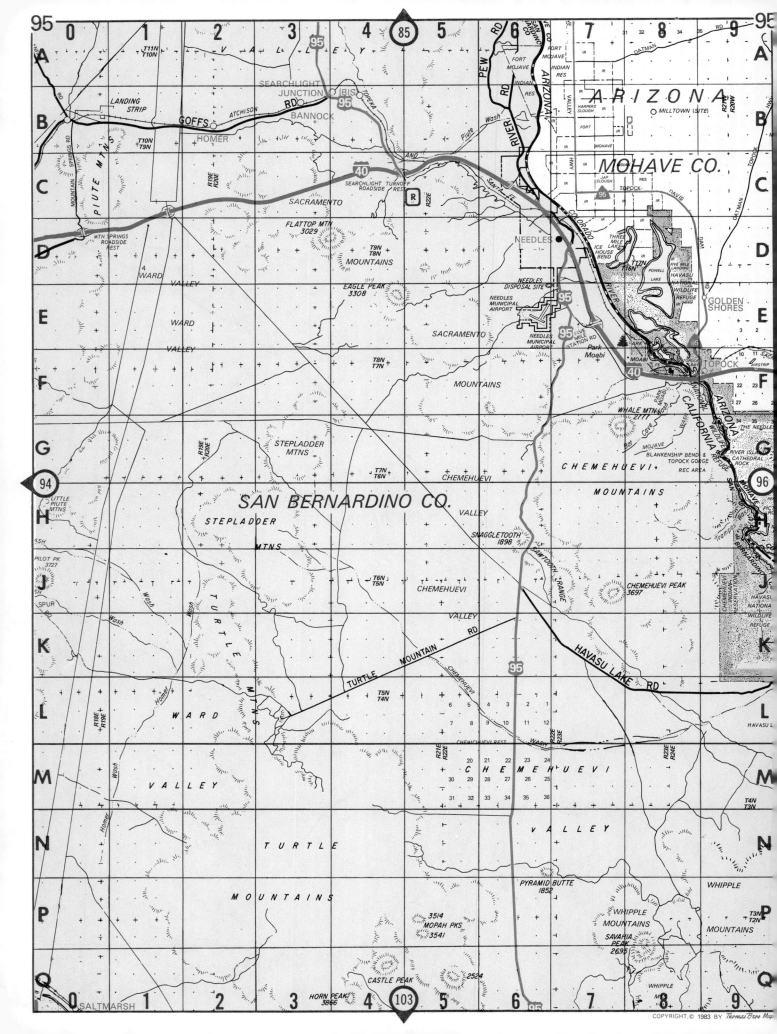

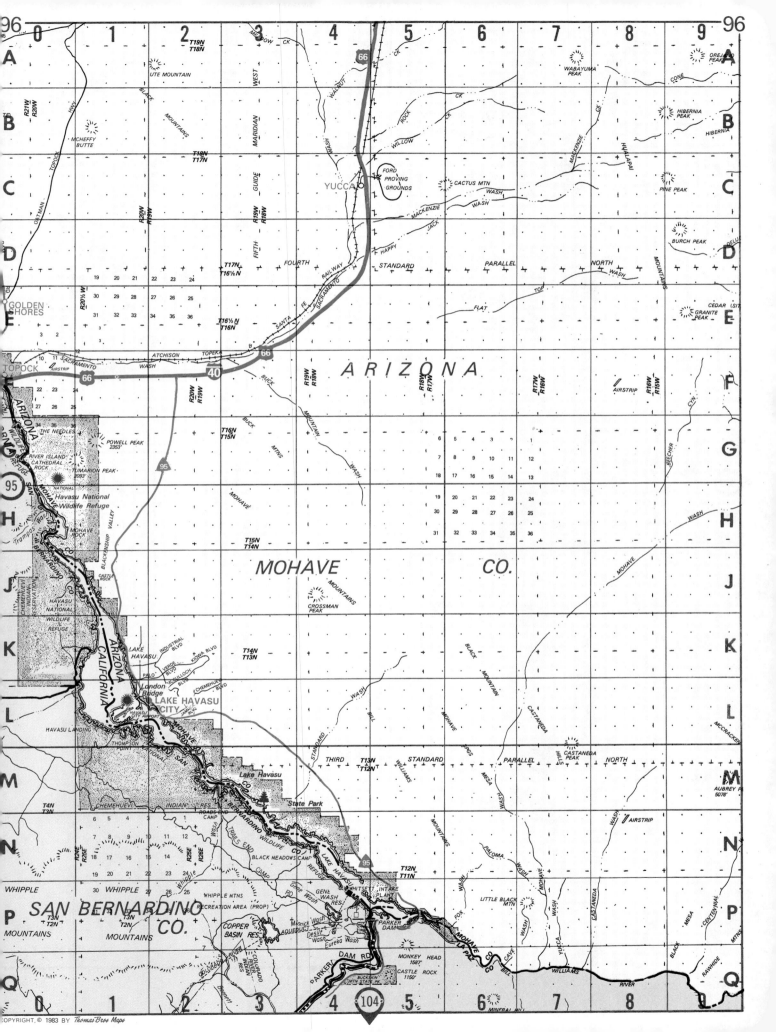

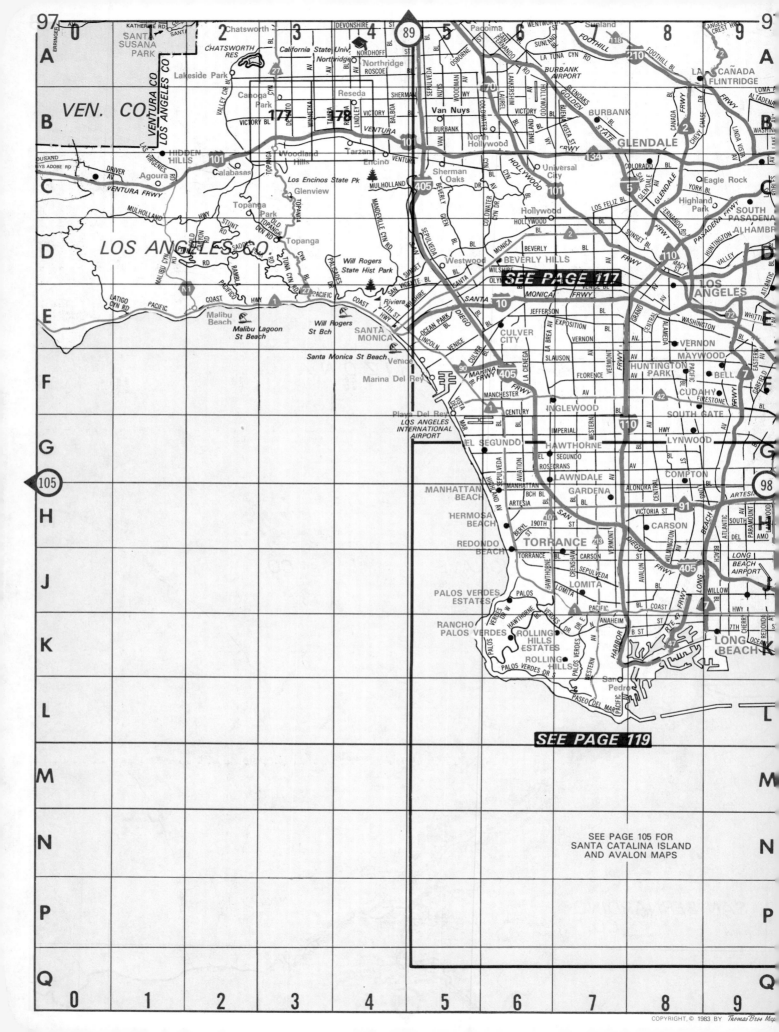

SEE PAGE 117

SEE PAGE 119

SEE PAGE 105 FOR
SANTA CATALINA ISLAND
AND AVALON MAPS

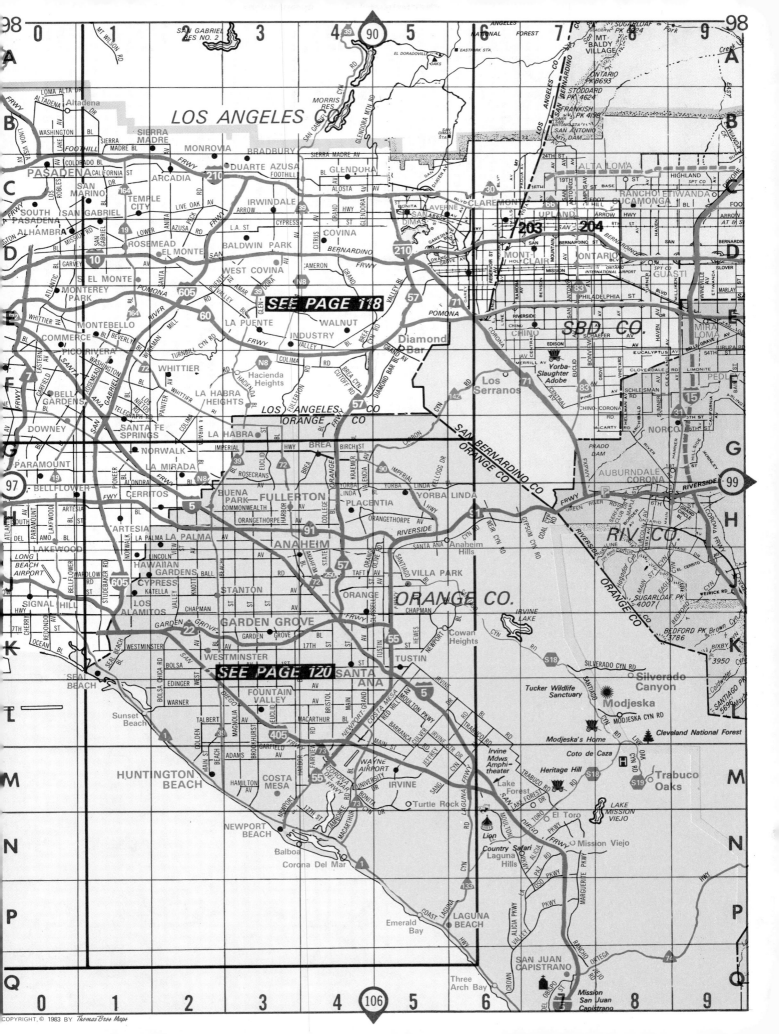

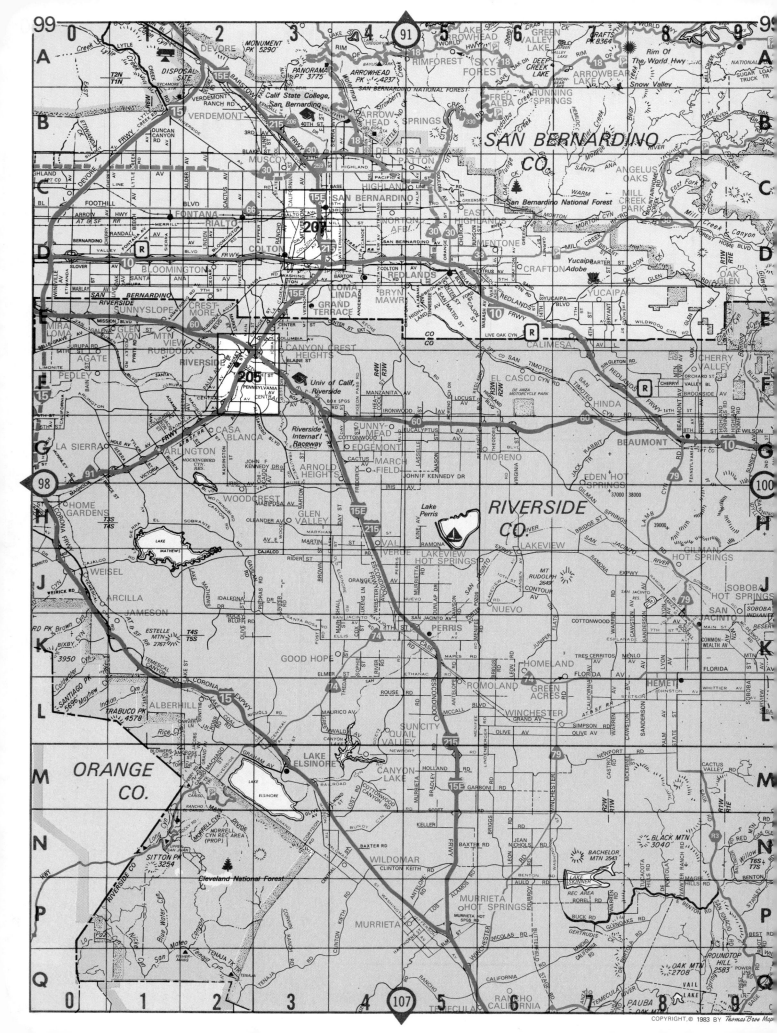

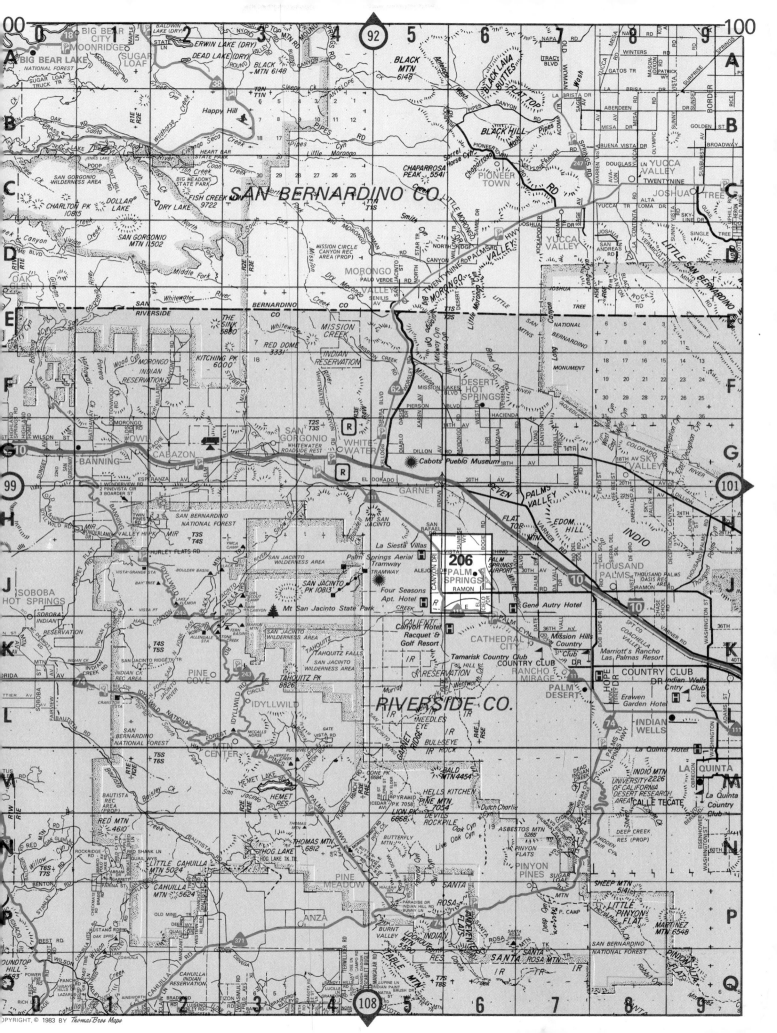

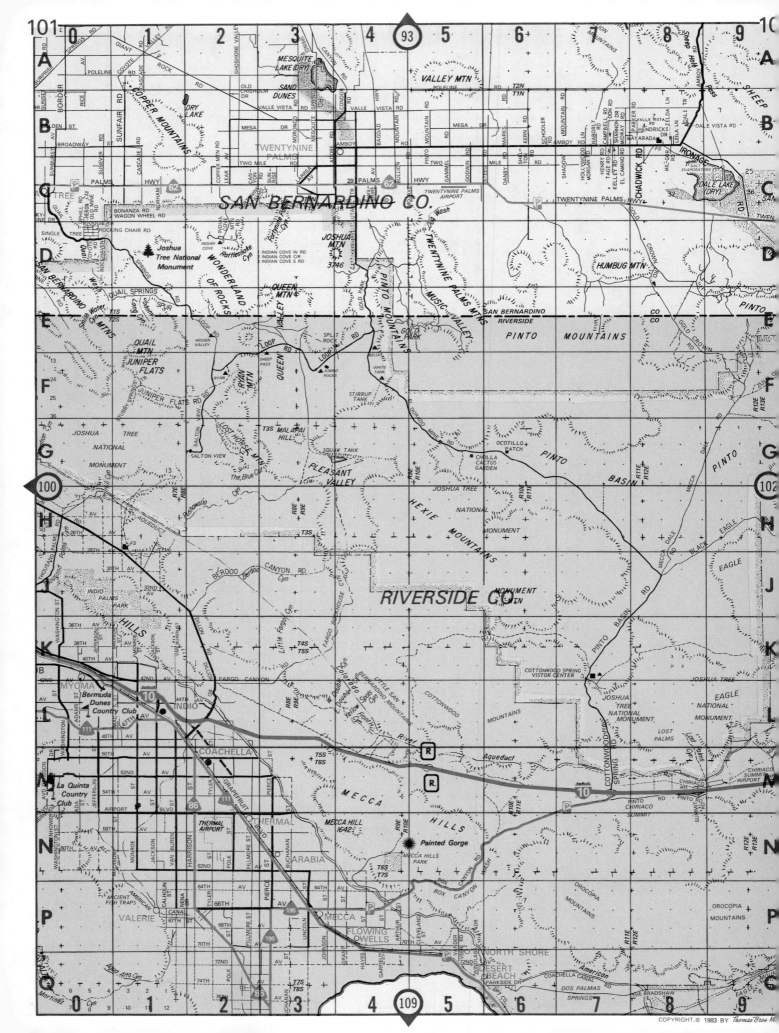

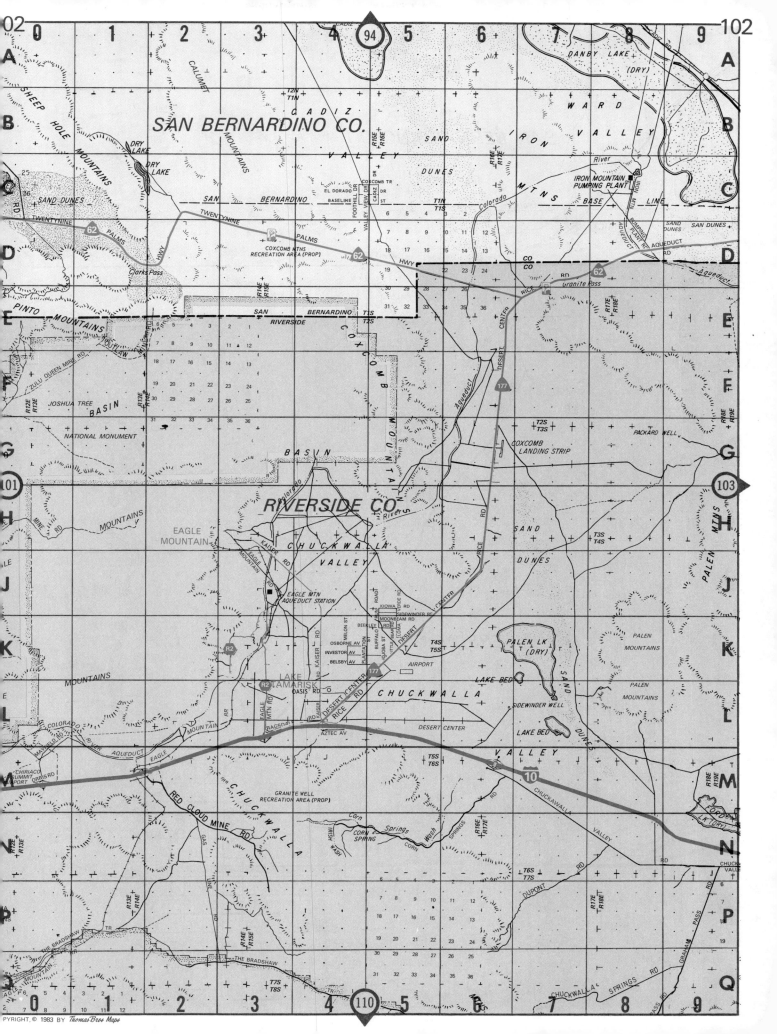

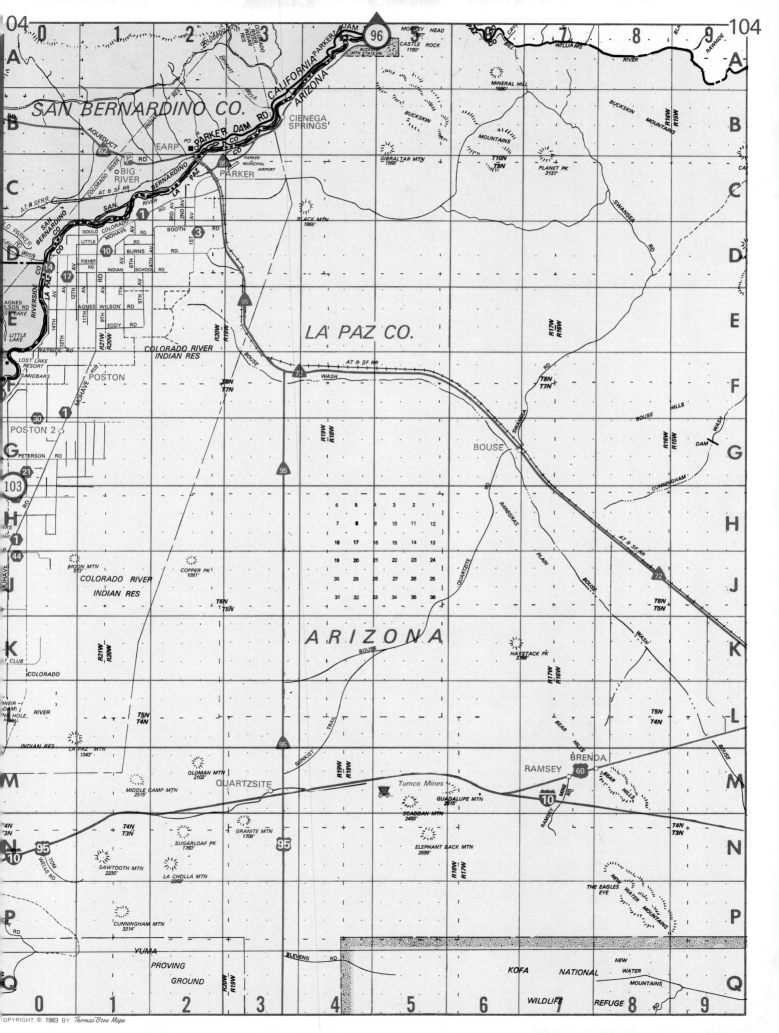

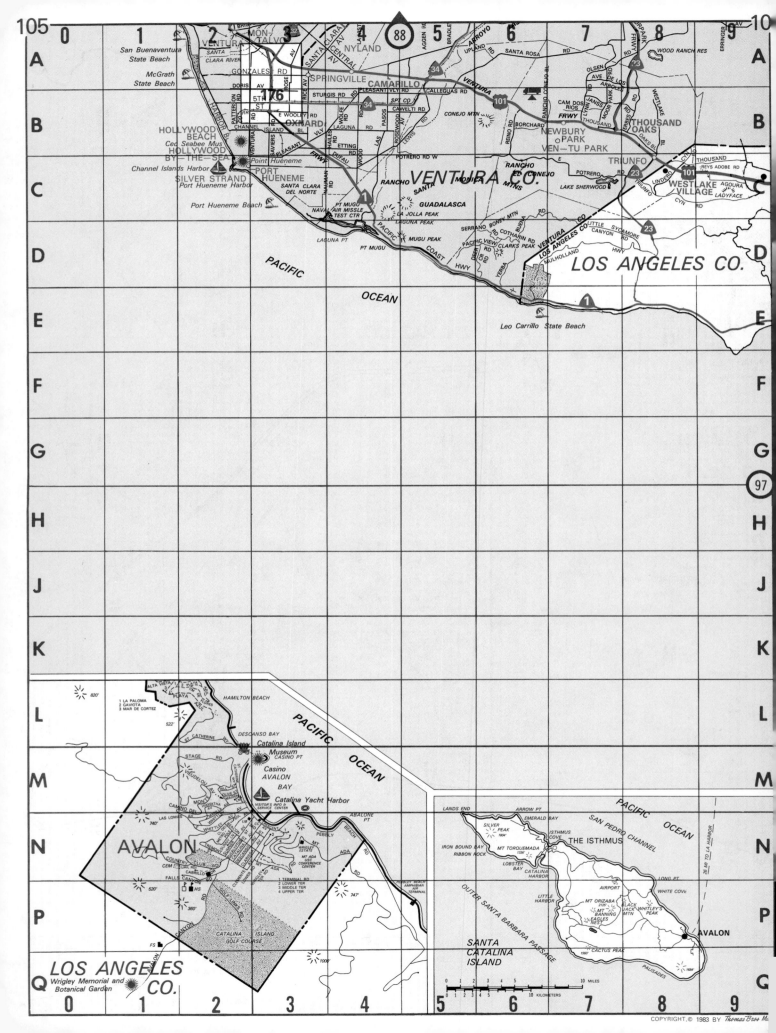

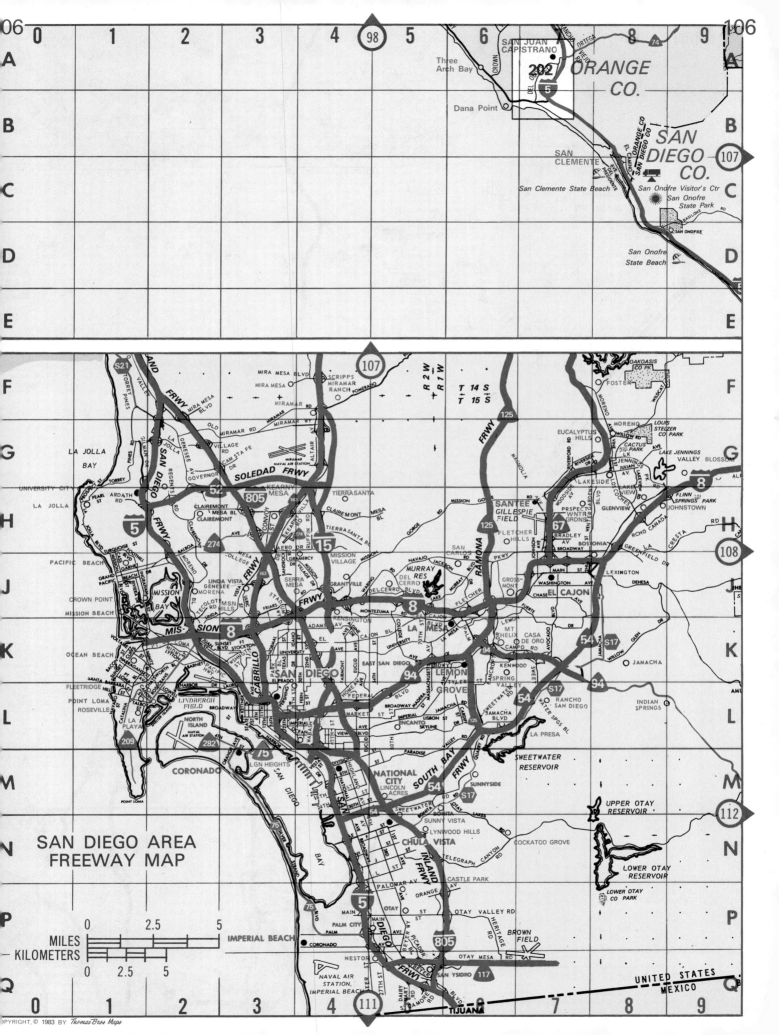

SAN DIEGO AREA
FREEWAY MAP

MILES
KILOMETERS

COPYRIGHT, © 1983 BY *Thomas Bros Maps*

SEE PAGE 106

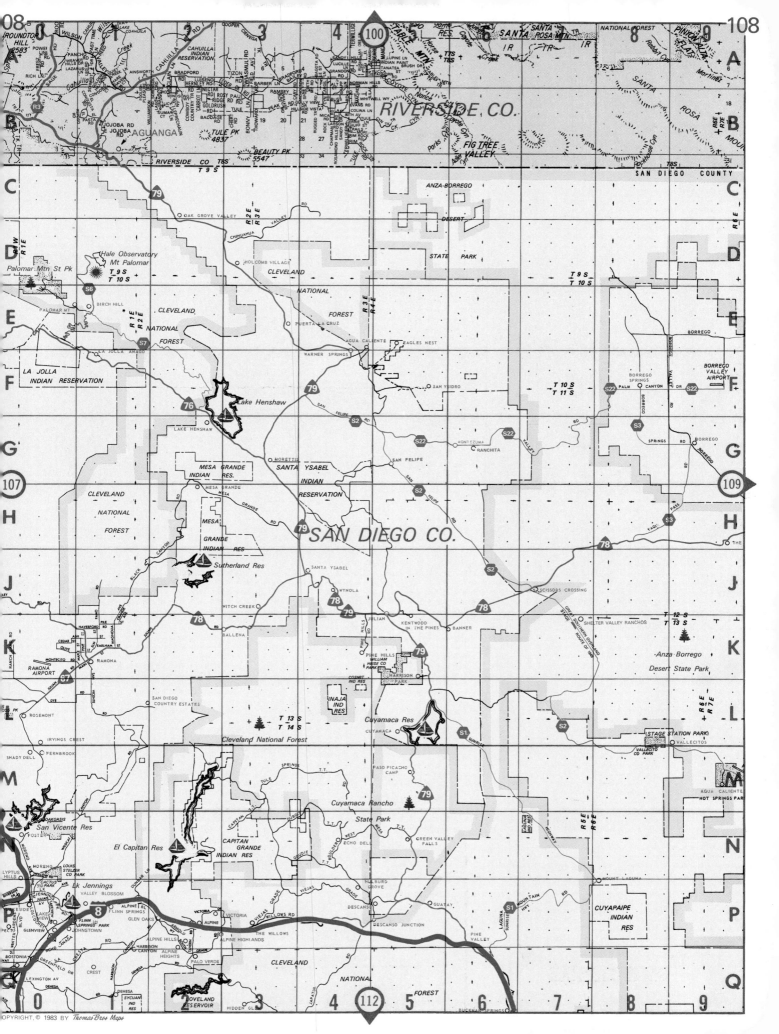

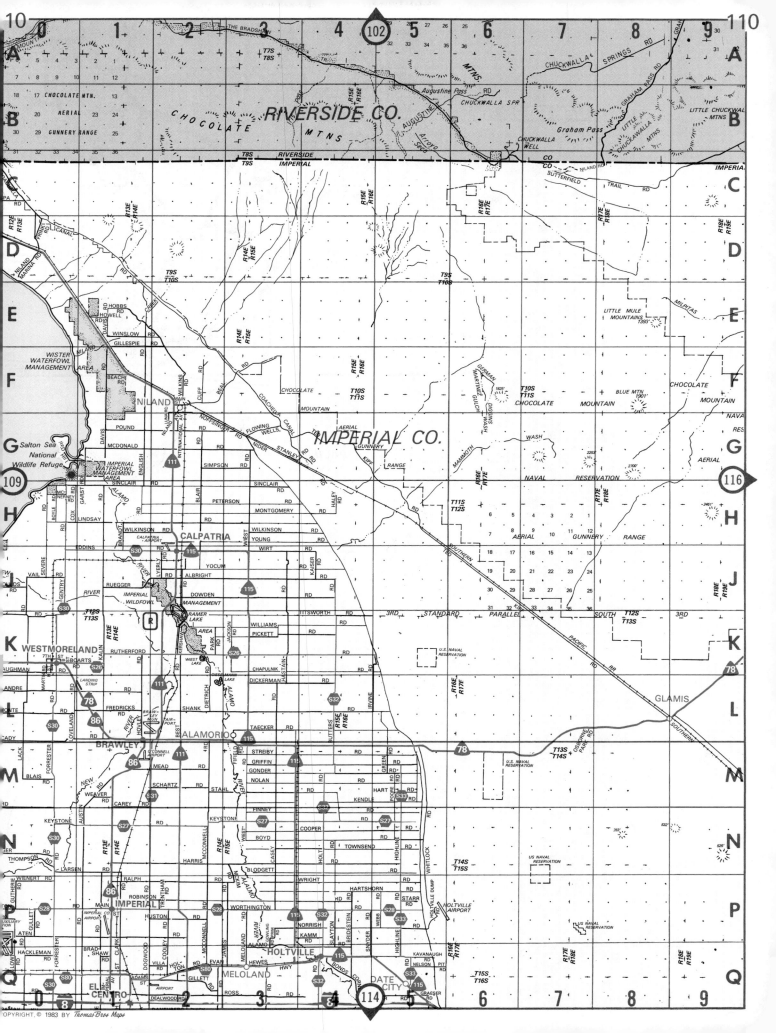

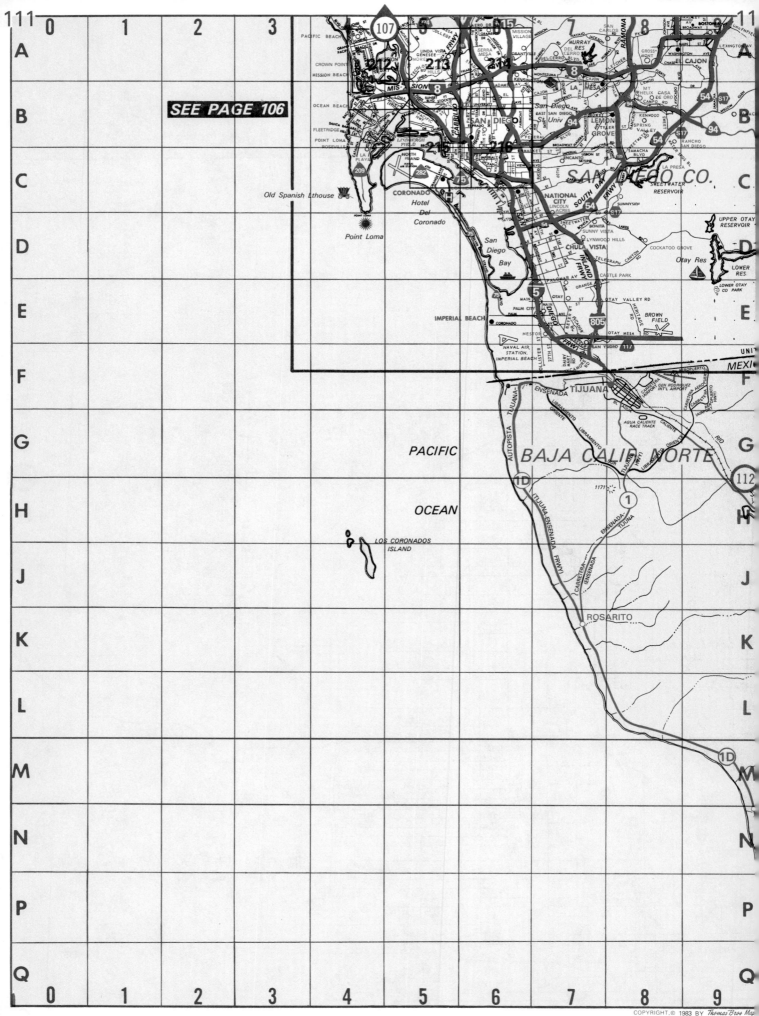

SEE PAGE 106

Old Spanish Lthouse

Point Loma

PACIFIC

OCEAN

LOS CORONADOS
ISLAND

BAJA CALIF. NORTE

SAN DIEGO CO.

ROSARITO

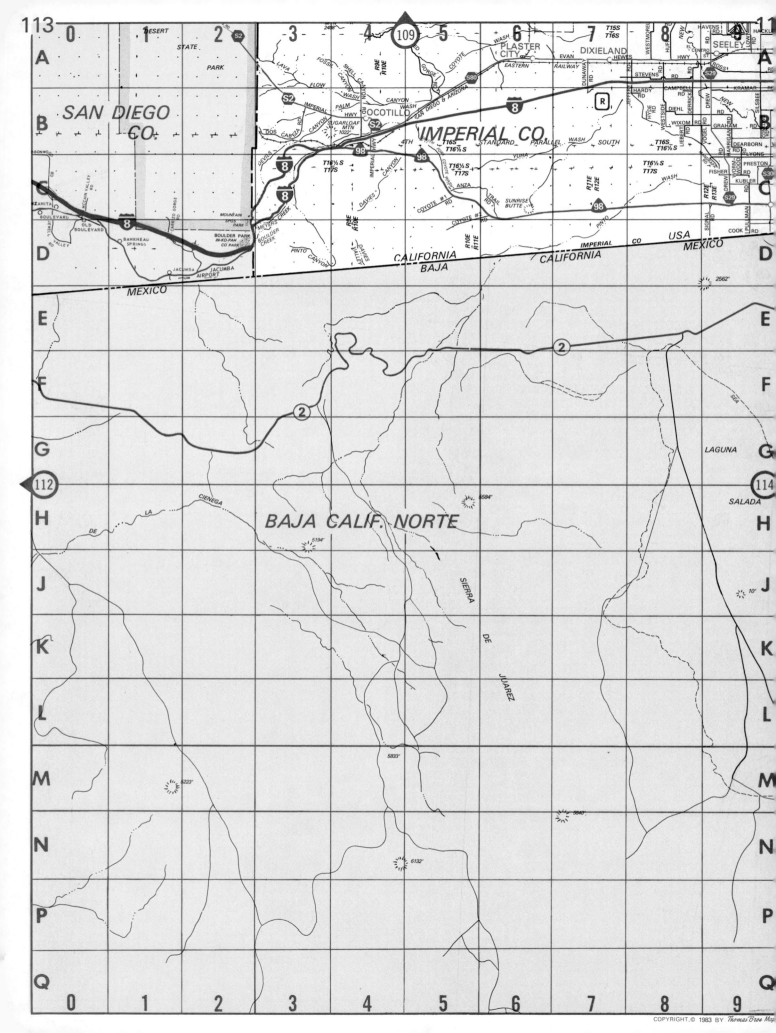

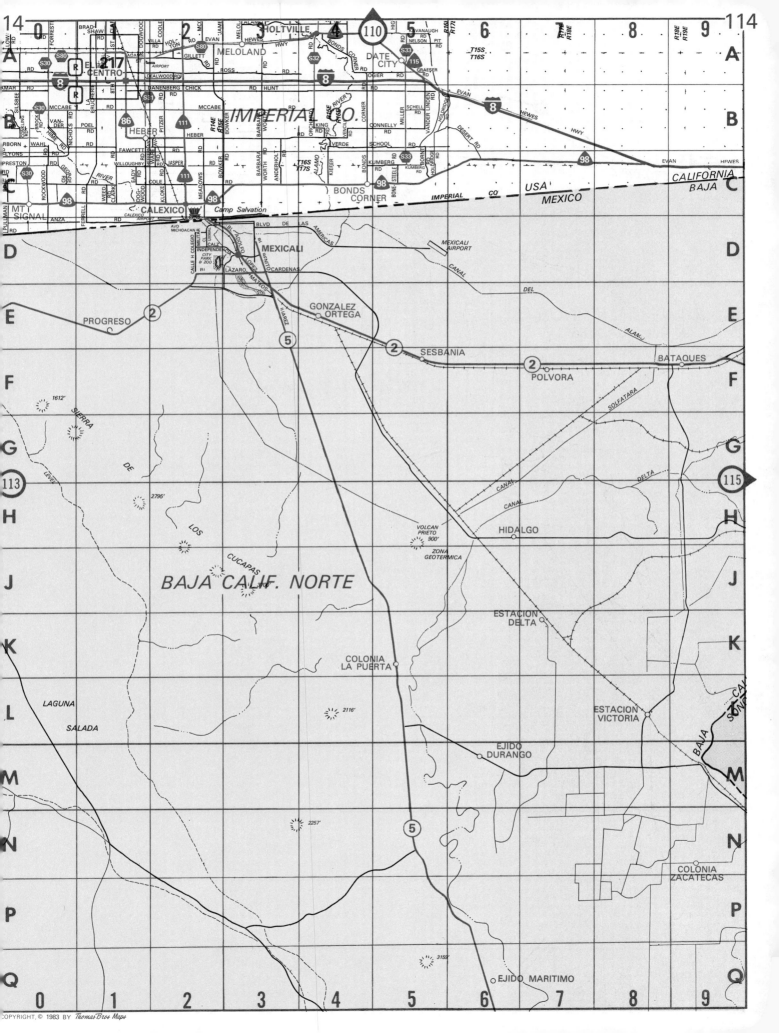

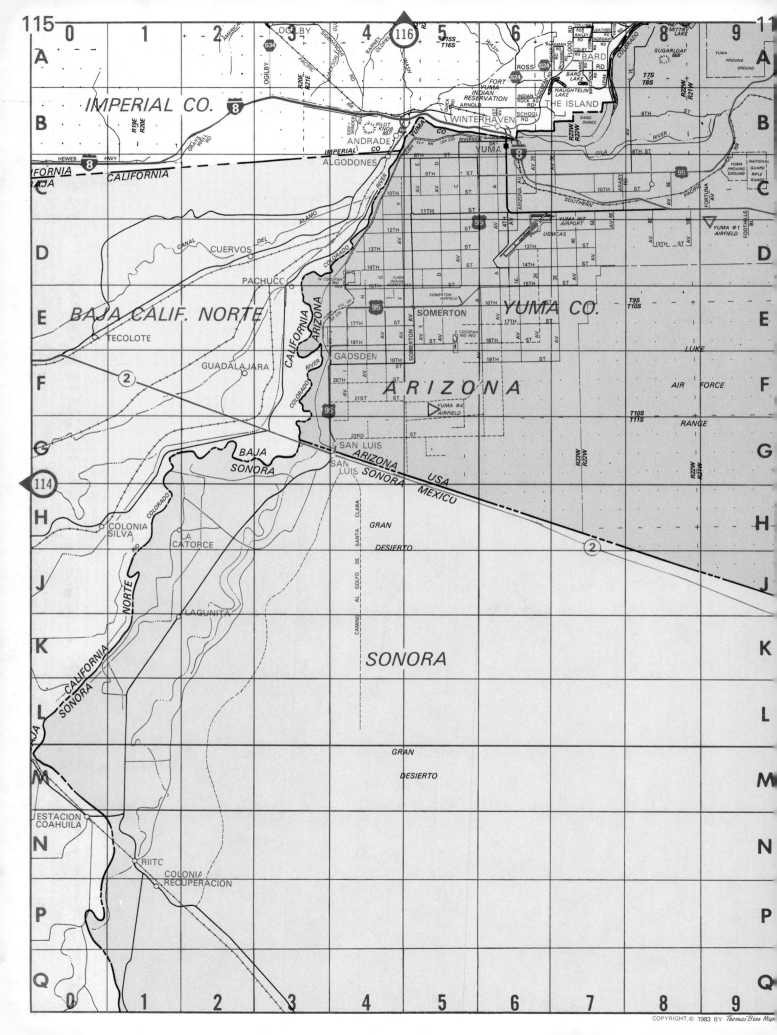

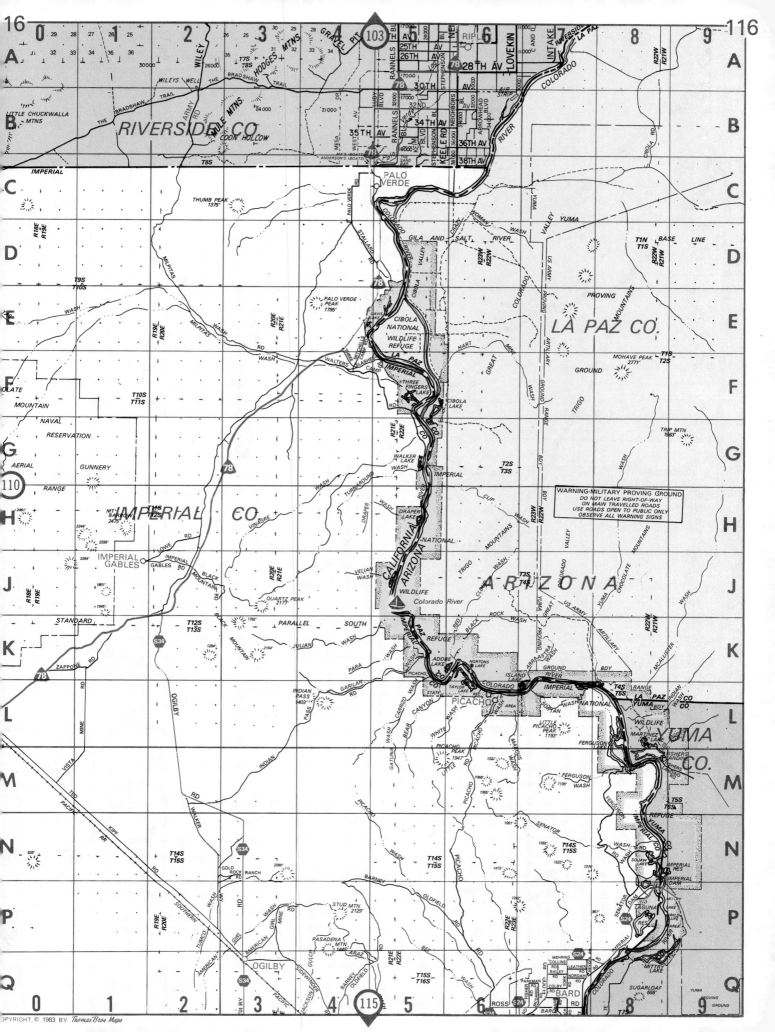

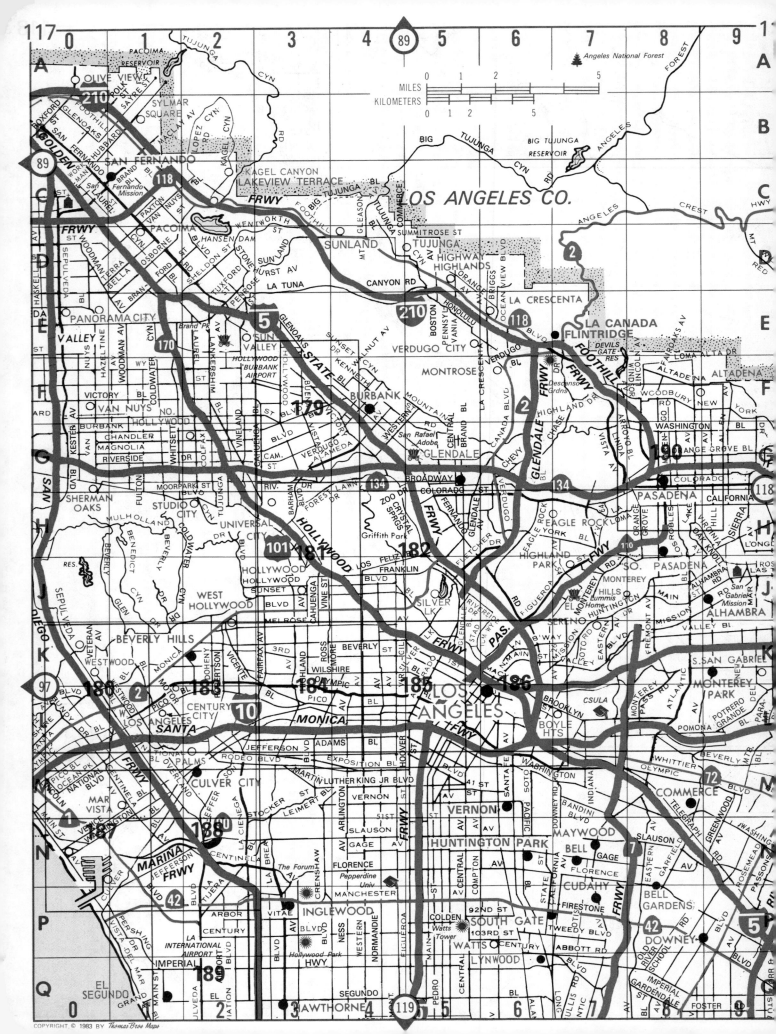

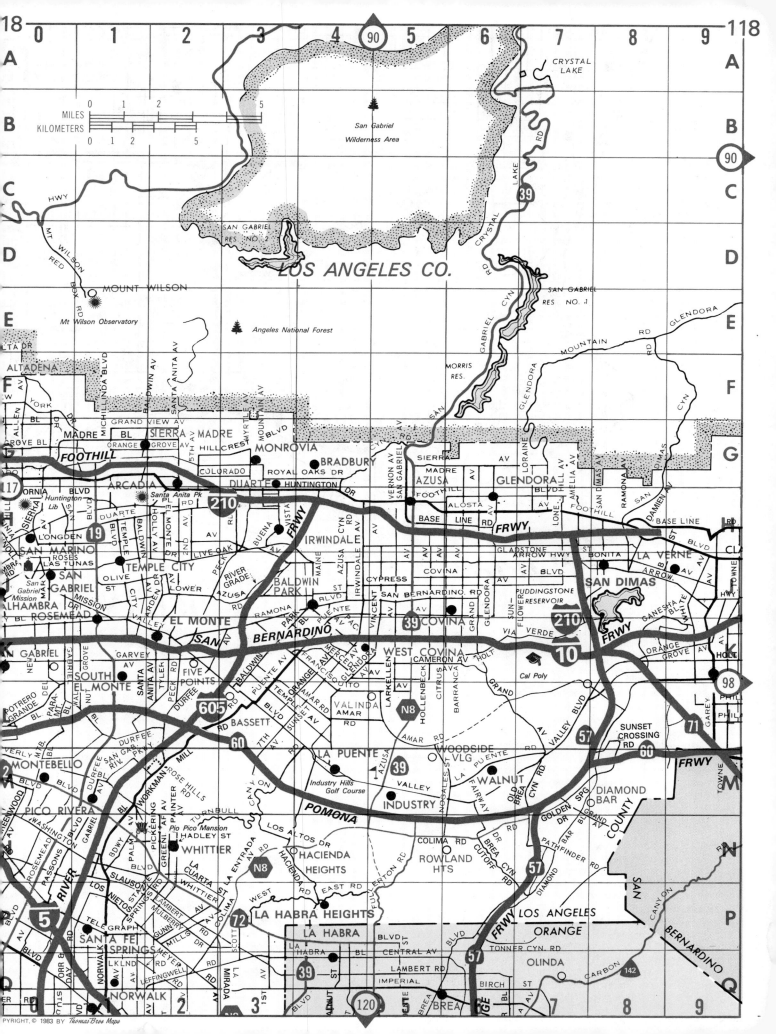

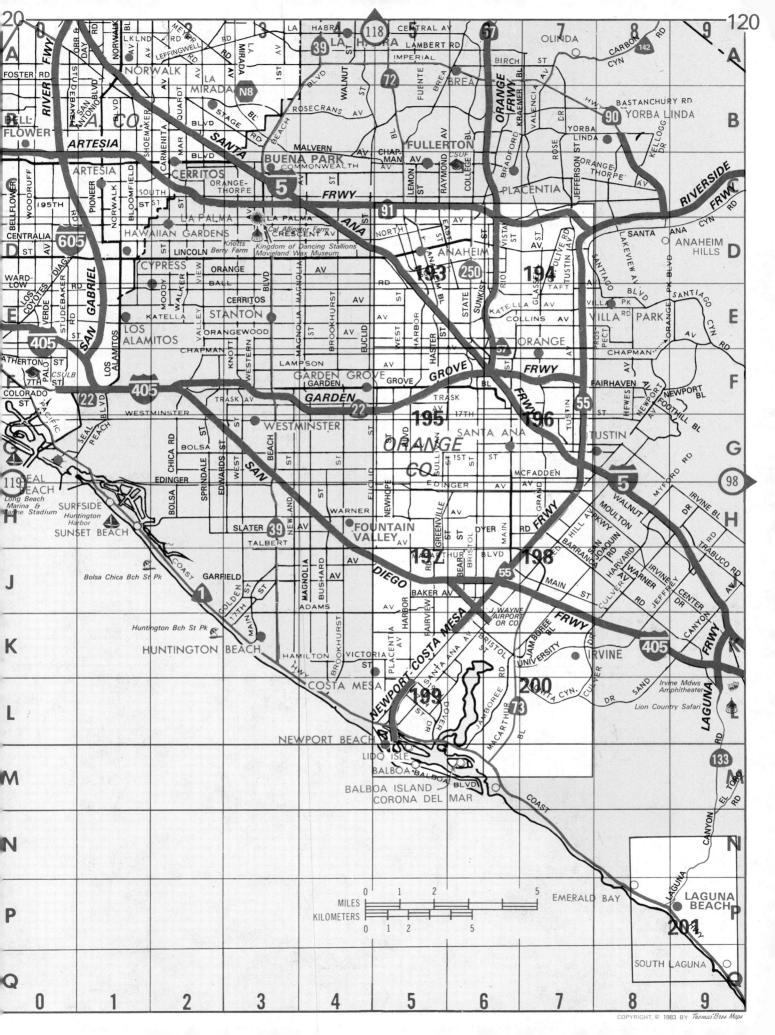

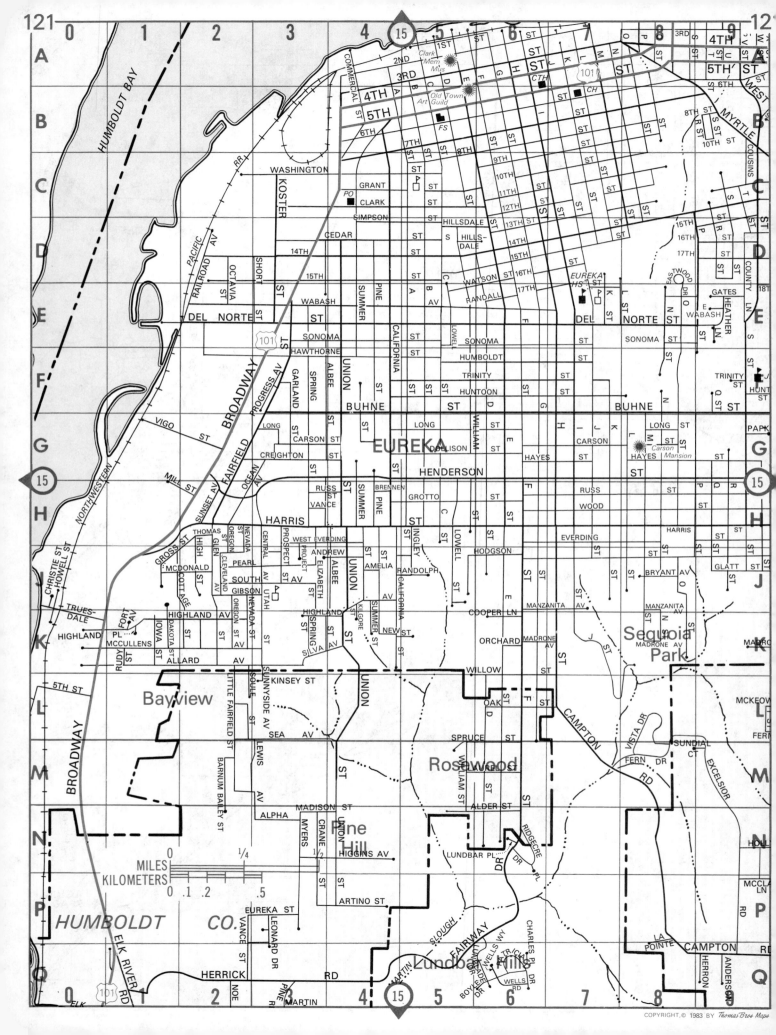

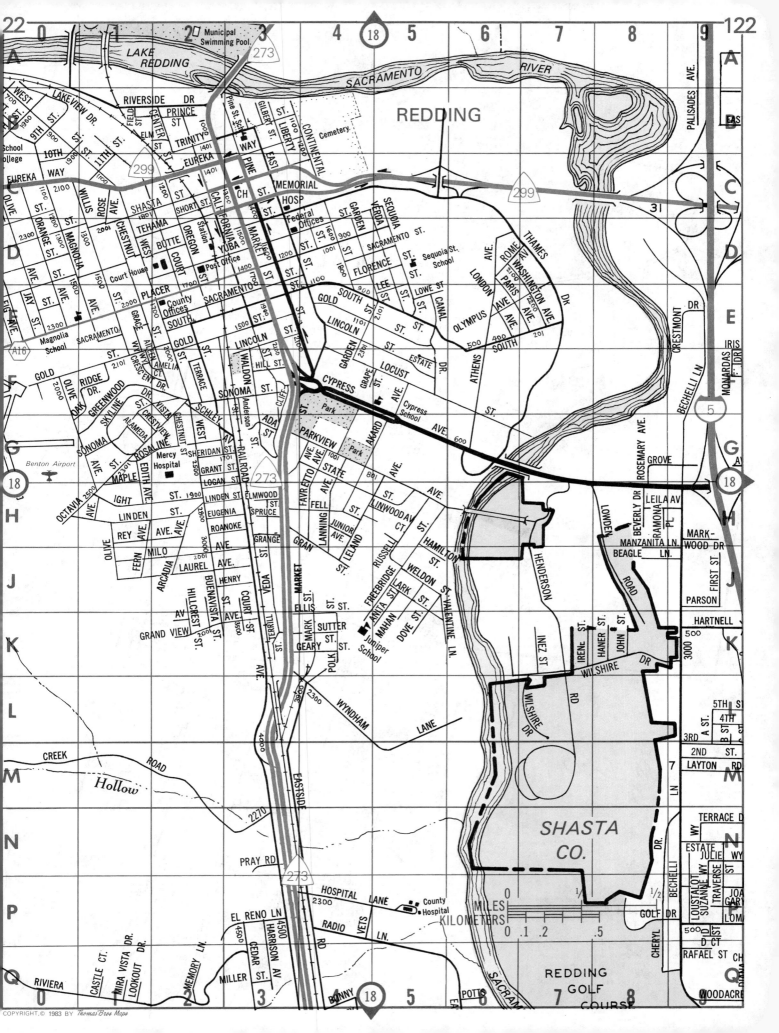

REDDING

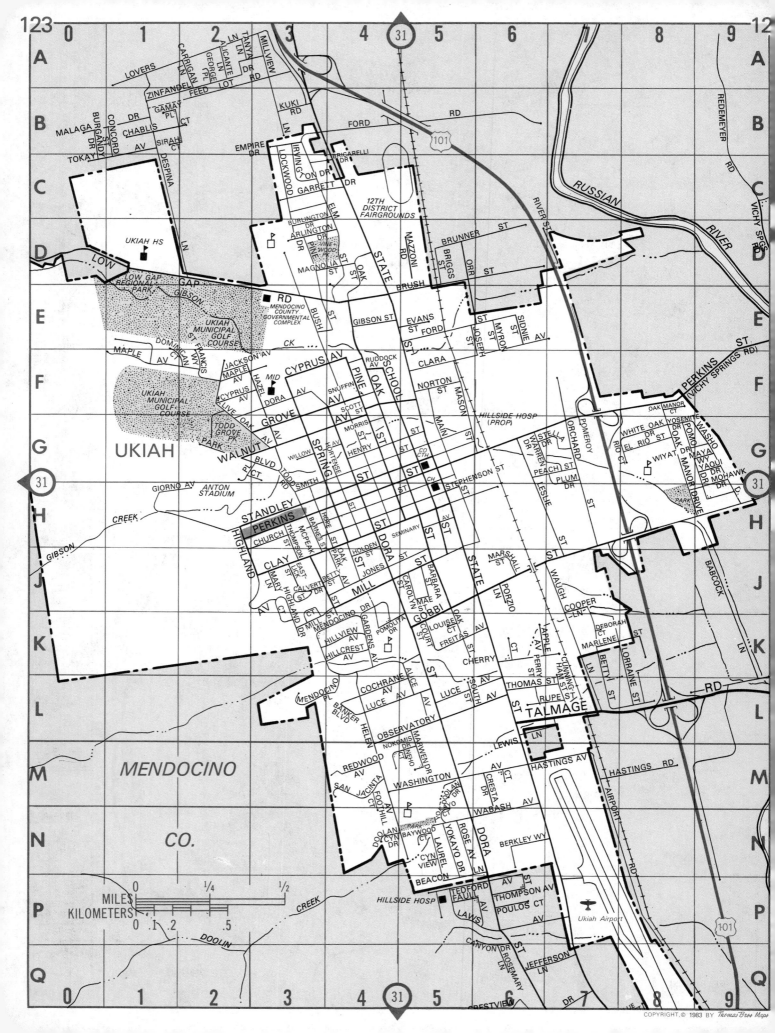

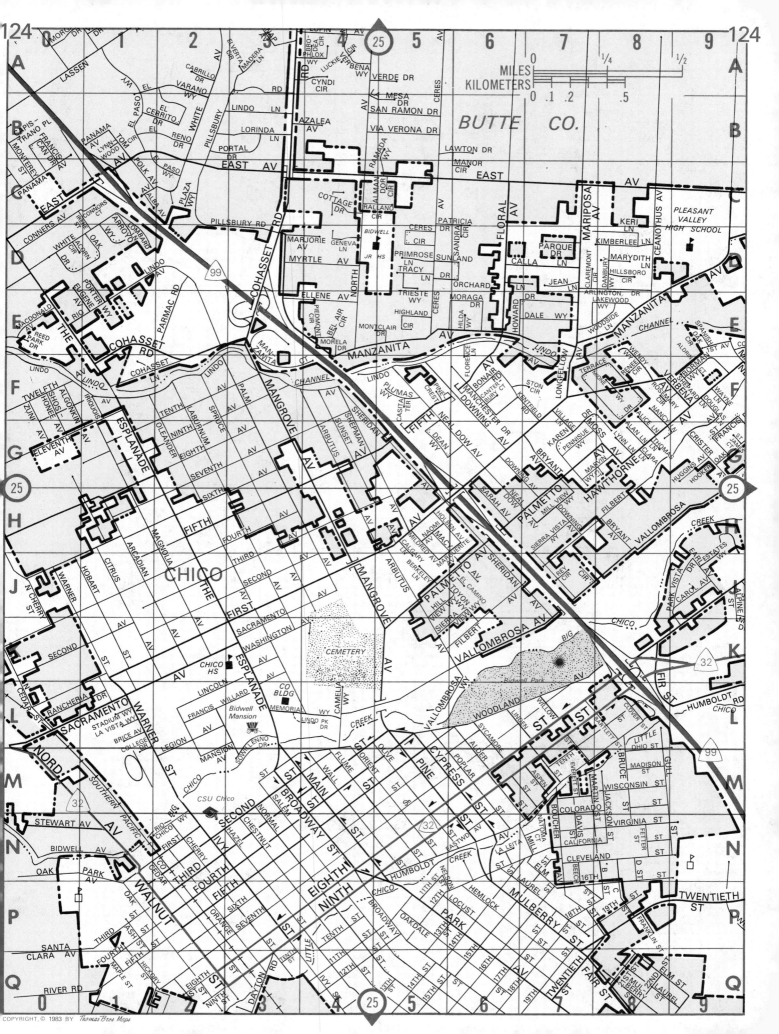

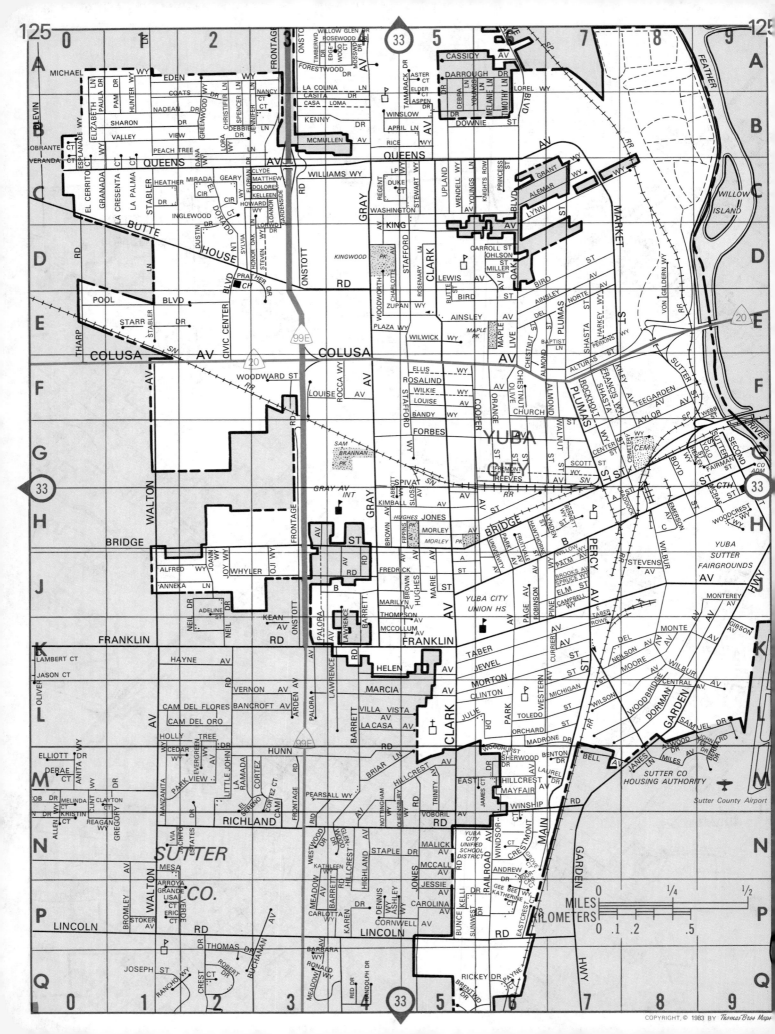

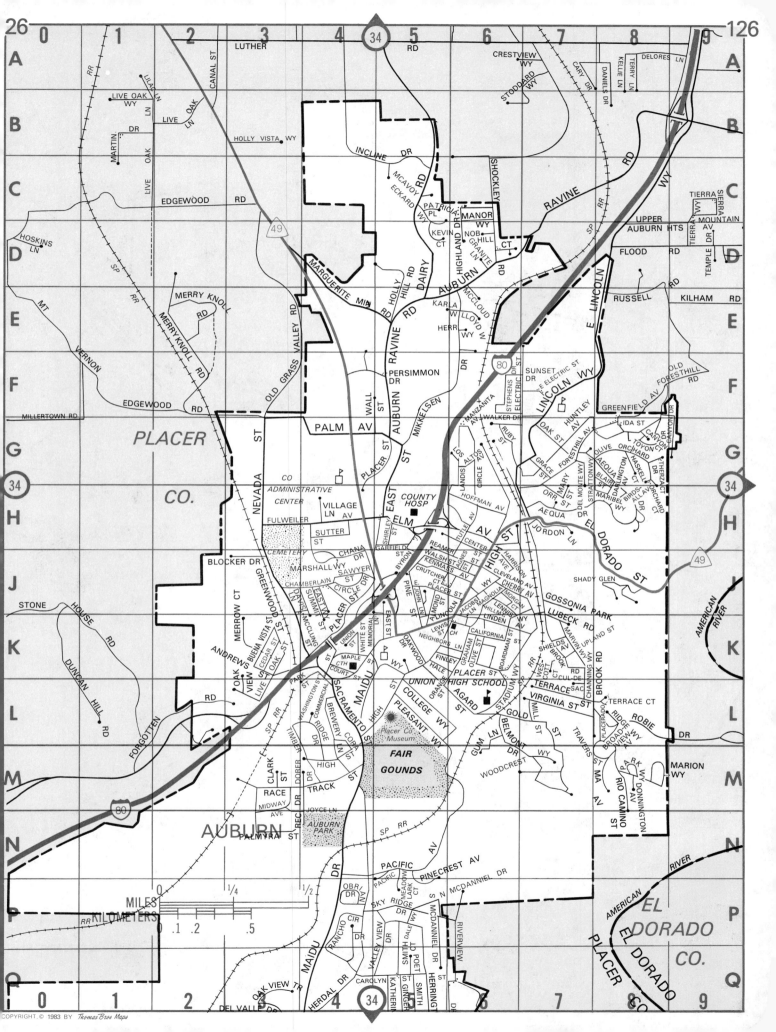

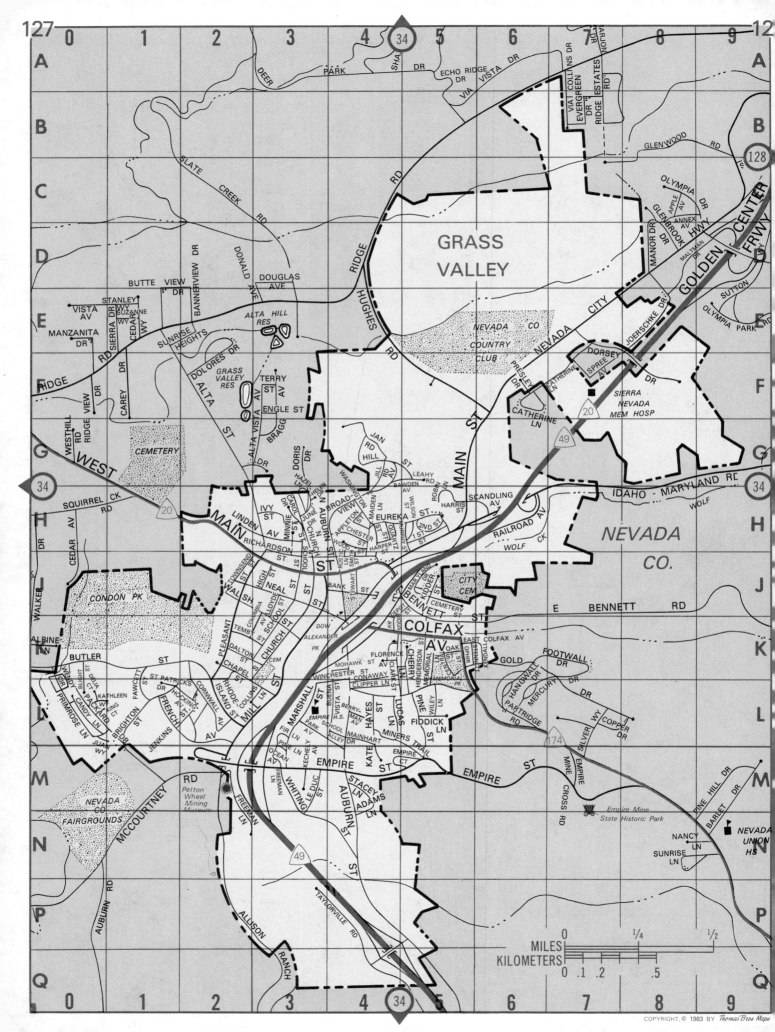

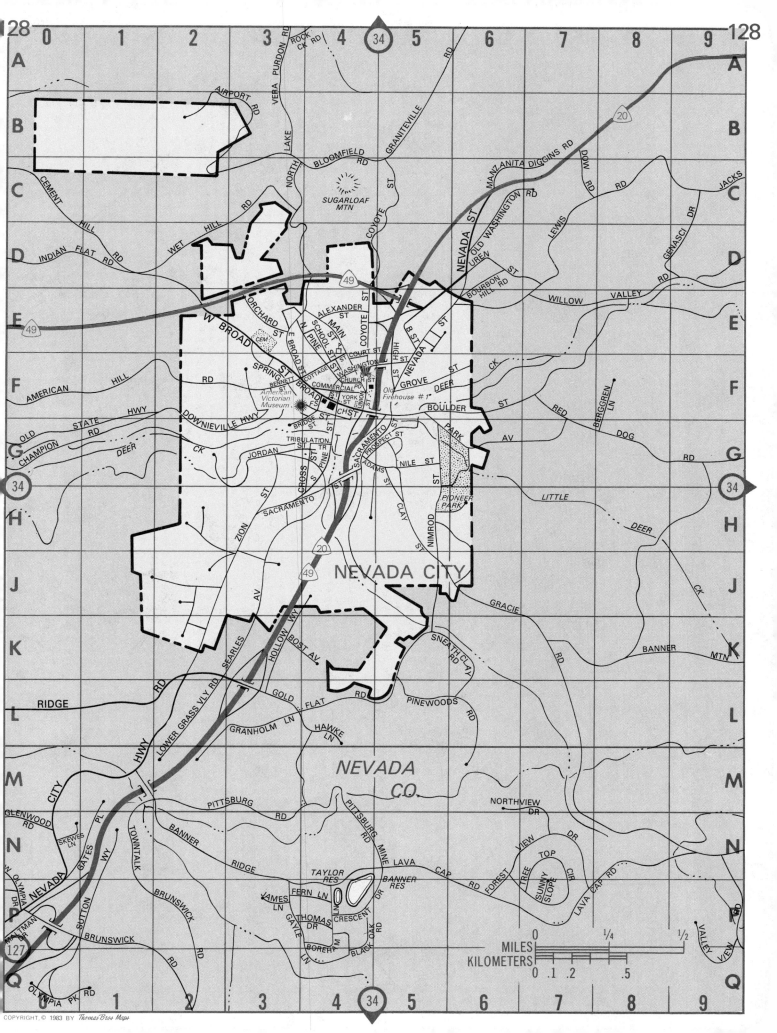

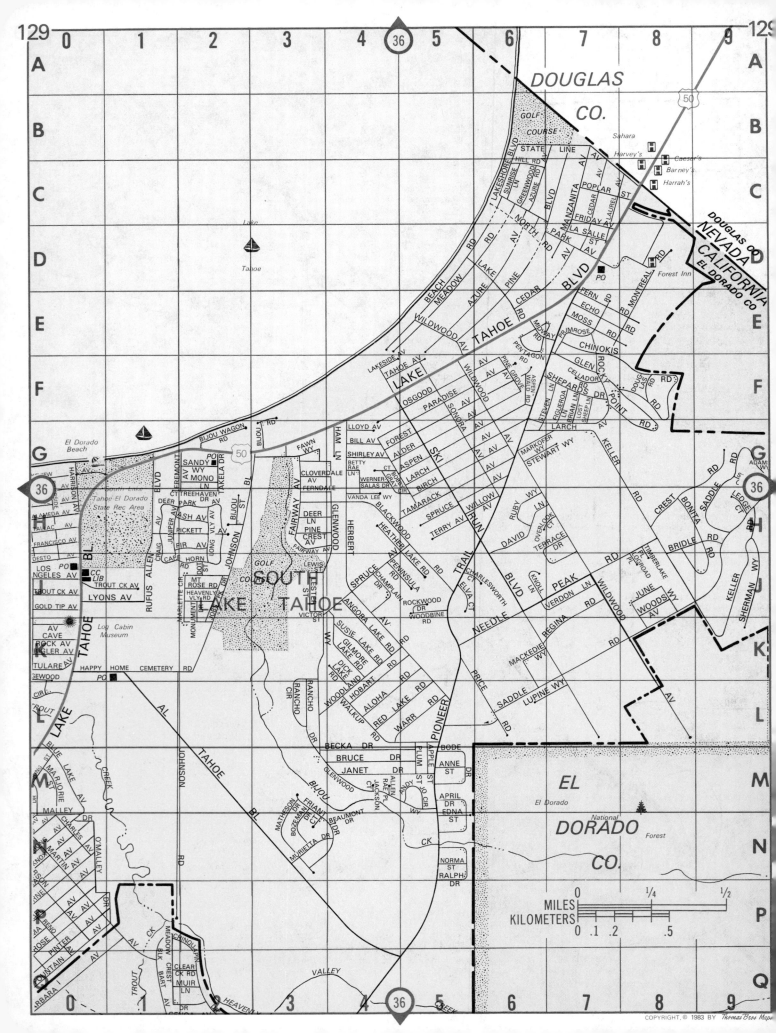

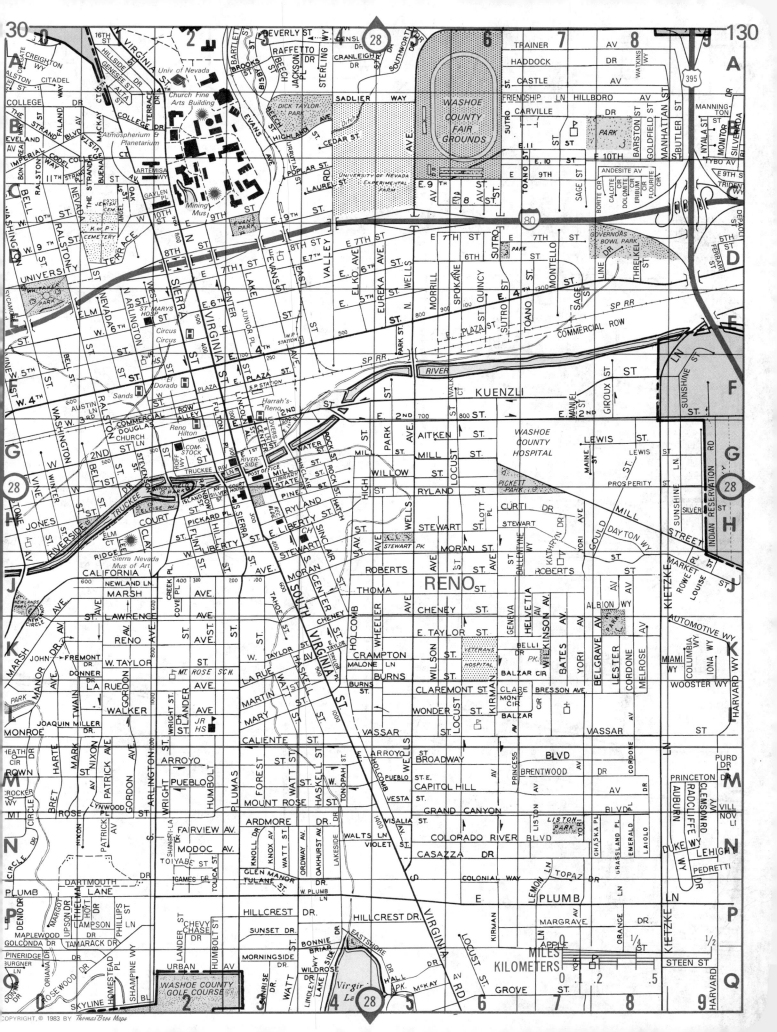

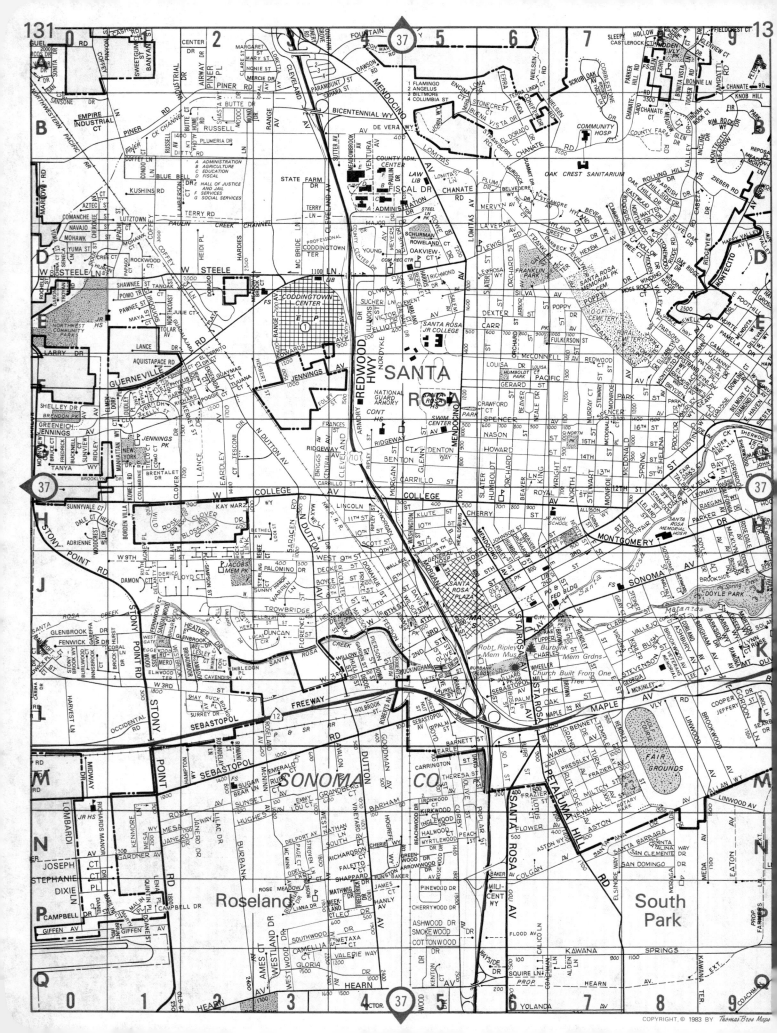

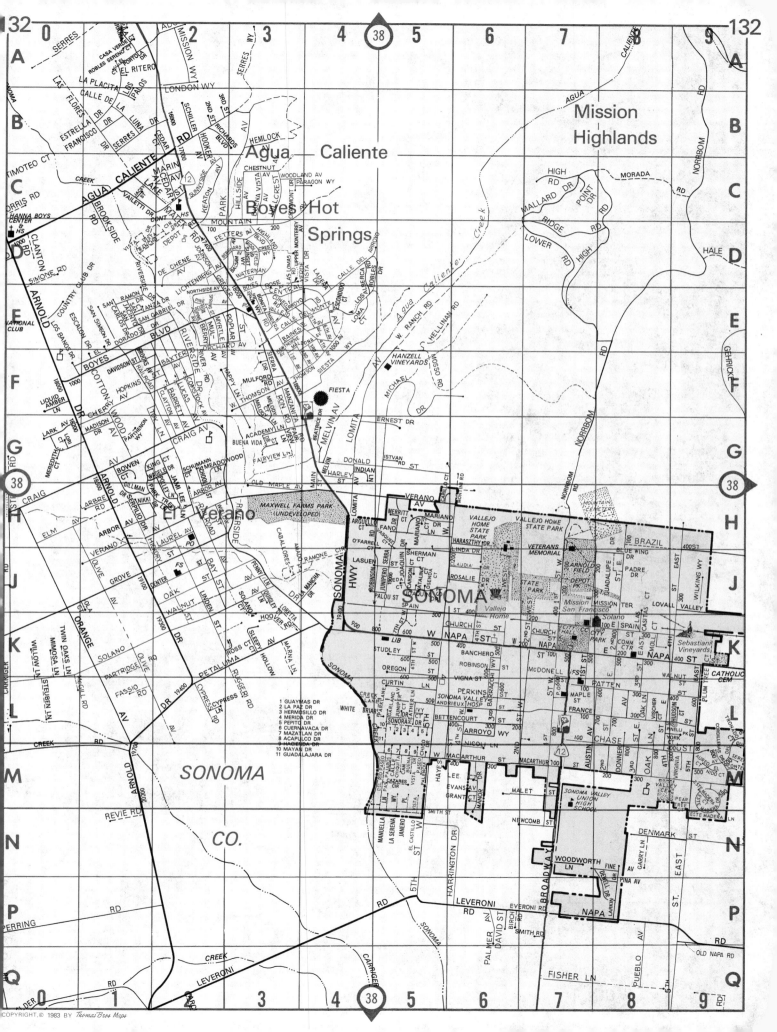

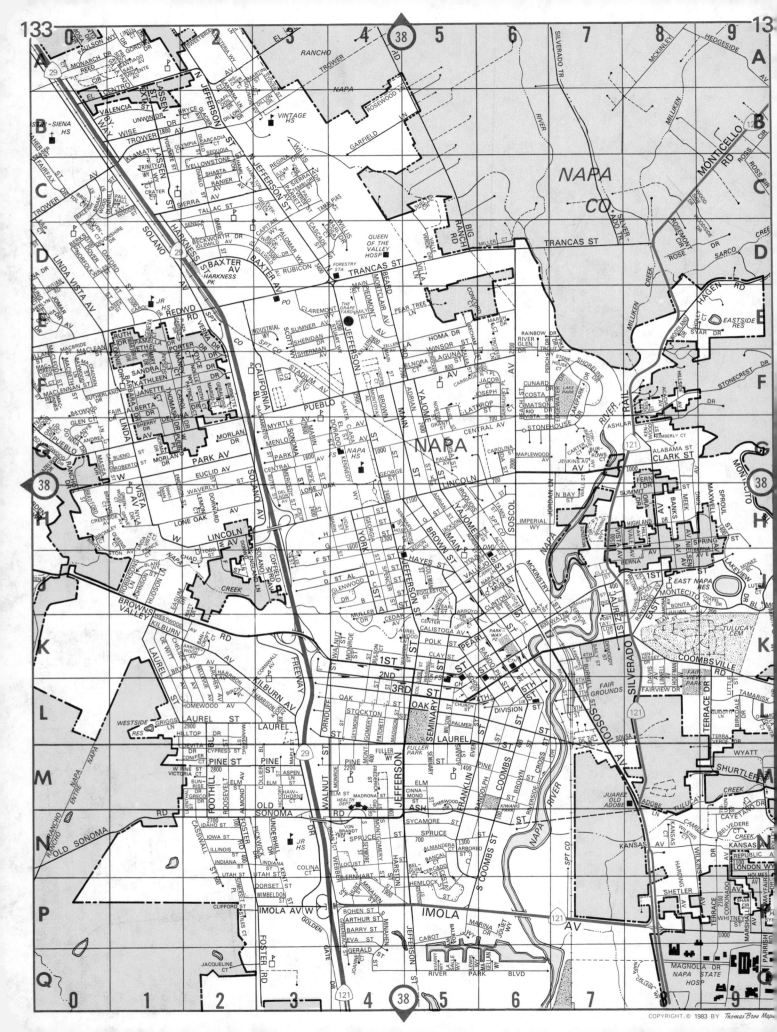

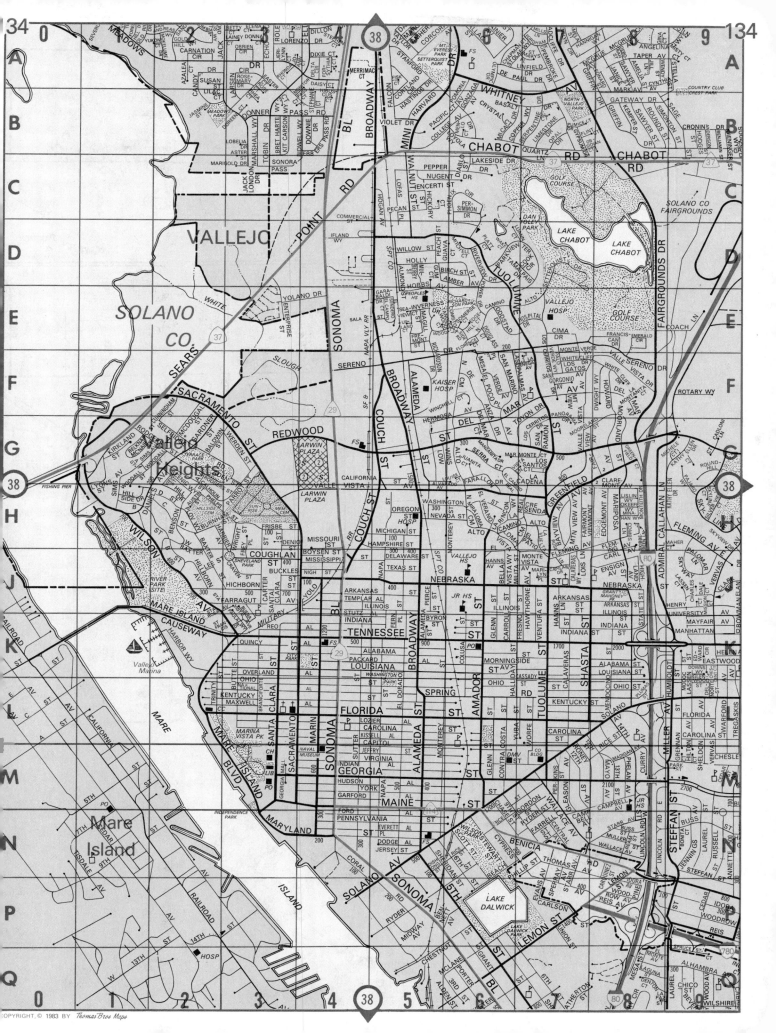

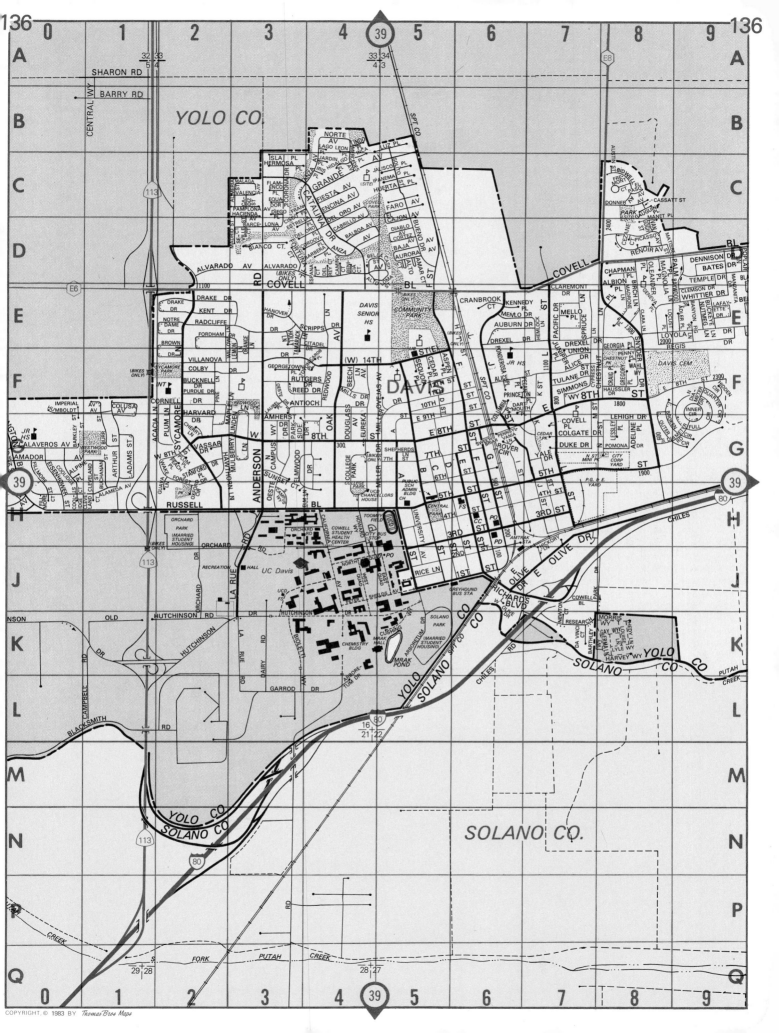

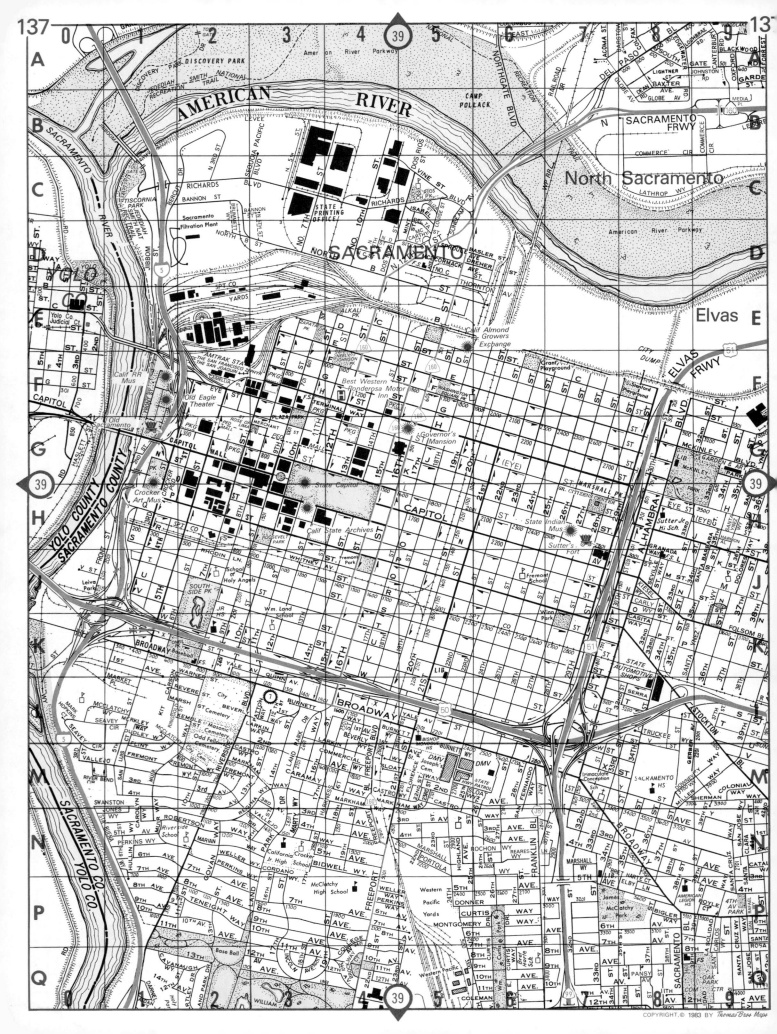

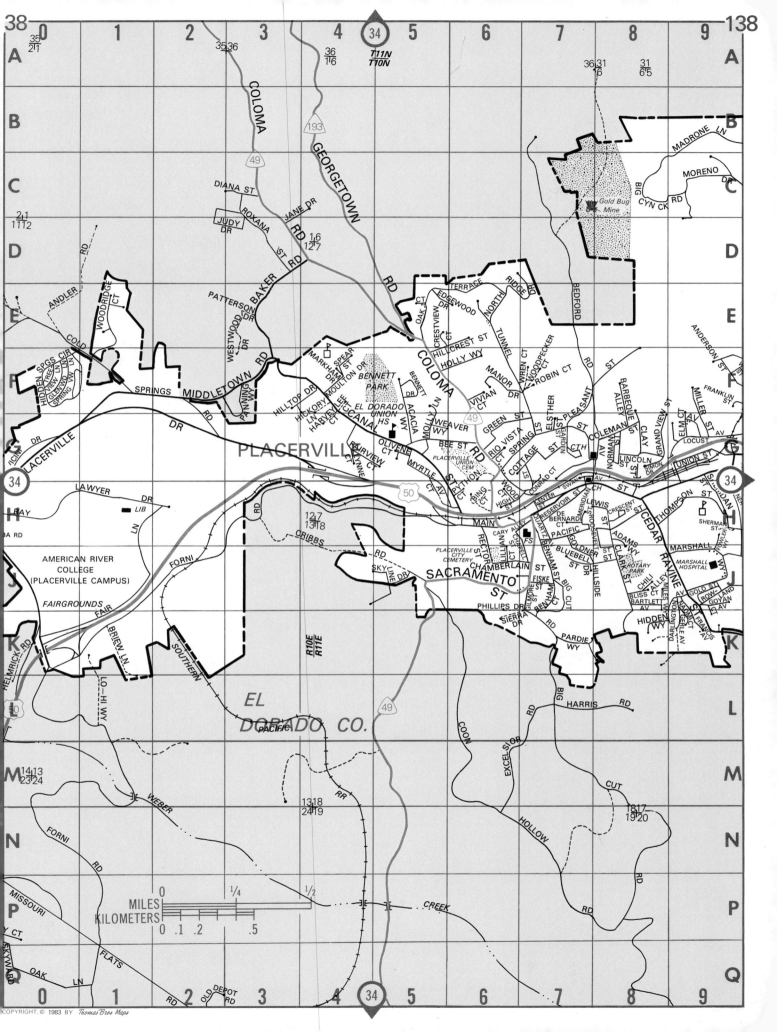

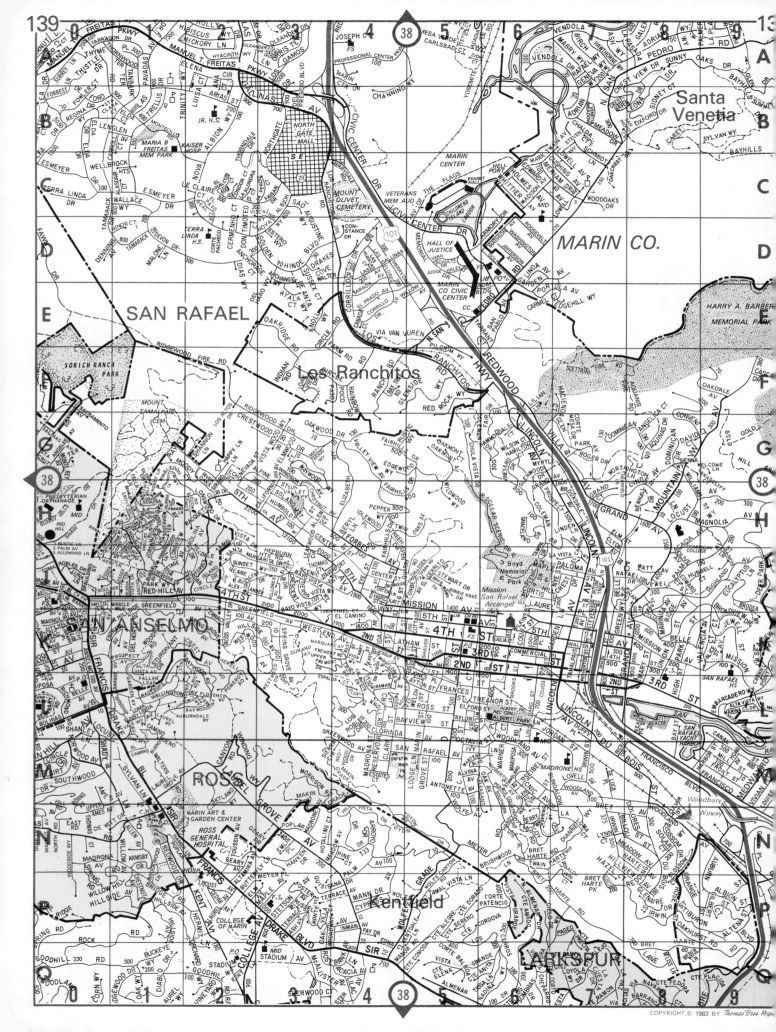

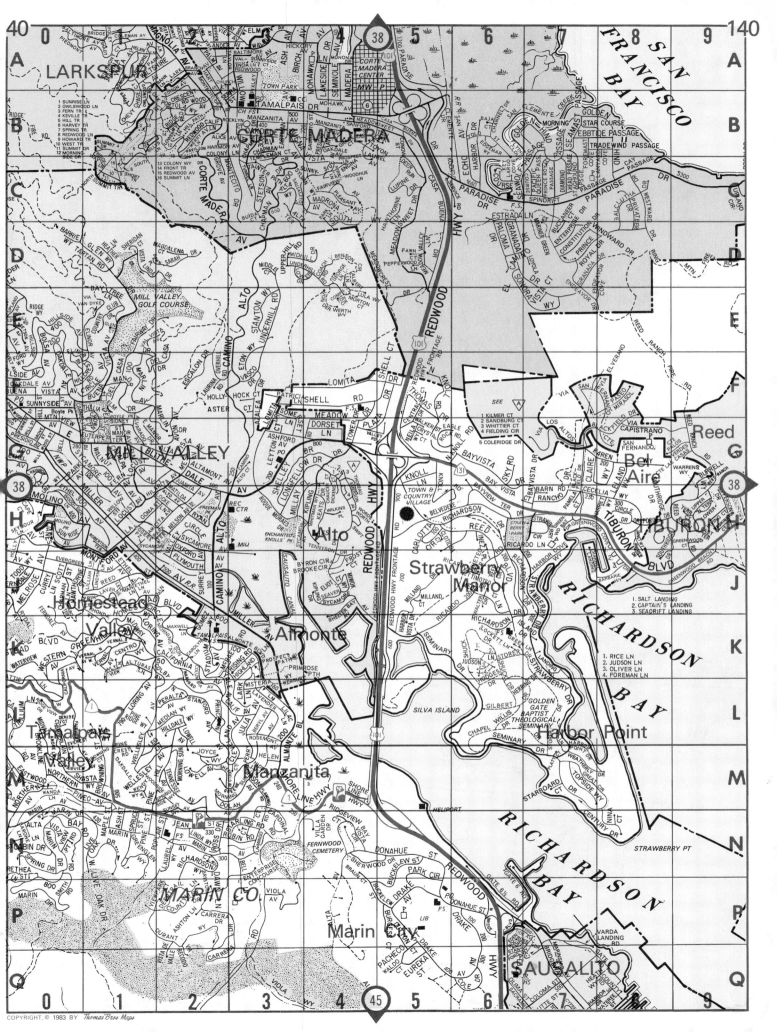

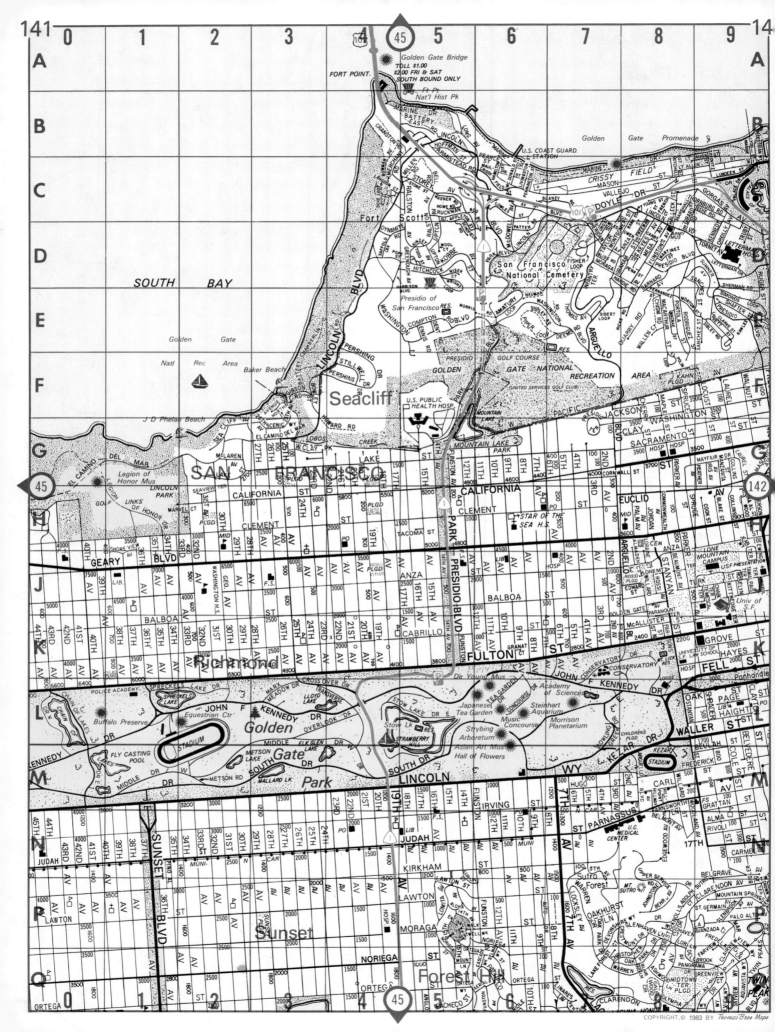

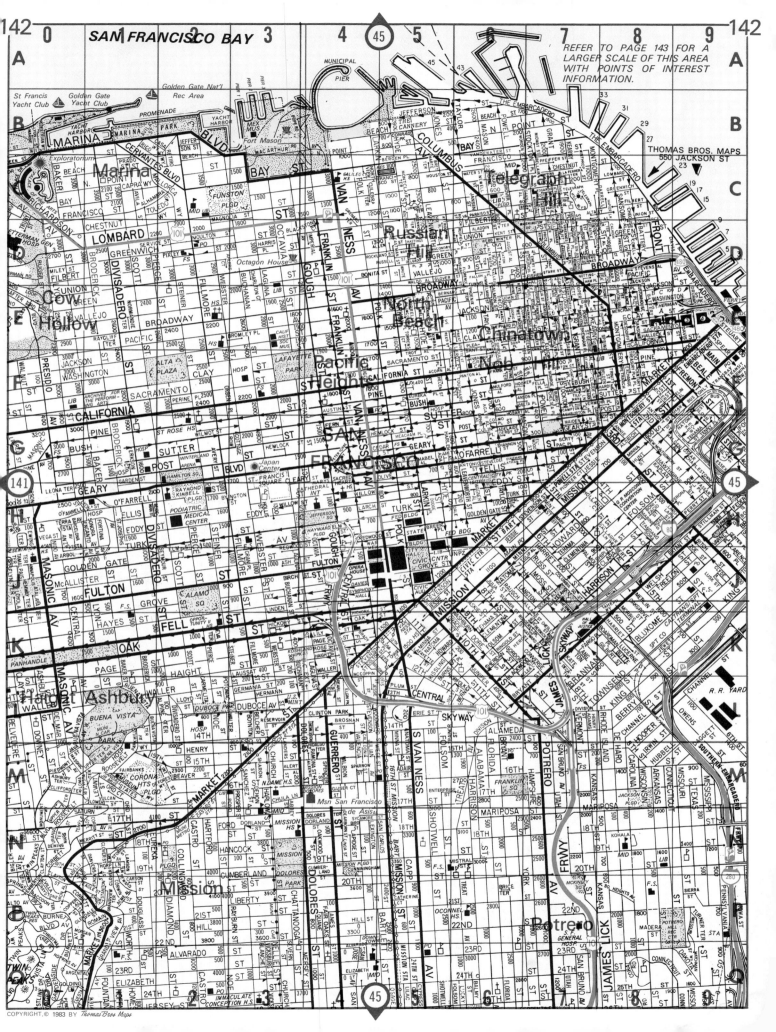

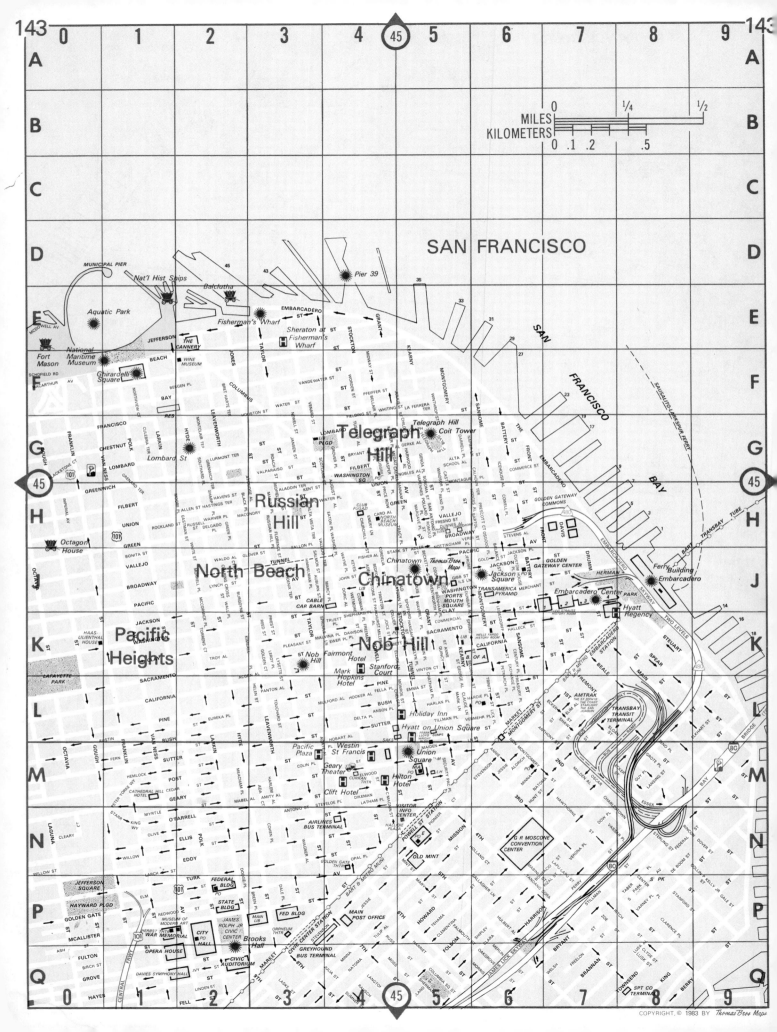

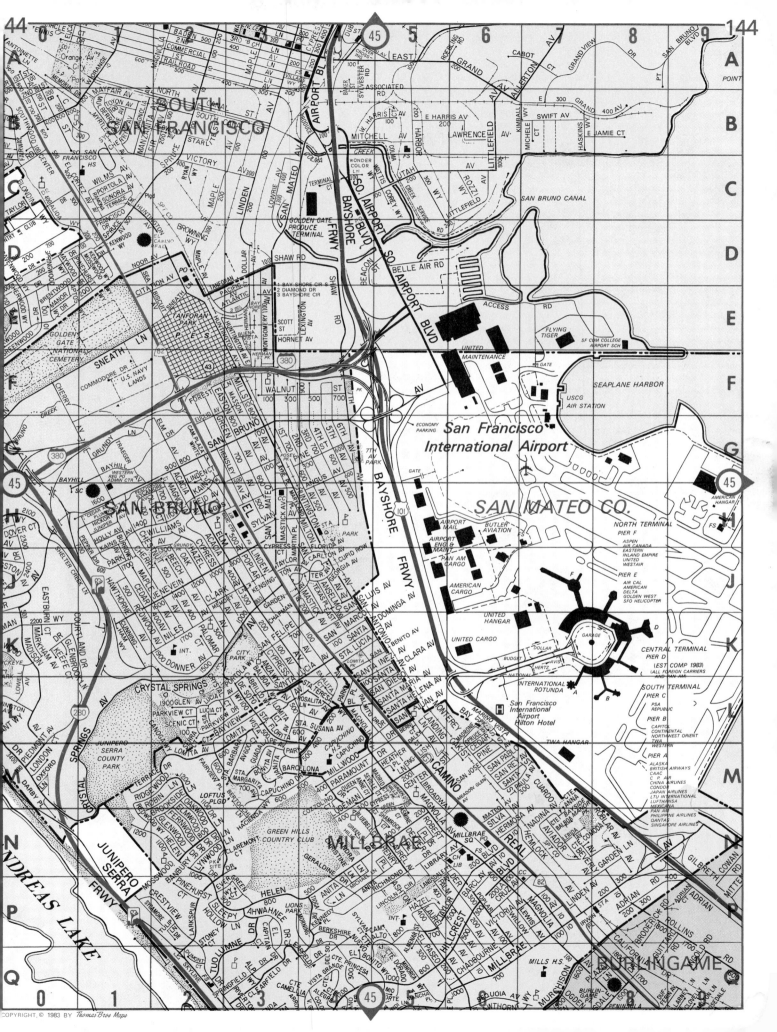

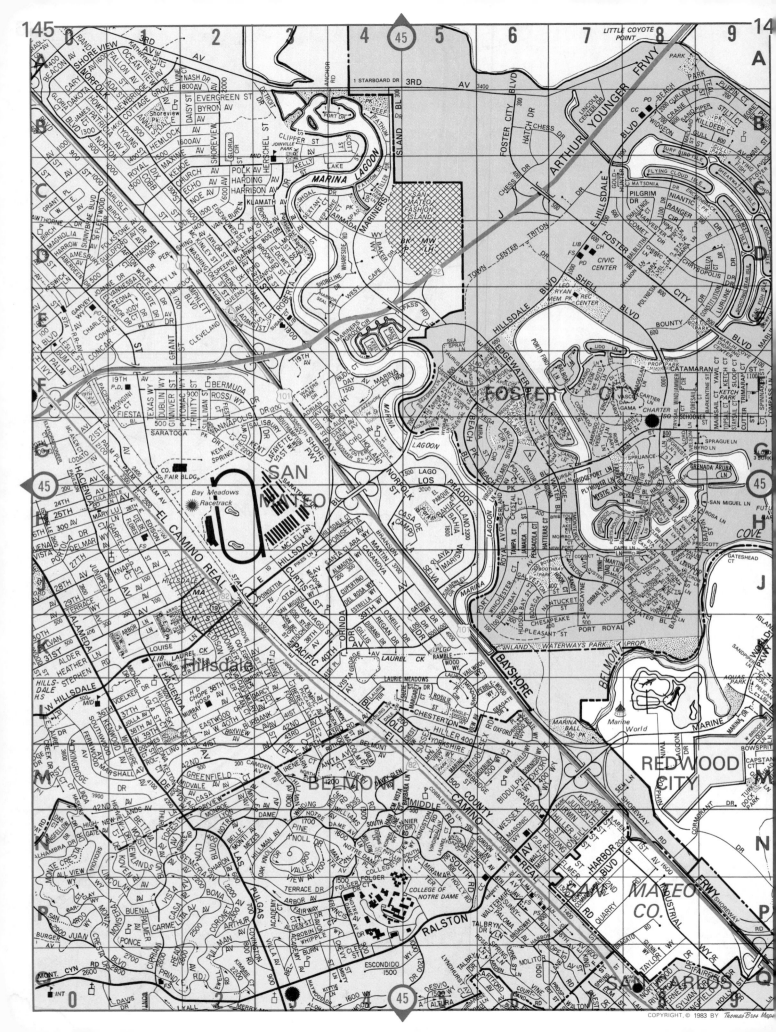

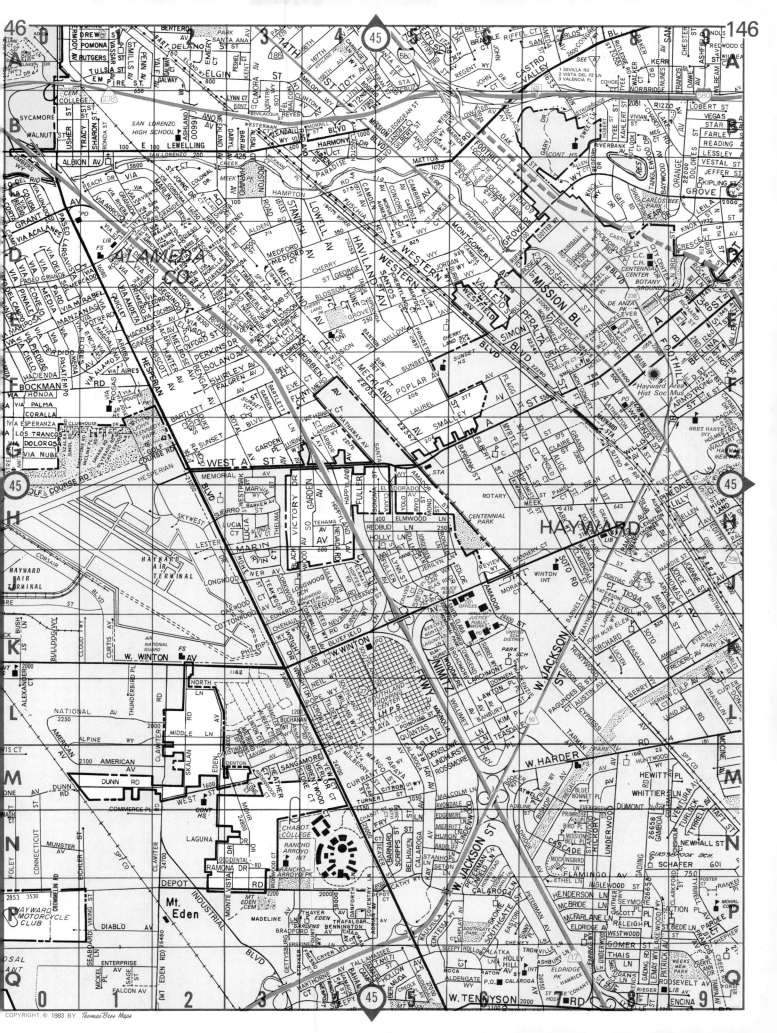

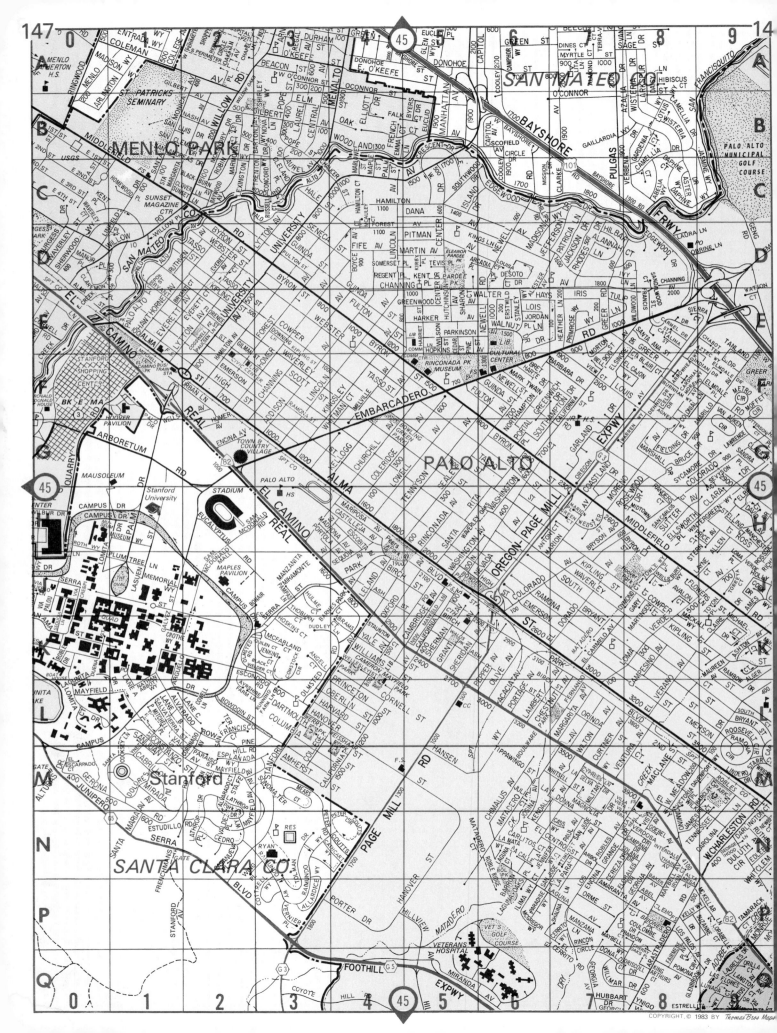

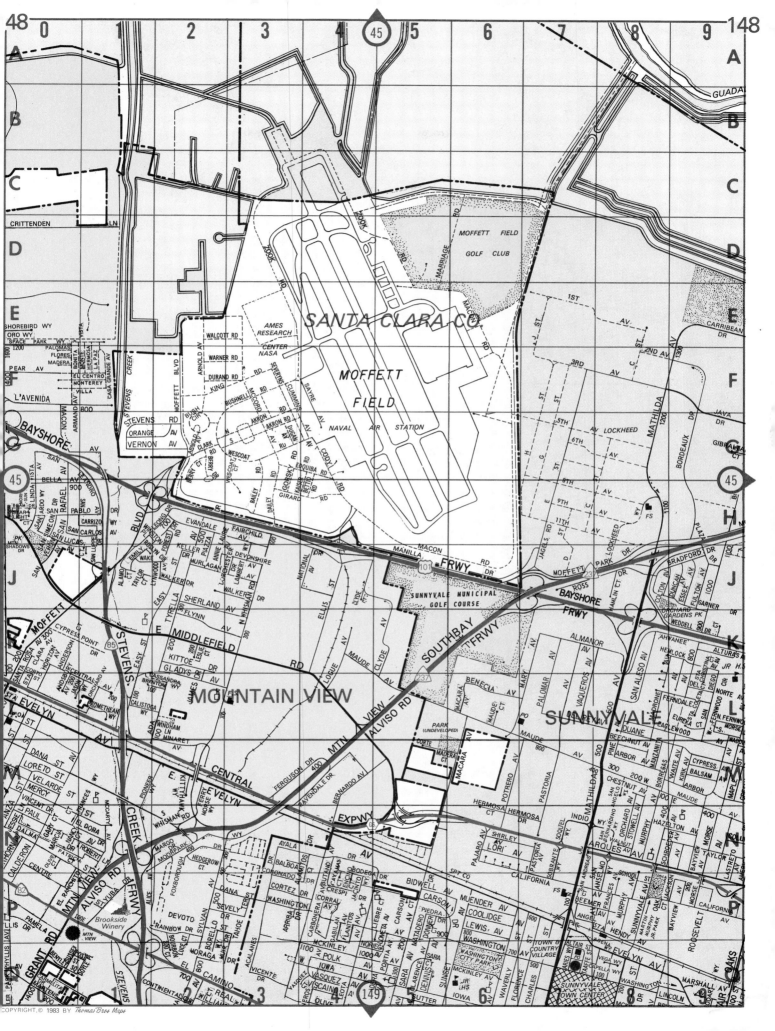

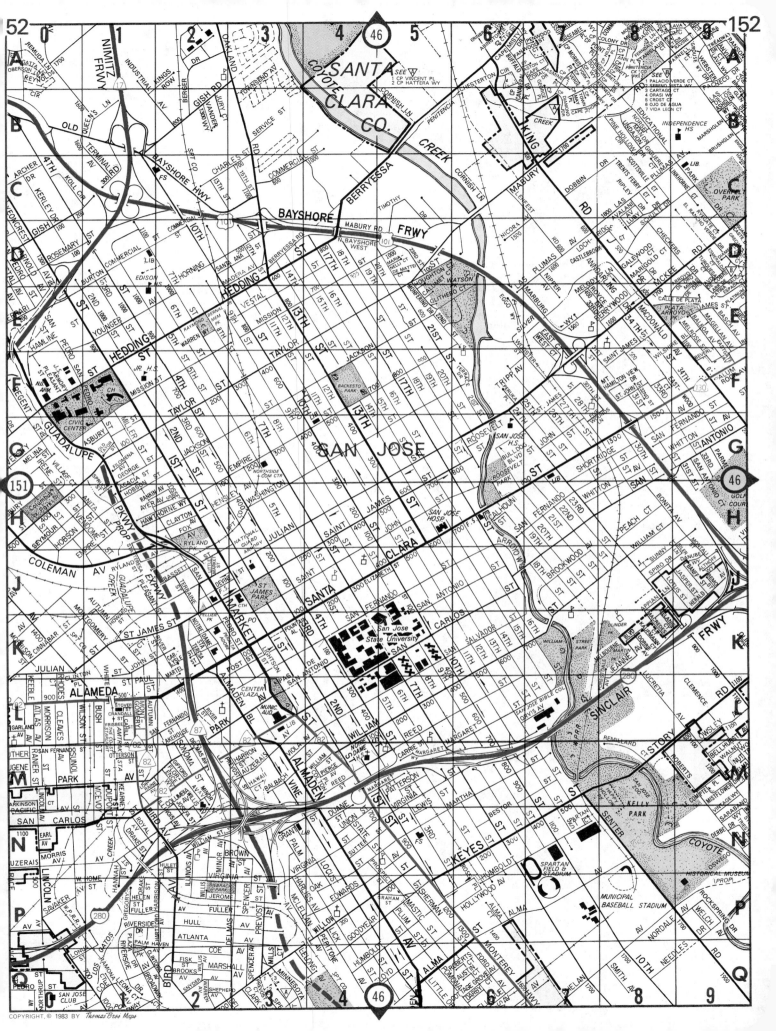

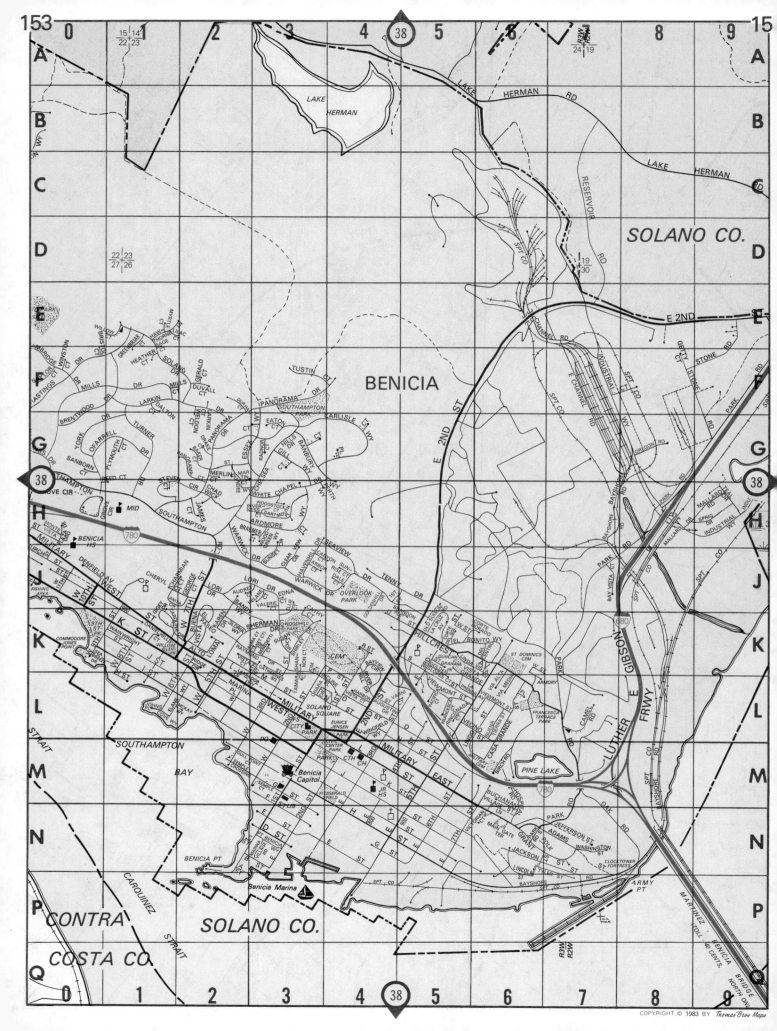

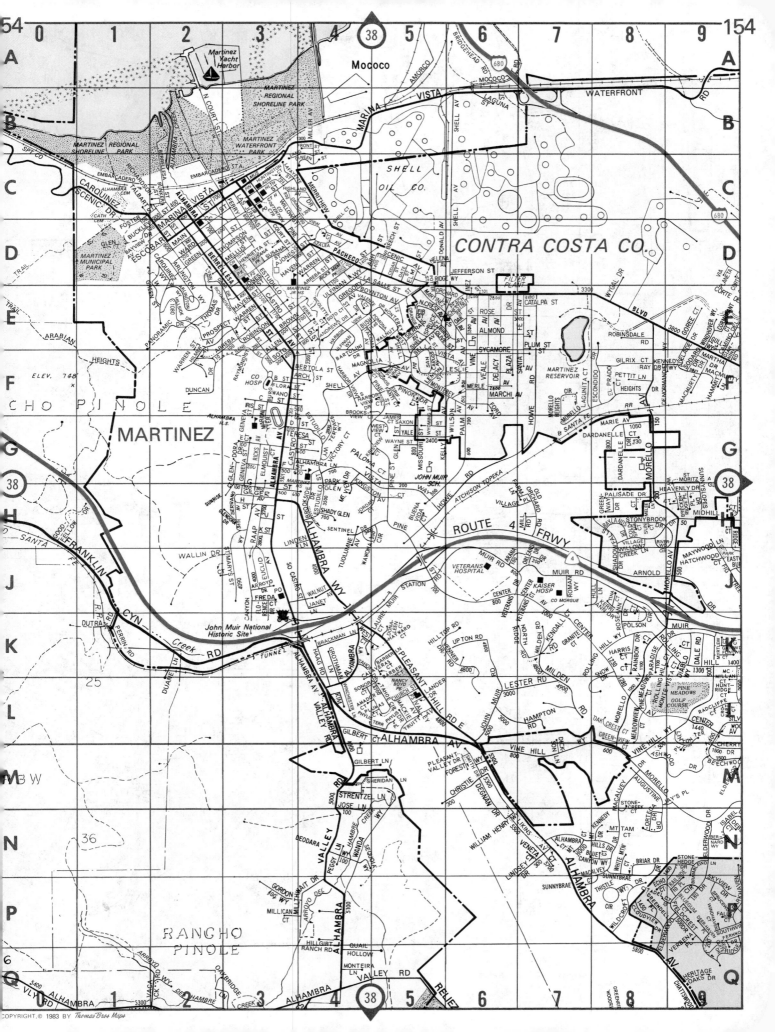

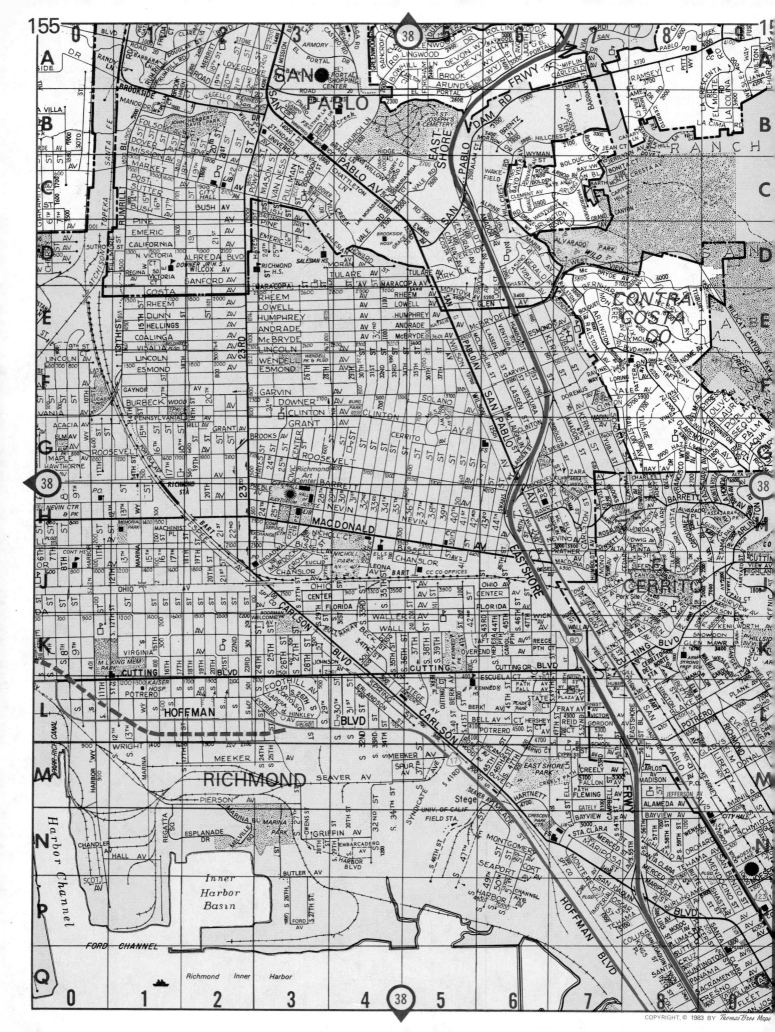

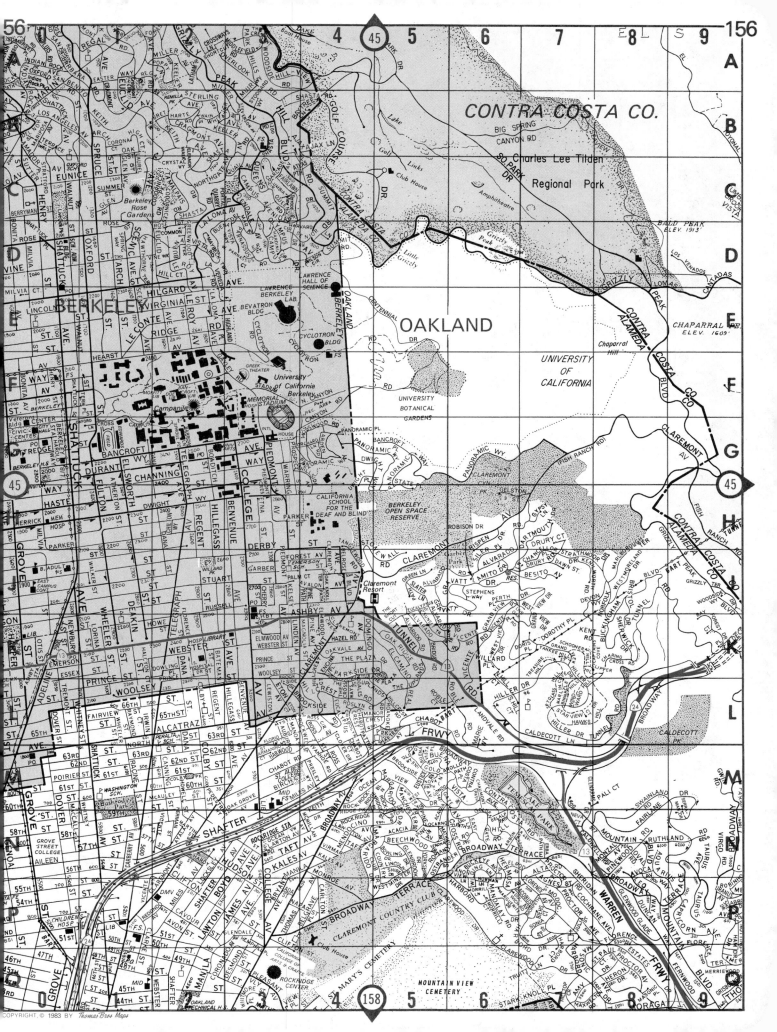

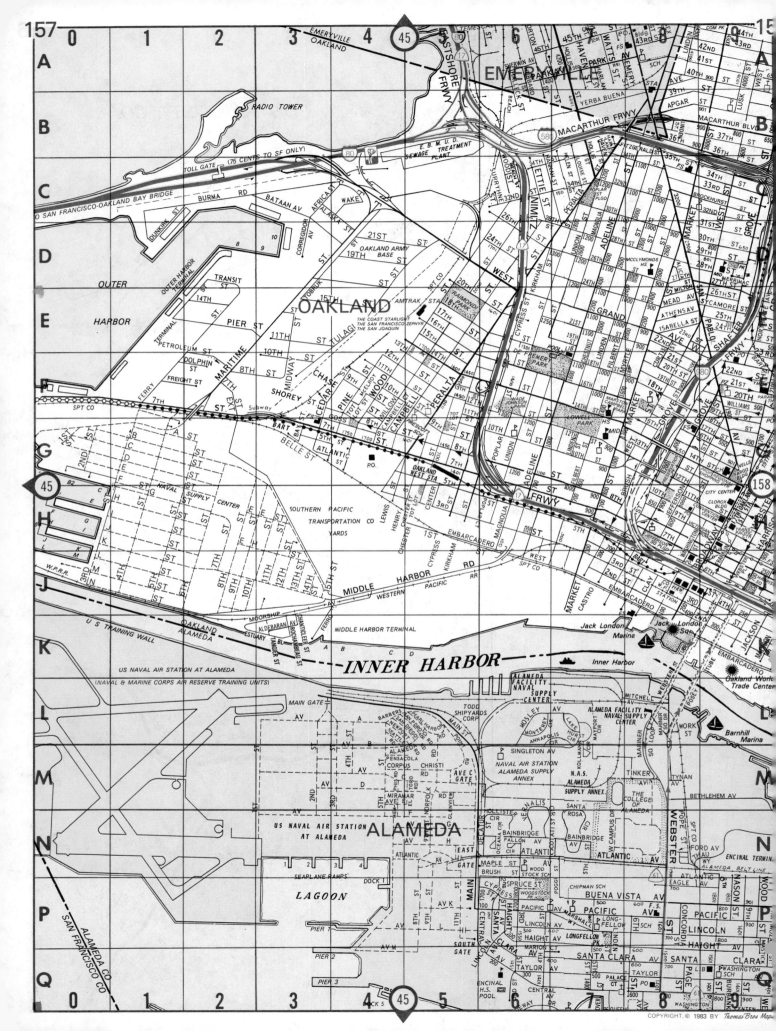

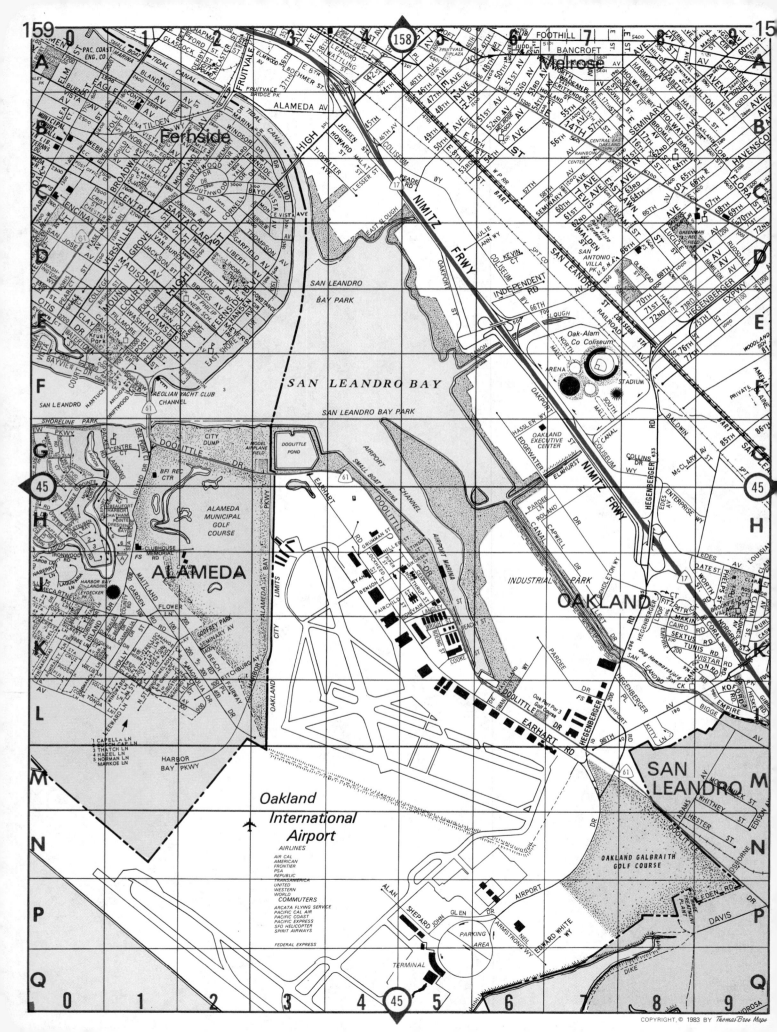

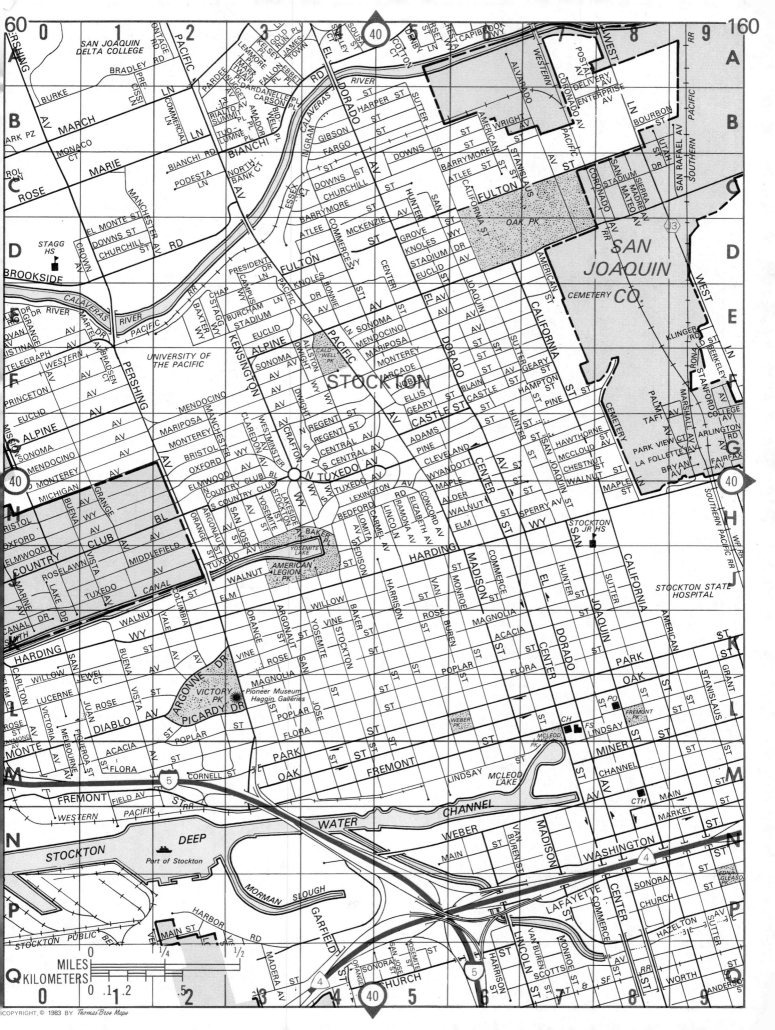

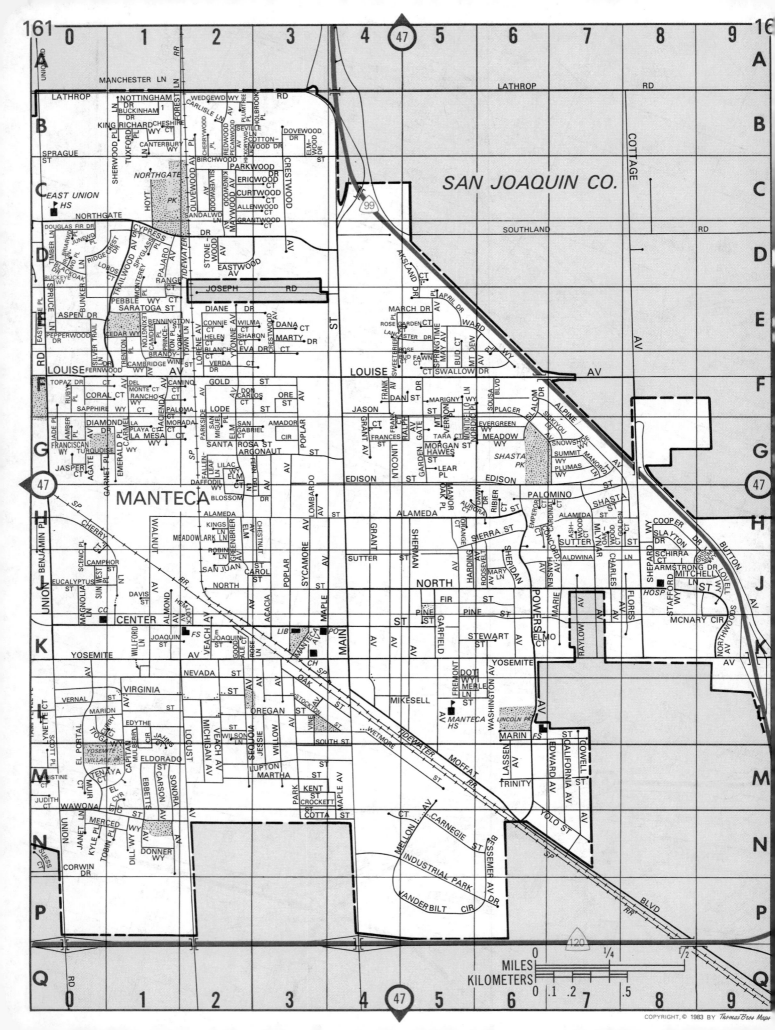

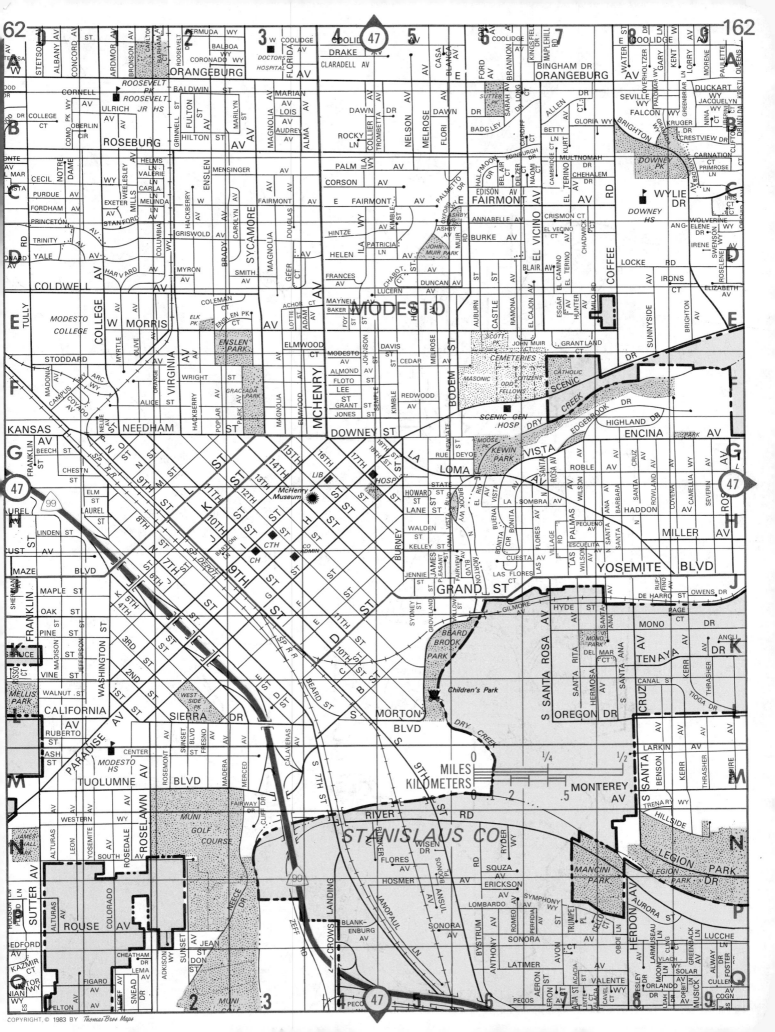

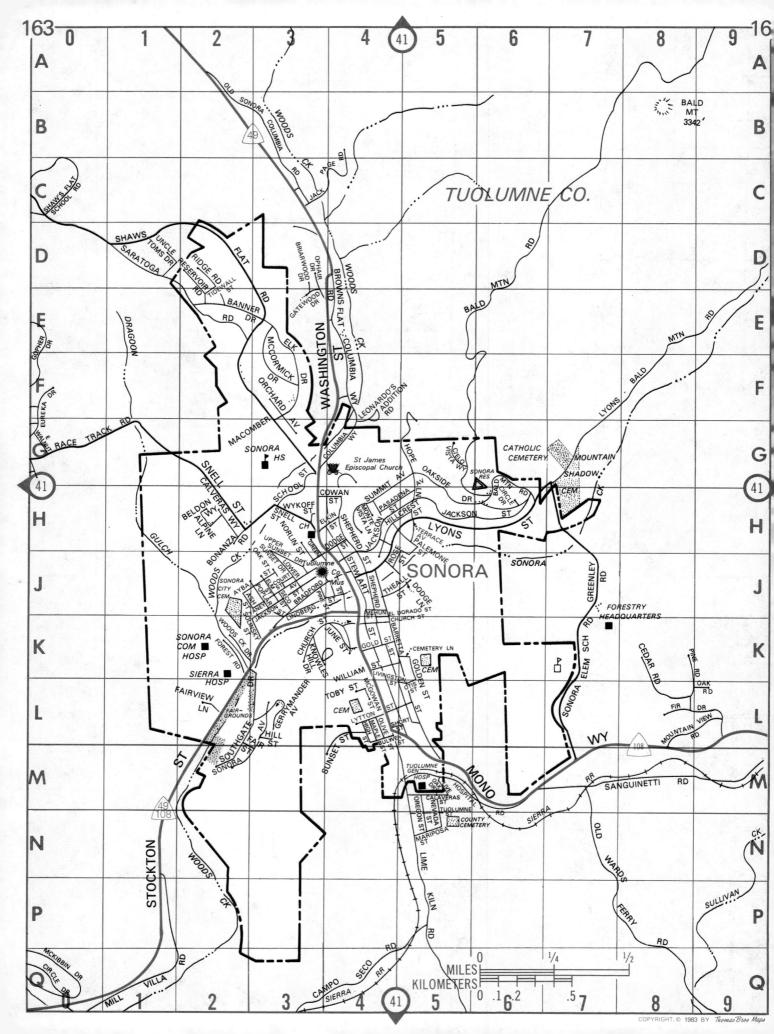

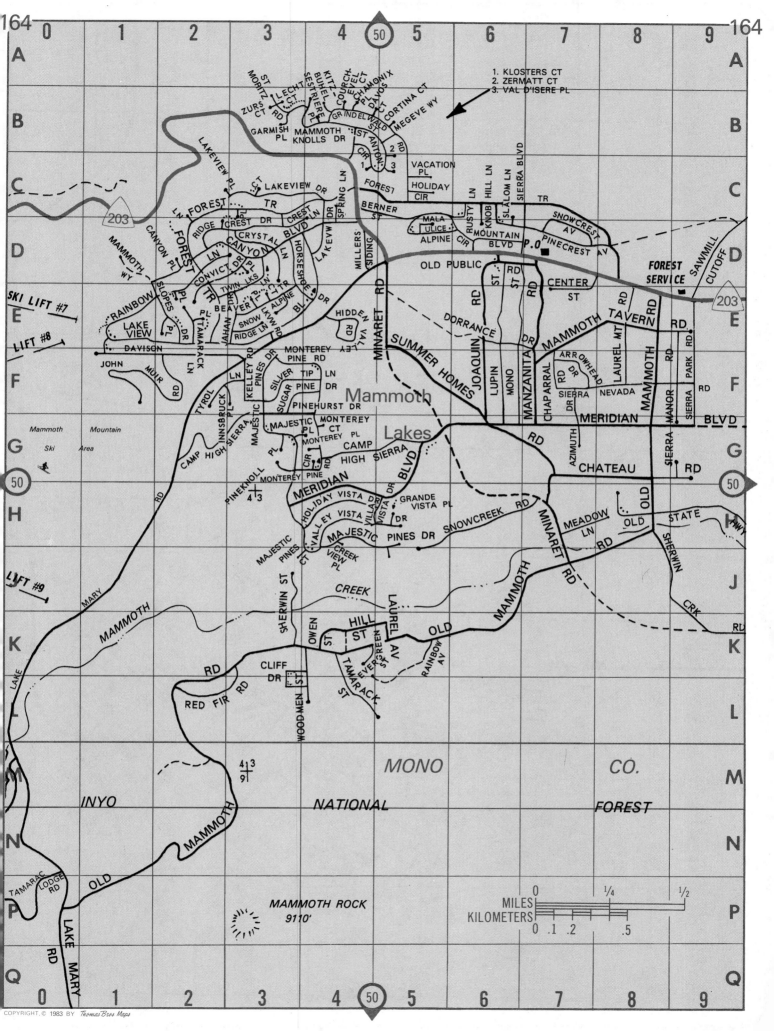

1. KLOSTERS CT
2. ZERMATT CT
3. VAL D'ISERE PL

ST MORITZ CT, LECHT CT, ZURS CT, BUHEL, SESTRIERE PL, KITZ, COURCH-EVEL, PL, CHAMONIX, DAVOS CT, CORTINA CT, MEGEVE WY, GARMISH PL, GRINDELWALD, MAMMOTH KNOLLS DR, ST ANTON, VACATION PL, HOLIDAY CIR

LAKEVIEW PL, CT, LAKEVIEW DR, FOREST TR, SPRING LN, FOREST, BERNER ST, MALA ULICE, ALPINE CIR, MOUNTAIN BLVD, OLD PUBLIC

RUSTY LN, KNOB HILL LN, SLALOM LN, SIERRA BLVD, TR, SNOWCREST AV, PINECREST AV

FOREST LN, RIDGE, CREST DR, CREST BLVD, LN, LAKEVW DR, MILLERS SIDING

FOREST SERVICE, SAWMILL CUTOFF, 203

CANYON PL, FOREST TR, CRYSTAL LN, CANYON LN, HORSESHOE DR, HIDDEN VALLEY

MAMMOTH WY, CONVICT DR, PL, TWIN LKS LN, CT, ALPINE, MINARET RD, SUMMER HOMES, CENTER ST, RD, ST, RD, MAMMOTH, TAVERN RD, LAUREL MT RD, RD, MAMMOTH PARK RD

RAINBOW SLOPES, LAKE VIEW, JAHAN, BEAVER PL, SNOW RIDGE LN, LKVW RD, DORRANCE, JOAQUIN RD, LUPIN, MONO, MANZANITA, CHAPARRAL, ARROWHEAD DR, SIERRA DR, NEVADA, SIERRA, SIERRA PARK RD

TAMARACK LN, DAVISON, JOHN MUIR RD, KELLEY RD, PINES DR, MONTEREY PINE RD, SILVER TIP LN, SUGAR PINE DR, PINEHURST DR, MAMMOTH, MERIDIAN, AZIMUTH, SIERRA MANOR RD

TYROL, CAMP HIGH, INNSBRUCK PL, SIERRA, MAJESTIC, MAJESTIC PL, MONTEREY PL, MONTEREY CT, MONTEREY PINE, CAMP HIGH SIERRA, BLVD, RD, CHATEAU, SIERRA RD, OLD

PINEKNOLL 4 3, MERIDIAN, HOLIDAY VISTA DR, VALLEY VISTA DR, VILLA DR, VISTA DR, GRANDE VISTA PL, SNOWCREEK RD, MEADOW LN, RD, OLD STATE, MINARET RD

MAJESTIC PINES CT, CREEK VIEW PL, MAJESTIC PINES DR, SNOWCREEK RD, SHERWIN

SKI LIFT #7, LIFT #8, LIFT #9

MARY, MAMMOTH, SHERWIN ST, CREEK, OWEN ST, HILL ST, LAUREL AV, EVERGREEN ST, OLD, RAINBOW AV, TAMARACK ST

LAKE, RED FIR RD, CLIFF DR, WOODMEN ST, MAMMOTH

MONO CO.

INYO NATIONAL FOREST

TAMARAC RD, LODGE RD, OLD MAMMOTH

LAKE MARY RD

MAMMOTH ROCK 9110'

Mammoth Mountain Ski Area

Mammoth Lakes

MILES
KILOMETERS
0 .1 .2 .5
0 1/4 1/2

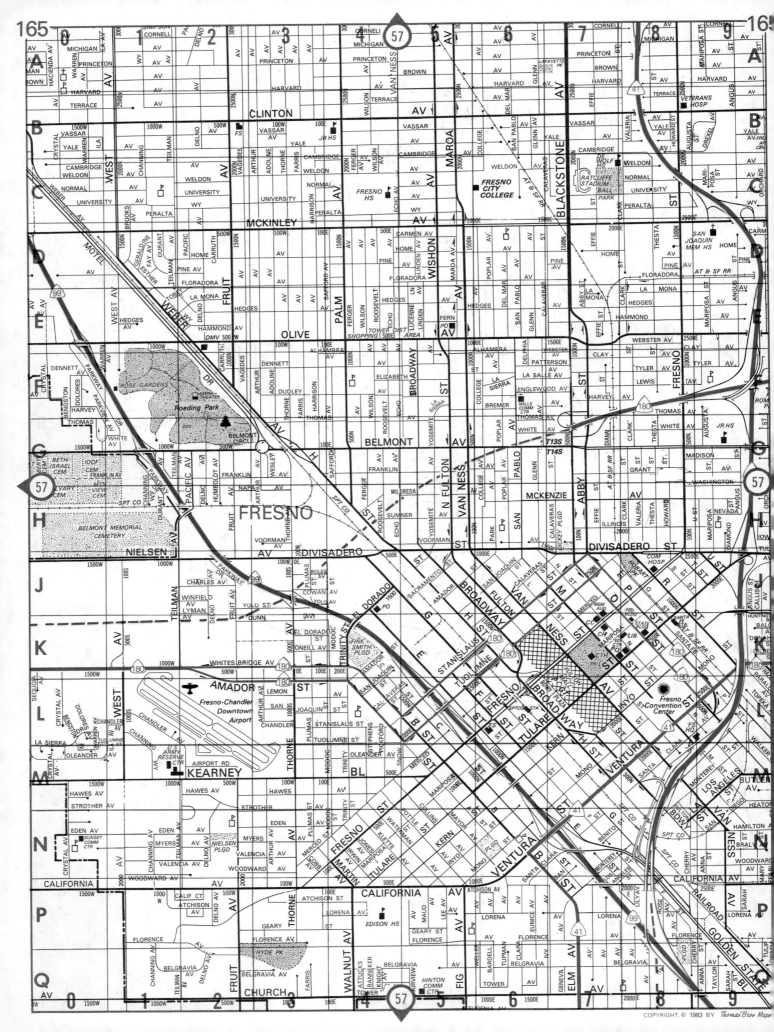

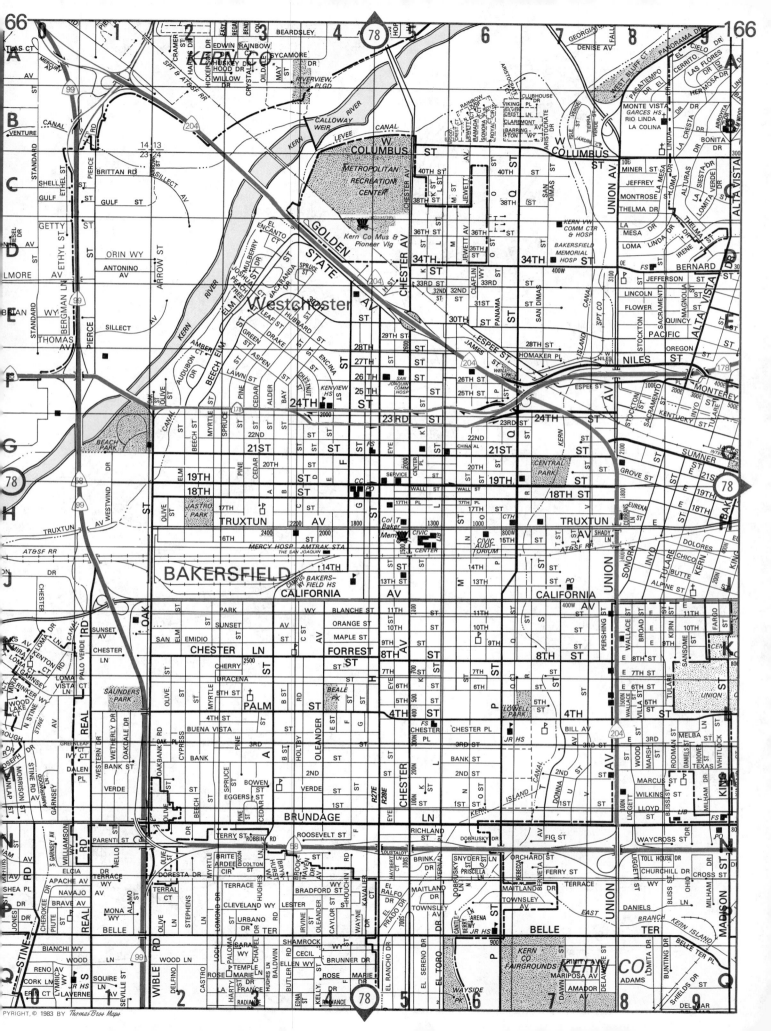

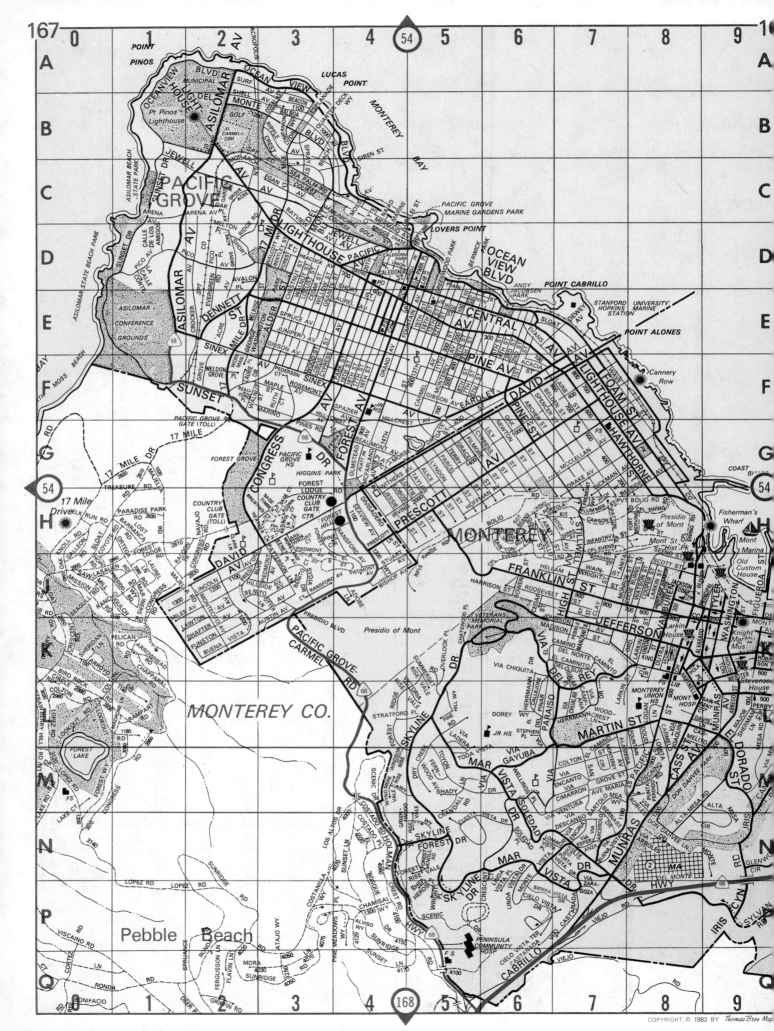

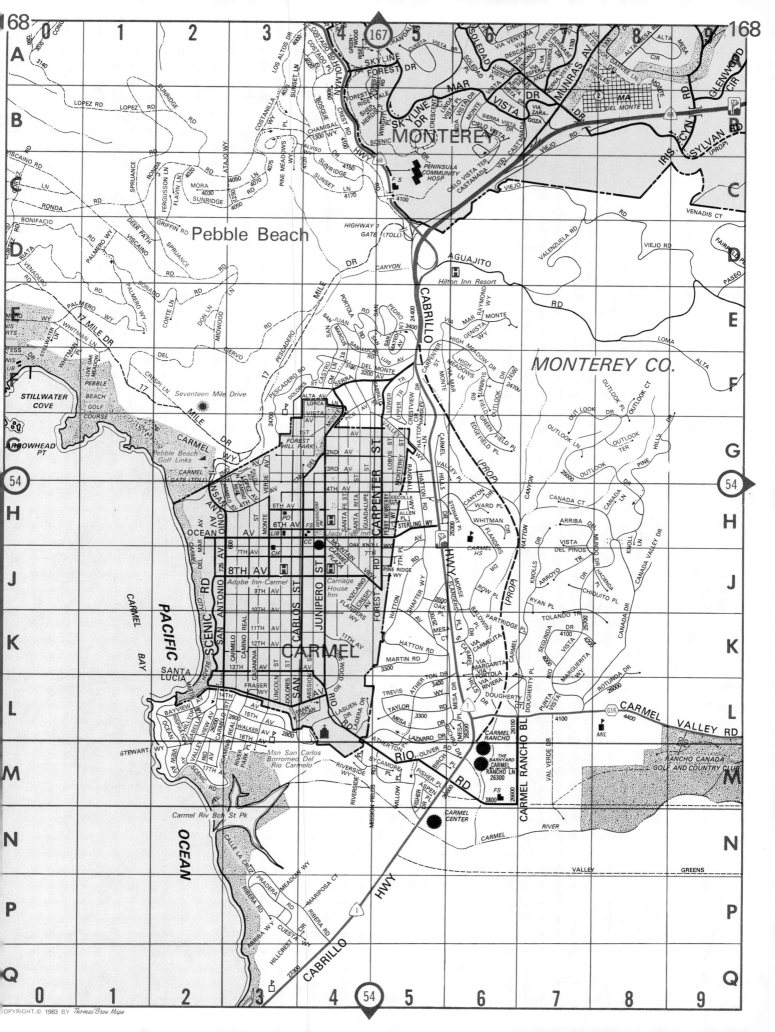

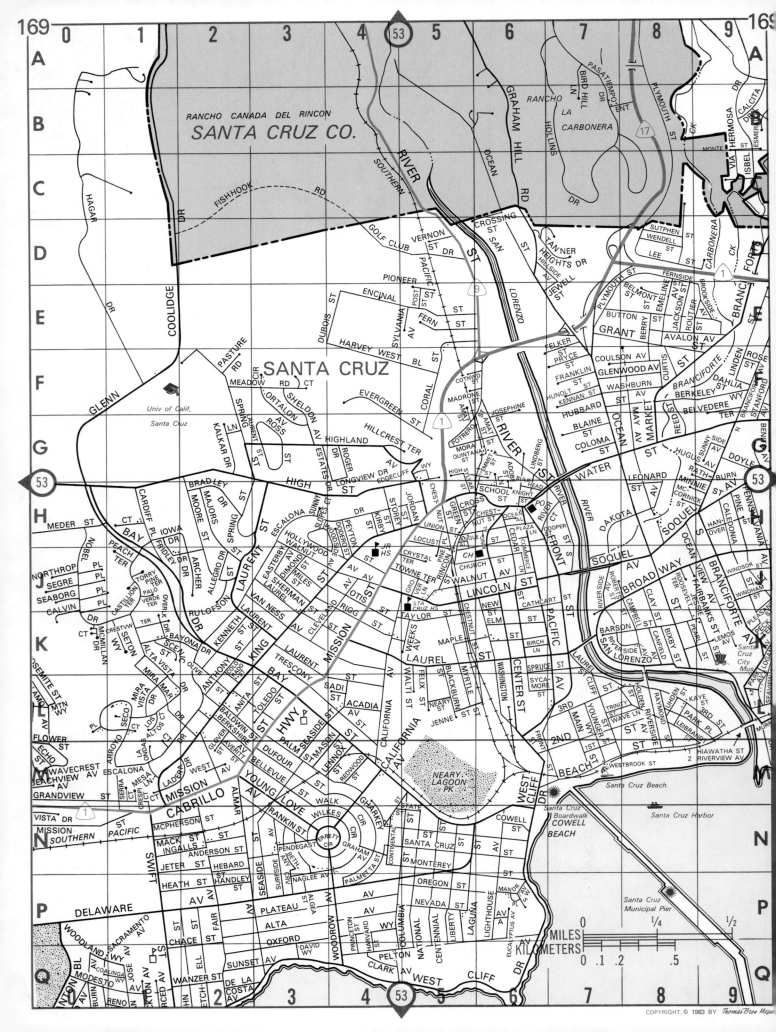

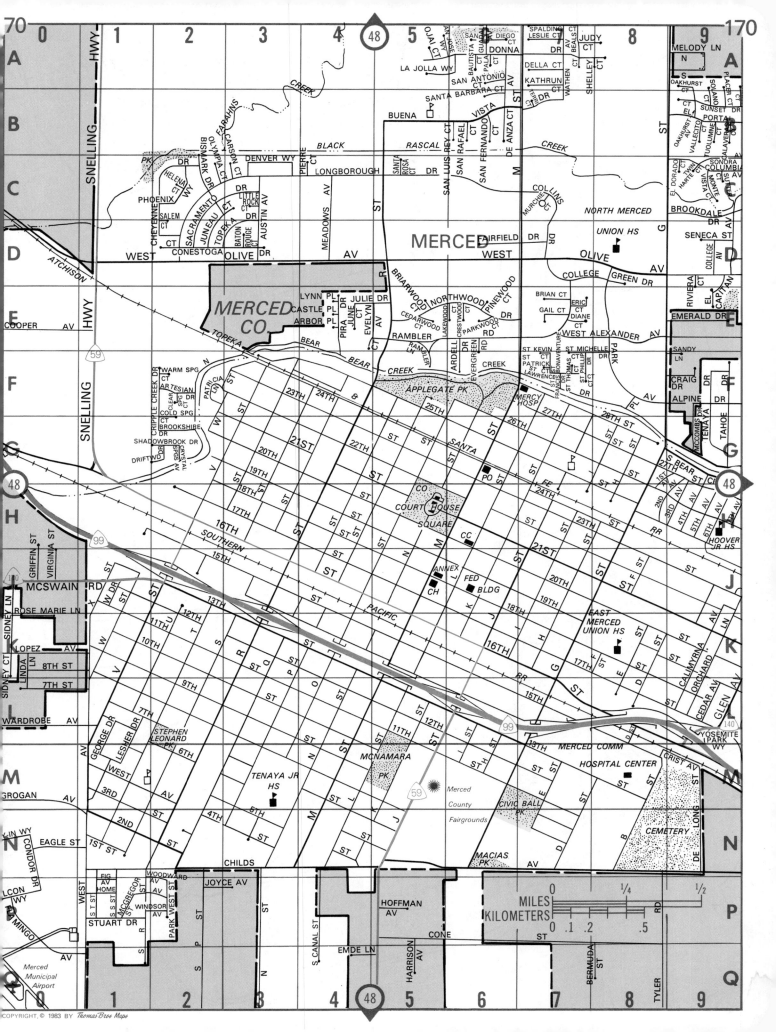

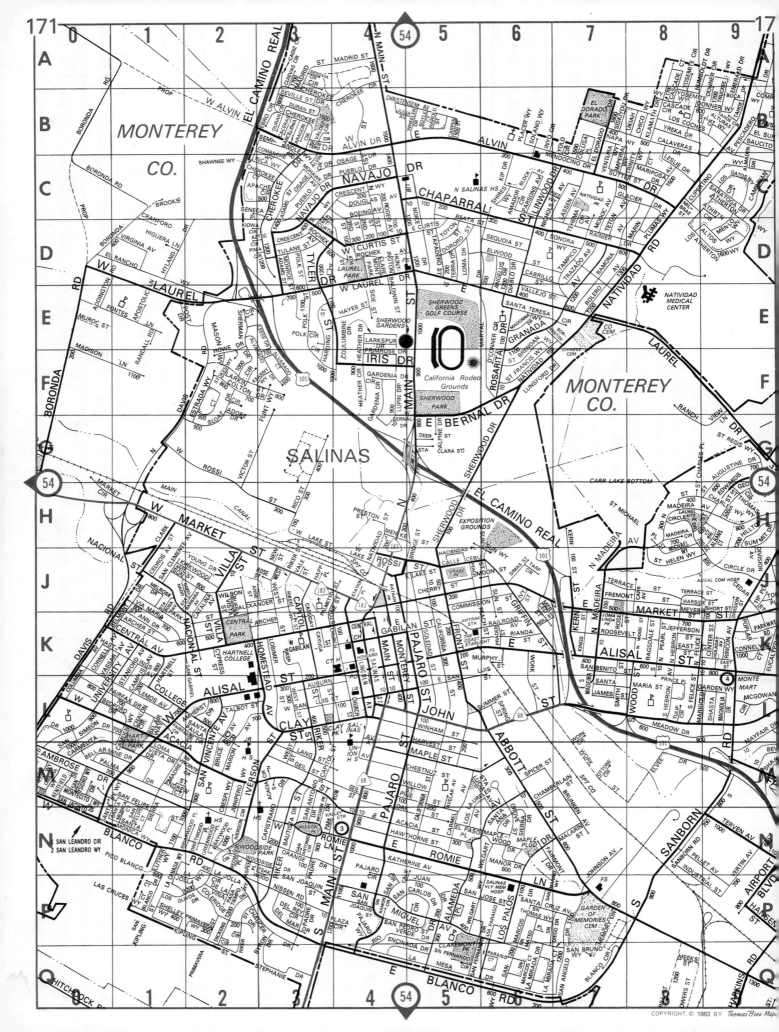

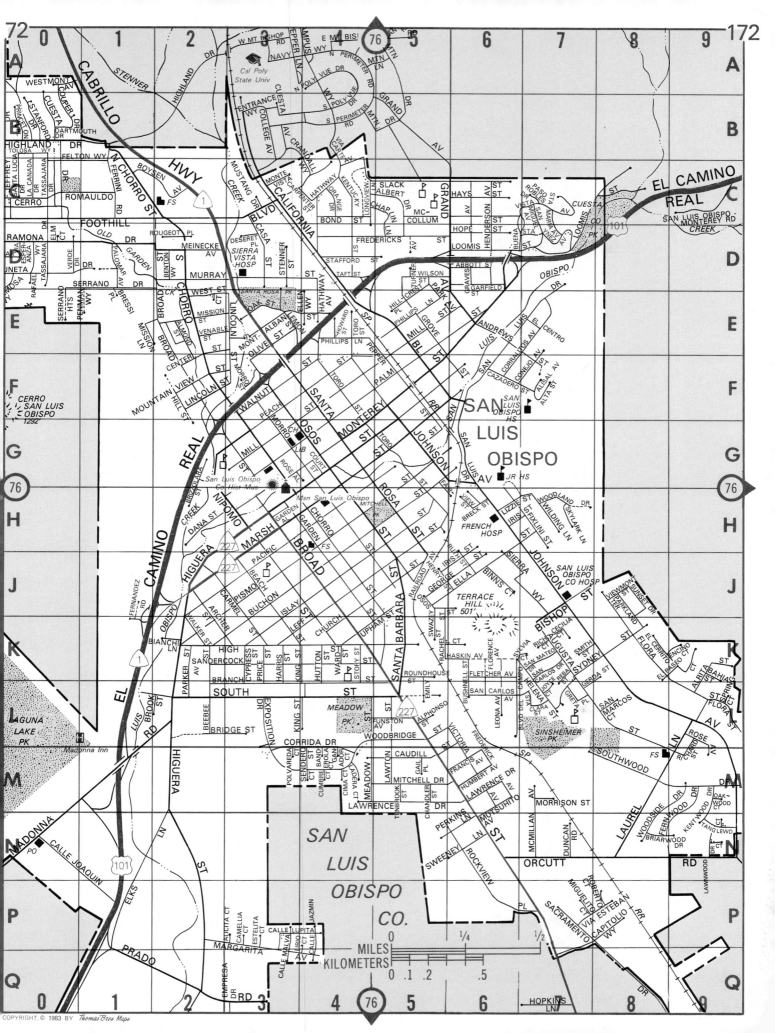

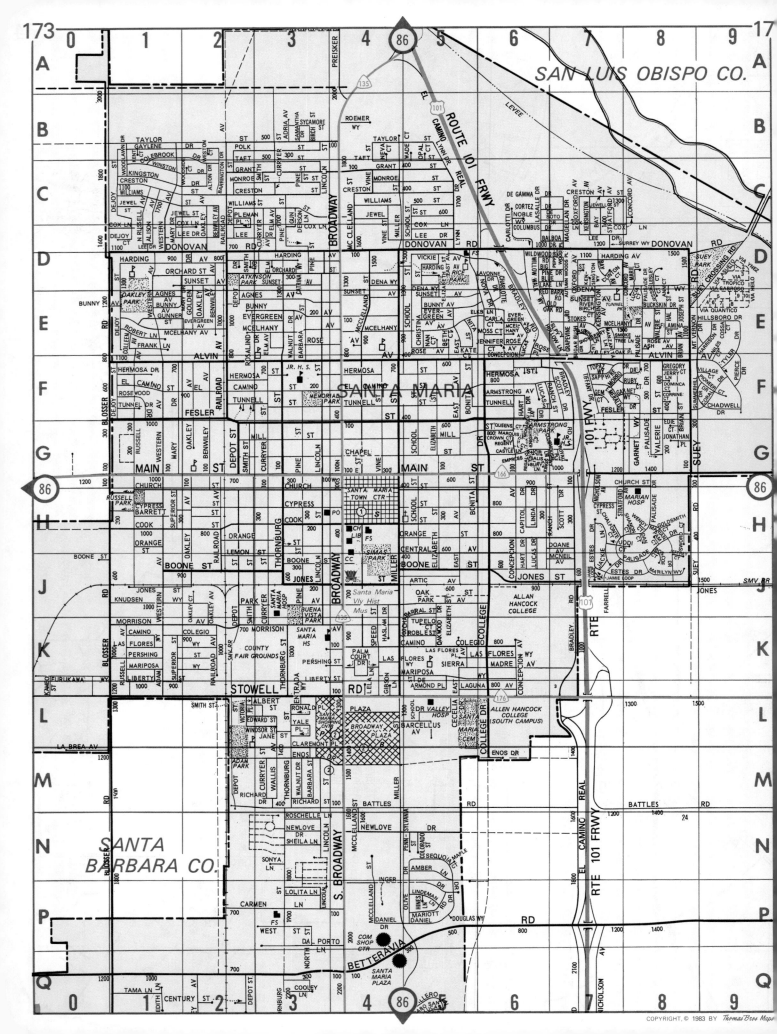

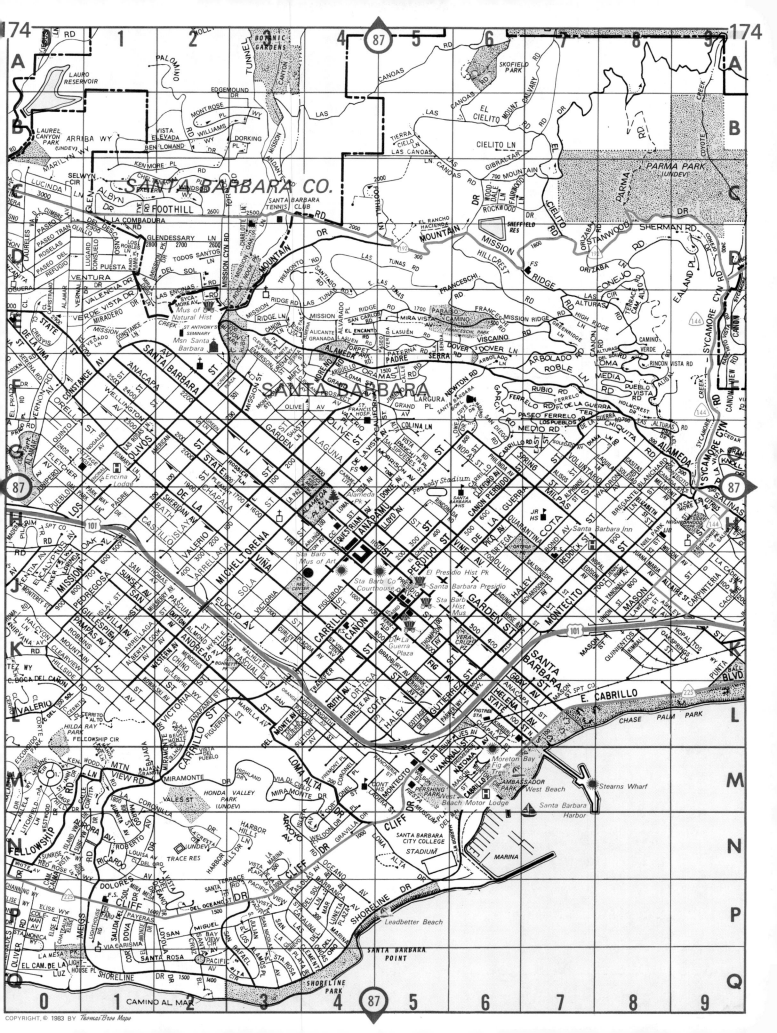

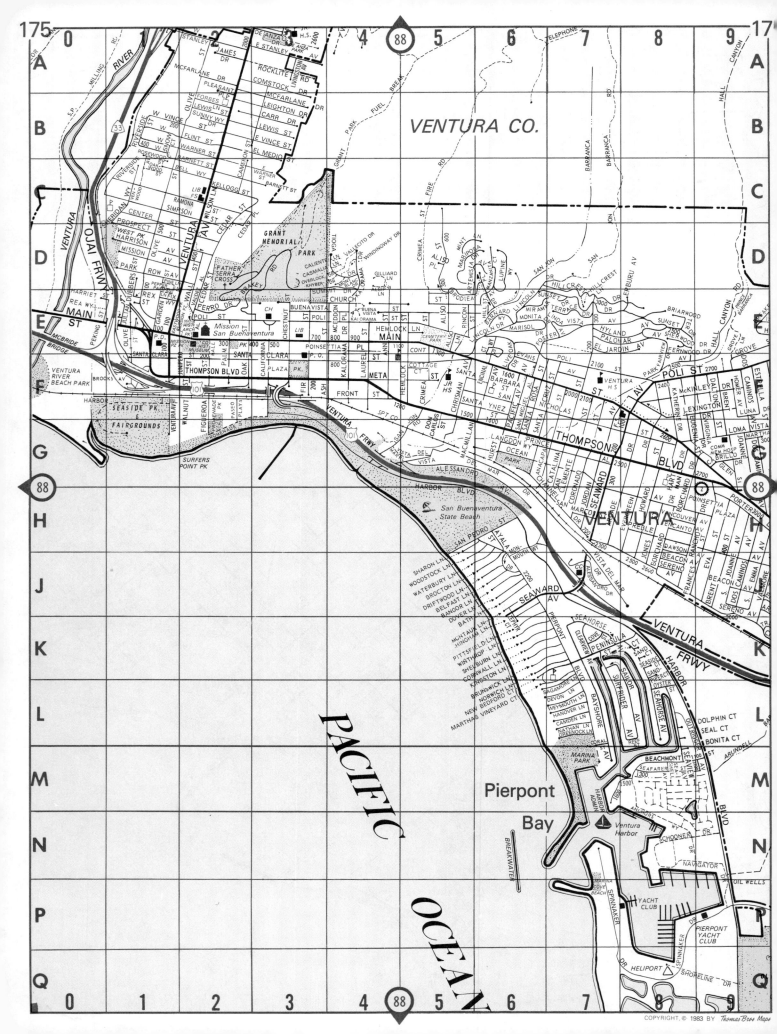

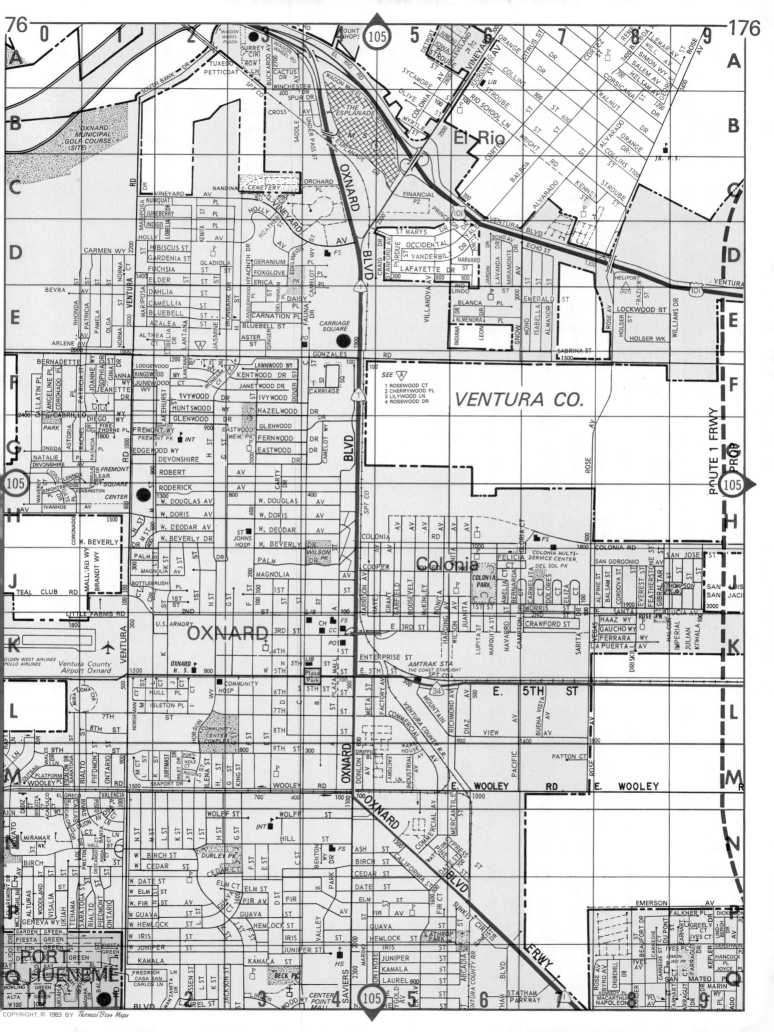

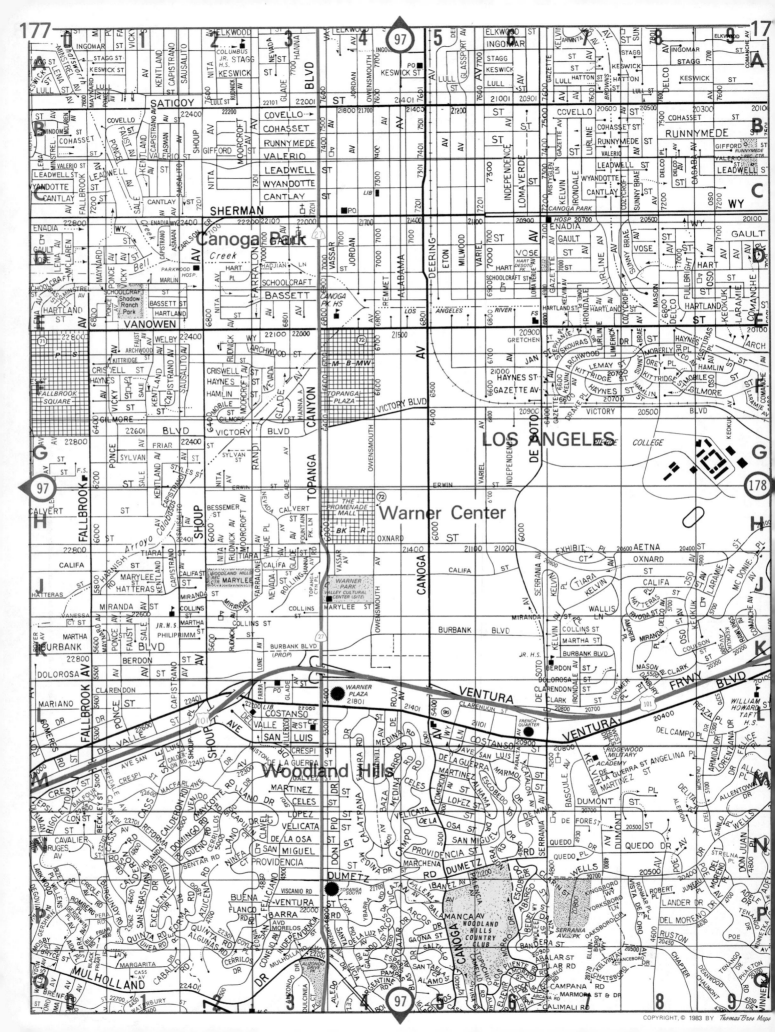

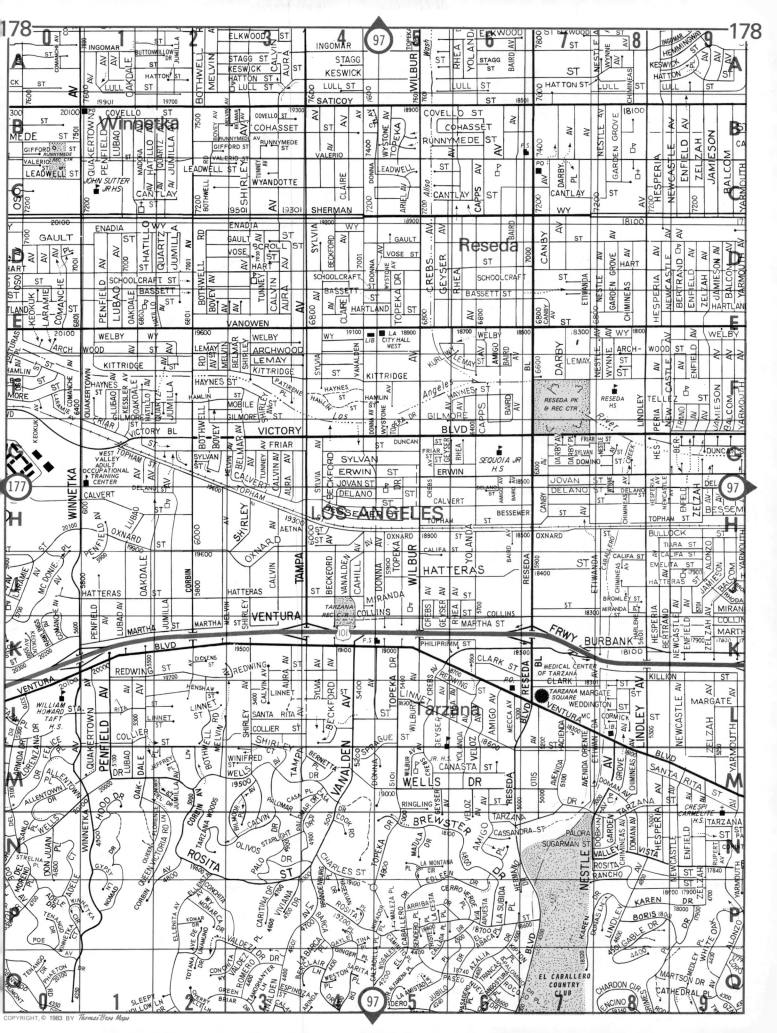

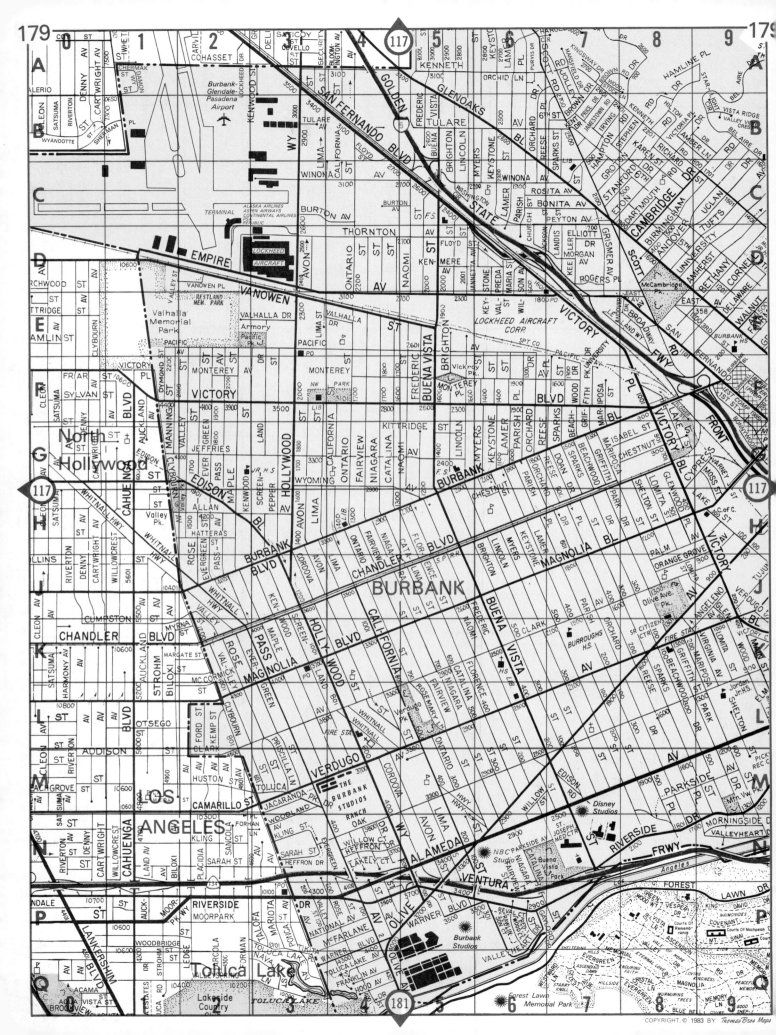

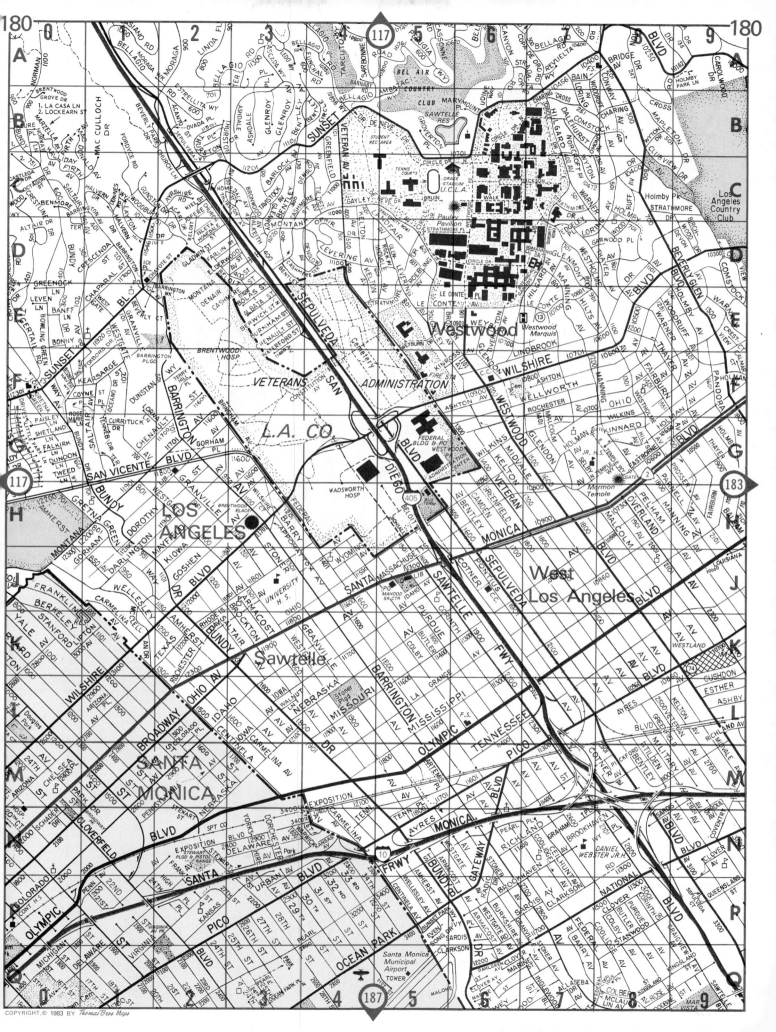

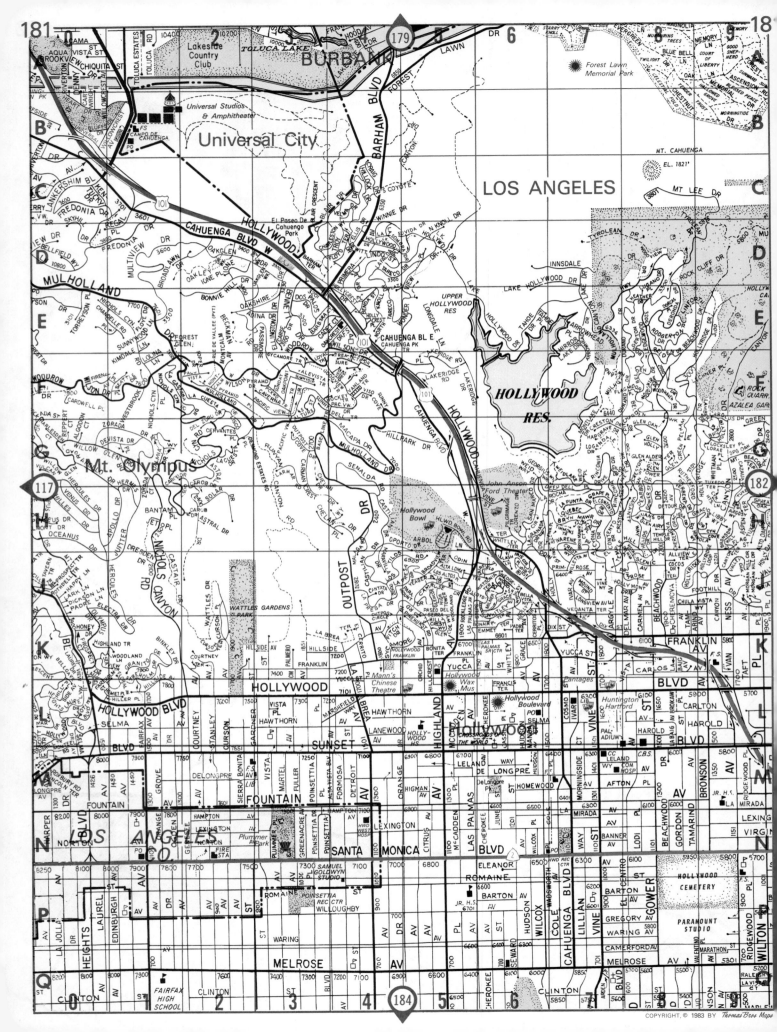

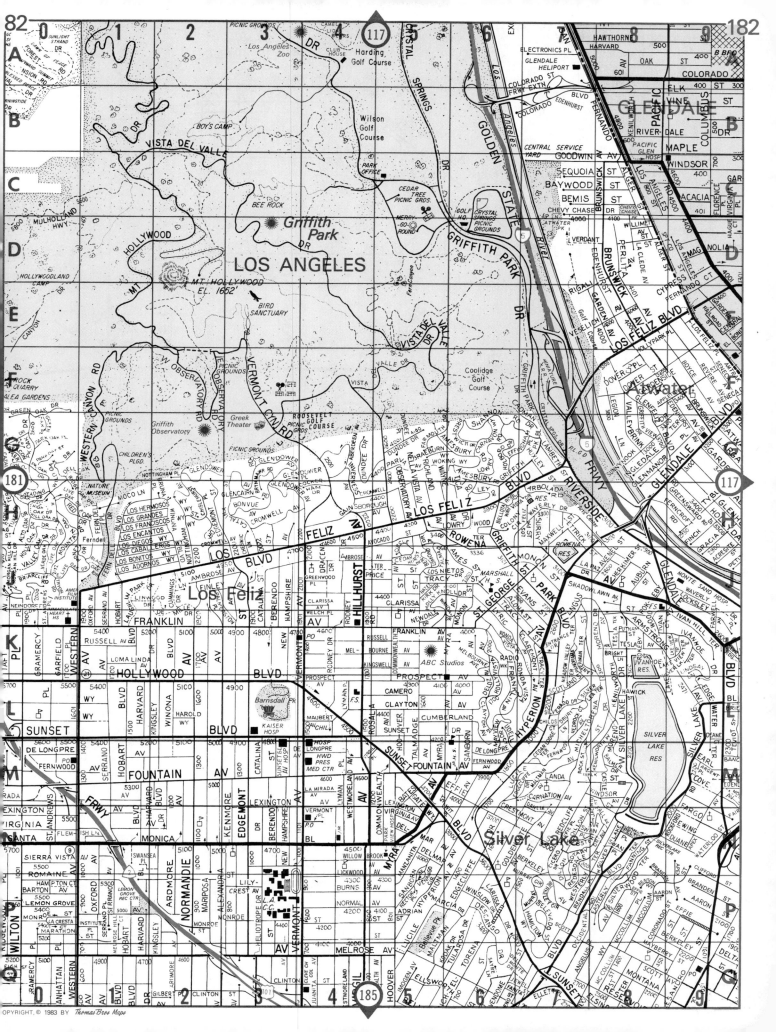

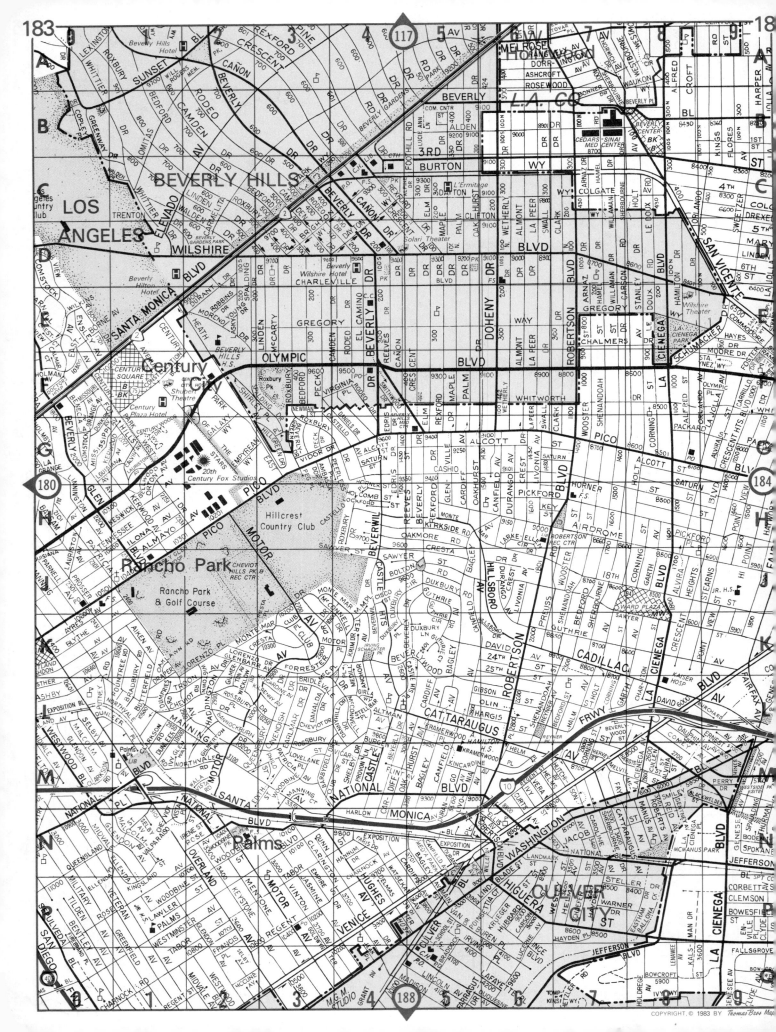

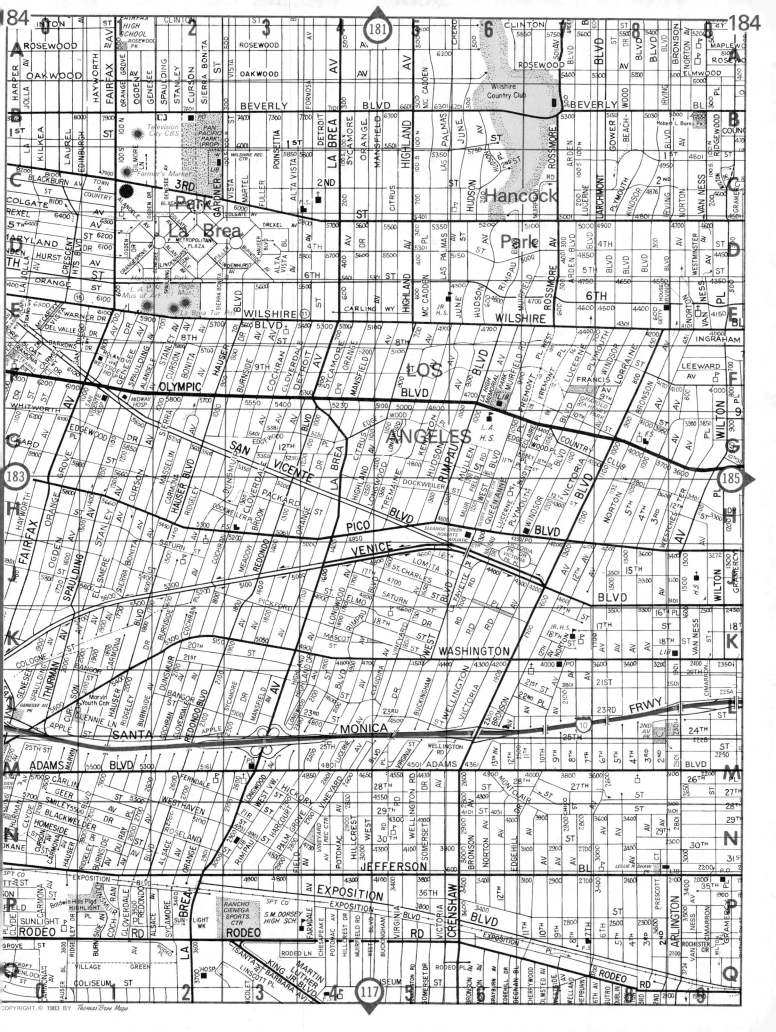

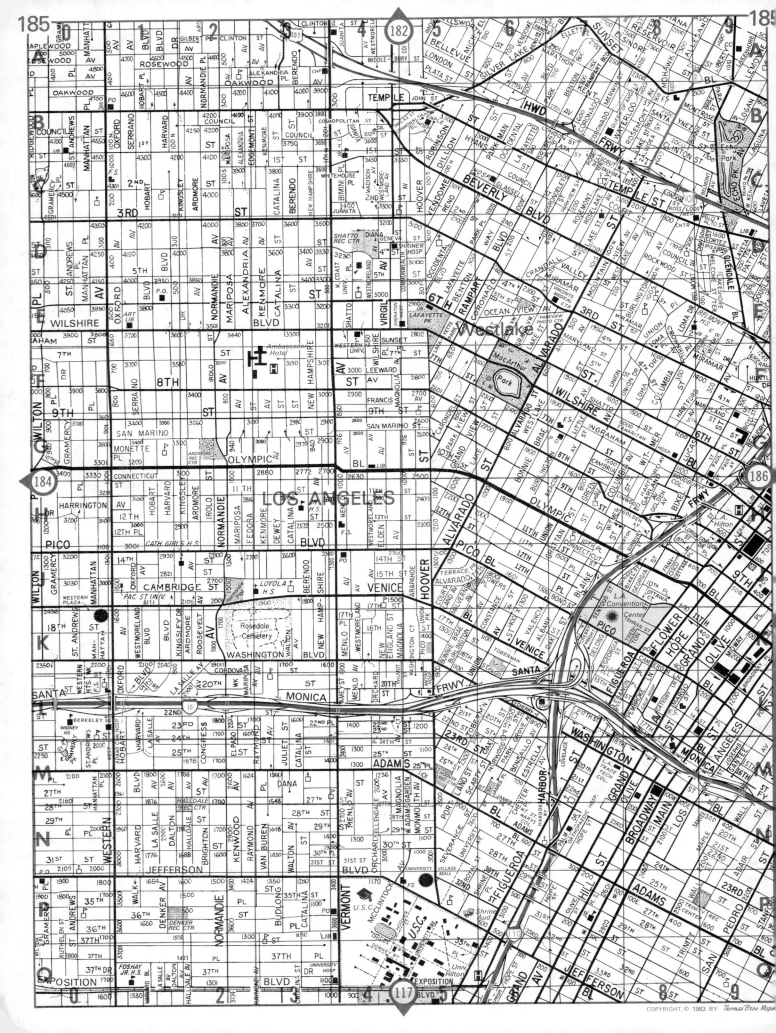

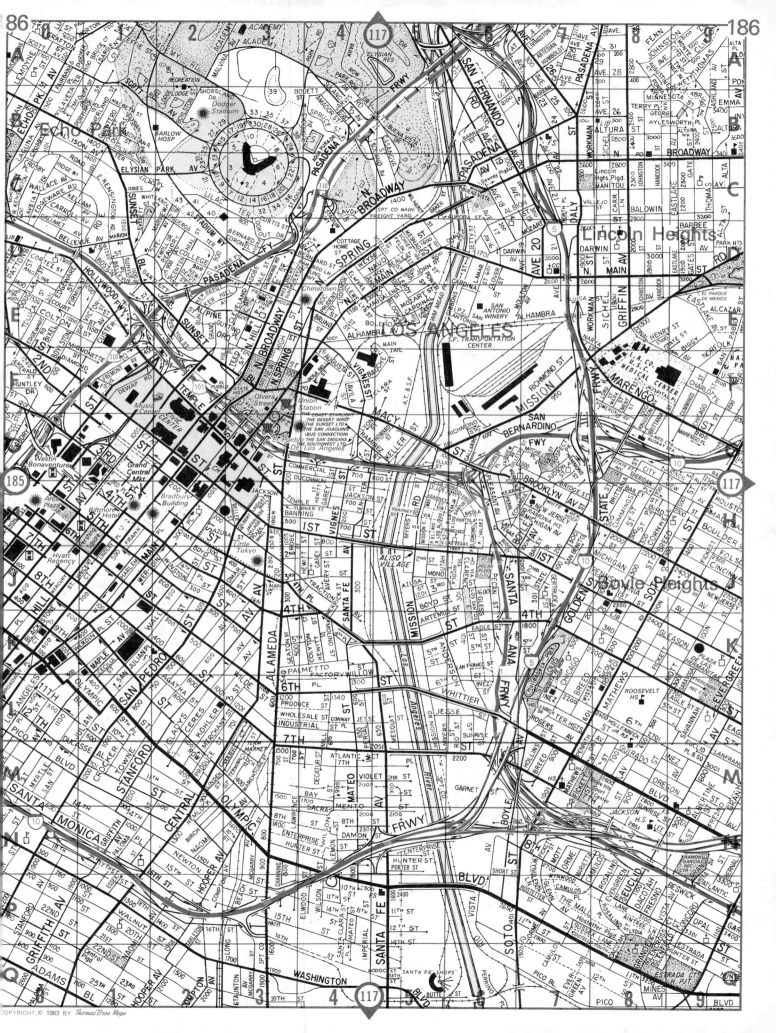

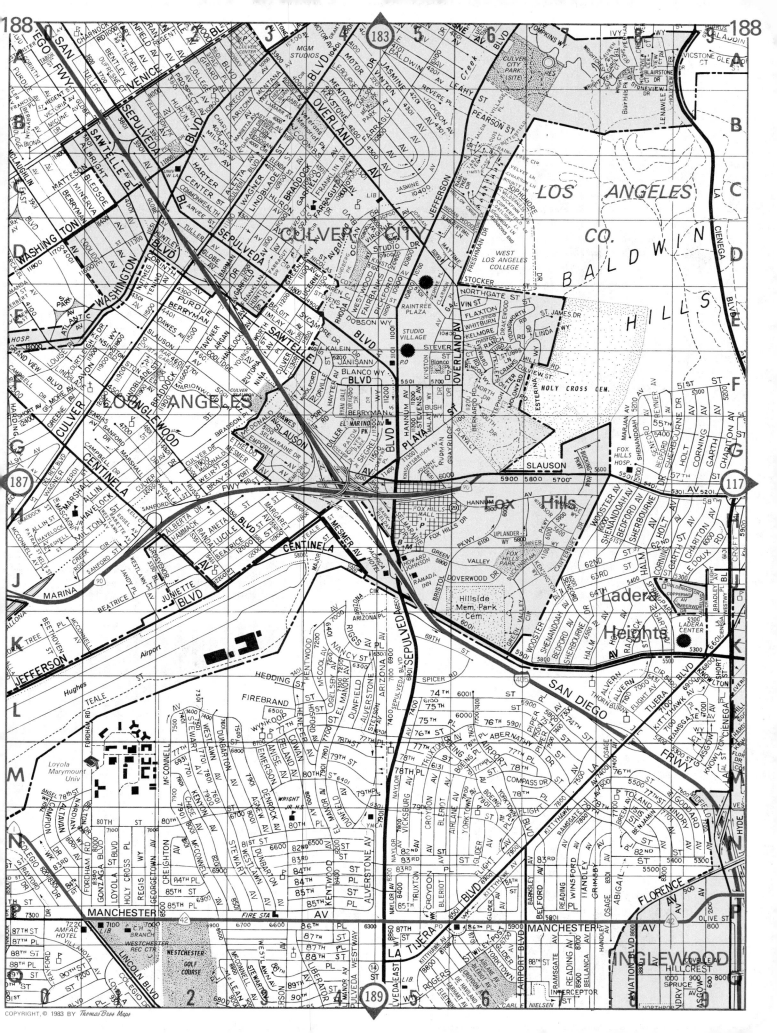

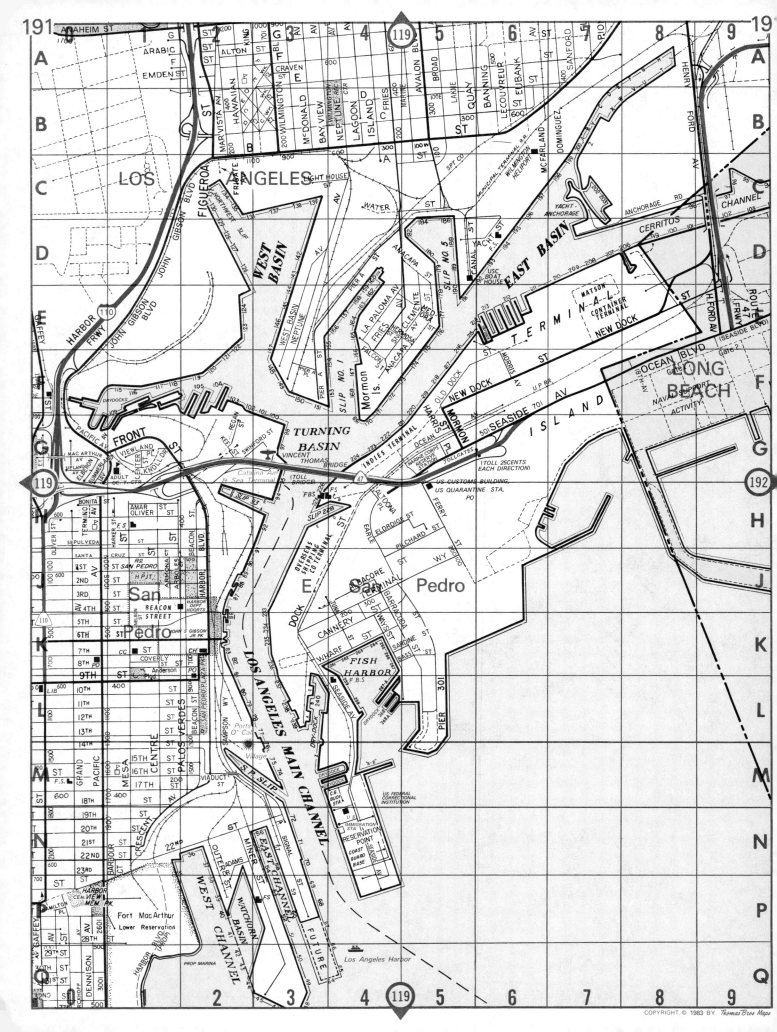

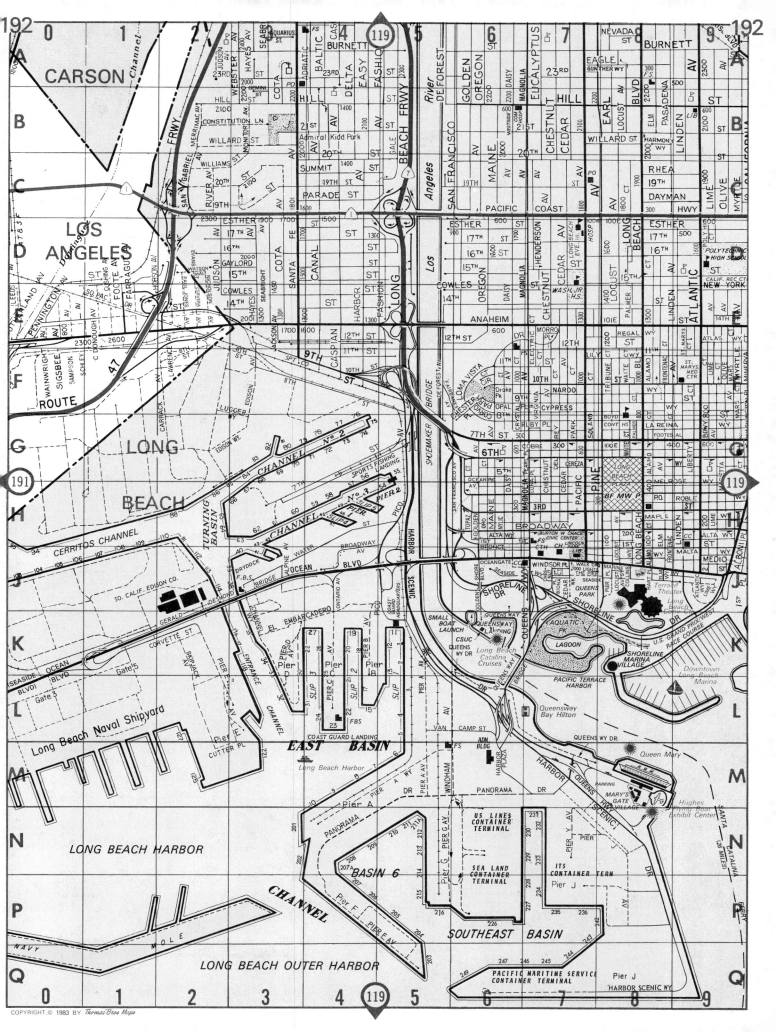

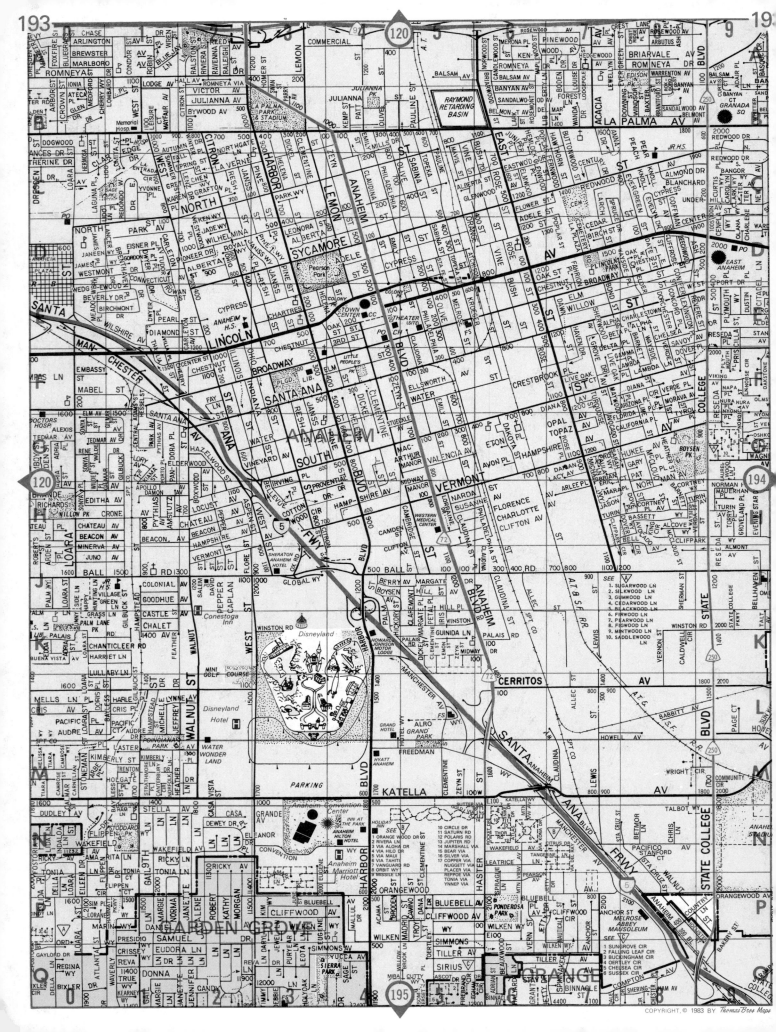

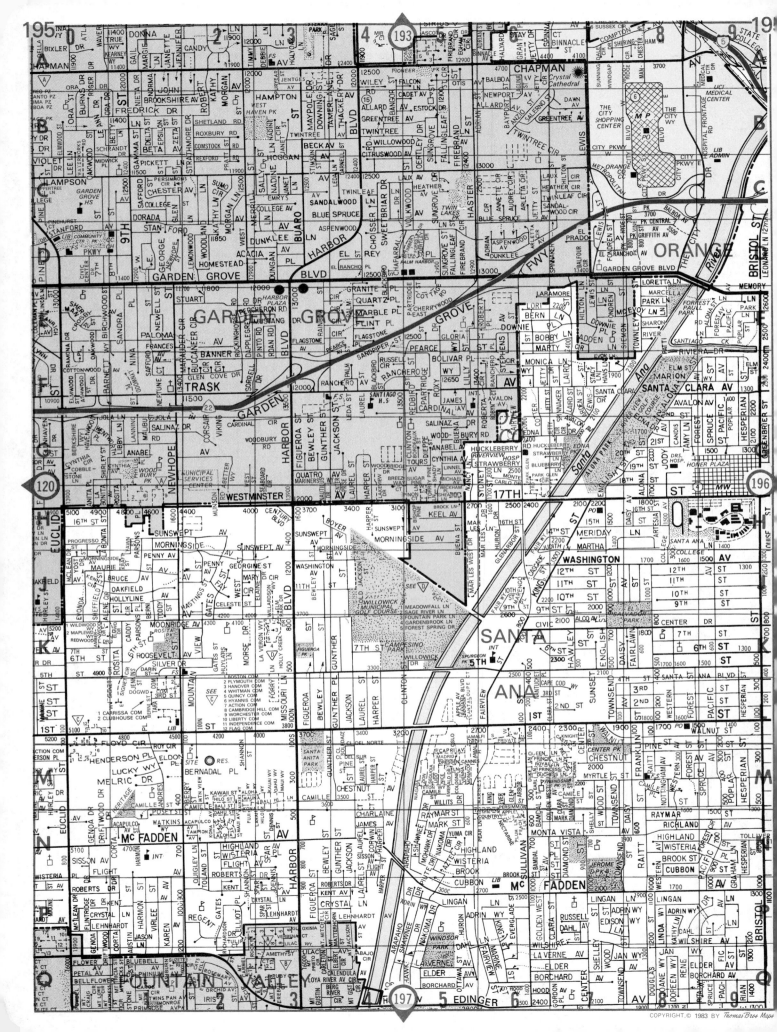

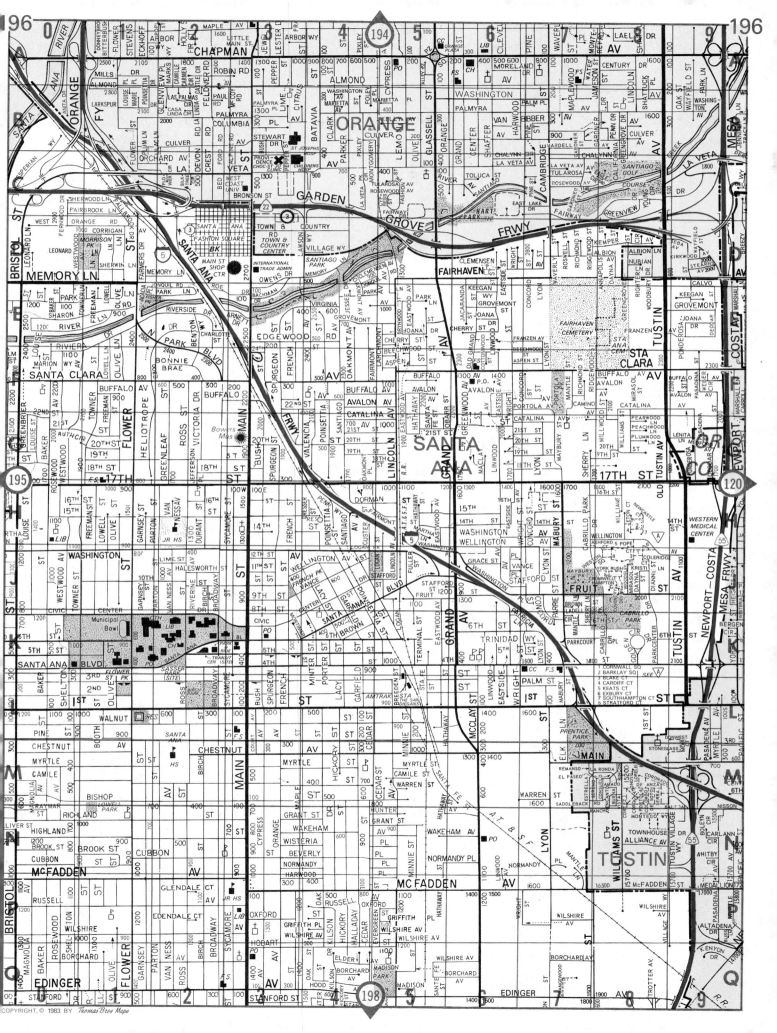

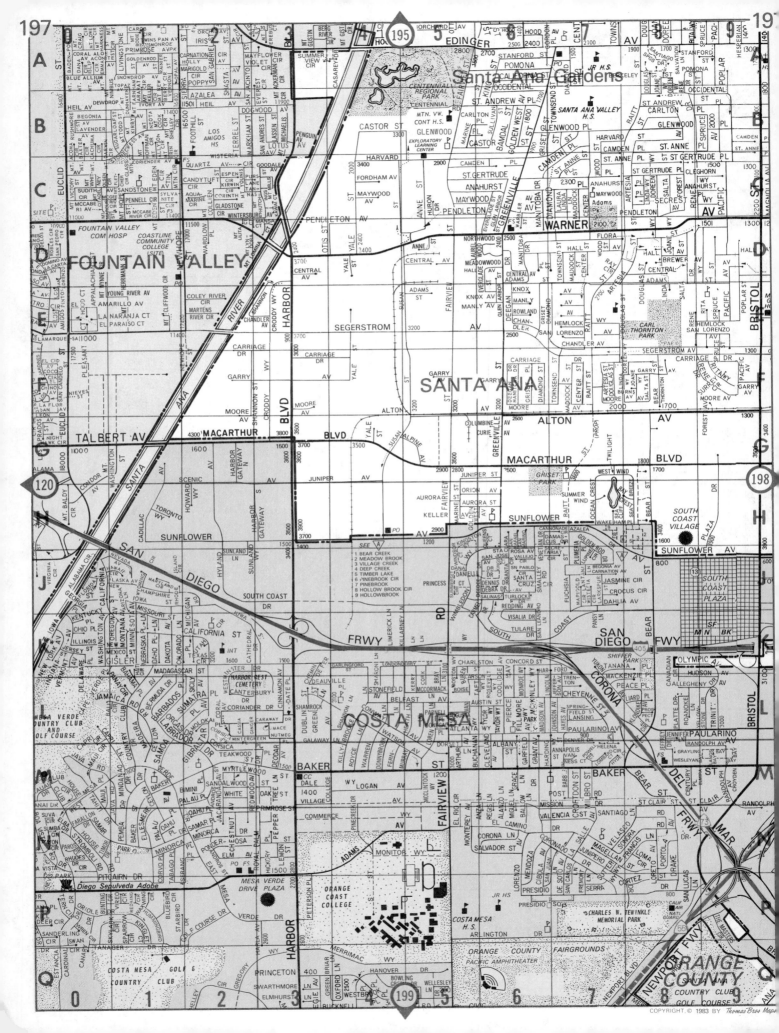

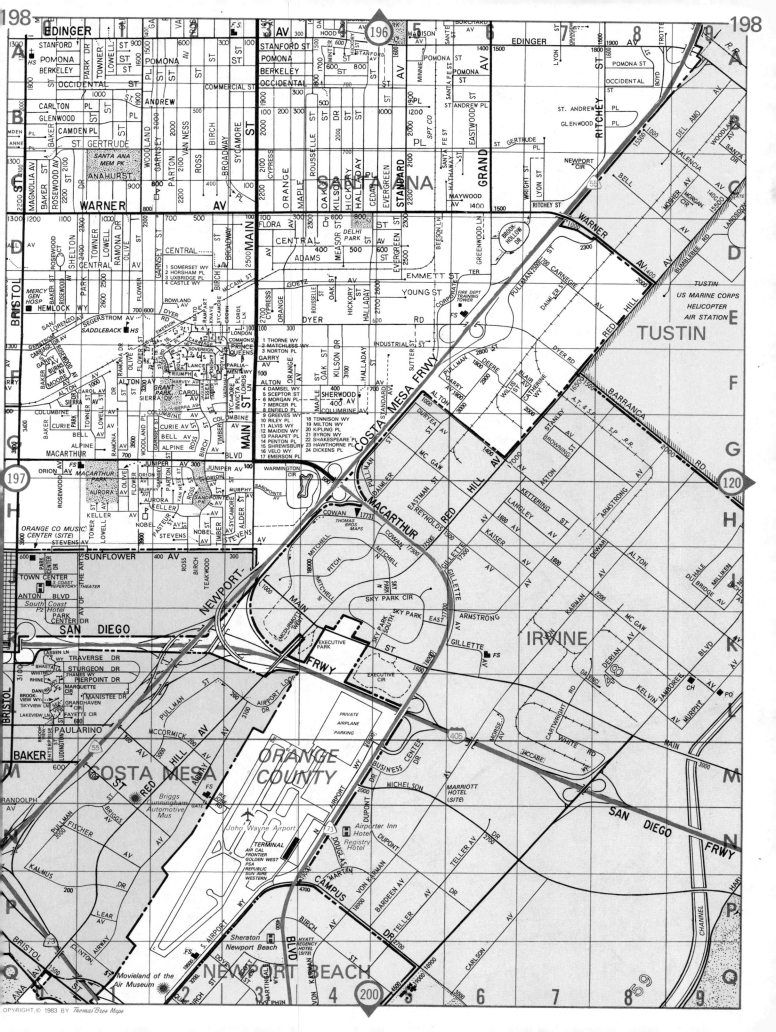

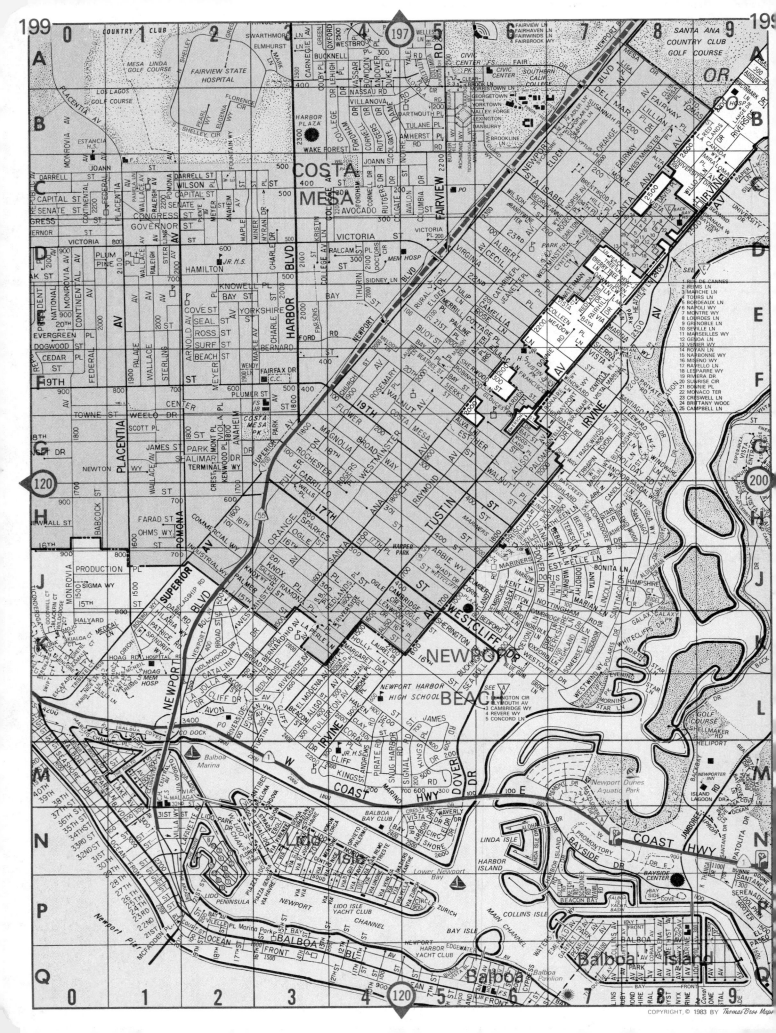

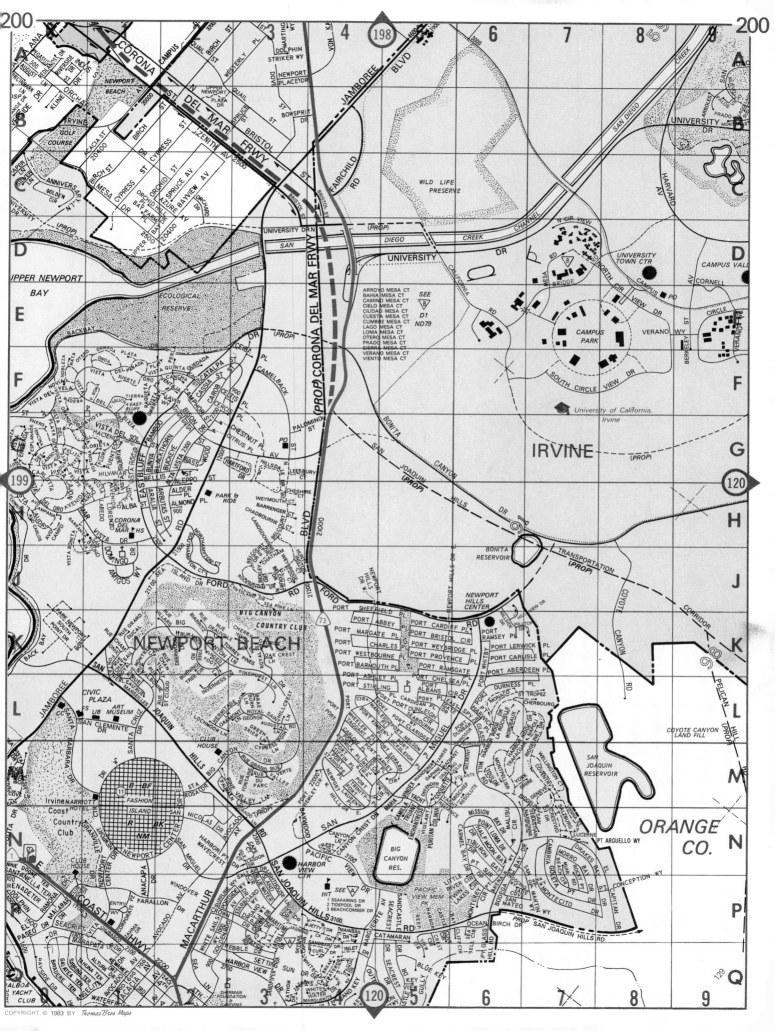

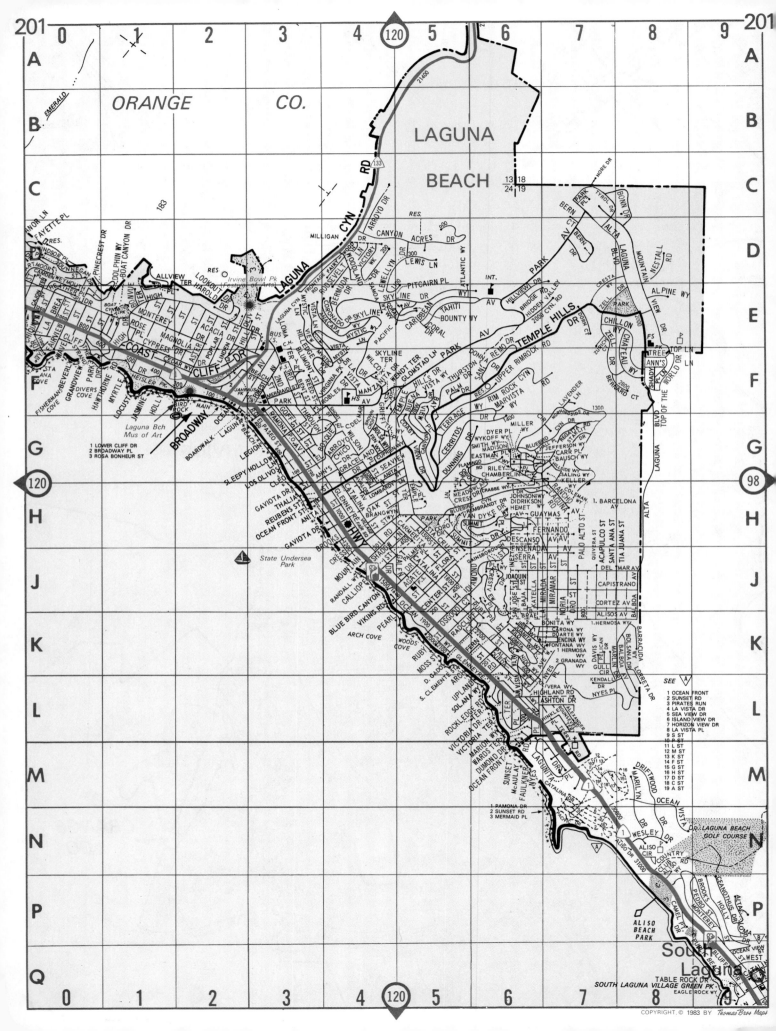

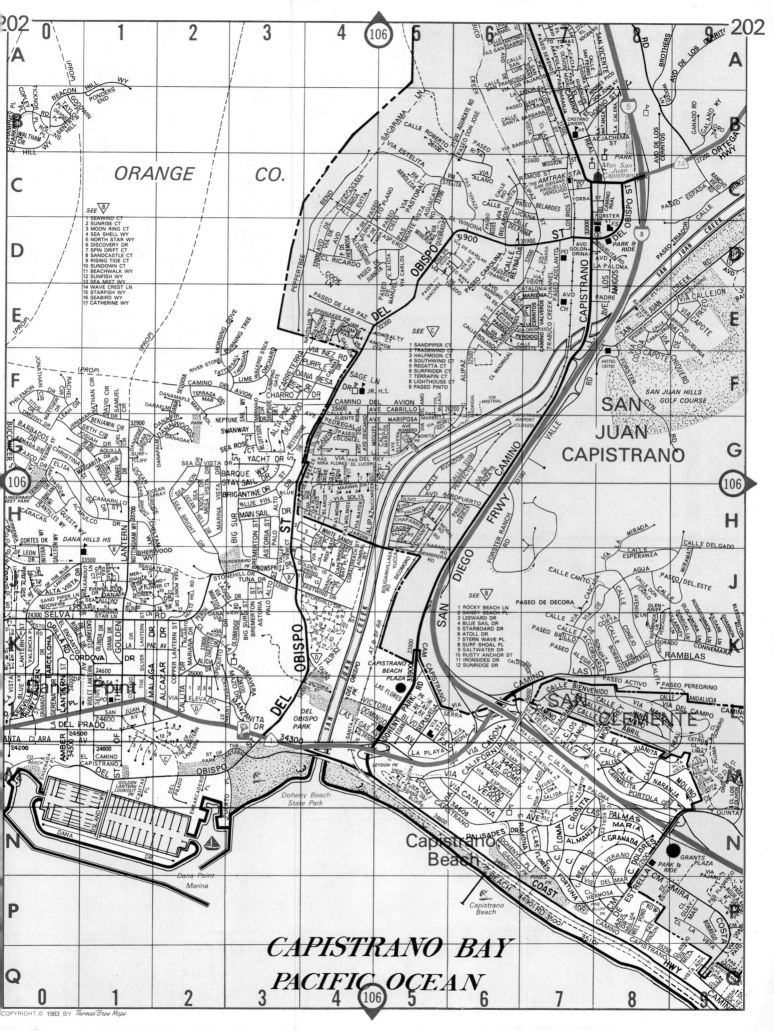

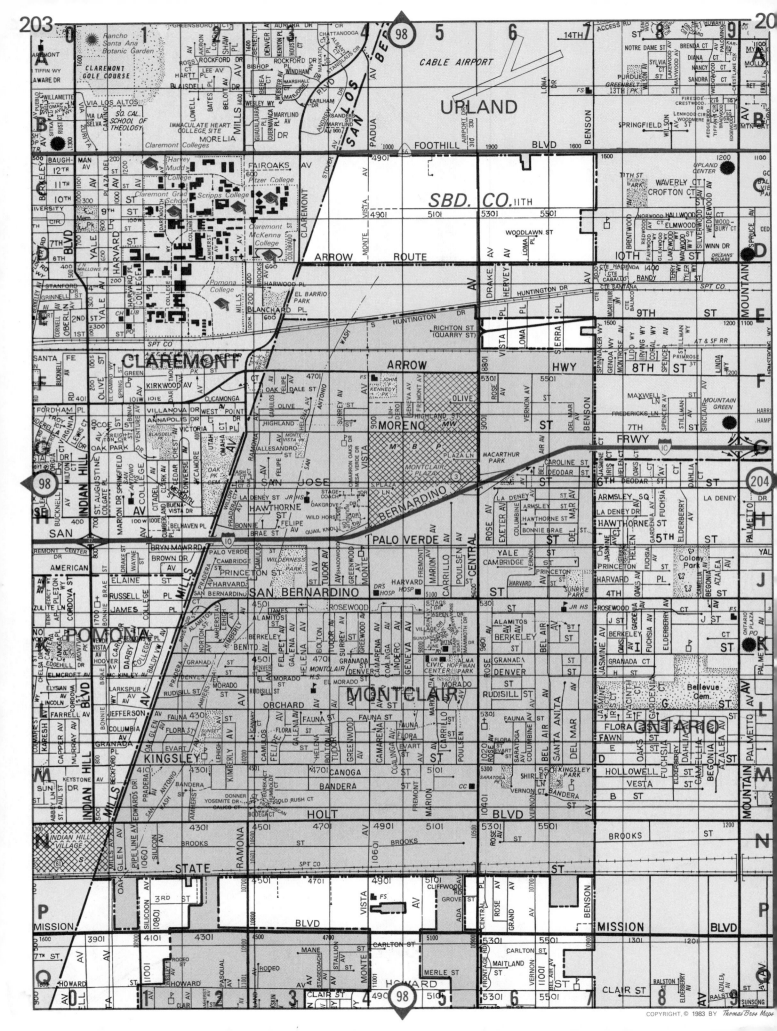

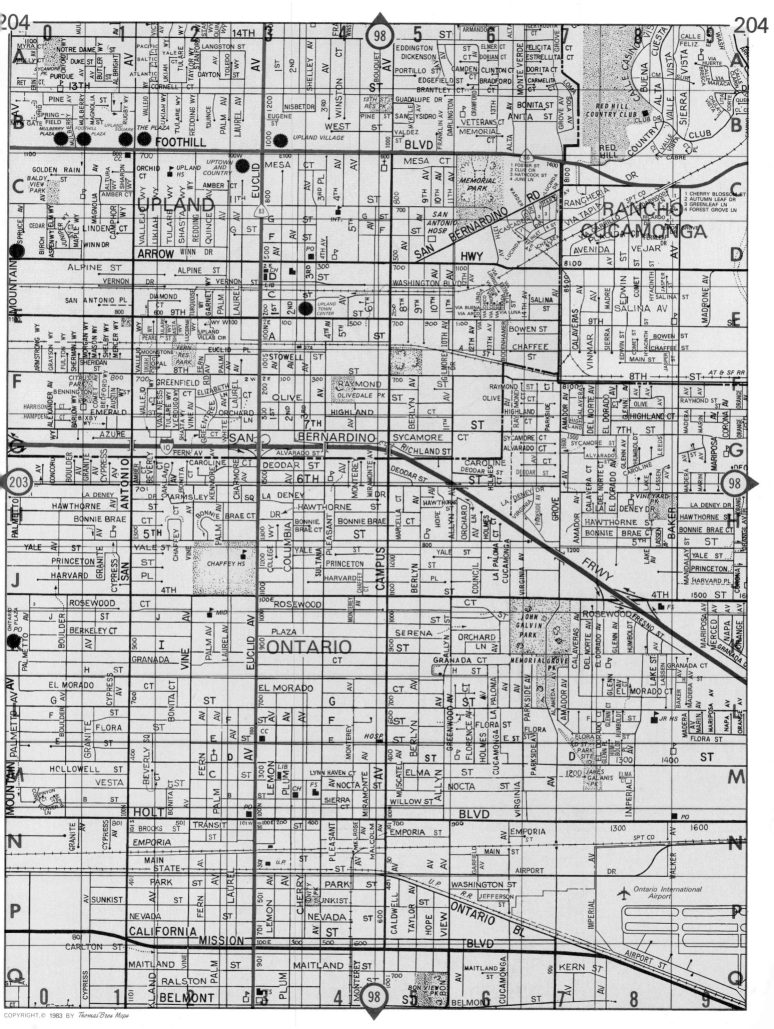

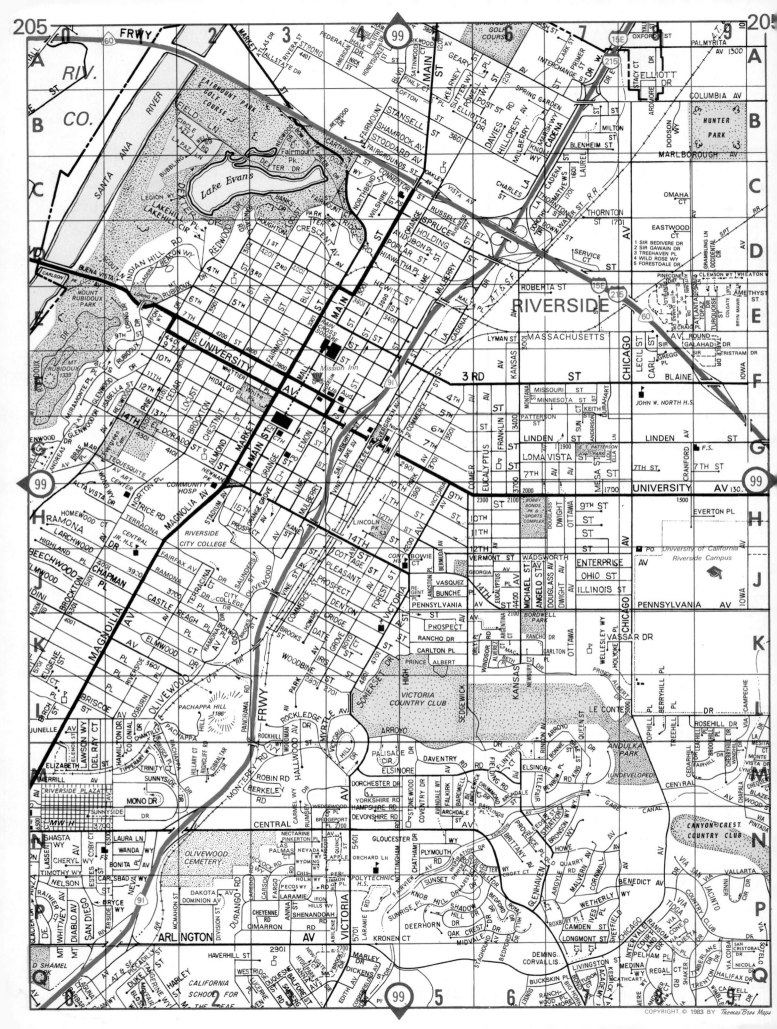

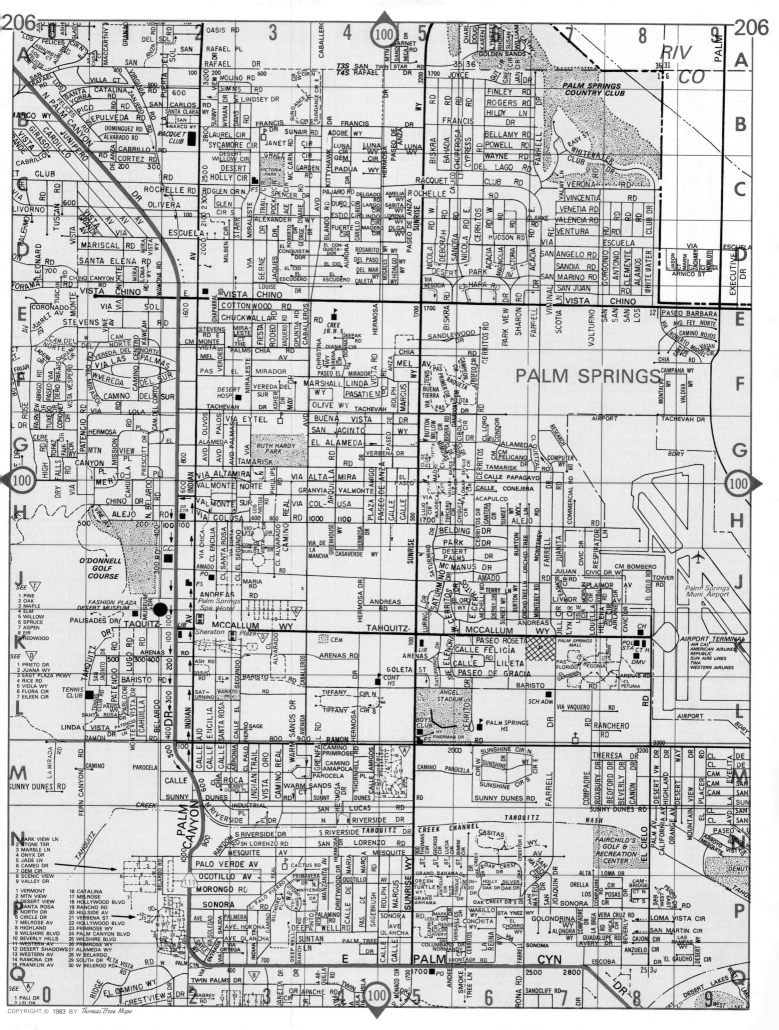

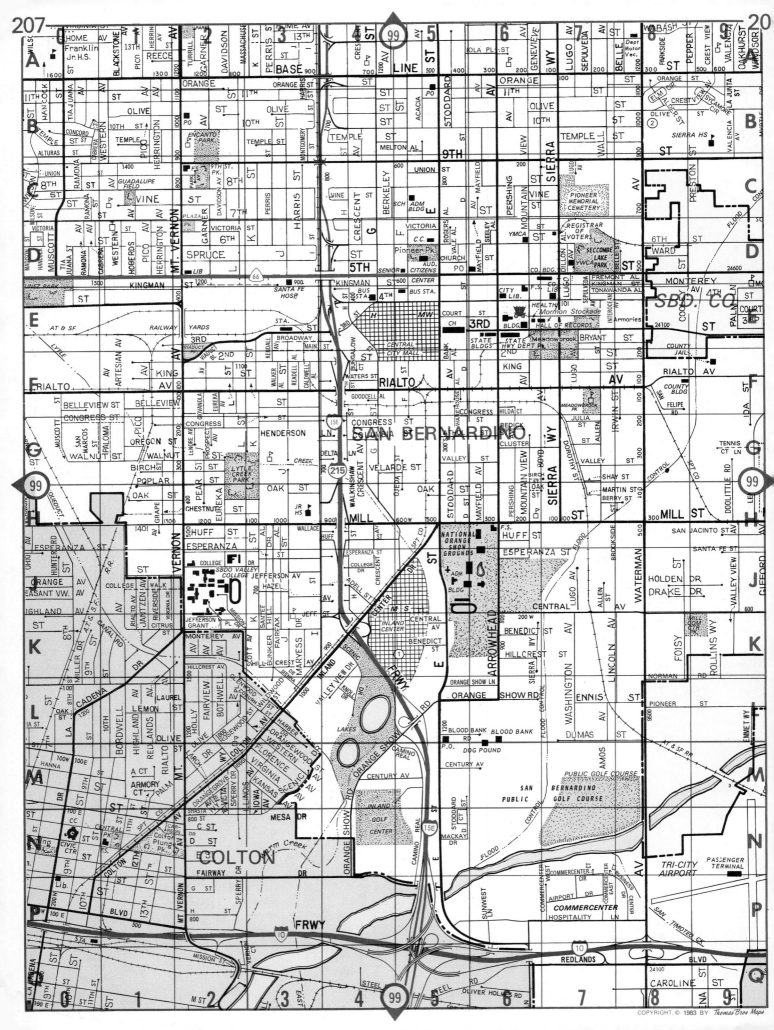

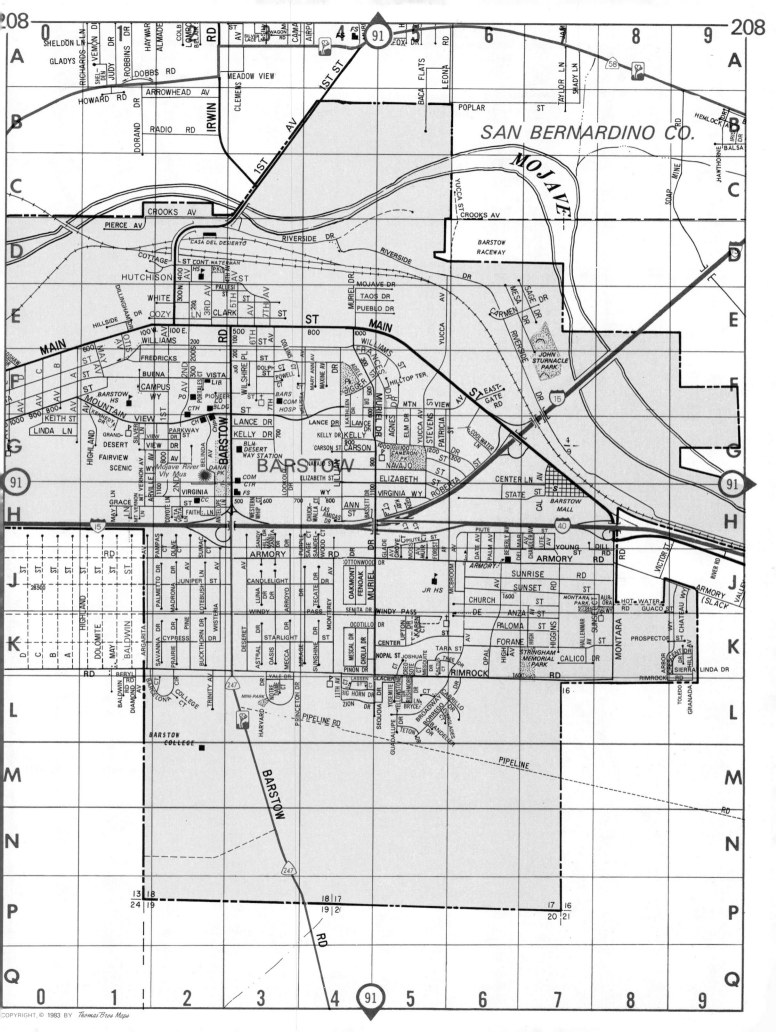

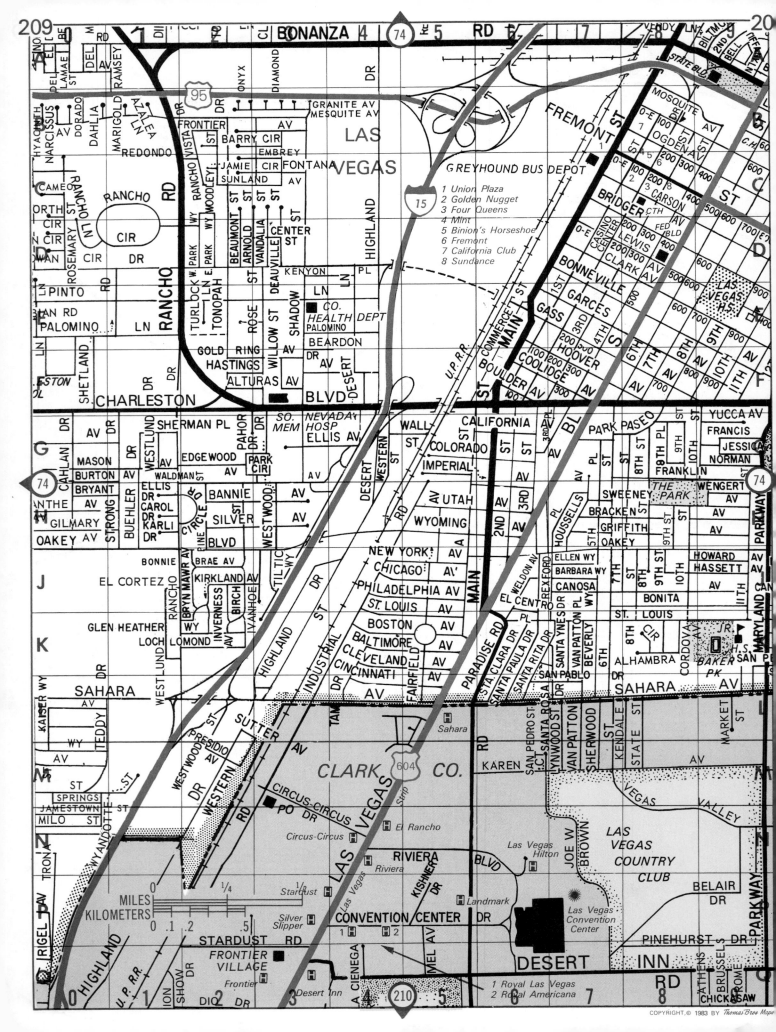

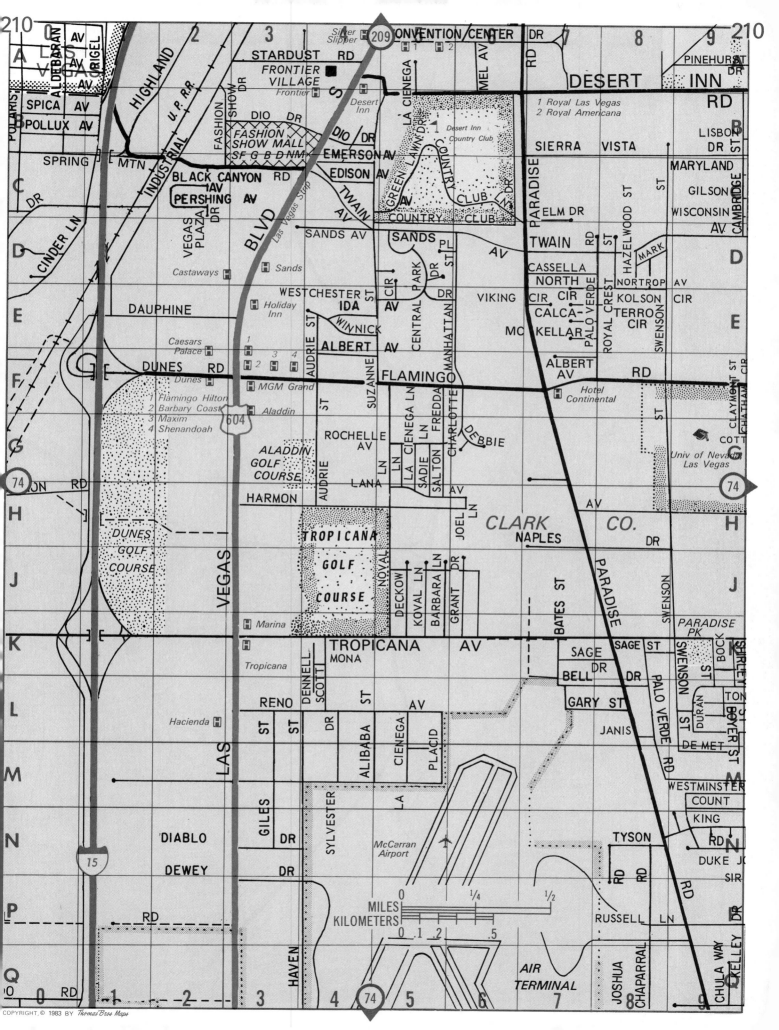

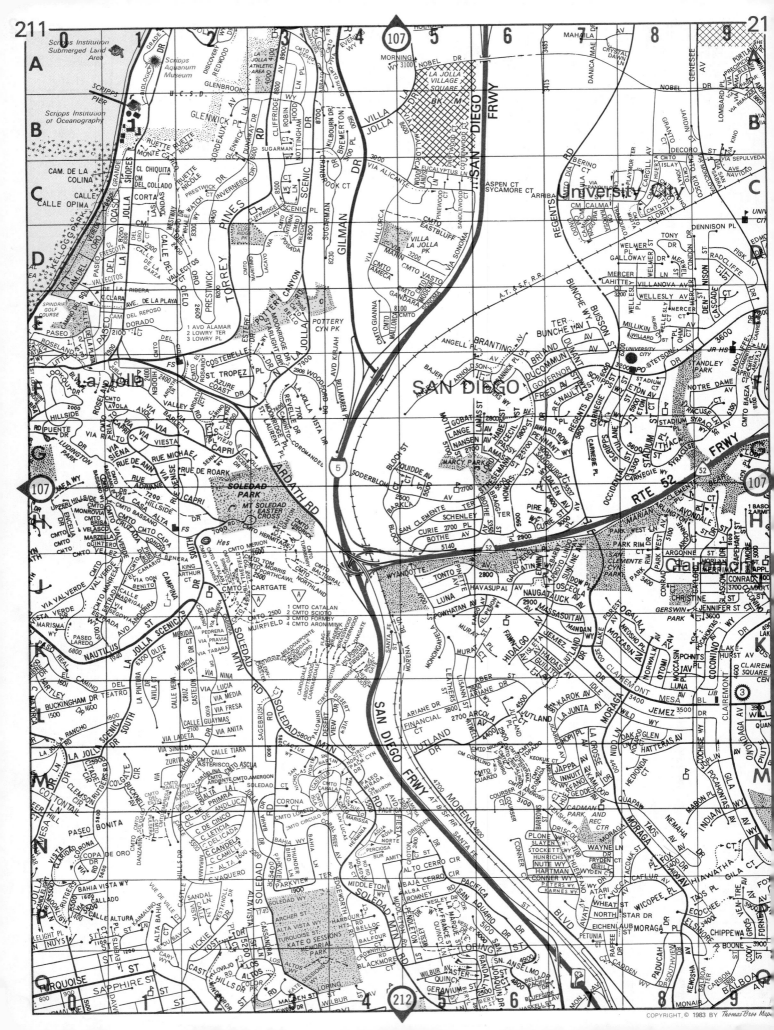

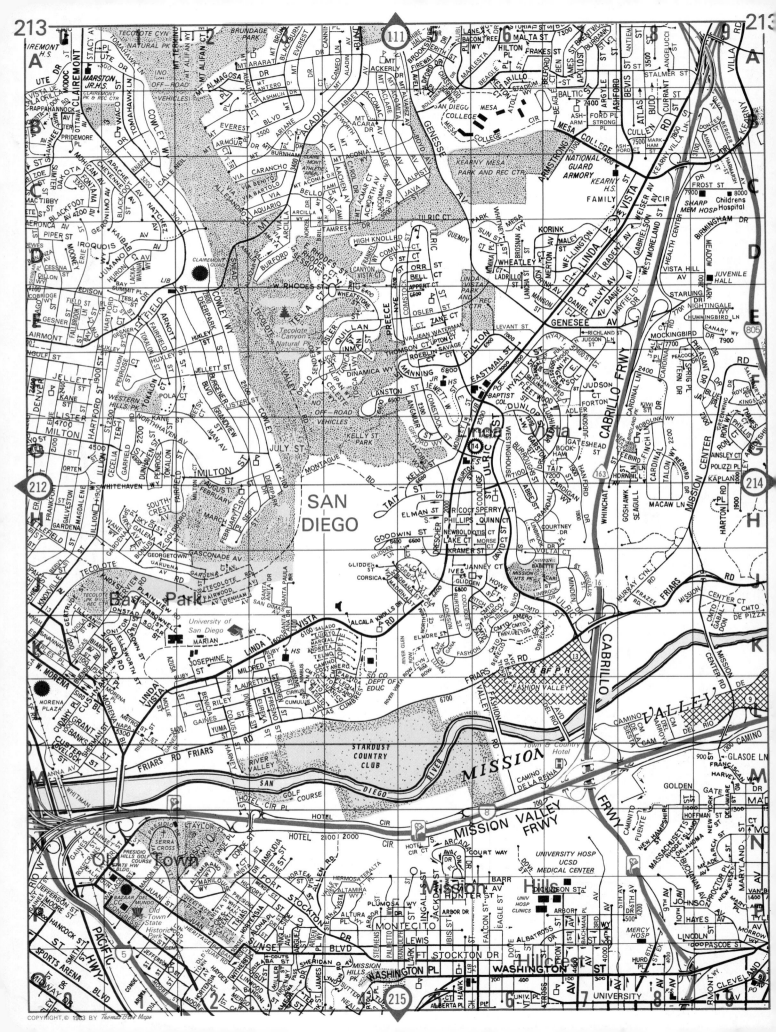

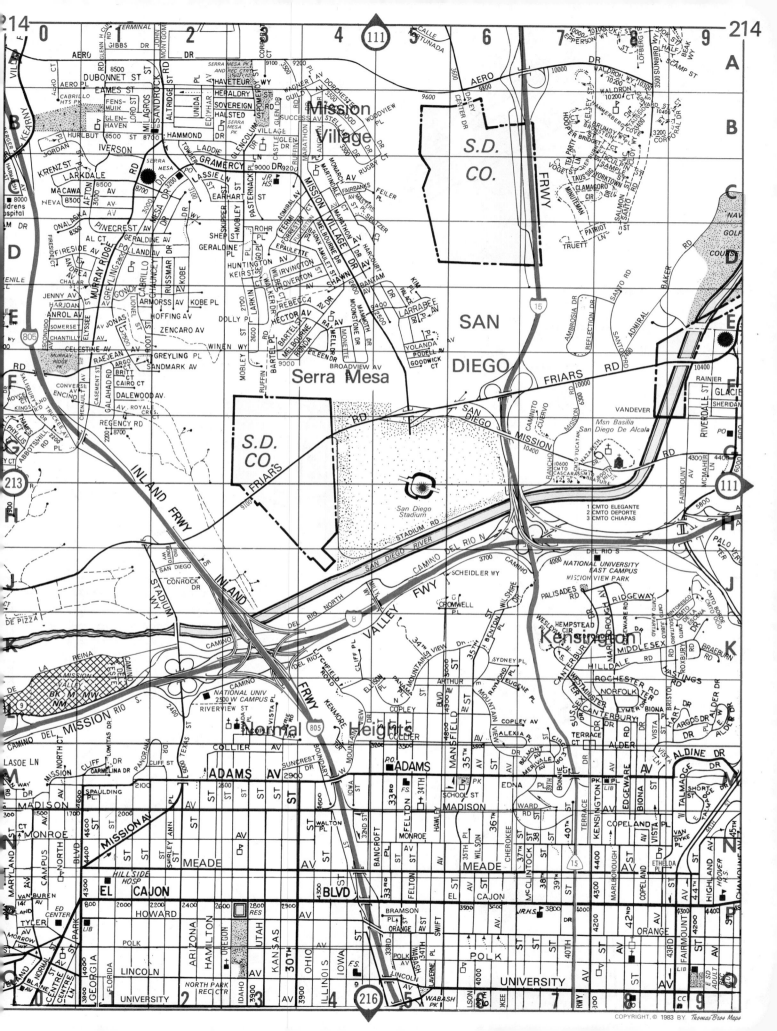

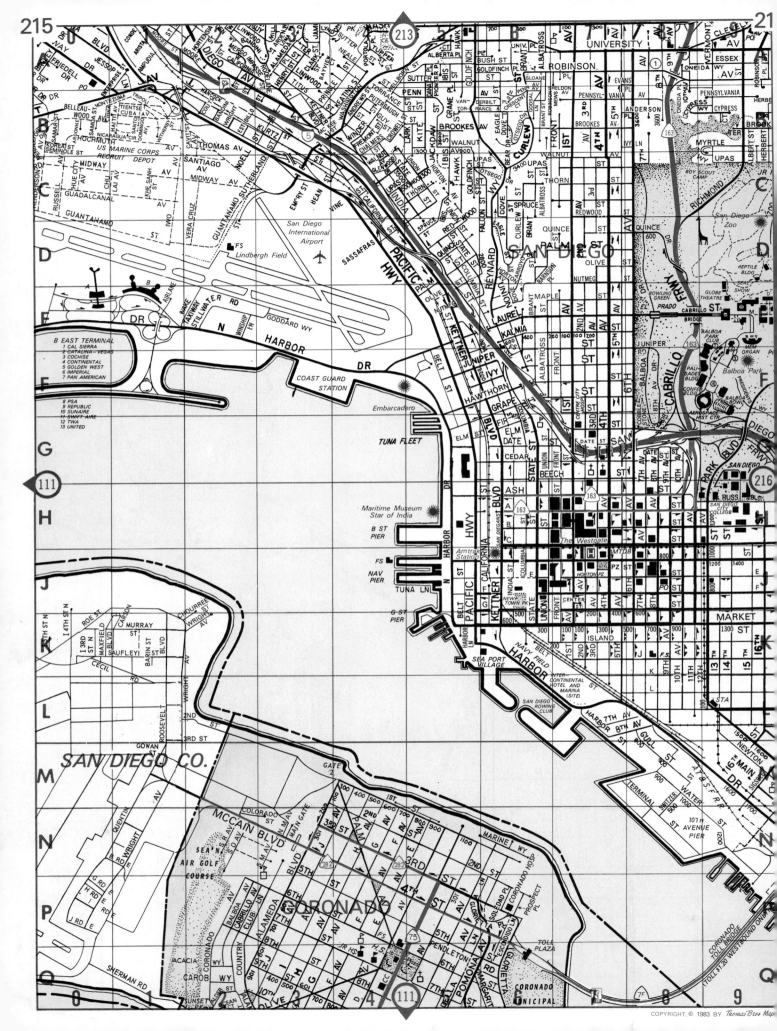

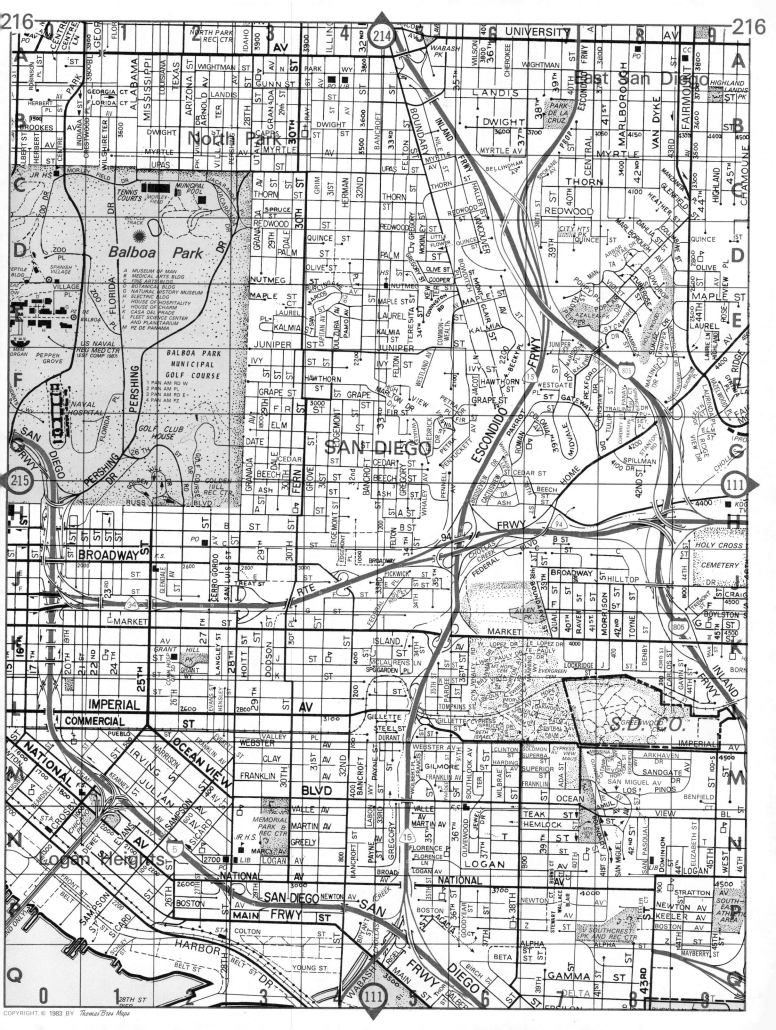

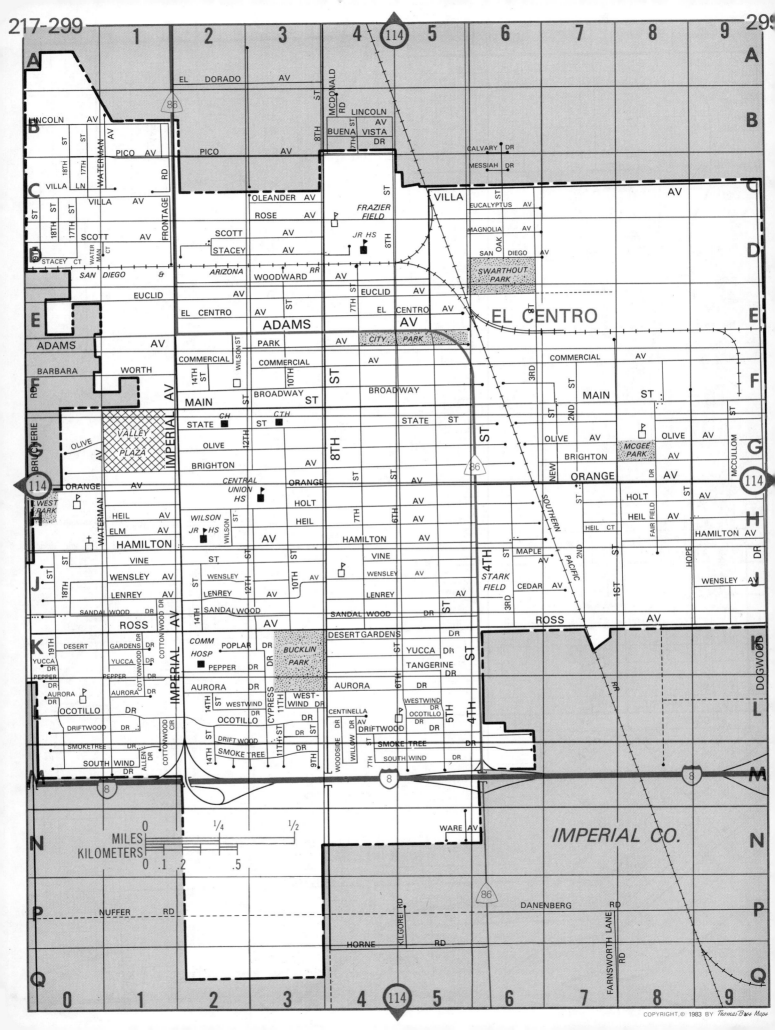

LIST OF ABBREVIATIONS

AL	ALLEY
AR	ARROYO
ARR	ARROYO
AV	AVENUE
AVD	AVENIDA
AVD D LS	AVENIDA DE LOS
BCH	BEACH
BL	BOULEVARD
BLVD	BOULEVARD
CEM	CEMETERY
CIR	CIRCLE
CK	CREEK
CL	CALLE
CL DL	CALLE DEL
CL D LS	CALLE DE LAS CALLE DE LOS
CL EL	CALLE EL
CLJ	CALLEJON
CL LA	CALLE LA
CL LS	CALLE LAS CALLE LOS
CM	CAMINO
CM D	CAMINO DE
CM D LA	CAMINO DE LA
CM D LS	CAMINO DE LAS CAMINO DE LOS
CMTO	CAMINITO
CN	CANAL
COM	COMMON
CR	CRESCENT
CRES	CRESCENT
CSWY	CAUSEWAY
CT	COURT
CTR	CENTER
CV	COVE
CY	CANYON
CYN	CANYON
D	DE
DL	DEL
DR	DRIVE
DS	DOS
E	EAST
EST	ESTATE
EXPWY	EXPRESSWAY
EXT	EXTENSION
FRWY	FREEWAY
FWY	FREEWAY
FY	FREEWAY
GN	GLEN
GRDS	GROUNDS
GRN	GREEN
GRV	GROVE
HTS	HEIGHTS
HWY	HIGHWAY
HY	HIGHWAY
JCT	JUNCTION
KPN	KEY PENINSULA NORTH
KPS	KEY PENINSULA SOUTH
L	LA
LN	LANE
LP	LOOP
LS	LAS, LOS
MDW	MEADOW
MT	MOUNT
MTN	MOUNTAIN
MTWY	MOTORWAY
MTY	MOTORWAY
N	NORTH
PAS	PASEO
PAS DE	PASEO DE
PAS DL	PASEO DEL
PAS D LS	PASEO DE LAS PASEO DE LOS
PGD	PLAYGROUND
PK	PARK
PKWY	PARKWAY
PL	PLACE
PT	POINT
PZ	PLAZA
RCH	RANCH
RCHO	RANCHO
RD	ROAD
RDG	RIDGE
RES	RESERVOIR
RIV	RIVER
RV	RIVER
RO	RANCHO
S	SOUTH
SN	SAN
SPG	SPRING
SPGS	SPRINGS
SQ	SQUARE
SRA	SIERRA
ST	SAINT
ST	STREET
STA	SANTA
STA	STATION
TER	TERRACE
THTR	THEATER
TK TR	TRUCK TRAIL
TR	TRAIL
VIA D	VIA DE
VIA D LS	VIA DE LAS VIA DE LOS
VIA DL	VIA DEL
VIS	VISTA
VLY	VALLEY
VW	VIEW
W	WEST
WK	WALK
WY	WAY

STREET INDEX

STREET	CO.	PAGE & GRID	
A			
A ST	ALA	45	E8
A ST	DVS	136	G5
A ST	DN	1	L7
A ST	H	146	E8
A ST	SBD	92	C0
A ST	SD	215	H6
A ST	TEH	18	P8
A ST W	H	146	G3
ABBOTT DR	KER	80	G3
ABBOTT RD	LACO	117	P7
ABBOTT ST	MON	54	L6
ABBOTT ST	SAL	171	M6
ABBY ST	FRE	165	H7
ABELOR RD	INY	51	K5
ABERDEEN DR	SBD	100	B8
ABERDEEN STA RD	INY	59	C8
ABERNATHY RD	SOL	38	H8
ABERNATHY RD	YUB	26	M2
ABLE RD	COL	32	E8
ABORN RD	SCL	46	M4
ABRAM DR	RCO	100	N1
ACACIA AV	ANA	193	B7
ACACIA AV	STA	47	J4
ACACIA AV	SUT	33	E4
ACACIA ST	SAL	171	L1
ACADEMY AV	FRCO	57	M8
ACAMPO	SJCO	40	K2
ACARI RD	KER	78	G3
ACKERMAN LN	HUM	16	H3
ACME RD	SUT	33	G3
ACOMA TR	SBD	100	B7
ADA RD	KER	78	G3
ADAIR RD	IMP	109	P8
ADAIR RD	STA	47	E4
ADAMS AV	CM	197	N4
ADAMS AV	EC	217	E3
ADAMS AV	FRCO	56	L7
ADAMS AV	FRCO	57	L4
ADAMS AV	FRCO	58	L1
ADAMS AV	ORA	120	J4
ADAMS AV	SD	214	M2
ADAMS AV	SDCO	106	K4
ADAMS AV	SDCO	111	B6
ADAMS BLVD	LA	184	M0
ADAMS BLVD	LA	185	M4
ADAMS BLVD	LACO	117	L3
ADAMS DR	KER	79	B8
ADAMS RD	TEH	18	K5
ADAMS ST	IMP	110	Q1
ADAMS ST	RCO	99	F1
ADAMS ST	RCO	101	L0
ADDISON RD	BUT	25	C5
ADELAIDA RD	SLO	75	B8
ADELINE ST	B	156	L0
ADELINE ST	O	157	D7
ADELANTO RD	SBD	91	H2
ADML CALLAHN LN	VAL	134	J8
ADOBE DR	KER	79	D9
ADOBE DR	KER	80	D0
ADOBE PL	MON	65	L4
ADOBE RD	BUT	25	K4
ADOBE RD	COL	25	Q1
ADOBE RD	KER	78	M7
ADOBE RD	SBD	101	B3
ADOBE RD	SLO	76	A1
ADOBE RD	SON	38	H1
ADOBE RD	TEH	18	M6
ADOBE CREEK RD	LAK	31	J7
ADOBE RANCH RD	MNO	44	Q1
ADOHR RD	KER	78	H1
ADOLFO LOPEZ BL	BAJA	114	D3
AERO DR	SD	214	A0
AERO DR	SDCO	106	H3
AERO DR	SDCO	111	A6
AEROPUERTO HWY	BAJA	111	F9
AFTON BLVD	GLE	25	M1
AFTON RD	BUT	25	P3
AFTON CANYON RD	SBD	82	N7
AGATE RD	SBD	91	B6
AGER BESWICK RD	SIS	4	H4
AGGEN RD	VEN	88	P5
AGNES WILSON RD	LPAZ	104	E1
AGNES WILSON RD	RCO	103	E9
AGOURA RD	LACO	105	C9
AGUA CALIENT BL	BAJA	111	G8
AGUA CALIENT RD	SB	87	K7
AGUA CALIENT RD	SON	132	C1
AGUA DULCE CYN	LACO	89	L6
AGUA FRIA	MPA	49	H1
AGUAJITO RD	MON	53	M8
AGUAJITO RD	MON	168	D6
AGUA MANSA RD	RCO	99	E2
AGUAS FRIAS RD	BUT	25	L2
AGUEREBERRY PT	INY	71	B6
AHERN RD	SJCO	47	E1
AINSWORTH PL	RCO	108	A1
AIR BASE PKWY	FRFD	135	D4
AIR BASE PKWY	SOL	38	H9
AIR BASE PKWY	SOL	39	H0
AIR BASE RD	SBD	91	H2
AIRD CIR	BUT	25	J8
AIROLA	CAL	41	M3
AIROSA DR	SBD	90	G8
AIROX RD	SB	86	C2
AIR PARK DR	IMP	109	F5
AIRPORT	SJCO	40	Q2
AIRPORT BLVD	LA	188	Q7
AIRPORT BLVD	LA	189	C6
AIRPORT BLVD	LACO	117	Q2
AIRPORT BLVD	RCO	101	M1
AIRPORT BLVD	SAL	171	P9
AIRPORT BLVD	SF	144	B4
AIRPORT BLVD	SJ	151	D8
AIRPORT BLVD	SCR	54	E3
AIRPORT BLVD	SON	37	C8
AIRPORT BLVD S	SSF	144	D5
AIRPORT DR	O	159	P6
AIRPORT RD	ALP	36	M4
AIRPORT RD	HUM	9	M9
AIRPORT RD	KER	78	L1
AIRPORT RD	MEN	30	C4
AIRPORT RD	MOD	8	A0
AIRPORT RD	MOD	14	A9
AIRPORT RD	NAPA	38	J5
AIRPORT RD	O	159	L7
AIRPORT RD	SLO	76	A2
AIRPORT RD	SHA	18	G5
AIRPORT RD	SOL	39	J5
AIRPORT RD	TRI	17	B6
AIRPORT WY	SJCO	47	D2
AIRPORT WY	SIS	12	A4
AIRPT WILLOW CK	SIS	4	K3
AIRWAY DR	KLAM	5	B4
AKER AV	STA	47	B7
AKRICH ST	SHA	18	D5
ALABAMA ST	SBD	99	E5
ALAMEDA AV	BUR	179	N6
ALAMEDA AV	LACO	117	G3
ALAMEDA AV	O	159	B3
ALAMEDA AV	SAL	171	P5
ALAMEDA AV	YOL	39	F6
ALAMEDA ST	LA	186	K3
ALAMEDA ST	LACO	97	E8
ALAMEDA ST	LACO	119	A6
ALAMEDA ST	LACO	119	E6
ALAMEDA ST	MAN	161	H5
ALAMEDA ST	VAL	134	M5
ALAMEDA, THE	SJ	151	F4
ALAMEDA, THE	SJ	152	L0
ALAMEDA, THE	SCLR	151	F4
ALAM D LS PULGS	BLMT	145	K0
ALAM D LS PULGS	SM	145	K0
ALAM D LS PULGS	SMCO	45	K6
ALAMEDA PAD SER	STB	174	E4
ALAMITOS AV	LACO	119	F7
ALAMO RD	IMP	110	P3
ALAMO ST	LACO	88	P9
ALAMO ST	VEN	89	P0
ALAMO CREEK RD	SLO	76	P7
ALAMO PINTADO	SB	86	H8
ALBA RD	SCR	53	B8
ALBAUGH RD	LAS	14	H5
ALBERS RD	STA	47	D8
ALBRT ETTER RCH	HUM	16	P1
ALBERTON AV	BUT	25	H1
ALBION LTL RIV	MEN	30	C3
ALBION RIDGE RD	MEN	30	C4
ALBRIGHT RD	IMP	110	J2
ALCALDE RD	FRCO	66	G6
ALCATRAZ AV	O	156	L2
ALDEN ST	KER	78	K8
ALDER AV	SBD	80	B8
ALDER AV	SBD	99	C2
ALDER ST	PAC	167	E3
ALDER CAMP RD	DN	1	Q9
ALDER CAMP RD	DN	9	A9
ALDER CAMP RD	DN	10	A0
ALDER CK BCH RD	MEN	30	H5
ALDRCRFT HTS RD	SCL	54	A1
ALDERPOINT RD	HUM	16	J4
ALDER PT BLUFF	TRI	16	N8
ALDER SPGS RD	GLE	23	G6
ALDER SPGS RD	GLE	23	J9
ALDER SPGS RD	GLE	23	J9
ALDER SPGS RD	GLE	23	J9
ALDERPOINT RD	HUM	16	H4
ALDINE DR	SD	214	M9
ALDINE DR	SDCO	106	K4
ALDRIDGE RD	SHA	19	F2
ALEJO DR	RCO	100	J5
ALESSANDRO BLVD	RCO	99	G3
ALEXANDER LN	LAS	21	J4
ALEXANDR VLY RD	SON	31	Q7
ALFALFA AV	STA	47	K5
ALFRD HARRL HWY	KER	78	F7
ALGERINE RD	TUO	41	P5
ALGRN WRDS FRRY	TUO	41	P5
ALGOMAN AV	SBD	91	H8
ALHAMBRA	CC	38	N8
ALHAMBRA AV	M	154	C2
ALHAMBRA BL	SCTO	137	H8
ALHAMBRA RD	LACO	117	J8
ALHAMBRA WY	M	154	H4
ALHAMBRA VLY RD	CC	38	P6
ALHAMBRA VLY RD	CC	154	Q4
ALHAMBRA VLY RD	M	154	L4
ALICE AV	HUM	16	Q4
ALICA PKWY	ORA	98	N7
ALISAL RD	MON	54	K6
ALISAL RD	SB	86	J8
ALISAL ST E	SAL	171	K7
ALISAL ST W	SAL	171	L2
ALISO CANYON RD	LACO	89	L9
ALISO CANYON RD	SB	87	B4
ALISO CANYON RD	VEN	88	N3
ALISO PARK RD	SB	87	B4
ALISOS AV	SB	87	H0
ALISOS CYN RD	SB	86	E7
ALLEGHANY RD	YUB	26	P4
ALLEN	SJCO	47	C4
ALLEN AV	LACO	117	G9
ALLEN AV	LACO	118	G0
ALLEN AV	MCO	48	H5
ALLEN RD	IMP	109	J7
ALLEN RD	KER	78	G5
ALLENDALE RD	SOL	39	D1
ALLERTON AV	SSF	144	A7
ALLIANCE RD	HUM	9	P9
ALLIANCE RD	HUM	10	P0
ALLRED	MPA	49	J3
ALLUVIAL AV	FRCO	57	G5
ALMA AV	KER	79	P7
ALMA ST	PA	147	E1
ALMA ST	SJ	152	Q5
ALMA ST	SCL	45	K7
ALMADEN AV	SJ	152	M3
ALMADEN BL	SJ	152	K2
ALMADEN EXPWY	SCL	46	N2
ALMANOR DR W	PLU	20	M3
ALMER RD	COL	32	D6
ALMOND AV	STA	47	J4
ALMOND DR	MCO	55	D7
ALMOND DR	MOD	76	D2
ALMOND RD	KER	77	A3
ALMOND ST	RCO	99	M4
ALMONTE BL	MAR	140	M3
ALMONWOOD	SJCO	47	D2
ALONA ST	KER	80	L1
ALONDRA	LACO	97	H8
ALONDRA BLVD	LACO	98	G1
ALOSTA	LACO	98	C4
ALOSTA AV	LACO	118	H6
ALPHA RD	NEV	26	Q8
ALPINE AV	FRCO	56	K7
ALPINE AV	SJCO	40	P0
ALPINE AV	S	160	G0
ALPINE BLVD	SDCO	108	P1
ALPINE DR	SDCO	111	B6
ALPINE RD	MOD	7	Q4
ALPINE RD	MOD	8	A4
ALPINE RD	SJCO	40	L2
ALPINE RD	SMCO	45	L7
ALPINE MINE RD	ALP	36	N1
ALPS DR	KER	79	N4
ALT CT	RCO	108	A4
ALTA	FRCO	58	L1
ALTA ST	MON	54	N8
ALTA ST	NEV	34	C4
ALTA BONNY NOOK	PLA	34	C7
ALTADENA	LACO	98	B0
ALTADENA DR	LACO	117	F8
AL TAHOE BL	SLT	129	L1
ALTAIR AV	SDCO	106	G4
ALTAIR AV	SDCO	107	P6
ALTA LOMA DR	SBD	100	C8
ALTA MESA DR	SHA	18	F5
ALTA MESA RD	SAC	40	F2
ALTAMONT PSS RD	ALA	46	D5
ALTA VISTA	AVLN	105	L1
ALTA VISTA	BKD	166	E9
ALTA VISTA	KER	78	G7
ALTHEA AV	FRCO	56	F1
ALTON AV	SA	197	G7
ALTUS AV	KER	80	N2
ALUM ROCK AV	SCL	46	L3
ALVARADO BLVD	ALA	45	G9
ALVARADO RD	MON	65	L7
ALVARADO RD	STA	47	D8
ALVARADO ST	LA	185	H5
ALVARADO ST	LA	185	H5
ALVARADO ST	LACO	117	L5
ALVARADO ST	SDCO	107	D4
ALVARADO TR	MCO	55	D7
ALVARADO-NILES	ALA	45	G9
ALVIN AV	SMA	173	F2
ALVIN DR E	SAL	171	B6
ALVIN DR W	SAL	171	B4
ALVISO-MLPTS RD	SCL	46	K1
ALVORD MTN RD	SBD	82	N4
ALWARD RD	SHA	19	G2
AMADOR AV	FRCO	56	P7
AMADOR ST	FRE	165	L2
AMADOR ST	VAL	134	L6
AMAR RD	LACO	98	E3
AMAR RD	LACO	118	L4
AMARGOSA RD	SBD	91	J3
AMARGOSA ST	SBD	92	D4
AMBOY RD	SBD	93	L7
AMBOY RD	SBD	101	B4
AMBOY RD	SBD	101	A8
AMBROSE DR	SAL	171	M0
AMBOY CUTOFF	SBD	93	J8
AMEDEE RD	LAS	21	K6
AMELIA AV	LACO	118	H7
AMEN LN	TEH	18	J5
AMERICAN AV	FRCO	57	K0
AMERICAN AV	FRCO	58	K2
AMERICAN AV	MCO	47	K6
AMERICAN AV	STA	47	D5
AMERICN CYN RD	NAPA	38	K6
AMERICN GIRL MN	IMP	116	P3
AMERICN MINE RD	SHA	18	B1
AMERIGO	SJCO	40	Q4
AMES ST	ALA	46	D4
AMESTI RD	SCR	54	E3
AMOROSE ST	RCO	99	M2
AMOUR RD	SUT	33	K5
AMSTERDAM RD	MCO	48	J3
ANAHEIM BLVD	ANA	193	C4
ANAHEIM BLVD	ORA	98	J4
ANAHEIM BLVD	ORA	120	D5
ANAHEIM ST	LB	192	E6
ANAHEIM ST	LA	191	A0
ANAHEIM ST	LA	192	E6
ANAHEIM ST	LACO	97	K7
ANAHEIM ST	LACO	119	F5
ANAPAMU ST	STB	174	H4
ANCHO ERIE MINE	NEV	26	P8
ANCHO MINE RD	NEV	26	P8
ANCHOR	FRCO	58	K2
ANDERHOLT RD	IMP	114	C3
ANDERSON DR W	SHA	18	H5
ANDERSON LN	HUM	15	F8
ANDERSON RD	DVS	136	H3
ANDERSON RD	SLO	76	C0
ANDERSON RD	SOL	39	K4
ANDERSON RD	STA	47	L4
ANDERSON ST	SBD	99	E4
ANDERSON CK RD	JKSN	3	B7
ANDERSON GRADE	SIS	4	H2
ANDERSON RCH RD	LAS	14	K6
ANDERSON VLY WY	MEN	30	G8
ANDESITE RD	SIS	4	Q6
ANDESITE RD	SIS	12	A6
ANDESITE LOG RD	SIS	12	B7
ANDRADE RD	ALA	46	G2
ANDRE RD	IMP	110	L0
ANDRESSEN RD	PLA	33	H9
ANDREW AV	SB	86	C5
ANDREWS RD	LAS	14	J4
ANGELES CRST HY	LACO	117	C7
ANGELES FRST HY	LACO	90	L0
ANGELES FRST HY	LACO	117	B7
ANITA RD	BUT	25	F0
ANNADALE AV	FRCO	57	K2
ANNADALE AV	FRCO	58	J0
ANNAPOLIS RD	SON	30	N9
ANNETTE RD	KER	76	A9
ANTELOPE DR	LAS	8	L2
ANTELOPE HWY	LACO	90	K6
ANTELOPE RD	MNO	42	B9
ANTELOPE RD	MNO	43	B0
ANTELOPE RD	RCO	99	L5
ANTELOPE RD	SAC	34	N1
ANTELOPE RD	SLO	66	P8
ANTELOPE SPGS	MNO	50	E8
ANTELOPE VLY FY	LACO	89	D9
ANTELOPE VLY RD	SIE	27	J5
ANTHONY RD	LACO	89	K7
ANTOLA RD	LAS	21	J5
ANZA RD	IMP	114	D0
ANZA RD	RCO	107	A7
ANZAR RD	SBT	54	F6
ANZA TRAIL RD	IMP	113	C5
APACHE TR	RCO	100	G2
APACHE CYN RD	VEN	88	E0
APPALOOSA RD	CAL	41	M1
APPIAN WY	CC	38	P5
APPLE RD	TEH	24	D5
APPLE CANYON RD	RCO	100	M4
APPLE COLONY RD	TUO	41	P7
APPLE RANCH RD	TUO	41	L8
APPLE SEED LN	RCO	100	N1
APPLE VALLEY RD	SBD	91	J4
APPLEWHITE	SBD	91	P0
APRICOT AV	STA	47	J4
APRIL LN	VEN	88	M4
AQUEDUCT RD	KER	79	N8
AQUEDUCT RD	SBD	103	D1
AQUEDUCT RD	SBD	104	B1
ARAMAYO WY	TEH	24	B8
ARASTRADERO RD	PA	147	Q8
ARATA LN	SON	37	B8
ARBINI RD	STA	47	C8
ARBOGA RD	YUB	33	F6
ARBOLEDA DR	MCO	48	N5
ARBOR AV	BLMT	145	P3
ARBOR RD	SLO	76	C1
ARBOR WY	MCO	56	A4
ARBORETUM RD	PA	147	G1
ARBOR VITAE	ING	189	A7
ARBOR VITAE	LA	189	A7
ARBOR VITAE ST	LACO	117	P2
ARBUCKL-GRIM RD	COL	33	G1
ARBURUA RD	MCO	55	E7
ARC RD	INY	51	Q7
ARCHER AV	SUT	33	B5
ARCHER RD	SHA	18	G2
ARCHERDALE	SJCO	40	N4
ARCHIBALD AV	RCO	98	G8
ARCHIE BROWN RD	SHA	13	K7
ARDATH RD	SD	211	G3
ARDATH RD	SDCO	106	H1
ARDATH RD	SDCO	107	P4
ARDEN DR	LACO	118	J2
ARDEN WY	SAC	40	A0
ARENA WY	MCO	48	L1
ARGO ST	KER	80	B6
ARGONNE DR	S	160	L2
ARGUELLO BL	SF	141	E7
ARGYLE RD	MON	65	J3
ARLINGTON AV	LA	184	P9
ARLINGTON AV	LACO	117	N4
ARLINGTON AV	LACO	119	E4
ARLINGTON AV	RIV	205	P1
ARLINGTON AV	RCO	99	F0
ARLINGTON AV S	RENO	130	N1
ARLINGTON RD	PLU	20	Q6
ARLINGTON MN RD	RCO	103	J2
ARMORY RD	BARS	208	J3
ARMOUR RD	SUT	33	L5
ARMOUR RANCH RD	SB	86	H9
ARMOUR RANCH RD	SB	87	H0
ARMSTRONG	SJCO	40	L1
ARMSTRONG AV	FRCO	57	F6
ARMSTRONG RD	CAL	41	J4
ARMSTRONG RD	LAS	14	H6
ARMSTRONG RD	RCO	99	E1
ARMSTRONG RD	STA	47	K4
ARMSTRONG RD	YUB	33	C6
ARMY RD	RCO	116	B2
ARMY ST	SFCO	45	D4
ARNO RD	SAC	40	G2
ARNOLD RD	IMP	115	B5
ARNOLD DR	SON	132	H1
ARNOLD DR	SON	38	G2
ARNOLD WY	SDCO	108	P2
AROSA RD	KER	79	M4
ARQUES AV	SVL	148	M8
ARRECHE RD	MOD	7	P7
ARRELLAGA ST	STB	174	J2
ARROW HWY	CLA	203	F4
ARROW HWY	LACO	98	C3
ARROW HWY	LACO	98	C8
ARROW HWY	LACO	118	J7
ARROW HWY	MTCL	203	F4
ARROW HWY	ROC	204	D1
ARROW HWY	SBD	98	C8
ARROW HWY	UPL	204	D1
ARROW ROUTE	SBD	203	D3
ARROWHEAD AV	SBDO	207	K6
ARROWHEAD BLVD	RCO	103	P6
ARROWHEAD BLVD	RCO	116	B6
ARROWHEAD RD	LAK	32	H0
ARROWHEAD TR	SBD	82	M9
ARROWHEAD TR	SBD	83	M0
ARROWHEAD LK RD	SBD	91	N4
ARROY AV	MCO	56	C1
ARROYO AV	KER	79	N9
ARROYO AV	KER	80	N0
ARROYO BLVD	LACO	117	G7
ARROYO BL	PAS	190	L1
ARROYO PKWY	PAS	190	P4
ARROYO RD	ALA	46	F4
ARROYO RD	SBD	92	L1
ARROYO BURRO RD	SB	87	K4
ARROYO GR GUADL	SLO	76	Q3
ARROYO GR GUADL	SLO	86	A1
AROYO GR HUASNA	SLO	76	M6
ARROYO SECO RD	MON	64	D9
ARROYO SECO RD	MON	65	B1
ARTESIA AV	SB	86	G2
ARTESIA BLVD	LACO	97	H6
ARTESIA BLVD	LACO	98	H0
ARTESIA BLVD	LACO	119	C2
ARTESIA FRWY	LACO	98	H0
ARTESIA FRWY	LACO	119	B6
ARTESIA FRWY	LACO	120	B1
ARTHUR	SJCO	47	B5
ARTHUR ST	RCO	101	P4
ARTICHOKE RD	SMCO	45	P4
ARTIC MINE RD	NEV	26	P8
ARTISTS DR	INY	72	B1
ASH AV	STA	47	H4
ASH ST	SD	215	H6
ASH ST	SDCO	108	K1
ASHBY AV	B	156	J3
ASHBY RD	SHA	18	D4
ASH CREEK RD	INY	60	Q2
ASH CREEK RD	SHA	18	H8
ASH CREEK RD	SHA	18	H7
ASH CREEK RD	SIS	4	J1
ASH CK SINK RD	SIS	13	E1
ASHE RD	KER	78	K6
ASHLAN AV	FRCO	56	H4
ASHLAN AV	FRCO	47	L1
ASH VALLEY RD	LAS	14	H7
ASH VALLEY RD	LAS	8	J0
ASHWORTH	MPA	49	J3
ASILOMAR AV	PAC	167	E1
ASPEN VALLEY RD	TUO	49	B4
ASPEN VALLEY RD	TUO	63	K1
ASSOCIATED RD	SB	86	C2
ASSOCIATED RD	SIS	5	G0
ASTER RD	SBD	91	J1
ASTORIA AV	KER	89	C5
ATEN RD	IMP	110	P0
ATHEL ST	KER	80	A5
ATHERTON BLVD	MAR	38	L2
ATHERTON ST	LACO	119	F9
ATHERTON ST	LACO	120	F0
ATHLONE RD	MCO	48	P6
ATLANTIC AV	A	157	N7
ATLANTIC AV	FRFD	135	C4
ATLANTIC AV	LB	192	E9
ATLANTIC AV	LACO	97	H9
ATLANTIC AV	LACO	119	B7
ATLANTIC AV E	FRFD	135	C6
ATLANTIC BLVD	LACO	98	E0
ATLANTIC BLVD	LACO	117	L8
ATLANTIC BLVD	LACO	119	F7
ATLAS	CC	38	N5
ATLAS PEAK RD	NAPA	38	D6
ATTERBERRY CT	KER	79	F8
ATTILA RD	SBD	84	K4
ATWATER	MCO	47	M8
ATWOOD	PLA	34	J4
AUBERRY RD	FRCO	57	C9
AUBERRY RD	FRCO	58	B0
AUBREY AV	MCO	56	D1
AUBURN BLVD	SAC	34	P0
AUBURN BLVD	SAC	34	P1
AUBURN RD	NEV	34	D4
AUBURN RD	PLA	34	H2
AUBURN-FOLSM RD	SAC	34	P3
AUBURN FRST HLL	PLA	34	G7
AUBURN RAVNE RD	AUB	126	G5
AUBURN RAVNE RD	PLA	126	G5
AUCTION SNIVELY	TEH	18	K6
AUGUST AV	MCO	47	K7
AUGUST RD	STA	47	K6
AUGUSTINE RD	RCO	110	B5
AUKLET RD	SBD	92	B5
AULD RD	RCO	99	P6
AURORA CYN RD	MNO	43	G3
AUSTIN	SJCO	40	Q3
AUSTIN	SJCO	47	A3
AUSTIN RD	IMP	110	N1
AUSTIN MDWS RD	NEV	27	M1
AUTOPSTA TIJ-EN	BAJA	111	G6
AVALON AV	SBD	100	C8
AVALON BLVD	LA	191	A5
AVALON BLVD	LACO	97	J8
AVALON BLVD	LACO	119	C5
AVALON CYN RD	AVLN	105	Q1
AVENA	SJCO	47	B4
AVENAL CUTOFF	KIN	67	G1
AVD BERMUDAS	RCO	100	M9
AVD DEL CAPITAN	SB	87	K0
AVD D LS ARBOLS	VEN	88	Q7
AVD DL PRESIDNT	ORA	106	C8
AVENIDA DEL SOL	KER	80	A5
AVENIDA ENCINO	RCO	100	N7
AVD LA CUMBRE	RCO	100	N7
AVD LOS FELIZ	RCO	100	N7
AVENIDA OBREGON	RCO	100	M9
AVENUE A	KER	89	C8
AVENUE A	YUMA	115	C6
AVENUE B	LACO	89	D7
AVENUE B	LACO	90	D5
AVENUE B	YUMA	115	E5
AVENUE C	LACO	89	D7
AVENUE C	LACO	90	D6
AVENUE C	YUMA	115	C5
AVENUE D	LACO	90	E2
AVENUE D	YUMA	115	D5
AVENUE E	LACO	90	E0
AVENUE E	RCO	99	H3
AVENUE E	YUMA	115	C5
AVENUE E-8	LACO	90	E2
AVENUE E-8	LACO	90	F5
AVENUE F	LACO	89	E3
AVENUE F	LACO	89	E7
AVENUE F	LACO	90	E5
AVENUE F	SBD	99	E7
AVENUE F	YUMA	115	E4
AVENUE F-4	LACO	90	E0
AVENUE F-8	LACO	90	E6
AVENUE F-8	LACO	89	F5
AVENUE G	LACO	89	F8
AVENUE G	YUMA	115	D4
AVENUE G-2	LACO	90	F4
AVENUE G-3	LACO	90	F4
AVENUE G-4	LACO	90	F4
AVENUE G-6	LACO	90	F4
AVENUE G-8	LACO	90	F2
AVENUE H	LACO	89	F5
AVENUE H	YUMA	115	E4
AVENUE I	LACO	89	F7
AVENUE I	YUMA	115	F4
AVENUE J	LACO	89	G9
AVENUE J	LACO	90	F5
AVENUE J	YUMA	115	E4
AVENUE J-8	LACO	90	G1
AVENUE K	LACO	89	G9
AVENUE K-8	LACO	89	G7
AVENUE L	LACO	89	G9
AVENUE L	RCO	99	E7
AVENUE M	LACO	90	G3
AVENUE M-8	LACO	89	G8
AVENUE N	LACO	89	H8
AVENUE N	LACO	90	G5
AVENUE O	LACO	90	H1
AVENUE P	LACO	90	H1
AVENUE P	LACO	90	J7
AVENUE P-8	LACO	90	H1
AVENUE P-8	LACO	90	H5
AVENUE Q	LACO	90	H4
AVENUE Q	LACO	90	H5
AVENUE R-8	LACO	90	J7
AVENUE S	LACO	90	J0
AV SAN LUIS	LA	177	L2
AV STANFORD	LACO	89	L3
AVENUE T	LACO	90	J3
AVENUE T	LACO	90	J5
AVENUE U	LACO	90	J5
AVENUE Z	LACO	90	L7
AVENUE 2	TUL	68	N6
AVENUE 4 1/2	MAD	56	H8
AVENUE 5	MAD	56	G9
AVENUE 5 1/2	MAD	57	G1
AVENUE 6	MAD	57	G1
AVENUE 6 1/2	MAD	57	G0
AVENUE 7 1/2	MAD	56	G6
AVENUE 7 1/2	MAD	57	G4
AVENUE 8	MAD	57	F1
AVENUE 8	MAD	57	F4
AVENUE 8	TUL	68	N3
AVENUE 8 1/2	MAD	57	F1
AVENUE 9	MAD	56	F9
AVENUE 9	MAD	57	F4
AVENUE 9 1/2	MAD	56	F9
AVENUE 10	MAD	56	F9
AVENUE 10	MAD	57	F2
AVENUE 10 1/2	MAD	56	F9
AVENUE 10 1/2	MAD	57	F0
AVENUE 11	MAD	56	F9
AVENUE 11	MAD	57	F0
AVENUE 12	MAD	56	F7
AVENUE 12	MAD	57	E2
AVENUE 12	TUL	68	N3
AVENUE 12	TUL	68	N4
AVENUE 13	MAD	56	E8
AVENUE 13 1/2	MAD	56	E9
AVENUE 14	MAD	56	E6
AVENUE 15	MAD	56	E8
AVENUE 15 1/2	MAD	56	D9
AVENUE 16	MAD	56	D8

SEE PAGE D FOR INSTRUCTIONS

STREET	CO.	PAGE & GRID
AVENUE 16	TUL	68 M3
AVENUE 16	TUL	68 M4
AVENUE 16 1/2	MAD	56 D8
AVENUE 17	MAD	56 D6
AVENUE 17 1/2	MAD	56 D6
AVENUE 18	MAD	56 D7
AVENUE 19	MAD	56 C6
AVENUE 19 1/2	MAD	56 C6
AVENUE 20	LA	186 D7
AVENUE 20	MAD	56 C6
AVENUE 20 1/2	MAD	56 C6
AVENUE 21	MAD	56 C6
AVENUE 21 1/2	MAD	56 C6
AVENUE 22	MAD	56 B6
AVENUE 23 1/2	MAD	56 B6
AVENUE 24	MAD	56 B6
AVENUE 24	TUL	68 M3
AVENUE 24 1/2	MAD	56 B8
AVENUE 25	MAD	56 B6
AVENUE 25 1/2	MAD	56 B6
AVENUE 26	MAD	56 A7
AVENUE 26 1/2	MAD	56 A9
AVENUE 27	MAD	48 Q9
AVENUE 27 1/2	MAD	48 Q9
AVENUE 28	MAD	48 Q9
AVENUE 28	TUL	68 M5
AVENUE 32	TUL	68 M3
AVENUE 32	TUL	68 M4
AVENUE 40	TUL	68 L4
AVENUE 40	TUL	68 L4
AVENUE 42	TUL	67 M9
AVENUE 44	TUL	68 L3
AVENUE 46	TUL	67 M9
AVENUE 48	TUL	68 L3
AVENUE 48	TUL	68 L3
AVENUE 50	TUL	68 L9
AVENUE 52	TUL	68 L3
AVENUE 52	TUL	67 L9
AVENUE 54	TUL	67 L9
AVENUE 56	TUL	68 L2
AVENUE 56	TUL	68 L2
AVENUE 58	TUL	68 L0
AVENUE 60	TUL	68 L0
AVENUE 62	TUL	68 L6
AVENUE 64	TUL	68 L6
AVENUE 66	TUL	68 L7
AVENUE 68	TUL	68 L6
AVENUE 68	TUL	68 L7
AVENUE 70	TUL	68 L7
AVENUE 72	TUL	68 K2
AVENUE 72	TUL	68 K2
AVENUE 76	TUL	68 K6
AVENUE 76	TUL	68 K3
AVENUE 80	TUL	68 K5
AVENUE 80	TUL	68 K1
AVENUE 84	TUL	68 K6
AVENUE 88	TUL	68 K0
AVENUE 88	TUL	68 K6
AVENUE 90	FRCO	55 G8
AVENUE 92	MCO	55 G7
AVENUE 94	TUL	68 K6
AVENUE 95	HAW	189 K7
AVENUE 95	TUL	68 K7
AVENUE 100	LA	188 Q8
AVENUE 100	TUL	68 J6
AVENUE 104	TUL	67 J9
AVENUE 104	LACO	97 G6
AVENUE 108	LACO	119 J2
AVENUE 108	RB	189 H2
AVENUE 112	TUL	68 J7
AVENUE 112	SDCO	106 K7
AVENUE 116	BUT	25 P8
AVENUE 116	SJCO	47 J3
AVENUE 120	TUL	67 J9
AVENUE 120	PLA	34 J3
AVENUE 124	TUL	67 J5
AVENUE 124	SOL	39 E2
AVENUE 128	TUL	68 H5
AVENUE 128	MCO	47 P6
AVENUE 132	LACO	118 M5
AVENUE 136	TUL	67 H9
AVENUE 136	LACO	118 M5
AVENUE 138	TUL	68 H4
AVENUE 138	TUL	68 H8
AVENUE 140	TUL	68 H7
AVENUE 144	TUL	68 H0
AVENUE 146	TUL	68 H7
AVENUE 148	TUL	68 H2
AVENUE 152	TUL	68 G6
AVENUE 156	TUL	68 G6
AVENUE 160	TUL	68 G1
AVENUE 164	TUL	68 G2
AVENUE 168	TUL	68 G4
AVENUE 169	TUL	68 G7
AVENUE 172	TUL	68 G6
AVENUE 176	TUL	68 G5
AVENUE 176	TUL	68 G3
AVENUE 178	TUL	68 G6
AVENUE 180	LAS	14 L4
AVENUE 180	TUL	68 F7
AVENUE 184	LAK	31 D5
AVENUE 184	TUL	68 F6
AVENUE 188	NEV	26 P6
AVENUE 190	TUL	68 F3
AVENUE 192	TUL	68 F3
AVENUE 192	KER	79 M5
AVENUE 196	KER	79 N7
AVENUE 196	STA	47 F7
AVENUE 198	SDCO	106 K1
AVENUE 200	SDCO	111 J4
AVENUE 204	RCO	108 J8
AVENUE 204	SIE	27 J7
AVENUE 208	SON	38 D0
AVENUE 208	MCO	55 C7
AVENUE 212	SBD	99 J1
AVENUE 212	SBD	98 E7
AVENUE 216	SBD	93 K6
AVENUE 216	TUL	68 E6
AVENUE 220	BUT	25 M6
AVENUE 224	KER	79 E3
AVENUE 224	MCO	48 M2
AVENUE 228	SB	52 Q3
AVENUE 228	TUL	68 E7
AVENUE 232	CC	39 N1
AVENUE 236	DN	10 P8
AVENUE 236	IMP	116 Q7
AVENUE 240	RCO	108 A3
AVENUE 244	SBD	84 D1
AVENUE 248	SCL	46 F7
AVENUE 252	TUL	68 D1
AVENUE 256	SIS	13 F1
AVENUE 256	KER	79 M3
AVENUE 260	RCO	99 P0
AVENUE 264	HUM	10 D0
AVENUE 264	SON	38 D0
AVENUE 272	SJCO	40 M4
AVENUE 272	ONT	204 A3
AVENUE 280	ROC	204 H8
AVENUE 280	TUL	68 C0
AVENUE 292	TUL	68 C0
AVENUE 304	COL	32 N2
AVENUE 308	SBD	85 B9
AVENUE 312	STA	47 B2
AVENUE 317	TUL	68 B2

STREET	CO.	PAGE & GRID
AVENUE 317	TUL	68 B6
AVENUE 318	TUL	68 B5
AVENUE 320	TUL	68 B6
AVENUE 320	TUL	68 B1
AVENUE 324	TUL	68 B5
AVENUE 328	TUL	68 A1
AVENUE 328	TUL	68 B5
AVENUE 332	TUL	68 A5
AVENUE 336	TUL	58 A3
AVENUE 336	TUL	58 A5
AVENUE 337	TUL	58 A5
AVENUE 340	TUL	58 A3
AVENUE 340	TUL	58 Q4
AVENUE 344	TUL	58 Q3
AVENUE 344	TUL	58 Q4
AVENUE 346	TUL	58 A6
AVENUE 348	TUL	58 Q6
AVENUE 350	TUL	57 Q9
AVENUE 352	TUL	57 Q9
AVENUE 352	TUL	58 Q4
AVENUE 356	TUL	58 Q4
AVENUE 356	TUL	57 P9
AVENUE 360	TUL	57 P5
AVENUE 360	TUL	58 P5
AVENUE 364	TUL	58 P2
AVENUE 364	TUL	58 P2
AVENUE 368	TUL	58 P2
AVENUE 368	TUL	58 M5
AVENUE 376	TUL	57 P9
AVENUE 376	TUL	58 P5
AVENUE 380	TUL	58 P5
AVENUE 384	TUL	58 P1
AVENUE 388	TUL	58 P1
AVENUE 390	TUL	57 N0
AVENUE 390	TUL	58 N0
AVENUE 392	TUL	58 N0
AVENUE 394	TUL	58 N3
AVENUE 396	TUL	57 N9
AVENUE 404	TUL	58 N2
AVENUE 404	TUL	58 N2
AVENUE 408	TUL	57 N9
AVENUE 410	TUL	58 P4
AVENUE 416	TUL	58 M3
AVENUE 428	TUL	58 M3
AVENUE 432	TUL	58 M3
AVENUE 436	TUL	58 M3
AVENUE 440	TUL	58 M2
AVENUE 448	TUL	58 L3
AVENUE 448	TUL	58 L3
AVENUE 450	TUL	58 L3
AVENUE 452	TUL	58 L3
AVENUE 456	TUL	58 L3
AVENUE 464	TUL	58 L3
AVENUE 472	TUL	58 L3
AVERY RD	FRCO	55 G8
AVERY RD	MCO	55 G7
AVERY SHEEP RCH	CAL	41 J4
AVIATION BLVD	ELS	189 K5
AVIATION BLVD	HAW	189 K7
AVIATION BLVD	ING	189 K7
AVIATION BL	LA	188 Q8
AVIATION BLVD	LACO	97 G6
AVIATION BLVD	LACO	119 J2
AVIATION BLVD	RB	189 H2
AVOCADO BLVD	SDCO	106 K7
AVOCADO BLVD	SDCO	111 J4
AVOCADO RD	BUT	25 P8
AYERS RD	SJCO	47 J3
AYRES HOLMES RD	PLA	34 J3
AZALEA TR	RCO	100 C9
AZEVEDO	MCO	47 P6
AZEVEDO RD	SOL	39 E2
AZEVEDO RD	STA	47 L5
AZTEC AV	TUL	67 H5
AZUSA AV	LACO	97 G6
AZUSA AV	LACO	118 M5
AZUSA CANYON RD	LACO	118 J4
B		
B ST	BUT	25 M6
B ST	DVS	136 G5
B ST	FRE	165 L5
B ST	H	146 E9
B ST	IMP	110 K0
B ST	KER	78 G0
B ST	LA	191 B4
B ST	LACO	98 D5
B ST	LACO	119 F5
B ST	SCTO	137 E5
B ST	SD	215 H6
B ST	SJCO	40 H2
B ST	YUBA	125 H7
B ST	YUB	33 J8
B ST N	SCTO	137 H8
BABCOCK RD	LAS	14 K1
BABCOCK CNDR RD	LAS	14 K2
BABEL SLOUGH RD	YOL	33 D1
BACHELOR VLY RD	LAK	31 D5
BACK BONE RD	NEV	26 P6
BACKBONE RD	SBD	18 B8
BACKBONE RD	SHA	13 Q9
BACKES LN	KER	79 M5
BACKUS RD	KER	79 F7
BACON ST	STA	47 F7
BACON ST	SDCO	106 K1
BACON ST	SDCO	111 J0
BACON ISLAND	SJCO	39 P8
BADDGE RD	RCO	108 J8
BADENOUGH CY RD	SIE	27 J7
BADGER	SON	38 D0
BADGER FLAT	MCO	55 C7
BAGDAD HWY	SBD	99 J1
BAGDAD HWY	SBD	98 E7
BAGDAD WY	SBD	93 K6
BAGDAD CHASE RD	SBD	99 H3
BAGGTT MARYSVLL	BUT	25 M6
BAILEY AV	KER	79 E3
BAILEY AV	MCO	48 M2
BAILEY RD	SB	52 Q3
BAILEY RD	CC	39 N1
BAILEY RD	DN	10 P8
BAILEY RD	IMP	116 Q7
BAILEY RD	RCO	108 A3
BAILEY RD	SBD	84 D1
BAILEY RD	SCL	46 F7
BAILEY HILL RD	SIS	13 F1
BAILY RD	KER	79 M3
BAILY RIDGE RD	SIS	13 F1
BAIN RD	RCO	99 P0
BAIRD RD	HUM	10 D0
BAIRD	SON	38 D0
BAKER	SJCO	40 M4
BAKER AV	ONT	204 A3
BAKER AV	ROC	204 H8
BAKER AV	TUL	68 C0
BAKER RD	COL	32 N2
BAKER RD	SBD	85 B9
BAKER RD	STA	47 B2
BAKER RD	TEH	18 N6

STREET	CO.	PAGE & GRID
BAKER RD	YUB	26 N3
BAKER ST	CM	197 M3
BAKER ST	CM	198 M0
BAKER CREEK RD	INY	51 P7
BAKER RCH SODA	PLA	34 F9
BAKER RCH SODA	PLA	35 D3
BAKER RILEY WY	CAL	41 H2
BAKRSFD GLVL RD	KER	78 E6
BAKRSFLD MCKITT	KER	78 G0
BALBOA AV	SD	211 Q9
BALBOA AV	SD	212 C5
BALBOA AV	SDCO	106 H2
BALBOA AV	SDCO	107 Q5
BALBOA BLVD	LACO	97 P3
BALBOA BLVD	NB	199 P3
BALBOA BLVD	ORA	120 M5
BALCH PARK RD	TUL	69 D1
BALCOM CYN RD	VEN	88 N6
BALDERSTON	ED	34 J9
BALD HILL RD	PLA	34 J4
BALD HILLS RD	DN	1 K9
BALD HILLS RD	DN	2 K0
BALD HILLS RD	HUM	10 F1
BALD MOUNTAIN N	CAL	41 E4
BALD MTN RD	CAL	41 E3
BALD MTN RD	HUM	10 P2
BALD MTN RD	MEN	23 D1
BALD MTN RD	MNO	50 B8
BALD MTN RD	SHA	13 M8
BALD MTN RD	YUB	33 C9
BALD MTN LKOUT	SIS	3 K6
BALD MT SPGS RD	MNO	50 B8
BALD ROCK RD	BUT	25 J8
BALFOUR RD	CC	39 P4
BALDWIN AV	LACO	118 M5
BALDWIN RD	STA	47 J3
BALDWIN RD	VEN	88 L1
BALDWIN ST	CAL	40 L7
BALDWIN PARK BL	LACO	118 K3
BALDY RD	SBD	90 P8
BALDY MCCULY RD	SHA	13 K9
BALDY MESA RD	SBD	91 M3
BALE LN	NAPA	29 D2
BALFLOUR RD	CC	39 P4
BALIS BELL RD	TEH	18 L3
BALL RD	ANA	193 J0
BALL RD	ANA	194 J0
BALL RD	ORA	98 J2
BALL RD	ORA	120 J2
BALL RD	TEH	17 K8
BALL MT LTL SHA	SIS	4 L3
BALL MT LTL SHA	SIS	5 K0
BALL MTN LKOUT	SIS	4 J7
BALL ROCK RD	TEH	23 B8
BALL ROCK RD	TEH	23 B8
BALLARAT RD	INY	71 H4
BALLINGER RD	RCO	99 N9
BALLINGR CYN RD	VEN	87 C9
BALLIS RD	TEH	18 P5
BALLS FERRY RD	SHA	18 H6
BALL FERRY PK RD	SHA	18 H7
BALSAM RD	SBD	91 L3
BALSAMO RD	SBD	81 N0
BALTIMORE MN RD	PLA	34 G8
BANCROFT AV	O	159 A7
BANCROFT DR	SDCO	106 P3
BANCROFT ST	SDCO	111 R8
BANCROFT RD	STA	47 G4
BANCROFT WY	B	156 Q1
BANDINI BLVD	LACO	117 M7
B AR L N	SOL	39 J5
BANDUCCI RD	KER	79 M3
BANGOR RD	KIN	57 N9
BANGOR PARK RD	BUT	25 P8
BANNER RD	CAL	41 G3
BANNER QUAKR RD	NEV	34 C5
BANNER RDG LAVA	NEV	34 C5
BANNING IDYLLWD	RCO	100 J3
BANNISTER RD	IMP	109 K8
BARBARA WRTH RD	IMP	114 C3
BARBARA WRTH RD	IMP	114 C3
BARBER	SJCO	39 H8
BARBER LN	RCO	108 A3
BARBER RD	ALP	36 M3
BARBER RD	SBD	92 M6
BARD RD	IMP	116 O7
BARDSDALE CV	VEN	88 N6
BARGLEY RD	COL	32 N3
BARHAM BL	LA	181 B4
BARHAM BLVD	LACO	117 H3
BAR K RD	TRI	17 D5
BARKER CREEK RD	KER	67 P2
BARKER MINE RD	INY	17 E3
BARKHOUSE CK RD	SIS	3 K7
BARKSHANTY RD	SIS	10 C6
BARNES LN	MEN	23 F2
BARNES RD	SBD	92 M6
BARNES RD	SLO	66 Q9
BARNETT AV	SDCO	106 C1
BARNETT RD	STA	48 E2
BARNEY GULCH RD	TRI	11 P3
BARNHART RD	STA	47 H4
BARNY OLDFLD RD	IMP	116 P5
BARR RD	HUM	10 Q3
BARRANCA AV	LACO	118 L5
BARRANCA AV	ORA	98 L5
BARRANCA RD	ORA	120 J7
BARRANCA RD	TUS	198 J7
BARREL SPGS RD	SBD	91 K3
BARREL SPGS RD	MOD	7 H2
BARRETT	CC	38 P5
BARRETT RD	FRCO	57 P2
BARRETT AV	STA	48 E2
BARRINGTON AV	LACO	180 G2
BARRINGTON AV	SIE	27 K4
BARRY RD	SBD	92 F9
BARRY CREEK RD	TRI	16 M1
BARRYS RD	HUM	16 C1
BARSTOW AV	FRCO	57 G1
BARSTOW AV	SB	92 G3
BARSTOW FRWY	KIN	57 N9
BARSTOW FRWY	SBD	91 H1
BARSTOW FRWY	SBD	99 A2
BARSTOW RD	BARS	208 G2
BARSTOW RD	KER	80 P6
BARSTOW RD	KER	80 F9
BARTELL RD	INY	51 P7
BARTH RD	IMP	109 H8
BARTLE GAP RD	SIS	13 G3
BARTLETT RD	SIS	3 G4
BARTLETT RD	INY	60 N8
BARTLETT SPG RD	LAK	31 F8
BARTLETT SPG RD	LAK	31 F8
BARTOLOMEI	SJCO	40 Q5
BARTOLOMEI	SJCO	47 Q5
BARTON	PLA	34 H2
BARTON ST	RCO	99 H3
BARTON HILL RD	SBD	90 P8
BAR W RD	FRCO	57 G1
BASCOM AV	SCL	46 N2
BASCOM AV	SJ	151 L5
BASE LINE AV	SB	86 G2

STREET	CO.	PAGE & GRID
BASELINE RD	LACO	98 C8
BASE LINE RD	LACO	118 H5
BASE LINE RD	LACO	118 H9
BASELINE RD	PLA	33 N8
BASELINE RD	SBD	101 C4
BASELINE RD	SBD	98 E7
BASELINE ST	SBD	102 C4
BASIC SCHOOL RD	KER	78 N2
BASILONE RD	SDCO	106 Q9
BASIN RD	SBD	82 N9
BASIN ST	KER	79 F5
BASLER RD	TEH	18 M3
BASS	FRCO	56 H5
BASS RD	LAS	14 H5
BASSET RD	SBD	91 H5
BASSETT AV	KER	68 N4
BASS HILL RD	LAS	21 K1
BASS LAKE RD	ED	34 F5
BASTANCHURY RD	ORA	120 D8
BATAVIA RD	SOL	39 E2
BATCHELDER RD	SB	86 F4
BATEMAN RD	SUT	33 M5
BATES	SUT	33 M5
BATTL CK BTM RD	SHA	13 H1
BAUGHMAN AV	KER	79 F5
BAUTISTA RD	RCO	100 L0
BAXTER AV	NAP	133 Q2
BAXTER RD	MCO	48 P9
BAXTER RD	RCO	99 N4
BAXTER RD	RCO	99 N5
BAXTERS RD	MNO	43 Q8
BAY DR	SC	169 H1
BAY HWY	SON	37 C2
BAY ST	SMCO	45 J7
BAY ST	SF	143 F1
BAY ST	SC	169 L3
BAYLES RES RD	MOD	8 E0
BAYLIS BLUE GUM	GLE	24 L7
BAYOU RD	SAC	33 Q4
BAYSHORE BLVD	SMCO	45 J4
BAYSHORE FRWY	BLMT	145 G3
BAYSHORE FRWY	BURL	144 H4
BAYSHORE FRWY	MLBR	144 H5
BAYSHORE FRWY	MVW	148 G0
BAYSHORE FRWY	SJ	152 C3
BAYSHORE FRWY	SJ	152 C1
BAYSHORE FRWY	SM	145 J4
BAYSHORE FRWY	SMCO	144 H5
BAYSHORE FRWY	SMCO	145 G3
BAYSHORE FRWY	SSF	144 H4
BAYSHORE FRWY	SVL	144 G1
BAYSIDE DR	NB	199 N7
BAYSIDE DR	NB	200 Q0
BAY VIEW AV	NAPA	38 J5
BAY VIEW RD	MCO	55 F9
BEACH	MPA	49 L2
BEACH BLVD	ORA	98 P5
BEACH BLVD	ORA	120 B3
BEACH RD	IMP	110 F1
BEACH RD	SCR	54 G3
BEACH ST	SF	143 F1
BEACH PARK BL	FCTY	145 G2
BEACON RD	SLO	76 J4
BEACON ST	AVLN	105 H2
BEAL RD	IMP	110 F2
BEALE RD N	YUB	33 J7
BEALE RD S	YUB	33 J7
BEALE ST	SF	143 K7
BEAL RANCH RD	CAL	41 H0
BEAL RANCH RD	KER	79 M3
BEALEVILLE RD	KER	79 J3
BEAMER ST	YOL	33 C4
BEAN CLIPPER RD	YUB	26 M3
BEAN CREEK RD	SCR	54 C0
BEAN HOLLOW RD	SMCO	45 P4
BEAR ST	CM	197 J4
BEAR ST	ORA	120 J6
BEAR BASIN RD	DN	1 N3
BEAR BUTTE RD	HUM	16 N3
BEAR CANYON RD	FRCO	66 P3
BEAR CREEK DR S	MCO	48 E9
BEAR CREEK LOOP	TRI	11 H1
BEAR CREEK RD	CC	38 P7
BEAR CREEK RD	LAK	31 B6
BEAR CREEK RD	SCR	45 J4
BEAR MTN BL	KER	78 K7
BEAR MTN RD	FRCO	57 J3
BEAR MTN RD	SHA	18 C5
BEAR MT LKOUT	SHA	18 C5
BEAR MT WINE RD	KER	78 J3
BEAR MT WINE RD	KER	79 H3
BEAR RANCH HILL	BUT	25 E9
BEAR RIVER	AMA	41 B6
BEAR RIVER S	SUT	33 H8
BEAR RIV RDG RD	HUM	15 Q3
BEAR RIV RDG RD	HUM	16 Q1
BEAR SPRINGS RD	LAS	14 H1
BEAR TRAP DR	MPA	49 H1
BEAR VALLEY	MPA	49 H1
BEAR VALLEY RD	COL	32 M3
BEAR VALLEY RD	KER	79 J3
BEAR VALLEY RD	SBD	91 H1
BEAR VALLEY RD	SIE	27 H4
BEAR VLY CUTOFF	SBD	91 K3
BEAR VLY PKWY	SDCO	107 K8
BEASON ST	COL	32 E7
BEAUCHAMP RD	COL	32 E7
BEAUMONT AV	RCO	99 H8
BEAUMONT ST	SBD	91 H8
BEAVER CREEK RD	SIS	3 G9
BECHELLI LN	RED	122 F9
BECHELLI LN	SHA	18 F5
BECKER	SUT	33 M5
BECKER RD	SOL	39 H4
BECKET CT	KER	79 N4
BECKWITH RD	STA	47 G4
BECKWITH FRWY	SIE	27 H4
BECKWRTH CALPNE	PLU	27 G4
BECKWRTH GENESE	PLU	27 G4
BECKWRTH LOYLTN	PLU	26 A7
BCKWRTH TYLRSVL	PLU	27 A7
BCKWRTH TYLRSVL	PLU	27 A7
BEDFORD DR	SBD	92 B2
BEECH AV	KER	78 E3
BEECH AV	KER	79 E3
BEECH ST	SBD	92 B2
BEE GULCH RD	ALP	42 Q1
BEEGUM GORGE RD	SHA	17 K6
BEEKLEY RD	RCO	99 H3
BEEKLEY RD	SLO	90 K1
BEEKMAN RD	SBD	90 P8
BEHYMER RD	FRCO	57 G1
BELCHER RD	MCO	48 L5
BELFAST RD	LAS	21 H3
BELFAST RD	LAS	21 H3

STREET	CO.	PAGE & GRID
BELL	MCO	48 L1
BELL RD	BUT	25 G1
BELL RD	KER	77 D9
BELL RD	KER	78 D0
BELL RD	SB	87 B5
BELL RD	STA	47 L4
BELL ST	MS	18 L6
BELLA ROSA DR	HUM	16 L4
BELLA VISTA DR	KER	79 B7
BELLE TER	KER	166 P7
BELLE GRAVE AV	RCO	99 G3
BELLEVUE RD	MCO	48 L3
BELLFLOWER BLVD	LACO	98 J1
BELLFLOWER BLVD	LACO	119 C9
BELLFLOWER BLVD	LACO	120 D0
BELLFLOWER ST	SBD	91 J2
BELL MTN RD	SBD	91 H5
BELL SPRINGS RD	HUM	16 Q5
BELL SPRINGS RD	MEN	22 C6
BELMONT AV	FRE	165 Q4
BELMONT AV	FRCO	56 J5
BELMONT ST	SCLR	151 H3
BELTLINE RD	SHA	18 C4
BEN WY	SON	37 C2
BENA RD	KER	79 H1
BENBOW DR	HUM	22 B4
BEND	TEH	18 L6
BENDER	SJCO	40 J1
BENDER AV	KER	78 D2
BENDER RD	SHA	18 Q8
BENEDICT CYN DR	LACO	117 H1
BENHAM LN	CUR	1 E3
BENICIA AV	KIN	57 P8
BENICIA RD	SOL	38 L6
BENICIA RD	VAL	134 N6
BENIT JUAREZ BL	BAJA	114 D3
BENNER AV	KER	68 P0
BENNET RD	VEN	88 P9
BENNETS WELL RD	INY	72 D3
BENNETT RD	BUT	25 F9
BENNETT RD	MCO	55 F9
BENNETT RD	NEV	34 C5
BENNETT RD	RCO	100 G7
BENNETT VLY RD	SON	38 E0
BENNETT VLY RD	STR	131 L7
BISIGNANI RD	MCO	55 B9
BENSON AV	MTCL	203 G7
BENSON AV	ONT	203 P7
BENSON AV	SBD	98 E7
BENSON AV	SBD	203 G7
BENSON AV	UPL	203 P7
BENSON DR	SHA	18 D3
BENTLEY RD	STA	47 E3
BENTON DR	SHA	18 L4
BENTON RD	RCO	99 N6
BENTON RD	RCO	99 N4
BENTON ST	SCLR	150 H5
BENTON CROSSING	MNO	51 D3
BERDOO CYN RD	RCO	101 J2
BERKELEY AV	STA	47 H8
BERKSHIRE RD	KER	79 J1
BERMUDA DR	SM	145 F2
BERNARD DR E	SAL	171 G5
BERNARD WY	SHA	18 C5
BERNELL ST	M	154 D2
BERRY AV	H	146 L8
BERRY CREEK RD	BUT	25 J9
BERRYESSA RD	SCL	152 C4
BERRYESSA KNX RD	NAPA	29 J7
BERT RD	LAS	27 B8
BERTAS RD	HUM	15 C8
BERTRAM CIR	KER	79 C4
BERYL	LACO	97 H6
BERYL ST	SD	212 B0
BERYL ST	LACO	119 C2
BERYLWOOD RD	VEN	88 P5
BESSEMR MINE RD	MNO	51 Q5
BEST AV	FRCO	57 K8
BEST RD	RCO	99 P9
BETHEL AV	FRCO	57 K8
BETHEL RD	SLO	76 D1
BETHEL ISLND RD	CC	39 N5
BETTERAVIA RD	STB	173 Q4
BETTERAVIA RD	SB	86 A2
BETTERAVIA RD	SMA	173 Q4
BETTS RD	FRCO	57 K8
BETZ RD	SUT	33 H7
BEVERLY	LACO	98 E1
BEVERLY BL	LA	183 B5
BEVERLY BLVD	LA	184 B3
BEVERLY BLVD	LA	185 C6
BEVERLY BLVD	LACO	97 K4
BEVERLY DR	LAS	20 J9
BEVERLY DR	LAS	20 J9
BEVERLY GLEN BL	LA	180 G2
BEVERLY GLEN BL	LA	183 G0
BEVERLY GLEN BL	LACO	97 G5
BEVERLY GLEN BL	LACO	117 H0
BEVERWIL DR	BH	183 H4
BEVERWIL DR	ORA	183 H4
BEYER BLVD	SDCO	106 Q5
BEYER RD	STA	48 E2
BEYER WY	SDCO	106 Q5
BIANCHI RD	S	160 B3
BIBLE RD	YUB	33 G7
BIDDLE	SLO	76 K2
BIDWELL AV	MAR	45 L3
BIDWELL CK RD	MOD	7 B7
BIEBER LKOUT RD	LAS	14 H3
BIG BAR MTN RD	BUT	25 F8
BIG BEND RD	MCO	55 C4
BIG BEND RD	SBD	98 M1
BIG CANYON	LAK	30 G7
BIG CREEK RD	TRI	17 D3
BIG CK SHAFT RD	TUO	48 B8
BIG DIPPER	SBD	92 B2
BIG DIPPER	SBD	92 B2
BIG FLAT RD	DN	1 P6
BIG FRCH CK RD	TRI	11 Q1
BIGGAR LN	MEN	23 F2
BIGGS EAST HWY	BUT	25 P5
BIG HILL RD	TUO	41 M6
BIG INCH PIPELN	KER	79 P9
BIG MEADOWS RD	SIS	3 N2
BIG OAK DR	MEN	31 P2

STREET	CO.	PAGE & GRID
BIG PN REPTR RD	INY	51 P9
BIG RANCH RD	NAPA	29 N9
BIG RANCH RD	NAPA	38 F5
BIG RANCH RD	NAPA	133 D5
BIG RESRVOIR RD	PLA	34 E9
BIG ROCK CK RD	LACO	90 M5
BIG SAGE RD	MOD	6 P9
BIG SAGE RD	MOD	7 P0
BIG SANDY RD	MON	66 K2
BIG SPRINGS RD	SHA	18 N9
BIG SPRINGS RD	PLU	22 L3
BIG SPRINGS RD	SIS	4 N9
BIG SPRINGS RD	SIS	13 F4
BIG SPGS CUTOFF	PLU	22 L3
BIG TRAILS DR	MEN	23 M0
BIG TREES RD	INY	51 M4
BIG TUJUNGA BL	LACO	117 C3
BIG TUJUNGA CYN	LACO	90 P5
BIG TUJUNGA CYN	LACO	117 B5
BILBY RD	SAC	39 F8
BILLIE ST	KER	78 K6
BILLINGS AV	KER	78 A2
BILLINGS LN	RCO	99 L2
BILLY WRIGHT RD	MCO	55 D5
BINET RD	BUT	26 L2
BINGHAMTON RD	SOL	39 F3
BIOLA AV	FRCO	57 H2
BIR RD	INY	51 L5
BIRCH ST	MON	65 C1
BIRCH ST	ORA	98 C4
BIRCH ST	ORA	118 Q6
BIRCH ST	ORA	120 A6
BIRCH CREEK RD	INY	59 N9
BIRCHIN LN	INY	51 L4
BIRCHIN FLAT RD	MNO	42 D9
BIRCHIN FLAT RD	MNO	43 E0
BIRCHVILLE RD	NEV	26 Q3
BIRD RD	SJCO	47 D0
BIRD AV	SJ	152 Q2
BIRDS LANDNG RD	SOL	39 K2
BIRD SPG CYN RD	KER	80 C0
BIRKENHEAD	FRCO	57 K3
BIRMINGHAM DR	SDCO	107 L3
BISCH CT	KER	79 F3
BISHOP AV	FRCO	57 K2
BISHOP AV	FRCO	67 K2
BISHOP ST	SNLO	172 K7
BISHOP CK RD E	INY	51 K9
BISHOP CK RD W	INY	51 K9
BISIGNANI RD	MCO	55 B9
BITNEY SPGS RD	NEV	34 B3
BITTERWATER RD	MON	65 E4
BITTRWTR VLY RD	KER	77 C1
BIXBY RD	VEN	88 N6
BIXLER RD	CC	39 P6
BLACK BART RD	BUT	25 M9
BLACK BUTTE RD	GLE	24 H3
BLACK BUTTE RD	SHA	18 N9
BLACK BUTTE RD	TEH	24 E4
BLACK CANYON	INY	51 M8
BLACK CANYON	MNO	44 Q2
BLACK CANYON	SBD	91 N4
BLACK CANYON	SBD	84 N3
BLACK CANYON	SBD	85 B4
BLACK CANYON RD	SDCO	108 J1
BLACK DIAMND MN	BUT	25 D5
BLACK DIAMND WY	CC	39 P2
BLACK FOX MTN	SIS	13 D2
BLACK GULCH RD	KER	79 B4
BLACK GULCH RD	LAS	14 P1
BLACK HAWK RD	CC	46 B4
BLACKHAWK RD	CC	46 C2
BLACK HILLS RD	RCO	100 M7
BLACKIE RD	MON	54 J4
BLACK LAKE RD	LAS	14 P2
BLACKMER	SUT	33 L2
BLACKMORE	SJCO	47 B5
BLACK MTN RD	IMP	116 J7
BLACK MTN RD	SDCO	107 M6
BLACK MTN RD	SMCO	45 N4
BLACK MTN TR	RCO	100 L2
BLACK MTN LO RD	SLO	75 G6
BLACK RANCH RD	SHA	15 M5
BLACK ROCK RD	RCO	103 N4
BLACK RCK MN RD	MNO	51 N2
BLACK ROCK SPGS	INY	59 E8
BLACKS CYN RD	MOD	14 A6
BLACKS RDG LKOT	LAS	14 N2
BLACKSTONE AV	FRE	165 C7
BLAINE ST	RCO	99 F3
BLAIR RD	IMP	110 M0
BLAIS RD	IMP	110 M0
BLAKE RD	SAC	40 H2
BLAKE ST	SBD	92 B2
BLAKER RD	STA	47 M5
BLANCHARD FT RD	TRI	17 E1
BLANCO	MON	54 K4
BLANCO RD E	MON	171 Q5
BLANCO RD	MON	171 Q5
BLANCO RD W	MON	171 N0
BLANCO RD W	SAL	171 N0
BLAND RD	SHA	17 M1
BLANEY AV	CPTO	149 P9
BLANKENSHIP AV	KER	78 N4
BLAZING-STAR AV	SBD	90 H2
BLEDSOE RD	SHA	18 H2
BLEVENS RD	LPAZ	104 Q4
BLEWETT RD	STA	47 F2
BLICKENSTAFF RD	LAS	21 L3
BLISS DR	RCO	108 J3
BLISS RD	MCO	48 Q5
BLISS RD	YUB	33 G7
BLITHEDALE AV	MV	140 H3
B L M DUMP RD	LAS	20 B8
B L M DUMP RD	LAS	20 B8
BLODGETT RD	IMP	110 N3
BLOODY CAMP RD	NEV	34 H4
BLOOMFIELD AV	SCL	54 L7
BLOOMFIELD AV	LACO	120 C1
BLOOMFLD GRNTVL	NEV	34 G7
BLOOMINGTON RD	SBD	99 D2
BLOSSER RD	MCO	47 P8
BLOSSER RD	SB	86 B3
BLOSSER RD	SMA	173 B4
BLOSSOM	SJCO	39 J8
BLOSSOM AV	MCO	56 J2
BLOSSOM HILL RD	SCL	46 N3
BLOWERS DR	RCO	99 M1
BLUE GUM AV	STA	47 E4
BLUE LAKE BLVD	HUM	8 H6
BLUE LAKE RD	LAS	21 H6
BLUE LAKE RD	MOD	14 D7
BLUE LAKE RD	MOD	8 C3
BLUE LAKES RD	ALP	36 N2
BLUE LK MPLE CK	HUM	16 C3

STREET INDEX

STREET	CO.	PAGE & GRID
BLUE LAKES RD	LAK	31 D5
BLUE MTN RD	CAL	41 E4
BLUE MTN LKT RD	KER	69 N6
BLUE RIDGE RD	TEH	19 J3
BLUE RIDGE RD	SOL	38 E8
BLUE SLIDE RD	HUM	15 G8
BLUFF ST	RCO	100 F0
BLUFF CREEK RD	TRI	16 N9
BLYTHE AV	FRCO	67 A3
BOARTS RD	IMP	110 K1
BOAT HARBOR RD	LAS	20 F8
BOB HOPE DR	RCO	100 K8
BOBCAT TR	RCO	100 N1
BOBS GAP RD	LACO	90 L5
BOB WHITE WY	INY	73 M1
BOCA RD	NEV	27 P8
BOCA SPRINGS RD	NEV	27 N8
BOCA SPGS RD E	NEV	27 N8
BOCKMAN RD	ALA	146 F7
BODEGA AV	SON	37 H8
BODEGA AV	SON	37 H9
BODEGA HWY	SON	37 F6
BODEM ST	MDO	162 H7
BODFISH CYN RD	KER	79 C6
BODIE CIR	FRCO	57 F6
BODIE RD	MNO	43 J5
BODIE MASONC RD	MNO	43 H5
BOESSOW RD	SAC	40 H2
BOGARD RD	LAS	14 P2
BOGGS RD	COL	24 P9
BOGGS & CHAMLIN	TEH	24 C4
BOGIE RD	RCO	100 H6
BOGUE RD	STA	47 H9
BOGUE RD	STA	48 H0
BOGUE RD	SUT	33 F4
BOHEMIAN HWY	SON	37 C2
BOHN DILLON RD	SON	37 C2
BOLAM RD	SIS	4 J1
BOLAM LN	SCL	12 A6
BOLAM LOGGNG RD	SIS	12 A6
BOLES RD	COL	32 H8
BOLEY RD	IMP	109 P8
BOLINGER CYN RD	CC	45 B9
BOLINGER CYN RD	CC	46 C1
BOLO RD	SBD	94 J1
BOLSA AV	ORA	98 K2
BOLSA CHICA RD	ORA	98 L3
BOLSA CHICA RD	ORA	98 L3
BONANZA AV	TRI	12 L1
BONANZA RD	CLK	74 E7
BONANZA TR	LV	209 A3
BONANZA TR	SBD	91 E4
BONANZA KING RD	TRI	12 L1
BOND RD	SJCO	40 K7
BOND RD	STA	47 D8
BONDS CORNER RD	IMP	114 C4
BONDS FLAT RD	TUO	48 D4
BONDURANT	MPA	48 D0
BONE STEEL RD	IMP	114 C5
BONITA	LACO	98 C5
BONITA AV	LACO	118 C9
BONITA RD	MCO	55 B6
BONITA RD	SDCO	106 M5
BONITA RD	SDCO	111 D7
BONITA CANYON	ORA	98 M4
BONITA CYN DR	IRV	200 G5
BONITA CYN DR	ORA	120 L1
BONITA LATERAL	SB	76 Q4
BONITA LATERAL	SB	76 A3
BONITA SCHL RD	SLO	76 L3
BONITA SCHL RD	SB	76 Q4
BONITA SCHL RD	SB	86 Q3
BONITA VISTA RD	SB	86 A4
BONNER RD	MCO	48 M6
BONNIE CT	KER	79 G5
BONNY LN	RCO	100 B3
BONNY DOON RD	SCR	53 D7
BONNYVIEW RD S	SHA	18 F4
BONVIEW AV	SBD	98 F7
BOOKER RD	TUO	41 P6
BOONE LN	SMA	173 J1
BOOTH RD	LPAZ	104 J7
BOOT JACK	MPA	49 J5
BORAX RD	KER	80 P7
BORAX MILL RD	INY	62 P0
BORBA	SJCO	40 Q0
BORBA	SJCO	47 Q0
BORCHARD	VEN	88 B6
BORDEN RD	SAC	40 J3
BORDER AV	SBD	98 F9
BORDER AV	SBD	100 P7
BOREL RD	RCO	99 P7
BORMAN LN	LAK	32 M2
BORNT RD	IMP	114 C4
BORON AV	KER	80 N8
BORREGO SLTN SEA	SDCO	109 E0
BORREGO SPGS RD	SDCO	108 F9
BORREGO VLY RD	SDCO	108 F9
BOSCOVICH RD	IMP	115 A7
BOSTON AV	LACO	117 E5
BOTTINI RD	TUO	41 L8
BOTTLE CREEK RD	BUT	25 B6
BOTTLE HILL RD	BUT	25 B6
BOTTLE ROCK RD	LAK	32 H4
BOUCHO RD	COL	32 H4
BOULDER AV	SBD	98 C5
BOULDER HWY	CLK	74 E7
BOULDER CK RD	SDCO	108 N4
BOULDER CK RD	SIS	3 N8
BOULEVARD, THE	GLE	24 M8
BL D L AMERICAS	BAJA	114 C1
BOUNDARY ST	SDCO	216 B3
BOUNDARY TR	DN	2 L1
BOUQUET CYN RD	LACO	89 L1
BOUQUET CYN RD	LACO	89 L4
BOUSE QUARTZITE	LPAZ	104 K1
BOW AV	KER	80 A5
BOWEN RD	COL	32 C6
BOWEN RANCH RD	SBD	90 M5
BOWERS AV	SCLR	150 A7
BOWKER RD	IMP	114 B9
BOWKER RD	IMP	114 C2
BOWL PL	SB	86 J8
BOWMAN RD	KER	80 B2
BOWMAN RD	KER	80 B4
BOWMAN RD	TEH	18 L5
BOX CANYON RD	RCO	101 J9
BOX CAR RD	MCO	55 C9
BOX ELDER ST	RCO	100 M5
BOX SPRINGS BL	RCO	99 F4
BOX SPRINGS RD	RCO	100 F1
BOYCE RD	SOL	39 H1
BOYD	CC	46 J7
BOYD RD	IMP	110 N4
BOYD SPRINGS RD	LAS	20 D7
BOYER RD	MPA	49 J1
BOYES BL	SON	132 F1
BOYLE RD	YUB	34 B0
BOYLE RD	SHA	18 E6
BOYLES AV	LAK	18 I1
BOY SCOUT CP RD	VEN	34 H7
BRACE RD	PLA	34 H2
BRADBURY RD	MCO	48 J1
BRADBURY RD	STA	47 J5
BRADFORD AV	ORA	120 C6
BRADFORD RD	BUT	25 M3
BRADFORD RD	RCO	108 A2
BRADLEY AV	SDCO	106 H7
BRADLEY AV	MON	65 M9
BRADLEY RD	RC0	99 M5
BRADLEY RD	VEN	88 P5
BRADLY HENLY RD	SIS	4 G2
BRADLEY LOCK RD	LAS	21 B7
BRADSHAW RD	IMP	110 Q1
BRADSHAW RD	SAC	40 D1
BRADSHAW RD	SAC	40 D1
BRADSHAW RD	YUB	33 G8
BRADSHW TR, THE	RCO	102 P0
BRADSHW TR, THE	RCO	103 A3
BRADY RD	TRI	17 E3
BRAGG RD	RCO	100 P1
BRAMLETT RCH RD	MNO	44 P4
BRAMLOT BL	TRI	17 J2
BRAMLOT RD	TRI	17 H3
BRANCH RD	SLO	76 B3
BRANCH RD E	HUM	22 A3
BRANCH RD W	SIS	3 L7
BRANCH CAMP W	BUT	25 A7
BRANCH MILL RD	SLO	76 M3
BRANCIFORTE RD	SCR	169 J9
BRANCIFORTE DR	SCR	54 D0
BRANCO RD	MCO	55 C5
BRAND BLVD	LACO	117 C1
BRAND BLVD	LACO	117 E1
BRANDON RD	ED	40 K6
BRANDT	IMP	110 H1
BRANDT RD	SJCO	40 K4
BRANDT RD	KER	78 F1
BRANDY CITY RD	SIE	26 L4
BRANDY CREEK RD	SHA	18 E1
BRANFORD ST	LACO	117 E1
BRANHAM LN	SCL	46 N2
BRANHAM ST	SJ	151 B7
BRANNAN ISL RD	SAC	39 L5
BRANNAN MTN RD	RD	10 M5
BRANNIGAN MN RD	SBD	84 E5
BRANNIN RD	TEH	24 E5
BRANNON AV	CC	46 C1
BRANSCOMB RD	MEN	22 K7
BRANSTETTER LN	SHA	18 F4
BRANT RD	SBD	84 H4
BRANT CIMA RD	SBD	84 J2
BRAWLEY	IMP	109 Q4
BRAWLEY AV	FRCO	57 N4
BRAWLEY AV	FRCO	57 N4
BRAZO RD	MCO	47 M6
BREA BLVD	ORA	98 Q4
BREA BLVD	ORA	120 A5
BREA CANYON RD	LACO	98 E4
BREA CYN CUTOFF	LACO	118 N6
BREA CUTOFF	LACO	98 E3
BRECKENRIDGE RD	KER	78 C8
BRECKENRIDGE RD	KER	79 F1
BREEDLOVE RD	ED	34 J8
BRENDA ST	KER	70 P1
BREUING RD	MCO	55 C7
BRENNAN	SJCO	47 B3
BRENTWOOD AV	CC	39 P5
BRETZ RD	FRCO	58 B2
BREUNER AV	COL	32 J2
BREWER RD	PLA	33 J8
BREWER RD	PLA	33 J8
BREWER CREEK RD	SIS	12 B8
BRICELAND RD	HUM	16 Q3
BRICELAND RD	MEN	22 C2
BRICELAND THORNE	HUM	16 Q2
BRIDESTEIN RD	IMP	110 P4
BRIDGE RD	MCO	55 C6
BRIDGE ST	COL	33 D0
BRIDGE ST	RCO	99 H7
BRIDGE ST	SUT	33 B5
BRIDGE ST	YUBA	125 H1
BRIDGE ARBOR	LAK	31 E6
BRIDGE CK SPGS	LAS	20 E8
BRIDGE GULCH RD	TRI	17 G4
BRDGPORT SCH RD	ED	41 B0
BRIDGEWAY	MAR	140 Q2
BRIGGS AV	LACO	117 D6
BRIGGS RD	RCO	99 K6
BRIGGS RD	VEN	88 N4
BRIGGS GRIDLY W	BUT	25 P4
BRIGGSMORE AV	STA	47 E5
BRIGHTON AV	MDO	162 B8
BRIM RD	COL	32 E8
BRIMHALL RD	KER	77 P5
BRINKERHOLD AV	SB	86 G9
BRINKERHOFF AV	SB	87 G0
BRIONES VLY RD	CC	39 Q3
BRISTOL ST	VEN	88 Q2
BRISTOL ST	SCL	46 C6
BRISTOL ST	ORA	98 L4
BRISTOL ST	ORA	120 J6
BRISTOL ST	ORA	197 L9
BRISTOL ST	RIV	205 D0
BRISTOL ST	SA	196 P9
BRISTOL ST	SA	197 P0
BRISTOL ST	SA	197 E9
BRISTOL ST	SBD	100 B8
BRISTOL ST N	SLO	198 A3
BRISTOL ST N	NB	200 A3
BRITE RD	MCO	55 D3
BRITTO RD	MCO	48 J1
BROAD ST	NEVC	128 B3
BROAD ST	SNLO	172 H4
BROAD ST	SLO	172 H4
BROAD ST W	SLO	128 E2
BROADWAY	ALA	45 B6
BROADWAY	ANA	193 F3
BROADWAY	EUR	121 M0
BROADWAY	FRE	165 J3
BROADWAY	LB	192 H7
BROADWAY	LA	185 N8
BROADWAY	LA	186 H7
BROADWAY	LACO	110 G5
BROADWAY	LACO	119 P8
BROADWAY	LACO	119 F8
BROADWAY	O	158 N4
BROADWAY	FRCO	57 N4
BROADWAY	FRCO	57 P7
BROADWAY	RCO	99 H7
BROADWAY	SA	196 D0
BROADWAY	SAC	40 D1
BROADWAY	SD	216 J1
BROADWAY	SCTO	137 A3
BROADWAY	SMON	172 H4
BROADWAY	SNMA	132 H7
BROADWAY	VAL	134 F5
BROADWAY N	LA	186 C4
BROADWAY N	LACO	117 K6
BROADWAY RD	LACO	118 N1
BROADWAY RD	VEN	88 P7
BROADWAY ST	FRFD	135 K2
BROADWAY ST	SBD	100 B0
BROADWAY TER	O	156 P4
BROCK RD	IMP	114 M9
BROCKMAN LN	INY	51 K6
BROCKMAN RD	KER	78 B5
BROCKMAN MLL RD	AMA	41 C1
BROCK MTN LKOUT	SHA	12 Q7
BROKAW RD	SJ	151 B7
BROKAW RD	SCL	46 L2
BROKEOF MDWS	SHA	19 F5
BROOKDALE RD	SHA	18 F7
BROOKHURST ST	ORA	120 E4
BROOKHURST ST	ORA	120 L3
BROOKLYN AV	LA	186 H7
BROOKLYN ST	LACO	117 L7
BROOKS ST	SON	37 B8
BROOKS ST	FRCO	58 K6
BROOKSIDE AV	RCO	99 F8
BROOKSIDE AV	SBD	99 E5
BROOKSIDE DR	SP	155 B1
BROOKSIDE RD	CAL	41 D4
BROOKSIDE RD	S	160 D0
BROWN RD	KER	70 N5
BROWN RD	SB	86 B1
BROWN RD	SLO	33 K7
BROWN RD	SOL	39 G3
BROWN RD	SUT	33 G4
BROWN ST	NAP	133 H5
BROWN WY	RCO	99 J3
BROWNING	PLA	33 N8
BROWNING RD	COL	33 N8
BROWNING RD	KER	68 P4
BROWN MATRL RD	KER	68 P4
BROWNS CREEK RD	TRI	17 E6
BROWNS MTN RD	TRI	17 C7
BROWNS RAVINE	BUT	25 B7
BROWNS VALLEY	SBT	25 K2
BROWNS VLY RD	NAP	133 J1
BROWN VALLEY RD	SOL	133 J1
BROYLE RD	STA	47 P4
BROYLES RD	BUT	25 C0
BROYLES RD	STA	47 F4
BRUCE CRUM	SHA	13 K9
BRUCEVILLE RD	SAC	40 H2
BRUGGA LN	HUM	15 E7
BRUNDAGE LN	BKD	166 N4
BRUNDAGE LN	KER	166 N4
BRUNSWICK AV	LA	182 D8
BRUNSWICK RD	NEV	34 C5
BRUSH LN	STA	47 G4
BRUSH CREEK RD	SIS	3 G3
BRUSH CREEK RD	SON	38 D0
BRYAN AV	FRCO	57 P3
BRYANT ST	SBD	99 D7
BRYANT ST	SF	142 L6
BRYANT RAVIN RD	BUT	26 K1
BRYANTS CYN RD	MON	55 G1
BRYANT WILLW CK	SIS	3 J3
BUARO ST	GGR	195 D3
BUCHANAN RD	CC	39 N2
BUCHANAN RD	TUO	41 N8
BUCHANAN ST	RCO	101 N3
BUCHANAN HLW RD	MCO	48 P6
BUCKEYE ARM RD	TRI	11 Q7
BUCKEYE CK RD	SON	31 N0
BUCKEYE CK RD	TRI	11 Q7
BUCKEYE CK RD	TRI	12 K0
BUCKEYE CK RD	TRI	17 C8
BUCKEYE RDG RD	TRI	11 Q7
BUCKHORN	TRI	24 F4
BUCKHORN AV	KER	89 C5
BUCKHORN STA LP	TRI	11 T8
BUCKLEY RD	SLO	76 H5
BUCKMAN FUNCK	SJCO	47 B3
BUCK MEADOWS	MPA	49 B1
BUCKS BAR RD	ED	34 P9
BUCKS FLAT RD	TEH	19 H4
BUCKNELL RD	KER	80 B3
BUCKS LAKE RD	PLU	26 C4
BUCKSKIN RD	CAL	41 M1
BUD RD	SHA	18 H7
BUELL RD	SHA	18 J8
BUENA CREEK RD	SDCO	107 H5
BUENA VISTA	LACO	97 H5
BUENA VISTA	SCL	46 C6
BUENA VISTA	A	157 P7
BUENA VISTA AV	MV	140 F1
BUENA VISTA AV	RIV	205 D0
BUENA VISTA BL	KER	78 K5
BUENA VISTA BL	KER	79 K1
BUENA VISTA DR	MER	138 F1
BUENA VISTA DR	SBD	100 B8
BUENA VISTA RD	SLO	76 B2
BUENA VISTA RD	SCR	54 F3
BUENA VISTA ST	LACO	117 F3
BUENA VISTA ST	VEN	88 M3
BUERER LN	SJCO	47 B3
BUERKLE RD	KER	78 B2
BUFFALO RUN RD	RCO	102 K5
BUFFUM LN	LAS	21 J2
BUFFUM RD	SHA	18 N3
BUHACH RD	MCO	48 N7
BUHNE ST	EUR	121 F4
BUKLEY RD	SOL	39 E4
BULLARD	MAD	56 G4
BULLARD AV	FRCO	57 F2
BULL CANYON RD	SLO	76 B2
BULL CREEK RD	MPA	49 C2
BULL HILL RD	BUT	19 L6
BULLION MTN RD	SBD	101 J6
BULLHEAD CITY	AZ	75 L6
BULLRIDGE WHEEL	KIN	67 K2
BULL RUN ST	KER	80 B4
BULL SKIN RIDGE	SHA	17 N8
BULLY CHOOP RD	SHA	17 M7
BUMMERVILLE RD	CAL	41 E2
BUNCE RD	KIN	67 Q2
BUNCH GRASS LKT	SHA	13 N4
BUNDY DR	LA	183 G5
BUNDY CANYON RD	RCO	99 N4
BUNKER RD	MCO	47 N5
BUNKER STATN RD	SOL	39 E4
BUNNY LN	RCO	100 P5
BUNSELMEIER RD	LAS	14 J3
BUNTE RD	MON	65 G5
BUNTGVLL CUMMGS	LAS	21 K3
BURBANK BLVD	BUR	179 H3
BURBANK BLVD	LACO	179 H3
BURBANK BLVD	LACO	197 B5
BURBANK BLVD	LACO	117 E0
BURCHELL AV	MCO	48 N7
BURCHELL RD	SCL	54 L5
BURCH HAVEN RD	MCO	55 E3
BURGESS RCH RD	TRI	16 N8
BURKE LN	SOL	39 G3
BURLANDO RD	KER	69 F6
BURMA RD	NEV	34 D5
BURNES VALLEY	LAK	32 H1
BURNETT	PLA	34 H2
BURNETT	VEN	88 M1
BURNS FRWY	HUM	9 Q3
BURNS FRWY	KER	78 A5
BURNS RD	LPAZ	104 D1
BURNS CANYON RD	SBD	100 A3
BURNSIDE LK RD	ALP	36 M2
BURNT TREE RD	SBD	81 P5
BURNT RCH DUMP	TRI	10 Q8
BURRELL RD	HUM	15 M9
BURRIS	SUT	33 B2
BURRIS LN	SBD	91 E4
BURROUGH N RD	FRCO	58 D1
BURROUGH VLY RD	FRCO	58 D1
BURSON	CAL	40 K7
BURTON WY	BH	183 G5
BURTON WY	LA	183 G5
BURTON MESA BL	SB	86 F3
BURWOOD RD	SJCO	47 D6
BUSCH LN	MEN	23 Q3
BUSH ST	SF	142 L4
BUSH ST	SF	143 L4
BUSHARD ST	ORA	120 L4
BUSHEY RD	MOD	14 C5
BUSSEL RD	KER	78 F2
BUSTER DR	COL	33 F1
BUTANO CUT-OFF	SMCO	45 F9
BUTCHER RCH RD	SIE	26 J9
BUTLER AV	FRCO	57 J3
BUTLER RD	COL	25 Q5
BUTLER RD	STA	47 F3
BUTLER VLY RD	HUM	16 K3
BUTTE AV	LAS	14 E7
BUTTE RD E	SUT	33 D4
BUTTE RD E	SUT	33 D3
BUTTE RD S	SUT	33 E2
BUTTE RD W	SUT	33 C2
BUTTE CREEK RD	HUM	16 D3
BUTTE HOUSE RD	SUT	33 D4
BUTTEMER RD	SBD	90 M9
BUTTE MTN RD	TEH	24 E4
BUTTERBREAD CYN	KER	79 F9
BUTTERCUP CT	KER	79 L4
BUTTERFLD STAGE	RCO	99 P6
BUTTERFLY PK RD	RCO	100 N4
BUTTRFLY VY TWN	PLU	26 B4
BUTTERMILK RD	INY	51 M3
BUTTERS RD	IMP	110 L4
BUTTE SLOUGH RD	COL	33 G2
BUTTE VALLEY RD	INY	72 J1
BUTTE VLY RD E	SIS	3 G1
BUTTE VLY RD W	SIS	3 J8
BUTTONHOOK RD	SB	86 J7
BUTTONWILLOW AV	FRCO	58 L0
BUTTONWILLOW DR	KER	78 G0
BUTTONWILLOW DR	KER	78 G0
BUTTS RD	MCO	55 A4
BUTTS CANYON RD	LAK	32 N0
BUZZARD ROOST	SHA	12 B0
BVD AV	KER	80 B5
BYERS PASS RD	LAS	21 J3
BYOFF RD	TRI	10 P8
BYRON HWY	CC	39 P6
BYRON RD	CC	46 B6
BYSTRUM RD	STA	47 F6
BYWOOD DR	TEH	18 K4
C		
C ST	KER	68 P2
C ST	SB	215 H6
C ST	YOL	137 E0
CABALLERO CT	LAK	32 K1
CABIN RD	LAS	14 M3
CABRILLO AV	LACO	119 D4
CABRILLO DR	AVLN	105 N2
CABRILLO DR	MV	140 F1
CABRILLO FRWY	SD	215 F2
CABRILLO FRWY	SD	215 G7
CABRILLO HWY	MON	54 Q1
CABRILLO HWY	MON	168 M3
CABRILLO HWY	SCR	53 B6
CABRILLO HWY	SMA	54 M6
CABRILLO ST	LACO	117 G3
CACHAGUA RD	MON	54 Q1
CACHUMA RD	SBD	91 J5
CACTUS AV	RCO	99 G4
CACTUS DR	MCO	55 D7
CACTUS FLATS	INY	70 D5
CACTUS VLY RD	RCO	100 G5
CADET RD	KER	78 M1
CADILLAC AV	SA	183 K7
CADIZ DR	SBD	102 C0
CADIZ RD	SBD	103 C0
CADY RD	IMP	110 L0
CAHUENGA BL	LA	179 L4
CAHUENGA BL	LACO	179 L4
CAHUENGA BL W	LA	181 D2
CAHUILLA RD	RCO	99 J5
CAHUILLA ST	RCO	91 J5
CAHUILLA HTS RD	RCO	100 G5
CAIRO	KIN	67 Q0
CAJALCO RD	RCO	99 N4
CAJON BL	SBD	99 E5
CAJON RD	SBD	99 E5
CALAVERAS AV	FRCO	66 F7
CALAVERAS AV	ALA	46 G3
CALAVERAS RD	SCL	46 K2
CALAVERITAS RD	CAL	41 J1
CALDOR RD	ED	41 A3
CAL-GROVE BL	SBD	89 N3
CALICO BLVD	SBD	92 B1
CALIENT-BODF RD	KER	79 J2
CALIENT-BODF RD	KER	79 H4
CALIENTE LK RD	KER	79 H4
CALIFORNIA AV	BKD	166 J3
CALIFORNIA AV	COL	32 J8
CALIFORNIA AV	FRE	165 P0
CALIFORNIA AV	FRCO	57 J5
CALIFORNIA AV	FRCO	56 J5
CALIFORNIA AV	LACO	117 N7
CALIFORNIA AV	MDO	162 L0
CALIFORNIA AV	RENO	130 J1
CALIFORNIA AV	RCO	98 F9
CALIFORNIA AV	RCO	99 L7
CALIFORNIA AV	SCL	54 B5
CALIFORNIA AV	SER	169 M4
CALIFORNIA BLVD	LACO	117 H9
CALIFORNIA BLVD	LACO	118 H0
CALIFORNIA BL	NAP	133 F3
CALIFORNIA BL	PAS	190 M1
CALIFORNIA BL	SNLO	172 C3
CALIFORNIA DR	SLO	172 C3
CALIFORNIA DR	IMP	109 E5
CALIFORNIA DR	NAPA	29 P7
CALIFORNIA ST	BUR	179 K4
CALIFORNIA ST	EUR	121 E4
CALIFORNIA ST	LACO	98 C1
CALIFORNIA ST	ONT	204 P1
CALIFORNIA ST	SBD	99 C3
CALIFORNIA ST	SF	142 G0
CALIFORNIA ST	SF	141 H6
CALIFORNIA ST	SFCO	45 C5
CALIFORNIA ST	S	160 E7
CALIF CITY BL	KER	80 M2
CALIFRNIA FARMS	SCL	47 A4
CALISTOGA RD	SON	38 C0
CALKINS RD	FRCO	57 J3
CALLAHAN RD	TEH	18 N5
CALLAHAN E	S	18 N5
CALLAHN CECLVLL	SIS	11 Q5
CALLE DEL SOL	AVLN	105 N2
CALLE ECUESTRE	SB	87 K1
CALLEGUAS RD	VEN	105 B5
CALLE H COLEGIO	BAJA	114 D2
CALLE LIPPIZANA	SB	87 K0
CALLENDR BLK LK	SLO	76 N3
CALLE QUEBRADA	SB	87 K1
CALLE REAL	SB	86 K8
CALLE REAL	SB	86 K8
CALLOWAY DR	KER	78 G5
CALNEVA RD	LAS	21 P9
CALVINE RD	SAC	40 D0
CALZ	BAJA	114 D2
CALZADA AV	SB	86 H9
CAMANCHE PKWY	CAL	40 J6
CAMANCHE PKWY N	AMA	40 H6
CAMARES DR	LACO	30 J0
CAMARILLO ST	LA	179 M2
CAMARILLO ST	LACO	117 G3
CAMBRIA AV	FRCO	56 F1
CAMBRIA RD	SBD	91 K9
CAMBRIDGE DR	BUR	179 D8
CAMBRIDGE ST	SHA	18 H4
CAMBRIDGE ST	OR	196 C7
CAMBRIDGE ST	SB	86 H4
CAMDEN AV	SCL	46 N2
CAMERON AV	LACO	98 D4
CAMERON AV	LACO	118 K5
CAMERON RD	MEN	30 A4
CAMERON CYN RD	KER	79 N7
CAMERON PARK DR	ED	34 P5
CAMINO AL GOLFO	SONR	115 K4
CAMINO ALTO	MV	140 J3
CM CAPISTRANO	SJC	202 G6
CAMINO CIELO	SB	87 J0
CM DE FLORES	AVLN	105 L2
CAMINO DIABLO	CC	46 A5
CM DOS RIOS	VEN	105 F7
CM LAS RAMBLAS	SJC	202 G6
CM MIRA COSTA	SCL	202 F9
CAMINO ORO	SHA	19 F0
CAMINO REAL	LACO	119 D1
CAMINO SANTA FE	SDCO	107 P5
CAM SANTA FE DR	SDCO	106 P3
CM TASSAJARA RD	ALA	46 C2
CM TASSAJARA RD	CC	46 C2
CAMINO VISTA	SHA	19 F0
CAMMATTI-SHN RD	SLO	76 G5
CAMP RD	CAL	41 J4
CAMP RD E	COL	32 G9
CAMP RD E	SAC	40 G9
CAMPBELL AV	SCL	46 N1
CAMPBELL DR	KER	79 K8
CAMPBELL RD	IMP	113 B8
CAMPBELL RD	SBD	101 B7
CAMPBELL RD	SOL	39 C2
CAMPBL HOT SPGS	TUO	41 P1
CAMPBL RDG RD	TRI	11 P5
CAMPBLLS LTT RD	TUO	41 P5
CAMP FAR WST RD	PLA	34 H0
CAMP FAR WST RD	YUB	34 F1
CAMPHORA RD	MON	54 Q1
CAMP KIMTU RD	HUM	15 B8
CAMPO RD	SDCO	106 P3
CAMP SECO RD	SOL	39 C2
CAMP SECO RD	TUO	41 J7
CAMP ROCK RD	SBD	92 J7
CAMP THREE RD	SIS	11 C8
CAMPTON RD	HUM	15 B8
CAMPTONVILLE RD	SIE	26 N5
CAMPUS AV	ONT	204 C7
CAMPUS DR	IRV	198 G1
CAMPUS DR	SCL	147 H0
CAMP WEOTT RD	HUM	14 F4
CMP 1 TEN MI RD	MEN	22 N7
CMP 2 TEN MI RD	MEN	22 M7
CAMP 8 RD	SLO	76 D4
CAMUESA RD	SB	87 J4
CANA HWY	BUT	25 F0
CANADA BLVD	LACO	97 B3
CANADA BLVD	LACO	117 G6
CANADA RD	SMCO	45 J5
CANADA RD	SCL	54 D8
CANAL AV	FRCO	57 C8
CANAL RD	KER	77 F9
CANAL ST	KER	78 F0
CANAL ST	PLCV	138 G4
CANAL BANK RD	STA	47 F9
CANAL BANK RD	STA	48 F0
CANAL SCHOOL RD	MCO	47 M5
CANA PINE CREEK	BUT	25 C0
C AND D BLVD	RCO	103 G7
CANFIELD RD	SON	37 G8
CANNIBAL RD	HUM	15 D6
CANNON RD	SDCO	107 J3
CANNON RD	SIS	3 N1
CANNON ST	SDCO	106 L1
CANOGA AV	LA	177 J3
CANON DR	BH	183 A2
CANON RD	SOL	39 G1
CANON ST	SDCO	111 B4
CANON PERDIDO	STB	174 K4
CANRIGHT RD	SOL	38 E9
CANTELOW RD	SOL	38 E8
CANTLOW RD	SOL	39 E1
CANTON RD	MCO	48 P4
CANYON DR	RCO	100 F5
CANYON DR	SBD	82 Q1
CANYON RD	INY	52 J3
CANYON RD	MEN	23 P1
CANYON RD	MNO	52 J3
CANYON RD	SBD	100 D5
CANYON RD	SBD	93 Q3
CANYON RD	SR	139 M2
CANYON RD	SHA	18 G4
CANYON RD	SON	36 P1
CANYON WY	PLA	34 G6
CANYON CREEK RD	MOD	14 Q2
CANYON CREEK RD	SIS	3 N3
CANYON CREST DR	RCO	99 F3
CANYON CREST DR	TRI	11 K3
CANYON VW LOOP	TEH	19 K3
CANYON VIEW RD	SBD	91 N7
CAPAY AV	GLE	24 G8
CAPAY RD	TEH	24 F3
CAPE GLOUCESTER	SBD	91 D8
CAPEZZOLI LN	LAS	21 K4
CAPITAL BLVD	GLE	24 M9
CAPITAN TK TR	SDCO	108 N5
CAPITOL AV	SCTO	137 A5
CAPITOL AV	SCL	46 L3
CAPITOL AV	YOL	137 B9
CAPITOL AV	YOL	39 B6
CAPITOL EXPWY	SCL	46 N2
CAPITOL ST	SAL	171 J3
CAPITOL ST	SCR	54 F3
CAPPELL RD	HUM	10 F4
CAPS CROSSING	ED	35 N3
CARBINE TR	TEH	18 N3
CARBON CYN RD	ORA	98 G5
CARBON CYN RD	ORA	118 Q8
CARBON CYN RD	SBD	118 Q8
CARDIFF ST	IMP	110 M1
CAREY RD	MCO	48 J1
CARGIL LN	ALA	45 A4
CARLETON	MPA	49 Q3
CARLOS RD	FRCO	56 F1
CARLSBAD BLVD	SDCO	107 H3
CARLSON	SBD	91 B8
CARLSON BL	R	155 K3
CARLTON RD	BUT	25 B6
CARLTON RD	SCR	54 E4
CARLUCCI RD	MCO	56 N1
CARLYLE RD	NEV	27 C7
CARMEL AV	LACO	98 D4
CARMELLIA AV	FRCO	56 D3
CARMEL MTN RD	SDCO	107 H4
CARMEL RCHO BL	MON	168 N2
CARMEL VLY RD	MON	54 N2
CARMEL VLY RD	MON	168 M4
CARMEL VLY RD	SDCO	107 M4
CARMELITA AV	SJCO	40 D3
CARMENCITA AV	SJCO	40 C1
CARMENITA RD	LACO	120 C1
CARMIRE RD	SUT	33 F3
CARNATION AV	MCO	47 N6
CARNELIAN BAY	PLA	35 H5
CARNEROS AV	NAPA	38 H5
CARPENTER RD	STA	47 J5
CARPENTER ST	CAR	168 J2
CARPENTER ST	CAR	168 H3
CARPENTERIA	MON	54 F5
CARPENTERIA RIDGE	SB	86 B6
CARR AV	SBT	54 F5
CARRIAGE LN	SHA	18 J3
CARRIER GLCH RD	TRI	17 G4
CARRILLO ST	STB	174 M2
CARRIZO GRGE RD	SDCO	113 D1
CARROLL RD	INY	60 N2
CARROLLTON	SJCO	47 B4
CARROT LN	RCO	108 B2
CARRVILLE LOOP	TRI	11 K9
CARRVILLE LOOP	TRI	11 K9
CARSON RD	ED	34 N9
CARSON ST	LACO	119 D3
CARSTENS	MPA	49 J3
CARTER ST	SOL	39 D7
CARUTHERS AV	FRCO	57 N4
CARVER LN	RCO	99 G4
CASA DIABLO CTF	MNO	51 F3
CASA DIABLO MN	MNO	51 E3
CASA LOMA RD	SCL	54 B3
CASCADE BLVD	SBD	101 A1
CASE RD	RCO	99 K5
CASE RD	SB	86 G9
CASEY AV	RCO	100 M1
CASEY RD	IMP	110 N4
CASEY RD	SOL	39 E3
CASPR LTL LK RD	MEN	22 Q4
CASS ST	MONT	167 M8
CASS ST	SDCO	111 B4
CASSEL RD	SHA	13 N4
CASSEL FALL RIV	SHA	13 M4
CASSELRY RD	SCR	54 C4
CASSIDY ST	SDCO	111 B4
CASTAIC RD	LACO	89 K1
CASTAIC CYN RD	LACO	89 L1
CASTERLINE RD	HUM	16 M6
CASTLE CT	S	160 G5
CASTLE CREEK RD	SIS	3 N3
CASTLE LAKE RD	SIS	12 B8
CASTRO	CC	38 P4
CASTRO	CC	38 P6

SEE PAGE D FOR INSTRUCTIONS

STREET	CO.	PAGE & GRID
CASTRO RD	RCO	99 M7
CASTRO VLY BL	ALA	146 A7
CASTROVILLE BL	MON	54 H4
CATALINA AV	AVLN	105 N2
CATALINA BLVD	SDCO	106 L1
CATALINA DR	DVS	136 C4
CAT CANYON RD	SB	86 E6
CATERPILLAR RD	SHA	18 D4
CATFISH BCH RD	PLU	20 K2
CATHEDRAL RD	ED	35 J9
CATHEY RD	HUM	16 L3
CATLETT RD W	SUT	33 L6
CATRINA RD	MCO	56 C2
CATTARAUGUS AV	CUL	183 L5
CATTARAUGUS AV	LA	183 L5
CATTLE DR	TUL	68 G9
CATTLE DRIVE RD	MNO	51 C4
CATTLEMEN RD	MON	65 G6
CATWAY RD	SB	87 E0
CAUGHLIN RD	SBD	91 H1
CAVE CITY RD	CAL	41 J3
CAVEDALE RD	SON	38 F3
CAVIN RD	VEN	88 M8
CAVITT & STLLMN	PLA	34 M3
CAWELTI RD	VEN	105 B5
CAWSTON AV	RCO	99 K8
CAYLEY DR	KER	79 M2
CAYTON VLY RD	SHA	13 K5
CAYUCOS CK RD	SLO	75 E7
CCMO RD	KER	77 J6
CEBADA CYN RD	SB	86 G4
CECIL AV	KER	68 N2
CECIL AV	KER	68 N5
CECIL RD	COL	33 G2
CEDAR AV	FRCO	57 H5
CEDAR AV	FRCO	57 P5
CEDAR AV	RCO	100 M5
CEDAR AV	SBD	99 D2
CEDAR ST	SBD	80 C8
CEDAR ST	SDCO	108 K0
CEDAR CAMP RD	HUM	10 D5
CEDAR CAMP RD	SIS	10 C5
CEDAR CAMP RD	TRI	17 M1
CEDAR CANYON RD	SBD	84 L2
CEDAR CREEK RD	ED	40 B9
CEDAR CREEK RD	ED	41 B0
CEDAR CREEK RD	HUM	10 N4
CEDAR CK LP RD	BUT	25 B5
CEDAR RAVINE RD	ED	34 N8
CEDAR RAVINE ST	PLCV	138 H8
CEDARVILLE DUMP	MOD	8 A8
CEDAR WELL	SIS	5 L1
CEDARWOOD CT	SHA	19 G1
CEDROS DR	SBD	90 F8
CEMENT HILL RD	FRFD	135 C5
CEMENT HILL RD	NEV	34 B4
CEMETERY DR	MOD	14 G5
CEMETERY RD	COL	32 B6
CEMETERY RD	HUM	16 L6
CEMETERY RD	MCO	47 M6
CEMETERY RD	MNO	43 M4
CEMETERY RD	SBD	81 Q9
CEMETERY RD	SBD	82 Q0
CEMETERY RD	SHA	19 D2
CEMETERY RD	SIS	5 F0
CENTENNIAL RD	HUM	15 H7
CENTER AV	MCO	56 D2
CENTER RD	LAS	21 H1
CENTER RD	STA	47 F2
CENTER ST	MAN	161 J1
CENTER ST	RCO	99 E3
CENTER ST	SBD	99 E5
CENTER ST	SC	169 L6
CENTER ST	S	160 G6
CENTER ST EXT	RCO	99 E4
CENTER ST S	TEH	24 B8
CTR SCH HOUSE	LAS	14 H4
CENTERVILLE LN	DGL	36 J3
CENTERVILLE LN	DGL	36 J3
CENTERVILLE RD	HUM	15 E6
CENTERVILLE RD	MOD	14 C8
CENTINELA AV	CUL	187 B6
CENTINELA AV	ING	188 J3
CENTINELA AV	LA	187 B6
CENTINELA AV	LACO	117 M1
CENTINELLA RD	MCO	55 B5
CENTRAL AV	A	158 Q0
CENTRAL AV	A	159 C1
CENTRAL AV	CLA	203 J5
CENTRAL AV	FRCO	56 K7
CENTRAL AV	FRCO	57 K3
CENTRAL AV	HUM	9 M9
CENTRAL AV	HUM	10 M0
CENTRAL AV	KER	78 D1
CENTRAL AV	LA	186 N2
CENTRAL AV	LACO	97 E8
CENTRAL AV	LACO	117 G5
CENTRAL AV	LACO	119 A5
CENTRAL AV	MCO	47 L6
CENTRAL AV	MON	65 D2
CENTRAL AV	ONT	203 J5
CENTRAL AV	ORA	118 Q5
CENTRAL AV	ORA	120 A5
CENTRAL AV	PAC	167 E5
CENTRAL AV	RCO	99 F2
CENTRAL AV	RCO	205 N3
CENTRAL AV	SAL	171 K1
CENTRAL AV	SBD	98 F7
CENTRAL AV	SBD	203 J5
CENTRAL AV	SB	86 G3
CENTRAL AV	STA	47 J6
CENTRAL AV	SUT	33 H3
CENTRAL AV	VEN	88 Q4
CENTRAL AV	YOL	39 E6
CENTRAL RD	SBD	91 J5
CENTRAL EXPWY	MVW	148 M2
CENTRAL EXPWY	SCL	46 L1
CENTRAL EXPWY	SVL	148 M2
CENTRAL FRWY	SF	143 Q1
CENTRAL SKYWAY	SF	142 L5
CENTRAL ST	RC0	99 N4
CENTRAL HILL RD	CAL	40 J9
CENTRAL HILL RD	CAL	41 J0
CENTRL HOUSE RD	BUT	25 Q6
CENTRALIA ST	LACO	119 D9
CENTRALIA ST	LACO	120 D0
CENTRAL VLY HWY	KER	78 C2
CENTURY BL	LA	189 C6
CENTURY BLVD	LACO	97 F6
CENTURY BLVD	LACO	117 P2
CERINI AV	FRCO	57 P2
CERINI AV	FRCO	57 P5
CERRITOS AV	ANA	193 L6
CERRITOS AV	ORA	120 E3
CERRO GORDO RD	INY	60 N5
CERRO GORDO RD	INY	60 M6
CERRO NOROESTE	KER	78 Q0
CERRO NOROESTE	KER	87 A9
CERVANTES BL	SF	142 B1
CHABOT RD	VAL	134 B6
CHADBOURNE RD	CC	39 P3
CHADBOURNE RD	SOL	38 J8
CHADWICK RD	SBD	101 C8
CHAHLIP LN	FRCO	58 C4
CHALET DR	KER	79 M4
CHALFANT RD	MNO	51 H6

STREET	CO.	PAGE & GRID
CHALFANT LP RD	MNO	51 H7
CHALK BLUFF RD	INY	51 K5
CHALK BLUFF RD	NEV	34 C7
CHALK HILL RD	SON	37 B8
CHALONE RD	SBT	55 N1
CHAMBERLAIN	PLA	34 J1
CHAMBERLAIN RD	MCO	48 Q3
CHAMBERS RD	HUM	15 K7
CHAMBERS WLS RD	SBD	103 C8
CHAMPAGNE AV	KER	89 B5
CHAMPS FLAT RD	LAS	20 D5
CHANAC RD	KER	79 M3
CHANDLER	YUB	33 B6
CHANDLER BL	BUR	179 J4
CHANDLER BLVD	LA	179 K0
CHANDLER BLVD	LACO	117 G1
CHANDLER RD	PLU	26 C6
CHANNEL ISLD BL	VEN	105 B2
CHAPARAJOS ST	CAL	41 L0
CHAPARRAL DR	SHA	18 F3
CHAPMAN AV	GGR	195 A0
CHAPMAN AV	OR	195 A6
CHAPMAN AV	OR	196 A2
CHAPMAN AV	ORA	84 J0
CHAPMAN AV	ORA	120 C5
CHAPMAN AV	ORA	120 F2
CHAPMAN DR	CRTM	140 D3
CHAPMAN RD	RCO	108 B4
CHAPPIUS LN N	LAS	21 J3
CHAPPIUS LN S	LAS	21 K3
CHAPULNIK RD	IMP	110 K3
CHARD AV	TEH	18 Q6
CHARLEBOIS RD	MNO	42 A8
CHARLES ST	KER	80 B6
CHARLESTON BLVD	LV	209 F1
CHARLESTON BL E	CLK	74 F7
CHARLESTON RD	MCO	55 D7
CHARLESTON RD	SCL	45 K8
CHARLESTON RD W	PA	147 N9
CHRLSTN VOLCANO	AMA	41 D1
CHAROLAIS RD	SLO	76 C1
CHARTER WY	SJCO	40 P2
CHASE AV	KER	79 D9
CHASE AV	KER	80 D0
CHASE AV	SDCO	106 J7
CHASE AV	SDCO	111 A8
CHASE DR	RCO	98 J9
CHASE SCHOOL RD	RCO	100 J8
CHATEAU DR	SMCO	45 H4
CHATEAU RD	ML	164 G8
CHATEAU FRESNO	FRCO	57 K3
CHATEAU FRESNO	FRCO	57 P3
CHATSWORTH BLVD	SDCO	106 K2
CHATSWORTH BLVD	SDCO	111 B4
CHECKMATE RD	RCO	100 P1
CHEMEHUEVI BLVD	MOH	96 L2
CHEMISE MTN RD	HUM	22 B1
CHEROKEE LN	SAC	40 H2
CHEROKEE RD	BUT	25 K6
CHEROKEE RD	MCO	55 B6
CHEROKEE RD	SBD	82 Q4
CHEROKEE RD	SJCO	40 N2
CHERRY AV	FRCO	57 L5
CHERRY AV	FRCO	57 P5
CHERRY AV	KER	78 F3
CHERRY AV	LACO	97 K9
CHERRY AV	LACO	119 D8
CHERRY AV	RCO	99 G9
CHERRY AV	SBD	99 D0
CHERRY AV	STA	47 K4
CHERRY CREEK RD	SON	31 L4
CHERRY GLEN RD	SOL	38 G9
CHERRY VLY BLVD	RCO	99 F8
CHERT RD	RCO	108 B3
CHESEBORO RD	LACO	90 K2
CHESTER AV	BKD	166 M5
CHESTER AV	KER	78 G6
CHESTER LN	BKD	166 K2
CHESTR JUNPR LK	PLU	20 H1
CHESTER SKI RD	PLU	20 L1
CHESTR WRNR VLY	PLU	19 H9
CHESTR WRNR VLY	PLU	20 H0
CHESTNUT AV	FRCO	57 F5
CHESTNUT AV	FRCO	57 N5
CHESTNUT AV	SA	196 M2
CHESTNUT AV	TEH	18 N6
CHESTNUT ST	SF	143 G0
CHESTNUT ST	SHA	18 H4
CHESTNUT ST	SHA	18 H4
CHESTNUT WY	CAL	41 N2
CHEVALIER RD	KER	78 K7
CHEVY CHASE DR	LACO	97 B8
CHEVY CHASE DR	LACO	117 G6
CHEZEM RD	HUM	10 N3
CHICAGO AV	RIV	205 K8
CHICK RD	IMP	114 B2
CHICK RD	RCO	109 C9
CHICKEN HAWK RD	PLA	34 F9
CHICKEN RCH RD	TUO	41 P4
CHICO AV	KIN	57 P8
CHICO CANYON RD	BUT	25 F4
CHICORB LN	SOL	39 F2
CHICO RIVER RD	BUT	25 H1
CHIDAGO LOOP	MNO	51 F4
CHIDAGO CYN RD	MNO	51 E3
CHIHUAHUA VLY	SDCO	108 D3
CHILDS AV	MER	170 N3
CHILDS AV	MCO	48 M5
CHILENO VLY RD	MAR	37 K9
CHILENO VLY RD	SON	37 K9
CHILES RD	YOL	39 B5
CHILES POPE VLY	NAPA	29 B6
CHILES POPE VLY	NAPA	38 B4
CHILI HILL	PLA	34 J3
CHIMNEY ROCK RD	SLO	75 B7
CHINA CAMP RD	MCO	55 B7
CHINA GRADE	SIS	3 K1
CHINA GRADE LP	KER	78 F7
CHINA GRADE RD	PLU	26 A7
CHINA GULCH DR	SHA	18 G3
CHINA LAKE BLVD	KER	80 C7
CHINA PK LO RD	SIS	3 J1
CHINA POINT RD	BUT	25 D6
CHINA RANCH RD	INY	73 N1
CHINO AV	SBD	98 E7
CHINO-CORONA RD	SBD	98 F8
CHINQUAPIN DR	MEN	23 Q1
CHIRIACO RD	RCO	101 M8
CHITTENDEN RD	TEH	24 D5
CHLORIDE RD	SBD	92 C2
CHLORIDE CLF RD	INY	62 J0
CHOLAME RD	MON	66 M5
CHOLAME VLY RD	SLO	66 P6
CHOLLA RD	SBD	91 L5
CHOLLA RD	SBD	92 N5
CHORRO ST N	SNLO	172 C1
CHORRO ST S	SNLO	172 E2
CHOWCHILLA	MAD	56 H6
CHOWCHILLA BLVD	MAD	56 A8
CHOWCHILLA MTN	MPA	49 J5
CHRISMAN RD	SJCO	47 E0
CHRISTENSEN RD	SAC	40 H1
CHRISTIAN RD	TEH	24 F7
CHRISTN VLY RD	PLA	34 H4
CHROME MINE RD	TRI	17 H2
CHUALAR RD	MON	54 M7

STREET	CO.	PAGE & GRID
CHUALAR CYN RD	MON	54 M8
CHUALAR RIV RD	MON	54 N7
CHUCKWALLA RD	SBD	91 J6
CHUCKWL SPGS RD	RCO	102 Q7
CHUCKWL SPGS RD	RCO	102 Q7
CHUCKWLA VLY RD	RCO	102 M7
CHUCKWLA VLY RD	RCO	103 N0
CHURCH AV	FRE	165 Q3
CHURCH AV	FRCO	57 J1
CHURCH AV	FRCO	57 J6
CHURCH AV	SCL	54 C6
CHURCH LN	HUM	15 F8
CHURCH LN	PLU	27 G4
CHURCH RD	SOL	39 K5
CHURCH ST	HUM	16 L6
CHURCH ST	SBD	99 D5
CHURCH ST	STA	47 F7
CHURCH ST	S	160 Q5
CHURCH HILL RD	CAL	41 J1
CHURCHILL MN RD	INY	51 J7
CIBOLA RD	LPAZ	103 P8
CIENAGA RD	KER	78 P1
CIENEGA RD	SBT	54 J9
CIENEGA RD	SBT	55 K1
CIMA RD	SBD	83 F9
CIMA RD	SBD	84 F0
CIMA MESA RD	LACO	90 L3
CINCHA ST	CAL	41 L1
CINDER RD	INY	70 J4
CINDER PIT RD	MOD	14 C6
CIRCLE DR	INY	70 C8
CIRCLE DR	RCO	100 L3
CIRCLEA CT	BUT	25 J5
CIRCLE C LN	SOL	39 F2
CITRACADO PKWY	SDCO	107 J6
CITRON ST	ANA	193 B2
CITRUS AV	LACO	98 D4
CITRUS AV	LACO	118 L5
CITRUS AV	SBD	99 D1
CITRUS AV	SBD	99 D6
CITRUS AV	SDCO	107 G4
CITRUS AV	SDCO	107 H7
CITY DR, THE	OR	195 D8
CITY CAMP	MNO	43 P5
CITY CREEK RD	SBD	99 B5
CITY CREEK RD	SBD	100 B5
CIVIC CENTER DR	SR	139 B4
CIVIC CENTER DR	SA	196 K0
CLAIREMONT DR	SD	211 L9
CLAIREMONT DR	SD	213 B0
CLAIREMONT DR	SDCO	106 H2
CLAIREMONT DR	SDCO	107 Q5
CLAIREMONT MESA	SD	211 K7
CLAIREMONT MESA	SDCO	106 H2
CLAIREMONT MESA	SDCO	107 P5
CLAIREMONT MESA	SDCO	107 P6
CLAREMONT AV	B	156 K4
CLAREMONT AV	O	156 P2
CLAREMONT BL	CLA	203 D3
CLARIBEL RD	STA	47 D6
CLARISSA AV	AVLN	105 N2
CLARK AV	COL	24 P8
CLARK AV	LACO	119 D8
CLARK AV	SB	86 C4
CLARK AV	TEH	24 F8
CLARK AV	YUBA	125 L5
CLARK RD	BUT	25 G5
CLARK RD	BUT	25 J5
CLARK RD	IMP	110 Q1
CLARK RD	IMP	114 C1
CLARK RD	MEN	30 F6
CLARK RD	MON	65 C1
CLARK RD	SLO	76 B5
CLARK RD	SOL	39 F2
CLARK RD	STA	47 F4
CLARK RD	SUT	33 C4
CLARK ST	NAP	133 G8
CLARKE RD	HUM	15 K6
CLARK MTN RD	SBD	84 E1
CLARK RANCH	MNO	51 B5
CLARKSBURG	YOL	39 E6
CLARKS FORK RD	ALP	42 E3
CLARKSON AV	FRCO	56 P6
CLARKSON AV	FRCO	57 N4
CLARKS VLY RD	GLE	24 L3
CLAUS RD	STA	47 F7
CLAUSEN RD	MCO	48 P8
CLAWITER RD	ALA	45 F8
CLAWITER RD	ALA	146 M2
CLAWITER RD	H	146 M2
CLAY RD	INY	72 B6
CLAY ST	SAL	171 L3
CLAY ST	U	123 J3
CLAY BANK RD	SOL	39 H0
CLAY MINE RD	KER	80 N5
CLAY RIVER RD	SBD	91 B8
CLAY STATION RD	SAC	40 H3
CLAYTON AV	FRCO	56 L7
CLAYTON AV	FRCO	58 L1
CLAYTON RD	CC	39 P1
CLAYTON RD	SON	32 Q0
CLAYTON CREEK	LAK	32 K1
CLEAR CREEK RD	KER	79 K3
CLEAR CREEK RD	SBT	66 B0
CLEAR CREEK RD	SHA	18 G2
CLEARFIELD DR	MLBR	144 Q3
CLEAR LAKE RD	MOD	6 J4
CLEGHORN RD	LAS	14 Q7
CLEGHORN CYN RD	SBD	91 P2
CLEM	SJCO	40 M4
CLEMENCEAU AV	FRCO	57 N6
CLEMENTE AV	AVLN	105 P2
CLEMENTS RD	SJCO	40 M4
CLEMENTS RD	SUT	33 F4
CLEVELAND AV	SBD	98 F8
CLEVELAND AV	SD	213 Q9
CLEVELAND RD	MCO	56 B4
CLEVELAND ST	RCO	101 P5
CLIFF DR	LAG	201 F2
CLIFF DR	STB	174 P1
CLIFF DR W	SC	169 M6
CLIFF RIDGE RD	MEN	30 E4
CLIMAX RD	AMA	30 K8
CLINE GULCH RD	SHA	18 C1
CLINT WY	SON	37 C1
CLINTON AV	FRE	165 B3
CLINTON AV	FRCO	56 H9
CLINTON AV	FRCO	57 H0
CLINTON AV	KIN	57 P8
CLINTON RD	AMA	40 F9
CLINTON RD	ED	41 F0
CLINTN KEITH RD	RC0	99 N4
CLOUGH RD	HUM	15 D7
CLOVER LN	SB	86 F9
CLOVER LN	SB	87 F0
CLOVER LN	SHA	18 G3
CLOVER CREEK RD	KLAM	5 B0
CLOVERDALE DR	SHA	18 G3
CLOVERDALE RD	RCO	98 F8
CLOVERDALE RD	SMCO	45 P5
CLOVERFIELD BL	SMON	180 N1
CLOVER VLY RD	LAK	31 E7
CLOVIS AV	FRCO	57 L6
CLOVIS AV	FRCO	57 N6
CLUB DR	DN	1 J8
COACHELLA CANAL	RCO	109 A6

STREET	CO.	PAGE & GRID
COACHLA CNAL RD	IMP	110 F3
COACHLLA CYN RD	RCO	101 Q7
COAL RD	RCO	99 L2
COAL CANYON RD	BUT	25 K6
COAL CANYON RD	ORA	98 H7
COALINGA RD	SBT	65 A6
COALNGA MNL SPG	FRCO	66 G3
COAST HWY	LAG	201 F1
COAST HWY	ORA	98 P5
COAST HWY	ORA	201 E1
COAST HWY	ORA	202 P7
COAST HWY	SON	30 Q9
COAST HWY	SON	30 N7
COAST HWY E	NB	199 M6
COAST HWY E	NB	200 N0
COAST HWY W	NB	199 M4
COAST RD	MON	64 B2
COAST RIDGE TR	MON	64 K8
COCHRAN RD	SCL	54 A5
COCK ROBIN ISL	HUM	15 D7
COCK RBN ISL RD	HUM	15 D7
COCOPAH RD	IMP	115 B6
COFFEE RD	MDO	162 D8
COFFEE RD	STA	47 E6
COFFEE CREEK RD	TRI	11 J6
COGSWELL RD	STA	47 F9
COGSWELL RD	STA	48 F0
COHASSET RD	BUT	25 D4
COHASSET RD	C	124 E1
COHN AV	FRCO	66 G7
COLBY RD	IMP	116 Q7
COLBY MTN LKOUT	TEH	19 N6
COLDEN AV	LACO	117 P5
COLD CANYON RD	LACO	97 D2
COLD CREEK RD	TRI	17 J3
COLD SPRINGS RD	ED	34 M7
COLD SPRINGS RD	LAS	8 M5
COLDWATR CYN AV	LACO	97 B5
COLDWATR CYN AV	LACO	117 F1
COLDWTR CYN DR	LACO	97 C6
COLDWELL AV	MDO	162 D0
COLDWELL LN	FRCO	66 G3
COLE RD	IMP	114 C2
COLE GRADE RD	SDCO	107 F7
COLEMAN AV	MP	147 A1
COLEMAN AV	SMCO	147 A1
COLEMAN AV	SCLR	151 D4
COLEMN FSH HTCH	SHA	18 J7
COLEMAN VLY RD	SON	37 E5
COLES RD	SUT	33 H3
COLES LEVEE RD	KER	78 K3
COLFAX	PLA	34 F7
COLFAX AV	GV	127 K5
COLFAX AV	LACO	117 G2
COLFAX AV	NEV	127 K5
COLFAX FRST HLL	PLA	34 F6
COLGATE RD	KER	80 J6
COLIMA RD	LACO	98 G2
COLIMA RD	LACO	118 N5
COLIMA RD	LACO	118 P3
COLIN RD	SBD	80 B8
COLLEGE	SON	37 E9
COLLEGE AV	B	156 G3
COLLEGE AV	MAR	139 Q2
COLLEGE AV	MDO	162 E1
COLLEGE AV	O	156 N3
COLLEGE AV	SDCO	106 K5
COLLEGE AV	SDCO	111 B7
COLLEGE AV	SIS	12 C4
COLLEGE AV	STR	131 H5
COLLEGE AV W	STR	131 H2
COLLEGE BLVD	PLA	34 K2
COLLEGE BLVD	SDCO	107 H3
COLLEGE DR	SAL	171 L1
COLLEGE DR	SMA	173 K6
COLLEGE CITY RD	COL	33 H0
COLLEGE HTS BL	KER	80 C8
COLLEGE VIEW DR	SHA	18 E5
COLLIER RD	SJCO	40 J2
COLLIER CYN RD	ALA	46 D3
COLLINS AV	OR	194 M7
COLLINS AV	ORA	120 E6
COLLINS RD	IMP	116 Q7
COLLINS RD	INY	51 M7
COLLINSVILLE RD	SOL	39 K2
COLLYER DR	SHA	18 D5
COLOMA RD	ED	34 L5
COLOMA RD	PLCV	138 B3
COLOMA RD	SAC	40 A1
COLOMBERO DR	SIS	12 F7
COLOMBUS AV	MCO	47 L7
COLONY RD	BUT	25 M4
COLONY RD	MON	64 B9
COLONY RD	MON	65 B0
COLONY RD	SAC	40 F2
COLORADO	LACO	98 C1
COLORADO	MPA	49 G2
COLORADO AV	RCO	99 G1
COLORADO AV	SMON	180 P0
COLORADO BLVD	LACO	97 C8
COLORADO BLVD	LACO	118 G2
COLORADO BL	PAS	190 K2
COLORADO RD	FRCO	57 N1
COLORADO ST	GLEN	182 A9
COLORADO ST	LACO	117 G5
COLORADO ST	LACO	119 F8
COLORADO ST	LACO	120 F0
COLOSEUM	INY	59 E9
COLSEN CYN RD	SB	86 B7
COLTON AV	CLTN	207 M2
COLTON AV	SBD	99 D3
COLUMBIA AV	RCO	99 E3
COLUMBIA RD N	KER	80 J7
COLUMBIA RD S	KER	80 K7
COLUMBUS AV	SF	143 F2
COLUMBUS AV	SFCO	45 C4
COLUMBUS PKWY	SOL	38 K6
COLUMBUS PKWY	SOL	38 L7
COLUSA AV	FRCO	56 M8
COLUSA AV	FRCO	66 B8
COLUSA AV	SUT	125 F0
COLUSA AV	YUBA	125 F0
COLUSA RD	SBD	91 G2
COLUSA CO RD	COL	31 B9
COLUSA-PRNTN RD	COL	32 B9
COLYEAR SPGS RD	TEH	17 Q9
COMANCHE DR	KER	78 K9
COMANCHE DR	KER	79 H0
COMANCHE PT RD	KER	79 M1
COMBIE RD	NEV	34 G4
COMBIE RD	PLA	34 G5
COMETA	SJCO	47 B6
COMM BLVD	SBD	91 B5
COMM BLVD	SBD	91 B5
COMMERCE AV	LACO	117 C4
COMMERCIAL ST	SD	216 L0
COMMONS	STA	47 J7
COMMONWEALTH	ORA	98 H3
COMMONWEALTH AV	ORA	120 C3
COMMONWEALTH AV	RCO	99 K9
COMPTCHE UKIAH	MEN	30 B3
COMPTON AV	LACO	117 N5
COMPTON BLVD	LACO	119 B2
COMSTOCK	SJCO	40 M4
CONARD RD	LAS	20 H6
CONCHO ST	CAL	41 K0

STREET	CO.	PAGE & GRID
CONCORD AV	CC	39 Q4
CONCORD BLVD	CC	39 N1
CONCOW RD	BUT	25 C7
CONDIT AV	STA	47 H3
CONDOR RD	SBD	92 B3
CONDOR RD	SBD	101 B4
CONDUIT	SUT	33 G4
CONE RD	INY	51 Q7
CONE RD 3	LAS	20 B3
CONE GROVE RD	TEH	18 N7
CONEJO AV	FRCO	57 N2
CONEJO AV	FRCO	57 N5
CONEJO DR	SBD	90 G9
CONE PEAK RD	MON	64 H8
CONGRESS AV	MONT	53 G6
CONGRESS AV	PAC	167 G3
CONGRESS ST	SD	213 P1
CONGRESS SPG RD	SCL	45 N8
CONKLIN RD	MOD	8 B7
CONKLIN CK RD	HUM	15 L7
CONKLING RD	IMP	114 B0
CONN CREEK RD	NAPA	29 K6
CONNECTION	LAS	21 L8
CONNELLY RD	IMP	114 B5
CONRAD GROVE LP	TEH	19 J6
CONSTANCE AV	STB	174 E2
CONSTANTIA RD	LAS	27 B8
CONSTELLATN AV	KER	89 B5
CONSUMNES MINE	ED	35 P2
CONTADAS	CC	38 Q7
CONTOUR AV	RCO	99 J6
CONTRA COSTA AV	FRCO	56 M7
CONVENTN CTR DR	CLK	209 P4
CONVICT CPGD RD	MNO	50 F9
CONVICT CPGD RD	MNO	51 F0
CONVICT CK EXP	MNO	51 F0
CONVICT LAKE RD	MNO	50 F9
CONVICT LAKE RD	MNO	51 F0
CONVOY ST	SDCO	106 H3
CONVOY ST	SDCO	107 P6
CONWAY RANCH RD	MNO	43 L3
COOK LN	SOL	39 H3
COOK ST	RCO	100 L8
COOK ST	SMA	173 H1
COOK CAMPBLL RD	SIS	4 K9
COOK PEAK LKOUT	KER	79 B6
COOKS CAMP RD	CAL	41 D4
COOKS SPRING RD	COL	32 C2
COOLEY RD	IMP	110 Q2
COOLEY RD	SIS	4 J3
COOLGARDIE RD	SBD	81 M7
COOLIDGE AV	O	158 M8
COOMBSVILLE RD	NAPA	38 G6
COON HOLLOW CK	BUT	25 A7
COOPER RD	IMP	110 N4
COOPER RD	MON	54 K4
COOPR CIENG T T	RCO	100 Q3
COOPERSTOWN RD	STA	48 D3
COPCO RD	SIS	4 G3
COPENHAGEN	HUM	15 D7
COPENHAGEN	HUM	15 D7
COPP AV	KER	89 C2
COPPER	FRCO	57 F6
COPPER AV	FRCO	56 F1
COPPER AV	FRCO	56 F1
COPPER CYN RD	SHA	18 C5
COPPER CITY RD	SBD	81 K7
COPPER HEAD RD	MON	65 M5
COPPER MTN RD	SBD	101 C2
COPPEROPOLIS	SJCO	40 N6
COPPER VISTA WY	SDCO	107 G4
COPUS RD	KER	78 M3
CORAL RD	MCO	47 Q8
CORAL RD	MCO	55 A8
CORAN RD	SHA	18 C3
CORBETT CYN RD	SLO	76 L3
CORBIN AV	LA	178 J2
CORBIN RD	COL	32 A7
CORCORAN RD	KER	77 B8
CORD	SJCO	40 J5
CORDA RD	MON	54 P8
CORDELIA RD	SOL	38 J8
CORDELIA RD	SOL	135 N2
CORDELIA RD	SUIS	135 N2
CORE RD	SAC	39 F8
CORKILL RD	RCO	100 G7
CORN CAMP RD	KER	77 G9
CORNELIA AV	FRCO	57 H3
CORNELIA AV	FRCO	57 M3
CORNELIUS AV	SUT	33 J7
CORNER RD	IMP	114 B4
CORNING RD	TEH	24 D6
CORNING-KIRKWD	TEH	24 E7
CORN SPRINGS RD	RCO	102 N6
CORONA AV	KIN	57 P8
CORONA EXPWY	RCO	98 G7
CORONA EXPWY	SBD	98 E6
CORONA FRWY	RCO	98 H9
CORONA RD	SON	38 H0
CORONA D MAR FY	CM	197 L7
CORONA D MAR FY	ORA	98 M4
CORONADO AV	SDCO	106 P4
CORONADO AV	SDCO	111 E6
CORRAL RD	SHA	19 D9
CORRAL BOTTM RD	TRI	17 C0
CORRL DE TIERRA	MON	54 N4
CORRAL HOLLW RD	SJCO	46 E8
CORRALITOS RD	SCR	54 E3
CORREIA	SJCO	39 L8
CORRELL RD	SUT	33 G3
CORTE MADERA AV	CRTM	140 C2
CORTEZ AV	MCO	47 J9
CORTEZ AV	MCO	48 J0
CORTEZ WY	KER	79 D9
CORTEZ WY	KER	80 D0
CORTINA SCH RD	COL	32 G7
CORTINA VNYD RD	COL	32 G7
CORTO RD	SBD	91 L7
CORWIN RD	SBD	91 H5
CORWIN RANCH RD	RC0	99 P3
CORYDON RD	RC0	99 N3
COSGROVE	CAL	41 L1
COSTA RD	YUB	26 M1
COSTNER RD	STA	47 D5
COTA ST	STB	174 L4
COTHARIN RD	VEN	105 D6
COTTAGE AV	MAN	161 B8
COTTAGE AV	SJCO	161 B8
COTTLE RD	STA	47 C7
COTTON RD	MCO	55 D8
COTTON CREEK	MPA	48 F7
COTTON GIN RD	MCO	55 E8
COTTNTAIL CK RD	SLO	75 E7
COTTONWOOD AV	RCO	99 G4
COTTONWOOD AV	RCO	99 K7
COTTONWOOD DR	SBD	92 C4
COTTONWOOD RD	INY	60 P2
COTTONWOOD RD	KER	78 H7
COTTONWOOD RD	MCO	47 P5
COTTONWOOD RD	RCO	100 F1
COTTONWOOD RD	SBT	55 K2
COTTONWD CYN RD	MNO	43 K5
COTTONWD CYN RD	RCO	99 M4
COTTONWD CYN RD	SB	77 Q3
COTTONWD CK RD	SIS	4 F1
COTTONWD SPG RD	RCO	101 M7

STREET	CO.	PAGE & GRID
COUCH ST	VAL	134 G5
COUGHLAN ST	VAL	134 J3
COUNCIL HILL RD	SIE	26 K5
COUNCILMAN RD	HUM	10 N7
COUNTRY	SJCO	40 Q4
COUNTRY CLUB BL	SJCO	40 P1
COUNTRY CLUB BL	SJCO	160 J0
COUNTRY CLUB DR	RCO	100 K7
COUNTRY CLUB RD	AVLN	105 N1
COUNTRYMAN DR	PLU	26 E2
COUNTY RD	INY	51 N7
COUNTY RD	MOD	8 C0
COUNTY RD	MOD	14 C9
COUNTY RD B	GLE	24 L5
COUNTY RD BB	GLE	24 M5
COUNTY RD C	GLE	24 J5
COUNTY RD D	GLE	24 L6
COUNTY RD F	GLE	24 J6
COUNTY RD H	GLE	24 H6
COUNTY RD H	GLE	24 K6
COUNTY RD I	GLE	24 H6
COUNTY RD J	GLE	24 H6
COUNTY RD M	GLE	24 J7
COUNTY RD MM	GLE	24 G7
COUNTY RD N	GLE	24 J7
COUNTY RD N	GLE	24 J7
COUNTY RD NN	GLE	24 H7
COUNTY RD P	GLE	24 G7
COUNTY RD P	GLE	24 J7
COUNTY RD PP	GLE	24 M7
COUNTY RD QQ	GLE	24 H7
COUNTY RD R	GLE	24 L8
COUNTY RD RR	GLE	24 G8
COUNTY RD S	GLE	24 L8
COUNTY RD SS	GLE	24 L8
COUNTY RD T	GLE	24 K8
COUNTY RD TT	GLE	24 L8
COUNTY RD U	GLE	24 J8
COUNTY RD U	GLE	24 J8
COUNTY RD V	GLE	24 J8
COUNTY RD V	GLE	24 L8
COUNTY RD VV	GLE	24 J8
COUNTY RD VV	GLE	24 L8
COUNTY RD W	GLE	24 L9
COUNTY RD WW	GLE	24 L9
COUNTY RD XX	GLE	25 H0
COUNTY RD XX	GLE	25 P0
COUNTY RD Y	GLE	25 N1
COUNTY RD YY	GLE	25 P1
COUNTY RD Z	GLE	25 M1
COUNTY RD ZZ	GLE	25 M2
COUNTY RD 5	YOL	33 K1
COUNTY RD 6	YOL	33 K1
COUNTY RD 7	YOL	33 K1
COUNTY RD 8	YOL	32 K9
COUNTY RD 9	GLE	24 G7
COUNTY RD 10	YOL	32 L9
COUNTY RD 11	GLE	24 G8
COUNTY RD 11	YOL	32 L9
COUNTY RD 11	YOL	33 L0
COUNTY RD 11A	YOL	33 L2
COUNTY RD 11B	YOL	33 L2
COUNTY RD 12	YOL	33 L2
COUNTY RD 12A	YOL	33 L1
COUNTY RD 13	YOL	32 M9
COUNTY RD 14	YOL	33 M0
COUNTY RD 14A	YOL	33 M2
COUNTY RD 15	GLE	24 G8
COUNTY RD 15	YOL	33 M3
COUNTY RD 15B	YOL	32 M9
COUNTY RD 15B	YOL	33 M0
COUNTY RD 16	GLE	24 G8
COUNTY RD 16	YOL	33 N0
COUNTY RD 16A	YOL	32 N9
COUNTY RD 17	YOL	33 N0
COUNTY RD 18	GLE	24 H8
COUNTY RD 18	YOL	33 N2
COUNTY RD 18B	YOL	33 N4
COUNTY RD 18C	YOL	33 N4
COUNTY RD 19	GLE	24 H8
COUNTY RD 19	GLE	25 H0
COUNTY RD 19	YOL	33 N2
COUNTY RD 19A	YOL	33 N0
COUNTY RD 20	GLE	24 H8
COUNTY RD 20	YOL	33 P4
COUNTY RD 20A	YOL	32 P9
COUNTY RD 21	GLE	24 H8
COUNTY RD 21	GLE	25 H0
COUNTY RD 21A	YOL	32 P9
COUNTY RD 23	GLE	25 H0
COUNTY RD 23	YOL	33 P1
COUNTY RD 24	GLE	24 H7
COUNTY RD 24	YOL	33 P3
COUNTY RD 25	GLE	24 H6
COUNTY RD 25	YOL	33 Q0
COUNTY RD 25A	YOL	33 Q1
COUNTY RD 26	GLE	24 H5
COUNTY RD 26	YOL	33 Q0
COUNTY RD 26A	YOL	33 Q4
COUNTY RD 27	GLE	24 J7
COUNTY RD 27	YOL	33 Q1
COUNTY RD 28	GLE	24 J6
COUNTY RD 28	YOL	33 Q1
COUNTY RD 28H	YOL	39 B4
COUNTY RD 29	GLE	24 J8
COUNTY RD 29	GLE	25 J0
COUNTY RD 29	YOL	39 B0
COUNTY RD 29A	YOL	39 B1
COUNTY RD 30	GLE	24 J6
COUNTY RD 30	GLE	25 J0
COUNTY RD 30	YOL	39 B3
CO RD 30 1/2	GLE	25 J0
COUNTY RD 31	GLE	24 J7
COUNTY RD 31	GLE	25 J0
COUNTY RD 31	YOL	39 B1
COUNTY RD 32	GLE	24 K9
COUNTY RD 32	GLE	25 K0
COUNTY RD 32	YOL	39 B2
CO RD 32 1/2	GLE	24 K8
COUNTY RD 33	GLE	24 K7
COUNTY RD 33	GLE	25 K0
COUNTY RD 34	GLE	24 K8
COUNTY RD 34	GLE	25 K0
COUNTY RD 35	GLE	24 K7
COUNTY RD 36	GLE	24 K9
COUNTY RD 36	YOL	39 D5
COUNTY RD 37	GLE	24 K9
COUNTY RD 38	GLE	24 K9
COUNTY RD 38	YOL	39 D5
COUNTY RD 38A	YOL	39 D5
COUNTY RD 39	GLE	24 L6
COUNTY RD 40	GLE	24 L9
COUNTY RD 41	GLE	24 L8
COUNTY RD 43	GLE	24 L8
COUNTY RD 43	YOL	32 L6
COUNTY RD 44	GLE	24 L8
COUNTY RD 44	YOL	32 L6
COUNTY RD 45	GLE	24 L7
COUNTY RD 45	YOL	32 L6
COUNTY RD 46	GLE	24 L8
COUNTY RD 47	YOL	32 L7
COUNTY RD 48	GLE	24 L6
COUNTY RD 49	GLE	24 L6
COUNTY RD 50	GLE	24 M8
COUNTY RD 50	GLE	25 M1
COUNTY RD 53	GLE	24 M8

STREET INDEX

STREET INDEX

STREET	CO.	PAGE & GRID
COUNTY RD 57	GLE	24 M6
COUNTY RD 58	GLE	24 M5
COUNTY RD 59	GLE	24 N5
COUNTY RD 59	YOL	32 L7
COUNTY RD 60	GLE	24 N7
COUNTY RD 61	GLE	24 N8
COUNTY RD 61	YOL	32 L7
COUNTY RD 62	GLE	24 N5
COUNTY RD 62	YOL	25 N1
COUNTY RD 63	YOL	32 M7
COUNTY RD 64	GLE	24 N9
COUNTY RD 65A	GLE	24 N8
COUNTY RD 65B	GLE	24 N8
COUNTY RD 65C	YOL	32 M9
COUNTY RD 66A	GLE	24 N6
COUNTY RD 66B	GLE	25 P2
COUNTY RD 67	GLE	25 P2
COUNTY RD 68	GLE	24 P6
COUNTY RD 69	GLE	24 P5
COUNTY RD 69	GLE	25 P5
COUNTY RD 70	GLE	24 P6
COUNTY RD 70	YOL	32 M7
COUNTY RD 71	GLE	24 P7
COUNTY RD 71	YOL	32 M7
COUNTY RD 75A	YOL	32 N7
COUNTY RD 76	YOL	32 N7
COUNTY RD 78	YOL	32 N7
COUNTY RD 78A	YOL	32 N7
COUNTY RD 79	YOL	32 N8
COUNTY RD 79A	YOL	32 P8
COUNTY RD 79B	YOL	32 P8
COUNTY RD 80	YOL	32 P8
COUNTY RD 81	YOL	32 P8
COUNTY RD 82	YOL	32 P8
COUNTY RD 82B	YOL	32 P8
COUNTY RD 84A	YOL	32 M9
COUNTY RD 84B	YOL	32 M9
COUNTY RD 85	YOL	32 M9
COUNTY RD 85B	YOL	32 M9
COUNTY RD 86	YOL	32 M9
COUNTY RD 86A	YOL	33 Q0
COUNTY RD 87	YOL	33 Q0
COUNTY RD 87B	YOL	33 M0
COUNTY RD 88	YOL	33 M0
COUNTY RD 88A	YOL	33 N1
COUNTY RD 88B	YOL	33 M1
COUNTY RD 89	YOL	33 M1
COUNTY RD 90	YOL	39 C1
COUNTY RD 90A	YOL	33 P1
COUNTY RD 91	YOL	39 B1
COUNTY RD 91A	YOL	39 B1
COUNTY RD 91B	YOL	33 L2
COUNTY RD 92	YOL	33 L2
COUNTY RD 92B	YOL	33 P2
COUNTY RD 92C	YOL	33 P2
COUNTY RD 92D	YOL	33 Q2
COUNTY RD 92F	YOL	33 Q2
COUNTY RD 93	YOL	33 Q2
COUNTY RD 93A	YOL	33 M2
COUNTY RD 93B	YOL	33 M2
COUNTY RD 94	YOL	33 Q2
COUNTY RD 94A	YOL	33 Q2
COUNTY RD 94B	YOL	33 M3
COUNTY RD 95	YOL	33 L2
COUNTY RD 95A	YOL	39 C3
COUNTY RD 96	YOL	33 N3
COUNTY RD 96B	YOL	33 Q3
COUNTY RD 97	YOL	33 N3
COUNTY RD 97D	YOL	33 B3
COUNTY RD 98	YOL	33 N3
COUNTY RD 99	YOL	33 N3
COUNTY RD 99E	YOL	33 N4
COUNTY RD 100	YOL	33 N4
COUNTY RD 101	YOL	39 N4
COUNTY RD 101A	YOL	39 Q4
COUNTY RD 102	YOL	33 Q4
COUNTY RD 102B	YOL	33 P4
COUNTY RD 103	YOL	33 P4
COUNTY RD 104	YOL	39 D5
COUNTY RD 105	YOL	39 D5
COUNTY RD 106	YOL	33 N5
COUNTY RD 107	YOL	33 N5
COUNTY RD 107A	YOL	33 M6
COUNTY RD 108	YOL	33 M4
COUNTY RD 116	YOL	33 M4
COUNTY RD 119	YOL	33 P6
COUNTY RD 122	YOL	33 P6
COUNTY RD 124	YOL	33 Q6
COUNTY RD 152	YOL	39 E5
COUNTY RD 155	YOL	39 E5
COUNTY RD 126	YOL	33 N6
COUNTY RD 128A	YOL	39 A6
COUNTY RD 303	GLE	24 K2
COUNTY RD 304	GLE	24 K2
COUNTY RD 307	GLE	24 L3
COUNTY RD 310	GLE	23 K9
COUNTY RD 314	GLE	24 N3
COUNTY RD 315	GLE	24 N3
COUNTY HOSP RD	PLU	20 L5
COUNTY LINE RD	KER	68 N3
COUNTY LINE RD	KER	68 N3
CO LINE RD E	TRI	17 F8
CO LINE RD	TRI	17 F8
CO LINE CK RD	TRI	16 G8
COURCHEVEL RD	PLA	35 D7
COURSE RD	KER	78 K2
COURT ST	RED	122 C2
COURTLAND RD N	YOL	39 F6
COURTLAND CT	KER	79 M4
COUTOLENC RD	KER	79 M3
COVE AV	FRCO	58 K2
COVE RD	SBD	91 K6
COVE RD	SHA	13 N1
COVELL BL	DVS	136 D3
COVELO RD	MEN	23 H1
COVELO RD	MEN	23 H1
COVELO REFUS RD	MEN	23 H1
COVERT RD	STA	47 D4
COVINA BLVD	LACO	108 H5
COWBOY CNTRY TR	RCO	108 B2
COWBOY JOE RD	LAS	21 Q7
COW CAMP RD	BUT	25 P8
COW CAMP RD	MNO	43 G5
COW CREEK RD S	SHA	14 A1
COWEL RD	CC	38 H4
COW GULCH RD	KER	79 J6
COW HAVEN CY RD	KER	78 J6
COW MTN ACCESS	MEN	31 E3
COX	SJCO	45 N9
COX AV	SCL	45 N9
COX LN	BUT	25 P8
COX RD	IMP	110 H0
COX RD	SHA	18 J2
COX RD	SBD	91 M6
COX ST	RCO	99 K4
COXCOMB TR	SBD	102 C5
COXEY	SBD	91 M6
COX FERRY RD	MCO	56 H3
COYOTE RD	MCO	56 H3
COYOTE RD	SBD	101 D0
COYOTE #1 RD	IMP	113 C5
COYOTE #2 RD	IMP	113 C5
COYOTE CYN RD	INY	71 L6
COYOTE CYN RD	RCO	108 A5
COYOTE GAP RD	BUT	25 F9
COYOTE LAKE RD	SBD	82 M9
COYOTE SPGS RD	MNO	43 K4
COYOTE VLY RD	INY	51 L5
COYOTE VLY RD	SBD	93 Q1
COYOTE VLY RES	LAS	14 N4
COZZI AV	MCO	56 C1
CRABTREE RD	LAS	8 M6
CRABTREE RD	LAS	25 N1
CRAFTON AV	SBD	99 D6
CRAIG	SJCO	47 C5
CRAIG AV	SON	132 Q3
CRAIG RD	SUT	33 B3
CRAMER	PLA	34 H3
CRANE AV	MCO	47 L7
CRANE RD	SIS	4 P1
CRANE RD	MCO	48 N2
CRANE RD	STA	47 D7
CRANE CANYON RD	SON	38 F6
CRANE FLAT	MPA	63 P2
CRANMORE RD	SUT	33 H3
CRANMORE RD	SUT	33 K3
CRANNELL RD	HUM	9 L9
CRANNELL RD	HUM	10 L0
CRATER RD	SBD	93 J3
CRATER HILL RD	PLA	34 J3
CRAWFORD AV	FRCO	58 C1
CRAY CROFT RDG	SIE	26 K7
CRAZY HORSE CYN	MON	54 H6
CREED RD	SOL	39 H2
CREEK RD	MCO	55 D7
CREEK RD	RED	122 M0
CREEK RD	VEN	88 M2
CREEKSIDE CT	KER	79 A4
CREEKSIDE LN	STA	47 E8
CREIGHTON DR	SHA	13 J7
CRENSHAW BLVD	LACO	117 N3
CRENSHAW BLVD	LACO	119 C3
CREOLE MINE RD	SBD	92 M8
CRESCENT AV	AVLN	105 N3
CRESCENT AV	ORA	120 D3
C RESERVOIR RD	MOD	6 M7
CRESSEY WY	MCO	48 M1
CREST DR	RCO	99 F3
CREST RD	LACO	119 F9
CRESTON RD	SLO	76 C2
CRESTON EUREKA	SLO	76 C2
CRESTN ODONOVAN	SLO	76 A4
CRESTVIEW RD	MNO	51 J9
CRESTVIEW ST	KER	80 A5
CREWS RD	SCL	54 D7
CRIPE	FRCO	58 C1
CRIPPEN RD	SBD	91 H1
CRIPPLE CK RD	SLO	76 D3
CRISPIN DR	MEN	30 H5
CRISS RD	SIS	4 J9
CRISWELL AV	MCO	55 B8
CROCKER SPGS RD	KER	77 K7
CROCKETT BLVD	CC	38 M7
CRONESE LAKE RD	SBD	82 M9
CRONESE LAKE RD	SBD	83 M0
CROOKED MDW RD	MEN	31 L3
CROSBY RD	HUM	15 O7
CROSBY RD	HUM	15 F7
CROSBY ST	SD	216 M3
CROSBY HAROLD	PLA	34 J2
CROSS RD	COL	32 H8
CROSS RD	MCO	48 Q6
CROSS RD	MON	55 K4
CROSS CYNS RD	SLO	66 P2
CROSS CTRVILLE	MEN	31 N3
CROSS CNTRY RD	MCO	56 M2
CROW RD	STA	47 A6
CROW CANYON RD	ALA	45 D9
CROWDER	PLA	33 N9
CROWDER FLAT RD	MOD	6 P9
CROWLEY RD	SUT	33 G4
CROWLEY LAKE DR	MNO	51 G1
CROWLEY LAKE PL	MNO	51 F1
CROWLY LK DM RD	MON	51 F1
CROWN & PICKLE	SIE	26 N7
CROWN POINT RD	BUT	25 N4
CROWN VLY PKWY	ORA	98 Q6
CROWN VALLEY RD	LACO	89 L8
CROWS LANDING	MDO	162 G4
CROWS LANDING	STA	162 F4
CROWS LANDNG RD	STA	47 B5
CROY RD	SCL	54 B4
CRUCERO RD	SBD	93 A2
CRUMP LN	FRCO	66 Q3
CRUZON GRADE RD	NEV	26 P3
CRYSTAL CK RD	SHA	18 D0
CRYSTAL LAKE RD	LACO	118 D6
CRYSTAL SPGS AV	SBD	134 M1
CRYSTAL SPGS DR	LA	182 A5
CRYSTAL SPGS RD	LACO	117 H4
CRYSTAL SPGS	KLAM	5 B4
CUDA DR	KER	78 K6
CUDDEBACK RD	SBD	80 J9
CUDDEBACK RD	SBD	81 J0
CUDDY VALLEY RD	KER	78 A3
CUDDY VALLEY RD	VEN	88 D4
CUFF RD	IMP	110 P9
CULL CANYON RD	ALA	45 D9
CULVER BLVD	CUL	183 C1
CULVER BLVD	CUL	108 K0
CULVER BLVD	LA	183 C1
CULVER BLVD	LA	188 D0
CULVER BLVD	LACO	97 F5
CULVER BLVD	LACO	187 H0
CULVER DR	ORA	98 L5
CULVER DR	ORA	120 L4
CUMMINGS RD	HUM	15 B9
CUMMINGS RD	MEN	31 N3
CUMMINGS SKYWAY	CC	38 M6
CUMMINGS SKYWAY	KER	79 M3
CUNEO RD	MPA	48 P8
CUNNINGHAM LN	MNO	42 M1
CUNNINGHAM RD	MCO	48 N7
CUNNINGHAM RD	MEN	31 N3
CUNNINHAM RD	CAL	41 H4
CURLEW ST	SD	215 B6
CURRIE RD	SOL	39 K4
CURRIER RD	BUT	25 N5
CURTIS RD	SM	145 J4
CURTIS ST W	SAL	171 A4
CURTNER AV	SCL	46 N2
CUSTER AV	FRCO	56 P4
CUSTER AV	SBD	91 M4
CUTCA TRUCK TR	RCO	107 P2
CUTLER AV	GLE	24 P8
CUT OFF RD	LAS	21 J4
CUTOFF RD	MEN	23 J9
CUTTING AV	GLE	24 P8
CUTTING BL	K	155 K4
CUTTNGS WHRF RD	NAPA	38 F5
CYA RD	MPA	49 H1
CYPRESS AV	LACO	118 J5
CYPRESS AV	SHA	18 E4
CYPRESS RD	CC	39 N5
CYPRESS RD	MCO	56 C1
CYPRESS RD	SBD	80 C8
CYPRESS ST	C	124 M5
CYPRESS MTN DR	SLO	66 B7
CYPRESS MTN DR	SCLR	151 D4
CYRMIC RD	KER	77 G6
CYRUS CANYON RD	KER	69 Q6
CYRUS CANYON RD	KER	79 A6

D

STREET	CO.	PAGE & GRID
D ST	MDO	162 K4
D ST	ONT	203 M9
D ST	SR	139 L5
D ST	SON	38 J9
DAGGETT YERMO	SBD	92 C1
DAGNINO RD	ALA	45 D9
DAHLSTROM RD	COL	32 J8
DAILEY RD	KER	99 J5
DAINTY AV	CC	39 P5
DAIRY AV	LACO	119 C7
DAIRY LN	MCO	56 C1
DAIRY RD	BUT	25 H1
DAIRY RD	KER	78 N7
DAIRY RD	STA	47 F2
DAIRY RD	YUB	33 G5
DAIRY MART	SDCO	106 Q3
DAIRY MART RD	SDCO	111 P7
DALBY	PLA	33 H9
DALE LN	SHA	18 G3
DALE RD	STA	47 D5
DALE TR	SBD	101 B8
DALE VISTA RD	SBD	101 B9
DALTON AV	ALA	46 D5
DALY ST	LACO	186 C7
DAMIEN RD	LACO	98 H8
DAMIEN RD	LACO	118 H8
DANA DR	SHA	18 S5
DANA FOOTHLL RD	SLO	76 N5
DANBY RD	SBD	101 L4
DANENBERG RD	IMP	114 B2
DANIELS AV	VAL	134 H4
DANLEY LATERAL	COL	32 C5
DANLEY RD	COL	32 C6
DAN MCNAMARA RD	MCO	48 F5
DANTES VIEW	INY	72 C3
DANVILLE BLVD	CC	45 D9
DANYS RD	SBD	91 H1
DARBY RD	CAL	41 J5
DARGATE RD	KER	77 F6
DARK CANYON RD	BUT	25 H7
DARLING RD	LACO	96 Q6
DARMS LN	NAPA	38 F4
DARRAH	MPA	49 H4
DATE ST	SB	86 B5
DATE PALM DR	RCO	100 K7
DATE ST	SMA	173 G2
DA VALL DR	RCO	100 K7
DAVENPORT RD	LACO	89 L6
DAVEY GLEN RD	SM	145 J4
DAVID AV	MONT	53 G5
DAVID AV	PAC	167 J2
DAVIDSON	HUM	9 E9
DAVIDSON RD	HUM	10 E0
DAVIS	SJCO	40 K1
DAVIS RD	FRCO	57 H5
DAVIS RD	STA	47 K4
DAVIS ST	ALA	45 D7
DAVIS ST	SUT	33 F3
DAVIS ST	LAK	32 J1
DAVS CK CEM RD	MOD	7 L4
DVS CK TRNS STA	MOD	7 L4
DAWN RD	KER	89 B9
DEADMAN CK RD	KER	78 A3
DEAD MANS GULCH	MON	65 K8
DEARBORN RD	BUT	25 F5
DEARDORFF RD	CAL	41 F2
DEARWOOD DR	MEN	31 D3
DEATH VALLEY RD	INY	52 P1
DEAVER AV	KER	70 P1
DECEPTION CYN RD	MNO	42 M1
DECKER RD	SBD	92 P8
DECORD DR	LACO	89 L1
DECOTO RD	ALA	45 D7
DEE KNOCH RD	SHA	13 L8
DEEP CREEK RD	MOD	7 M4
DEEP CREEK RD	SBD	101 B9
DEEP SPRING RD	SBD	84 J1
DEEP SPGS RANCH	INY	52 L5
DEEP SPGS RD	INY	52 L5
DEER WY	MCO	100 P2
DEER CREEK RD	GLE	24 P8
DEER CREEK RD	SBD	101 B9
DEER CREEK RD	VEN	106 M5
DEER FLAT RD	SHA	109 F4
DEER LICK SPGS	TRI	17 G6
DEER MTN RD	LAS	21 P7
DEER PARK RD	BUT	26 J4
DEER PARK RD	NAPA	26 C3
DEER PARK RD	NAPA	38 C3
DEER SPRING RD	MNO	51 M5
DEER VALLEY	ED	34 N5
DEER VALLEY RD	CC	39 Q4
DEER VALLEY RD	RCO	103 P6
DE HARVEY RD	KER	78 N4
DEHESA RD	SDCO	106 Q0
DEHESA RD	SDCO	108 Q0
DE LA CRUZ BL	SCLR	151 D4
DE LA GUERRA ST	STB	174 H6
DEL AMO BLVD	LACO	98 H0
DEL AMO BLVD	LACO	119 C0
DE LA VINA ST	STB	174 H4
DELAWARE AV	SC	169 P0
DELCERRO BLVD	SDCO	106 J5
DELCERRO BLVD	SDCO	111 K0
DEL DIOS HWY	SDCO	107 K6
DELEVAN RD	COL	32 A6
DELFATTI LN	KLAM	5 C3
DELFERN RD	KER	77 F6
DELIRIUM RD	KER	77 D7
DELHI RD	SOL	39 P5
DELIMA RD	SJCO	47 B1
DEL MAR AV	LACO	117 L9
DEL MAR AV	LACO	118 L9
DEL MAR RD	VAL	134 G6
DEL MAR BLVD	PAS	190 L5
DEL MONTE BL	MONT	167 B2
DEL MONTE AV	SUT	33 K4
DEL NORTE AV	FRCO	57 K1
DEL NORTE DR	TEH	18 K4
DEL NORTE ST	EUR	121 C2
DEL OBISPO ST	ORA	98 Q7
DEL OBISPO ST	ORA	202 L3
DEL OBISPO ST	SJC	202 L5
DEL ORO RD	SBD	91 L5
DEL ORTO RD	CAL	40 G9
DEL ORTO RD	CAL	41 G0
DEL PASO RD	SAC	33 P9
DEL PUERTO AV	STA	47 A6
DEL PUERTO CYN	STA	46 K9
DEL PUERTO CYN	STA	47 J1
DEL REY AV	FRCO	57 G8
DEL REY AV	FRCO	57 N8
DEL ROSA AV	SBD	99 B4
DELTA RD	CC	39 P5
DELTA RD	MCO	55 C9
DEMAREST MNE RD	CAL	41 L1
DENISE AV	SBD	91 L7
DENNETT ST	PAC	167 E2
DENNISON RD	KER	79 M6
DENNY RD	KER	78 N7
DENNY RD	TRI	11 M0
DENTON RD	MCO	56 F1
DENTON RD	STA	48 F1
DENTN & LEAK RD	MCO	56 F1
DENVER AV	FRCO	57 D8
DENVER AV	KIN	57 Q0
DENVERTON RD	SOL	39 H2
DE PORTOLA RD	RCO	99 N4
DEPOT AV	SB	86 C5
DEPOT AV	ALA	146 P2
DEPOT RD	H	146 P2
DEPOT ST	SMA	173 G2
DERBY ST	B	156 H3
DERRICK BLVD	FRCO	66 F5
DERRICK RD	FRCO	66 F5
DERRICK RD	IMP	113 B8
DERRICK RD	LAS	14 J3
DERRICK FT RD N	TRI	11 M9
DERRICK FT RD S	TRI	12 D0
DE RUYTER AV	JOL	105 N2
DESCANSO AV	AVLN	105 N2
DESCHUTES RD	SHA	18 B6
DESERT RD	IMP	114 B6
DESERT CTR RICE	RCO	102 L4
DESERT INN RD	CLK	209 Q6
DESERT INN RD	CLK	210 A0
DESERT SHORS DR	SBD	100 L7
DESERT VIEW AV	SBD	91 L7
DESERT WILLW TR	SBD	100 L7
DESEVADO RD	SIS	4 M4
DE SOTO AV	LA	177 Q6
DE SOTO AV	LACO	96 P6
DESSIE DR	LAK	97 B5
DETLOW RD	BUT	25 H7
DETOUR	GLE	24 P8
DETOUR RD	GLE	24 J7
DEVILS CORRL RD	LAS	21 L1
DEVILS DEN RD	KER	67 P2
DEVILS DEN RD	KER	78 A1
DEVONSHIRE BLVD	LACO	96 N4
DEVORE FRWY	SBD	99 C4
DEVORE DR	LAS	8 L1
DE VRIES	SJCO	40 K0
DE WOLF AV	FRCO	57 F7
DE WOLF AV	SB	86 G2
DAY AV	MOD	13 K8
DAY RD	SOL	54 C5
DAY RD	SHA	13 H9
DIABLO RD	CC	46 B1
DIABLO MINE RD	INY	51 H5
DIABLO MINE RD	MNO	51 H5
DIABLO OASIS DR	RCO	100 C3
DIAGONAL 7	MAD	56 P4
DIAGONAL 11	MAD	56 P4
DIAGONAL 232	TUL	68 F6
DIAGONAL 252	TUL	68 F6
DIAGONAL 254	TUL	68 F6
DIAMOND BAR BL	LACO	98 H8
DIAMOND BAR BL	LACO	118 H8
DIAMOND MTN RD	PLU	20 M8
DIAMOND VLY RD	ALP	36 M4
DIAZ LN	INY	51 K6
DIAZ ST	KER	118 L0
DICK COOK	PLA	34 K4
DICKERSON RD	IMP	110 L3
DICKINSON AV	FRCO	57 H5
DICKNSN FRRY RD	MCO	48 N7
DIDO AV	SBD	92 J1
DIEHL RD	STA	47 A4
DIENSTAG RD	STA	48 F1
DIERSSEN RD	SAC	39 P5
DIETRICH	SJCO	40 P5
DIETRICH RD	SJCO	40 P5
DIGGER RAVNE RD	PLU	26 J7
DI GIORGIO RD	KER	79 M6
DILLARD RD	SAC	40 C1
DILLON RD	RCO	100 H3
DILLON RD	SIS	4 A3
DINABA AV	HUM	15 E7
DINUBA AV	FRCO	57 P7
DINKELSPIEL RD	SOL	39 L2
DINKEY CREEK RD	FRCO	58 D3
DINUBA AV	KIN	57 P7
DIPS RD	TRI	17 H3
DIRKS RD	TRI	11 H0
DISTRICT CTR RD	BUT	25 H7
DITCH AV	KER	78 N7
DITCH RD	KER	78 N7
DITCH RD	SIE	26 M5
DITCH CREEK RD	SIS	4 G1
DIVISADERO ST	FRE	165 J3
DIVISADERO ST	SF	142 D1
DIVISION ST	LACO	89 F9
DIVISION ST	SDCO	106 M4
DIVISION ST	SDCO	111 F9
DIVISION CK RD	INY	59 L3
DIXIE RD	SBD	91 B6
DIXIE CYN RND VY	PLU	20 P5
DIXIE VALLEY RD	LAS	14 M6
DIXON AV E	SOL	39 E3
DIXON AV W	SOL	39 D3
DIXON LN	INY	51 K6
DIXON HILL RD	YUB	26 Q1
DIXON MINE RD	ALP	42 A6
DOBBINS ST	KER	70 P1
DOBIE LN	MEN	23 M8
DOBIE MEADOWS	MNO	43 Q4
DOBIE MEADOWS	MNO	44 Q2
DOBSON RD	SBD	81 M8
DODDS	SJCO	40 K5
DODDS RD	STA	47 K5
DODGE RD	COL	32 Q9
DODGE RDG LP RD	TUO	42 J3
DODGE RD	BUT	25 D5
DOERKSEN RD	STA	47 C8
DOE MILL RD	BUT	25 D5
DOG BAR RD	NEV	34 F3
DOGE CREEK RD	SHA	12 M2
DOGGIE TR	SBD	101 D0
DOGTOWN RD	CAL	41 K2
DOGTOWN RD	MPA	48 K9
DOGWOOD RD	ALP	36 M4
DOGWOOD RD	IMP	110 O1
DOGWOOD RD	IMP	114 C1
DOHENY DR	BH	183 K1
DOHENY DR	LA	183 K1
DOHENY DR	LACO	117 K2
DOHENY PARK RD	ORA	202 L5
DOLAN RD	MON	54 H3
DOLLARHIDE RD	NAPA	38 A9
DOLORES ST	SF	142 F2
DOLPHIN AV	KER	80 L1
DOLPHIN DR	IMP	109 K4
DOME AV	TUL	68 L6
DOME ST	SB	86 C6
DOMINION RD	SB	86 C5
DOMINO CT	KER	79 L3
DON RD	SBD	101 B7
DONNER PASS RD	NEV	27 N4
DONOVAN RD	SMA	173 D1
DONS RD	MOD	6 P7
DOOLITTLE DR	A	159 D6
DOOLITTLE DR	ALA	45 D6
DOOLITTLE DR	O	159 H4
DOOLITTLE CK RD	SIS	2 J8
DOON GRADE	BUT	25 D6
DORA RD	SBD	133 F2
DORAN SCENIC DR	SBD	82 Q1
DORFF LN	HUM	15 E7
DORIS AV	VEN	105 J4
DORNES RD	PLA	34 H1
DORRIS AV	FRCO	66 D8
DORRIS BROWNELL	SIS	2 J8
DORRIS TEHNER	SIS	3 J1
DORSEY RD	STA	47 A4
DOS CABEZA RD	IMP	113 A7
DOSE RD	TRI	10 Q8
DOS PALMAS RD	SBD	90 K4
DOS REIS RD	SJCO	40 B1
DOS RIOS	STA	47 G3
DOS RIOS DR	BUT	25 H5
DOSTER RD	CAL	41 H1
DOTTA LN	PLU	27 F7
DOTTO GUIDCI RD	PLU	27 F7
DOTY RD	SHA	13 M9
DOUBLE SPGS RD	CAL	40 P4
DOUGHERTY RD	CC	46 C2
DOUGLAS	SUT	33 A4
DOUGLAS AV	FRCO	56 L4
DOUGLAS AV	SB	86 C5
DOUGLAS LN	SBD	100 C8
DOUGLAS AV	SAC	40 B8
DOUGLAS ST	ELS	189 J7
DOVEER DR	ORA	120 L5
DOVER AV	KIN	57 Q0
DOVER DR	SBD	99 D4
DOVER CANYON RD	SLO	75 C8
DOVE SPG CYN RD	KER	69 P2
DOW BUTTE RD	LAS	20 B7
DOW BUTTE LO RD	LAS	20 B7
DOW FLAT RD	LAS	20 C6
DOW RD	PLA	34 K9
DOWD RD	PLA	33 K9
DOWD CAMP RD	PLA	33 K9
DOWDEN RD	IMP	110 J2
DOWNEY AV	LACO	119 L9
DOWNEY AV	INY	73 M1
DOWNEY ST	STA	48 G0
DOWNIE ST	SF	141 C7
DOYLE GRADE	FRCO	57 N5
DOYLE RD	MCO	48 N7
DOYLE RANCH RD	MEN	23 C2
DRAIS	SJCO	40 P5
DRAKE AV	COL	32 H9
DRAKE RD	LACO	118 P4
DRAKE ST	ANA	193 D6
DRAPER DR	TEH	18 J5
DREDGE CP MORGN	TRI	17 H4
DRESSER AV	KER	78 A3
DREW RD	IMP	113 A9
DREXLER	SUT	33 A2
DRIVE 168	TUL	58 L6
DRIVE 212	TUL	58 L6
DRIVE 243	TUL	68 L6
DRIVE 244	TUL	68 L6
DRIVE 246	TUL	68 L6
DRIVE 1688	TUL	58 L7
DRIVER RD	KER	78 N7
DRIVER RD	KER	78 B4
DROBISH	BUT	25 D6
DROGE	BUT	25 D6
DRUM CANYON RD	SB	86 G6
DRUMMOND AV	KER	80 B5
DRY CREEK RD	LAK	32 N0
DRY CREEK RD	MCO	48 J2
DRY CREEK RD	MNO	50 D7
DRY CREEK RD	NAPA	24 B3
DRY CREEK RD	NAPA	38 E3
DRY CREEK RD	PLA	34 H4
DRY CREEK RD	SLO	76 B2
DRY CREEK RD	SHA	18 D6
DRY CREEK RD	SIS	4 G2
DRY CREEK RD	SON	31 N5
DRY CK BASIN RD	MOD	8 J4
DRY CK CMP GRND	LAS	8 J2
DRY GENESEO RD	SLO	76 B3
DRY SLOUGH RD	COL	33 G1
DU BOIS ST	SR	139 M7
DUBOIS TK TR	SDCO	108 N3
DUCK LAKE RD	LAS	21 M8
DUDLEY RD	MON	65 J7
DUFAU	VEN	105 C4
DUGGANS RD	NEV	34 F4
DUMETZ RD	HUM	16 G2
DUMP RD	IMP	60 G0
DUMP RD	LAK	31 E7
DUNAWAY RD	IMP	113 A7
DUNBAR LN	NAPA	29 D1
DUNBAR LN	SDCO	108 P1
DUNCAN	SJCO	40 N4
DUNCAN CYN RD	SBD	90 K8
DUNCAN CREEK RD	SHA	17 H8
DUNDERBURG MDW	MNO	43 K3
DUNE RD	SBD	92 C3
DUNES RD	CLK	210 F2
DUNFORD RD	KER	78 G1
DUNLAP DR	RCO	99 J5
DUNLAP DR	FRCO	58 J5
DUNLAP RD	KER	69 P2
DUNN LN	CAL	41 N2
DUNN RD	STA	47 E3
DUNNE AV	SCL	54 A6
DUNSTONE DR	BUT	25 N8
DUNTON RD	STA	40 P8
DUPONT RD	RCO	102 P7
DURANT AV	B	156 G1
DURFEE AV	LACO	118 L1
DURHAM RD	SIS	5 G0
DURHAM DAYTN HY	BUT	25 J2
DURHAM FERRY RD	SJCO	47 Q0
DURKEE RD	LAS	14 H1
DURNEL RD	BUT	25 L3
DUSTIN RD	SJCO	40 K2
DUSTIN AKERS RD	KER	78 K1
DUSTY LN	STA	47 E7
DUSTY WY	TEH	18 Q6
DUSTY MILE RD	SBD	92 N7
DUTCH CREEK RD	SON	31 N5
DUTCHER CK RD	SON	31 N5
DUTCH MINE RD	TUO	51 P4
DUTTON AV	SON	131 M4
DUTTON AV N	STR	131 M1
DUVALL ST	KER	78 N1
DUZEL CREEK RD	SIS	3 Q8
DUZEL CREEK RD	SIS	11 A8
DUZEL RCK LO RD	SIS	3 Q8
DUZEL RCK LO RD	SIS	11 A8
DWIGHT WY	MCO	48 M1
DWINNELL WY	SIS	4 F3
DWINNELL WY	SIS	12 A4
DYE RD	SDCO	108 L0
DYER LN	PLA	20 L4
DYER LN	PLA	33 N9
DYER ST	TEH	18 J5
DYER RD	PLU	34 J7
DYERVILLE LOOP	HUM	16 K3
DYERVILLE LP RD	HUM	16 L4
DYSON LN	PLU	27 L4

E

STREET	CO.	PAGE & GRID
E ST	DVS	136 G6
E ST	EUR	121 A5
E ST	FRE	165 K5
E ST	SCTO	137 D4
E ST	SBDO	207 K5
E ST	SDCO	106 N4
E ST	SDCO	111 D7
E ST	YUB	33 D6
EABY RD	SBD	90 L9
EADY RD	IMP	114 C1
EAGLE RD	FRCO	57 F1
EAGLE AV	SB	86 C5
EAGLE BORAX WLL	INY	72 K9
EAGLE CK LP RD	TRI	11 J9
EAGLE FIELD RD	MCO	55 F9
EAGLE LAKE RD	LAS	20 H8
EAGLE LAKE RD	LAS	20 E7
EAGLE LAKE RD	NEV	27 L3
EAGL PEAK LKOUT	TEH	24 D0
EAGLE ROCK BLVD	LACO	117 H6
EAGLE RCK LKOUT	SIS	4 H6
EAGLES NEST RD	LAS	20 B7
EAGLES NEST RD	SAC	40 D2
EAGLEVLLE DUMP RD	MOD	8 M8
EAGLEVILLE LOOP	MOD	8 M8
EARDLEY AV	PAC	167 F5
EARHART RD	CO	159 L6
EARL RD	MCO	48 M1
EARL RD	YUB	33 F5
EARL ST	SDCO	106 K1
EARLHAM ST	SDCO	106 K1
EARP AV	COL	33 F1
EARP ST	ALA	46 E4
EAST AV	BUT	25 J2
EAST AV	BUT	124 C3
EAST AV	C	124 C3
EAST FORK RD	SHA	18 B1
EAST FORK RD	TRI	17 H4
EAST FORK RD	TRI	11 P5
EAST GRADE RD	TRI	17 H4
E FK HAYFORD RD	TRI	17 H4
E FK STUART CPG	TRI	11 H0
EASTMAN RD	STA	47 Q7
EASTMAN RD	KER	78 A9
EASTMONT AV	KER	78 E4
EASTBLUFF DR	SBD	98 E6
EASTERN	ALA	98 K7
EASTERN AV	LACO	117 K7
EASTSHORE FRWY	SP	155 J6
EASTSHORE FRWY	K	155 J6

SEE PAGE D FOR INSTRUCTIONS

STREET INDEX

STREET	CO.	PAGE & GRID
EAST SIDE	PLU	20 P7
EASTSIDE LN	MNO	42 A8
EASTSIDE RD	INY	51 L7
EASTSIDE RD	MEN	23 F1
EASTSIDE RD	MEN	31 F3
EASTSIDE RD	MNO	42 B9
EASTSIDE RD	RED	18 F4
EASTSIDE RD	SHA	18 F4
EASTSIDE RD	SIS	3 B7
EASTSIDE RD	SIS	11 B7
EAST SIDE RD	TRI	12 L1
E SIDE CALPELLA	MEN	31 D2
EASTSDE PORTR V	MEN	31 C3
E SDE REDWD VLY	MEN	31 B2
EAST WEST RD	SIS	5 F6
EASY ST	KER	79 M4
EASY ST	SHA	18 D6
EATON RD	BUT	25 G2
EATON RD	STA	47 C8
EBERLE RD	KER	78 K5
ECHO PARK AV	LA	185 C9
ECHO PARK AV	LA	186 B9
ECHO VALLEY RD	MON	54 L3
EDDINS RD	IMP	110 J1
EDDY RD	COL	33 H9
EDDY RD	LPAZ	104 E1
EDDY ST	SF	143 N2
EDDYS GULCH RD	SIS	11 F2
EDDYS GLH LKOUT	SIS	11 G3
EDGEMONT ST	LA	182 N3
EDGER RD	IMP	109 M4
EDGEWATER BLVD	FCTY	145 F6
EDGEWOOD AV	MAR	45 A2
EDGEWOOD AV	SMCO	45 J6
EDGEWOOD RD	SIS	12 B4
EDGEWD BIG SPGS	SIS	12 B4
EDINGER AV	ORA	98 L2
EDINGER AV	ORA	120 G2
EDINGER AV	SA	196 Q0
EDINGER AV	SA	197 A5
EDINGER AV	SA	198 A5
EDINGER ST	FTNV	195 Q5
EDINGER ST	SA	195 Q5
EDISON AV	SBD	98 F7
EDISON BL	BUR	179 G2
EDISON RD	KER	78 H8
EDISON ST	SB	86 H9
EDMINSTER	MCO	47 M7
EDMUNDSON AV	SCL	54 B5
ED POWERS RD	INY	51 L5
ED RAU RD	SAC	39 F8
EDWARD ST	KER	79 N3
EDWARDS	SJCO	47 B6
EDWARDS ST	ORA	120 H2
EEL RIVER RD	MEN	23 Q3
EEL ROCK RD	HUM	16 L4
EGAN RD	TUO	41 P4
EGGERT RD	SOL	39 D4
EHRLICH RD	STA	47 J5
EICKHOFF RD	LAK	31 N4
EIGHMY RD	TEH	18 K4
EIGHTH ST	C	124 P4
EIGHT MILE RD	SJCO	39 M9
EIGHT MILE RD	SJCO	40 M8
EISENHOWER DR	RCO	100 N9
EISENHOWER ST	FRFD	135 L6
EISENHOWER ST	KER	89 C9
ELBERTA ST	KER	89 C9
EL CAJON BLVD	SD	214 P1
EL CAJON BLVD	SDCO	106 H6
EL CAJON BLVD	SDCO	111 B7
EL CAMINO AV	SAC	40 A9
EL CAMINO AV W	SAC	33 Q7
EL CAMINO DR	SIS	18 J5
EL CAMINO CIELO	SBD	87 K4
EL CAMINO REAL	BLMT	145 L4
EL CAMINO REAL	BUR	144 K1
EL CAMINO REAL	MP	147 F4
EL CAMINO REAL	MLBR	144 M5
EL CAMINO REAL	MON	54 L6
EL CAMINO REAL	MON	65 B1
EL CAMINO REAL	MON	66 P1
EL CAMINO REAL	MON	71 B2
EL CAMINO REAL	MVW	148 Q2
EL CAMINO REAL	ORA	106 C8
EL CAMINO REAL	PA	147 F3
EL CAMINO REAL	SBT	54 D7
EL CAMINO REAL	SCL	171 H4
EL CAMINO REAL	SDCO	107 H3
EL CAMINO REAL	SNLO	172 L1
EL CAMINO REAL	SLO	76 E2
EL CAMINO REAL	SLO	76 L2
EL CAMINO REAL	SLO	172 C9
EL CAMINO REAL	SM	145 H1
EL CAMINO REAL	SMCO	45 L6
EL CAMINO REAL	STB	173 N7
EL CAMINO REAL	SCLR	195 Q3
EL CAMINO REAL	SCLR	151 F1
EL CAMINO REAL	SCL	46 L1
EL CAMPO	MCO	55 E8
EL CAMPO RD	RCO	100 G4
EL CAMPO RD	SLO	76 N3
EL CAPITAN WY	MCO	47 K9
EL CAPTN SCH RD	MCO	48 J0
EL CAPTN TK TR	RCO	90 M2
EL CARISO TK TR	RCO	90 M2
EL CENTRO AV	NAPA	38 G5
EL CENTRO RD	SAC	33 P7
EL CENTRO ST	IMP	113 A8
EL CERRITO RD	RCO	99 K4
EL CIELITO RD	STB	174 B7
EL CIELO DR	PMSP	206 N8
EL CIELO RD	RCO	108 B2
EL CONQUISTA DR	KIN	67 D3
ELDER AV	KER	79 P7
ELDER CREEK RD	RCO	108 A3
ELDER CREEK RD	SAC	40 C0
EL DIABLO RD	SBD	92 P8
EL DORADO AV	FRCO	66 M8
EL DORADO AV	FRCO	66 M8
EL DORADO AV	S	160 A4
EL DORADO DR	RCO	100 G5
EL DORADO RD	BUT	25 M7
EL DORADO ST	FRE	165 J4
EL DORADO ST	SJCO	40 P1
EL DRDO HLLS RD	ED	40 A4
EL DRADO MN RD	RCO	101 G5
ELDRIDGE	LAS	14 C4
ELEANOR AV	STA	47 D7
ELEVADO AV	MEN	31 D2
ELEVADO RD	SBD	101 J3
ELEVADOR RD	SOL	53 H6
ELEVATOR ST	STA	47 L4
ELFERS RD	SBD	101 J3
ELGIN	KIN	67 B3
ELGIN AV	KIN	67 B3
ELHOLM RD	MCO	47 N3
ELINOR RD N	HUM	16 H1
ELINOR RD S	HUM	16 H1
ELIZA GULCH RD	SIS	3 K8
ELIZABETH LK RD	LACO	89 G4
ELZBTH LK P CYN	LACO	89 E2
ELK	MCO	48 L1
ELK CT	KER	79 L3
ELK CREEK RD	HUM	16 L3
ELK CREEK RD	SIS	3 K0
ELK GROVE BLVD	SAC	39 E8
ELK GROVE FLORN	SAC	40 D0
ELK HILLS RD	KER	77 J9
ELK HILLS RD	KER	78 J0
ELKHORN AV	FRCO	56 P7
ELKHORN BLVD	MEN	31 L1
ELKHORN BLVD	SAC	33 P7
ELKHORN BLVD	SAC	40 A0
ELKHORN GRAD RD	KER	78 P0
ELKHORN GRADE	FRCO	57 P2
ELK MOUNTAIN RD	LAK	31 A6
ELK RIVER RD	HUM	121 H1
ELK RIVER RD	HUM	15 B8
ELK VALLEY RD	DN	1 L7
ELK VLY RD	SIS	10 A4
ELK VLY CRSS RD	DN	1 K8
ELLA RICHTER RD	SIS	18 G1
ELLENA ST	FRCO	57 L5
ELLEN SPGS DR	LAK	32 K1
ELLENWOOD DR	STA	47 E9
ELLENWOOD RD	STA	48 E0
ELLER LN	SIS	3 Q7
ELLER LN	SIS	11 A6
ELLIOT	SJCO	40 J3
ELLIOT ST	SBD	93 E1
ELLIOT RCH RD	PLA	34 D8
ELLIOTT CK RD	SIS	3 F3
ELLIOTT RCH RD	SAC	39 E8
ELLIS AV	RCO	99 K4
ELLIS RD	AMA	41 L3
ELLIS RD	YUB	33 D6
ELLIS ST	FTNV	197 Q2
ELLIS ST	SA	195 Q5
ELLSWORTH ST	B	156 G1
ELM AV	FRCO	57 L4
ELM AV	FRCO	57 P5
ELM AV	MON	53 D1
ELM AV	MON	65 C2
ELM AV	SBR	144 H2
ELM ST	BKO	166 F2
ELM ST	RCO	99 M9
ELM ST	SDCO	108 K1
ELMER ST	RCO	99 K3
ELMIRA RD	SOL	39 F1
EL MIRAGE RD	SBD	90 H8
ELMO HWY	KER	78 A1
EL MONTE AV	LACO	118 H4
EL MONTE AV	SVL	148 M1
EL MONTE RD	SCL	45 L8
ELNA RD	INY	59 C8
EL NIDO RD	MCO	48 Q4
EL NIDO PKWY	SDCO	107 H7
EL PASTA DR	RCO	99 B1
EL POMAR DR	SLO	76 D1
EL POMAR RD	SLO	76 D2
EL PORTAL	CC	38 C7
EL POZO GRADE	SLO	76 H6
EL PRADO	SDCO	106 K3
EL RANCHO DR	KER	79 C9
EL REPOSO RD	RCO	108 B4
EL ROBLAR RD	VEN	88 B1
EL ROBLAR ST	SB	87 C3
EL SEGUNDO BLVD	ELS	189 K6
EL SEGUNDO BLVD	LACO	97 Q2
EL SEGUNDO BLVD	LACO	117 Q2
EL SEGUNDO RD	SBD	73 A3
EL SERENO AV	MPA	48 G7
EL SOBRANTE RD	RCO	99 H2
EL TEJON HWY	KER	78 K9
EL TEJON HWY	KER	78 K0
EL TORO DR	BKD	166 P3
EL TORO RD	ORA	98 N7
ELVAS FRWY	SCTO	137 P4
ELVERTA RD	SAC	33 Q7
EL VICINO AV	MDO	162 D7
ELWOOD ST	FRCO	58 G2
ELY RD	SUT	33 M5
ELYSIAN VLY RD	LAS	21 K1
EMBARCADERO, THE	SF	143 L3
EMBARCADERO RD	PA	147 F4
EMBRCDRO SKYWAY	SF	143 H7
EMERALD AV	SDCO	107 H3
EMERALD AV	SDCO	106 N1
EMERALD RD	SBD	91 M8
EMERSON RD	MOD	7 E2
EMERSON RD	TEH	18 F1
EMERY RD	STA	47 D9
EMERY RD	STA	48 C0
EMIGH RD	SOL	39 E0
EMIGRANT RD	PLU	26 A6
EMIGRANT TR	SHA	18 B5
EMMERT RD	COL	33 J1
EMMIGRANT TR	ALP	36 L3
EMPIRE	CC	39 M4
EMPIRE AV	BUR	179 D2
EMPIRE AV	NEV	127 M3
EMPIRE GRADE	SCR	53 B7
EMPIRE MINE RD	CC	39 L3
ENCINAL	MON	54 L1
ENCINAL AV	ALA	44 L3
ENCINAL AV	SA	196 M3
ENCINITAS BLVD	SDCO	107 H3
ENCINITAS RD	SDCO	107 H5
ENDERTS BCH RD	DN	1 L8
ENGLEHART AV	FRCO	58 L1
ENGLISH COLONY	PLA	34 L2
ENGLISH HILLS	SOL	39 D1
ENNIS RD	FRCO	58 J4
ENNIS RD	SUT	33 F3
EN OAKS	LACO	118 H1
ENOS LN	KER	78 E7
ENSNADA-TIJ HWY	BAJA	111 H3
ENSLEY RD	STA	33 M5
ENTERPRISE	MON	54 L1
ENTERPRISE RD	BUT	25 M4
ERBES RD	VEN	105 D4
EREISTIN DR	SBD	92 N7
ERHIT RD	TUO	48 D2
ERHIT RD	TUO	48 D2
ERNST	MPA	48 D2
ERNST	SB	87 C3
ERRECA RD	MCO	47 Q8
ERRINGER RD	CM	199 N4
ERSKINE RD	IMP	109 M4
ERSKINE CK RD	KER	79 M4
ERTESZEK RD	ORA	120 K5
ESCALON BELLOTA	SJCO	40 G9
ESCALON BELLOTA	SJCO	47 A9
ESCHINGER RD	VEN	88 L1
ESCOBAR ST	M	154 G1
ESCOLLE RD	MON	54 P7
ESCONDIDO AV	SDCO	107 G4
ESCONDIDO FRWY	RCO	99 J4
ESCONDIDO FRWY	SD	216 G6
ESCONDIDO FRWY	SDCO	107 F6
ESMERALDA RD	CAL	41 K3
ESPERANZA AV	RCO	100 G2
ESPERANZA RD	MON	54 M7
ESPINOSA RD	MON	54 J4
ESPINOSA RD	MON	65 C2
ESPLANADE	BUT	25 F1
ESPLANADE AV	BUT	25 F1
ESPLANADE THE	C	124 J2
ESPOLA RD	SDCO	107 L7
ESQUON RD	BUT	25 K3
ESSEX LN	HUM	10 N0
ESSEX RD	SBD	94 E6
ESTRELLA RD	SLO	66 P1
ESTRELLA RD	SLO	76 A3
ETHANAC RD	RCO	99 K5
ETHEREDGE ST	KER	78 J6
ETIWANDA AV	SBD	98 D9
ETTERBG HONEYDW	HUM	16 P1
ETTING RD	VEN	105 B4
ETZEL ST	SOL	39 L3
EUCALYPTUS AV	RCO	99 G1
EUCALYPTUS AV	STA	47 H3
EUCALYPTUS RD	BUT	25 N4
EUCALYPTUS RD	MCO	56 G1
EUCALYPTUS RD	AVLN	105 N2
EUCALYPTUS ST	SBD	91 L3
EUCLID AV	SDCO	111 B6
EUCLID AV	SDCO	111 C6
EUCLID ST	SF	141 H8
EUCLID ST	SA	120 E4
EUCLID ST	SA	195 H0
EUREKA RD	PLA	34 N2
EUREKA RD	INY	52 F6
EUREKA WY	RED	122 C2
EUREKA WY	SHA	18 C4
EUREKA HILL RD	MEN	31 J3
EUREKA MINE RD	SIE	26 L5
EUREKA VLY RD	INY	52 M6
EUROPE AV	KER	79 P7
EVAN HEWES HWY	IMP	113 K7
EVAN HEWES HWY	IMP	114 B6
EVANS AV	FRCO	56 D7
EVANS RD	COL	32 F7
EVANS RD	RCO	100 B4
EVANS REIMER RD	BUT	25 Q4
EVELYN AV	MVW	148 M2
EVELYN AV	SVL	148 Q8
EVERETT AV	KIN	67 A4
EVERETT ST	KER	86 P4
EVERETT MEM HWY	SIS	12 D5
EVERGLADE	SUT	33 H4
EVERGREEN RD	TEH	18 K4
EVERGREEN RD	TUO	42 Q3
EVERGREEN RD	TUO	43 J0
EVERITT RD	SUT	33 D4
EXCELSIOR AV	FRCO	67 A9
EXCELSIOR AV	SAC	40 D1
EXCELSIOR MN RD	SBD	73 A3
EXCELSIOR MN RD	SBD	73 A3
EXCELSIOR ST	PT NEV	34 H3
EXCHEQUER DR	FRCO	58 C4
EXCHEQUER DAM	MPA	48 C1
EXP MINE RD	TUO	41 M5
EXPOSITION AV	LA	185 Q5
EXPOSITION BL	LA	185 Q5
EXPOSITION BLVD	LACO	97 E7
EXPOSITION BLVD	LACO	117 M4
EXPOSITION BLVD	SAC	39 B8
F ST	DVS	136 F6
F ST	EUR	121 H6
F ST	FRE	165 L1
F ST	HUM	15 H1
F ST	SBD	90 B3
F ST	SDCO	106 N4
F ST	SDCO	111 D7
FABRY RD	MON	55 J9
FAHEY RD	KER	78 K9
FAIR ST	BUT	25 H3
FAIRBANKS RD	MEN	23 G2
FAIRCHILD	SJCO	40 J2
FAIRFAX	FRCO	56 G3
FAIRFAX AV	LA	181 K1
FAIRFAX AV	LA	184 D1
FAIRFAX AV	LACO	181 K1
FAIRFAX BOLINAS	MAR	38 J0
FAIRFIELD AV	C	121 H4
FAIRFIELD AV	C	124 K8
FAIRFIELD RD ST	LACO	118 J3
FAIRGROUNDS DR	MON	54 F3
FAIRHAVEN AV	OR	196 D5
FAIRHAVEN AV	SA	196 D5
FAIRLANE RD	SBD	91 J2
FAIRMONT AV	LACO	106 K4
FAIRMONT AV	LA	182 P3
FAIRMONT AV E	MDO	162 D7
FAIRMOUNT AV	SD	214 Q9
FAIRMOUNT RD	IMP	110 M4
FAIR OAKS	SIS	3 F3
FAIROAKS AV	LACO	117 H2
FAIR OAKS AV	PAS	190 M3
FAIR OAKS BLVD	SAC	34 P1
FAIR OAKS BLVD	SAC	34 Q1
FAIR PLAY RD	ED	41 D2
FAIRVIEW AV	RCO	99 P4
FAIRVIEW AV	SB	87 P3
FAIRVIEW RD	COL	32 C6
FAIRVIEW RD	MEN	54 Q8
FAIRVIEW RD	SCL	54 C6
FAIRVIEW CK RD	SBD	91 P0
FAIRWAY DR	CLTN	207 N2
FAIRWAY DR	EUR	121 H4
FAIRWAY DR	LACO	118 M6
FAITH HOME RD	MCO	47 K6
FAITH HOME RD	STA	47 J6
FALLBROOK AV	LA	177 L0
FALL CREEK RD	SIS	4 F5
FALLEN LEAF RD	ED	35 J9
FALLING LEAF RD	SHA	18 D5
FALLON RD	SBT	54 D4
FALLON RD	SBT	55 F0
FALL RIVER RD	SHA	13 M8
FALLS CYN RD	AVLN	105 N3
FAMOSO HWY	KER	78 C5
FAMOSO-PRTVL HY	KER	78 C5
FANDANGO PSS RD	MOD	7 H5
FANNING	SJCO	40 N3
FANOE RD	MON	54 N8
FARGO AV	KIN	67 B4
FARGO CANYON RD	RCO	101 K2
FARINA ST	RCO	99 P1
FARLEY MINE RD	SBD	91 G6
FARMER RANCH RD	TRI	17 E3
FARMILAN RD	SUT	33 D2
FARMLN RD	ED	41 C1
FARNHAM RDG RD	ED	41 C1
FARQUHAR RD	TEH	18 K3
FARRIS RD	BUT	25 P4
FASIG RD	SUT	33 H3
FAUST RD	STA	47 H4
FAWCETT RD	IMP	114 B1
FAWN LODGE RD	TRI	17 C7
FAXON RD	COL	33 G2
FAY LN	SIS	11 G7
FAY RD	MCO	47 L7
FAY RANCH RD	KER	69 P8
FAY RANCH RD	KER	79 A8
FAY RIDGE RD	KER	78 A5
FEATHER LK HWY	LAS	20 H7
FEATHER LK HWY	LAS	20 H7
FEATHER RIV BL	SHA	18 H9
FEATHER BLVD	UPL	204 C3
FEDERAL BLVD	SDCO	106 L4
FEE RD	MOD	7 J7
FEE RESRVOIR RD	MOD	7 H7
FEENSTRA RD	SLO	76 D3
FELDSPAR AV	KER	80 C5
FELICITA RD	SDCO	107 J7
FELIZ CREEK RD	MEN	31 H3
FELL ST	SF	142 H8
FELL ST	SFCO	45 C3
FELLOWSHIP RD	STB	174 N1
FELTER RD	SCL	46 K3
FELTON EMPRE RD	SCR	53 C8
FENDERS FERRY	SHA	13 D0
FENTEM RD	MCO	47 N5
FERGUSON RD	IMP	116 M8
FERN RD	SHA	19 C1
FERN ST	SD	216 H3
FERN ST	SDCO	106 L4
FERN ST	SDCO	111 B6
FERN CANYON DR	MEN	31 F3
FERNDALE DMP RD	MEN	31 H5
FERRELL RD	IMP	114 C1
FERRETTI RD	TUO	41 Q7
FERRETTI RD	TUO	42 A7
FERRY RD	SBD	99 C0
FERRY RD E	HUM	15 F8
FESLER ST	SDCO	106 L2
FICKLE HILL RD	HUM	10 D4
FIDDLETOWN RD	AMA	41 D8
FIDDLTWN SLV LK	AMA	41 C0
FIDDYMENT RD	PLA	33 M9
FIELD RD	SBD	82 P5
FIELDBROOK RD	HUM	10 M1
FIELDS RD	MCO	48 M1
FIELDS RD	RCO	100 G1
FIELDS RIDGE RD	BUT	26 L2
FIESTA ISLND RD	SD	212 L9
FIFIELD RD	IMP	110 M3
FIFIELD RD	SUT	33 H4
FIFTH AV	C	124 H2
FIFTH ST	C	124 K8
FIG AV	FRE	165 G5
FIG AV	FRCO	57 L5
FIG AV	STA	47 J4
FIGMOND AV	MCO	47 K4
FIGUEROA ST	LA	185 P6
FIGUEROA ST	LA	191 C2
FIGUEROA ST	LACO	97 E7
FIGUEROA ST	LACO	118 K2
FIGUEROA MTN RD	SB	87 E7
FILBURN RD	KER	79 C9
FILIPPINI RD	SIE	27 H5
FILLMAN RD	STA	47 H4
FILLMORE ST	LAS	14 H1
FILLMORE ST	RCO	101 K1
FILLMORE ST	SF	142 D2
FILLY LN	CAL	41 N1
FINE AV	STA	47 N5
FINE RD	MCO	48 M1
FINK RD	MCO	48 K1
FINLEY LN	LAS	14 H4
FINNELL RD	IMP	116 C0
FINNEY AV	TEH	24 L7
FINNEY RD	SJCO	40 M7
FINNING HILL RD	PLA	34 H4
FIR ST	C	124 K8
FIRE CAMP RD	BUT	25 M1
FIRESTONE	MCO	66 G5
FIRESTONE BLVD	LACO	97 F6
FIRESTONE BLVD	LACO	117 F7
FIRETHORN ST	SBD	92 J2
FIRST AV	C	124 J3
FISCHER RD	IMP	113 A7
FISH & GAME RD	LAS	15 J3
FISH RD	STA	47 D4
FISHER RD	HUM	15 B0
FISHER RD	LPAZ	104 D1
FISHER RD	MCO	48 K2
FISHERS LANDING	YUMA	116 H3
FISH HATCHRY RD	INY	59 C9
FORGAY RD	PLU	20 P6
FISH ROCK RD	MEN	30 N6
FISH ROCK RD	MEN	31 N6
FISH SLOUGH RD	INY	59 B8
FISH SPRINGS RD	INY	59 B8
FISKE	MPA	48 C9
FISKE RD	SDCO	106 C3
FITCH MTN RD	SON	37 A7
FITZGERALD DR	CC	38 K6
FITZGERALD RD	SCL	54 C6
FITZHUGH CK RD	MOD	8 C8
FIVE BRIDGES RD	INY	51 K6
FIVE MILE RD	SBD	91 N8
FIVE MI NTH RD	SBD	91 N8
FIVE MILE DR	SJCO	40 P1
FIVE MILE RD	SDCO	108 L1
FLAMINGO RD	CLK	210 F5
FLANAGAN RD	SHA	18 C4
FLANNERY RD	SOL	39 J3
FLATTOP MTN RD	KIN	67 L0
FLEA VALLEY RD	BUT	25 E7
FLEMING AV E	VAL	134 H9
FLEMING RD	PLA	34 H1
FLETCHER DR	LACO	117 J5
FLETCHER PKWY	SDCO	106 J6
FLETCHER PKWY	SDCO	111 D6
FLINT AV	KIN	67 B5
FLINT ST	KER	80 D9
FLOOD	SJCO	40 N4
FLOOD RD	IMP	116 Q7
FLORADALE AV	SB	86 G3
FLORAL AV	C	124 D6
FLORAL AV	FRCO	56 M6
FLORAL AV	FRCO	57 M6
FLORAL AV	FRCO	57 M4
FLORENCE	LACO	97 F7
FLORENCE AV	ING	188 B7
FLORENCE AV	LACO	97 F7
FLORENCE AV	LACO	117 N4
FLORES RD	TEH	18 G2
FLORIDA RD	RCO	99 K7
FLORIDA DR	SD	216 J1
FLORIDA ST	VAL	134 H1
FLORIN RD	SAC	40 C0
FLORIN MILL RD	SHA	13 H6
FLORIN PERKINS	SAC	40 D0
FLOWER ST	LA	185 K8
FLOWING WELLS	IMP	116 G1
FLOYD AV	FRCO	57 J2
FLOYD AV	STA	47 E6
FLYNN RD	INY	51 K7
FLYNN CREEK RD	MEN	30 N6
FOAM AV	MONT	167 F7
FOAM ST	MON	53 F9
FOGARTY	STA	47 C9
FOGARTY	STA	48 C0
FOGG RD	SAC	39 F8
FOLETTA RD	VEN	88 N6
FOLLETT AV	KER	79 N6
FOLSOM BLVD	SAC	39 B8
FOLSOM BLVD	SAC	40 B0
FONSECA RD	COL	32 Q9
FONTANA AV	SBD	99 F8
FOOLISH PLSR RD	SBD	108 B1
FOOLISH PLSR RD	RCO	108 B1
FOOTE RD	SIE	26 N6
FOOTHILL	INY	59 A8
FOOTHILL AV	O	159 H6
FOOTHILL BLVD	ALA	46 L2
FOOTHILL BLVD	BUT	25 M7
FOOTHILL BLVD	LACO	98 A3
FOOTHILL BLVD	LACO	118 H1
FOOTHILL EXPWY	SCL	45 L8
FOOTHILL EXPWY	SCCO	149 K1
FOOTHILL FRWY	LACO	97 Q7
FOOTHILL FRWY	LACO	98 A3
FOOTHILL FRWY	LACO	117 F7
FOOTHILL RD	ALA	46 K1
FOOTHILL RD	DGL	46 L3
FOOTHILL RD	MNO	51 B3
FOOTHILL RD	MON	65 B0
FOOTHILL RD	SBD	99 C0
FOOTHILL RD	SB	174 G4
FOOTHILL RD	SCL	45 F8
FOOTHILL RD	SUT	33 F8
FOOTHILL RD	TEH	18 F8
FOOTHILL RD	VEN	88 P5
FORBES AV	LACO	118 H5
FORBES S	PLA	34 H1
FORBES RANCH RD	RCO	100 H6
FORBESTOWN RD	BUT	25 M5
FORBESTOWN RD	BUT	26 M1
FORD RD	NB	200 J4
FORD ST	RCO	100 G1
FORD ST	SBD	99 C0
FORDYCE LAKE RD	NEV	27 Q2
FOREMAN CIR RD	BUT	25 M1
FOREST	MPA	48 H6
FOREST CIR	ED	35 E4
FOREST DR	BUT	25 E4
FOREST DR	CAR	168 J5
FOREST HOME BL	SBD	99 D0
FOREST HOUSE	SIS	3 M8
FOREST LAWN	SJCO	40 Q0
FOREST LAWN DR	LA	179 P3
FOREST LAWN DR	LACO	117 H2
FOREST RANCH RD	BUT	25 D4
FOREST RANCH WY	BUT	57 H1
FORESTA RD	MPA	48 P6
FORREST ST	BKD	166 K4
FORRESTER RD	IMP	110 M4
FORSYTHE RD	MEN	22 H6
FORT BRAGG SHERWD	MEN	22 H6
FT CADY RD	SBD	92 D5
FORT INDEPNDNCE	INY	59 D7
FORT ROMIE RD	MON	54 A0
FORT ROSS RD	SON	37 D4
FORT SAGE RD	LAS	21 P4
FORT SEWARD RD	HUM	16 M0
FT STOCKTN DR	SD	213 P3
FORT STOCKTON	SD	213 P3
FORT TEJON RD	LACO	90 D7
FT TEJON CHSBRO	LACO	90 D7
FORTUNA BLVD	HUM	15 H2
FORTY MILE RD	YUB	33 G7
FORTYNINE LN	MOD	7 N7
FORTYNINE PALMS	SBD	101 C2
FORWARD RD	TEH	19 H2
FORWARDS MILL	SHA	19 H1
FOSS RD	JKSN	3 A7
FOSS HILL	SON	32 A0
FOSSIL BED RD	SBD	81 P5
FOSSIL BED RD	SBD	81 P7
FOSTER	MON	54 L5
FOSTER AV	HUM	9 N9
FOSTER RD	LACO	117 Q8
FOSTER RD	LACO	119 A9
FOSTER RD	NAP	133 J2
FOSTER RD	SHA	18 J2
FOSTER CITY BL	FCTY	145 D7
FOSTER CITY BL	SMCO	45 H6
FOSTER MTN RD	MEN	23 N2
FOULDS RD	IMP	109 J9
FOULKE LN	LA	182 M1
FOUNTAIN AV	LA	182 M1
FOUNTN HOUSE RD	YUB	26 F2
FOUR CORNERS RD	LAS	14 J1
FOUR MILE RD	COL	32 B8
FOUR MIL RDG RD	BUT	25 G9
FOURTEENTH ST	EUR	121 D3
FOURTH ST	C	124 P2
FOUSSAT RD	SDCO	107 G3
FOUTS SPRGS RD	SOL	39 F6
FOWLER AV	FRCO	57 F6
FOWLER AV	FRCO	57 P6
FOWLER AV	PLA	34 J2
FOWLER PBLC CMP	SIS	13 F0
FOX RD	LAS	21 K3
FOX RD	SOL	39 F2
FOXEN CANYON RD	SB	86 C6
FOXWORTHY AV	SCL	46 N2
FRAGUERO RD	TUO	41 N4
FRANCESCHI RD	KER	79 G7
FRANCISCO ST	SF	143 G0
FRANCISQUITO AV	LACO	118 K4
FRANCISQITO CYN	LACO	89 J4
FRANCIS SPGS RD	SBD	83 F5
FRANCO WSTRN RD	KER	77 G7
FRANK	KER	70 N1
FRANKENHEIMR RD	STA	47 N9
FRANKLIN AV	LA	181 K1
FRANKLIN AV	LA	182 K1
FRANKLIN AV	LACO	117 H4
FRANKLIN BLVD	SAC	39 B8
FRANKLIN RD	MCO	48 M3
FRANKLIN RD	SBD	84 K4
FRANKLIN RD	SUT	33 B3
FRANKLIN ST	MDO	162 K0
FRANKLIN ST	MONT	167 H4
FRANKLIN ST	MON	53 H8
FRANKLIN ST	SF	143 M1
FRANKLIN CYN RD	M	154 H0
FRANKLIN LEVEE	SUT	33 Q5
FRANK SNATRA DR	RCO	100 K3
FRANKWOOD AV	FRCO	58 B0
FRANZ VALLEY RD	SON	38 B0
FRANZ VLY SCHL	SON	38 B0
FRASER RD	KER	78 H5
FRATES RD	SON	38 H1
FRAZIER	SJCO	40 M4
FRAZIER RD	FRCO	57 H5
FRAZIER MTN	KER	88 D5
FRAZR MTN PK RD	KER	88 D5
FREDERICK ST	RCO	99 G4
FREDERICKSBURG	ALP	36 K4
FREDERICKSON RD	LAS	8 N6
FRED HAIGHT DR	DN	1 H8
FREDRICKS RD	IMP	110 L1
FREEBORN	KER	78 H0
FREEDOM BLVD	SCR	54 D2
FREEMN SCH HSE	TEH	24 L5
FREEPORT BLVD	SCTO	137 P4
FREITAS PKWY	MAR	38 H2
FREITAS RD	STA	47 L5
FREMONT AV	KER	79 K4
FREMONT AV	KIN	67 K3
FREMONT AV	LSAL	149 F3
FREMONT AV	LACO	117 K8
FREMONT AV	SCL	45 L4
FREMONT AV	SVL	148 P3
FREMONT BLVD	ALA	46 M1
FREMONT RD	SBD	92 P5
FREMONT RD	SJCO	40 N2
FREMONT ST	CLK	74 F7
FREMONT ST	LV	209 B7
FREMONT ST	SBD	99 C0
FREMONT ST	SF	143 L1
FREMONT	S	160 M0
FREMONT PEAK RD	SB	162 K0
FRENCH&SUGAR CK	SIS	11 D4
FRENCH CAMP RD	HUM	10 D4
FRENCH CAMP RD	SJCO	47 A2
FRENCH CREEK RD	ED	40 B6
FRENCH CREEK RD	SIS	3 B6
FRENCH FLAT RD	TUO	41 H4
FRENCH GULCH RD	CAL	41 L9
FRENCH GULCH RD	SHA	18 J3
FRENCH HILL RD	DN	2 J1
FRENCHMAN LK RD	PLU	27 D7
FRENCHTOWN RD	YUB	26 N1
FRENZEN RD	COL	32 F5
FRESH WATER RD	COL	32 F5
FRESHWTR KNEELD	HUM	15 A9
FRESHWATER POOL	HUM	16 B0
FRESNO AV	KER	78 M7
FRESNO RD	MEN	54 Q8
FRESNO ST	FRE	165 H5
FRESNO ST	FRCO	57 H5
FRESNO-COALINGA	RCO	107 A9
FRESZ RD	COL	32 F5
FREY AV	KER	78 D0
FREY RANCH RD	PLU	20 P6
FRIANT RD	FRE	165 H3
FRIANT RD	FRCO	58 C0
FRIARS RD	SD	213 M7
FRIARS RD	SDCO	106 J6
FRIARS RD	SDCO	214 H1
FRICOT CITY RD	CAL	41 K8
FRIDAY RIDGE RD	HUM	16 N5
FRIEDRICH RD	TRI	16 L1
FRINK RD	IMP	116 H1
FRISBY RD	SHA	19 A1
FRONT ST	MON	53 H8
FRONT ST	SAL	171 K5
FRONT ST	SB	174 G4
FRONT ST	SC	169 H7
FRONT ST	SOL	39 K4

SEE PAGE D FOR INSTRUCTIONS

STREET INDEX

StreetGuide INDEX

STREET	CO.	PAGE & GRID		STREET	CO.	PAGE & GRID
FRONTAGE RD	CAL	40 H9		GARVEY AV	LACO	98 D0
FRONTAGE RD	CAL	41 H0		GARVEY AV	LACO	118 K1
FRONTIER RD	SBD	91 E4		GARVEY RD	IMP	109 K9
FRUCHTENICHT RD	COL	33 G2		GARWOOD RD	SUT	33 L6
FRUDDEN RD	MON	65 L7		GARZOLI AV	KER	89 A3
FRUIT AV	FRE	165 E2		GASKELL RD	KER	89 C2
FRUIT AV	FRCO	57 L4		GASKELL RD	KER	89 C6
FRUIT AV	FRCO	57 P4		GAS LINE RD	RCO	102 N3
FRUIT AV	STA	47 H3		GASPERS RD	SHA	18 D6
FRUIT ST	5A	196 J7		GAS POINT RD	SHA	18 G5
FRUITLAND AV	MCO	48 L1		GAS POINT RD	SHA	18 E5
FRUITLAND RD	YUB	33 B7		GASQUET FLAT RD	DN	2 J1
FRUITRIDGE RD	ED	34 M9		GASTENBIDE RD	MCO	55 E5
FRUITRIDGE RD	SAC	40 C0		GASTON RD	NEV	26 P8
FRUITVALE	O	159 H2		GATES RD	STA	47 F3
FRUITVALE AV	ALA	45 C6		GATES RD	TRI	16 C7
FRUITVALE AV	KER	78 G6		GATES CANYON RD	SOL	38 F3
FRUITVALE AV	O	158 K8		GATEWAY	CC	39 N6
FRUITVALE RD	BUT	25 M4		GATEWAY BLVD	LA	180 D4
FRY RD	SOL	39 E3		GATEWAY BLVD	KER	80 B8
FRYMIRE RD	STA	48 B1		GATOS TR	SBD	100 A8
FUENTE ST	ORA	120 B5		GAVILAN DR	RCO	99 J2
FUERTE DR	SDCO	106 J7		GAVIOTA	AVLN	105 L1
FUERTE DR	SDCO	111 A8		GAVIOTA BCH RD	SB	86 K6
FUGLER RD	SB	86 B5		GAVIOTA RD	SB	86 K7
FULKERTH RD	STA	47 H5		GAWNE CARTER RD	SJCO	40 J8
FULLEN RD	CAL	41 J4		GAWNE CARTER RD	SJCO	40 K8
FULLER RD	INY	59 J5		GAZELLE CALLAHN	SIS	11 D9
FULLER RD	LACO	98 F3		GAZELLE CALLAHN	SIS	12 B2
FULLERTON RD	LACO	118 F5		GAZELLE MTN LKT	SIS	12 C0
FULLERTON RD	ORA	118 P6		GAZOS CREEK RD	SMCO	45 J8
FULMOR RD	HUM	15 E7		G-BAR-T RCH RD	MNO	44 Q4
FULMOR TOPPEN	HUM	15 E7		G-BAR-T RCH RD	MNO	51 A3
FULTON AV	SAC	40 B0		GEARY	CC	38 P8
FULTON LN	NAPA	29 F4		GEARY BLVD	SF	141 J4
FULTON RD	SON	37 E8		GEARY BLVD	SF	142 H1
FULTON ST	B	156 H1		GEARY BLVD	SFCO	45 C4
FULTON ST	SF	141 K6		GEARY ST	SF	143 J4
FULTON ST	SF	142 H1		GEER AV	MCO	48 M1
FULTON ST	SF	143 Q0		GEER RD	STA	47 G8
FULTON ST	SFCO	45 C4		GELDING RD	CAL	41 M2
FULTON ST	S	160 D3		GENASCI RD	SIE	27 M1
FULTON ST N	FRE	165 H5		GENERL BEALE RD	KER	79 J1
FULWEILER AV	AUB	126 H3		GENRL PETROLEUM	KER	79 Q8
FURNACE CK RD	SBD	91 M9		GENERALS HWY	TUL	58 N0
FURNC CK WSH RD	INY	72 D4		GENERALS HWY	TUL	59 N0
FURNC CK WSH RD	INY	73 L1		GENESEE AV	SD	211 A8
G				GENESEE AV	SD	213 A5
G ST	DVS	136 G6		GENESEE AV	SDCO	107 P5
G ST	FRE	165 K5		GENESEE INDN CK	PLU	26 G9
G ST	HUM	9 P9		GENEVA AV	SF	142 J0
G ST	HUM	10 P0		GENEVA AV	SFCO	45 C4
G ST	MER	170 K7		GENEVIEVE RD	SHA	18 D5
G ST	MCO	48 K4		GENOA LN	DGL	36 J5
G ST	MCO	48 M4		GENTRY RD	INY	72 M9
G ST	SCTO	137 F4		GENTRY RD	INY	73 M0
GABY AV	COL	32 H9		GEORGE RD	IMP	114 C0
GADDINI	SOL	39 C1		GEORGE SMITH RD	FRCO	57 A8
GAFFERY RD	STA	47 G3		GEORGETOWN	ED	34 J8
GAFFEY ST	LA	191 P0		GEORGETOWN RD	ED	34 J8
GAFFEY ST	LACO	119 G4		GEORGETOWN RD	PLCV	138 C4
GAFFNEY RD	YOL	39 E6		GEO WSHNTN BL S	SUT	33 J8
GAGE AV	LACO	117 N4		GEORGIA RD	SBD	91 C2
GAGE RD	BUT	25 M2		GEORGIA RD	SBD	81 H4
GALE AV	FRCO	56 D3		GEORGIA ST	VAL	134 M4
GALE RD	SBD	91 E9		GEORGIA SLID RD	ED	34 J7
GALENA ST	RCO	99 E0		GEPHART RD	KER	80 Q7
GALENA CYN RD	INY	72 H0		GERARD AV	MCO	48 M5
GALEPPI RD	LAS	21 K4		GERBER RD	SAC	40 C0
GALLAGHER AV	TEH	24 D6		GERBER RD	TEH	18 Q7
GALLAGHER RD	SUT	33 H8		GERKIN RD	INY	51 M6
GALLATIN RD	LAS	20 F8		GERRIE LN	RCO	108 K4
GALLATIN RD	TEH	18 Q4		GETTYSBURG AV	FRCO	57 A1
GALLAWAY RD	SIE	26 L1		GETTYSBURG AV	FRCO	57 H4
GALLINAS AV	SR	139 B2		GEYSERS RD	SON	31 M7
GALLOPADE TR	SBD	80 C5		GEYSRS RESRT RD	SON	31 M7
GALVEZ AV	FRCO	56 D3		GHOST TOWN RD	SBD	92 N8
GAMBLE RD	MCO	48 J3		GIANT ROCK RD	SBD	92 B0
GAMMEL RD	SBD	101 C5		GIANT ROCK RD	SBD	93 Q1
GANESHA BLVD	LACO	98 D5		GIBRALTAR RD	SB	86 J8
GANESHA BLVD	LACO	118 J8		GIBSON LN	MEN	23 Q3
GANN RD	CAL	40 L9		GIBSON RD	COL	32 Q7
GAP FOLSOM RD	CAL	41 D4		GIBSON RD	YOL	33 P7
GARAPATOS RD	MON	64 B2		GIBSON CYN RD	SOL	39 F1
GARATE RD	LAS	21 Q5		GIDDINGS AV	TUL	59 F5
GARBAGE DUMP RD	LAS	14 H2		GIELOW LN	MEN	31 F2
GARBAGE PIT RD	MNO	43 G3		GIFFORD RD	SUT	33 N5
GARBAGE PIT RD	MNO	50 B6		GILBERT RD	STA	47 C7
GARBONI RD	RCO	99 M6		GILLAM RD	CAL	41 H4
GARBONI RD	RCO	99 N6		GILLESPIE RD	IMP	110 E1
GARCES HWY	KER	67 P9		GILLESPIE ST	STB	174 M1
GARCES HWY	KER	68 N5		GILLETT RD	IMP	110 Q2
GARCIA RIVER RD	MEN	30 L5		GILLETT RD	MON	65 L4
GARDEN HWY	SAC	33 P6		GILLETTE RD	KER	79 Q6
GARDEN HWY	SUT	33 L6		GILLILAND RD	MCO	48 N6
GARDEN HWY	SUT	125 N7		GILLILAND RD	LAS	8 J8
GARDEN HWY	YUBA	33 L8		GILLIS CYN RD	SLO	76 C6
GARDEN RD	SDCO	107 M8		GILL STA COSO	INY	70 F6
GARDEN ST	STB	174 G3		GILMAN RD	SD	211 D4
GARDENA BLVD	LACO	119 B5		GILMAN RD	SDCO	106 C3
GARDEN BAR	PLA	34 L2		GILMAN RD	SCL	54 D7
GARDEN BAR RD	NEV	34 G3		GILMAN RD	SHA	12 A6
GARDENDALE ST	LACO	117 Q8		GILMAN SPGS RD	RCO	99 H7
GARDENDALE ST	LACO	117 N8		GILMORE	SJCO	40 M5
GARDEN GROVE BL	GGR	195 D1		GILROY HT SP RD	SCL	54 C7
GARDEN GROVE BL	ORA	195 D7		GIRARD RD	SHA	12 C7
GARDEN GROVE FY	GGR	195 D1		GIRARD LOOKOUT	SHA	12 H5
GARDEN GROVE FY	GGR	195 D7		GIRARD RIDGE RD	SHA	12 H6
GARDEN GROVE FY	ORA	196 K2		GIRAUDO RD	KER	79 M3
GARDEN GROVE FY	ORA	120 F4		GIRDNER RD	SUT	33 F2
GARDEN VLY RD	ED	34 J7		GISH RD	SJ	152 D0
GARDEN VLY RD	YUB	26 N3		GIVENS LUSTR RD	MCO	48 N5
GARDNER ST	LA	184 D1		GLACIER PT RD	MPA	63 Q5
GARDNER ST	VAL	134 M2		GLADDING RD	PLA	34 K1
GARDNER FLD RD	KER	78 M1		GLADSTONE ST	LACO	118 H6
GAREY AV	LACO	98 E6		GLASS CREEK RD	MNO	50 G4
GAREY AV	LACO	118 L9		GLASSELL ST	OR	194 K5
GAREY AV	SB	86 G5		GLASSELL ST	OR	196 B5
GARFIELD AV	LACO	98 F6		GLASSELL ST	ORA	120 E7
GARFIELD AV	FRCO	57 J3		GLASS FLOW RD	MNO	50 F5
GARFIELD AV	FRCO	57 P3		GLEASON RD	SBD	92 P7
GARFIELD AV	LACO	117 N8		GLEN AV	MER	170 L9
GARFIELD AV	LACO	119 B7		GLEN RD	SHA	18 H7
GARFIELD AV	ORA	120 A6		GLEN ALPINE RD	ED	35 B7
GARFIELD ST	SAC	40 L6		GLEN ANNIE RD	SB	86 K3
GARFIELD ST	RCO	101 Q4		GLEN ARBOR RD	SCR	54 K7
GARLAND RD	MON	54 F4		GLENBURN RD	SHA	13 K8
GARLOCK RD	KER	80 D5		GLEN CANYON RD	SCR	54 K7
GARNER LN	BUT	25 J3		GLENCO	GLE	24 J2
GARNER RD	SD	212 L1		GLENDALE AV	LACO	97 F6
GARNET AV	SDCO	106 J1		GLENDALE BLVD	LA	182 J6
GARNET ST	SDCO	107 D6		GLENDALE BLVD	LA	185 N9
GARNETT LN	SOL	39 D6		GLENDALE FRWY	LACO	117 J6
GARNIER RD	LAS	21 P7		GLENDORA AV	LACO	118 J6
GARRARD	CC	38 P4		GLENDORA MTN RD	LACO	98 J2
GARRETT DR	PLA	34 J2				
GARRETT DR	RCO	100 N1				
GARST RD	IMP	110 H1				

STREET	CO.	PAGE & GRID		STREET	CO.	PAGE & GRID
GLENDORA MTN RD	LACO	118 F7		GRAND AV	ELS	189 J0
GLENISON GAP RD	TRI	11 A5		GRAND AV	LA	185 M7
GLENN AV	FRCO	66 G9		GRAND AV	LACO	97 E8
GLENN DR	GLE	24 K1		GRAND AV	LACO	118 F5
GLENN RD	TEH	24 K8		GRAND AV	LACO	118 J0
GLENN RD W	COL	24 P6		GRAND AV	O	158 A0
GLENN-ALLEN AV	KER	89 N6		GRAND AV	ORA	120 H7
GLENN COOLDG DR	SC	169 A1		GRAND AV	PAS	190 P1
GLENN COOLDG DR	SC	169 J3		GRAND AV	P	158 B4
GLENNDENNING RD	SIS	3 P6		GRAND AV	RCO	99 L6
GLENOAKS BLVD	BUR	179 A5		GRAND AV	RCO	99 M2
GLENOAKS BLVD	LA	179 A5		GRAND AV	RCO	99 K6
GLENOAKS BLVD	LACO	97 B0		GRAND AV	SA	196 K8
GLENOAKS BLVD	LACO	117 B0		GRAND AV	SA	198 C6
GLENOAKS RD	RCO	99 P7		GRAND AV	SD	212 D2
GLENSHIRE DR	NEV	27 Q7		GRAND AV E	SB	86 G8
GLENWOOD DR	SCR	54 B0		GRAND AV W	O	157 P0
GLENWOOD LN	FRCO	58 C2		GRAND ST	MDO	162 J6
GLOBE DR	TUL	58 B3		GRAND CIRCLE BL	RCO	98 H9
GLOBE MINE RD	SBD	84 N1		GRANDE AV	DVS	136 C4
GLORIA RD	MON	55 P0		GRANDE PUMICE	MOD	8 C0
GLORIETTA BLVD	SDCO	45 B7		GRAND PUMICE	MOD	14 C0
GOAT MTN RD	COL	32 C1		GRAND ISLAND RD	SAC	39 K6
GOBBI ST	U	123 K5		GRANDON RD	RCO	108 A9
GOBLE LN	HUM	15 E7		GRAND VIEW AV	LACO	118 G1
GOBLE LN	HUM	15 E7		GRAND VIEW RD	LAK	32 M2
GODDELL RD	CAL	40 H8		GRANGE RD	SON	38 F0
GODFREY RCH RD	SLO	75 A8		GRANGER CK RD	MOD	8 B7
GODLEY	PLA	34 H2		GRANGEVILLE BL	KIN	67 J3
GODWIN RD	SBD	101 C5		GRANGEVLLE BYPS	KIN	67 B3
GOETZ RD	RCO	99 L4		GRANITE RD	KER	78 A1
GOFFS RD	SBD	94 C7		GRANITE RD	MAD	49 P3
GOGNA	SJCO	40 N3		GRANITE RD	SBD	92 K0
GOLD CROWN RD	RCO	101 D3		GRANITE RD	SCR	54 N0
GOLD CROWN RD	SBD	101 D3		GRANITE PARK RD	TRI	11 N7
GOLDEN ST	SBD	100 B9		GRANITE VIEW RD	INY	60 M1
GOLDEN CYN RD	INY	72 A1		GRANITEVILLE RD	NEV	27 M1
GOLDEN CTR FRWY	NEV	127 E8		GRANIT WELLS RD	SBD	93 L7
GOLDEN CTR FRWY	NEV	127 E8		GRANT AV	ALCO	146 D6
GOLDEN EAGLE RD	PLU	26 C5		GRANT AV	COL	32 H9
GOLDEN GATE AV	SF	142 J0		GRANT AV	SF	143 J4
GOLDEN GATE AV	SF	143 P0		GRANT RD	LSAL	149 H0
GOLDEN GATE DR	HUM	16 H3		GRANT RD	MCO	56 D2
GOLDEN LK FOREST	PLU	26 G9		GRANT RD	MVW	148 Q0
GOLDENROD AV	FRCO	57 K1		GRANT RD	SCL	54 N5
GOLDEN SPG DR	LACO	118 K7		GRANT ST	RCO	101 Q4
GOLDEN STATE FY	BKD	166 D4		GRANT ST	SMA	173 C2
GOLDEN STATE FY	BUR	179 A4		GRANT LAKE RD	MNO	50 B4
GOLDEN STATE FY	LA	179 A4		GRANTLAND AV	FRCO	57 A3
GOLDEN STATE FY	LA	182 J6		GRAND LINE RD	SAC	40 D0
GOLDEN STATE FY	LA	186 J7		GRAND LINE RD	SJCO	40 D0
GOLDEN STATE FY	LACO	89 B7		GUNN AV	LACO	118 E2
GOLDEN STATE FY	LACO	97 B7		GRAPEFRUIT BLVD	RCO	101 M2
GOLDEN STATE FY	LACO	117 B0		GRAPEVNE CYN RD	KER	70 P4
GOLDEN TROUT CRS	BUT	26 K3		GRAPEVNE CYN RD	SBD	81 N7
GOLDEN WEST ST	SMA	173 C2		GRAPP LN	RCO	108 A8
GOLDEN WEST ST	SMA	173 C2		GRASS RD	SBD	100 B0
GOLD HILL	ED	34 M6		GRASSHOPPR RD S	LAS	8 P9
GOLD HILL RD	PLA	34 M6		GRASSHOPPR RD S	LAS	14 P9
GOLD HILL RD	SOL	38 K3		GRASSHOPPER FLT	TRI	11 P4
GOLD LAKE RD	SIE	27 J1		GRASSLAND	SJCO	40 L3
GOLD PARK	SBD	101 E4		GRASS VALLEY RD	SBT	54 J0
GOLD RCK RCH RD	IMP	116 N3		GRASS VALLEY RD	SBT	55 J0
GOLD RUN RD	LAS	14 L8		GRATON RD	SON	37 H4
GOLDRUSH	SBD	101 E4		GRATTON RD	STA	47 H8
GODSBOROUGH GL	SHA	17 J7		GRAVEL PIT RD	RCO	103 D4
GOLD STONE LN	SHA	18 F3		GRAVEN RES RD	MOD	8 E1
GOLDSTONE RD	SBD	81 J8		GRAVEN RES RD	MOD	14 E9
GOLD STRIKE RD	CAL	41 J0		GRAY AV	YUBA	33 H4
GOLER RD	KER	80 F8		GRAYSON	CC	38 P4
GOLF RD	MCO	48 L4		GRAYSON RD	STA	47 G3
GOLF COURSE RD	HUM	9 P9		GREAT HWY	SFCO	45 D3
GOLF LINK RD	AVLN	105 P2		GREAT NORTHERN	MOD	5 N1
GOLF LINKS RD	ALA	45 D8		GREAT SO OVRLND	SDCO	109 N1
GOMAN RD	TUL	70 J1		GREELEY RD	KER	78 N4
GOMER AV	KER	78 N5		GREELY HILL	MPA	49 C0
GOMEZ RD	SHA	13 K7		GREEN	COL	32 P8
GONDER RD	IMP	110 M3		GREEN AV	IMP	110 M5
GONSALVES RD	TEH	18 P4		GREEN ST	SBD	90 M9
GONZAGA RD	MCO	55 J9		GREENBACK LN	SAC	34 P2
GONZALES RD	KER	89 C0		GREENBAY RD	COL	32 N4
GONZALES RD	VEN	105 A2		GREENFIELD AV	VAL	134 M5
GONZALES RIV RD	MON	64 L5		GREENFIELD DR	SDCO	108 Q0
GOODALE RD	INY	59 D3		GREENHORN RD	NEV	34 C5
GOODE HILL RD	LACO	89 H4		GREEN HOUSE RD	MCO	48 N0
GOODENOUGH RD	VEN	88 L7		GREEN HOUSE RD	MCO	48 N0
GOODFELLOW AV	FRCO	57 N9		GREEN LAKES RD	LACO	118 M1
GOODWIN DR	SBD	91 L1		GREENLEAF AV	LACO	118 N5
GOODYEAR RD	SBD	90 L8		GREENLEY RD	TUO	41 N5
GOOLSBY RCH RD	MNO	51 B5		GREENLEY RD	TUO	41 N5
GOOSE HAVEN RD	SOL	39 J5		GREENVILLE RD	PLU	27 C2
GOOSE RANCH RD	TRI	17 C7		GREENVILLE ST	ORA	120 P5
GOOSE VALLEY RD	SHA	13 N9		GREENVILLE ST	SA	197 Q6
GOPHER CYN RD	SDCO	107 F5		GRNVLL RND VLY	PLU	19 P5
GOPHR HLL LNDFL	PLU	26 F5		GREENWALD AV	RCO	99 L3
GORDONS FRRY RD	SIS	3 K0		GREENWOOD	ED	34 K7
GORDON VLY RD	NAPA	38 G7		GREENWOOD AV	FRCO	57 K9
GORDON VLY RD	NAPA	38 P7		GREENWOOD HTS DR	HUM	10 C7
GORGE RD	INY	51 J4		GREENWOOD RD	MEN	30 L9
GORMAN RANCH	PLA	34 N7		GREGORY AV	YUB	33 E7
GOSS RD	SBD	90 L8		GREGORY CK RD	SHA	12 H3
GOSSFORD RD	KER	78 H5		GRIDER RD	SIS	2 J2
GOUDIE TRUCK TR	SDCO	108 N4		GRIDER CREEK RD	SIS	3 J3
GOUGER NECK RD	MOD	14 Q7		GRIDLEY RD	RCO	99 K3
GOUGH ST	SF	142 J4		GRIDLEY-COLUSA	BUT	25 Q1
GOULD AV	LACO	119 C2		GRIEVE RD	INY	60 J4
GOULD RD	COL	25 H9		GRIFFIN AV	LA	186 B6
GOULD ST	SF	143 J4		GRIFFIN RD	DN	2 J4
GOVER RD	SHA	18 H7		GRIFFITH AV	YUB	33 E7
GOVERNOR DR	SDCO	106 A7		GRIFFITH PK BL	LA	182 H6
GOVERNOR DR	SDCO	107 A5				
GOVERNOR MN RD	LACO	89 K8				
GOWER RD	TEH	24 E7				
GOWING RD	IMP	110 P3				
GRACE RESORT RD	SIS	19 G2				
GRACIE RD	NEV	34 G1				
GRACIOSA RD	SB	86 L4				
GRAEAGL JHNSVLL	PLU	26 F8				
GRAESER RD	IMP	114 A5				
GRAHAM	SIS	11 A5				
GRAHAM AV	FRCO	57 M0				
GRAHAM AV	FRCO	57 M0				
GRAHAM HILL RD	SCR	54 C6				
GRAHAM HILL RD	SCR	54 K7				
GRAHAM PASS RD	RCO	110 J3				
GRAHAM PASS RD	RCO	110 D3				
GRAINLAND RD	BUT	25 C2				
GRAMERCY AV	SBD	214 C2				
GRAMERCY PL	LACO	117 A6				
GRAMERCY PL	SDCO	111 A6				
GRANADA AV	SAL	171 N4				
GRAND	ORA	120 L4				
GRAND	YUB	33 F6				

STREET	CO.	PAGE & GRID		STREET	CO.	PAGE & GRID
GRIFFITH PK DR	LA	182 D6		HAMLIN GULCH RD	SIS	3 P8
GRIFFITH PK DR	LACO	117 H4		HAMLOW RD	STA	47 G8
GRIMES CYN RD	VEN	88 P6		HAMMER LN	SJCO	40 N1
GRIMSEL DR	KER	79 N4		HAMMER LOOP RD	TEH	18 P0
GRINDSTONE RD	GLE	23 J9		HAMMETT RD	STA	47 F3
GRIZZLY BLUF RD	HUM	15 E7		HAMMIL RD	MNO	51 M6
GRIZZLY FLAT RD	ED	35 P1		HAMMOND GRV RD	YUB	33 C6
GRIZZLY FLAT RD	ED	35 P1		HAMMONTON RD	YUB	33 E8
GRIZLY HLL RD N	NEV	26 Q5		HAMNER AV	RCO	98 G9
GRIZZLY ISLD RD	SOL	39 J9		HANAUPAH CYN RD	INY	72 E0
GRIZZLY ISLD RD	SOL	39 L1		HANAWALT AV	KER	78 B1
GRIZZLY ISLD RD	SOL	135 P7		HANCOCK RD	SBD	84 K4
GRIZZLY PEAK BL	B	156 A2		HANEY VIEW DR	SHA	13 K8
GRIZZLY PEAK BL	CC	156 D8		HANFORD ARMONA	KIN	67 C5
GRIZZLY PEAK BL	CC	156 D8		HANKINS RD	COL	32 E6
GRZZLY PK LKOUT	SIS	13 G2		HANSEN	FRCO	58 L2
GROOMS	SJCO	40 B6		HANSEN AV	RCO	99 J6
GROS JEAN	MPA	49 K9		HANSEN RD	LAS	21 C3
GROTTO CANYON	INY	61 L6		HANSEN ST	SAL	171 P9
GROUSE RIDGE RD	NEV	27 P0		HAPGOOD RD	SB	86 G5
GRUBBS RD	BUT	25 N7		HAPPY TR	SBD	92 P7
GSCHWEND RD	MEN	31 A8		HAPPY CAMP LKOT	SIS	3 J0
GUADALUPE PKWY	SJ	151 A6		HAPPY CAMP RD	VEN	88 N7
GUADALUPE PKWY	SJ	152 G3		HAPPY CANYON RD	SB	87 H0
GUALALA LOOKOUT	MEN	30 L7		HAPPY GAP RD	TUL	58 J7
GUALALA RDG RD	MEN	30 L9		HAPPY VALLEY RD	CC	55 A7
GUERNEVILLE HWY	SON	37 C5		HAPPY VALLEY RD	ED	35 P1
GUERNEVILLE RD	STR	131 F1		HAPPY VALLEY RD	ED	35 P1
GUERNEVILLE RD	SON	37 B8		HAPPY VALLEY RD	SHA	18 H4
GUERRERO ST	SF	142 L4		HARBERS LN	HUM	15 E7
GUERRERO ST	SFCO	45 C4		HARBOR BLVD	ANA	193 J0
GUIBERSON RD	VEN	88 M7		HARBOR BLVD	CM	197 Q3
GUIDIVILLE RES	MEN	31 E3		HARBOR BLVD	CM	199 E3
GUINTOLI LN	HUM	9 N9		HARBOR BLVD	FTNV	195 P3
GUINTOLI LN	HUM	10 N0		HARBOR BLVD	FTNV	197 P3
GULCH RD	TRI	17 H2		HARBOR BLVD	GGR	195 G3
GULLETT RD	IMP	110 P0		HARBOR BLVD	LA	191 J2
GULLEY VIEW RD	RCO	108 B4		HARBOR BLVD	LACO	119 G5
GUM AV	GLE	25 N0		HARBOR BLVD	ORA	196 H3
GUN CLUB RD	KER	77 E9		HARBOR DR	SD	215 K6
GUN CLUB RD	MCO	47 N6		HARBOR DR	SDCO	216 P2
GUNN AV	LACO	118 E2		HARBOR DR N	SD	215 K6
GUNST RD	HUM	9 P9		HARBOR FRWY	LA	185 M5
GUNST RD	HUM	10 P0		HARBOR FRWY	LA	191 J2
GURR RD	MCO	48 P3		HARBOR FRWY	LACO	119 K7
GUTHERIE RD	IMP	109 P9		HARBOR FRWY	LACO	119 J5
GUTIERREZ ST	STB	174 L5		HARBOR SCNIC DR	LB	192 F6
GUTTRY RD	SBD	91 C5		HARBOR WY	SB	86 J4
GUY KER RCH RD	HUM	10 C4		HARDEN FLAT	TUO	49 K8
GWIN MINE RD	CAL	40 H9		HARDER RD	ALA	45 F8
GYLE RD	TEH	24 B6		HARDER RD W	H	146 M1
GYPSUM CYN RD	ORA	98 H7		HARDING AV	STA	47 H9
H				HARDING WY	SJCO	40 P1
H ST	BKD	166 L5		HARDY RD	S	160 K0
H ST	BEN	153 N4		HARE CANYON RD	MON	66 M0
H ST	EUR	121 K6		HARDY RD	IMP	113 B8
H ST	FRE	165 K5		HARKINS RD	SAL	171 P9
H ST	IMP	110 K0		HARKINS SLGH RD	SCR	54 L7
H ST	KER	78 H6		HARKNESS DR	PLU	20 J1
H ST	SCTO	137 F3		HARKNESS ST	LAPAZ	133 D1
H ST	SAC	39 B8		HARLAN AV	FRCO	66 A6
H ST	SBD	91 E9		HARLAN AV	FRCO	57 E4
H ST	SDCO	111 D7		HARLAN RD	COL	32 E5
H ST	SR	139 J4		HARLAN MTN RD	SBT	55 K0
H ST	SB	86 J4		HARMON RD	MCO	56 B5
HACIENDA AV	RCO	100 E5		HARMONY GRVE RD	SDCO	107 C3
HACIENDA AV	SM	145 Q0		HARMONY VLY RD	SLO	75 Q0
HACIENDA BLVD	LACO	98 F3		HARNEY	SDCO	40 L1
HACKAMORE PL	MNO	43 H1		HARP RD	TEH	18 J4
HACKLEMAN RD	IMP	110 N3		HARPER LN	MCO	55 D3
HACKMAN RD	SOL	39 E4		HARPER LAKE RD	SBD	81 Q3
HACKNEY DR	MNO	42 C8		HARPOLD RD	KLAM	2 B7
HACKSTAFF RD	LAS	21 H1		HARRIGAN RD	IMP	113 B8
HAGATA RD	LAS	21 F1		HARRINGTON AV	COL	32 J9
HAGEMAN RD	KER	78 A5		HARRIS	MPA	49 P3
HAGEN RD	RCO	100 E5		HARRIS RD	BUT	25 M3
HAGEN FLAT RD	SHA	13 L2		HARRIS RD	HUM	10 K3
HAHN RD	SBD	92 K1		HARRIS RD	IMP	110 N2
HAIGHT MTN RD	SIS	3 P1		HARRIS RD	MON	54 L5
HAILES RD	VEN	105 B4		HARRIS RD	SUT	33 N8
HAILE RD	TEH	24 E7		HARRIS ST	EUR	121 H3
HALE AV	COL	32 N4		HARRIS ST	HUM	9 A8
HALE RD	AMA	41 A0		HARRISON AV	HUM	15 A4
HALEY AV	IMP	110 H4		HARRISON RD	MON	54 M2
HALEY ST	STB	174 L5		HARRISON ST	O	157 E3
HALF MOON BY RD	SMCO	45 F8		HARRISON ST	RCO	101 N4
HALL AV	SJCO	47 L5		HARRISON ST	SF	143 J4
HALL RD	LAS	21 B8		HARRIS GLCH RD	SHA	17 J1
HALL RD	MON	54 L5		HARRIS RANCH RD	MNO	51 A4
HALL RD	SON	37 C4		HARROD	SBD	92 K1
HALL RD	STA	47 H9		HARRY CASH RD	SJCO	55 M4
HALL RD	TEH	24 E7		HART AV	KER	68 P3
HALL WY	SHA	13 L2		HART RD	IMP	110 M3
HALL CITY CK RD	SHA	17 J1		HART RD	STA	47 H9
HALLEY RD	SOL	39 N4		HART FLAT RD	KER	79 J3
HALLOCK	VEN	105 B4		HARTLEY DR	BUT	25 K7
HALLORAN SUMMIT	SBD	83 G2		HART MINE RD	SBD	84 J1
HALLOWELL RD	LAS	14 B8		HARTMANN RD	LAK	32 M2
HALLS FLAT RD	LAS	20 J7		HARTNELL	RED	122 K9
HALLWOOD BLVD W	YUB	33 H3		HARTNELL	MON	54 L5
HALSTEAD	DN	2 J4		HART OAKS DR	KER	78 A5
HAMBONE RD	SIS	5 F4		HARTSHORN RD	IMP	110 P4
HAMBURG RD	MCO	55 N0		HARTS MEADOW	SBD	92 K1
HAMES RD	SCR	54 M5		HARTS MTN RD	SIS	5 F4
HAMILTON	YOL	39 F7		HARTVICKSON LN	CAL	40 H8
HAMILTON AV	SCL	46 N1		HARVARD AV	IRV	200 C4
HAMILTON AV	STA	47 H9		HARVARD AV	ORA	98 C4
HAMILTON RD	KER	78 A5		HARVARD RD	SBD	92 C4
HAMILTON RD	TEH	24 E7		HARVARD MINE RD	TUO	41 P0
HAMILTON RD E	BUT	25 J4		HARVEY RD	LAS	21 J3
HAMILTON RD W	BUT	25 J4		HARVEY RD	SAC	40 H1
HAMLTN NORD CNA	ORA	98 M3		HARVEY RD 3	LAS	21 J3
HAMLTN VICTORIA	ORA	98 M3		HARVEY RD 4	LAS	21 J3
HAMLIN RD	BUT	25 J4		HARVY MTN LO RD	LAS	20 C4
				HARVEY PETTIT RD	KER	79 J3
				HARVY VLY RD	LAS	20 C4
				HARWOOD RD	SCL	54 C7
				HASKINS RD	SIS	5 F4
				HASKINS VALLEY	BUT	26 C6
				HASLEY CYN RD	LACO	89 K1
				HASS RD	COL	32 D7

SEE PAGE D FOR INSTRUCTIONS

HASSLER RD

STREET INDEX

JEFFERSON ST

STREET	CO.	PAGE & GRID
HASSLER RD	ED	34 M9
HASTAIN RD	IMP	110 K3
HASTE ST	B	156 H0
HASTER ST	ANA	193 P6
HASTER ST	ANA	195 C5
HASTER ST	ORA	120 F5
HATCHET CK RD	TRI	11 L9
HAT CREEK PK RD	SHA	13 L6
HAT CK PWRHOUSE	SHA	13 M6
HAT CK PWRHS #2	SHA	13 M6
HATCH RD	BUT	25 Q2
HATCH RD	STA	47 F5
HATCHERY RD	HUM	10 P1
HATCHET CK RD	TRI	12 L0
HATHAWAY ST	RCO	100 G1
HAUSER BLVD	LA	184 H2
HAUSER BR RD	SON	37 B1
HAVASU LAKE RD	SBD	95 K7
HAVEN AV	SBD	98 D8
HAVEN RD	SBD	80 P9
HAVENS RD	IMP	109 Q9
HAVERFORD RD	SDCO	108 K1
HAVLINA ST	SIS	5 F7
HAWEE CANYON RD	INY	70 F2
HAWKEYE AV	STA	47 H8
HAWKINS RD	SOL	39 F2
HAWKINS RD	STA	48 G1
HAWKNVL HMBG RD	SIS	3 K9
HAWKS HILL RD	HUM	15 D7
HAWKS HILL RD	HUM	15 D7
HAWLEY RD	SHA	18 E5
HAWTHORNE AV	C	124 G8
HAWTHORNE AV	SHA	18 G3
HAWTHORNE BLVD	LACO	97 J6
HAWTHORNE BLVD	LACO	119 E3
HAWTHORNE ST	MONT	167 G7
HAWTHORNE ST	RCO	99 P5
HAWVER RD	CAL	41 H1
HAYDEN RD	MCO	48 M6
HAYDEN HILL RD	LAS	14 M4
HAYDN HLL CTOFF	LAS	14 L7
HAYDN HLL LKOUT	LAS	14 L6
HAYES AV	FRCO	57 H3
HAYES AV	FRCO	57 Q3
HAYES ST	NAP	133 J5
HAYES ST	RCO	101 Q4
HAYNES RD	SBD	91 J9
HAYNES RD	SHA	13 P4
HAYS CANYON RD	MOD	8 E8
HAYWARD RD	MCO	48 F5
HAZEL AV	SAC	34 P2
HAZELDEAN RD	STA	48 E1
HAZELTINE AV	LACO	117 F0
HAZELTON AV	S	160 P8
HAZEN RD	TEH	19 H2
HEACOCK ST	RCO	99 F4
HEAD DAM RD	BUT	25 C6
HEALDSBURG AV	SON	37 E7
HEALY RD	MCO	48 P5
HEARST RD	MCO	47 Q6
HEARST RD	MCO	55 A6
HEARST POST OFC	MEN	23 M2
HEARST WLLTS RD	MEN	23 N1
HEATHER AV	KER	70 P5
HEATHER DR	FRFD	135 D4
HEBER RD	IMP	114 B2
HECKER PASS HWY	SCL	54 D5
HECTOR RD	SBD	92 D7
HEDDING ST	SJ	151 L5
HEDDING ST	SJ	152 E3
HEFFERNAN AV	IMP	114 C1
HEGENBRGR EXPWY	ALA	45 D7
HEGENBRGR EXPWY	O	159 E8
HEGENBERGER RD	ALA	45 D7
HEGENBURGER RD	O	159 H8
HEIDI RD	TUL	68 A8
HEINSEN RD	MON	65 M7
HEITT AV	KER	68 Q3
HELEN DR	MLBR	144 P3
HELENDALE RD	SBD	91 F2
HELLMAN AV	RCO	98 F8
HELLS HALF ACRE	SIE	26 M7
HELLS HALF ACRE	TUO	41 G7
HELLS HALF ACRE	TUO	42 G0
HELLS HOLLOW RD	TUO	48 B8
HELMS CT	KER	79 G5
HEMET LAKE RD	RCO	100 M3
HEMPHILL RD	LAS	21 L3
HENDERSON RD	FRCO	57 L3
HENDERSON RD	FRCO	57 M4
HENDERSON RD	FRCO	57 M4
HENDERSON RD	RED	122 J7
HENDERSON ST	EUR	121 G5
HENDRICKS DR	SBD	101 B8
HENDRICKS RD	LAK	31 F5
HENLEY RD	KLAM	5 C4
HENNESSEY RD	HUM	10 P7
HENNESSEY RD	TRI	10 P8
HENNESS PASS RD	SIE	26 M6
HENNESS PASS RD	SIE	27 M2
HENRY RD	SBD	101 C7
HENRY RD	SJCO	40 Q6
HENRY RD	SJCO	47 C6
HENRY ST	B	156 C0
HENRY DOTA RD	SIE	27 K4
HENRY FORD AV	LA	191 A8
HENRY FORD AV	LB	191 E9
HENRY MILLER AV	MCO	56 B0
HENRY MILLER RD	MCO	55 B5
HEREFORD RD	MCO	47 Q9
HEREFORD RD	MCO	48 Q0
HEREFORD RD	MCO	55 A9
HEREFORD RD	SBD	92 B3
HERIOT LN	PLU	27 H5
HERIOT LN	SIE	27 H5
HERITAGE CT	SHA	18 F3
HERITAGE RD	SDCO	106 P6
HERITAGE RD	SDCO	111 E8
HERLONG ACCESS	LAS	21 N6
HERMOSA AV	LACO	119 C1
HERMOSA RD	KER	78 H8
HERMOSA RD	VEN	88 L2
HERNANDEZ DR	LACO	90 J0
HERNDON AV	FRCO	56 G3
HERNDON AV	FRCO	56 G3
HERNDON AV	FRCO	57 G5
HERNLEY RD	RCO	108 A2
HERON AV	SBD	101 C0
HERRICK RD	HUM	121 Q2
HERRING RD	KER	78 L5
HERZOG RD	SAC	39 G7
HESPELER RD	SOL	38 F9
HESPERIA RD	MON	65 N5
HESPERIA RD	SBD	91 L3
HESPERIAN BLVD	ALA	45 F8
HESPERIAN BLVD	ALCO	146 F1
HESPERIAN BLVD	H	146 F1
HESSE RD	TEH	18 P3
HETTENSHAW RD	TRI	16 L9
HETZEL RD	IMP	109 P8
HEWES AV	ORA	98 K5
HEWES AV	ORA	120 F8
HEWITT	SJCO	40 P5
HEWLTT STURTVNT	MEN	31 H3
HEYSER RD	IMP	116 Q7
HIALEAH WY	RCO	100 P5

STREET	CO.	PAGE & GRID
HIATT RD	SUT	33 K3
HIAWATHA AV	AVLN	105 M1
HIBBARD RD	MEN	31 K1
HICKEY BLVD	SMCO	45 E3
HICKMAN LN	TEH	18 L5
HICKMAN RD	STA	47 H9
HICKMAN RD	STA	48 H0
HICKS	LAS	21 L3
HICKS LN	BUT	25 F2
HICKS RD	SUT	33 J8
HIDDEN HILLS RD	SBD	94 D1
HIDDEN OAKS DR	KER	79 M3
HIDDEN VLY RD	SB	87 K3
HIDEAWAY HAVEN	SHA	13 J6
HIEROGLYPH RD	MNO	51 E5
HIETT AV	KER	78 A3
HIGDON RD	CAL	41 E2
HIGGINS PURSM RD	SMCO	45 J4
HIGH RD	SBD	91 L7
HIGH RD	SIS	3 K8
HIGH ST	A	159 E1
HIGH ST	AUB	126 J6
HIGH ST	MONT	167 J7
HIGH ST	MON	53 H8
HIGH ST	O	159 B3
HIGH ST	SC	169 H3
HIGH ST	SCR	53 D9
HIGHGRADE RD	MOD	7 F6
HIGHLAND AV	FRCO	57 F7
HIGHLAND AV	LA	181 L5
HIGHLAND AV	LA	184 C5
HIGHLAND AV	LACO	97 H6
HIGHLAND AV	LACO	117 K3
HIGHLAND AV	LACO	119 E0
HIGHLAND AV	MB	189 P1
HIGHLAND AV	SBD	98 C9
HIGHLAND AV	SBD	99 E5
HIGHLAND AV	SDCO	106 M4
HIGHLAND AV	SDCO	111 C6
HIGHLAND AV	U	123 H2
HIGHLAND BLVD	RCO	99 F6
HIGHLAND DR	CLK	209 Q0
HIGHLAND DR	LACO	117 F6
HIGHLAND DR	SNLO	172 B1
HIGHLAND RD	CC	46 C3
HIGHLND HOME RD	RCO	99 G9
HIGHLAND LK RD	ALP	42 B3
HIGHLAND SPG RD	LAK	31 J6
HIGHLND SPGS RD	RCO	99 G9
HIGHLND VLY RD	SDCO	107 K8
HIGHLANDS LK RD	SHA	12 K3
HIGHLINE RD	IMP	110 N5
HIGHLINE RD	KER	79 M3
HIGHLINE RD	KER	79 M5
HIGH PRAIRIE RD	HUM	10 P4
HIGHRIDGE RD	LACO	119 G2
HIGH ROCK RD	LAS	21 L9
HIGH SCHOOL RD	SON	37 E7
HIGH VALLEY RD	KER	88 B6
HIGH VALLEY RD	LAK	31 F8
HIGH VALLEY RD	LAK	31 G9
HIGUERA ST	SLO	76 K1
HIGUERA ST	SNLO	172 J2
HILL	FRCO	58 L2
HILL AV	PAS	190 D9
HILL RD	COL	32 F7
HILL RD	CC	38 P8
HILL RD	KER	78 L4
HILL RD	KLAM	5 E4
HILL RD	MEN	23 G2
HILL RD	SCL	54 A6
HILL RD	SIS	5 J6
HILL RD	YUB	33 B8
HILL RD E	MEN	23 P0
HILL ST	AVLN	105 M2
HILL ST	LA	185 P7
HILL ST	LA	186 J0
HILL ST	LACO	119 E7
HILL ST	ML	164 K4
HILL ST	SDCO	106 L1
HILL ST	SDCO	107 G2
HILL ST	SDCO	111 B4
HILLCREST AV	BEN	153 K5
HILLCREST AV	CC	39 N4
HILLCREST BLVD	LACO	118 G2
HILLCREST BLVD	MLBR	144 P6
HILLCREST BLVD	SMCO	45 G3
HILLCREST ST	KER	80 B8
HILLDALE AV	MCO	55 C5
HILLER RD	HUM	9 M9
HILLER ST	BLMT	145 L5
HILLGATE RD	COL	32 H8
HILLHURST AV	LA	182 J4
HILLMAN AV	BLMT	145 M3
HILLSBORO AV	LA	183 J6
HILLSDALE BL E	FCTY	145 E6
HILLSDALE BL E	SM	145 J3
HILLSDALE BL W	SM	145 L0
HILLS FERRY RD	MCO	47 M5
HILLSIDE AV	RCO	98 G9
HILLSIDE BLVD	SMCO	45 E3
HILLSIDE DR	MPA	49 J4
HILLSIDE DR	SMCO	45 G4
HILL SIDE STA	LAS	14 J2
HILLSIDE VIS RD	RCO	108 B4
HILLS VALLEY RD	FRCO	58 K3
HILLTOP	SHA	18 E4
HILL VIEW TK TR	SBD	91 D4
HILMAR RD	STA	47 K6
HILT RD	SIS	4 E1
HILT HUNGRY RD	SIS	4 F0
HILTON PACK STA	MNO	51 G1
HILTONS RD	HUM	9 F9
HILTONS RD	HUM	10 F0
HIME RD	IMP	114 B0
HI MOUNTAIN RD	SLO	76 J5
HINDS RD	STA	47 B7
HINKLEY RD	SBD	81 Q5
HIRSCH	MPA	49 K3
HIRSCHDALE RD	NEV	27 P8
HITCHCOCK RD	MON	54 L5
HI YOU GULCH RD	SIS	5 L7
HOADLEY PKS RD	SHA	17 C9
HOAG RD	TEH	24 D7
HOAGLAND RD	HUM	16 N7
HOAGLIN RD	TRI	16 P9
HOAGLIN SCH RD	TRI	16 P8
HOBART AV	FRCO	56 D2
HOBART MILLS RD	NEV	27 N7
HOBBS RD	IMP	110 E1
HOBBS RD	SUT	33 H5
HOBO GULCH RD	TRI	11 P3
HOBSON AV	MON	65 D3
HOBSON WY	RCO	103 N5
HOFFMAN BLVD	R	155 L1
HOFFMAN LN	CC	39 Q5
HOFFMAN RD	SBD	80 H9
HOFFMAN RD	SBD	81 J0
HOGAN BUCKEYE	MPA	49 J2
HOGAN DAM RD	CAL	40 K8
HOGAN DAM RD	CAL	40 L8
HOGBACK RD	INY	60 L0
HOG CANYON RD	KER	79 J6
HOG CANYON RD	SLO	76 A2
HOG CANYON EXT	SLO	66 Q3
HOGIN RD	STA	47 K5

STREET	CO.	PAGE & GRID
HOG LAKE TK TR	RCO	100 N3
HOGSBACK RD	TEH	18 N7
HOGSBACK RD	TEH	19 L2
HOKE RD	SUT	33 F4
HOLBROOK RD	MCO	48 P7
HOLCOMB CK RD	SBD	91 P8
HOLCOMB VLY RD	SBD	91 P9
HOLCOMBS RD	SIE	27 M6
HOLDEN	SJCO	40 P4
HOLDNER RD	SOL	39 F2
HOLDRIDGE DR	TUL	68 G8
HOLDRIDGE RD	IMP	114 B5
HOLDRIDGE RD	IMP	114 B5
HOLE AV	RCO	99 G1
HOLENBECK	SJCO	40 P4
HOLIDAY AV	KER	89 C5
HOLIDAY RD	DN	2 G2
HOLLAND	YOL	39 E7
HOLLAND AV	BUT	25 J3
HOLLAND RD	RCO	99 M5
HOLLAND RD	SOL	39 G5
HOLLAND TRACT RD	CC	39 N6
HOLLENBECK AV	LACO	118 L5
HOLLENBECK AV	SVL	149 D6
HOLLISTER AV	SB	87 L2
HOLLISTER ST	SDCO	106 Q5
HOLLISTER ST	SDCO	111 F7
HOLLOW RD	CC	39 P1
HOLLOWAY RD	KER	77 A4
HOLLOW LOG RD	PLA	34 E8
HOLLY AV	LACO	118 H2
HOLLY RD	SBD	91 J1
HOLLY RD	TRI	17 L0
HOLLYWOOD BLVD	LA	181 L1
HOLLYWOOD BLVD	LA	182 L1
HOLLYWOOD BLVD	LACO	97 D6
HOLLYWOOD BLVD	LACO	117 J3
HOLLYWOOD FRWY	LA	181 D3
HOLLYWOOD FRWY	LA	185 B6
HOLLYWOOD FRWY	LA	186 D1
HOLLYWOOD FRWY	LACO	97 C6
HOLLYWOOD FRWY	LACO	117 H3
HOLLYWOOD LN	SBD	101 C7
HOLLYWOOD WY	BUR	179 G3
HOLLYWOOD WY	LA	179 G3
HOLLYWOOD WY	LACO	97 B6
HOLLYWOOD WY	LACO	117 F3
HOLMAN HWY	MONT	167 N4
HOLMAN HWY	MON	53 K7
HOLMAN HWY	MON	168 A4
HOLMES AV	KER	78 N2
HOLMES LN	SOL	39 D1
HOLMES RD	SBD	84 K4
HOLMES ST	ALA	46 E4
HOLMS FLAT RD	HUM	16 J2
HOLOHAN RD	SCR	54 E4
HOLSTEAD RD	SBD	81 P5
HOLT	SJCO	39 P9
HOLT AV	LACO	118 K6
HOLT BLVD	MTCL	203 N3
HOLT BLVD	ONT	203 N3
HOLT BLVD	ONT	204 N1
HOLT BLVD	POM	203 N3
HOLT BLVD	SBD	98 D6
HOLT RD	IMP	110 N4
HOLT RD	KER	79 P9
HOLT RD	KER	80 N0
HOLTON RD	IMP	110 Q2
HOLTVLE DUMP RD	IMP	110 P5
HOLTZWL	MPA	48 D9
HOLTZWL	MPA	49 D0
HOLZHAUSER LN	SIS	11 A6
HOME AV	SD	216 G7
HOME AV	SDCO	106 L4
HOME AV	SDCO	111 B6
HOME RD	STA	47 B7
HOMEDALE RD	KLAM	5 B4
HOMES RD	SBD	91 K8
HOMESTEAD AV	SAL	171 K3
HOMESTEAD RD	SLO	76 D2
HOMESTEAD RD	SCLR	150 J5
HOMESTEAD RD	SCL	45 M9
HOMESTEAD RD	SCLR	151 H1
HOMESTEAD RD	SVL	150 J5
HOMEWOOD CYN RD	INY	71 L2
HONDA RD	SB	86 H2
HONEY BEE RD	SHA	18 G3
HONEY RUN RD	BUT	25 G4
HONEY SPGS RD	SDCO	112 C2
HONEY WAGON RD	IMP	109 D8
HONOLULU AV	IMP	109 E5
HONOLULU AV	LACO	117 E5
HONOLULU RD	KER	78 L1
HOOD FRANKLN RD	SAC	39 F8
HOOKER CREEK RD	HUM	16 N4
HOOKER CREEK RD	TEH	18 L5
HOOKTON RD	HUM	15 C7
HOOKTON RD	HUM	15 C7
HOOPER RD	YUB	33 D7
HOOVER RD	MCO	56 B4
HOOVER ST	LA	185 J5
HOOVER ST	LACO	117 M4
HOOVER FLAT RD	LAS	14 L4
HOPE AV	MCO	55 G8
HOPE ST	KLAM	5 B4
HOPE ST	LA	185 K8
HOPLAND ST	SBD	91 J3
HOPPER RD	STA	47 F8
HOPYARD RD	ALA	46 E2
HORIZON RD	SBD	91 B2
HORIZON ST	SBD	91 M4
HORN LN	SIS	11 B7
HORN RD	LAS	8 P7
HORNBROOK RD	SIS	4 G2
HORNBROOK AGER	SIS	4 G2
HORNITOS RD	MPA	48 H7
HORR RD	SHA	13 J7
HORSE CANYON RD	KER	80 C2
HORSE CREEK RD	SIS	3 H4
HORSE LAKE RD	LAS	21 C4
HORSE LINTO RD	HUM	10 M6
HORSE RDG LKOUT	TRI	17 K0
HORSESHOE RD	STA	47 B9
HORSESHOE RD	STA	48 B0
HORSESHOE BND RD	PLA	34 L3
HORSESHOE HL RD	MAR	37 P9
HORSESHOE MDWS	INY	60 M1
HORTON CREEK RD	INY	51 K4
HOSLER AV	BUT	25 G1
HOSPITAL LN	RED	122 P4
HOTCHKISS RD	TRI	22 B9
HOT CK RANCH RD	MNO	50 F9
HOT CK RANCH RD	MNO	51 E0
HOTLUM	SIS	12 B5
HOT SPRINGS RD	ALP	36 N3
HOT SPRINGS RD	RCO	109 C7
HOT SPRINGS RD	TUL	69 L0
HOUGHTON AV	TEH	24 D7
HOUGHTON RD	KER	78 K5
HOUSE RD	IMP	109 P8
HOUSE RD	LAS	14 H5
HOUSTON AV	KIN	67 C6
HOUSTON AV	TUL	68 B2
HOVLEY RD	IMP	110 L1
HOWARD	SJCO	47 A0
HOWARD AV	FRCO	57 P1

STREET	CO.	PAGE & GRID
HOWARD AV	FRCO	57 H1
HOWARD AV	MCO	47 M8
HOWARD AV	MCO	48 M0
HOWARD AV	SD	214 P1
HOWARD RD	RCO	108 B3
HOWARD RD	STA	47 H2
HOWARD RD	TUL	68 M3
HOWARD CREEK RD	SIE	27 H1
HOWARD MTHWS RD	SJCO	40 Q0
HOWRDS GLCH FTG	MOD	14 B5
HOWE AV	SAC	39 A9
HOWE CREEK RD	HUM	15 G8
HOWELL AV	KER	80 B5
HOWELL RD	IMP	110 E1
HOWELL MTN RD	NAPA	29 D5
HOWELL MTN RD	NAPA	38 B3
HOWELLS RD	PLU	26 B2
HOWLAND HILL RD	DN	1 B5
HOWSLEY RD	SUT	33 L7
HOY RD	SIS	12 B4
HOY RD	TEH	18 N7
HOYER RD	STA	47 M4
HUASNA RD	SLO	76 M4
HUASNA TOWNSITE	SLO	76 M6
HUBBARD	PLA	34 H3
HUBBARD RD	LACO	89 L8
HUBBARD RD	LACO	89 P5
HUBBARD ST	LACO	117 B0
HUDSON AV	FRCO	56 E3
HUDSON RD	CAL	41 N0
HUDSON RD	MON	65 C1
HUDSON RD	SIS	4 J1
HUDSON RD	SUT	33 H8
HUERHUERO L PNZ	SLO	76 E4
HUEY RD	SLO	76 A1
HUFF RD	IMP	109 Q8
HUFF RD	SBD	91 J9
HUFF ST	RCO	108 B4
HUFFAKER RD	SUT	33 H8
HUFFMEISTER RD	COL	32 D4
HUFFORD RD	HUM	9 F9
HUFFORD RD	HUM	10 E0
HUGHES AV	CUL	183 P4
HUGHES AV	FRCO	57 M4
HUGHES AV	FRCO	67 A4
HUGHES AV	LA	183 P4
HUGHES RD	GV	127 E4
HUGHES RD	NEV	127 E4
HUGHES RD	SUT	33 F4
HULEN RD	MCO	47 Q5
HULEN RD	MCO	55 A5
HULL AV	MCO	48 M2
HULL RD	GLE	24 G0
HULL CREEK RD	TRI	23 C1
HULL MTN RD	LAK	23 N6
HULL VALLEY	MEN	23 E1
HULTBURG RD	STA	47 J7
HUMBOLDT AV	FRCO	56 J9
HUMBOLDT AV	FRCO	57 H0
HUMBOLDT RD	BUT	19 Q7
HUMBOLDT RD	BUT	25 G3
HUMBOLDT RD	C	124 L9
HUMBOLDT RD	DN	1 L8
HUMBOLDT RD	PLU	19 N8
HUMBOLDT RD	PLU	20 N1
HUMBLDT HILL RD	HUM	15 C8
HUMBUG RD	BUT	25 A7
HUMBUG RD	PLU	19 P8
HUMBUG RD	PLU	20 P1
HUMBUG CREEK RD	SIS	4 J0
HUMBUG HUMBOLDT	PLU	20 M2
HUMBUG WALKR RD	SIS	4 K0
HUME AV	KIN	67 C9
HUME RD	FRCO	58 H8
HUMPHREY CIR	PLU	20 P6
HUN RD	SBD	84 K4
HUNEWILL RCH RD	MNO	43 H2
HUNGRY CK MTRWY	PLU	20 N9
HUNGRY CK LO RD	SIS	4 F0
HUNGRY VLY RD	VEN	88 E7
HUNT RD	CAL	40 M8
HUNT RD	CAL	41 M0
HUNT RD	IMP	114 B3
HUNT RD	LAS	14 H4
HUNT RD	MCO	47 P5
HUNTER	MON	54 L5
HUNTER BLVD	RCO	103 L7
HUNTER ST	CAL	41 N1
HUNTER CREEK RD	DN	1 P9
HUNTER CREEK RD	DN	2 P0
HUNTER MTN RD	INY	61 M0
HUNTERS VALLEY	MPA	48 F8
HUNTINGTON AV	SBR	144 H4
HUNTINGTON DR	LACO	97 D9
HUNTINGTON DR	LACO	117 J7
HUNTINGTON DR	LACO	118 G4
HUNTLEY MINE RD	MNO	50 D8
HUNTSMAN AV	FRCO	56 M9
HUNTSMAN AV	FRCO	57 M4
HUNTSMAN AV	FRCO	58 M1
HUPP COUTOLENC	BUT	25 D6
HURDS GULCH RD	SIS	3 P7
HURLES CIR	BUT	25 M9
HURLETON RD	BUT	25 M8
HURLTN SWDS FLT	BUT	25 M9
HURLEY FLATS RD	RCO	100 H2
HURRICANE RD	SLO	77 K6
HUSMAN RD	MCO	47 Q5
HUSMAN RD	MCO	55 A5
HUSTED RD	COL	32 F8
HUSTON RD	IMP	110 P2
HUTCHINS	MCO	56 B2
HUTSELL RD	MEN	30 H9
HYAMPOM RD	TRI	17 J0
HYDE RD	IMP	113 B8
HYDE ST	FRCO	57 P2
HYDRIL RD	KIN	67 J0
HYPERION AV	LA	182 L7
I		
I AV	SBD	91 L4
I ST	BEN	153 K1
I ST	EUR	121 B6
I ST	MDO	162 H3
IBEX SPRING RD	SBD	72 N7
ICE HOUSE RD	ED	35 J5
ICE HOUSE RD	ED	35 M4
ICELAND RD	NEV	27 P8
IDA	MCO	56 D2
IDAHO AV	KIN	67 D6
IDAHO ST	SDCO	106 K3
IDAHO ST	SDCO	111 B6
IDAHO-MARYLAND	NEV	34 C5
IDAHO-MARYLD RD	GV	127 H7
IDAHO-MARYLD RD	NEV	127 H7
IDALEONA DR	RCO	99 J2
IDLEWOOD LN	HUM	9 G9
IDLEWOOD LN	HUM	10 G0
IKE CROW RD	STA	47 K4
ILLINOIS AV	TEH	24 E8
IMLER RD	IMP	109 M8
IMOLA AV	NAP	133 P5
IMOLA AV W	NAP	133 P3
IMPERIAL AV	EC	217 L2
IMPERIAL AV	IMP	110 Q1
IMPERIAL AV	SD	216 L1
IMPERIAL AV	SDCO	106 L4

STREET	CO.	PAGE & GRID
IMPERIAL AV	SDCO	111 C6
IMPERIAL HWY	IMP	113 B3
IMPERIAL HWY	LA	189 F2
IMPERIAL HWY	LACO	97 G7
IMPERIAL HWY	LACO	98 G2
IMPERIAL HWY	LACO	117 Q1
IMPERIAL HWY	LACO	118 Q5
IMPERIAL HWY	ORA	118 A1
IMPERIAL HWY	ORA	118 Q5
IMPERIAL HWY	ORA	120 A5
IMPERIAL ST	KER	77 E8
IMPERIAL ST	KER	78 E2
IMPERIAL DAM RD	IMP	116 P8
IMPERL GABLS RD	IMP	116 J2
INCLINE RD	MPA	49 E3
INCLINE RD	MPA	63 Q0
INDEPENDENCE RD	CAL	41 F2
INDPNDCE CEM RD	CAL	41 F3
INDEPNDNC LK RD	SIE	27 N5
INDEPNDNCIA MAT	BAJA	114 D2
INDIA ST	SD	215 C4
INDIAN AV	PMSP	206 L2
INDIAN AV	RCO	100 H5
INDIAN RD	LAS	21 K1
INDIANA AV	MCO	56 C2
INDIANA AV	STA	47 F8
INDIANA ST	LACO	117 M7
INDIANA RCH RD	YUB	26 N2
INDIANA SCH RD	YUB	26 P1
INDIAN CYN RD	KER	70 P3
INDIAN CEM RD	ALP	36 M3
INDIAN CV MT RD	SBD	101 D2
INDIAN CREEK RD	ALP	36 P4
INDIAN CREEK RD	KER	79 K6
INDIAN CREEK RD	MNO	51 E6
INDIAN CREEK RD	PLU	20 P9
INDIAN CREEK RD	RCO	100 K1
INDIAN CREEK RD	SIS	2 F7
INDIAN CREEK RD	SIS	3 M7
INDIAN CREEK RD	TRI	17 D6
INDIAN DIGGINS	ED	41 B2
INDIAN GULCH	MPA	48 H8
INDIAN GLCH EXT	MPA	48 K7
INDIAN HILL BL	CLA	203 H0
INDIAN HILL BL	LACO	98 D6
INDIAN HILL BL	POM	203 N0
INDIAN HILL RD	RCO	100 P5
INDIAN HILL RD	SIE	26 M5
INDIANOLA AV	FRCO	57 L8
INDIANOLA CTOFF	HUM	9 Q9
INDIANOLA CTOFF	HUM	10 Q0
INDIANOLA RESRV	HUM	15 D7
INDIAN OLE RD	LAS	20 L4
INDIAN PAINT DR	RCO	100 Q5
INDIAN PASS RD	IMP	116 M3
INDIAN PEAK	MPA	49 J3
INDIAN POINT RD	KER	79 K2
INDIAN RANCH RD	INY	71 F4
INDIAN ROCK RD	IMP	115 B6
INDIANS RD	MON	64 F7
INDIAN SCHOL RD	LPAZ	104 D1
INDIAN SRVCE RD	TUL	69 H1
INDIAN SPGS RD	ALP	36 N7
INDIAN SPGS RD	NEV	34 D3
INDIAN SPGS RD	SBD	81 K7
INDIAN TOM LAKE	SIS	5 F2
INDIAN VLY RD	MAR	38 L1
INDIAN VLY RD	MON	66 N1
INDIAN VLY RD	SLO	66 P1
INDIAN VLY RD	TRI	17 F0
INDIAN WELLS ST	KER	80 B6
INDUSTRIAL BLVD	MOH	96 K2
INDUSTRIAL PKWY	ALA	45 F9
INDSTRL FARM RD	KER	78 E5
INGHRAM RD	TEH	24 F7
INGLEWOOD AV	LACO	119 C3
INGLEWOOD BLVD	LA	188 F1
INGOMAR GRADE	MCO	55 B7
INGOMAR RD	MCO	47 Q6
INGOMAR RD	MCO	55 A6
INGRAHAM ST	SD	212 B3
INGRAHAM ST	SDCO	106 J1
INGRAM LN	SUT	33 B3
INGRAM CREEK RD	STA	47 H1
INGRAM CREEK RD	STA	47 H1
INK GRADE	NAPA	32 Q3
INLAND DR	SJCO	40 P0
INLAND FRWY	SD	214 G1
INLAND FRWY	SD	216 B5
INLAND FRWY	SDCO	106 N5
INLAND FRWY	SDCO	107 N4
INLAND FRWY	SDCO	111 D7
INLAND CTR DR	SBDO	207 L3
INSKIP RD	TEH	19 K1
INTAKE BLVD	RCO	103 Q7
INTERLAKE RD	SLO	65 P6
INTERNATIONL AV	FRCO	57 F6
INTERNATIONL AV	IMP	110 G2
INWOOD RD	SHA	19 G0
INYO N	INY	51 J7
INYO ST	DN	1 K7
INYOKERN RD	KER	80 B7
IONA AV	KIN	67 D6
IONE RD	SAC	40 E5
IOWA AV	RCO	99 E3
IOWA AV	STA	47 G4
IOWA CITY RD	YUB	33 B7
IOWA HILL	PLA	34 F7
IRIS AV	RCO	99 H2
IRIS CT	KER	79 C5
IRIS DR	SAL	171 F4
IRIS LN	SDCO	107 H6
IRIS RD	LAS	13 J9
IRIS RD	LAS	14 J0
IRIS WY	CAL	41 E2
IRIS CANYON RD	MONT	167 P9
IRIS CANYON RD	MONT	168 C8
IRMULCO RD	MEN	22 P8
IRONAGE RD	SBD	101 B8
IRONE AV	KER	89 C5
IRON MTN RD	SBD	91 C4
IRON MTN RD	SHA	18 C2
IRON MTN PUMPNG	SBD	102 C8
IRONWOOD AV	RCO	99 F4
IRONWOOD CT	KER	79 L3
IRVINE AV	CM	199 L4
IRVINE AV	ORA	199 C9
IRVINE AV	NB	199 L4
IRVINE BLVD	ORA	98 L5
IRVINE BLVD	ORA	120 H9
IRVINE RD	IMP	110 L4
IRVINE CENTR DR	ORA	98 L5
IRVINE CENTR DR	ORA	120 J8
IRVINE LODGE RD	MEN	22 K9
IRWIN RD	SBD	81 Q8
IRWIN RD	SBD	82 B7
IRWIN RD	SBD	208 B2
IRWIN RD	TEH	24 F4
IRWINDALE AV	LACO	118 J4
ISABELA-WLKR PS	KER	79 B6
ISABELA-WLKR PS	KER	80 A2
ISHI PISHI RD	HUM	10 D7
ISLAND RD	SHA	13 J7
ISLAND RD	SIS	3 Q7
ISLAND RD	SIS	11 B7
ISLAND BAR HILL	BUT	25 K9

STREET	CO.	PAGE & GRID
ISLAND MTN RD	HUM	22 B6
ISLAND MTN RD	TRI	22 B7
ISLAND PARK RD	FRCO	58 F2
ISPEN AV	MCO	48 N8
ITALIAN BAR RD	FRCO	50 Q1
ITALIAN BAR RD	TUO	41 L5
IVANHOE RD	SBD	91 M8
IVANPAH RD	SBD	84 G4
IVANPAH CIMA RD	SBD	84 J2
IVERSON LN	LAS	14 J3
IVERSON RD	MEN	30 L6
IVERSON RD	MON	54 N8
IVERSON ST	SAL	171 M2
IVESGROVE DR	LACO	89 G7
IVORY MILL RD	GLE	24 L0
IVY AV	MCO	56 B5
J		
J ST	DVS	136 F6
J ST	MDO	162 H2
J ST	MER	170 N5
J ST	SCTO	137 H9
J ST	SDCO	106 N5
J ST	SDCO	111 D7
JACALITOS CK RD	FRCO	66 H6
JACARANDA DR	KER	79 L3
JACK AV	KER	78 D2
JACKASS GRADE	SBT	55 M9
JACKASS HILL RD	TUO	41 N4
JACK CREEK RD	SLO	75 D9
JACK CREEK RD	SLO	76 D0
JACKLIN RD	SCL	46 K2
JACK PINE AV	KER	79 P8
JACK RABBIT TR	RCO	99 G7
JACK RANCH RD	KER	69 P2
JACK RANCH RD	KER	80 B7
JACKS RD	MON	54 N8
JACK SHAW RD	HUM	16 D3
JACK SLOUGH RD	YUB	33 D6
JACKSNIPE RD	SOL	38 J8
JACKSON	PLA	33 M8
JACKSON AV	KER	77 C9
JACKSON AV	KER	78 C2
JACKSON AV	KIN	67 D6
JACKSON AV	SJCO	47 C6
JACKSON DR	SDCO	106 J5
JACKSON DR	SDCO	107 Q7
JACKSON RD	IMP	110 K3
JACKSON RD	SAC	40 C1
JACKSON RD	SBD	91 J6
JACKSON RD	STA	47 E4
JACKSON ST	ALA	45 F8
JACKSON ST	RCO	99 G1
JACKSON ST	RCO	101 K1
JACKSON ST	SF	143 J6
JACKSON ST W	H	146 K7
JACKSON GATE RD	AMA	40 F8
JACKSON MDWS RD	SIE	27 M4
JACKSON RCH RD	HUM	9 P8
JACKSON VLY RD	AMA	40 G6
JACKSONVILLE RD	TUO	41 P4
JACK TONE	SJCO	40 N3
JACOBS	FRCO	58 L2
JACOBS WY	RCO	99 M2
JACOBY CREEK RD	HUM	10 P0
JACQUELINE	SIS	4 F5
JAHANT	SJCO	40 J1
JAIL RD	AVLN	105 N2
JAKE RD	RCO	100 N1
JALAMA RD	SB	86 K3
JAMACHA BLVD	SDCO	106 L6
JAMACHA RD	SDCO	106 K8
JAMACHA RD	SDCO	111 B7
JAMAICA BLVD	MOH	96 L2
JAMBOREE BLVD	IRV	198 L8
JAMBOREE BLVD	IRV	200 B4
JAMBOREE BLVD	ORA	120 K7
JAMBOREE RD	IRV	198 L8
JAMBOREE RD	NB	200 L0
JAMBOREE RD	ORA	98 N4
JAMES RD	FRCO	56 K8
JAMES RD	IMP	110 Q3
JAMES RD	KER	78 E6
JAMES LICK FRWY	SF	142 Q8
JAMES LICK SKWY	SF	142 L7
JAMES LICK SKWY	SF	143 Q6
JAMES LICK FRWY	SFCO	45 D4
JAMESON AV	FRCO	57 M2
JAMESON AV	FRCO	57 K2
JAMESON RD	KER	79 M6
JANE RD	SBD	92 M7
JANES RD	HUM	9 N9
JANES RD	HUM	10 N0
JANESVLLE CTOFF	LAS	21 L2
JANESVLLE GRADE	LAS	21 L2
JANICE AV	KER	79 C9
JANICE RD	SIS	4 F5
JANICE ST	KER	80 M1
JANSS RD	VEN	105 B7
JAPATUL RD	SBD	91 M5
JAPATUL RD	SBD	91 J6
JAPATUL RD	SDCO	108 Q4
JAQUIMA DR	CAL	41 L0
JARDINE RD	SLO	76 B2
JARED LN	SB	86 F9
J ARTHR YNGR FY	SMCO	45 G6
J ARTHR YNGR FY	FCTY	145 C6
J ARTHR YNGR FY	SM	145 C6
JARVIS AV	ALA	45 H9
JARVIS RD	ALP	36 L4
JASMINE RD	SBD	92 J2
JASPER LN	YUB	33 G8
JASPER RD	IMP	114 C2
JASPER RD	TUO	48 B3
JASPER SEARS BR	MCO	55 C5
JASPER SEARS RD	MCO	55 C5
JAVA AV	KIN	67 E4
JAVA DR	SVL	148 F9
JAVIS AV	KER	80 C5
JAVIS AV	KER	80 C8
JAWBONE CYN RD	KER	79 F8
JAWBONE CYN RD	KER	80 G0
JAY DEE LN	RCO	100 Q4
JAYMAR RD	HUM	16 G3
JAYNE AV	FRCO	66 G7
JEAN BLANC RD	INY	51 J6
JEAN NICHOLS RD	RCO	99 N6
JEANESE	TUO	41 P4
JEFF ST	KER	80 B5
JEFFERSON AV	FRCO	56 L8
JEFFERSON AV	FRCO	57 K4
JEFFERSON AV	FRCO	58 K0
JEFFERSON AV	RCO	99 P5
JEFFERSON BLVD	CUL	183 Q7
JEFFERSON BLVD	CUL	188 C5
JEFFERSON BLVD	LA	183 Q7
JEFFERSON BLVD	LA	185 N1
JEFFERSON BLVD	LACO	97 E6
JEFFERSON BLVD	LACO	117 L3
JEFFERSON BLVD	LACO	187 M7
JEFFERSON BLVD	LACO	188 K0
JEFFERSON BLVD	YOL	39 E6
JEFFERSON ST	MONT	167 K7
JEFFERSON ST	NAP	133 M4
JEFFERSON ST	ORA	120 C7
JEFFERSON ST	RCO	101 K0
JEFFERSON ST	SDCO	107 G3

JEFFERSON ST STREET INDEX LINCOLN AV

STREET	CO.	PAGE & GRID
JEFFERSON ST	SF	143 E1
JEFFERSON ST N	NAP	133 C3
JEFFERY RD	IMP	113 B8
JEFFREY RD	ORA	98 M5
JEFFREY RD	ORA	120 J8
JEFFREY RCH RD	MNO	51 F6
JELLYS FERRY RD	TEH	18 M6
JENEVEIN AV	SBR	144 J2
JENKS LAKE RD	SBD	100 B0
JENNINGS RD	STA	47 H4
JENNINGS PK RD	SDCO	106 G8
JENSEN AV	COL	32 H8
JENSEN AV	FRCO	56 K5
JENSEN AV	FRCO	57 J1
JENSEN RD	SLO	75 C8
JERROLD AV	FRCO	56 D3
JERRY COLLNS AV	MCO	48 N3
JERSEY	MCO	55 D8
JERSEY AV	KIN	67 D5
JERSEYDALE	MPA	49 G4
JERSEY ISLAND	CC	39 M5
JERUSALEM GRADE	LAK	32 L2
JESS VALLEY RD	MOD	8 G3
JESUS MARIA RD	CAL	41 G1
JETTY RD S	HUM	15 B7
JETTY RD S	HUM	15 B7
JEWELL AV	PAC	167 B1
JEWELL RD	TEH	18 K5
JEWELL VLY RD	SDCO	113 D0
JEWETT RD	HUM	16 Q6
JEWETT RD	SUT	33 J4
J HELT RD	HUM	15 D7
J HELT RD	HUM	15 D7
JIM DAY RD	SHA	13 K8
JIM HARVEY RD	SHA	18 D5
JIMMY DURNTE BL	SDCO	107 M4
JIM NEGRA RD	MCO	55 E5
JOAQUIN RD	ML	164 F6
JOAQUIN RDG LKT	FRCO	66 D5
JOEGER	PLA	34 H4
JOE SMITH RD	INY	51 K7
JOHANSEN RD	STA	47 F7
JOHN ST	RCO	100 H9
JOHN ST	SAL	171 L5
JOHN DALY BLVD	SMCO	45 E3
J F KENNEDY DR	RCO	99 G5
J F KENNEDY DR	SF	141 L2
JOHN FOX RD	STA	47 F8
JOHN GIBSON BL	LA	191 D1
JOHN LADD CHROM	SIS	3 J3
JOHN MUIR PKWY	CC	38 N7
JOHNNY MDW RD	MNO	43 Q8
JOHNNY MDW RD	MNO	50 A9
JOHNNY MDW RD	MNO	51 A0
JOHNS DR	TUL	68 G6
JOHNS RD	KER	79 G4
JOHN SCHOOL RD	COL	33 J1
JOHN SCHOOL RD	YOL	33 J1
JOHN SMITH RD	SBT	55 G0
JOHNSON	MCO	55 C7
JOHNSON AV	MCO	47 K7
JOHNSON AV	SDCO	106 H7
JOHNSON AV	SDCO	107 Q8
JOHNSON AV	SNLO	172 G5
JOHNSON AV	SLO	76 J2
JOHNSON CT	KER	79 M4
JOHNSON DR	TUL	58 M3
JOHNSON RD	HUM	10 F2
JOHNSON RD	HUM	15 F9
JOHNSON RD	KER	78 G4
JOHNSON RD	LAS	21 J3
JOHNSON RD	LACO	89 G6
JOHNSON RD	LACO	89 K7
JOHNSON RD	SBD	90 G9
JOHNSON RD	SBD	91 H5
JOHNSON RD	SBD	90 M9
JOHNSON RD	TEH	18 P3
JOHNSON RD	TEH	18 M6
JOHNSON ST	RCO	101 P3
JOHNSON ST	RCO	109 B3
JOHNSON ST	SBD	91 H8
JOHNSON ST	SB	87 B6
JOHNSON CYN RD	INY	72 G0
JOHNSON CYN RD	MON	54 N9
JOHNSON CYN RD	MON	55 N0
JOHNSON RCH RD	PLU	20 Q6
JOHNSON RCH RD	LAS	21 J3
JOHNSTON AV	KER	80 B6
JOHNSTON AV	RCO	99 L5
JOHNSVILLE RD	SIE	26 G6
JOHNSVLL MCCREA	PLU	26 G8
JOINES RD	YUB	33 C8
JOINT HWY 14	LAS	20 H9
JOINT HWY 14	LAS	21 G1
JOINT RD	TEH	18 P3
JOJOBA RD	RCO	108 B1
JOJOBA RD E	RCO	108 B1
JOLON RD	MON	65 H3
JOLON PLEYTO	MON	65 K3
JONATA PARK RD	SB	86 H7
JONATHAN ST	SBD	91 G2
JONES AV	COL	32 J9
JONES LN	MOD	8 C2
JONES RD	LAS	8 K3
JONES RD	MCO	48 K2
JONES ST	FRCO	57 P2
JONES ST	SF	143 F2
JONES ST	SMA	173 J6
JONES BAR RD	NEV	34 B4
JONES BRADWAY	SBD	92 J1
JONES VALLEY RD	SIE	27 L8
JORDAN RD	HUM	16 H3
JORDAN RD	MCO	47 M9
JORDAN RD	MCO	48 L0
JORDAN CREEK RD	MPA	48 C9
JORDAN CREEK RD	MPA	49 C0
JORDON HILL RD	BUT	25 F6
JORGENSEN RD	MCO	47 P5
JORGENSEN RD	STA	47 L4
JOSE BASIN RD	FRCO	50 Q1
JOSEPH PL	SIS	4 F5
JOSEPH CREEK RD	MOD	7 N4
JOSHUA DR	SBD	100 D7
JOSHUA LN	SBD	100 B8
JOSHUA RD	SBD	91 J5
JOSHUA RD	SBD	91 L7
JOSHUA RD	SBD	91 N5
JOSHUA WY	KER	79 P7
JOSHUA TREE RD	SBD	92 N5
JOY ST	KER	70 P1
J T CROW RD	STA	47 L5
JUAN ST	SD	213 P1
JUAN ST	SDCO	106 K2
JUBILEE PASS RD	INY	72 L4
JUDSON ST	SBD	99 D5
JUDSON ST	SBD	99 D5
JULIAN AV	SDCO	106 G8
JULIAN AV	SDCO	108 P0
JULIAN RD	SDCO	108 L0
JULIAN ST	SCL	46 M2
JULIAN ST	SJ	152 K0
JULIE ST	KER	79 G5
JUMAR CT	RCO	108 B2
JUMPER AV	KER	78 E1
JUNCAL RD	SB	87 K7
JCT CAMPGRND RD	MNO	43 P2
JUNE ST	SBD	99 B3

STREET	CO.	PAGE & GRID
JUNE LK BCH RD	MNO	50 B5
JUNIPER LN	SIS	4 N4
JUNIPER RD	LAS	14 J3
JUNIPER RD	RCO	99 J3
JUNIPER ST	SDCO	107 D4
JUNIPER FLTS RD	RCO	101 F1
JUNIPER FLTS RD	RCO	99 K6
JUNIPER HILL RD	LACO	90 L3
JUNIPR KNOLL RD	SIS	5 J0
JUNIPER LAKE RD	LAS	20 G1
JUNIPERO ST	CAR	168 K4
JUNIPERO SRA BL	SCL	45 K7
JUNIPERO SRA FY	CPTO	149 K5
JUNIPERO SRA FY	CPTO	150 L0
JUNIPERO SRA FY	MLBR	144 N1
JUNIPERO SRA FY	SJ	150 L0
JUNIPERO SRA FY	SMCO	45 J5
JUNIPERO SRA FY	SCL	149 K5
JUNIPER STA RD	MOD	7 P3
JUNKANS RD	SHA	18 G1
JURS RD	CAL	41 E3
JURUPA AV	RCO	99 F1
JURUPA AV	SBD	99 E0
JURUPA RD	RCO	99 E0
JUSTICE CT	KER	79 F7
JUSTICE RD	TRI	16 N8
JUTLAND DR	SD	211 M5
J W BARR	SIS	12 F5
K		
K ST	BEN	153 K1
K ST	MDO	162 H2
KADOTA AV	MCO	48 N6
KAGEL CANYON RD	LACO	117 B2
KAISER	SJCO	40 P3
KAISER RD	IMP	110 J4
KAISER RD	RCO	102 K4
KAISER RD	STA	47 G6
KALIN RD	IMP	110 K1
KAMM AV	FRCO	56 N9
KAMM AV	FRCO	57 N4
KAMM AV	TUL	57 N7
KAMM RD	IMP	110 P4
KANDRA RD	SIS	5 F6
KANE RD	HUM	9 G9
KANE RD	HUM	10 G0
KANE RD	SBD	91 E9
KANSAS AV	KIN	67 E6
KANSAS AV	MDO	162 G0
KANSAS AV	STA	47 F4
KAPAPA RD	SBD	80 B8
KAPRANOS RD	LAK	23 P5
KARCHNER RD	PLA	34 H0
KARCHNER RD	PLA	34 G1
KAREN AV	RCO	100 G5
KARLO RD	LAS	21 F5
KARNAK RD	SUT	33 M5
KASSON RD	SJCO	47 D1
KATELLA AV	ANA	193 M4
KATELLA AV	ANA	194 L3
KATELLA AV	OR	194 L3
KATELLA AV	ORA	98 J2
KATELLA AV	ORA	120 E6
KATHERINE RD	VEN	97 A1
KAUFENBERG RD	LAS	14 K1
KAUFFMAN AV	TEH	18 P8
KAUFMAN RD	STA	47 D8
KAUT RD	TRI	10 Q8
KAVANAUGH RD	IMP	114 A5
KEARNEY AV	FRCO	57 J1
KEARNEY BLVD	FRE	165 M2
KEARNY ST	SF	143 E5
KEARNY VILLA RD	SD	213 B9
KEARNY VILLA RD	SD	214 B0
KEARNY VILLA RD	SDCO	106 H3
KEARNY VILLA RD	SDCO	107 P6
KEATON	MCO	47 M7
KECKS RD	KER	77 A1
KEEFER RD	BUT	25 F1
KEEGAN RD	COL	32 E4
KEELE RD	RCO	116 B5
KEIM BLVD	RCO	116 B5
KELBAKER RD	SBD	83 J5
KELBAKER RD	SBD	84 N0
KELBAKER RD	SBD	94 C1
KELLEMS LN	SIS	3 Q6
KELLEMS LN	SIS	11 A6
KELLER RD	RCO	99 N5
KELLEY RD	SBD	101 C7
KELLOG RD	SUT	33 D3
KELLOGG DR	ORA	98 G5
KELLOGG DR	ORA	120 B8
KELLOGG RD	DN	1 H7
KELLOGG SRRA BL	RCO	100 G5
KELLY	SJCO	47 B6
KELLY RD	HUM	16 P1
KELLY RD	NAPA	38 F9
KELLY RD	TEH	24 D1
KELLY RD	YUB	26 P3
KELLY GULCH RD	SIS	11 E3
KELSEY CREEK RD	SIS	3 N3
KELSEY CREEK RD	LAK	31 J7
KELSO AV	KER	79 B8
KELSO RD	ALA	46 C6
KELSO RD	KER	79 B8
KELSO RD	SBD	83 K4
KELSO AMBOY RD	SBD	94 B0
KELSO CIMA RD	SBD	83 P9
KELSO CIMA RD	SBD	84 L1
KELSO CK VLY RD	KER	79 B8
KELSO VALLEY RD	KER	79 E9
KELSO VALLEY RD	KER	80 E0
KEMP CT	HUM	16 H3
KEMPER RD	KER	80 J1
KEMPER RD	STA	47 E7
KEMPTON RD	SUT	33 H8
KENDALL AV	KER	80 C7
KENDALL DR	SBD	99 B3
KENDLE RD	IMP	110 M4
KENMAR LN	KER	79 L0
KENNEBRAW LN	HUM	16 L4
KENNEDY AV	BUT	25 G1
KENNEDY RD	TRI	17 B2
KENNEDY MEADOW	TUL	70 J1
KENNEDY MEM DR	SHA	18 E2
KENNETH AV	SAC	34 P2
KENNETH RD	LACO	117 F4
KENNETT RD	SHA	18 C4
KENNEY AV	TEH	18 M5
KENNY AV	MCO	48 K3
KENNY CAMP RD	TRI	11 P6
KENO WORDEN RD	KLAM	5 C1
KENSINGTON WY	S	160 E3
KENT AV	KIN	67 E3
KENT AV	KIN	67 E4
KENT AV	MAR	139 P2
KENT RD	SUT	33 C5
KENTUCKY AV	YOL	33 P3
KENTUCKY ST	FRFD	135 J3
KENWOOD	SDCO	111 B8
KENWOOD DR	SDCO	106 K6
KEOUGH HOT SPGS	INY	51 N6
KERN RD	SBD	101 B6
KERN ST	SAL	171 K7
KERN CANYON RD	KER	79 F0
KERN RIV CYN RD	KER	79 D3
KERSHAW RD	IMP	110 K2

STREET	CO.	PAGE & GRID
KERTO RD	KER	78 N1
KESTER AV	LACO	117 G0
KESWICK DAM RD	SHA	18 D3
KETTLEMAN LN	SJCO	40 L1
KETTNER BLVD	SD	215 K6
KETTNER BLVD	SDCO	106 L3
KEYES RD	MCO	48 G2
KEYES RD	STA	47 G7
KEYES RD	STA	48 G0
KEYES ST	SJ	152 N6
KEYS RD	SUT	33 M8
KEYSTONE RD	IMP	110 N0
KEYSVILLE RD	KER	79 B5
KEZAR DR	SF	141 M7
KIBBE RD	YUB	33 C7
KICKAPOO TR	SBD	100 D7
KIDDER AV	FRFD	135 G5
KIDDER CREEK RD	SIS	3 Q5
KIDDER CK RD S	SIS	3 Q6
KIDDER CK RD S	SIS	11 A6
KID LAKES	PLA	35 A4
KIDWELL RD	SOL	39 C3
KIEFER BLVD	SAC	40 C2
KIEFER RD	IMP	114 C4
KIELY BLVD	SJ	150 N8
KIELY BLVD	SCLR	150 H7
KIERNAN AV	STA	47 D3
KIETZKE LN	RENO	130 J8
KIFER RD	SCLR	150 A6
KIFER RD	SVL	150 A1
KILAGA SPGS RD	PLA	34 H2
KILAGA SPG RD N	PLA	34 H2
KILBURN AV	NAP	133 K1
KILBURN RD	STA	47 K5
KILER CANYON RD	SLO	75 C9
KILER CANYON RD	SLO	76 C0
KILGORE	SUT	33 E1
KILKARE RD	ALA	46 F2
KILROY	STA	47 J7
KIMBALL AV	SBD	98 F7
KIMBALL LN	YUB	33 D7
KIMBERLINA RD	KER	78 C3
KIMBERLY CT	KER	79 P4
KIMBERLY DR	KER	79 N4
KIMBERLY RD	SHA	18 H6
KIMTU CT	HUM	16 Q3
KINCAID RD	SCL	46 L5
KINE AV	RCO	99 H5
KINEVAN RD	SB	87 K3
KING AV	KIN	67 E5
KING RD	COL	32 E5
KING RD	IMP	114 B4
KING RD	KER	67 P4
KING RD	PLA	34 L3
KING RD	SJ	152 B7
KING RD	SCL	46 M3
KING RD	SCL	152 B7
KING RD	SOL	39 E5
KING RD	TRI	12 K1
KING ST	BKD	166 M9
KING CITY RD	SBT	65 C5
KINGDON	SJCO	40 L0
KING RANCH RD	BUT	25 P8
KING RIDGE RD	SON	37 A1
KINGS AV	FRCO	66 F6
KINGS RD	SBD	90 L9
KINGS RD	TUO	48 A9
KINGS RD	TUO	49 A0
KINGSBURY RD	TRI	17 F3
KINGS CANYON RD	FRCO	58 J1
KINGS HILL RD	PLA	34 E3
KINGSLEY ST	MTCL	203 M1
KINGS MTN RD	SMCO	45 K5
KINGS PEAK RD	HUM	16 Q0
KINGSTON RD	SBD	83 D8
KINGS VALLEY RD	DN	1 J8
KINNEY RD	MEN	30 H4
KIOWA BLVD	MOH	96 K2
KIOWA RD	RCO	102 J5
KIOWA RD	SBD	91 L5
KIP ST	KER	80 B5
KIRBY RD	MCO	48 M5
KIRKER PASS	CC	39 P2
KIRKVILLE RD	SUT	33 J4
KIRSCHENMANN RD	SB	87 B6
KIT CARSON CPGD	ALP	36 L2
KLAMATH BCH RD	DN	1 Q9
KLAMATH BCH RD	DN	9 A9
KLAMATH BCH RD	DN	10 A0
KLAMATH MILL RD	DN	1 Q9
KLAMATH RIV RD	SIS	3 J7
KLASSETTE ST	KER	80 L1
KLAU MINE RD	SLO	75 B7
KLIPSTEIN ST	KER	78 N1
KLIPSTEIN CY RD	KER	78 P1
KLOKE RD	IMP	114 C2
KLONDIKE RD	SBD	93 G4
KLONDIKE MINE RD	TRI	17 J0
KNEELAND RD	HUM	16 C2
KNIGHTON RD	SHA	18 G4
KNIGHTS RD	SUT	33 H4
KNIGHTSEN AV	CC	39 N5
KNOB PK LKOT RD	SHA	17 J6
KNOTT AV	ORA	98 J2
KNOTT AV	ORA	120 F3
KNOW	PLA	33 N9
KNOWLES RD	MCO	56 A5
KNOX RD	STA	47 C8
KNOXVL DVLHD RD	NAPA	32 L5
KOALA RD	SBD	91 H1
KOCH RD	KER	78 F3
KOENIGSTEIN RD	VEN	88 K6
KOESTER RD	KER	79 K6
KOSTER ST	EUR	121 C3
KOWOLOWSKI RD	MOD	6 F1
KRAEMER BLVD	ORA	120 B6
KRAFT RD	KER	78 P8
KRAMAR RD	IMP	113 B9
KRAMER BLVD	ORA	98 G4
KRAMER RD	LAS	14 H2
KRAMER RD	SBD	91 B1
KRATZMEYER RD	KER	78 F4
KROSENS RD	YUB	25 Q8
KRUSE RD	COL	32 B7
KRUSE RANCH RD	SON	37 B0
KT RD	SBT	54 H9
KT RD	SBT	55 H0
KUBLER RD	IMP	113 C9
KUENZLI ST	RENO	130 F6
KUMBERG RD	IMP	114 C5
KURT RD	KER	77 C8
KUTZ RD	IMP	109 P8
KYLE AV	KER	70 P1
KYTE AV	KER	78 D5
L		
L ST	DVS	136 G7
L ST	DN	1 L7
L ST	MDO	162 H2
L ST	SCTO	137 G2
L ST	SDCO	106 N5
L ST	SDCO	111 D7
LA BARR MDWS RD	NEV	34 D4
LABP & L RD	SBD	91 M1
LA BREA AV	LA	181 K4
LA BREA AV	LA	184 H4
LA BREA AV	LACO	97 E6

STREET	CO.	PAGE & GRID
LA BREA AV	LACO	117 N3
LA BREA CK RD	SB	77 Q0
LA BRISA DR	SBD	100 A8
LA BRUCHERIE RD	IMP	114 B1
LA CADENA DR	CLTN	207 L0
LA CADENA DR	SBD	90 G8
LA CADENA DR	SBD	99 E3
LACEY BLVD	KIN	67 C4
LA CIENEGA BLVD	BH	183 E8
LA CIENEGA BLVD	CUL	183 Q9
LA CIENEGA BLVD	ING	188 M9
LA CIENEGA BLVD	ING	189 F0
LA CIENEGA BLVD	LA	183 L8
LA CIENEGA BLVD	LACO	97 F6
LA CIENEGA BLVD	LACO	117 N2
LA CIENEGA BLVD	LACO	183 E8
LA CIENEGA BLVD	LACO	188 C9
LA CIENEGA BLVD	LACO	189 F9
LACK RD	IMP	110 M0
LA COLINA	TUL	68 G9
LA COLINA LN	RCO	108 B4
LA CONTENTA RD	SBD	100 D8
LA COSTA AV	SDCO	107 J4
LA CRESCENTA AV	LACO	117 F6
LA CRESTA DR	SDCO	108 Q1
LA CRESTA RD	SDCO	106 H9
LA CUARTA ST	LACO	118 N2
LADD RD	STA	47 D5
LADDER RIDGE RD	LAK	31 D7
LA ENTRADA AV	LACO	118 N3
LAFAYETTE RD	SIE	26 N7
LAFAYETTE ST	SCL	46 K1
LAFAYETTE ST	SCLR	151 A2
LAFAYETTE ST	S	160 P7
LAG JAC	FRCO	58 L0
LA GLORIA RD	SBT	55 N2
LAGOMARSINO AV	MON	65 D3
LAGOON DR	KER	78 F1
LA GRANADA	SDCO	107 L5
LA GRANDE RD	COL	32 D5
LA GRANGE RD	MCO	48 F4
LA GRANGE RD	STA	48 E4
LA GRANGE RD	TUO	48 B4
LAGUE RD	YUB	26 N0
LAGUNA AV	FRCO	67 A2
LAGUNA FRWY	ORA	98 M6
LAGUNA FRWY	ORA	120 L9
LAGUNA RD	SON	37 D7
LAGUNA RD	VEN	105 B4
LAGUNA CYN RD	LAG	201 D3
LAGUNA CYN RD	ORA	98 P6
LAGUNA CYN RD	ORA	120 P9
LAGUNA CREEK TR	SOL	38 G9
LAGUNA MTN RD	SDCO	108 P6
LAGUNA SECA DR	SBD	91 L6
LAGUNA SECA RD	MCO	55 G7
LA HABRA BLVD	ORA	118 Q4
LA HABRA BLVD	ORA	120 A4
LA HONDA RD	SMCO	45 M6
LAIRD RD	PLA	34 M3
LAIRD RD	STA	47 G4
LAIRO RED ROCK	SIS	5 H3
LA JOLLA AV	SDCO	107 P5
LA JOLLA BLVD	SDCO	106 H1
LA JOLLA BLVD	SDCO	107 P4
LA JOLLA AMAGO	SDCO	108 F1
LA JOLLA S DR N	SD	211 F3
LA JOLLA S RD S	SD	211 M0
LA JOLLA SHR DR	SD	211 D1
LA JOLLA VLG RD	SDCO	106 G2
LAKE AV	FRCO	56 J9
LAKE AV	FRCO	57 J0
LAKE AV	KER	79 F4
LAKE AV	LACO	98 B0
LAKE AV	LACO	117 H8
LAKE AV	PAS	190 M7
LAKE AV	SCR	54 E4
LAKE BLVD	SHA	18 D4
LAKE DR	SBD	91 Q4
LAKE RD	FRCO	50 P3
LAKE RD	KER	80 H4
LAKE RD	MCO	48 L4
LAKE RD	STA	47 F9
LAKE RD	STA	48 F3
LAKE RD N	INY	51 N3
LAKE RD S	INY	51 P4
LAKE RD S	KER	78 M2
LAKE RD S	KER	78 L4
LAKE ST	MAD	57 D1
LAKE ST	RCO	99 L2
LK ALMANOR W DR	PLU	20 M2
LK ALMANR RD E	PLU	20 M4
LK ALPINE RD E	ALP	42 C1
LK ALPINE RD W	ALP	42 D1
LAKE ANNIE RD	MOD	7 H7
LK BRITTON LOOP	SHA	13 L6
LK BRITTON RAMP	SHA	13 L6
LAKE CALIF DR	TEH	18 J6
LAKE CANYON RD	LACO	89 H3
LAKE CANYON RD	LACO	89 G4
LAKE CHABOT RD	ALA	45 D8
LK CITY DUMP RD	MOD	7 N7
LAKE CREST RD	LAS	21 L3
LAKE DAVIS RD	PLU	27 E2
LAKE EARL DR	DN	1 K7
LAKE FOREST DR	ORA	98 M7
LAKE FRANCES RD	YUB	26 P2
LAKE HERMAN RD	SOL	38 L7
LAKE HERMAN RD	SOL	153 B5
LK JENNINGS PK	SDCO	108 P0
LAKELAND RD	LACO	118 Q1
LAKELAND RD	LACO	120 A1
LAKE LEAVITT RD	LAS	21 J3
LAKE MARY RD	ML	164 L0
LAKE MARY RD	MNO	50 F7
LAKE MATHEWS DR	RCO	99 J2
LAKE MCCUMBER	SHA	19 F3
LAKE MORENA DR	SDCO	112 C6
LAKE MURRAY BL	SDCO	106 J5
LAKE MURRAY BL	SDCO	107 Q7
LAKE POWAY RD	SDCO	107 L7
LAKERIDGE RD	SHA	19 G1
LAKE SHORE AV	O	158 J2
LAKESHORE BLVD	LAK	31 G6
LAKESHORE DR	KLAM	5 A2
LAKESHORE DR	LAK	32 H0
LAKESHORE DR	SHA	12 N4
LAKESHORE RD	MOD	7 L3
LAKESIDE DR	O	158 G1
LAKE STATION RD	KER	78 M2
LAKE TAHOE BLVD	SLT	129 L0
LAKEVIEW	KIN	67 F4
LAKEVIEW	PLA	34 G1
LAKEVIEW AV	ORA	120 D8
LAKEVIEW AV	RCO	99 J6
LAKE VIEW DR	LAS	21 L3
LAKE VIEW DR	SLO	75 B6
LAKEVIEW RD	SCR	54 E4
LAKEVIEW RD	SDCO	106 G8
LAKEVIEW RD	SDCO	108 P0
LAKEVIEW RD	SON	38 K2
LAKEVIEW CEM RD	SIS	5 J0
LAKEWOOD BLVD	LACO	98 H0
LAKEWOOD BLVD	LACO	119 D8
LAKEWOOD DR	MEN	23 Q1
LAKIN DAM RD	SIS	13 F0

STREET	CO.	PAGE & GRID
LA LOMA AV	B	156 D2
LA LOMA AV	MDO	162 G5
LA LOMA AV	VEN	88 P4
LA LOMA RD	LACO	117 H7
LAMB BLVD	CLK	74 F8
LAMB CANYON RD	RCO	99 H8
LAMBERT LN	LAS	21 K4
LAMBERT RD	LACO	118 P2
LAMBERT RD	ORA	118 Q5
LAMBERT RD	ORA	120 A5
LAMBERT RD	SAC	39 G8
LAMBIE' RD	SOL	39 J2
LAMBUTH RD	STA	47 B7
LAMERT LN	GLE	24 P7
LA MESA BLVD	SDCO	106 K6
LA MESA RD	SBD	90 K8
LA MIRADA AV	LACO	118 Q3
LA MIRADA AV	LACO	120 A3
LA MIRADA BLVD	LACO	98 G2
LAMPLEY RD	STA	48 F1
LAMPSON AV	GGR	195 C0
LAMPSON AV	ORA	120 F3
LANCASTER BLVD	KER	90 C3
LANCASTER BLVD	LACO	90 F1
LANCASTER RD	LACO	88 D9
LANCASTER RD	LACO	89 E0
LANCASTER RD	STA	47 C9
LANCASTER RD	STA	48 C0
LANDACRE RD	TRI	17 F2
LANDAU BLVD	RCO	100 J6
LANDECENA DR	TRI	17 B6
LANDER AV	MCO	47 N7
LANDER AV	STA	47 J8
LANDERGEN RD	HUM	15 M9
LANDES RD	TEH	18 K5
LANDESS RD	SCL	46 K2
LANDIS GULCH	TRI	17 J4
LANDRAM AV	MCO	48 M2
LANES RD	FRCO	57 F5
LANES VALLEY RD	TEH	19 J0
LANFAIR RD	SBD	84 J6
LANFAIR RD	SBD	94 A9
LANGDON RD	MCO	55 E7
LANGLL VLY RD E	KLAM	5 B8
LANGLL VLY RD E	KLAM	6 C1
LANGLL VLY RD W	KLAM	5 B8
LANGLL VLY RD W	KLAM	6 D1
LANGTRY RD	NAPA	38 C2
LANGWORTH RD	STA	47 E7
LANINI RD	MON	54 P8
LANKERSHIM BLVD	LA	179 P0
LANKERSHIM BLVD	LACO	97 B6
LANKERSHIM BLVD	LACO	117 E2
LANNAGAN RD	TRI	11 Q3
LANNAGAN RD	TRI	17 A3
LANPHERE RD	HUM	9 N9
LANSING AV	KIN	67 E4
LA PALMA AV	ANA	193 B7
LA PALMA AV	ANA	194 B0
LA PALMA AV	KER	80 N1
LA PALMA AV	ORA	98 H1
LA PALMA AV	ORA	120 D3
LA PALOMA	AVLN	105 L1
LA PALOMA DR	TUL	68 G9
LA PALOMA RD	MCO	48 K4
LA PANZA AV	SB	87 D8
LA PAZ RD	ORA	98 N7
LA PORTE RD	BUT	25 Q8
LA PORTE RD	BUT	26 L2
LA PORTE RD	SIE	26 N1
LA PORTE RD	YUB	26 Q4
LA POSTA RD	SDCO	112 C7
LA PUENTE RD	LACO	118 M6
LARCHMONT BLVD	LA	184 C8
LARGO GRANDE	RCO	108 B2
LARGO VISTA RD	LACO	90 L6
LARKELLEN AV	LACO	118 L5
LARKIN RD	BUT	25 M6
LARKIN RD	SUT	33 C5
LARKIN VALLEY	SCR	54 E3
LARKMEAD LN	NAPA	29 D2
LARKSPUR DR	MLBR	144 P2
LARREA AV	SBD	101 C3
LARRY FLAT	MOD	7 G6
LARSON LN	MNO	42 B8
LARSON RD	IMP	110 N0
LARSON RD	RCO	108 B4
LA RUE RD	YOL	136 J3
LA SALLE CANYON	SB	86 H2
LAS AMIGAS RD	NAPA	38 J5
LAS FLORES AV	KER	80 B5
LA SIERRA AV	RCO	99 G1
LAS LOMAS AV	AVLN	105 N1
LAS PALMAS AV	STA	47 J4
LAS PASOS	VEN	105 B4
LAS PLGAS CY RD	SDCO	107 E1
LAS ROCAS	RCO	100 M7
LASSELLE ST	RCO	99 G5
LASSEN	TEH	25 D0
LASSEN AV	BUT	25 G2
LASSEN AV	FRCO	67 B0
LASSEN AV	FRCO	57 J0
LASSEN ST	LAS	8 K2
LASSEN ST	NAP	133 B1
LASSEN TRAIL	TEH	19 M6
LASSEN CREEK RD	MOD	7 M5
LASSEN PARK HWY	SHA	19 F6
LASSICS LKOT RD	TRI	16 L8
LASSICS LOOKOUT	TRI	16 L8
LAST CHANCE CYN	KER	80 E4
LAST CHANCE MNE	NEV	26 Q9
LAS TUNAS DR	LACO	118 J0
LAS VARAS RD	SB	87 L1
LAS VEGAS BLVD	CLK	74 H7
LAS VEGAS BL S	CLK	209 N4
LAS VEGAS BL S	CLK	210 M2
LAS VEGAS BL S	LV	209 N4
LAS VEGAS EXPWY	CLK	74 E6
LAS VIRGENES RD	LACO	97 B1
LATHAM	SUT	33 G3
LATHROP RD	MAN	161 A0
LATHROP RD	SJCO	47 B1
LATHROP RD	SJCO	161 A6
LATIGO CYN RD	LACO	97 E1
LA TIJERA BLVD	LA	188 Q5
LA TIJERA BLVD	LACO	117 P2
LATKA LN	TEH	19 K2
LATROBE RD	AMA	40 C6
LATROBE RD	ED	40 A5
LATROBE RD	SAC	40 C3
LA TUNA CYN RD	LACO	97 A7
LA TUNA CYN RD	LACO	117 D3
LAUFFER RD	HUM	2 A7
LAUGHLIN RD	STA	47 D8
LAURA DR	LAS	27 B8
LAUREL AV	KIN	67 E3
LAUREL AV	KIN	67 E4
LAUREL AV	ML	164 K5
LAUREL AV	MLBR	144 N5
LAUREL DR W	SAL	171 E1
LAUREL DR W	MON	171 E1
LAUREL LN	YUB	33 B6
LAUREL ST	NAP	133 K1
LAUREL ST	SD	215 E6
LAUREL ST	SDCO	106 L3
LAUREL ST	SC	169 K5
LAUREL WY	TEH	18 L5

STREET	CO.	PAGE & GRID
LAUREL CYN BLVD	LACO	97 B6
LAUREL CYN BLVD	LACO	117 C0
LAUREL DELL RD	LAK	31 E5
LAURELES GRADE	MON	54 N4
LAUREL GROVE AV	MAR	139 M2
LAUREL GROVE AV	ROSS	139 M1
LAURENT ST	SC	169 J2
LAURJOE RD	SBD	91 H8
LAUSTEN RD	COL	32 B7
LAUX RD	COL	33 C1
LAVA BED RD	BUT	25 G3
LAVA BDS NAT MN	MOD	6 M0
LAVA BDS MED LK	SIS	5 P5
LAVAL RD	KER	78 P8
LAVER CROSSING	LAS	21 Q8
LAVERNE AV	MAR	140 J1
LA VETA AV	OR	196 C2
LAVEZZOLA RD	SIE	26 K7
LAVIC RD	SBD	92 F9
LA VISTA AV	VEN	88 Q4
LAWRENCE EXPWY	SCLR	150 K4
LAWRENCE EXPWY	SJ	150 K4
LAWRENCE EXPWY	SVL	150 K4
LAWSON LN	HUM	15 F8
LAXAQUE RD	MOD	8 B7
LAYTNVL DOS RIO	MEN	22 J8
LAZARO CARDENAS	BAJA	114 D3
LAZARUS LN	RCO	100 Q0
L B CROW RD	STA	47 K5
LEAR AV	SBD	101 C2
LEARY RD	SAC	39 H7
LEASTALK AV	SBD	84 H4
LEATHER RD	IMP	116 Q7
LEAVENWORTH ST	SF	143 F2
LEAVESLEY RD	SCL	54 C7
LEAVITT RD	LAS	21 J2
LEE RD	MCO	48 J1
LEE RD	SHA	13 K9
LEE RD	SUT	33 K6
LEEDS	MCO	48 M5
LEEGE AV	SB	86 G3
LEE SCHOOL RD	SAC	40 E2
LEESVILLE RD	COL	32 E4
LEESVL-LODGA RD	COL	32 C3
LEFF RD	RCO	108 B2
LEFFINGWELL RD	LACO	118 Q2
LEFFINGWELL RD	LACO	120 A2
LEGION PARK DR	MDO	162 N8
LE GRAND RD	MCO	48 N6
LEGRAY RD	KER	78 P8
LEILA LN	SBD	101 B8
LEIMERT BLVD	LACO	117 M3
LEININGER RD	TEH	25 C0
LEISER RD	SUT	33 L4
LEISURE TOWN RD	SOL	39 F1
LELITER RD	KER	70 P5
LEMON AV	SDCO	106 K6
LEMON AV	SDCO	111 B8
LEMON AV	SJCO	47 C6
LEMON AV	STA	47 H3
LEMON RD	SBD	91 L4
LEMON ST	ORA	120 C5
LEMON ST	VAL	134 P7
LEMON CANYON RD	SIE	27 K5
LEMOS RD	SIS	4 F1
LENAHAN RD	COL	32 A6
LENARD RD	LAS	14 H4
LENGER	SUT	33 F2
LENINGER RD	BUT	25 F0
LENTELL RD	HUM	15 B8
LENWOOD RD	SBD	91 B6
LEO RD	RCO	108 A1
LEON AV	MCO	56 D2
LEON RD	RCO	99 K6
LEONA AV	LACO	89 H7
LEONARD AV	FRCO	57 L7
LEONARD AV	KER	78 E1
LEONARD RD	MPA	49 J4
LEONI RD	ED	41 A3
LEOTA ST	MCO	55 B6
LEPRECHAUN LN	RCO	108 B2
LERDO HWY	KER	77 E6
LERDO HWY	KER	78 E0
LESSING ST	SBD	91 H0
LETTS VALLEY RD	COL	31 B9
LEVEE RD	IMP	115 A7
LEVEE RD	YOL	39 E5
LEVERONI RD	SON	38 J3
LEVERONI RD	SON	132 Q2
LEVIATHAN LKOUT	ALP	36 N6
LEVIATHAN RD	ALP	36 N6
LEWELLING BLVD	ALA	146 B2
LEWIS RD	MON	54 F4
LEWIS RD	SHA	13 K8
LEWIS RD	SOL	39 G2
LEWIS RD	STA	47 L5
LEWIS RD	VEN	105 B5
LEWIS RD	YUB	33 G8
LEWIS CREEK RD	MON	65 D7
LEWISTON AV	FRCO	67 A4
LEWISTON RD	SHA	18 C0
LEWISTON RD	TRI	17 C7
LEWISTON TURNPK	TRI	17 C8
LEXINGTON AV	SDCO	106 J8
LEXINGTON AV	SDCO	107 Q9
LEXINGTON ST	SCLR	151 G3
LEXINGTN HLL RD	PLU	26 H5
LIBERAL AV	TEH	24 E6
LIBERTY RD	SJCO	40 H2
LIBERTY RD W	BUT	25 Q3
LIBERTY ISLD RD	SOL	39 J4
LIBRAMIENTO SUR	BAJA	111 G7
LIBRAMNT ORIENT	BAJA	111 F7
LICHEN WY	RCO	108 B2
LIEBERT RD	IMP	113 B8
LIGGET AV	COL	32 H8
LIGHTHILL RD	SIS	3 P6
LIGHTHOUSE AV	MONT	167 F7
LIGHTHOUSE AV	MON	53 F9
LIGHTHOUSE AV	PAC	167 D3
LIGHTHOUSE RD	HUM	15 L6
LIKELY DUMP RD	MOD	8 G3
LILLY VALLEY WY	CAL	41 D4
LILY GAP RD	CAL	41 D4
LIM RD	LAS	14 H5
LIME CREEK RD	CAL	40 J8
LIMEDYKE LKOUT	TRI	16 F9
LIME GULCH RD	SIS	4 Q1
LIME GULCH RD	SIS	12 A1
LIMEKILN RD	MON	54 P7
LIME KILN RD	NEV	34 A4
LIMEKILN RD	SBT	54 K9
LIMEKILN RD	SBT	55 K0
LIME KILN RD	TUO	38 C3
LIME SADDLE RD	BUT	25 H6
LIMONITE AV	RCO	99 F0
LINCOLN	LACO	97 E5
LINCOLN	MCO	48 Q3
LINCOLN AV	ANA	193 E2
LINCOLN AV	ANA	194 D2
LINCOLN AV	FRCO	56 L7
LINCOLN AV	FRCO	57 L1
LINCOLN AV	FRCO	58 L1
LINCOLN AV	KIN	67 F4
LINCOLN AV	LACO	117 F8
LINCOLN AV	LACO	190 C2

SEE PAGE D FOR INSTRUCTIONS

STREET INDEX

STREET	CO.	PAGE	GRID
LINCOLN AV	OR	194	E8
LINCOLN AV	ORA	98	J2
LINCOLN AV	ORA	120	D2
LINCOLN AV	PAS	190	D2
LINCOLN AV	RCO	98	H8
LINCOLN AV	SAL	171	K4
LINCOLN AV	SD	214	Q1
LINCOLN AV	SDCO	107	H7
LINCOLN AV	SR	139	G6
LINCOLN AV	SA	196	G5
LINCOLN AV	SCL	46	M2
LINCOLN AV	YUB	33	C8
LINCOLN AV W	NAP	133	H1
LINCOLN BLVD	BUT	25	N7
LINCOLN BLVD	LA	187	C0
LINCOLN BLVD	LACO	117	M0
LINCOLN BLVD	LACO	187	J7
LINCOLN BLVD	MCO	47	M9
LINCOLN BLVD	MCO	48	M0
LINCOLN BLVD	SMON	187	C0
LINCOLN RD	SBD	91	L9
LINCOLN RD	SUT	33	E4
LINCOLN RD	SUT	125	P0
LINCOLN RD	YUBA	125	P0
LINCOLN ST	NAPA	29	C0
LINCOLN ST	NAPA	38	B1
LINCOLN ST	RCO	101	P3
LINCOLN ST	S	169	L2
LINCOLN ST	S	160	P6
LINCOLN ST N	KER	77	L9
LINCOLN ST N	KER	78	L0
LINCOLN WY	AUB	126	F7
LINCOLN WY	SF	141	M5
LINCOLN WY	SFCO	45	C3
LINCOLN WY E	PLA	126	E7
LINCOLN WY E	PLA	126	F7
LINDA VISTA AV	LACO	98	B0
LINDA VISTA AV	LACO	117	G2
LINDA VISTA DR	NAP	133	D0
LINDA VISTA DR	SB	87	H0
LINDA VISTA RD	SBD	91	C7
LINDA VISTA RD	SD	213	K3
LINDA VISTA RD	SDCO	111	A5
LINDBERGH BLVD	KER	89	L7
LINDBLOOM RD	MCO	55	G7
LINDEN AV	MCO	56	C1
LINDEN AV	SBD	99	D2
LINDEN AV	SSF	144	C3
LINDENBERGER RD	RCO	99	N6
LINDERO CYN RD	LACO	105	M6
LINDLEY AV	LA	178	L3
LINDLEY AV	LACO	97	B4
LINDLEY RD	HUM	15	M8
LINDSAY RD	IMP	110	H1
LINDSAY RD	KER	78	K5
LINDSEY AV	GLE	24	G8
LINE RD	YOL	39	J3
LINEA DEL CIELO	SDCO	107	L3
LINNE AV	MCO	48	N1
LINNE RD	SJCO	46	E9
LINSON AV	SBD	76	C2
LINWOOD AV	STA	47	J5
LINWOOD RD	MCO	47	J9
LINWOOD RD	MCO	48	J0
LISBON ST	MCO	48	N1
LISBON ST	SDCO	106	L5
LISCOMB HILL RD	HUM	10	L1
LITT RD	LPAZ	104	D1
LITTLE RD	RCO	102	K5
LITTLE BEAR RD	TRI	17	L4
LITL BLACK ROCK	TRI	17	A6
LTL BRWNS CK	TRI	11	Q6
LTL BRWNS CK RD	TRI	17	A6
LITTLE GIANT ML	TEH	19	K3
LITTL GRASS VLY	PLU	26	K1
LITTL HONKR BAY	SOL	39	J2
LITTLE JOHN	SJCO	40	Q4
LITTLE LAKE RD	INY	70	N4
LITTLE LAKE RD	MEN	30	A4
LITL MORONGO DR	SBD	100	C6
LITL PANOCHE RD	FRCO	55	L7
LITL PANOCHE ST	SLO	55	L1
LITTLE RIVER	MEN	30	C3
LTL SLATE CK RD	SHA	12	L3
LTL TUJUNGA RD	LACO	105	D7
LITTLE VLY RD	LAS	14	L0
LITTLE VLY RD	MEN	22	M4
LITTL VLY DUMP	LAS	14	L5
LITL VIRGINIA LK	MNO	43	M2
LITTLE WALKR RD	MNO	42	G7
LITTLE WALKR RD	MNO	43	G7
LIVELY RD	BUT	25	P4
LIVE OAK AV	LACO	98	B0
LIVE OAK DR	SBD	99	A1
LIVE OAK DR	ORA	98	L8
LIVE OAK RD	SBT	55	L3
LIVE OAK RD	SJCO	40	Q4
LIVEOAK DR	BUT	25	P4
LIVE OAK CYN RD	SBD	99	A1
LIVERMORE RD	NAPA	38	J1
LIVERY RD	IMP	110	J2
LIVNGSTN CRESSY	MCO	47	K9
LIVNGSTN CRESSY	MCO	48	K0
LLAGAS RD	SCL	54	M4
LLANO RD	SON	37	F8
LOBATA RD	YUB	33	B9
LOCAN AV	FRCO	57	K5
LOCH LOMOND RD	LAK	31	A9
LOCKHART RD	SBD	81	M3
LOCKWOOD CEM RD	MON	65	N5
LOCKWD JOLON RD	MON	65	K5
LOCKWD SN LUCAS	MON	65	J5
LOCKWD VLY RD	VEN	88	G5
LOCKWD VLY RD	VEN	88	D5
LOCO BILL RD	KER	79	G2
LOCUST AV	RCO	99	F5
LOCUST AV	SBD	81	M3
LOCUST AV	SBD	91	L9
LOCUST AV	STA	47	J4
LOCUST ST	SHA	18	G4
LODGE RD	FRCO	58	C0
LODI AV	NAPA	29	F3
LODI ST	COL	33	C8
LOFGREN RD	BUT	25	M8
LOGAN AV	SD	216	N9
LOG CABIN MINE	MEN	43	N4
LOGGING CAMP RD	MNO	50	B7
LOG HOUSE RD	SIS	4	F9
LOKERN RD	KER	77	L9
LOKOYA RD	NAPA	38	F3
LOLETA AV	TEH	24	C7
LOMA ALTA DR	MCO	56	B2
LOMA ALTA DR	LACO	98	B0
LOMA ALTA DR	LACO	117	F8
LOMA ALTA DR	STB	174	M3
LOMA RICA RD	YUB	33	C7
LOMAS CONTADAS	CC	45	A6
LOMAS CANTADAS	CC	156	D8
LOMA VERDE RD	RCO	102	K5
LOMA VISTA DR	NAPA	38	L9
LOMBARD ST	SF	142	D1
LOMBARD ST	SFCO	45	C3
LOMBARD ST	SB	143	G3
LOMITA	VEN	88	L1
LOMITA BLVD	LACO	97	J7
LOMITA BLVD	LACO	119	F3
LOMITA BLVD	SB	86	E2
LONDALE RD	STA	47	F4
LONE BUTTE RD	KER	80	Q1
LONE COMPANY RD	MNO	42	M9
LONE MTN RD	SUT	33	L5
LONE PINE LN	SON	38	C1
LONE PINE CYN	SBD	90	N8
LONE STAR MN RD	MNO	51	D4
LONE STAR RD	COL	32	F8
LONE STAR RD	MNO	51	E4
LONE STAR RD	PLA	34	G3
LONE STAR RD	SBD	91	C5
LONE TREE RD	BUT	25	G3
LONE TREE RD	BUT	26	G6
LONE TREE RD	MCO	48	Q2
LONE TREE RD	SBT	55	L3
LONE TREE WY	CC	39	P3
LONG BARN	TUO	41	L8
LONG BEACH BLVD	LB	192	J8
LONG BEACH BLVD	LACO	97	J8
LONG BEACH BL N	LACO	119	C7
LONG BEACH BL N	LB	192	J5
LONG BEACH FRWY	LACO	97	J8
LONG CANYON RD	SB	86	J6
LONG CANYON RD	RCO	100	G7
LONGCOR RD	TEH	18	K3
LONGDEN AV	LACO	118	H0
LONG HAY FLAT	BUT	25	G3
LONG HOLLOW DR	TEH	24	E4
LONG HOLLOW RD	MAD	49	Q5
LONGHORN LN	KER	79	H2
LONGHORN DR	LAS	32	K2
LONG RIDGE RD	TRI	16	P9
LONG VALLEY RD	ALP	36	L4
LONG VALLEY RD	LAK	32	G1
LONG VALLEY RD	SIE	27	K9
LONG VALLEY RD	PLU	33	B9
LONGVIEW AV	MCO	47	L8
LONGVIEW AV	MCO	48	L0
LONOAK RD	MON	65	K4
LOOKOUT RD	SHA	19	F4
LKOUT-HACKMR RD	LAS	6	O1
LKOUT-HACKMR RD	MOD	6	Q2
LKOUT INDIAN RD	SIS	5	J5
LOOKOUT MTN RD	SLO	76	L3
LOONEY RD	MCO	48	H1
LOOP RD	SHA	19	F4
LOOP RD	RCO	101	L6
LOPES RD	SOL	38	M8
LOPEZ DR	SLO	76	L3
LOPEZ CANYON RD	LACO	105	D7
LOPEZ CANYON RD	LACO	117	B2
LOQUAT AV	STA	47	F4
LORAINE AV	LACO	118	G7
LORENSON RD	SBD	92	F7
LORRAINE RD	SBD	92	F7
LOS ALAMITOS BL	ORA	120	F1
LOS ALAMOS RD	RCO	99	P7
LOS ALTOS DR	LACO	118	N3
LOS ANGELES AV	VEN	89	O1
LOS ANGELES ST	LA	185	N4
LOS CERRITOS RD	MCO	48	C3
LOS CERRITOS RD	STA	48	F3
LOS COCHES RD	MON	65	H1
LOS COCHES RD	SDCO	108	J7
LOS COCHES RD	TEH	18	G4
LS COYOTES DIAG	LACO	119	E9
LS COYOTES DIAG	LACO	120	E0
LOS FELIZ BLVD	GLEN	182	J2
LOS FELIZ BLVD	LA	182	J2
LOS FELIZ BLVD	LACO	117	J4
LOS FLORES RD	SBD	91	N3
LOS GATOS BLVD	LACO	118	N3
LOS GATOS RD	FRCO	66	E9
LOS GATOS RD	SBD	91	J5
LOS NIETOS RD	LACO	98	J5
LOS OLIVOS ST	STB	174	H0
LOS OSOS VLY RD	SLO	76	H5
LOS PADRES DR	SAL	171	K4
LOS PALOS DR	SBD	91	H5
LOS PINOS DR	RCO	100	N7
LOS PRADOS	SM	145	Q5
LS RANCHITOS RD	SR	139	C3
LOS ROBLES	LACO	90	G1
LOS ROBLES AV	PAS	190	D5
LOST RD	RCO	99	M4
LOST CREEK RD	TEH	19	K8
LOST CK DAM RD	YUB	26	L3
LOST HILLS RD	FRCO	66	E9
LOST HILLS RD	KER	77	M5
LOST LAKE RD	KER	80	P1
LOST LAKE RD	FRCO	57	H5
LOST SECTION S	INY	72	N8
LOST SECTION S	INY	72	H5
LOS VERJELES RD	BUT	25	P9
LOS VERJELES RD	YUB	25	P9
LOTT RD	BUT	25	L3
LOTUS RD	ED	34	N6
LOUIE RD	SIS	12	A8
LOUIE RD	SJCO	47	B4
LOUISE	MAN	161	H4
LOUISE ST	SUIS	135	L2
LOUISIANA ST	VAL	134	L3
LOUMAS LN	KER	79	J4
LOVEKIN BLVD	RCO	103	Q6
LOVELAND RD	IMP	110	J0
LOVENESS RD	MOD	14	A9
LOWDEN RD	RED	12	L1
LOWDEN RD	SHA	122	H4
LOW DIVIDE RD	DN	1	Q3
LOWER RD	AVLN	105	M1
LOWER TER	AVLN	105	P3
LOWER AZUSA RD	LACO	98	D2
LOWER AZUSA RD	LACO	118	J2
LOWER CHILES VLY	NAPA	29	E8
LOWER CHILES VLY	NAPA	38	C5
LOWER COLFAX RD	NEV	34	D5
LOWER DORRAY RD	CAL	41	F1
LOWR ENTRPRS RD	BUT	25	L9
LOWER FIRE RD	LAK	31	J8
LOWER FORBESTWN	BUT	26	M0
LOWER GAS PT RD	SHA	18	H2
LOWER GAS PT RD	SHA	18	H2
LOWER GLACIER RD	INY	51	Q8
LOWER HONCUT RD	BUT	25	Q8
LOWER JONES	SJCO	39	P7
LOWER KLAMTH HY	KLAM	5	C3
LOWER KUCK RD	SIS	4	J4
LOWER LAKE RD	DN	1	H7
LWR LITL SHASTA	SIS	4	L3
LOWER MAD RIVER	TRI	17	K0
LOWER RATLSNAKE	TRI	17	J1
LOWER SACRAMNTO	SJCO	40	M1
LOWER SACRAMNTO	SJCO	40	M1
LOWER SPGS RD	SHA	18	G3
LOWER WSIDE RD	TRI	16	K9
LOWR WYANDTT RD	BUT	25	M7
LOWERY RD	HUM	15	H7
LOWERY CEM RD	TEH	24	C7
LOWES CANYON RD	SLO	66	P2
LOW GAP RD	MEN	30	D8
LOW GAP RD	U	123	D0
LOYALTON RD	SIE	27	H6
LOYALTON RD	SIE	27	H6
LOZANOS RD	PLA	34	K3
LUBKEN RD	INY	60	M2
LUCAS	SJCO	40	N1
LUCAS VALLEY RD	MAR	38	M0
LUCE GRISWLD RD	TEH	18	K3
LUCILLE	FRCO	66	G6
LUCILLE LN	LB	192	H7
LUCINDA RD	SBD	81	N4
LUCY BROWN RD	RCO	116	B4
LUDLOW RD	RCO	99	F2
LUDY BLVD	RCO	116	C3
LUIS AV	MCO	55	B5
LUISENO RD	SDCO	107	P8
LUKENS LN	RCO	99	J4
LULU MINE RD	TUO	41	M5
LULU MINE RD	TUO	48	A4
LUMGREY RD	SIS	3	M7
LUMPKIN RD	BUT	25	L9
LUMPKIN RD	BUT	26	K2
LUMPKIN LA P RD	BUT	26	K1
LUMPKIN RDG RD	BUT	26	J2
LUNA RD	IMP	110	Q2
LUNDY LAKE RD	MNO	43	M2
LUNT RD	BUT	25	H6
LUPE RD	SLO	76	N4
LUPINE LN	RCO	100	Q5
LURLINE AV	COL	32	D6
LUTHER RD	PLA	34	J4
LUTHER RD	SBD	91	M3
LUTHER E GIBSON	SOL	38	M8
LUTHER GIBSN FY	BEN	153	M7
LUTIE AV	KER	80	M1
LUX AV	MCO	56	B2
LYNCH RD	NAPA	38	J6
LYNCH CANYON DR	SLO	65	P6
LYNCH MDWS RD	BUT	25	E7
LYNN RD	VEN	105	J7
LYON AV	FRCO	56	P4
LYON AV	RCO	99	F1
LYON ST	STA	47	F9
LYON ST	STA	48	F0
LYONS AV	LACO	89	M3
LYONS RD	COL	32	C7
LYONS RD	IMP	114	C0
LYONS RD	IMP	113	C9
LYONS ST	SNRA	163	H5
LYTLE AV	KER	68	K2
LYTLE CREEK RD	SBD	99	A1
LYTTON ST	SDCO	106	K2
LYTTON SPG RD	SON	31	P6
M			
M ST	EUR	121	A7
M ST	FRE	165	M7
M ST	MER	170	N4
M 1	TUL	69	N2
M 1	TUL	69	L0
M 8	LACO	90	H9
M 10	TUL	69	N2
M 15	TUL	69	M8
M 33	TUL	69	M7
M 52	TUL	69	L8
M 99	TUL	69	N2
M 107	TUL	69	N2
M 109	TUL	69	L8
M 117	TUL	69	N2
M 176	TUL	69	N8
M 220	TUL	69	E1
M 231	TUL	69	E1
M 240	TUL	69	C1
M 296	TUL	69	C1
M 348	TUL	69	N8
M 357	TUL	58	N8
M 453	TUL	58	P6
M 461	TUL	58	N8
M 465	TUL	58	P1
M 468	TUL	58	O3
M 468	TUL	58	O3
MABURY RD	SJ	152	C6
MABURY ST	SA	196	H7
MAC RD	RCO	108	A8
MAC RD	RCO	108	B4
MACARTHUR BLVD	ALA	45	G7
MACARTHUR BLVD	CM	197	G2
MACARTHUR BL	IRV	198	H5
MACARTHUR BL	IRV	200	P2
MACARTHUR BL	NB	198	H5
MACARTHUR BL	NB	200	P2
MACARTHUR DR	O	157	B7
MACARTHUR FRWY	ORA	120	L4
MACARTHUR FRWY	LACO	120	L4
MACARTHUR FRWY	SA	197	J4
MACARTHUR FRWY	A	157	B7
MACARTHUR FRWY	O	157	B7
MACDONALD AV	RCO	99	H3
MACDONALD AV	SB	86	Q4
MACE RD	YOL	39	M5
MACHADO LN	SIS	4	N4
MACLAY AV	LACO	89	P6
MACLAY AV	LACO	117	B1
MACY ST	LA	186	G5
MACY ST	LACO	97	D8
MACY ST	LACO	117	K6
MADDALENA RD	PLU	27	F5
MADDOCK RD	SUT	33	L5
MADEIRA AV N	MON	171	J7
MADEIRA AV N	SAL	171	J7
MADERA AV	FRCO	57	L1
MADERA AV	KER	78	D3
MADERA AV	KER	78	D3
MADERA RD	MCO	57	E1
MADERA RD	SBD	90	G9
MADISON AV	SAC	33	P0
MADISON AV	SAC	34	P0
MADISON AV	SBR	144	K0
MADISON ST	SD	214	M0
MADISON ST	KER	166	P9
MADISON ST	RCO	99	F2
MADISON ST	S	160	J6
MADONNA RD	SLO	76	K1
MADONNA RD	SNLO	172	N0
MADRE BLVD	LACO	118	G3
MAD RIVER ROCK	TRI	16	M8
MADRONA ST	NAPA	29	G3
MADRONE RD	SON	38	G2
MADSEN	SBD	80	N9
MADSEN	FRCO	57	F8
MAGEE CANYON RD	MNO	44	Q1
MAGIC MTN PKWY	LACO	89	D0
MAGNOLIA AV	FRCO	56	M3
MAGNOLIA AV	GLE	24	H6
MAGNOLIA AV	KER	78	F7
MAGNOLIA AV	LB	192	H7
MAGNOLIA AV	RCO	99	M4
MAGNOLIA AV	RIV	205	K0
MAGNOLIA AV	SDCO	107	P8
MAGNOLIA AV	SDCO	108	L1
MAGNOLIA BLVD	BUR	176	K3
MAGNOLIA BLVD	LA	179	K3
MAGNOLIA BLVD	LACO	117	L1
MAGNOLIA RD	YUB	33	K3
MAGNUS ORCHD RD	SIE	26	N6
MAGONIGAL RD	NEV	27	Q3
MAHER RD	MON	54	Q3
MAHOGANY FLAT	INY	71	N0
MAHOGANY PK RD	SIS	5	K7
MAHONEY RD	SLO	75	A9
MAHONEY RD	SB	86	B3
MAIL RD	SBD	92	C1
MAIL RT	LAS	8	Q5
MAIN AV	STR	139	L3
MAIN AV E	SCL	54	Q5
MAIN RD S	KLAM	5	B5
MAIN RD S	MOD	7	H0
MAIN ST	A	157	B7
MAIN ST	BARS	208	Q4
MAIN ST	CAL	41	H4
MAIN ST	EC	217	H9
MAIN ST	ELS	189	J1
MAIN ST	GV	127	G5
MAIN ST	IMP	110	Q2
MAIN ST	IRV	198	H3
MAIN ST	KER	78	J3
MAIN ST	LAK	31	L6
MAIN ST	LV	209	J5
MAIN ST	LA	185	N4
MAIN ST	LACO	117	Q1
MAIN ST	LACO	117	P5
MAIN ST	ALA	46	F4
MAIN ST	MON	171	N0
MAIN ST N	LA	186	H6
MAIN ST N	LACO	117	M0
MAIN ST N	MON	171	K5
MAIN ST N	SAL	171	F5
MAIN ST S	A	157	B7
MAIN ST S	LACO	117	M0
MAIN ST S	MON	171	K5
MAIN ST S	SA	197	J4
MAIN ST E	SCL	54	Q5
MAIN ST W	MON	171	N0
MAIN ST W	VENT	18	J6
MAIN DRAIN RD	KER	77	M0
MAINE ST	LACO	117	Q1
MAINE ST	SOL	38	L5
MAINE ST	VAL	134	M5
MAIN EAST WEST	MOD	5	G8
MAIN PRAIRIE RD	SOL	39	G3
MALAGA AV	FRCO	56	K8
MALAGA AV	KER	78	H9
MALIBU CYN RD	LACO	97	D1
MALIN HWY	KER	78	D3
MALLARD RD	MCO	55	D9
MALLARD RD	YOL	39	G3
MALLOTT RD	SUT	33	D4
MALVERN AV	ORA	120	B4
MAMELUKE HLL RD	ED	34	J3
MAMMOTH TVRN RD	ML	164	E7
MANCHESTER AV	ANA	193	E0
MANCHESTER AV	ING	188	P7
MANCHESTER AV	LA	187	G6
MANCHESTER AV	LACO	117	F6
MANCHESTER AV	LACO	117	P4
MANCHESTER AV	SDCO	107	L4
MANDEVILL CYN RD	LACO	97	D4
MANDRAPA RD	RCO	100	D5
MANGALAR RD	RCO	100	Q5
MANGO RD	SBD	80	N9
MANGROVE AV	BUT	124	F3
MANGROVE AV	C	124	J4
MANHATTAN AV	LACO	97	H6
MANHATTAN AV	LACO	119	C0
MANHATTAN BLVD	LACO	97	H6
MANHATTAN BLVD	LACO	119	B2
MANIER DR	TUL	69	G0
MANILLA AV	AVLN	105	N2
MANKAS CORNR RD	SOL	38	Q1
MANNEL AV	KER	78	D3
MANNING AV	FRCO	56	M3
MANNING AV	FRCO	57	L8
MANNING RD	ALA	46	D4
MANOR RD	COL	32	E5
MANOR ST	KER	78	F7
MANTECA AV	SJCO	47	D2
MANTON AV	KER	78	H1
MANTON RD	TEH	18	M3
MANTON RD	TEH	19	H1
MANTON SCH RD	TEH	19	H2
MANUAL DOMINGOS	SJCO	47	D2
MANZANA RD	RCO	100	G6
MANZANA RD	RCO	100	G6
MANZANITA AV	BUT	25	G3
MANZANITA AV	BUT	124	F4
MANZANITA AV	RCO	99	F4
MANZANITA RD	RCO	100	P2
MANZANITA RD	TRI	16	C7
MANZANITA LKOUT	MOD	14	C1
MANZNR REWRD RD	INY	60	H1
MAPES RD	LAS	21	J3
MAPES RD	RCO	99	K5
MAPLE AV	FRCO	67	A5
MAPLE AV	STR	139	L3
MAPLE LN	NAPA	29	D2
MAPLE ST	RCO	98	H0
MAPLE ST	SDCO	108	K1
MAPLE CREEK RD	HUM	10	P2
MARCH LN	SJCO	40	B0
MARCONI AV	SAC	90	B0
MARCONI POLO AV	RCO	100	N1
MARCUM RD	SUT	33	K6
MAR DE CORTEZ	AVLN	105	M1
MARE ISLAND BL	VAL	134	L2
MARE ISL CAUSWY	VAL	134	L2
MARENGO RD	LACO	117	G8
MARENGO ST	COL	32	D6
MARGUERITE AV	KER	78	F7
MARGUERITE PKWY	ORA	98	P7
MARGUERITE RD	MCO	48	G6
MARGUERTE MN RD	AUB	126	D4
MARICOPA HWY	KER	78	N3
MARIE AV	KER	78	N3
MARIE DR	PLU	20	Q6
MARIE AV	KER	89	L7
MARIN ST	VAL	134	L4
MARIN ST	ALA	46	F4
MARINA AV	ALA	46	E4
MARINA BLVD	SF	142	B0
MARINA BLVD	SUIS	135	M5
MARINA DR	IMP	109	E5
MARINA EXPWY	LACO	187	J7
MARINA FRWY	CUL	188	J0
MARINA FRWY	LA	188	J0
MARINA FRWY	LACO	97	J8
MARINA VISTA	VAL	134	H8
MARINE AV	MB	189	P4
MARINE AV	RCO	99	K9
MARINE PKWY	RC	145	L9
MARINERS ISL BL	SM	145	L8
MARINETTE	TUL	68	C3
MARIN WRLD PKY	SOL	153	B7
MARIPOSA AV	BUT	25	G2
MARIPOSA AV	C	124	D7
MARIPOSA AV	RCO	99	E2
MARIPOSA RD	SJCO	47	B5
MARIPOSA RD	SLO	76	J7
MARIPOSA DUMP	MPA	49	H2
MARITIME ST	COL	33	D0
MARKET ST	COL	33	D0
MARKET ST	SA	198	M3
MARKET ST	RIV	205	K0
MARKET ST	RCO	99	E2
MARKET ST	SB	86	Q4
MARKET ST	SD	216	K1
MARKET ST	SF	142	M2
MARKET ST	SMA	173	C2
MARKET ST	SIE	26	L7
MARKET ST	SJ	152	J3
MARKET ST	SCLR	151	N2
MARKET ST S	S	160	N8
MARKET ST S	YUBA	125	C7
MARKET ST W	MON	171	M3
MARKET ST W	VENT	18	J6
MARKHAM ST	RCO	99	H3
MARKLEEVLLE LKT	ALP	36	J3
MARKLEEVLLE	FRCO	57	P4
MARK SPGS W RD	SON	37	G3
MARKWEST STA RD	SBD	100	B6
MARLAY AV	SBD	101	B8
MAR MONTE AV	KER	89	K4
MARNI CT	KER	79	K4
MAROA AV	FRE	165	B5
MARQUARDT AV	LACO	120	B2
MARSH ST	SNLO	172	H3
MARSH ST	SLO	76	J1
MARSHALL RD	ED	34	L7
MARSHALL RD	STA	47	K4
MARSHALL RD	RCO	99	J3
MARSHALL-PETALMA	MAR	37	K7
MARSHALL RCH RD	TRI	17	D5
MARSHES FLAT RD	TUO	48	C6
MARSHVIEW RD	SOL	38	K7
MARSH RD	STA	47	F8
MARTIN AV	FRE	165	N4
MARTIN AV	KER	78	F7
MARTIN RD	FRCO	56	L7
MARTIN RD	IMP	110	L0
MARTIN RD	MON	64	J9
MARTIN RD	YUB	25	M9
MARTIN ST	MONT	167	L7
MARTIN ST	MON	53	J9
MARTIN ST	RCO	99	H3
MARTIN RD	MON	65	K4
MARTN LTHR KING	LA	184	J4
MARTN LTHR KING	LACO	89	M1
MARTIS PEAK RD	PLA	35	B9
MARTIS RD	CAL	41	M1
MAR VISTA	SDCO	107	H4
MAR VISTA DR	MONT	168	B6
MAR VISTA DR	MONT	167	M6
MAR VISTA DR	MON	53	J9
MARX RD NO 1	SHA	18	H0
MARX RD NO 2	SHA	18	H0
MARYLAND ST	VAL	134	N3
MARYSVILLE BLVD	SAC	33	N8
MARYSVILLE RD	YUB	26	Q1
MARYSVILLE RD	YUB	26	Q1
MASON ST	SF	143	J8
MASON ST	STB	174	J8
MASON DIXON RD	SBD	100	A8
MASONIC AV	SF	142	J0
MASONIC RD	MNO	43	F4
MASSACHUSTTS AV	SDCO	106	L5
MASSACHUSTTS AV	SDCO	111	B7
MASSACK RD	PLU	26	D7
MASSEY	MPA	49	J4
MAST AV	KER	78	B3
MASTERS AV	FRCO	56	M7
MASTERSONS RD	SIS	4	E3
MATHER ST	O	158	A3
MATHER FIELD RD	SAC	34	B1
MATHESON RD	SHA	18	H4
MATHEWS	SJCO	40	Q1
MATHEWS RD	SJCO	47	A1
MATHEWS RD	LAS	14	K3
MATHEWS RD	SIS	5	F1
MATHILDA AV	SCL	45	K9
MATILIJA AV	VEN	88	K0
MATLOCK LP	TEH	18	L5
MATTERHORN DR	KER	79	N4
MATTHEWS LN	YUB	33	K7
MATTOLE RD	HUM	15	M8
MATTOLE RD	HUM	9	G2
MAUI RD	SBD	92	C5
MAURICO AV	RCO	99	L4
MAWSON RD	SUT	33	D1
MAXSON RD	FRCO	58	D2
MAXWELL LN	SON	39	B4
MAXWELL CYN RD	NAPA	38	N4
MAXWLL SITES RD	COL	32	B5
MAY	C	124	P5
MAYARADA	SBD	101	B8
MAYARO LODGE RD	BUT	26	E8
MAYBECK	SJCO	40	J3
MAYBERT RD	NEV	26	Q8
MAYER AV	KER	78	F7
MAYER RD	YUB	33	D6
MAYFIELD RD	RCO	102	M9
MARY SCHOOL RD	LA	185	H7
MARYS CANYON RD	SON	37	D5
MAZE BL	MDO	162	Q0
MAZE BLVD	STA	47	F4
MAZOURKA CANYON	INY	60	G0
MCADAMS CK RD	SIS	3	N7
MCADAMS INDN CK	SIS	3	M7
MCARTHUR RD	SHA	19	H5
MCARTHUR RD	SUT	33	E2
MCAULIFFE RD	SBD	100	P9
MCAUSLAND RD	COL	32	A9
MCBEAN PKWY	LACO	89	D0
MCCABE RD	IMP	114	B9
MCCAHILL LN	HUM	15	L9
MCCAIN BLVD	COR	215	N2
MCCAIN VLY RD	SDCO	111	C6
MCCALL AV	FRCO	57	G7
MCCALL BLVD	RCO	99	C8
MCCANN RD	HUM	16	K3
MCCARTHY RES RD	CAL	41	F4
MCCARTY AV	RCO	98	B8
MCCARTY RD	TEH	24	E3
MCCATER RD	MCO	47	L3
MCCLAIN LN	RCO	108	A4
MCCLATCHY RD	SUT	33	F3
MCCLELLAN RD	CPTO	149	P3
MCCLELLAND LN	LAS	21	J4
MCCLELLN MTN RD	HUM	16	L3
MCCLINTOCK RD	STA	47	L5
MCCLOSKEY RD	SBT	54	G9
MCCLOSKEY RD	SBT	55	G9
MCCLOUD DUMP RD	SIS	12	H4
MCCLURE SUB RD	MEN	30	A4
MCCOMBS RD	KER	89	M3
MCCOMBS RD	KER	79	N4
MCCONAHUE GL RD	SIS	11	C8
MCCONNALT RD	IMP	110	N2
MCCORMACK RD	SON	37	J3
MCCOURTNEY RD	PLA	34	E3
MCCOY AV	LACO	120	J0
MCCOY RD	LAS	20	H5
MCCOY RD	LAS	14	P9
MCCOY RD	MON	53	P9
MCCOY RD	TEH	18	M5
MCCRACKEN RD	STA	47	J4
MCCREERY RCH RD	SBT	54	G5
MCCRORY RD	SON	39	J4
MCCULLAGH RD	SUT	39	E3
MCCULLOCK BLVD	MOD	7	P7
MCCULLY RD	MCO	47	K9
MCDANIEL RD	IMP	115	A7
MCDERMOTT RD	RCO	99	K9
MCDOEL DIST	SIS	5	K9
MCDOEL DORRS RD	SIS	5	K9
MCDONALD	SJCO	39	P7
MCDONALD RD	IMP	110	Q2

STREET INDEX

STREET	CO.	PAGE & GRID
MCEWEN RD	CC	38 M7
MCEWEN RD	STA	47 F8
MCFADDEN	MON	54 K4
MCFADDEN AV	SA	195 N1
MCFADDEN AV	SA	196 P5
MCFARLND-WDY RD	KER	78 A5
MCGARY RD	SOL	38 K7
MCGEE AV	STA	47 D7
MCGEE CREEK RD	MNO	51 G0
MCGOWAN	YUB	33 F6
MCGRATH RD	SUT	33 F3
MCHENRY AV	MDO	162 G6
MCHENRY AV	SJCO	47 E5
MCINTOSH RD	HUM	10 M6
MCKEAN RD	SCL	46 P4
MCKEE RD	MCO	48 M4
MCKEE RD	SJ	152 D8
MCKEE RD	SCL	46 L3
MCKEEN RD	SIS	11 F7
MCKELL RD	LAK	32 P1
MCKENZIE LN	FRE	165 H6
MCKENZIE RD	SAC	40 G1
MCKERNIE ST	RCO	99 M8
MCKIBBEN RD	KER	78 C0
MCKIM RD	IMP	110 P3
MCKINLEY AV	FRE	165 D3
MCKINLEY AV	FRCO	57 H1
MCKINLEY AV	FRCO	57 H1
MCKINLEY ST	RCO	99 G0
MCKINNEY CK RD	SIS	3 K6
MCLAIN RD	YUB	26 M3
MCLAUGHLIN AV	LA	187 A8
MCMASTER RD	MCO	48 N4
MCMILLAN CYN RD	SLO	76 A5
MCMULLIN	SJCO	47 D1
MCMULLIN GRADE	FRCO	57 M1
MCMURRY MDWS RD	INY	59 B7
MCNAMARA RD	MCO	48 N4
MCNEILL LN	SOL	39 C2
MCNELLA LN	PLU	27 G5
MCNERNEY RD	IMP	110 M2
MCRAE RD	BUT	25 M3
MCRAE RD	TUO	41 J4
MCSWAIN RD	MER	170 J0
MCSWAIN RD	MCO	170 J0
MEACHAM RD	KER	78 B2
MEAD RD	IMP	110 M2
MEADE AV	SD	214 N2
MEADOW DR	MCO	48 K1
MEADOW RD	TRI	17 B6
MEADOW GLEN RD	CAL	41 H2
MEADOW LAKE RD	NEV	26 N9
MEADOW LAKE RD	NEV	27 M2
MEADOWS DR	VAL	134 K2
MEADOWS RD	IMP	114 C2
MEADOWSWEET DR	CRTM	108 M9
MEADOW VLY RD	YUB	26 P2
MEADOW VIEW DR	SHA	18 A3
MEADOWVIEW RD	SAC	39 D8
MEADOW VISTA RD	PLA	34 G4
MEALEY RD	IMP	109 P3
MEARS RIDGE RD	SHA	12 J4
MECCA DALE RD	RCO	101 J8
MECHAM RD	SON	37 H8
MEDFORD AV	KIN	67 D3
MEDFORD RD	FRCO	57 C9
MEDICINE LK RD	SIS	5 P4
MEDLIN RD	STA	47 H7
MEEKS RD	SBD	92 N7
MEHRING RD	IMP	116 Q7
MEIER RD	STA	47 F0
MEIER RD	STA	47 F0
MEIGS RD	STB	174 F1
MEIKLE RD	STA	47 F0
MEIKLE RD	STA	48 F0
MEISS RD	SAC	40 H3
MEISS LK SAM NK	SIS	4 H3
MEISS LK SAM NK	SIS	4 H3
MELCHER RD	KER	78 A3
MELLO	SJCO	47 C9
MELLOR RD	STA	48 F1
MELODY CT	HUM	10 P0
MELOLANO RD	IMP	110 Q3
MELONES CT	TUO	41 N3
MELROSE AV	LA	181 Q3
MELROSE AV	LA	182 Q4
MELROSE AV	LACO	181 Q3
MELROSE DR	RCO	99 H2
MEMORY LN	SA	195 E9
MEMORY LN	SA	196 D0
MENALTO AV	MP	147 B4
MENDIBOURE RD	LAS	8 L3
MENDIBURN	KER	79 N6
MENDOCINO AV	FRCO	57 F6
MENDOCINO AV	STR	130 A1
MENDOCINO PASS	MEN	23 F3
MENIFEE RD	RCO	99 K5
MENIFEE RD	RCO	99 K5
MENLO AV	KER	78 D0
MERCED AV	KER	78 E0
MERCED AV	LACO	118 N4
MERCED FALLS RD	MPA	48 E6
MERCED FALLS RD	TUO	48 E6
MERCED WOODS	FRCO	56 E8
MERIDIAN AV	SCL	151 P8
MERIDIAN BLVD	MNO	50 B9
MERIDIAN RD	BUT	25 G1
MERIDIAN RD	SCL	46 N2
MERIDIAN RD	SOL	39 D1
MERIDIAN RD	SUT	33 D1
MERIDIAN ST	SJ	151 P8
MERLE AV	STA	47 F9
MERRIAM RD	YUB	26 P2
MERRILL AV	FRCO	56 C4
MERRILL RD	TEH	24 E4
MERRILL RD S	KER	79 N5
MERRILL FLAT RD	LAS	20 F6
MERRILLVILLE RD	LAS	20 F6
MERRIMAC CTF RD	BUT	25 G9
MERRITT LN	PLA	34 G4
MERVEL AV	MCO	55 E8
MESA DR	RCO	103 P5
MESA DR	RCO	116 A9
MESA DR	SBD	100 B8
MESA DR	SDCO	107 G3
MESA RD	MAR	37 N3
MESA RD	SBD	92 N8
MESA TK TR W	SDCO	108 N5
MESA COLLEGE DR	SD	212 K2
MESA COLLEGE DR	SDCO	106 J3
MESA GRANDE RD	SDCO	107 H2
MESQUITE RD	INY	61 D3
MESQUITE CYN RD	SBD	91 A5
MESQUITE SPG RD	INY	62 F1
MESQUITE VLY RD	INY	73 J4
MESSICK RD	KER	78 A3
MESSILLA VLY RD	BUT	25 J6
MESTMAKER ST	SCL	46 P4
METCALFE RD	AVLN	105 N2
METROPOLE AV	AVLN	105 N2
METTER RD	SUT	33 B5
METTLER AV	KER	78 D3
METTLER RD	KER	78 D3
METTLER RD	STA	47 B7
METZ RD	MON	65 B2
METZGER RD	SHA	13 J6
MEXICAN LAKE RD	SBT	66 B2
MEYER RD	LACO	118 Q2
MEYER RD	LACO	120 A2
MEYERS LN	SUT	33 B3
MEYERS GRADE RD	SON	37 C2
MICA RD	RCO	108 B4
MICHAEL RD	MCO	48 P3
MICHEL RD	CAL	41 J2
MICHELSON DR	IRV	198 M5
MICHELTORENA ST	STB	174 J2
MICHIGAN BAR RD	AMA	40 E5
MICHIGAN AVD	BAJA	114 Q2
MIDDLE AV	SCL	46 L4
MIDDLE RD	BLMT	145 B5
MIDDLE TER	AVLN	105 P3
MIDDLE CREEK RD	SIS	3 H4
MIDDLEFIELD RD	MP	147 B0
MIDDLEFIELD RD	PA	147 H8
MIDDLEFLD RD E	MVW	148 K2
MIDDLE FORK RD	MON	66 M3
MIDDL FK GASQUET	DN	2 J1
MIDDLE FK HUMBG RD	SIS	3 N9
MIDDLE HARBR RD	O	157 J4
MIDDLE HONCUT RD	BUT	26 G6
MIDDLE RIDGE RD	MEN	30 D4
MIDDLETON RD	SUT	33 A3
MIDDLETON RD	TRI	11 J8
MIDDLETWN PK DR	SHA	18 F2
MIDDLE 2 RCK RD	SON	37 H4
MIDLAND AV	SDCO	107 M7
MIDLAND RD	RCO	103 P3
MIDLAND RD	KER	80 D4
MIDOIL RD	KER	77 L9
MIDWAY	BUT	25 H3
MIDWAY DR	SD	213 Q0
MIDWAY DR	SDCO	106 K2
MIDWAY RD	SBD	91 B7
MIDWAY RD	SOL	39 C2
MIDWAY WELLS	INY	61 H6
MIKISHA BLVD	SBD	92 N7
MILAN RD	KER	77 E8
MILE END	MON	64 B9
MILE END	MON	65 B0
MILFORD CEM RD	LAS	21 N4
MILFORD GRADE	LAS	21 N5
MILGEO RD	SJCO	47 D4
MIL-GOR RD	SBD	101 C4
MILHAM AV	KIN	67 J2
MILITAR	BAJA	114 D2
MILITARY E	BEN	153 N4
MILITARY W	BEN	153 L3
MILITARY RD	SIS	13 E1
MILITARY PASS	SIS	12 A7
MILITARY PASS	SIS	13 A7
MILL AV	KER	78 B3
MILL RD	BUT	26 K2
MILL RD	MNO	52 H4
MILL RD	SLO	76 B2
MILL RD	TEH	19 K4
MILL RD	YUB	26 P1
MILL ST	RENO	130 G5
MILL ST	SBDO	207 H4
MILL ST	U	123 J4
MILLARD CYN RD	RCO	100 F2
MILLBRAE AV	MLBR	144 Q6
MILLBRAE AV	SMCO	45 G3
MILLBROOK AV	FRCO	57 F5
MILL CANYON RD	MNO	42 D8
MILL CREEK RD	HUM	10 P0
MILL CREEK RD	MEN	31 L3
MILL CREEK RD	SBD	99 A4
MILL CREEK RD	SIS	3 P5
MILL CREEK RD	SIS	4 H9
MILL CK PWR HS	MNO	43 M3
MILLER	MAR	45 Q2
MILLER AV	CPTO	150 Q1
MILLER AV	FRCO	56 E3
MILLER AV	MV	140 M1
MILLER AV	VAL	134 M9
MILLER RD	FRCO	57 Q2
MILLER RD	IMP	114 B5
MILLER RD	TRI	23 B0
MILLER RD	YOL	39 E4
MILLER RANCH RD	SIE	26 M6
MILLERTON RD	FRCO	57 D0
MILLS AV	CLA	203 N1
MILLS RD	LACO	118 P2
MILLS ORCHDS RD	COL	32 C5
MILLS PARK RD	SIE	27 F4
MILLUX AV	KER	78 L4
MILLUX RD	KER	78 L4
MILLWOOD RD	FRCO	58 J5
MILNES RD	STA	47 E7
MILTON	SJCO	48 A0
MILTON RD	CAL	41 A9
MILTON RD	NAPA	38 J5
MILTON ST	SLA	171 H3
MINA RD	VEN	89 N1
MINE RD	CC	45 A7
MINER RD	SBD	92 A9
MINER ST	S	160 M8
MINERAL RD	IMP	109 M9
MINERAL RD	SHA	18 Q4
MINERAL KING AV	TUL	57 N9
MINERAL KING AV	TUL	57 N9
MINERAL SCHOOL	ML	164 N6
MINERET RD	ML	164 N6
MINERS CREEK RD	SIS	11 A7
MINES RD	ALA	46 A7
MINES RD	SJCO	47 A7
MINNELOA RD	SBD	92 B9
MINNEOLA AV	FRCO	57 F4
MINNEWAWA AV	FRCO	57 F4
MINNIETTA RD	INY	71 D2
MINT RD	MCO	56 C2
MINTURN RD	MCO	48 Q7
MIRABEL RD	SON	37 D6
MIRAMAR RD	SDCO	107 N6
MIRAMAR RD	STA	47 G9
MIRAMAR WY	SDCO	106 G3
MIRA MESA BLVD	SDCO	107 N5
MIRA MESA BLVD	SDCO	107 F2
MIRA MESA BLVD	SDCO	107 N6
MIRASOL AV	KER	77 G9
MIRASOL AV	KER	77 G9
MISSION AV	MCO	48 M1
MISSION AV	SD	214 N1
MISSION AV	SDCO	107 G2
MISSION AV	SR	139 J5
MISSION BLVD	ALA	45 F9
MISSION BL	H	146 E7
MISSION BL	MTCL	203 P0
MISSION BLVD	ONT	203 P1
MISSION BL	POM	204 P2
MISSION BLVD	RCO	99 G0
MISSION BLVD	SBD	203 P0
MISSION BL	SD	212 B0
MISSION BLVD	SDCO	106 J1
MISSION BLVD	SDCO	107 Q4
MISSION DR	LACO	118 J1
MISSION FRWY	SDCO	106 K2
MISSION RD	LA	186 F7
MISSION RD	LACO	117 D0
MISSION RD	LACO	117 J8
MISSION RD	MON	65 J2
MISSION RD	STA	47 K5
MISSION ST	SF	142 N5
MISSION ST	STB	143 N5
MISSION ST	SC	169 M2
MISSION TR	RCO	99 N3
MISSION BAY DR	SD	212 A7
MISSN BAY DR W	SD	212 K2
MISSION CK RD	SDCO	100 F5
MISSION CTR RD	SD	213 H8
MISSION GORG RD	SDCO	106 J4
MISSION GRGE RD	SDCO	107 Q6
MISSION LKS BL	RCO	100 F5
MISSN OLIVE RD	BUT	25 N6
MISSION RDGE RD	STB	174 D6
MISSION VLY FWY	SD	213 N5
MISSION VLY FWY	SD	213 L0
MISSION VLLG DR	SD	214 C4
MISSION VLGE DR	SDCO	107 Q6
MISSION VLGE DR	MCO	214 J4
MISTLETOE DR	VEN	88 M4
MIX CANYON RD	SOL	38 E8
MOANING CAVE RD	CAL	41 L3
MOBLEY	SJCO	40 Q5
MOBLEY	SJCO	47 A5
MOCAL RD	KER	77 K6
MOD JESKA CYN RD	ORA	98 L8
MODESTO AV	FRCO	56 J0
MODOC COUNTY RD	MOD	5 H7
MOFFAT BLVD	MAN	161 M5
MOFFAT RD	KER	78 N6
MOFFAT RANCH RD	INY	60 K1
MOFFATT RD	MCO	47 P6
MOFFETT RD	STA	47 J6
MOFFETT CK RD E	S	3 N8
MOFFETT CK RD W	SIS	3 N8
MOHAVE RD	LPAZ	103 J8
MOHAVE ROSE DR	LACO	90 J7
MOJAVE DR	SBD	91 J2
MOJAVE RD	SBD	91 J2
MOJAVE-RANDSBRG	KER	80 L6
MOJAVE TRPCO RD	KER	79 Q9
MOKE HILL CAMPO	CAL	41 L1
MOLERA RD	MON	54 H3
MOLINO AV	MV	140 N0
MONO WY	TUO	163 M5
MONROE	MCO	55 N7
MONROE AV	FRCO	57 Q2
MONROE AV	FRCO	57 F4
MONROE ST	RCO	101 N6
MONROE ST	TEH	18 N6
MONSON	FRCO	58 N7
MONTAGUE AGER RD	SIS	4 H0
MONTGUE GRNADA	SIS	4 H0
MONTAGUE AV	LA	180 H0
MONTANA ST	LACO	180 A5
MONTANA ST	PAS	190 B1
MONTARA RD	SBD	91 N4
MONTE RD	MP	110 H0
MONTEBELLO BLVD	LACO	118 Q0
MONTEBELLO BLVD	LACO	118 Q0
MONTE BELLO RD	SCL	150 H9
MONTE BLVD RD	MON	30 F7
MONTECITO RD	SLO	75 P9
MONTECITO ST	STB	174 H7
MONTE DIABLO AV	S	160 P9
MONTEREY AV	FRCO	56 L6
MONTEREY AV	MDO	162 E1
MONTEREY AV	RCO	99 M8
MONTEREY RD	SDCO	107 N9
MONTEREY RD	SCL	54 B6
MONTEREY RD	LACO	117 N3
MONTEREY HWY	SCL	54 B6
MONTEREY PSS RD	LACO	117 K4
MONTEREY PSS RD	LACO	172 K4
MONTE VERDE RD	CAR	168 M1
MONTE VISTA AV	MCO	48 F1
MONTE VISTA AV	STA	48 F1
MONTE VISTA RD	SHA	18 Q5
MONTE VISTA ST	LACO	118 D0
MONTE VISTA AV	STA	47 M1
MONTEZUMA	SHA	13 Q0
MONTEZUMA HL RD	SOL	39 K9
MONTFORD RD	SCL	46 N8
MONTGOMERY AV	FRCO	56 G0
MONTGOMERY AV	SBD	92 B0
MONTGOMERY ST	SF	143 F5
MONTGOMERY ST	MCO	48 G4
MONTGOMRY CK RD	TRI	11 Q7
MONTICELLO RD	NAPA	133 C9
MONTPELIER RD	STA	47 G9
MONTPELIER RD	STA	48 G9
MONUMENT RD	HUM	15 H8
MOODY RD	MEN	22 D3
MOODY ST	ORA	196 F2
MOONBEAM RD	RCO	102 K5
MOON BEND RD	COL	33 G1
MOONEY RD	MCO	48 J1
MOONEY RD	LAS	20 F4
MONEY FLAT RD	NEV	34 C1
MOONRIDGE RD	SBD	100 A1
MOONSHINE RD	YUB	26 P3
MOONWIND ST	KER	80 B6
MOORE RD	LAS	21 L9
MOORE RD	SUT	33 B3
MOOREHEAD RD	STA	47 N4
MOOREHEAD RD	SUT	47 N4
MOORES RD	NEV	26 N7
MOORPARK FRWY	VEN	88 B7
MOORPARK ST	LACO	110 D0
MOORVILL RDG RD	BUT	26 K3
MOOSE CAMP RD	SHA	13 P2
MORAGA AV	ALA	45 B6
MORAGA AV	O	158 A8
MORAGA AV	P	158 A6
MORAGA RD	SD	211 N8
MORAGA RD	SD	211 N8
MORAGA WY	CC	45 B7
MORAN AV	MCO	48 M1
MORAN RD	STA	47 K5
MORCOURT AV	KER	80 B4
MOREHEAD RD	DN	1 J7
MOREHEAD RD	SUT	33 N5
MORELLO AV	CC	154 G8
MORELLO AV	M	154 L8
MORENA BLVD	SD	211 M5
MORENA BLVD	SD	212 C9
MORENA BLVD	SD	213 L1
MORENA BLVD W	SD	213 K0
MORENA RES DR	SDCO	112 C6
MORENO AV	SDCO	106 F8
MORENO AV	SDCO	107 N9
MORENO BLVD	SDCO	106 J3
MORENO RD	STB	174 F4
MORENO ST	MTCL	203 Q4
MORENO BEACH DR	RCO	99 F5
MORGAN RD	CAL	41 M2
MORGAN RD	HUM	15 E6
MORGAN RD	LAS	21 N5
MORGAN RD	SBD	101 C7
MORGAN CYN RD	FRCO	57 D8
MORGAN TERRITORY	CC	39 Q2
MORGAN VLY RD	LAK	32 K1
MORGAN VLY RD	LAK	32 K1
MORMN EMGRNT TR	ED	35 N4
MORMON	KER	78 N5
MORNING STAR RD	ALP	36 N5
MORNING STAR CTO	SBD	84 J2
MORNING STAR RD	SBD	84 J2
MORONGO RD	RCO	100 Q1
MORONGO RD	SBD	101 B3
MORONI	SUT	33 F2
MORRETTI CYN RD	SIS	3 L3
MORRIS AV W	MDO	162 E1
MORRIS RD	COL	33 F1
MORRIS RD	STA	47 K5
MORRIS MINE RD	MNO	51 E4
MORRISON RD	STA	48 B1
MORRISN CYN RD	ALA	46 G1
MORRIS RANCH RD	RCO	100 N4
MORSE RD	YOL	39 G6
MORTAGA	MCO	55 C6
MORTON BL S	SBD	100 A4
MOSAIC CANYON	INY	61 L6
MOSHER	KER	80 D4
MOSQUITO RD	ED	34 M8
MOSQUITO RDG RD	PLA	34 N8
MOSS OLD MLL RD	TRI	10 Q8
MOTHER DR	ED	34 P7
MOTOR AV	LA	183 H2
MOTOR AV	LACO	183 H2
MOULTAN LOOP	TEH	19 L1
MOULTON PKWY	ORA	98 L5
MOULTON PKWY	ORA	120 H8
MOUND SPGS RD	SBD	100 A4
MOUNTAIN AV	LACO	118 Q0
MOUNTAIN AV	RCO	100 K0
MOUNTAIN AV	UPL	203 N7
MOUNTAIN BLVD	O	156 P9
MOUNTAIN DR	STB	174 D3
MOUNTAIN ST	LACO	117 N3
MOUNTAIN VW AV	FRCO	56 J0
MOUNTAIN VW AV	RCO	99 M8
MOUNTAIN RCH RD	CAL	41 J2
MTN CLIMBER WY	KER	79 N4
MTN HOME CK RD	SBD	99 C2
MTN HOME RCH RD	SON	38 N0
MTN HOUSE RD	ALA	46 A1
MTN HOUSE RD	MEN	31 K4
MTN HOUSE RD	MEN	31 B8
MTN LEMON RD S	VEN	88 M4
MTN MEADOW RD	MEN	22 Q8
MTN RCH RD	CAL	41 J2
MTN SCHOOL RD	SHA	13 Q2
MTN SPRINGS RD	SBD	94 C9
MTN SPRINGS RD	SDCO	113 N5
MTN VW ALVSO RD	SCL	46 K1
MTN VW-ALVSO RD	MVW	148 K1
MT AUKUM RD	ED	34 N9
MT AUKUM RD	ED	34 N9
MT BALDY LKOUT	SIS	2 H1
MT BULLION CTFF	MPA	48 F9
MT EATON RD	SCL	54 J4
MT EMMA RD	LACO	91 A8
MT GAINES	MPA	48 H8
MT GLEASON AV	LACO	117 Q4
MT HAMILTON RD	SCL	46 K4
MT HOUGH CRYSTL	PLU	27 Q7
MT HOLLYWOOD DR	LA	182 A1
MT MADONNA RD	SCL	54 D4
MT OLIVE RD	NEV	34 E5
MT OPHIR RD	MPA	49 H1
MT PIERCE LKOUT	HUM	15 H9
MT PINOS RD	KER	88 D5
MT PINOS RD	VEN	88 C1
MT REBA RD	ALP	42 C0
MT VEEDER RD	NAPA	29 M5
MT VEEDER RD	NAPA	38 F3
MT VERNON AV	CLTN	207 M2
MT VERNON AV	KER	78 G7
MT VERNON AV	RCO	99 E3
MT VERNON AV	SBD	91 C7
MT VERNON AV	SBD	99 E3
MT VERNON AV	SBDO	207 D2
MT VERNON RD	PLA	34 J3
MT WHITNEY	FRCO	57 Q5
MT WHITNEY AV	FRCO	66 A7
MT WHITNEY RD	KER	70 P4
MT WILSON RD	LACO	98 A1
MT WILSON RD	LACO	118 D0
MOVIE RD	INY	60 H1
M T FREITAS PKY	SR	139 J1
MUCK VALLEY RD	LAS	14 K2
MUD LAKE RD	ALP	36 L4
MUD LAKE RD	MOD	14 A1
MUELLER	SJCO	40 Q0
MUELLER	SJCO	47 A0
MUIR AV	BUT	25 G1
MUIR MILL RD	MEN	22 Q9
MUIR WOODS RD	MAR	45 A1
MULBERRY DR	LACO	118 P2
MULBERRY ST	C	124 P6
MULE CANYON RD	SBD	92 A1
MULE CREEK RD	TRI	11 N7
MULE TOWN RD	SHA	18 F2
MULHOLLAND DR	LA	177 Q0
MULHOLLAND DR	LA	181 D0
MULHOLLAND RD	LACO	97 C4
MULHOLLAND HWY	LACO	97 C1
MULLER LN	SCL	54 C6
MULLER RD	KER	78 H9
MUMMA RD	COL	33 J1
MUNRAS AV	MONT	167 N7
MUNRAS AV	MON	65 K9
MUNSEY RD	KER	80 J4
MUNCY RD	STA	47 G4
MUNJAR RD	SBD	25 E1
MUNRAS AV	MONT	168 A7
MURCHISON DR	MLBR	144 Q7
MURIEL DR	BARS	208 F4
MURPHY LN	SCL	54 C6
MURPHY RD	SHA	19 C0
MURPHY RD	MON	54 F5
MURPHY RD	NEV	26 Q4
MURPHY RD	STA	47 P5
MURPHY RD	TUO	41 P5
MURPHYS GRD RD	CAL	41 L3
MURRAY	SJCO	40 N4
MURRAY RD	HUM	10 M9
MURRAY RD	KER	78 N6
MURRAY RD	SUT	33 H5
MURRAY CK RD E	CAL	41 K3
MURRAY CK RD W	CAL	41 J3
MURRAY RIDGE RD	SD	214 C1
MURRIETA HT SPG	RCO	99 P5
MURRIETA HT SPG	RCO	99 P5
MURRIETTA RD	RCO	99 P5
MUSCAT AV	FRCO	57 K2
MUSCAT AV	FRCO	57 K7
MUSCAT AV	SBDO	207 D0
MUSTANG RD	MCO	48 Q3
MUSTANG SPGS RD	SLO	76 A1
MUTAU FLAT RD	VEN	88 F4
MYERS RD	COL	32 F4
MYERS RD	COL	32 F7
MYERS ST	BUT	25 M7
MYFORD RD	ORA	120 H5
MYKLE OAKS RD	MPA	49 H1
MYRTLE AV	RCO	99 M4
MYRTLE AV	LA	182 N5
MYRTLE AV	EUR	121 D9
MYRTLE AV	HUM	10 P9
MYRTLE AV	LACO	117 H1
NABORLY RD	SBD	101 B7
NACIMNTO-FER RD	MON	64 B7
NACIMNTO-FER RD	MON	64 B7
NACIMIENTO LAKE	MON	75 Q9
NACIMIENTO LN	SLO	75 A8
NACIMIENTO LN	SLO	75 A8
NACIONAL ST	SAL	171 H0
NADEAU RD	INY	60 H0
NADER RD	PLA	34 N8
NAGLEE AV	SJ	151 N8
NANTES AV	MCO	55 N8
NAPA AV	SBD	92 B0
NAPA RD	SON	132 G3
NAPA ST E	SNMA	38 T1
NAPA ST W	SNMA	132 W1
NARBONNE AV	LACO	119 F4
NARRAGANSETT AV	SDCO	106 A7
NARRAGANSETT AV	SDCO	111 B4
NASHUA RD	MON	54 J4
NASON ST	RCO	99 F5
NATIONAL AV	SD	216 M0
NATIONAL BLVD	CUL	183 M4
NATIONAL BLVD	LA	183 M4
NATIONAL BLVD	LA	183 A5
NATL TRAILS HWY	KER	80 L9
NATL TRAILS HWY	SBD	84 M9
NATL TRAILS HWY	SBD	93 L1
NATL TRAILS HWY	SBD	94 G7
NATL TRAILS HWY	SBD	100 C1
NATOMAS	SUT	33 M0
NATURAL BRDG RD	INY	70 Q8
NAUMANN RD	VEN	105 J1
NAUTILUS ST	SD	211 B2
NAVAJO DR	SAL	171 G7
NAVAJO RD	RCO	99 K4
NAVAJO RD	SDCO	107 N7
NAVARRO RDG RD	MEN	30 B3
NAVELENCIA AV	FRCO	58 J3
NAVY ST	LACO	184 N2
NEAL RD	BUT	25 L6
NEAL SPRING RD	SBD	91 A8
NEBO ST	RCO	99 A9
NEBRASKA AV	FRCO	57 M1
NEBRASKA AV	SCL	46 N7
NEBRASKA AV	TUL	68 H1
NEBRASKA AV	VAL	134 J5
NECTAR AV	RCO	108 B2
NEEDHAM RD	STA	47 H2
NEEDHAM ST	MDO	162 G1
NEEDLE PEAK RD	SLT	129 K6
NEELEY	SJCO	40 L0
NEENACH RD	LACO	89 D1
NEES AV	FRCO	56 G4
NEGRO CREEK DR	TUL	58 L4
NEGRO HOLE RD	SIS	5 L4
NEIGHBORS BLVD	RCO	103 P6
NEIGHBORS BLVD	RCO	116 A9
NEILSON RD	CAL	40 H9
NELANDER	MCO	47 M8
NELSON	SJCO	47 A4
NELSON AV	SBD	25 L5
NELSON RD	BUT	25 L2
NELSON RD	TRI	17 E4
NELSON BAR RD	BUT	25 H6
NELSON CREEK RD	SHA	13 K2
NELSON PIT RD	IMP	114 A5
NELSON RES RD	LAS	8 J2
NELSON SHPPEE RD	BUT	26 J2
NELSONS CROSSNG	BUT	26 J2
NELSON SHPPEE RD	BUT	26 J2
NELTON RD	CC	39 N4
NESS AV	FRCO	57 G5
NESTLE AV	LA	178 N7
NETHERLANDS RD	YOL	39 F7
NEUGERBAUER	SJCO	39 N8
NEUMARKEL RD	KER	79 J1
NEURALIA RD	KER	80 K3
NEVA AV	TEH	24 D7
NEVADA AV	KIN	67 F2
NEVADA ST	AUB	126 H3
NEVADA ST	NEVC	128 F5
NEVADA ST	NEV	128 D6
NEVADA CITY HWY	GV	127 E6
NEVADA CITY HWY	NEV	127 E6
NEVADA CITY HWY	NEV	128 P0
NEVIS AV	KER	78 A5
NEW AV	LACO	117 A5
NEW AV	SCL	54 C7
NEWARK	FRCO	57 F8
NEWARK	FRCO	57 F8
NEWARK BLVD	NA	46 M3
NEWBERRY RD	SBD	92 C4
NEW BIG OAK FLT	MPA	49 M2
NEW BIG OAK FLT	MPA	63 M2
NEW CEMETERY RD	LAS	14 J2
NW CHESTER DUMP RD	KER	79 K3
NW CHG QRTZ MTN	AMA	40 P8
NEWCOMB ST	FRCO	56 K4
NEW DOCK ST	LA	191 F5
NEW DOCK ST	LACO	119 F5
NEWHALL AV	MCO	48 Q3
NEWHALL RD	SUT	33 J3
NEW HOPE RD	SJ	151 G7
NEW HOPE RD	SAC	40 H0
NEWHOPE ST	GGR	195 G1
NEWHOPE ST	SA	195 G1
NEW IDRIA RD	SBT	55 N8
NEWLAND ST	ORA	120 H3
NEWMARK AV	FRCO	57 F8
NEW NVY BASE RD	HUM	9 Q8
NEW PLEYTO RD	MON	65 L6
NEW PEORIA FLAT	TUO	41 P3
NEWPORT AV	ORA	98 K5
NEWPORT BL	CM	199 E4
NEWPORT BL	NB	199 L1
NEWPORT BLVD	ORA	98 K5
NEWPORT BLVD	ORA	120 F9
NEWPORT BLVD	SBD	100 J1
NEWPORT BLVD	RCO	99 M4
NEWPORT-CM FRWY	CM	197 Q8
NEWPORT-CM FRWY	CM	198 J2
NEWPORT-CM FRWY	OR	194 K9
NEWPORT-CM FRWY	ORA	196 K9
NEWPORT-CM FRWY	SA	196 K9
NEWPORT-CM FRWY	TUS	196 K9
NEWRIVER RD	TRI	11 M0
NEW ROME RD	NEV	34 N3
NEWTON AV	KIN	67 G4
NEWTON RD	GLE	24 N3
NEWVILLE RD	TEH	24 F1
NEW YORK DR	LACO	118 F0
NEW YRK FLAT RD	YUB	26 M1
NEW YRK HOUS RD	YUB	26 N1
NEW YORK ST	RCO	99 B0
NIACASIO VLY RD	MAR	37 K6
NICE LUCERNE	LAK	31 F6
NICHOLAS RD	FRCO	57 D9
NICHOLS AV	FRCO	57 F8
NICHOLS RD	RCO	99 B0
NICHOLS CYN RD	LA	181 J1
NICHOLS MILL RD	SIE	13 L3
NICKEL AV	FRCO	57 H1
NICLAS RD	RCO	99 P6
NIDEER RD	SLO	75 G9
NIDEER RD	SLO	76 G9
NIELSEN AV	FRE	165 J1
NIELSEN RD	FRCO	57 J1
NILAND AV	IMP	114 D0
NILES BL	KER	78 G7
NILES ST	BKD	166 F8
NILES CANYON RD	ALA	46 A1
NIMITZ BLVD	SD	212 Q4
NIMITZ FRWY	ALA	146 K5
NIMITZ FRWY	ALA	157 J9
NIMITZ FRWY	O	157 G2
NIMITZ FRWY	O	158 L2
NIMITZ FRWY	SJ	152 A1
NINE MILE CYN	INY	70 M3
NINTH ST	C	124 P4
NIPOMO ST	SLO	76 H2
NIPOMON CT	SNLO	172 P4
NIPTON DESRT RD	SBD	84 G3
NIPTON RD	SBD	84 E3
NIPTON MOORE RD	SBD	84 G3
NISQUALLY RD	HUM	15 E7
NM 1	TUL	68 M8
NM 14	TUL	68 M8

SEE PAGE D FOR INSTRUCTIONS

STREET INDEX

STREET INDEX

STREET INDEX

PEACHY CANYON RD

STREET INDEX

RICHARDSON AV

STREET	CO.	PAGE & GRID
PEACHY CYN RD	SLO	76 C0
PEAK RD	TRI	16 P8
PEAR AV	GLE	25 L0
PEAR AV	STA	47 K5
PEARBLOSSOM HWY	LACO	90 K1
PEARL ST	SDCO	106 H1
PEARL ST	SDCO	107 P4
PEAR MAIN ST	SBD	91 G2
PEARSON RD	BUT	25 G5
PEARSON RD	INY	70 N5
PEASE RD	SUT	33 D5
PEAVINE RDG RD	ED	35 L3
PEBBLE BEACH DR	DN	1 K6
PEBBLY BEACH RD	AVLN	105 N3
PECHO VALLEY RD	SLO	75 J8
PECK RD	LACO	98 C2
PECK RD	LACO	118 L2
PEDERSON	FRCO	58 H1
PEDLEY RD	RCO	99 E1
PEDRICK RD	SOL	39 F3
PEDRICK RD	SOL	39 C3
PEDRO RANCH RD	MNO	51 A5
PEDROS RD	STA	47 H6
PEGASUS ST	KER	79 M3
PELGER RD	SUT	33 J3
PELICAN RD	STA	47 F2
PELLET RD	IMP	109 L9
PELLISER RD	KER	79 M3
PELTIER	SJCO	40 J0
PENCIL RD	MOD	7 P2
PENDLETON RD	SBD	92 C0
PENDOLA RD	YUB	26 M4
PENDOLA EXT	YUB	26 M4
PENDOLA GARDEN	MPA	48 H9
PENFIELD AV	LA	178 M1
PENINSULA DR	PLU	20 L3
PENMAN SPGS RD	SLO	76 C2
PENNINGTON RD	BUT	25 Q3
PENNINGTON RD	SUT	33 B4
PENNSYLVANIA AV	FRFD	135 G2
PENNSYLVANIA AV	LACO	117 E5
PENNSYLVANIA AV	RIV	205 J8
PENNSYLVANIA AV	RCO	99 G8
PENNSYLVANIA AV	SOL	135 M2
PENNSYLV GCH RD	CAL	41 K4
PENON LOOKOUT	MPA	48 C7
PENOYAR GRAS LK	SIS	4 N8
PENOYAR TENNANT	SIS	5 N0
PENROSE ST	LACO	117 E2
PENTLAND RD	KER	78 N2
PENTZ RD	BUT	25 J5
PENTZ MAGALIA	BUT	25 G6
PEORIA RD	YUB	34 B0
PEPPER	SON	37 H9
PEPPER AV	SBD	99 D3
PEPPER RD	SON	37 H8
PEPPER ST	MCO	47 J9
PEPPER ST	MCO	48 J0
PEPPER ST	SBD	80 N9
PEPPER ST	SBD	81 P0
PERALTA BLVD	ALA	46 G1
PERALTA ST	O	157 F5
PERCH ST	KER	79 M4
PERCY AV	YUBA	125 H7
PERCY RD	KER	79 A6
PERI RD	MON	65 L7
PERIMETER RD	NEV	34 F2
PERINI RD	LAK	32 K1
PERINI RD	LAK	32 K1
PERKINS AV	KER	78 A2
PERKINS RD	SB	87 B5
PERKINS ST	U	123 H3
PERRAL RD	KER	77 E7
PERRIN	SJCO	47 D2
PERRIN AV	FRCO	57 F6
PERRIS BLVD	RCO	99 J4
PERRY RD	COL	32 A7
PERRY RD	RCO	99 M2
PERRY CREEK RD	ED	41 A0
PERSHING AV	S	160 A0
PERSHING DR	LA	187 P6
PERSHING DR	LACO	117 P1
PERSHING DR	SD	216 G1
PERSHING DR	SDCO	106 L3
PESCADERO CK RD	SMCO	45 N5
PETALUMA AV	SON	132 K2
PETALUMA HLL RD	STR	131 M7
PETALUMA HLL RD	SON	38 E0
PETALUMA HLL RD	SON	131 M7
PETE MILLER RD	STA	47 N4
PETERSBOURGH S	CAL	40 J8
PETERSBURG RD	SIS	11 J3
PETERSON DR	NAPA	29 E2
PETERSON LN	LAK	31 J6
PETERSON RD	COL	32 A5
PETERSON RD	FRCO	58 C2
PETERSON RD	IMP	110 H3
PETERSON RD	KER	68 Q4
PETERSON RD	KER	77 A9
PETERSON RD	KER	78 A2
PETERSON RD	LPAZ	104 G0
PETERSON RD	LACO	89 K6
PETERSON RDG RD	YUB	26 N2
PETRIFIED FORST	NAPA	38 B0
PETRIFIED FORST	SON	38 B0
PETRO RD	INY	72 D5
PETROGLYPH RD	MNO	51 G6
PETRLEUM CLB RD	KER	78 M0
PETTYJOHN RD	TEH	17 N8
PEW RD	SBD	85 P5
PFE RD	PLA	33 N9
PFITZER RD	MCO	47 P6
PHEASANT CT	KER	79 L3
PHELAN RD	HUM	15 C7
PHELAN RD	HUM	15 C7
PHELAN RD	SBD	91 L0
PHELPS AV	FRCO	66 F7
PHILADELPHIA ST	LACO	98 E8
PHILADELPHIA ST	SBD	98 E8
PHILBRIC RD	SB	86 B4
PHILBROOK RD	BUT	25 A7
PHILDOW RD	LAS	20 H8
PHILIP	PLA	33 M8
PHILLIPE LN	SIS	4 L1
PHILLIPS	LAK	32 J1
PHILLIPS DR	SBD	82 Q1
PHILLIPS RD	KER	78 B4
PHILLIPS RD	KER	78 K2
PHILLIPS RD	KER	80 K6
PHILLIPS RD	SHA	19 B1
PHILLIPS RD	SOL	39 C3
PHILLIPSVLLE RD	HUM	16 M4
PHILO GRNWD RD	MEN	30 E5
PHOENIX LAKE RD	TUO	41 B6
PHYLLIS RD	TEH	18 K5
PICACHO RD	IMP	116 N6
PICADOR BLVD	SDCO	106 P5
PICADOR BLVD	SDCO	111 E7
PICARD RD	SIS	4 F9
PICRD SAMS NECK	SIS	4 F9
PICARDY DR	S	160 L2
PICKENS RD	LAS	21 Q7
PICKERING AV	LACO	118 N2
PICKETT RD	IMP	110 K3
PICO BLVD	LA	180 M6
PICO BLVD	LA	183 H2
PICO BLVD	LA	184 H4
PICO BLVD	LA	185 H0
PICO BLVD	LACO	117 L1
PICO BLVD	SMON	180 P2
PICO BLVD	SMON	187 A0
PICO CANYON RD	LACO	89 M2
PIEDMONT AV	B	156 G3
PIEDMONT AV	O	158 C2
PIEDMONT RD	SCL	46 K3
PIEDRA RD	FRCO	58 H1
PIEDRA AZUL	MCO	55 G6
PIEDRAS DR	RCO	99 J3
PIER AV	LACO	119 C2
PIERCE LN	SOL	38 L8
PIERCE RD	SCL	45 N9
PIERCE ST	BKD	166 E1
PIERCE ST	RCO	99 H1
PIERCE ST	RCO	101 M3
PIERCE CK MTRWY	PLU	20 L9
PIERCE POINT RD	MAR	37 K6
PIERI RD	KER	78 L3
PIERLE RD	IMP	109 N9
PIERSON BLVD	RCO	100 F5
PIGEON PASS RD	RCO	99 F4
PIGEON SPG RD	KER	79 N5
PIKE RD	STA	47 H6
PIKE CITY RD	SIE	26 N5
PIKE CITY RD	YUB	26 N4
PILE ST	SDCO	108 K1
PILITAS HUERHRO	SLO	76 F4
PILOT SPRING RD	MNO	43 Q7
PILOT SPRING RD	MNO	50 A8
PIMLICO DR	RCO	100 P5
PINAL ST	SB	86 C6
PINE AV	LB	192 H7
PINE AV	MEN	31 B4
PINE AV	PAC	167 F5
PINE AV	SBD	98 F7
PINE DR	HUM	16 M3
PINE DR	LAS	20 E9
PINE DR	MPA	48 C8
PINE ST	C	124 M5
PINE ST	MONT	167 F6
PINE ST	MON	53 F8
PINE ST	NAP	133 M2
PINE ST	RED	122 C3
PINE ST	RCO	100 M5
PINE ST	SDCO	108 K1
PINE ST	SF	142 G1
PINE ST	SF	143 L4
PINE ST	SHA	18 H4
PINE ST	U	123 F4
PINE CANYON RD	MON	65 G2
PINE CANYON RD	SB	76 P9
PINE COVE TR	KER	79 F7
PINE CREEK BL	MOD	8 C2
PINE CREEK RD	INY	51 L2
PINE CREEK RD	HUM	10 H5
PINE CREEK RD	SIS	2 J8
PINE FLAT	SON	31 P8
PINE FLAT RD	SBD	91 N8
PINE FLAT RD	SCR	53 C7
PINE GROVE	VEN	88 M4
PINE GROVE RD	KLAM	5 B5
PINE HILLS RD	SDCO	108 K4
PINEHURST RD	CC	45 B7
PINE MTN RD	KER	78 B9
PINE MTN RD	KER	79 B0
PINE MTN RD	MEN	31 L6
PINE NUT RD	MNO	42 C8
PINE RIDGE	FRCO	58 H5
PINE RIDGE RD	HUM	10 J4
PINE RIDGE RD	MEN	31 E1
PNES TO PLMS HY	RCO	100 M4
PINE TREE CY RD	KER	80 K1
PINE VALLEY RD	MON	65 H7
PINEWOOD LN	FRCO	58 G2
PINEY CK LOOP	MON	64 D7
PINKSTON CYN RD	BUT	25 G7
PINNACLE RD	SBD	81 C1
PINON CANYON RD	KER	79 L5
PINON VILLGE RD	TUL	70 H1
PINTO DR	CAL	41 M2
PINTO RD	RCO	101 M8
PINTO BASIN RD	RCO	101 K7
PINTO MTN RD	SBD	101 B5
PIONEER AV	STA	47 C7
PIONEER BLVD	LACO	98 G1
PIONEER BLVD	LACO	120 G1
PIONEER DR	KER	78 G8
PIONEER RD	DN	2 J2
PIONEER RD	MCO	55 C7
PIONEER TR	SLT	129 L5
PIONEERTOWN RD	SBD	100 B6
PIONEERTOWN RD	SBD	100 B6
PIONEER TR RD	ED	36 K1
PIONEER TR RD	ED	36 K1
PIPE CREEK RD	RCO	100 N4
PIPE LINE AV	SBD	98 E6
PIPES RD	SBD	100 B4
PIPES CANYON RD	SBD	100 B6
PIPES CANYON RD	SBD	100 B6
PIPI RD	ED	41 A4
PIRCEN RD	LAS	14 H2
PIRU CANYON RD	LACO	89 L0
PIRU CANYON RD	VEN	88 L9
PISGAH CRATR RD	SBD	92 E8
PISTACHIO RD	KER	77 B3
PIT RD	MNO	51 D1
PIT #1 PWRHS RD	SHA	13 L7
PITTMAN HILL RD	FRCO	58 E0
PITT RIV CYN RD	LAS	14 K0
PITT SCHOOL RD	SOL	39 E3
PITTVILLE RD	LAS	20 A1
PITTVILLE RD	SHA	13 K9
PITTVILLE BENCH	LAS	14 K1
PITTZER RD	IMP	114 B2
PIUMA RD	LACO	97 D1
PIUTE MTN RD	KER	79 F6
PIUTE PINES RD	KER	79 G7
PLACENTIA AV	CM	199 G1
PLACENTIA AV	NB	199 G1
PLACENTIA AV	ORA	120 K5
PLACER AV	FRCO	56 M8
PLACER CT	KER	79 F7
PLACER RD	SHA	18 J4
PLACER RD	SUT	33 H8
PLACER ST	RED	122 E1
PLACER ST	SHA	18 E3
PLACER ST	TRI	17 B6
PLACER HILLS RD	PLA	34 G5
PLACERITA CYN	LACO	89 N2
PLACERVILLE DR	PLCV	138 G0
PLACERVILLE RD	SAC	34 P3
PLAINS RD	CC	39 P5
PLAINSBURG RD	MCO	48 P6
PLANT FIVE RD	INY	51 L5
PLASKETT RDG RD	MON	64 L8
PLATEAU CIR	SHA	18 F3
PLATEAU PINE RD	SHA	19 G3
PLATFORM RD	MAR	37 M8
PLATINA RD	SHA	18 J6
PLATINA RD	SHA	17 J7
PLATINA RD	SHA	17 H8
PLATINA SCH RD	SHA	17 K6
PLAYA AZUL	AVLN	105 L2
PLAZA ST	SDCO	107 L4
PLEASANT	CC	38 Q8
PLEASANT AV	SON	37 C8
PLEASANT RD	SLO	66 Q2
PLEASANT GROVE	PLA	33 M7
PLEASANT GROVE	SUT	33 M7
PLEASANT HILL	SON	37 F7
PLEASNT HL RD E	M	154 K5
PLEASANT OAK DR	TUL	68 G9
PLEASANTN SUNOL	ALA	46 F2
PLEASANT PT RD	HUM	15 E8
PLEASANT VLY AV	O	156 Q3
PLEASNTS VLY RD	SOL	38 F9
PLEASANT VLY RD	ALP	36 P3
PLEASANT VLY RD	ED	34 P8
PLEASANT VLY RD	NEV	34 C2
PLEASANT VLY RD	STA	47 B7
PLEASANT VLY RD	VEN	105 B4
PLEASNT VLY DAM	INY	51 J4
PLESANTE RD	MON	54 H5
PLEYTO CEM RD	MON	65 M5
PLINCO MINE RD	PLU	21 Q5
PLUMAS AV	FRCO	57 G0
PLUMAS ST	RENO	130 M2
PLUMAS ARBGA RD	YUB	33 G6
PLUMB LN E	RENO	130 P6
PLUMB LN W	RENO	130 P4
PLUMBAGO RD	SIE	26 N7
PLUM CREEK RD	TEH	19 K1
PLUMMER LKOT RD	TRI	17 G2
PLUM VALLEY RD	MOD	7 L5
PLUNKETT RD	HUM	10 P1
PLYMIRE RD	TEH	18 N5
PLYMOUTH AV	KIN	67 H1
PLYMOUTH RD	AMA	40 D8
PLYMOUTH RD	SBD	80 P9
P MOCUS LKOT RD	TEH	17 L7
POCK LN	SJCO	40 F2
POCKET RD	SAC	39 D7
POE RD	IMP	109 J8
POE POWERHOUSE	BUT	25 G8
POINSETTIA LN	SDCO	107 J3
PT LAKEVIEW RD	LAK	32 J0
PT LOMA AV	SDCO	106 K1
POINT LOMA AV	SDCO	111 B4
PT LOMA BLVD	SDCO	106 K6
POINT LOMA BL W	SD	212 P2
PT OF TIMBER RD	CC	39 Q6
PT PLEASANT RD	SAC	39 G8
POINT RANCH RD	MNO	43 H2
PT REYES RD	MAR	37 L9
PT REYES PETLMA	MAR	37 M8
POINT SAL RD	SB	86 B1
POKER BAR RD	TRI	17 C6
POKER FLAT RD	SIE	26 H7
POLE LINE RD	LAS	20 A0
POLE LINE RD	MCO	55 F9
POLELINE RD	SBD	93 Q0
POLE LINE RD	SHA	13 N8
POLETA RD	INY	51 L6
POLETA LAWS RD	INY	51 L7
POLI ST	VENT	175 F8
POLK AV	FRCO	57 H3
POLK AV	FRCO	67 A3
POLK AV	FRCO	57 P3
POLK ST	LACO	117 A1
POLK ST	RCO	101 N2
POLLACK FLAT	SIS	5 N1
POLSON RD	NAPA	38 J6
POMEGRANATE AV	STA	47 J4
POMELO AV	STA	47 J4
POMERADO RD	SDCO	106 F5
POMERADO RD	SDCO	107 N7
POMEROY AV	SCLR	150 J5
POMEROY LS BERS	SLO	76 N4
POMONA AV	COR	215 Q5
POMONA AV	CM	199 H2
POMONA BLVD	LACO	117 L8
POMONA FRWY	LACO	98 E1
POMONA FRWY	LACO	118 M4
POMONA ST	CC	38 M7
POND RD	KER	68 P1
POND RD	KER	68 P4
PONDER WY	SHA	18 J3
PONDEROSA BL	LAS	21 L3
PONDEROSA RD	CAL	41 L4
PONDEROSA WY	AMA	41 G2
PONDEROSA WY	BUT	25 D4
PONDEROSA WY	BUT	25 G7
PONDEROSA WY	BUT	25 J8
PONDEROSA WY	BUT	26 L0
PONDEROSA WY	CAL	41 J3
PONDEROSA WY	MPA	49 G3
PONDEROSA WY	PLA	34 G6
PONDEROSA WY	SHA	19 D2
PONDEROSA WY	TEH	19 J3
PONDOSA WY	SIS	13 G4
PONY RD	SBD	92 M5
PONY WY	SHA	41 M1
POOLE AV	KER	80 A5
POOLE LN	SIE	27 H6
POOLE RD	HUM	15 F6
POOLE RD	MCO	48 P6
POOL STATION RD	CAL	41 J0
POONKINNEY RD	MEN	23 H1
POOP OUT HL RD	SBD	100 C1
POOR BOY CK RD	ALP	36 P4
POORE RD	IMP	110 M5
POPE ST	NAPA	29 F4
POPE CANYON RD	NAPA	38 A4
POPE VALLEY RD	NAPA	29 G5
POPE VALLEY RD	NAPA	32 Q3
POPLAR AV	KER	78 D2
POPLAR AV	MLBR	144 P6
POPPET FLAT RD	RCO	100 J1
PORTAL RD W	MNO	43 Q5
PORTER	FRCO	58 L1
PORTER AV	RCO	99 J5
PORTER AV	RCO	99 J5
PORTER RD	SOL	39 E3
PORTER CREEK RD	SON	37 B9
PORTERVILLE HWY	KER	78 A6
PORTERVILLE WY	KER	78 A4
PORT KENYON RD	HUM	15 E6
PORTOLA AV	RCO	100 L8
PORTOLA BLVD	ALA	46 E4
PORTOLA DR	SFCO	45 D3
PORTOLA RD	SLO	76 E1
PORTOLA RD	SMCO	45 L6
PORTOLA STAT PK	SMCO	45 N6
PORTOLA MCLEARS	PLU	27 G2
PORTUGUESE CYN	MON	64 M2
PORT WINE RIDGE	PLU	26 H5
PORT WINE RIDGE	SIE	26 K5
PORTY ST	KER	78 K6
POSO AV	KER	77 C8
POSO FLAT RD	KER	79 B1
POST ST	SF	142 G2
POST ST	SF	143 M1
POST MTN RD	TRI	17 H2
POTRERO AV	SF	142 M7
POTRERO RD E	VEN	105 C7
POTRERO RD W	VEN	105 C5
POTRERO GRDE BL	LACO	118 L0
POTRERO GRDE DR	LACO	117 L9
POTTER RD	MON	54 M7
POTTEROFFS RD	CAL	41 G2
POUND RD	IMP	110 G1
POUNDSTONE RD	COL	33 H2
POURROY RD	RCO	99 P6
POVERTY RD	SAC	39 J6
POVERTY HILL RD	SIE	26 K5
POWAY RD	SDCO	107 M6
POWELL AV	SON	37 A7
POWELL RD	SBD	92 N7
POWELL RD	SUT	33 B3
POWELL RD	VEN	88 M8
POWER HOUSE RD	FRCO	57 A9
POWER HOUSE RD	MEN	23 Q3
POWERHOUSE RD	TRI	11 Q8
POWERHOUSE RD S	TEH	19 H2
POWER INN RD	SAC	40 C0
POWER LINE RD	MNO	52 H4
POWER LINE RD	RCO	107 A9
POWER LINE RD	SAC	33 P6
POWER LINE RD	SBD	83 G1
POWER LINE RD	SBD	91 G4
POWER LINE RD	SHA	18 F3
POWER LINE RD	SUT	33 L6
POWERS AV	MAN	161 J6
POZOS RD	RCO	99 J5
POZOS RD	RCO	99 J5
PRADO RD	SNLO	172 Q1
PRAHSER RD	SJCO	40 N4
PRAIRIE AV	LACO	119 C3
PRAIRIE AV	SBD	91 C5
PRAIRIE DR	LAS	8 P1
PRAIRIE WY	MEN	30 A3
PRAIRIE CK RD	TRI	17 B1
PRAIRIE FLOWER	STA	47 K6
PRATT RANCH RD	MEN	31 H4
PRATVLL BTT RES	PLU	20 N2
PREFUMO CYN RD	SLO	76 K0
PRELL RD	SB	86 B4
PRESCOTT AV	MONT	167 H5
PRESCOTT AV	MON	53 G7
PRESCOTT AV	PAC	167 H4
PRESIDIO AV	SF	142 F0
PRESIDIO BLVD	SFCO	45 C3
PRESTON	MPA	49 N0
PRESTON RD	BUT	25 K5
PRESTON RD	IMP	113 C9
PRESTON RD	MCO	47 M5
PRICE CREEK RD	HUM	15 G8
PRICE CK CAMPBL	TRI	17 C2
PRICE CK SCH RD	HUM	15 F8
PRICE CANYON RD	SLO	76 L2
PRIEST COLTRVLL	MPA	48 C7
PRIEST COLTRVLL	TUO	48 C7
PRIEST VLY RD	MON	66 F1
PRIM RD	IMP	110 P3
PRIMROSE MN RD	SIE	26 K9
PRINCE AV	FRCO	56 F1
PRINCE RD	MCO	47 N5
PRINCESS PAT MN	SBD	90 E9
PRINCETON	FRCO	58 H1
PRINCETON RD	MCO	48 J2
PROGRESS RD	SUT	33 F3
PROSPECT AV	KER	78 C1
PROSPECT AV	ORA	120 E8
PROSPECT AV	SDCO	106 H7
PROSPECT BLVD	PAS	190 G1
PROSPECT RD	SCL	45 M9
PROSPECT ST	SDCO	106 H1
PROSPECT ST	SDCO	107 P4
PROSSER DAM RD	NEV	27 Q7
PROVIDENCE RCH	SBD	84 M3
PRUNE AV	STA	47 J4
PRUNERIDGE AV	CPTO	150 K1
PRUNERIDGE AV	SJ	151 L1
PRUNERIDGE AV	SCLR	150 L4
PRUNERIDGE AV	SCL	151 L1
PRUSSIAN HLL RD	CAL	41 G2
PUEBLO AV	KIN	67 H5
PUEBLO AV	NAP	133 F3
PUENTE AV	LACO	98 D2
PUENTE AV	LACO	118 L3
PULGA RD	BUT	25 E8
PULLMAN RD	IMP	113 D9
PUMICE MILL RD	MNO	51 H6
PUMICE MINE RD	MNO	51 C4
PUMICE MINE RD	MNO	50 E6
PUMP RD	MCO	55 E8
PUMP RD	STA	47 L5
PUMPHOUSE RD	COL	32 E6
PUMPHOUSE RD	YOL	39 D7
PUNKIN CTR RD	LAS	14 K3
PURDON RD	NEV	26 Q4
PURDY AV	KER	80 P0
PURDYS RD	PLU	26 C5
PURISIMA RD	SB	86 G3
PURISIMA CK RD	SMCO	45 K4
PURITAN MINE RD	LACO	89 L8
PUTAH LN	LAK	32 M1
PUTAH CREEK RD	SOL	39 C1
PUTNAM RD	COL	25 Q1
PUTNAM WY	COL	32 G8
PY RD	CAL	41 N2
PYLE RD	LAK	31 E7
PYRAMID HILLS	KIN	67 H1
PYRITE RD	RCO	99 F1
Q		
QUAIL AV	KIN	67 H2
QUAIL DR	RCO	100 P2
QUAIL HILL RD	HUM	16 F0
QUAIL ST	KER	80 A5
QUAIL WY	RCO	100 N1
QUAIL SPGS RD	SBD	101 C0
QUAIL SPGS SPUR	SBD	101 E1
QUAKER ST	HUM	9 Q9
QUAKR HL CRS RD	NEV	34 B6
QUALITY RD	KER	78 B1
QUARRY RD	PA	147 G0
QUARRY RD	SDCO	106 M6
QUARRY RD	SDCO	111 C8
QUARRY RD S	HUM	10 Q0
QUARTZ ST	BUT	25 D6
QUARTZ ST	SBD	84 H4
QUARTZ ST	TUO	41 P4
QUARTZ HILL RD	SHA	18 E4
QUARTZ MT LKOUT	SIS	3 N6
QUARTZ VLY DR	SIS	3 N5
QUARTZ VLY RD	SIS	3 P5
QUARTZ VLY RD E	SIS	3 N5
QUATAL CYN RD	KER	87 D8
QUATAL CYN RD	SB	87 D8
QUATAL CYN RD	VEN	88 C1
QUEBEC AV	KIN	67 H8
QUEBEC AV	KIN	67 H1
QUEEN OF SHEBA	INY	72 J0
QUEENS AV	YUBA	125 C1
QUEENS WY	LB	192 K7
QUESTHAVEN RD	SDCO	107 J5
QUICK RD	IMP	115 B5
QUIEN SABE RD	SBT	55 H2
QUIEN SABE RCH	SBT	55 H3
QUIMBY RD	SCL	46 M4
QUINCY RD	SIE	26 G6
QUINCY JCT RD	PLU	26 C6
QUINCY LA PORTE	PLU	26 F6
QUINCY LA PORTE	PLU	26 K4
QUINLEY AV	MCO	48 N2
QUINN RD	HUM	15 C7
QUINN RD	HUM	15 C7
QUINN RD	KER	68 N6
QUISENBERRY RD	STA	47 G4
QUITO RD	SCL	46 N1
R		
R ST	FRE	165 J8
R ST	MER	170 K3
RABBIT RANCH RD	MNO	51 D4
RABBIT SPGS RD	SBD	91 L8
RABER ST	KER	80 P1
RACE ST	SJ	151 L9
RACE TRACK RD	SAC	39 J7
RACE TRACK RD	TUO	163 G0
RACETRACK VLY	INY	61 E1
RACINE AV	KIN	67 J8
RACQUET CLUB DR	SR	139 H2
RADIO LN	RED	122 P4
RADIO STATN RD	SOL	39 F3
RAGAN MEADWS RD	TRI	17 G1
RAG DUMP RD	BUT	25 E7
RAGLIN RIDGE RD	TEH	24 B0
RAGSDALE RD	RCO	102 L3
RAHILLY RD	MCO	48 P3
RAIL CANYON RD	COL	24 Q3
RAIL CANYON RD	GLE	24 P2
RAIL CREEK RD	SIS	12 D0
RAILROAD AV	SOL	135 H8
RAILROAD AV	HUM	16 M6
RAILROAD AV	RED	122 G3
RAILROAD AV	SMA	173 F2
RAILROAD AV	SUT	33 F5
RAILROAD AV	VAL	134 K0
RAILROAD AV	SBD	84 H4
RAILROAD CYN RD	RCO	99 M4
RAILRD FLAT RD	CAL	41 H3
RAINBOW	FRCO	57 J9
RAINBOW BASN RD	SBD	81 P7
RAINBOW CYN RD	SBD	93 L2
RAINBOW LAKE RD	SHA	18 G0
RAINES RD	STA	47 H3
RAINIER RD	TRI	11 N7
RAIN TREE LN	BUT	25 F1
RAJNUS RD	KLAM	5 E8
RALPH RD	IMP	110 P1
RALSTON AV	BLMT	145 P5
RALSTON AV	SMCO	45 G4
RAMAL RD	SON	38 J4
RAMBLA PACIFICO	LACO	97 D2
RAMELI GREIG RD	PLU	27 F7
RAMIREZ RD	YUB	33 C6
RAMON RD	PMSP	206 L4
RAMON RD	RCO	100 J6
RAMON RD	RCO	100 J8
RAMONA AV	LACO	118 H8
RAMONA AV	MTCL	203 N2
RAMONA AV	SBDO	203 N2
RAMONA AV	SBD	91 J5
RAMONA AV	SBD	98 E6
RAMONA BLVD	LACO	118 J3
RAMONA BLVD	RCO	99 J8
RAMONA DR	SNLO	172 D0
RAMONA EXPWY	RCO	99 H5
RAMONA EXPWY	RCO	99 J7
RAMONA FRWY	SDCO	106 J6
RAMONA FRWY	SDCO	107 Q8
RAMOS RD	MCO	55 C7
RAMP RD	MNO	43 G3
RAMSEY RD	RCO	108 B3
RAMSEY RD	RCO	108 B3
RAMSEY RD	SOL	38 J8
RAMSEY MINE RD	LPAZ	104 M7
RAMSHORN RD	TRI	12 H1
RAMS HORN GRADE	AMA	41 D1
RAMSHN MUMBO CK	TRI	12 J2
RANCH RD	HUM	15 C8
RANCH RD	MCO	48 P5
RANCH RD	MNO	52 H4
RANCH RD	SBD	92 P8
RANCHERIA RD	KER	78 F9
RANCHERIA RD	KER	79 F0
RANCHERIA RD	MEN	30 J5
RANCHERIA CK RD	SIS	4 G1
RANCHERIAS RD	SBD	91 J4
RANCHERIA-SAWML	KER	79 B3
RANCHERO	SBD	91 M4
RANCHITA CYN RD	MON	66 N4
RANCHITA CYN RD	SLO	66 P2
RANCHLAND DR	SHA	18 F3
RANCH LAND RD	SDCO	107 K9
RANCHO AV	SBD	99 D3
RANCHO DR	KER	78 M9
RANCHO DR	KER	79 M0
RANCHO DR	SBD	91 J1
RANCHO RD	KER	78 N9
RANCHO RD	KER	79 N0
RANCHO RD	LV	209 E1
RANCHO RD	SB	76 P5
RANCHO RD	SB	86 C2
RANCHO RD	SHA	18 F5
RNCHO ALISAL RD	SB	86 J8
RCHO BAUTSTA RD	RCO	100 P2
RO BERNARDO RD	SDCO	107 L7
RANCHO CALIF RD	RCO	99 Q6
RANCHO CALIF RD	RCO	107 A5
RANCHO CANADA	SDCO	108 P0
RCHO CANADA RD	SDCO	106 H8
RNCHO CONEJO BL	VEN	105 B6
RO SANTA FE RD	SDCO	107 J4
RANDALL AV	SBD	99 D1
RANDALL RD	KER	77 L8
RANDOLPH RD	SAC	40 E1
RANDSBURG RD	SBD	81 D4
RANDSBRG CUTOFF	KER	80 M0
RANDSBRG CUTOFF	SBD	80 H8
RANDSBG INYOKRN	KER	80 C6
RANDSBG WASH RD	SBD	80 B9
RANDSBG WASH RD	SBD	81 B0
RANGER STA RD	INY	51 J3
RANGER STA RD	INY	60 M0
RANGER STA RD	TRI	17 B2
RANNELS BLVD	RCO	103 Q5
RANNELS BLVD	RCO	116 B5
RASOR RD	SBD	83 M1
RATTLESNAKE RD	NEV	34 D5
RATTLESNAKE RD	TRI	17 H2
RATTLSNK BTT RD	MOD	14 B8
RATTLSNK CYN RD	SBD	92 N4
RATTLSNAK CK RD	SIS	3 N6
RAWHIDE RD	TUO	41 N4
RAWSON RD	TEH	18 P6
RAY	SJCO	40 J0
RAY	SJCO	40 L0
RAY RD	SB	86 A2
RAYHOUSE RD	YOL	32 K4
RAYMOND AV	ORA	120 C5
RAYMOND RD	ALA	46 D4
RAYNOR RANCH	MCO	48 N9
REAL RD	BKD	166 L1
REAL RD	KER	166 P1
RECALDE RD	SBT	55 M8
RECHE RD	SBD	92 P7
RECHE RD	SDCO	107 D5
RECHE CANYON RD	RCO	99 E4
RECLAMATION RD	LAK	31 E7
RECLAMATION RD	SUT	33 J4
RECLAMATION RD	SUT	33 L5
RECTOR RD	NEV	34 B5
RED BANK RD	TEH	18 P3
RED BOX RD	LACO	118 D0
RED CAP RD	HUM	10 F6
RED CLOUD MN RD	RCO	102 M2
REDDING AV	KIN	67 J7
REDDING CYN RD	INY	51 L8
REDDING CK RD	TRI	17 E7
REDDINGTON AV	COL	32 H8
RED DOG RD	NEV	34 C6
RED GRADE RD	TRI	17 C7
RED HEAD CYN RD	MON	65 H7
RED HILL AV	CM	198 M1
RED HILL AV	IRV	198 H6
RED HILL AV	ORA	120 J7
RED HILL BLVD	ORA	98 L5
REDHILL RD	CAL	41 M3
RED HILL RD	IMP	110 G0
RED HILL RD	INY	51 L5
REDHILL RD	TUO	48 B4
REDLANDS BLVD	RCO	99 F5
REDLANDS BLVD	RCO	99 F5
REDLANDS BLVD	SBDO	207 Q7
REDLANDS BLVD	SBD	99 D5
REDLANDS FRWY	RCO	99 F7
REDLANDS FRWY	SBD	99 E6
REDLANDS ST	SBD	99 D6
RED MOUNTAIN RD	KER	80 G8
RED MOUNTAIN RD	MCO	55 B2
RED MOUNTAIN RD	RCO	100 N0
RED MOUNTAIN RD	SBD	80 G8
RED MOUNTAIN RD	SHA	13 J5
RED MOUNTAIN RD	TRI	17 K3
RED MTN LKOUT	GLE	24 H0
RED MTN MOTORWY	TRI	17 K3
RED MTN TK TR	RCO	107 B5
RED OAK CYN RD	SIE	26 J8
REDONDO AV	LACO	98 K0
REDONDO AV	LACO	119 F8
REDONDO BLVD	LACO	184 L2
REDONDO BCH BL	LACO	119 B3
RED ROCK RD	LAS	8 K6
RED ROCK RD	LAS	27 D9
RED ROCK RD	SIS	5 J0
REDROCK-INYOKRN	KER	80 B5
REDROCK-INYOKRN	KER	80 E4
REDROCK-RANDSBG	KER	80 H3
RED ROVER MN RD	LACO	89 K8
RED SHANK LN	RCO	100 N1
REDSTONE AV	KER	79 G5
RED TOP RD	SOL	38 J7
RED VISTA RD	ALP	36 N1
REDWING RD	SBD	91 J6
REDWOOD DR	HUM	16 P4
REDWOOD HWY	DN	1 H8
REDWOOD HWY	HUM	16 G0
REDWOOD HWY	HUM	16 L2
REDWOOD HWY	MAR	38 K1
REDWOOD HWY	MAR	140 E5
REDWOOD HWY	MEN	22 F6
REDWOOD HWY	MEN	22 K9
REDWOOD HWY	CRTM	140 E5
REDWOOD HWY	SR	139 F6
REDWOOD HWY	STR	131 F4
REDWOOD HWY	SON	31 M5
REDWOOD HWY	SON	37 F9
REDWOOD RD	NAPA	29 P6
REDWOOD RD	NAPA	38 F4
REDWD HOUSE RD	HUM	41 N5
REDWOOD ST	VAL	134 G3
REDWOOD RETREAT	SCL	54 C4
REED	FRCO	58 K0
REED AV	KER	80 P1
REED AV	SVL	150 C2
REED RD	KER	68 N4
REEDER RD	KLAM	5 B4
REED MTN RD	HUM	22 B4
REED ORCHARD RD	TEH	25 C0
REEDS CREEK RD	TEH	18 N3
REEDS TURNPIKE	CAL	41 N1
REED VALLEY RD	RCO	100 Q1
REESE RD	BUT	25 E1
REEVES RD	VEN	88 L3
REEVES CYN RD	MEN	31 B0
REFUGIO RD	SB	86 J9
REGENTS RD	SD	211 D7
REGENTS RD	SDCO	106 G2
REGENTS RD	SDCO	107 P5
REGLI LN	HUM	15 F8
REICHART RCH RD	MNO	51 C5
REID RD	KER	79 D9
REID RD	KER	80 D0
REILLY RD	MCO	48 N4
REINO RD	VEN	105 B6
RELIEF HILL RD	NEV	26 Q7
RELIEZ RD	CC	38 P8
RELIZ CANYON RD	MON	65 D1
REMANN AV	SHA	19 C8
REMBACH WY	KER	79 C5
RENWICK AV	SB	86 G2
REQUA RD	DN	1 Q9
RESEDA BLVD	LA	178 J7
RESEDA BLVD	LACO	97 B4
RESERVATION RD	MON	54 K3
RESERVATION RD	TUL	68 H8
REIS AV	VAL	134 P9
RESERVE RD	KER	77 H7
RESERVOIR RD	BUT	25 N7
RESERVOIR RD	ED	34 J7
RESERVOIR RD	SOL	38 L7
RESERVOIR RD	STA	48 E1
RESERVOIR ST	LACO	98 D6
RETSON RD	BUT	25 C7
REWARD RD	KER	77 H6
REYES ADOBE RD	LACO	105 C9
REYNARD WY	SD	215 D6
REYNOLDS AV	MCO	56 D2
REYNOLDS HWY	MEN	23 N0
REYNOLDS RD	SHA	13 L8
REYNOLDS FRRY RD	TUO	41 N3
RHELM	CC	38 P5
RIALTO AV	SBD	99 C3
RIALTO AV	SBDO	207 F4
RIATA RD	LAK	32 K1
RIATA WY	CAL	41 L1
RICE AV	SBD	101 B0
RICE AV	VEN	105 B5
RICE RD	FRCO	57 F5
RICE RD	STA	47 D8
RICE RD	VEN	88 L1
RICE CANYON RD	LAS	21 G2
RICE CANYON RD	LAS	21 H2
RICE CREEK RD	LAK	23 P7
RICES CROSNG RD	YUB	26 Q1
RICES TEX HL RD	YUB	26 Q1
RICETON HWY	BUT	25 N4
RICH LN	RCO	107 A9
RICH RD	KER	68 P5
RICHARD ST	KER	70 P1
RICHARDS BL	DVS	136 J6
RICHARDSON AV	KER	142 C0

SEE PAGE D FOR INSTRUCTIONS

STREET INDEX

STREET	CO.	PAGE & GRID	
RICHARDSON RD	SBD	91	H1
RICHARDSON RD	SIS	4	G9
RICHARDSON SPGS	BUT	25	F2
RICH BAR RD	PLU	26	B2
RICH GULCH RD	PLU	26	B3
RICHLAND RD	SUT	125	N2
RICHMOND RD	LAS	21	J0
RICHMOND ST	SD	215	C9
RICHVALE HWY	BUT	25	M3
RIDER ST	RCO	99	J3
RIDGE DR	SHA	18	E3
RIDGE RD	CAL	41	F3
RIDGE RD	NEV	127	F0
RIDGE RD	NEV	128	L0
RIDGE RD	NEV	34	C4
RIDGE RD	SIE	26	N5
RIDGE RD	SIS	3	K8
RIDGE RD	TEH	18	P4
RIDGECREST BL	KER	80	B7
RIDGEWAY HWY	MEN	23	P3
RIDGEWOOD	MEN	23	Q1
RIDGEWOOD DR	HUM	15	B8
RIEBLI RD	SON	37	C9
RIEFF RD	LAK	32	K3
RIEGO RD	SUT	33	N6
RIGGIN AV	TUL	68	B1
RIGGINS RD	SUT	33	K4
RIGGS RD	SBD	83	E2
RIKER ST	SAL	171	N3
RILEY RD	BUT	25	P4
RILEY RD	SB	86	H8
RILEY RD	SAC	40	F1
RIM O T WRLD HY	SBD	91	Q4
RIM O T WRLD HY	SBD	99	A7
RIMPAU BLVD	LA	184	G5
RIMROCK RD	BARS	208	K6
RIM ROCK RD	RCO	108	B4
RIMROCK RD	SBD	91	C7
RIMROCK RD	SBD	100	B5
RIM ROCK CANYON	RCO	108	B4
RINCON	SON	38	C1
RINCON AV	SDCO	107	H7
RINCON RD	SBD	91	K4
RINCNADA LS PIL	SLO	76	H4
RIO RD	CAR	168	L4
RIO RD	MON	168	M5
RIO BLANCO	SJCO	40	M0
RIO DEL SOL RD	RCO	100	J8
RIOLINDA AV	FRCO	57	K2
RIO LINDA BLVD	SAC	33	N8
RIORDON RD	COL	32	B6
RIOSA	PLA	33	H9
RIOSA RD	PLA	34	H1
RIO VISTA AV	FRCO	58	M0
RIO VISTA AV W	TEH	18	N6
RIO VISTA RD	SUIS	135	K4
RIO VISTA ST	ORA	120	D6
RIPPON RD W	SJCO	47	D2
RITCHEY ST	SA	198	B8
RITCHIE	MPA	49	H3
RITTER RD	SHA	13	J6
RITTS MILL RD	SHA	19	F3
RIVER BLVD	KER	78	G7
RIVER RD	BUT	25	H1
RIVER RD	BUT	25	J1
RIVER RD	COL	33	C0
RIVER RD	HUM	15	G7
RIVER RD	HUM	16	P6
RIVER RD	MCO	47	L6
RIVER RD	MON	54	M6
RIVER RD	RCO	98	G8
RIVER RD	RCO	99	K4
RIVER RD	SBD	85	N5
RIVER RD	SJCO	47	C4
RIVER RD	SLO	76	B0
RIVER RD	SLO	76	H5
RIVER RD	SON	37	D7
RIVER RD	STA	47	G2
RIVER RD	STA	47	C7
RIVER RD	TEH	24	C7
RIVER RD S	YOL	39	D7
RIVER ST	SC	169	C5
RIVER ST	SCR	169	C5
RIVER ST	SON	31	M5
RIVER BENCH RD	LAS	20	H8
RIVERBEND AV	FRCO	57	H9
RIVERCREST DR	HUM	16	Q3
RIVERDALE RD	MEN	22	L9
RIVERFORD RD	SDCO	106	G7
RIVERFORD RD	SDCO	107	P9
RIVER GRADE RD	LACO	118	J3
RIVER ROCK RD	TRI	17	B7
RIVERSIDE AV	MCO	47	L7
RIVERSIDE AV	RCO	103	N5
RIVERSIDE AV	SBD	99	B2
RIVERSIDE AV	SHA	18	G5
RIVERSIDE BLVD	SCTO	137	M2
RIVERSIDE BLVD	SAC	39	C7
RIVERSIDE DR	LA	179	P2
RIVERSIDE DR	LA	182	H7
RIVERSIDE DR	LACO	117	J5
RIVERSIDE DR	LACO	117	G1
RIVERSIDE DR	RED	122	B1
RIVERSIDE DR	RCO	99	M2
RIVERSIDE DR	SBD	98	E7
RIVERSIDE DR	SDCO	106	G7
RIVERSIDE DR	SDCO	107	P9
RIVERSIDE DR	SON	132	H3
RIVERSIDE FRWY	ANA	194	A5
RIVERSIDE FRWY	ORA	98	H5
RIVERSIDE FRWY	ORA	120	C9
RIVERSIDE FRWY	RCO	99	H0
RIVERSIDE RD	HUM	10	P1
RIVERSIDE RD	INY	51	K6
RIVERSIDE RD	SBD	92	B4
RIVERSIDE ST	KER	78	E0
RIVERSIDE PK RD	HUM	16	G1
RIVER SPRINGS	MNO	44	P2
RIVER VIEW RD	SBD	91	B5
RIVIERA	RED	122	Q0
RIVIERA DR	SD	212	E3
RIVIERA DR	SDCO	106	J1
RIVIERA RD	SUT	33	B4
ROAD 1	LAS	20	B2
ROAD 1	MAD	56	C3
ROAD 4	LAS	20	B4
ROAD 4	MAD	56	C4
ROAD 5	MAD	56	B4
ROAD 5 1/2	MAD	56	F4
ROAD 6	MAD	56	C5
ROAD 7	MAD	56	C5
ROAD 8	MAD	56	C5
ROAD 8 1/2	MAD	56	G5
ROAD 9	LAS	20	C2
ROAD 9	MAD	56	C5
ROAD 10	MAD	56	B6
ROAD 10 1/2	MAD	56	D6
ROAD 11	MAD	56	C6
ROAD 12	MAD	56	C6
ROAD 12	TUL	57	N8
ROAD 13	MAD	56	B6
ROAD 14	MAD	56	C7
ROAD 14 1/2	MAD	56	C7
ROAD 15	MAD	56	C7
ROAD 16	MAD	56	D7
ROAD 16	TUL	57	N8

STREET	CO.	PAGE & GRID	
ROAD 16 1/2	MAD	56	D7
ROAD 17	MAD	56	E7
ROAD 18	MAD	56	C8
ROAD 18 1/2	MAD	56	C8
ROAD 19	MAD	56	C8
ROAD 19 1/2	MAD	56	E8
ROAD 20	MAD	56	D8
ROAD 20 1/2	MAD	56	E8
ROAD 21	MAD	56	E8
ROAD 21 1/2	MAD	56	E9
ROAD 22	MAD	48	Q9
ROAD 22 1/2	MAD	48	Q9
ROAD 23	MAD	48	Q9
ROAD 23 1/2	MAD	56	A9
ROAD 24	MAD	56	B9
ROAD 24	TUL	57	N9
ROAD 24 1/2	MAD	56	F9
ROAD 24 1/2	MAD	57	F0
ROAD 25	LAS	20	B2
ROAD 25	MAD	57	E0
ROAD 26	MAD	57	E1
ROAD 26 1/2	MAD	57	E1
ROAD 27	MAD	57	C1
ROAD 28	MAD	57	F1
ROAD 28	TUL	57	N9
ROAD 28 1/2	MAD	57	C1
ROAD 29	MAD	49	P2
ROAD 29 1/2	MAD	57	F2
ROAD 30	MAD	57	F2
ROAD 30 1/2	MAD	57	E2
ROAD 31	MAD	57	F2
ROAD 31 1/2	MAD	57	F2
ROAD 32	MAD	57	E2
ROAD 32	TUL	57	N9
ROAD 33	MAD	57	F2
ROAD 33 1/2	MAD	57	F3
ROAD 34	MAD	57	G3
ROAD 35	MAD	57	F3
ROAD 36	MAD	57	F3
ROAD 36	TUL	57	N9
ROAD 38	MAD	57	F4
ROAD 38	TUL	67	L9
ROAD 39	MAD	57	F4
ROAD 39 1/2	MAD	57	E4
ROAD 40	MAD	57	F4
ROAD 40	TUL	57	N9
ROAD 40 1/2	MAD	57	F4
ROAD 42	TUL	57	M9
ROAD 44	TUL	57	N9
ROAD 46	TUL	68	L0
ROAD 48	TUL	57	M9
ROAD 50	TUL	68	L0
ROAD 52	TUL	58	M0
ROAD 56	TUL	58	N0
ROAD 60	TUL	58	P0
ROAD 64	TUL	58	M1
ROAD 68	TUL	68	C1
ROAD 72	TUL	58	M1
ROAD 74	TUL	58	N1
ROAD 76	TUL	58	P1
ROAD 78	TUL	58	M1
ROAD 80	TUL	58	P1
ROAD 84	TUL	58	N1
ROAD 88	TUL	68	H1
ROAD 92	TUL	68	B1
ROAD 96	TUL	58	M1
ROAD 100	TUL	58	Q2
ROAD 104	TUL	58	N2
ROAD 108	TUL	68	A2
ROAD 109	TUL	58	M2
ROAD 110	MEN	31	J2
ROAD 112	TUL	58	N2
ROAD 114	TUL	58	M2
ROAD 120	TUL	58	N2
ROAD 124	TUL	58	M2
ROAD 124	TUL	68	F2
ROAD 128	TUL	58	L3
ROAD 128	TUL	68	G3
ROAD 132	TUL	58	L3
ROAD 132	TUL	68	A3
ROAD 136	TUL	58	L3
ROAD 136	TUL	68	G3
ROAD 138	TUL	68	B3
ROAD 140	TUL	58	L3
ROAD 140	TUL	68	A3
ROAD 143	TUL	58	L3
ROAD 144	TUL	58	N3
ROAD 148	TUL	68	A3
ROAD 152	TUL	68	A3
ROAD 156	TUL	58	P3
ROAD 158	TUL	68	B3
ROAD 164	TUL	68	A4
ROAD 168	TUL	68	B4
ROAD 172	TUL	68	F4
ROAD 176	TUL	68	J4
ROAD 180	TUL	58	N4
ROAD 182	TUL	58	Q4
ROAD 184	TUL	58	Q4
ROAD 188	TUL	68	A4
ROAD 190	TUL	68	B5
ROAD 192	TUL	68	C5
ROAD 194	TUL	58	P5
ROAD 196	TUL	58	P5
ROAD 197	TUL	58	P5
ROAD 200	TUL	58	P5
ROAD 202	TUL	68	G5
ROAD 204	MAD	57	E5
ROAD 204	TUL	58	P5
ROAD 205	MAD	57	D5
ROAD 206	TUL	58	N5
ROAD 208	MAD	57	C4
ROAD 208	TUL	58	N5
ROAD 209	MAD	57	C5
ROAD 210	MAD	57	B6
ROAD 211	MAD	57	B6
ROAD 212	TUL	58	P5
ROAD 216	TUL	68	F5
ROAD 220	TUL	58	P6
ROAD 224	TUL	68	K6
ROAD 225	MAD	50	P1
ROAD 228	TUL	68	B6
ROAD 232	TUL	68	F6
ROAD 233	MAD	50	N0
ROAD 235	MAD	50	Q0
ROAD 236	TUL	68	B6
ROAD 240	TUL	68	K6
ROAD 244	TUL	68	B6
ROAD 248	TUL	68	B7
ROAD 252	TUL	68	F7
ROAD 256	TUL	68	F7
ROAD 264	TUL	68	J7
ROAD 267	TUL	68	K7
ROAD 268	TUL	68	H7
ROAD 272	TUL	68	K7
ROAD 276	TUL	68	F7
ROAD 296	TUL	68	J8
ROAD 320	TUL	68	G9
ROAD 400	MAD	57	C3
ROAD 406	MAD	57	B4
ROAD 411	MAD	49	P3
ROAD 416	MAD	49	P5
ROAD 434	MAD	49	K8
ROAD 601	MAD	49	K6
ROAD 602	MAD	57	B2
ROAD 606	MAD	49	N3
ROAD 607	MAD	49	P2

STREET	CO.	PAGE & GRID	
ROAD 612	MAD	49	N4
ROAD 800	MAD	49	L4
ROAD 800	MAD	49	L4
ROAD 810	MAD	49	M4
ROAD 812	MAD	49	L4
ROAN RD	CAL	41	M2
ROBB RD	RCO	99	L2
ROBBEN RD	SOL	39	G3
ROBBEN RD	SOL	39	E3
ROBBINS RD	SUT	33	G3
ROBBINS RNCH RD	NEV	26	P7
ROBBY RD	KER	79	M3
ROBERTA AV	LAKE	7	B4
ROBRTNO RIGHETI	SLO	76	K3
ROBERTS	SJCO	40	Q0
ROBERTS	SJCO	47	A0
ROBERTS LN	KER	78	F6
ROBERTS FRRY RD	STA	48	F2
ROBERTSON BL	BH	183	F7
ROBERTSON BLVD	CUL	183	N6
ROBERTSON BL	LA	183	L6
ROBERTSON BLVD	LACO	117	K2
ROBERTSON BLVD	LACO	183	F7
ROBERTSON BLVD	MAD	56	C6
ROBERTS RES RD	MOD	14	G3
ROBINSON	SJCO	47	B4
ROBIN AV	MCO	47	M9
ROBIN AV	MCO	48	M0
ROBINSON RD	IMP	110	P1
ROBINSON RD	MCO	48	H4
ROBINSON RD	SOL	39	H3
ROBINSON CYN RD	MON	54	P3
ROBINSON CK RD	MEN	31	F1
ROBINSN MILL RD	BUT	25	N9
ROBNSN RCHRIA W	LAK	31	E6
ROBISON RD	SIS	5	L3
ROBLAR	SON	37	G7
ROBLAR AV	SB	86	G9
ROBLEY POINT RD	BUT	25	D7
ROBS RD	MOD	8	G2
ROCA LN	SBD	90	F9
ROCK CANYON RD	LAS	14	H0
ROCK CANYON RD	RCO	108	B4
ROCK CREEK DR	BUT	25	E2
ROCK CREEK RD	CAL	40	M8
ROCK CREEK RD	CAL	41	M0
ROCK CREEK RD	ED	34	M8
ROCK CREEK RD	INY	51	J1
ROCK CREEK RD	MNO	51	J1
ROCK CREEK RD	NEV	34	B5
ROCK CREEK RD	SHA	18	E3
ROCK CREEK RD	SHA	19	H3
ROCK CK GRBG PT	MNO	51	G2
ROCKERFELLER RD	BUT	25	J9
ROCKHAVEN	SBD	101	D0
ROCKING CHR RD	SBD	101	D1
ROCKLIN	PLA	34	M2
ROCK PILE RD	KER	79	K0
ROCKPILE RD	SON	31	M3
ROCKRIDGE RD	RCO	100	N1
ROCK RIVER RD	STA	48	C2
ROCK RIVER RD	TUO	48	C3
ROCK SPRINGS RD	SBD	91	L4
ROCKVILLE	SOL	38	H7
ROCKWOOD RD	IMP	114	C0
ROCKY CT	KER	79	N7
ROCKY LN	KER	79	G7
ROCKY RD	RCO	99	N2
ROCKY BAR RD	ED	41	A1
ROCKY BLUFF RD	RCO	99	K2
ROCKY CANYON RD	SLO	76	E2
ROCKYDALE RD	JOS	2	C5
ROCKY PT CMPGRD	PLU	20	N3
RODDEN RD	STA	47	C8
RODEO BLVD	LACO	117	M2
RODEO RD	LA	184	P0
RODEO RD	SBD	91	E4
RODUNER RD	MCO	48	N3
ROEN RD	STA	48	F1
ROGERS RD	KER	80	H3
ROGERS RD	STA	47	J3
ROGERS CREEK RD	SIS	10	B8
ROHNERVILLE RD	HUM	15	E8
ROLINDA AV	FRCO	57	P2
ROLLING HLLS RD	LACO	119	F3
ROLLINS RD	MLBR	144	P9
ROLLINS LAKE RD	PLA	34	E6
ROMEL ST	CAL	41	L1
ROMERO	MCO	55	A5
ROMERO RD	MCO	47	Q5
ROMERO CYN RD	SB	87	K6
ROMERS DAIRY RD	MEN	31	G2
ROMIE LN E	SAL	171	N5
RONNIE AV	KER	79	N3
ROOP RD	SCL	54	C7
ROOSEVELT RD	MCO	48	Q4
ROOST AV	KER	79	M3
ROOT AV	KER	78	C2
ROOT RD	RCO	99	P9
ROSA RD	MCO	47	M7
ROSAMOND BLVD	KER	89	C6
ROSAMOND RD	KER	90	B3
ROSAMND HLLS RD	RCO	108	B4
ROSARITA DR	SAL	171	F6
ROSCOE BLVD	LACO	97	A4
ROSCOE RD	HUM	15	L8
ROSCOE RD	STA	47	F8
ROSE AV	FRCO	56	M9
ROSE AV	FRCO	57	M4
ROSE AV	FRCO	56	M9
ROSE AV	FRCO	57	M4
ROSE AV	LAK	32	H0
ROSE AV	LA	187	E0
ROSE AV	MCO	48	M2
ROSE AV	VEN	105	A3
ROSE DR	ORA	120	B7
ROSE RD	KER	79	D9
ROSE RD	KER	80	D0
ROSE RD	MCO	47	M8
ROSE RD	SIS	5	F7
ROSE RD	TRI	17	B2
ROSE RD	YOL	39	D7
ROSE ST	SDCO	107	H7
ROSEBURG AV	MDO	162	B1
ROSECRANS	LACO	97	G7
ROSECRANS AV	ELS	189	N2
ROSECRANS AV	MB	189	N2
ROSECRANS AV	ORA	98	G3
ROSECRANS AV	ORA	120	B4
ROSECRANS BLVD	SDCO	111	B4
ROSECRANS ST	SDCO	106	L2
ROSE GARDEN RD	MCO	47	N5
ROSEDALE HWY	KER	78	G4
ROSE HILLS RD	LACO	118	M2
ROSELAWN AV	MDO	162	N1
ROSELLE AV	STA	47	E6
ROSE MARIE LN	S	160	B0
ROSEMARY RD	SB	86	B4
ROSEMEAD BLVD	LACO	98	F1
ROSEMEAD BLVD	LACO	117	N9
ROSEMEAD BLVD	LACO	118	N0
ROSE MINE RD	SBD	92	P3
ROSER RD	TEH	24	F5
ROSES RD	LACO	118	J0
ROSE VALLEY RD	VEN	88	J3
ROSEWOOD AV	VEN	105	B4

STREET	CO.	PAGE & GRID	
ROSITA ST	LA	178	N2
ROSS AV	EC	217	K1
ROSS RD	IMP	113	A9
ROSS RD	IMP	115	A6
ROSSI ST	SAL	171	J4
ROSSMORE AV	LA	184	E7
ROSSMORE AV	LACO	117	K3
ROSY RIDGE RD	RCO	108	B2
ROUGH & REDY RD	NEV	34	C3
ROULTS RD	MNO	51	G2
ROUND MTN LKOUT	SIS	13	C7
ROUND MTN RD	KER	78	D7
ROUND MTN RD	MNO	51	F2
ROUND ROBIN DR	RCO	100	K2
ROUND VALLEY RD	SBD	100	A3
ROUND VALLEY RD	TEH	23	F7
ROUND VLY RD N	INY	51	K3
ROUND VLY RD S	INY	51	K4
RND VLY TUNGSTN	INY	51	K4
ROUNDY RD	TRI	11	Q6
ROUNDY RD	TRI	17	A6
ROUSE AV	STA	162	P0
ROUSE RD	RCO	99	L4
ROUTE 101 FRWY	STB	173	P7
ROUTE 101 FRWY	SB	86	K7
ROUTE 101 FRWY	SB	87	L6
ROUTE 101 FRWY	SMA	173	B5
ROUTE 4 FRWY	CC	154	H6
ROUTE 4 FRWY	M	154	H6
ROUTE 47 FRWY	LB	191	E9
ROUTE 47 FRWY	LB	192	F0
ROUTE 47 FRWY	LA	191	E9
ROUTE 47 FRWY	LA	192	F0
ROUTE 47 FRWY	LACO	97	K8
ROUTE 47 FRWY	LACO	119	F5
ROUTE 94 FRWY	SD	216	J4
ROUTE 52 FRWY	SD	211	H8
ROWDY CREEK RD	DN	1	G8
ROWENA AV	LA	182	H6
ROWLEE RD	KER	77	E9
ROWLEE RD	KER	78	E0
ROXBURY DR	SIS	3	K4
ROXBURY RD	MCO	56	C2
ROXFORD ST	LACO	89	P5
ROXFORD ST	LACO	117	B0
ROYAL AV	VEN	88	Q9
ROYAL OAKS DR	LACO	118	G3
RUBIDOUX BLVD	RCO	99	E2
RUBLE RD	STA	47	J5
RUCKER AV	SCL	54	C6
RUDDICK	MEN	31	E2
RUDNICK RD	KER	80	L5
RUDOLPH DR	KER	79	M4
RUDOLPH RD	INY	51	J7
RUEGGER RD	IMP	110	J1
RUFF LN	GLE	24	M8
RUFFIN RD	SDCO	106	H4
RUFFIN RD	SDCO	107	Q6
RUGGED TRAIL RD	RCO	108	B4
RUNGE RD	SOL	39	D4
RUSH ST	RCO	108	A4
RUSH CREEK DR	TRI	11	Q7
RUSH CREEK RD	MNO	43	P5
RUSH CREEK RD	TRI	17	A7
RUSH CK SHORTCT	TRI	17	B7
RUSH CK CAMP RD	TRI	11	Q6
RUSHNG HILL LKT	TUO	48	B3
RUSS LN	HUM	15	E6
RUSSELL AV	FRCO	56	J1
RUSSELL BL	DVS	136	H2
RUSSELL BLVD	YOL	39	C0
RUSSELL RD	CAL	41	J0
RUSSELL RD	SAC	39	G7
RUSSELL RD	TEH	18	J4
RUTH AV	BLMT	145	M4
RUTH DUMP RD	TRI	17	L1
RUTHERFORD	NAPA	29	H6
RUTHERFORD AV	PLU	26	C5
RUTHERFORD RD	IMP	110	K1
RUTH HILL RD	FRCO	58	J4
RUTH HILL RD	FRCO	58	J3
RUTH ZENIA RD	TRI	16	M9
RUTHERFORD RD	BUT	25	Q3
RYAN AV	KER	80	M1
RYAN RD	LAS	21	J2
RYAN RD	SLO	76	D4
RYAN CREEK RD	MEN	23	N0
RYE CANYON RD	LACO	89	L2
RYE GRASS SWALE	MOD	8	C0
RYE GRASS SWALE	MOD	14	C9
RYER RD E	SOL	39	H6
S			
S ST	EUR	121	E9
SABINANA RD	YUB	33	B9
SABODAN ST	KER	78	P7
SACHREITER RD	COL	33	F0
SACRAMENTO AV	BUT	25	H0
SACRAMENTO AV	C	124	L0
SACRAMENTO AV	FRCO	56	L7
SACRAMENTO BLVD	SCTO	137	Q8
SACRAMNTO FWY N	SCTO	137	B8
SACRAMENTO ST	AUB	126	L4
SACRAMENTO ST	PLA	34	C7
SACRAMENTO ST	PLCV	138	J5
SACRAMENTO ST	VAL	134	F2
SACRMNTO VLY RD	SUT	33	G4
SACRMNTO VLY BL	SUT	33	L5
SADDLE CT	KER	79	N5
SADDLEBACK RD	SIE	26	K7
SADDLEHORN RD	SBD	84	G5
SADDLE PEAK RD	LACO	97	D2
SADDLE TRAIL RD	SHA	18	G3
SADDLE VIEW CT	SHA	13	K8
SAGE AV	SBD	100	B7
SAGE RD	RCO	99	M9
SAGEBRUSH LN	SIS	4	J9
SAGE CANYON RD	KER	80	C2
SAGE FLATS DR	INY	70	E2
SAGE HEN RD	MNO	51	D0
SAGE HEN RD	NEV	27	N6
SAGE HEN MDW RD	MNO	43	Q8
SAGE HEN MDWS	MNO	50	A9
SAGE HEN MDWS	MNO	51	A0
SAGEHORN RD	MOD	7	J7
SAGELAND CT	KER	79	L3
SAGINAW AV	FRCO	57	M8
SAHARA AV	LV	209	L0
SAHARA AV E	CLK	74	F7
SAHARA AV W	CLK	74	F5
ST CATHERINE WY	AVLN	105	L2
ST FRANCIS AV	STA	47	D5
ST GEORGE ST	LA	182	J6
ST HELENA HWY	NAPA	29	K6
ST HELENA RD	SON	38	C1
ST JAMES ST	SJ	152	H4
ST JOHN RD	TRI	16	E9
ST JOHN LOOP RD	TRI	16	E9
ST LOUIS AV	KER	80	L1
ST LOUIS RD	HUM	10	N0
ST LOUIS RD	HUM	9	P9
ST LOUIS RD	PLU	26	H5
ST MARYS AV	TEH	18	N7
ST MARYS RD	CC	45	B8
SALE LN	TEH	18	N6
SALEM AV	KIN	67	J8
SALEM RD	SOL	39	G3

STREET	CO.	PAGE & GRID	
SALINAS RD	MON	54	F4
SALINAS ST	STB	174	H9
SALINE RD	INY	60	E4
SALINE VLY ALT	INY	70	A8
SALINE VLY RD	INY	60	G4
SALINE VLY RD	INY	60	Q7
SALMON CREEK RD	HUM	16	M3
SALMON FALLS RD	ED	34	N4
SALT RD N	SHA	12	K5
SALT CREEK RD	MCO	55	E6
SALT CREEK RD	SHA	12	Q7
SALTDALE RD	KER	80	G5
SALTON DR	IMP	109	E5
SALTON RD	SBD	80	P9
SALTON RD	SBD	81	P0
SALTON BAY DR	IMP	109	E5
SALTON VIEW RD	RCO	101	G2
SALT POOL RD	INY	72	C1
SALT SPG VLY RD	CAL	40	M9
SALT SPG VLY RD	CAL	41	M0
SALTUS RD	SBD	93	J9
SALVADORI RD	SIS	4	N3
SAM ALLEY RIDGE	LAK	31	D7
SAMEL DR	SBD	100	D6
SAMPLE RD	FRCO	57	F9
SAMPSON ST	SD	216	N2
SAMSON AV	TEH	18	Q7
SAN ANDREAS RD	SCR	54	F3
SAN ANDREAS RD	SBD	100	D8
SAN ANDREAS ST	STB	174	J1
SN ANTONE CP RD	CAL	41	K3
SAN ANTONIO AV	CAR	53	Q6
SAN ANTONIO AV	ONT	204	J1
SAN ANTONIO AV	SBD	98	C7
SAN ANTONIO AV	UPL	204	J1
SN ANTONIO AV N	CAR	168	K2
SAN ANTONIO DR	LACO	119	D7
SAN ANTONIO DR	LACO	120	B1
SAN ANTONIO RD	MON	65	N6
SAN ANTONIO RD	MON	65	N6
SAN ANTONIO RD	SB	86	E3
SAN ANTONIO RD	SCL	45	L8
SAN ANTONIO ST	SJ	152	H8
SAN ANTONIO VLY	SCL	46	L6
SAN BENACIO RD	MON	54	M4
SAN BENITO AV	FRCO	56	K6
SAN BENITO AV	TEH	18	Q7
SAN BERNRDNO AV	FRCO	56	H5
SAN BERNRDNO AV	SBD	98	D7
SAN BERNRDNO FY	CLA	203	H0
SAN BERNRDNO FY	LA	186	G7
SAN BERNRDNO FY	LACO	98	D2
SAN BERNRDNO FY	LACO	118	K2
SAN BERNRDNO FY	MTCL	203	H0
SAN BERNRDNO FY	ONT	203	H0
SAN BERNRDNO FY	ONT	204	G3
SAN BERNRDNO FY	SBD	98	D8
SAN BERNRDNO FY	UPL	204	G3
SAN BERNRDNO RD	LACO	118	J5
SAN BERNRDNO RD	SBD	80	B8
SAN BERNRDNO RD	UPL	204	D5
SAN BERNRDNO ST	MTCL	203	J3
SAN BERNRDNO ST	POM	203	J5
SN BERNARDNO CK	SLO	75	G9
SN BERNARDNO CK	SLO	76	G0
SANBORN RD S	SAL	171	N8
SAN BRUNO AV	SBR	144	G2
SAN BRUNO AV	SMCO	45	F3
SAN CARLOS AV	SMCO	45	H6
SAN CARLOS RD	MCO	55	E6
SAN CARLOS ST	CAR	168	L3
SAN CARLOS ST	SJ	151	N7
SAN CARLOS ST	SJ	152	K5
SAN CARLOS ST	SCL	151	N7
SANCHES RD	MCO	47	M5
SANCHEZ RD	MON	54	Q8
SAND CANYON AV	ORA	98	M5
SAND CANYON AV	ORA	120	L8
SAND CANYON RD	INY	51	M4
SAND CANYON RD	KER	70	N4
SAND CANYON RD	KER	79	L7
SAND CANYON RD	LACO	89	M5
SAND CANYON RD	SBD	99	E6
SAND CREEK RD	COL	32	J6
SAND CREEK RD	FRCO	58	L3
SAND CREEK RD	TUL	58	L3
SAND CREST DR	IMP	109	E5
SANDERS RD	STA	47	G5
SANDERSON AV	RCO	99	K8
SAND FLAT RD	SIS	12	D6
SAND FLAT CTOFF	MNO	50	B8
SAND HILL RD	SMCO	45	K6
SAN DIEGO AV	FRCO	56	K5
SAN DIEGO AV	SD	213	Q2
SAN DIEGO FRWY	CUL	188	A0
SAN DIEGO FRWY	HAW	189	G9
SAN DIEGO FRWY	ING	188	L7
SAN DIEGO FRWY	IRV	198	N8
SAN DIEGO FRWY	LA	180	F4
SAN DIEGO FRWY	LA	188	L7
SAN DIEGO FRWY	LACO	97	D5
SAN DIEGO FRWY	LACO	119	C3
SAN DIEGO FRWY	LACO	180	F4
SAN DIEGO FRWY	LACO	189	G9
SAN DIEGO FRWY	ORA	98	N7
SAN DIEGO FRWY	ORA	120	G3
SAN DIEGO FRWY	ORA	197	J1
SAN DIEGO FRWY	ORA	198	K0
SAN DIEGO FRWY	ORA	202	K5
SAN DIEGO FRWY	SD	211	C6
SAN DIEGO FRWY	SD	212	J9
SAN DIEGO FRWY	SD	215	G7
SAN DIEGO FRWY	SD	216	G0
SAN DIEGO FRWY	SDCO	106	G2
SAN DIEGO FRWY	SDCO	107	J3
SAN DIEGO FRWY	SDCO	111	E7
SAN DIEGO FRWY	SJC	202	K5
SAN DIEGO ST	KER	78	E2
SN DIEGO MSN RD	SD	214	F6
SAN DIMAS AV	LACO	118	H8
SN DIMAS CYN RD	LACO	118	H8
SANDMOUND BLVD	CC	39	N6
SAN DOMINGO RD	CAL	41	K3
SAND RIDGE RD	ED	40	A8
SANDRINI RD	KER	78	M7
SANDROCK RD	SD	214	B2
SANDROCK RD	SDCO	106	J3
SANDROCK RD	SDCO	107	Q6
SAND SLOUGH RD	MCO	47	P9
SAND SLOUGH RD	MCO	48	P0
SANDY AV	KER	80	A5
SANDY DR	RCO	108	B4
SANDY RD	MON	66	K2
SANDY ST	KER	80	B5
SANDY HILLS RD	RCO	108	A4
SANDYMUSH RD	MCO	48	P1
SANDY MUSH RD	MCO	48	P3
SANDY PRAIRIE	HUM	15	F8
SAN FELIPE RD	SBT	54	E9
SAN FELIPE RD	SBT	55	E0
SAN FELIPE RD	SDCO	108	F4
SAN FELIPE RD	SCL	46	M4
SAN FERNANDO BL	BUR	179	B4
SAN FERNANDO BL	LA	179	B4
SAN FERNANDO RD	BUR	179	E8
SAN FERNANDO RD	GLEN	182	A7

STREET	CO.	PAGE & GRID	
SAN FERNANDO RD	LA	186	A6
SAN FERNANDO RD	LACO	89	N3
SAN FERNANDO RD	LACO	89	P5
SAN FERNANDO RD	LACO	97	C8
SAN FERNANDO RD	LACO	117	B0
SANFORD PASS	SHA	12	H2
SANFORD RCH RD	MEN	31	E3
SN FRANCSQT CYN	LACO	89	L3
SAN GABRIEL BL	LACO	98	D1
SAN GABRIEL BL	LACO	118	H0
SAN GABRIEL FWY	LACO	98	F1
SAN GABRIEL FWY	LACO	119	C9
SAN GABRIEL RD	LACO	118	G5
SAN GABRIEL CYN	LACO	98	B4
SAN GABRIEL CYN	LACO	118	F5
SAN GABRL R FWY	LACO	120	E1
SN GABRL RV PKY	LACO	118	M1
SAN GORGONIO AV	RCO	100	G0
SN GUILLERMO RD	VEN	88	F3
SANHEDRIN RD	GLE	24	J0
SAN IGNACIO RD	RCO	99	P9
SANITARIUM RD	NAPA	29	E4
SAN JACINTO RD	RCO	99	K4
SAN JACINTO ST	SBD	100	D5
SAN JACINTO RDG	RCO	100	K1
SAN JOAQUIN AV	FRCO	66	G7
SAN JOAQUIN AV	LAK	32	H0
SAN JOAQUIN RD	ORA	120	J8
SAN JOAQUIN ST	S	160	H7
SN JQUIN HLS RD	NB	200	K1
SAN JOSE BLVD	MAR	38	M1
SN JOSE AVNALES	SLO	76	H7
SN JOSE L PANZA	SLO	76	G5
SN JOSE-STA MAR	SLO	76	G3
SN JS ST MAR LK	SLO	76	H4
SN JS ST MAR MT	SLO	76	H6
SAN JUAN AV	SAC	34	P1
SAN JUAN HWY	SBT	54	F7
SAN JUAN RD	MCO	56	C1
SAN JUAN RD	MON	54	F4
SAN JUAN CYN RD	SBT	54	H7
SAN JUSTO RD	SBT	54	G7
SANKEY RD	SUT	33	M6
SAN LUCAS RD	MON	65	G4
SAN LUIS BAY DR	SLO	76	L1
SAN LUISITO CK	SLO	75	H9
SAN LUISITO CK	SLO	76	H0
SAN MARCOS RD	SLO	76	A0
SAN MARCOS RD	SB	87	L3
SN MARCOS PS RD	SB	87	J2
SAN MARTIN AV	SCL	54	B6
SN MARTNZ CHQT	LACO	89	L1
SN MARTNZ GD CN	LACO	89	L1
SAN MATEO AV	FRCO	56	L6
SAN MATEO AV	FRCO	56	N6
SAN MATEO AV	SBR	144	C3
SAN MATEO AV	SSF	144	C3
SAN MATEO ST	SBD	99	E5
SAN MIGUEL	CC	45	A9
SAN MIGUEL AV	SAL	171	P4
SAN MIGUEL DR	NB	200	N4
SN MGUEL CYN RD	MON	54	G5
SN MIGUELITO RD	SB	86	H3
SAN PABLO	CC	38	P5
SAN PABLO AV	ALA	45	B6
SAN PABLO AV	ELC	155	L8
SAN PABLO AV	O	157	E9
SAN PABLO AV	R	155	F6
SAN PABLO AV	SP	155	B3
SN PABLO DAM RD	CC	38	P5
SN PABLO DAM RD	SP	155	C5
SAN PASQUAL RD	SDCO	107	J7
SAN PASQUAL RD	SB	86	H3
SAN PASQUAL VLY	SDCO	107	J8
SAN PEDRO AV	SBD	84	H4
SAN PEDRO RD N	MAR	38	N2
SAN PEDRO RD N	MAR	139	E5
SAN PEDRO RD N	SR	139	E5
SAN PEDRO ST	LA	185	Q9
SAN PEDRO ST	LA	186	L1
SAN PEDRO ST	LACO	119	B5
SAN RAFAEL AV	PAS	190	L0
SAN RAFAEL DR	RCO	100	H5
SN RAMON VLY BL	CC	46	D1
SANS BAKER RD	FRCO	58	J5
SN SIMEON CK RD	SLO	75	C5
SANTA ANA AV	CM	199	J4
SANTA ANA AV	NB	199	J4
SANTA ANA AV	ORA	120	K5
SANTA ANA AV	ORA	199	C8
SANTA ANA AV	SBD	99	D1
SANTA ANA BL	SA	196	K0
SANTA ANA FRWY	ANA	193	E0
SANTA ANA FRWY	ANA	193	M6
SANTA ANA FRWY	LA	186	J6
SANTA ANA FRWY	LACO	98	F0
SANTA ANA FRWY	LACO	120	B3
SANTA ANA FRWY	ORA	98	F0
SANTA ANA FRWY	ORA	120	B3
SANTA ANA FRWY	SA	196	D2
SANTA ANA RD	VEN	88	N1
SANTA ANA ST	ANA	193	F3
STA ANA CYN RD	ORA	98	H5
STA ANA CYN RD	ORA	120	D8
STA ANA VLY RD	SBT	55	G0
STA ANA VLY RD	SBT	55	G0
SANTA ANITA AV	LACO	98	D2
SANTA ANITA AV	LACO	118	F2
SANTA ANITA AV	LACO	118	L1
SANTA ANITA RD	SBT	55	H2
STA BARBARA ST	SDCO	111	B4
STA BARBARA ST	STB	174	F2
STA BARBARA CYN	SB	87	B7
SANTA BARBRA ST	SDCO	106	K1
SANTA CLARA	A	159	C1
SANTA CLARA AV	O	158	D3
SANTA CLARA AV	SA	195	F8
SANTA CLARA AV	SA	196	F0
SANTA CLARA AV	VEN	88	Q3
SANTA CLARA ST	SJ	152	J4
SANTA CLARA ST	SCL	46	M2
SANTA CLARA ST	VAL	134	L3
SANTA CLARA WY	SM	145	J4
STA CRZ GUN CLB	MCO	55	D8
SANTA FE	MCO	48	M4
SANTA FE AV	LB	192	D3
SANTA FE AV	LA	186	Q5
SANTA FE AV	LACO	117	M6
SANTA FE AV	LACO	119	E6
SANTA FE AV	MCO	48	N7
SANTA FE AV	SBD	81	P3
SANTA FE AV	SDCO	107	F4
SANTA FE AV	STA	47	E7
SANTA FE DR	MCO	48	J1
SANTA FE DR	SDCO	107	K4
SANTA FE GRADE	FRCO	56	H5
SANTA FE GRADE	MCO	47	M5
SANTA FE RD	SBD	92	L2
SANTA FE ST	SBD	92	C1
SANTA FE WY	KER	78	D2
STA FE FIRE RD	SBD	91	P1
STA FE SPGS RD	LACO	118	P1
SANTA INEZ AV	SMCO	45	G5
SANTA ISABEL	CM	199	C6
SANTA LUCIA	SBR	144	L3
SANTA LUCIA AV	CAR	168	K2

SEE PAGE D FOR INSTRUCTIONS

SANTA LUCIA RD

STREET INDEX

STEVENS CREEK BLVD

STREET	CO.	PAGE & GRID
SANTA LUCIA RD	SLO	76 E1
SANTA MARIA WY	SB	86 B4
STA MAR MESA RD	SB	86 B5
SANTA MONICA BL	BH	183 E1
SANTA MONICA BL	LA	180 J4
SANTA MONICA BL	LA	181 N4
SANTA MONICA BL	LA	182 N0
SANTA MONICA BL	LA	183 E1
SANTA MONICA BL	LACO	97 D6
SANTA MONICA BL	LACO	181 N4
SANTA MONICA BL	LACO	183 E1
SANTA MONICA BL	SMON	180 J4
SANTA MONICA FY	LA	184 L1
SANTA MONICA FY	LA	185 L0
SANTA MONICA FY	LA	186 M0
SANTA MONICA FY	LACO	97 E5
SANTA MONICA FY	LACO	117 L1
SANTA MONICA FY	SMON	180 P2
SANTA PAULA FWY	VEN	88 P3
SANTA PAULA ST	VEN	88 N4
STA RITA GRADE	MCO	56 C2
SANTA RITA RD	ALA	46 E2
STA RITA OLD CK	SLO	75 E8
SANTA ROSA AV	SON	37 F9
SANTA ROSA AV	STR	131 K6
SANTA ROSA RD	INY	60 P7
SANTA ROSA RD	RCO	99 K3
SANTA ROSA RD	SBD	91 M7
SANTA ROSA RD	SB	86 H4
SANTA ROSA RD	VEN	88 Q6
SANTA ROSA ST	SNLO	172 F4
STA ROSA CK RD	SLO	75 D5
STA ROSA MTN TK	RCO	100 P6
STA ROSA MTN TT	RCO	100 P6
STA SUSANA PASS	LACO	59 Q1
STA TERESA BL	SCL	46 P3
SANTA TERESA BL	SCL	54 D6
SANTA YSABEL RD	SLO	75 H8
SANTIAGO BLVD	OR	194 F9
SANTIAGO BLVD	ORA	98 J5
SANTIAGO BLVD	ORA	120 D8
SANTIAGO CYN RD	ORA	98 J6
SANTIAGO CYN RD	ORA	120 E9
SAN TIMOTEO CYN	SBD	99 F6
SAN TIMOTEO CYN	RCO	99 F7
SAN TOMAS EXPWY	SJ	150 P9
SAN TOMAS EXPWY	SCLR	150 F9
SAN TOMAS EXPWY	SCLR	151 B0
SAN TOMAS EXPWY	SCL	46 N1
SANTOS RD	SB	86 H6
SANTOS ST	SB	86 C2
SAN VICENTE BL	'A	180 G1
SAN VICENTE BL	LA	183 D9
SAN VICENTE BL	LA	184 G3
SAN VICENTE BL	LACO	97 E4
SAN VICENTE BL	LACO	117 K2
SAN VICENTE RD	MON	55 Q1
SAN VICENTE RD	SDCO	108 L1
SAN VINCENTE AV	SAL	171 M2
SAPAQUE RD	MON	65 N4
SARATOGA AV	KER	80 C8
SARATOGA AV	SJ	150 P8
SARATOGA AV	SCLR	150 P8
SARATOGA AV	SCLR	151 L0
SARATOGA AV	SCL	45 N9
SARTGA-LS GATOS	SCL	45 N9
SARATOGA SPGS	LAK	31 D5
SARATOGA SPG RD	SBD	72 P7
SARATOGA SPG RD	SBD	82 B7
SARATGA-SNNYVLE	SCL	45 N9
SARATOGA-SVL RD	SVL	149 E7
SARBO RD	MCO	55 B7
SARGENT RD	SJCO	40 K1
SARGENTS RD	MON	65 L9
SARIDA AV	KER	79 M4
SARINA RD	DN	1 H7
SARON FRUIT COL	TEH	18 K7
SASIA RD	KER	79 M3
SATICOY AV	VEN	88 P3
SATICOY ST	LA	177 B1
SATICOY ST	LA	178 B4
SAUGUS VNTRA RD	LACO	89 M1
SAVANA	MCO	48 N7
SAVIERS RD	OXN	176 Q4
SAWMILL	INY	51 K5
SAW MILL RD	ALP	36 P3
SAWMILL RD	KER	79 A4
SAWMILL RD	MNO	50 E8
SAW MILL CREEK	SBT	66 C2
SAWMILL CRSSOVR	MNO	51 B2
SAWMILL CUTOFF	MNO	50 D7
SAWMILL FLAT RD	TUO	41 M5
SAWMILL MDWS RD	MNO	51 B2
SAWTELLE AV	SUT	33 H5
SAWTELLE BLVD	CUL	188 B1
SAWTELLE BL	LA	180 J5
SAWTELLE BLVD	LA	188 E3
SAWTOOTH PEAK	KER	80 A5
SAWYER AV	STA	47 C7
SAYRE ST	LACO	117 B1
SCALES RD	YUB	26 K4
SCANDIA RD	SOL	39 H1
SCARFACE RD	SIS	3 P8
SCARFACE RD	SIS	4 P0
SCARLT BUGLE RD	RCO	100 Q4
SCARONI AV	KER	78 F2
SCENIC DR	STA	47 E6
SCENIC DR	MDO	162 F7
SCENIC DR	STA	162 F7
SCHADD RD	CAL	41 E4
SCENIC RD	CAR	168 K2
SCHAAD RD	COL	32 E6
SCHAEFER AV	SBD	98 E8
SCHAEFFER RD	SB	87 B7
SCHAFER	MPA	49 J3
SCHAGLE RD	SUT	33 H5
SCHALLOCK RD	KER	78 N5
SCHARTZ RD	IMP	110 M2
SCHATZ RD	KER	79 M4
SCHELL RD	IMP	114 B5
SCHILLING	MPA	48 E9
SCHILLING AV	FRCO	67 A3
SCHLAG RD	SUT	33 F4
SCHLEISMAN RD	RCO	98 F8
SCHMIDT DR	RCO	108 A1
SCHMIDT RD	MCO	47 P5
SCHOBER LN	INY	51 L6
SCHOOL RD	IMP	115 B6
SCHOOL RD	MNO	50 E9
SCHOOL RD	MNO	51 E0
SCHOOL ST	HUM	15 F8
SCHOOL ST	MEN	60 J4
SCHOOL ST	U	123 F4
SCHOOLER RD	SBD	101 B6
SCHOOL HOUSE RD	LAS	8 Q4
SCHOOL HOUSE RD	MPA	49 K0
SCHOTT RD	BUT	25 E5
SCHOTT RD	LAS	14 J3
SCHROEDER MINE	SIS	3 L8
SCHUETTE RD	LAK	31 D4
SCHULTZ RD	KER	80 P6
SCHUSTER RD	KER	68 P3
SCIARONE RD	ED	35 P3
SCOFIELD AV	KER	78 C1
SCOTT AV	LACO	118 P3
SCOTT BLVD	SCLR	151 D1
SCOTT RD	CAL	41 J4
SCOTT RD	LAS	27 E8
SCOTT RD	MPA	49 G4
SCOTT RD	RCO	99 M5
SCOTT RD	SAC	40 C4
SCOTT BAR RD	SIS	3 L6
SCOTT CREEK RD	ALA	46 J2
SCOTT DAM RD	LAK	23 P5
SCOTT FORBES RD	YUB	34 C1
SCOTT GRANT RD	YUB	25 Q9
SCOTT LUMBER RD	SHA	19 C4
SCOTT MTN RD	SIS	11 E8
SCOTT RIVER RD	SIS	3 M3
SCOTTS CREEK RD	LAK	31 G5
SCOTTS FLAT RD	NEV	34 B6
SCOTTS VLY RD	LAK	31 E5
SCOTTS VLY RD	SCR	54 C0
SCOTT VALLEY RD	SIS	3 Q6
SCOTT VALLEY RD	SIS	11 A6
SCOTT VLY AIRPT	SIS	3 P7
SCOUT RD	BUT	19 Q6
SCOUT ST	SHA	18 H3
SCOVELL AV	RCO	99 K8
SCRANTON AV	TUL	68 H6
SEAL BEACH BLVD	ORA	98 K1
SEAL BEACH BLVD	ORA	120 G1
SEARLES STA RD	KER	80 E8
SEARLES STA RD	SBD	80 E8
SEARLES STA CTO	SBD	80 D9
SEARS RD	LAS	21 K2
SEARS POINT RD	SOL	38 L5
SEARS POINT RD	SOL	134 F2
SEARS POINT RD	VAL	134 F2
SEASIDE AV	LA	191 G6
SEASIDE BLVD	LACO	119 G5
SEATTLE AV	KIN	67 J6
SEA VIEW DR	IMP	109 F5
SEAVIEW RD	SON	37 B1
SEAVW QUARRY RD	SON	37 C2
SEAWARD AV	VENT	175 J6
SEBASTIAN RD	KER	78 N8
SEBASTOPOL AV	STR	131 L5
SEBASTOPOL FRWY	STR	131 L2
SEBASTOPOL FRWY	SON	131 L2
SEBASTOPOL RD	SON	131 M2
SECO ST	PAS	190 H1
SECOND ST	C	124 N2
SECRETARIAT RD	KER	79 M3
SECRET SPGS RD	SIS	4 G8
SECTION OLD RED	PLU	19 J8
SEE CANYON RD	SLO	76 K0
SEIAD CREEK	SIS	3 H3
SEIAD OAKS RD	SIS	3 J2
SEIDNER	SJCO	47 C6
SEIGLER CYN RD	LAK	32 K0
SEIGLER CYN RD	LAK	32 K0
SEIGLER SPGS RD	LAK	31 K9
SELLERS AV	CC	39 P5
SELMADOLPH ST	SBD	91 H8
SELVA RD	ORA	202 K0
SEMINARY AV	ALA	45 C7
SEMINARY AV	O	159 B8
SEMINARY DR	MAR	140 K5
SEMINARY DR	MV	140 K5
SENATOR WASH RD	IMP	116 P8
SENECA RD	PLU	20 P3
SENECA RD	SBD	91 K2
SENECA RD	SBD	91 H8
SENILIS AV	SBD	100 E5
SENTER RD	SJ	152 N8
SENTER RD	SCL	46 M3
SEPULVEDA BLVD	CUL	188 B1
SEPULVEDA BLVD	ELS	189 H4
SEPULVEDA BLVD	LA	180 J6
SEPULVEDA BLVD	LA	183 P0
SEPULVEDA BLVD	LA	188 K5
SEPULVEDA BLVD	LA	189 H4
SEPULVEDA BLVD	LACO	97 A5
SEPULVEDA BLVD	LACO	117 D0
SEPULVEDA BLVD	LACO	119 D3
SEPULVEDA BL	LACO	180 E3
SEPULVEDA BLVD	MB	189 H4
SEQUOIA BLVD	KER	80 M0
SEQUOIA RD	FRCO	58 J7
SEQUOIA RD	HUM	16 L4
SERENADE DR	SBD	80 B8
SERENE DR	SHA	18 F3
SERENO DR	VAL	134 F4
SERFAS CLUB DR	RCO	98 H8
SERPA LN	SIS	3 P7
SERPA LN	SOL	39 E2
SERRANO RD	VEN	105 D5
SERVICE RD	SIE	26 L5
SERVICE RD	STA	47 G5
SESPE ST	VEN	88 N6
SESPE RIVER RD	VEN	88 J2
SEVEN HILLS RD	ALA	45 D8
SEVEN MILE LN	BUT	25 L2
SEVEN MI SLOUGH	HUM	15 D7
SEVEN OAK RD	SBD	100 B0
SEVERE RD	IMP	110 J0
SEWARD DR	HUM	16 M5
SEXTON	SJCO	47 C5
SEYMOUR RD	SUT	33 K3
SEYMOUR RD	VEN	88 D4
SHABELL LN	INY	59 G9
SHACKELFORD RD	STA	47 E3
SHADOW CYN RD	SLO	75 D8
SHADOW MTN RD	SBD	83 D7
SHADOW MTN RD	SBD	90 E9
SHADOW MTN RD	SBD	101 C7
SHADY LN	SR	139 M0
SHADY DELL RD	SIS	5 H1
SHAFFER RD	MCO	48 J2
SHAFFER ST	OR	194 H6
SHAFTER AV	KER	78 E3
SHAFTER RD	KER	78 K5
SHAIN AV	FRCO	56 E2
SHAIN AV	FRCO	56 E3
SHAKE RIDGE RD	AMA	40 E8
SHAKE RIDGE RD	AMA	41 D1
SHALE RD	KER	77 K8
SHANDON CEM RD	SLO	76 B6
SHANDON-SN JUAN	SLO	76 B6
SHANK RD	IMP	110 L2
SHANNON DR	SBD	101 B7
SHANNONDALE RD	LACO	89 K8
SHANNON VLY RD	LACO	89 K8
SHARON RD	MCO	55 F9
SHARON RD	YOL	136 A1
SHARPE RD	SON	38 C1
SHARP PARK RD	SMCO	45 F3
SHASTA AV	FRCO	56 J9
SHASTA AV	FRCO	57 J0
SHASTA BL	TEH	18 Q8
SHASTA ST	VAL	134 K7
SHASTA WY	KLAM	5 A4
SHA CAVERNS RD	SHA	12 Q5
SHASTA CO RD	MOD	13 G8
SHA DAM ACCS RD	SHA	18 C3
SHA SPG MCCLOUD	SIS	12 F6
SHASTA VIEW DR	MOD	14 C9
SHASTA VLY RD	SIS	12 C3
SHATTUCK AV	B	156 D0
SHATTUCK AV	O	156 M1
SHAVES AV	SBD	91 B5
SHAW AV	FRCO	57 G5
SHAW AV	FRCO	57 G5
SHAWMUT RD	TUO	41 Q4
SHAWMUT RD	TUO	48 A5
SHAWS FLAT RD	SNRA	163 D1
SHAWS FLAT RD	TUO	163 D1
SHAWS FLAT RD	TUO	41 N5
SHAWS FT JMSTWN	TUO	41 N4
SHAY CREEK RD	ALP	36 N3
SHEE CAMP RD	MNO	51 F3
SHEEP CREEK RD	SBD	90 J8
SHEEP CK SPG RD	SBD	82 C8
SHEEP CK TK TR	SBD	90 N8
SHEEP MTN RD	SIS	5 H0
SHEEP RANCH RD	CAL	41 H3
SHEEPY CREEK RD	SIS	5 F2
SHEEPY ISLND RD	SIS	5 F2
SHEFFIELD RD	SUT	33 G4
SHEKELL	VEN	88 N7
SHELBY ST	KER	78 P2
SHELDON RD	SAC	39 D8
SHELDON ST	LACO	117 D2
SHELL AV	MCO	56 B1
SHELL BLVD	CC	38 N8
SHELL BLVD	FCTY	145 D7
SHELL RD	FRCO	66 E6
SHELL RD	TUO	41 P4
SHELL CANYON RD	IMP	113 A4
SHELLCO RD	KER	67 Q5
SHELL GULCH RD	SIS	11 A7
SHELL NO 2	YUB	33 C6
SHELLEY	SJCO	40 M6
SHELLEY RD	SIS	4 K2
SHELTER COVE RD	HUM	22 B0
SHELTER ISLD DR	SDCO	106 L2
SHELTON RD	SBD	101 C6
SHELTON RD	SJCO	40 M5
SHELTN BUTTE RD	HUM	10 F6
SHENANDOAH RD	AMA	40 C8
SHENANDOAH SCHL	AMA	40 C8
SHEPHERD AV	FRCO	57 F5
SHEPHERD RD	MOD	14 G2
SHEPPARD RD	VEN	88 N4
SHERIDAN	FRCO	58 M1
SHERIDAN RD	ALA	46 H2
SHERIDAN RD	SLO	76 P3
SHERLOCK	MPA	49 G2
SHERMAN RD	SBD	100 D5
SHERMAN WY	LA	177 C2
SHERMAN WY	LA	178 C4
SHERMAN WY	LACO	97 B4
SHERWIN CK RD	MNO	50 F8
SHERWOOD AV	KER	77 A8
SHERWOOD AV	KER	78 A2
SHERWOOD BLVD	TEH	24 B8
SHERWOOD DR	SAL	171 H5
SHERWOOD RD	MEN	22 L8
SHERWD RNCHERIA	MEN	22 L8
SHETLAND CT	CAL	41 N2
SHIELDS AV	FRCO	56 H1
SHIELDS AV	FRCO	56 H1
SHIELDS AV	FRCO	57 H1
SHIELDS RD	SHA	17 J5
SHIELLS RD	STA	47 M4
SHILOH RD	SOL	39 K2
SHILOH RD	SON	37 C8
SHIMMINS RDG RD	MEN	23 M0
SHINGLE RD	ED	40 B6
SHINGLE RD S	ED	40 B5
SHINGLETWN DUMP	SHA	19 G3
SHINGLETOWN RDG	SHA	19 G0
SHINN RANCH RD	LAS	21 E6
SHIPPEE RD	BUT	25 L4
SHIPPEE RD	MCO	48 N2
SHIRLAND	PLA	34 L4
SHIRLEY RD	CAL	41 P0
SHIRLEY MDWS RD	KER	79 A4
SHIRT TAIL CYN	PLA	34 F7
SHIVELY RD	HUM	16 H1
SHOEMAKE AV	STA	47 E3
SHOEMAKER AV	LACO	120 B1
SHOEMAKER RD	SIS	4 K9
SHOP RD	MNO	42 B8
SHORE RD	SBT	54 E8
SHORELINE DR	LB	192 J6
SHORELINE DR	STB	174 P4
SHORELINE HWY	MAR	37 H6
SHORELINE HWY	MAR	37 P9
SHORELINE HWY	MEN	22 J4
SHORELINE HWY	MEN	22 P4
SHORELINE HWY	MEN	30 L5
SHORELINE HWY	MAR	140 M3
SHORT RD	KER	78 P1
SHORT CREEK RD	MEN	23 F2
SHORTYS WELL RD	INY	72 D0
SHOSHONE VLY RD	SBD	93 Q2
SHOUP AV	LA	177 H2
SHOUP RD	SHA	18 H1
SHOWER PASS RD	HUM	16 D3
SHRODE LN	LAS	21 J4
SHULTZ RD	MCO	56 B4
SHUMWAY RCH RD	RCO	100 N7
SHUTE MTN RD	BUT	25 H9
SHY ST	MCO	47 Q5
SHY ST	MCO	55 A5
SICARD FLAT RD	YUB	34 C0
SIDDING RD	KER	78 G3
SIDEWINDER RD	IMP	116 Q4
SIDEWINDER RD	RCO	102 J5
SIDEWINDER RD	SBD	91 D6
SIERRA	FRCO	56 G5
SIERRA AV	NAP	133 C1
SIERRA AV	SBD	99 D1
SIERRA DR	MPA	48 C8
SIERRA DR	MDO	162 L2
SIERRA HWY	KER	80 Q1
SIERRA HWY	LACO	89 L5
SIERRA RD	LAS	20 J9
SIERRA RD	SCL	46 L3
SIERRA RD	STA	47 C8
SIERRA ST	RENO	130 D2
SIERRA WY	KER	69 Q7
SIERRA WY	KER	79 A7
SIERRA WY	SBDO	207 H7
SIERRA WY	SBD	99 B4
SIERRA WY	TUL	58 N1
SIERRA CTR DR	SHA	13 K8
SIERRA CLG BL	PLA	34 N2
SIERRA DEL SOL	RCO	100 J8
SIERRA MADRE AV	LACO	98 C5
SIERRA MADRE AV	LACO	118 G5
SIERRA MADRE BL	LACO	117 H9
SIERRA MADRE BL	LACO	118 H0
SIERRA VISTA ST	KER	80 C5
SIERRA VLY RD	PLU	27 G5
SIEVERS RD	SOL	39 D2
SIGNAL RD	IMP	113 D9
SIGNAL BUTTE RD	LAS	20 C8
SIGNAL RIDGE RD	MEN	30 G7
SIKES RD	SOL	39 E4
SILAXO AV	FRCO	56 F4
SILLS RD	COL	32 J7
SILSBEE RD	IMP	114 B0
SILURIAN LK RD	SBD	83 D2
SILVA	MPA	49 H3
SILVA RD	SIS	4 J4
SILVER LN	MPA	49 K3
SILVER BAR	MPA	49 K2
SILVERA CT	BUT	25 H6
SILVERADO TR	NAP	133 L8
SILVERADO TR	NAPA	29 C2
SILVERADO TR	NAPA	38 D4
SILVER CYN RD	INY	51 K8
SILVRADO CYN RD	ORA	98 K8
SILVER CREEK RD	SCL	46 M3
SILVER CK CMPGD	ALP	42 A4
SILVER HILL RD	ALP	36 P5
SILVER KING RD	SHA	18 F3
SILVER LAKE BL	LA	182 M9
SILVER LAKE BL	LA	185 A6
SILVER LAKE BL	LACO	117 K5
SILVER LAKE RD	LAS	20 G3
SILVER QUEEN RD	KER	79 P9
SILVER QUEEN RD	KER	80 P0
SILVR STRAND BL	SDCO	106 N3
SILVR STRAND BL	SDCO	111 D6
SILVERTHORN RD	SHA	18 B6
SLVR TIP CPGRD	ALP	42 D0
SILVER VLY RD	SBD	92 C2
SILVEYVILLE RD	SOL	39 D2
SIMAS ST	SB	86 A2
SIMMERHORN RD	SAC	40 H1
SIMMLER RD	SLO	77 E1
SIMMLR BITTRWTR	SLO	76 C9
SIMMLR BITTRWTR	SLO	77 C0
SIMMLR SN DIEGO	SLO	77 H2
SIMMLR SN DIEGO	SLO	77 K4
SIMMLER SODA LK	SLO	77 J4
SIMMONS RD	LAK	23 P5
SIMMONS RD	SHA	18 F3
SIMMONS RD	STA	47 J5
SIMPSON LN	YUB	33 E6
SIMPSON RD	IMP	110 G2
SIMPSON RD	RCO	99 L7
SIMPSON RD	TEH	24 C5
SIMS RD	TUO	41 Q4
SIMS RD	TUO	48 A4
SIMS CREEK RD	TRI	17 G5
SIMS LOOKOUT RD	SHA	12 K4
SINCLAIR FRWY	ALA	46 H2
SINCLAIR FRWY	SJ	151 P6
SINCLAIR FRWY	SCL	46 H2
SINCLAIR FRWY	SCL	151 P6
SINCLAIR RD	IMP	110 H1
SINEX AV	PAC	167 E2
SINGLE SPRINGS	SIS	4 P8
SINGLETON RD	RCO	99 F7
SINGLE TREE	SBD	100 D9
SINTON RD	SB	86 B2
SIR FRNCS DRAKE	MAR	37 M8
SIR FRNCS DRAKE	MAR	38 N0
SIR F DRAKE BL	ROSS	139 K0
SIR F DRAKE BL	SANS	139 K0
SISK RD	STA	47 D4
SISKIYOU AV	FRCO	57 J1
SISKIYOU AV	FRCO	67 F1
SITES-LODOGA RD	COL	32 A4
SIX MILE RD	CAL	41 L3
SKAGGS ISLND RD	SOL	38 K4
SKIDOO RD	INY	71 A6
SKI HILL	MOD	7 P5
SKI RUN BLVD	SLT	129 G5
SKULL FLAT RD	CAL	41 E3
SKUNK RANCH RD	CAL	41 K4
SKY HARBOUR AV	FRCO	57 D7
SKYLINE BLVD	ALA	45 C7
SKYLINE BLVD	KIN	67 J0
SKYLINE BLVD	SMCO	45 J5
SKYLINE DR	KER	79 L2
SKYLINE DR	MONT	167 L5
SKYLINE DR	MON	53 J7
SKYLINE DR	SBD	100 C9
SKYLINE DR	SDCO	106 L5
SKYLINE DR	SDCO	111 C7
SKYLINE MOTORWY	PLU	20 L7
SKYLINE RD	KER	77 J8
SKYLINE RD	KIN	67 J0
SKYLINE RD	SON	31 Q1
SKY LINE DR	VAL	134 H9
SKYLINE FRST DR	MONT	167 N5
SKYLINE FRST DR	MONT	168 A4
SKYLINE FRST DR	MON	53 K7
SKYLINE RCH RD	SBD	100 C7
SKY RANCH RD	MON	54 Q5
SKY VALLEY RD	RCO	100 H8
SKY VALLEY RD	SOL	38 L7
SKY VIEW DR	IMP	109 F5
SKYWAY	BUT	25 F5
SKYWAY DR	SB	86 B3
SLACKS CYN RD	MON	66 H2
SLASH X RCH RD	SBD	91 F5
SLATE RD	YUB	26 M1
SLATE CREEK RD	SHA	12 L2
SLATE CREEK RD	TRI	11 Q7
SLATE GULCH	MPA	48 J8
SLATE MTN RD	TRI	12 L1
SLATE MTN LO RD	SHA	12 L2
SLATER AV	ORA	120 H3
SLATER RD	HUM	16 D2
SLATE RANGE	INY	71 F3
SLATER BUTTE LO	SIS	2 H9
SLAUGHTERHOUSE	MPA	49 H2
SLAUSON AV	CUL	188 G7
SLAUSON AV	LACO	97 F7
SLAUSON AV	LACO	117 N4
SLAUSON AV	LACO	118 N1
SLAUSON AV	LACO	188 G7
SLAYTON RD	IMP	110 P4
SLIGER MINE RD	ED	34 J6
SLOAT BLVD	SFCO	45 D3
SLOAT RD	PLU	26 E9
SLOUGH RD	SIS	4 P3
SLOUGHHOUSE RD	SAC	40 D2
SLOVER AV	SBD	99 D0
SLUG GULCH RD	ED	41 A1
SLUSSER RD	SON	37 D7
SLY PARK RD	ED	35 P1
SLY PARK RD	ED	35 N2
SMALLEY RD	FRCO	57 B8
SMARTS RANCH RD	SBD	92 P2
SMARTVILLE RD	YUB	34 C1
SMITH AV	FRCO	57 M9
SMITH AV	KER	78 C3
SMITH AV	KER	70 P1
SMITH GRADE	SCR	53 C7
SMITH RD	MON	65 N5
SMITH RD	SBD	80 B8
SMITH MTN RD	MON	66 H2
SMITH PK LKOUT	TUO	48 B9
SMITH PK LKOUT	TUO	49 B0
SMITHNECK RD	SIE	27 K7
SMITHSON RD	SBD	91 E2
SMITH STA RD	MPA	48 C9
SMITH STA RD	MPA	49 C0
SMITH STA RD	TUO	48 B9
SMITH STA RD	TUO	49 B0
SMOKE CK RCH RD	LAS	21 G6
SMOKE TREE RD	SBD	90 L8
SNAVELY RD	DN	1 G8
SNEATH LN	SMCO	45 F3
SNEATH LN	SBR	144 F1
SNELL ST	SNRA	163 G2
SNELLING HWY	MER	170 G1
SNELLING RD	MCO	48 J4
SNELL VALLEY RD	NAPA	32 N3
SNOW RD	KER	77 F9
SNOW RD	KER	78 F5
SNOW ST	KER	79 C9
SNOW CAMP RD	HUM	10 N3
SNOWDN HOVEY GL	SIS	4 L4
SNOWS RD	ED	35 N1
SNOWSHOE SPGS	ALP	36 M2
SNYDER RD	IMP	110 P4
SNYDER RD	MCO	47 P5
SOAP CREEK RD	SIS	3 N8
SOBOBA RD	RCO	99 J9
SOBOBA ST	RCO	100 L0
SOBRANTE AV	CC	38 N5
SODA BAY RD	LAK	31 H7
SODA CANYON RD	NAPA	38 E5
SODA CREEK RD	SHA	12 H5
SODA LAKE RD	KER	78 Q0
SODA LAKE RD	KER	87 A8
SODA LAKE CK RD	SLO	77 H2
SODA LK SN DIEG	SLO	77 J3
SODA LK SN DIEG	SLO	77 L6
SODA ROCK LN W	SON	31 Q7
SODA SPRINGS RD	BUT	19 Q6
SODA SPRINGS RD	SON	30 N9
SOETH RD	GLE	24 N2
SOLANO AV	NAP	133 D1
SOLANO AV	VAL	134 P4
SOLDIER MTN DR	SHA	13 J7
SOLDIER MTN RD	SHA	13 J6
SOLEDAD DR	MONT	167 N6
SOLEDAD DR	MONT	168 A6
SOLEDAD DR	MON	53 K8
SOLEDAD FRWY	SDCO	106 G3
SOLEDAD FRWY	SDCO	107 P5
SOLEDAD CYN RD	LACO	89 M8
SOLEDAD MTN RD	SD	211 K2
SOLOMAN RD	SB	86 C3
SOMAVIA RD	MON	54 M6
SOMEO ST	SB	86 C2
SOMERSVILLE RD	CC	39 P2
SOMERTON AV	YUMA	115 E5
SOMES BAR ETNA	SIS	10 E9
SOMES BAR ETNA	SIS	11 F1
SONOMA AV	FRCO	56 M7
SONOMA AV	FRCO	66 A7
SONOMA AV	STR	131 J8
SONOMA BL	VAL	134 M4
SONOMA HWY	SNMA	132 J4
SONORA	SJCO	40 P6
SONORA	STA	41 Q0
SONORA RD	STA	40 Q7
SONORA RD	STA	47 A7
SONORA RD	STA	48 A0
SONORA ELEM SCH	TUO	163 L7
SOPHIE ST	RCO	99 K4
SOQUEL AV	SC	169 J7
SOQUEL-SAN JOSE	SCR	54 D1
SORENSON RD	HUM	16 J2
SORENSON RD	RCO	108 B2
SORENSON RD	RCO	108 B2
SORREL WY	CAL	41 M1
SORRENTO VLY	SDCO	107 M4
SOSCOL AV	NAP	133 H6
SOSCOL RD	NAPA	38 H5
SOTO ST	LA	186 Q6
SOTO ST	LACO	117 K7
SOULSBYVILLE RD	TUO	41 N7
SOUTH AV	FRCO	56 L8
SOUTH AV	FRCO	57 L3
SOUTH AV	TEH	24 D8
SOUTH DR	SF	141 M3
SOUTH RD	MNO	51 B5
SOUTH RD	BLMT	145 N5
SOUTH ST	ANA	193 G3
SOUTH ST	ANA	194 E0
SOUTH ST	GLE	24 H7
SOUTH ST	LACO	98 H0
SOUTH ST	LACO	119 C7
SOUTH ST	LACO	120 C1
SOUTH ST	ORA	120 D5
SOUTH ST	RED	122 E2
SOUTH ST	SBD	90 K8
SOUTH ST	SNLO	172 L3
SOUTH ST	SHA	18 H5
SOUTHAM RD	COL	24 P8
SOUTHAMPTON RD	BEN	153 H1
S BNK CHETKO RD	CUR	1 E6
SOUTH BAY FRWY	SDCO	106 M5
SOUTH BAY FRWY	SDCO	111 C7
SOUTHBAY FRWY	SVL	148 K5
SOUTHERN AV	SIS	12 F8
S EMBARCDRO FWY	SF	142 M9
S EMBARCADRO FY	SFCO	45 D4
S FORK MTN RD	LAS	8 H2
S FORK MTN RD	TRI	16 G8
SOUTH FORK RD	DN	2 K0
SOUTH FORK RD	SHA	18 G2
SOUTH FORK RD	SIS	2 H8
SOUTH FORK RD	TRI	10 P7
SOUTH FORK RD	TRI	16 D8
SOUTH FORK RD	TUO	41 L7
S FK LOOKOUT RD	SHA	18 D2
S FK MAD RIV RD	TRI	17 P2
S FK SALMON RIV	SIS	11 F1
SOUTH GRADE RD	SDCO	108 P2
SOUTHSIDE DR	MPA	63 E2
SOUTHSIDE RD	SBT	54 H9
SOUTHSIDE RD	SBT	55 H0
SOUTH VLY FRWY	SCL	54 B5
SOUZA RD	TRI	17 M1
SPA RD	IMP	109 C9
SPACER DR	TUL	68 F3
SPALDING RD	LAS	20 C7
SPANGLER RD	KER	68 P5
SPANISH DAGGER	RCO	100 Q4
SPANISH DRY DGN	ED	34 J7
SPANISH RCH RD	PLU	26 C4
SPANISH RCH BTT	PLU	25 E9
SPANISH RCH BUT	PLU	26 F0
SPANISH VALLEY	NAPA	32 P4
SPARKS RD	MCO	47 P4
SPARKS RANCH RD	SOL	39 C2
SPEAR AV	HUM	9 N9
SPEAR AV	HUM	10 N0
SPENCE RD	MON	54 L6
SPENCER LN	SON	32 Q0
SPENCER RD	COL	24 P8
SPENCER RD	STA	47 F1
SPENCEVILLE RD	NEV	34 D2
SPENCEVILLE RD	YUB	33 G9
SPERGEON RD	SON	37 B8
SPERRY AV	STA	47 J3
SPIES RANCH RD	MNO	51 A5
SPILLWAY RD	MNO	51 F2
SPINK RD	CAL	41 E2
SPLICER RD	COL	33 G0
SPOONER RD	LAS	8 K0
SPOONER RD	LAS	14 K9
SPORTS ARENA BL	SD	212 P7
SPORTS ARENA BL	SD	213 Q0
SPRECKELS BLVD	MON	54 L5
SPRING RD	VAL	134 L5
SPRING ST	LACO	119 E8
SPRING ST	NAPA	29 G4
SPRING ST	U	123 G3
SPRING ST N	LA	186 F3
SPRING TR	LAK	31 D7
SPRING BRNCH RD	TEH	18 J7
SPRING BRNCH RD	TEH	19 J0
SPRING CREEK RD	SHA	13 J7
SPRINGDALE ST	ORA	120 H2
SPRINGER RD	SCL	45 L8
SPRINGFIELD AV	FRCO	56 M8
SPRINGFIELD AV	FRCO	57 M3
SPRING GAP RD	TUO	41 J9
SPRING GAP RD	TUO	42 J0
SPRING GARDEN	PLA	34 G7
SPRING GULCH RD	LAS	14 L3
SPRING HILL RD	LAS	14 M8
SPRING HILL RD	SON	37 J9
SPRING LAKE RD	KLAM	5 C3
SPRING MTN RD	NAPA	29 F1
SPRING MTN RD	NAPA	38 C2
SPRINGS RD	SOL	38 L6
SPRING VLY LTRL	COL	32 F6
SPRING VLY RD	COL	32 F5
SPRING VLY RD	MEN	31 B3
SPRING VLY RD	YUB	33 C8
SPRINGVLLE MILO	TUL	69 E0
SPROUL CREEK RD	HUM	22 B3
SPRUCE AV	SSF	144 C2
SPRUCE RD EXT	LAK	32 M1
SPRUCE ST	B	156 B1
SPRUCE CAMP RD	MCO	55 D8
SPRUCE GROVE RD	LAK	32 L2
SPUNKY CYN RD	LACO	89 H5
SPUR ST	CAL	41 K0
SPYROCK RD	MEN	22 F7
SQUAW BUSH RD	SBD	92 K2
SQUAW FLAT RD	VEN	88 J7
SQUAW GULCH RD	SIS	11 D7
SQUAW VALLEY RD	SIS	12 G7
SQUAW VLY LP RD	SIS	12 G7
SQUIRREL CK RD	PLU	26 D7
STADIUM WY	LACO	117 K5
STADIUM WY	SD	214 J2
STADIUM WY	SDCO	106 J3
STADIUM WY	SDCO	111 A6
STAFFORD RD	HUM	16 H0
STAG RD	AVLN	105 M2
STAGE RD	BUT	25 D5
STAGE RD	LAS	8 P7
STAGE RD	LACO	120 B3
STAGE RD	SMCO	45 N4
STAGE COACH LN	SDCO	107 D4
STAGECOACH RD	HUM	9 K8
STAGECOACH RD	SB	87 J2
STAGECOACH CYN	NAPA	32 P4
STAGHORN RD	RCO	108 A5
STAHL RD	IMP	110 M2
STALLARD RD	IMP	116 D4
STALLION WY	CAL	41 M2
STAMPEDE DAM RD	SIE	27 N8
STAMPFLI LN RD	PLU	20 P6
STANDARD RD	TUO	41 N6
STANDARD MNE RD	PLU	20 P5
STANDLEY ST	U	123 H3
STANFORD RD	SON	37 E8
STANISLAUS AV	FRCO	66 A6
STANISLAUS RD W	STA	47 G3
STANLEY	SJCO	40 Q5
STANLEY AV	VEN	88 P1
STANLEY BLVD	ALA	46 E3
STANLEY RD	CAL	41 E2
STANLEY RD	IMP	110 G3
STANLEY RD	RCO	100 P0
STANWOOD DR	STB	174 D8
STANYAN ST	SF	141 J8
STAPP RD	HUM	16 E4
STARBRIGHT MINE	SBD	82 M0
STARDUST RD	CLK	210 A3
STARK	SJCO	40 Q0
STARK	SJCO	47 A0
STARK RD	STA	47 H2
STARKEY RD	SLO	76 B5
STARLING ST	LACO	90 E4
STARLITE DR	INY	51 L4
STARLITE DR	INY	51 M4
STARR RD	IMP	110 P5
STATE LN	SBD	100 A2
STATE ST	LACO	117 P6
STATE ST	MTCL	203 N2
STATE ST	ONT	203 N2
STATE ST	POM	203 N2
STATE ST	RCO	99 L8
STATE ST	SB	87 L4
STATE ST	SD	215 K6
STATE ST	SDCO	106 L3
STATE ST	STB	174 G2
STATE ST	U	123 D4
STATE ST N	MEN	31 D3
STATE COL BL N	ANA	193 P9
STATE COLLGE BL	ORA	98 H4
STATE COLLGE BL	ORA	120 E6
STATE COL BL N	OR	193 P9
STATE COL PKWY	SBD	99 C3
STATE FRSTRY RD	SON	31 P1
STATE LINE RD	MNO	52 H5
STATE LINE RD	INY	72 C7
STATE LINE RD	SIS	5 F2
STATEN ISLAND	SJCO	39 K7
STATION RD	KER	78 H1
STAVERVILLE RD	SIE	27 H7
STEAMWELLS RD	SBD	80 G9
STEARNS RD	STA	47 D8
STEARNS ST	LACO	119 E7
STEARNS ST	VEN	89 P1
STEEG RD	SBD	101 C6
STEEL BRIDGE RD	TRI	17 C6
STEELE LN	MEN	22 J8
STEELE LN W	STR	131 D2
STEELE CYN RD	NAPA	38 D7
STEELHEAD CIR	TRI	17 C7
STEELHEAD RD	HUM	16 N6
STEEL SWAMP RD	MOD	6 H5
STEFFAN ST	VAL	134 N9
STEINEGUL	SJCO	47 B6
STEINER RD	AMA	40 C8
STEINER RD	SUT	33 H3
STEINER FLAT RD	TRI	17 C5
STELLAR RD	SBD	92 K1
STELLING RD N	CPTO	149 K5
STELLING RD S	CPTO	149 Q6
STENT CUTOFF	TUO	41 P4
STEPHENS MNE RD	SBD	80 D9
STEPHENS MNE RD	SBD	81 D0
STEPHENSON BLVD	RCO	116 A5
STEPHENSON BLVD	RCO	116 B5
STEPHENS RIDGE	BUT	25 H8
STERLING AV	SBD	99 C4
STERLING RD	INY	70 M4
STERLING LAKE	NEV	27 Q2
STETSON AV	RCO	99 L8
STEVEN ST	KER	78 N2
STEVENS RD	IMP	113 A8
STEVENS CK BLVD	CPTO	149 N5
STEVENS CK BLVD	CPTO	150 N0
STEVENS CK BLVD	SCLR	150 N0
STEVENS CK BLVD	SCL	46 M1

SEE PAGE D FOR INSTRUCTIONS

STEVENS CREEK FRWY

STREET INDEX

USONA RD

STREET	CO.	PAGE & GRID
STEVENS CK FRWY	MVW	148 K1
STEVENS CK RD	SCL	45 N8
STEVENSN BDG RD	SOL	39 C2
STEVENS PASS RD	SIS	5 P1
STEVENS PASS RD	SIS	13 A2
STEWART	MOD	14 B7
STEWART AV	BUT	124 N0
STEWART LN	INY	51 Q8
STEWART LN	SOL	39 L4
STEWART RD	HUM	16 L4
STEWART RD	INY	51 K7
STEWART ST	SB	86 B5
STWRTS PT SKAGG	SON	31 P0
STEWART RCH RD	HUM	16 M7
STEWART SPGS RD	SIS	12 C3
STICE RD	TEH	18 M7
STILLWELL AV	MONT	167 H7
STILLWELL AV	MON	53 G8
STILSON CYN RD	BUT	25 G3
STIMPSON RD	BUT	25 P6
STINE RD	BKD	166 Q0
STINE RD	KER	78 J6
STINGY LN	SHA	18 G5
STOCKDALE HWY	KER	78 G1
STOCKDALE RD	SLO	76 B1
STOCKER ST	LACO	117 M3
STOCKTON AV	SJ	151 J9
STOCKTON BLVD	SCTO	137 L9
STOCKTON BLVD	SAC	39 B8
STOCKTON RD	VEN	88 N6
STOCKTON ST	SF	143 E4
STOCKTON ST	SNRA	163 P1
STOCKWLL MNE RD	INY	71 M3
STODDARD RD	STA	47 D4
STODDARD RD	STA	47 D8
STODDARD MTN RD	SBD	91 D5
STODDARD WELLS	SBD	91 H4
STODDARD WELLS	SBD	91 E7
STOEKEL RD	SHA	18 H2
STONE AV	STA	47 F4
STONE RD	LAS	20 C8
STONE RD	MCO	55 C7
STONEBORO RD	MEN	30 J4
STONE CANYON RD	MON	66 J2
STONE COAL RD	MOD	14 D3
STONEHEDGE DR	YUB	25 Q9
STONEHILL DR	ORA	202 J2
STONE HOUSE RD	SAC	40 C4
STONEHURST AV	LACO	117 D2
STONE VALLEY RD	CC	46 B0
STONEWLL CYN RD	MON	55 Q1
STONEWLL CYN RD	MON	55 Q1
STONEY CREEK RD	LAS	21 E6
STONY CREEK RD	AMA	40 H7
STONYFD-LDGA RD	COL	24 Q2
STONY POINT RD	STR	131 J1
STONY POINT RD	SON	37 F9
STONY POINT RD	SON	37 G9
STONY POINT RD	SON	131 L1
STORRIE RD	PLU	25 E8
STORY RD	SJ	152 M8
STORY RD	SCL	46 M3
STOVALL RD	COL	32 F7
STOVEPIPE WELLS	INY	61 K7
STOVER RD	HUM	10 K3
STOW	SJCO	40 Q4
STOW	SJCO	47 A4
STOWELL RD	STB	173 L2
STOWELL RD	SB	86 A3
STOWELL RD	SMA	173 L2
STRADLEY AV	KER	68 P3
STRAND, THE	LAS	20 C8
STRATTON LN	SOL	39 M3
STRAWBERRY RD	MON	54 H4
STRAWBERRY DR	MAR	140 J7
STREETER AV	RCO	99 F2
ST OF GL LNTERN	ORA	202 M1
STREET 145	MAD	57 D5
STREET 200	MAD	57 A6
STREET 206	MAD	57 D6
STREET 222	MAD	49 P9
STREET 223	MAD	49 N8
STREET 225	MAD	50 P0
STREET 274	MAD	49 M8
STREET 415	MAD	49 N5
STREET 426	MAD	49 M7
STREET 600	MAD	49 L5
STREET 600	MAD	57 A3
STREET 600	MAD	57 A3
STREET 603	MAD	57 A2
STREET 613	MAD	49 N3
STREET 820	MAD	49 N3
STREIBY RD	IMP	110 M3
STRINGTOWN RD	BUT	25 L9
STRIPLIN RD	SUT	33 K6
STROUD AV	FRCO	57 N4
STRUCKMAN RD	CAL	41 H2
STUBBLEFIELD RD	KER	78 Q0
STUBBLEFIELD RD	KER	87 A8
STUBBY SPRGS TR	RCO	101 F1
STUDEBAKER RD	LACO	98 J1
STUDEBAKER RD	LACO	119 A9
STUDEBAKER RD	LACO	119 E9
STUDEBAKER RD	LACO	120 A0
STUDEBAKER RD	LACO	120 E0
STUHR RD	STA	47 M4
STUMPFIELD MTN	MPA	49 J4
STUMPTOWN RD	HUM	9 K8
STUNT RD	LACO	97 D2
STURGIS RD	VEN	105 B3
STURM RD	HUM	16 H4
SUBACO RD	SUT	33 J3
SUBSTATION RD	MNO	50 E8
SUCCESS VLY DR	TUL	68 G9
SUCKER RUN RD	BUT	26 L1
SUCKOW RD	KER	80 B7
SUDDEN RD	SB	86 J2
SUE AV	KER	89 C5
SUE ST	KER	80 Q2
SUEY RD	SMA	173 G8
SUEY CREEK RD	SLO	76 N6
SUGAR CREEK RD	SIS	11 D7
SUGARLOAF RD	FRCO	58 B1
SUGAR LOAF RD	INY	51 Q7
SUGRLF LKSHR RD	SHA	12 N3
SUGARLOAF LKT RD	SHA	12 Q8
SUGARLOAF TK TR	SBD	99 A9
SUGAR PINE	PLA	34 E8
SUGAR PINE PL	BUT	25 D5
SUGAR PINE RD	TUO	41 L8
SUGAR PINE SPG	LAS	14 H0
SUISUN VLY RD	SOL	38 G8
SULFUR RD	INY	52 N7
SULLIVAN	MPA	49 J3
SULLIVAN RD	KER	78 F0
SULLIVAN RD	STA	47 N4
SULLIVAN ST	ORA	120 G5
SULLIVAN ST	SA	195 N6
SULPHUR BANK DR	LAK	32 H0
SULPHUR MTN RD	VEN	88 L3
SULPHR MTN RD E	VEN	88 L4
SULPHUR SPGS RD	MON	65 J2
SULTANA DR	MCO	48 M1
SULTZE AV	KER	78 P2
SUMMERHILL DR	TUO	42 J0
SUMMER HOMES RD	ML	164 E5

STREET	CO.	PAGE & GRID
SUMMERS LN	KLAM	5 B4
SUMMERS RD	LAS	21 P8
SUMMERSET RD	SBD	91 A5
SUMMERSET RD	SBD	91 A5
SUMMIT AV	SBD	99 B0
SUMMIT RD	BUT	25 N7
SUMMIT RD	SCR	54 C3
SUMMIT CREEK RD	TRI	17 E4
SUMMIT LAKE DR	NAPA	32 Q3
SUMMIT LEVEL RD	CAL	41 G5
SUMMITROSE ST	LACO	117 D5
SUMMIT TRUCK TR	SBD	91 N2
SUMMY	SUT	33 E2
SUMNER AV	AVLN	105 N2
SUMNER AV	FRCO	56 L7
SUMNER AV	FRCO	58 L2
SUMNER AV	RCO	98 F8
SUMNER ST	BKD	166 G9
SUNBURST AV	SBD	100 B9
SUNEVER RD	SBD	101 C0
SUNFAIR RD	SBD	101 B1
SUNFLOWER AV	CM	197 H6
SUNFLOWER AV	CM	198 J1
SUNFLOWER AV	LACO	118 J6
SUNFLOWER RD	SBD	94 F7
SUNFLOWR SPG RD	SBD	94 H8
SUNKIST ST	ANA	194 F0
SUNKIST ST	ORA	120 E6
SUNKIST TR	LPAZ	104 M4
SUNLAND BL	LACO	97 A6
SUNLAND BLVD	LACO	117 D3
SUNLAND DR	INY	51 M6
SUNNY LN	AVLN	105 N2
SUNNY ACRES AV	MCO	47 J9
SUNNY ACRES AV	MCO	48 J0
SUNNYBRAE BL	SM	145 D0
SUNNYBREA LN	HUM	10 P3
SUNNY HILL RD	SHA	18 G0
SUNNYSIDE AV	FRCO	57 G6
SUNNYSIDE AV	FRCO	57 M6
SUNNYSIDE AV	MV	140 F0
SUNNYSIDE RD	LAS	21 K2
SUNNYSLOPE	FRCO	58 F2
SUNNYSLOPE RD	SBD	90 M8
SUNNYVALE AV	CPTO	149 B7
SUNNYVALE AV	SVL	148 P8
SUNNY VISTA RD	SBD	100 B9
SUNRISE	SBD	101 C3
SUNRISE BLVD	SAC	34 P1
SUNRISE BLVD	SJCO	40 D2
SUNRISE HWY	SDCO	108 L6
SUNRISE HWY	SDCO	108 P6
SUNRISE WY	PMSP	206 P5
SUNRISE WY	RCO	100 H6
SUNRISE SPGS RD	SBD	93 P1
SUNSET	SAC	34 P2
SUNSET AV	FRFD	135 G7
SUNSET AV	KER	79 P8
SUNSET AV	LACO	118 L4
SUNSET AV	MCO	55 C7
SUNSET AV	RCO	99 G9
SUNSET AV	SOL	135 G7
SUNSET BL	BH	183 A1
SUNSET BLVD	KER	79 K0
SUNSET BLVD	LA	181 M3
SUNSET BLVD	LA	182 L0
SUNSET BLVD	LA	185 A7
SUNSET BL	LA	186 C1
SUNSET BLVD	LACO	97 D5
SUNSET BLVD	LACO	117 J3
SUNSET BL	SD	213 P3
SUNSET BLVD	SDCO	106 K3
SUNSET BLVD	SF	141 N1
SUNSET BLVD	SFCO	45 D3
SUNSET BL	LA	180 B4
SUNSET BL W	PLA	33 L8
SUNSET DR	IMP	109 F5
SUNSET DR	INY	60 M2
SUNSET DR	MAD	57 C5
SUNSET DR	MCO	47 L8
SUNSET DR	MCO	48 L0
SUNSET DR	MONT	53 F5
SUNSET DR	PAC	167 F2
SUNSET DR	SDCO	107 G4
SUNSET PKWY	MAR	38 M1
SUNSET RD	CC	39 P5
SUNSET RD	CLK	74 G7
SUNSET RD	GLE	24 H6
SUNSET RD	SBD	100 B9
SUNSET CYN DR	LACO	117 E4
SUNSET CLIFFS BL	SD	212 P3
SUNSET CLIFS BL	SDCO	106 K1
SUNSET CLIFS BL	SDCO	111 B4
SUNSET CRSNG RD	LACO	118 L8
SUNSET LAKE RD	ALP	42 A8
SUNSHINE MNE RD	KER	80 H8
SUPERIOR AV	CM	199 J1
SUPERIOR AV	NB	199 J1
SUPERIOR RD	KER	78 G3
SURPRISE CYN RD	INY	71 G5
SURPRISE SPG RD	SBD	100 A9
SURPRISE VLY RD	LAS	8 G8
SURPRISE VLY RD	MOD	7 H8
SURPRISE VLY RD	MOD	8 G8
SUSAN HILL DR	LAS	20 J9
SUSANVILLE RD	LAS	14 H3
SUTTER AV	FRCO	56 M8
SUTTER AV	FRCO	66 G8
SUTTER AV	MDO	162 P0
SUTTER RD	HUM	9 M9
SUTTER RD	HUM	10 M0
SUTTER RD	YOL	39 G6
SUTTER ST	SF	142 G2
SUTTER ST	SF	143 L4
SUTTER ISLND RD	SAC	39 H6
SUTTERVILLE RD	SAC	39 B7
SWAN RD	SOL	39 J2
SWAN MTN RD	PLU	20 J3
SWANSEA RD	LPAZ	104 G6
SWANSON AV	FRCO	57 N8
SWANSON AV	FRCO	57 N4
SWANSON RD	STA	47 G8
SWARTHOT CYN RD	SBD	91 D7
SWASEY DR	SHA	18 E3
SWEDE CREEK RD	SHA	18 H4
SWEDE CREEK RD	TRI	11 Q0
SWEDES FLAT RD	BUT	25 N8
SWEENEY RD	ED	35 P2
SWEENEY RD	SB	86 G4
SWEENEY RD	SOL	39 D1
SWEENY RD	MCO	55 F4
SWEENEY PASS RD	SDCO	109 P1
SWEETEN LN	SBD	91 C6
SWEETLAND RD	NEV	26 Q3
SWEETSER RD	KER	89 B7
SWEETWATER RD	SDCO	106 M5
SWEETWATER RD	SDCO	111 B8
SWEETWATER RD	SDCO	111 D7
SWEETWTR SPG BL	SDCO	106 N7
SWEETWTR SPG RD	SON	37 C6
SWEITZER LN	SBD	92 N7
SWENSEN RD	MCO	47 L6
SWETZER RD	SUT	33 H8
SWIFT AV	MCO	56 D1
SWIFT RD	SBD	80 P9
SWIFT ST	SC	169 N1
SWIFT CREEK	TRI	11 M8

STREET	CO.	PAGE & GRID
SWISS RANCH RD	CAL	41 H3
SX RD	MOD	14 A8
SYCAMORE AV	FRCO	57 K1
SYCAMORE AV	SDCO	107 H4
SYCAMORE DR	LACO	88 P9
SYCAMORE LN	DVS	136 G2
SYCAMORE RD	KER	79 L0
SYCAMORE RD	SDCO	106 Q5
SYCAMORE RD	SDCO	111 F7
SYCAMORE RD	VEN	88 M6
SYCAMORE ST	ANA	193 D3
SYCAMORE CYN RD	SB	87 L5
SYCAMORE CYN RD	STB	174 G9
SYCAMRE FLAT RD	MON	65 D0
SYCAMORE SL RD	COL	33 G0
SYCAMORE VLY RD	CC	46 C1
SYDNOR AV	KER	80 B6
SYKES RD	INY	70 H3
SYLVAN AV	STA	47 E6
SYLVESTER RD	MCO	55 B7
SYMMES RD	INY	59 J8
T		
T ST	BKD	166 M7
TABL MTN OVRCRS	BUT	25 L5
TABLE BLUFF RD	HUM	15 C7
TABLE BLUFF RD	HUM	15 C7
TABLE MTN BL	BUT	25 L5
TABLE MTN RD	FRCO	57 D7
TABLE MTN RD	RCO	100 N5
TABLE MTN TK TR	RCO	108 A5
TABLEROCK RD	SIS	4 L4
TABOOSE CK RD	INY	59 C8
TABOR AV	FRFD	135 F3
TABOR AV	SOL	39 H0
TABOR AV E	FRFD	135 F5
TAECKER RD	IMP	110 L3
TAFT	ORA	98 J4
TAFT AV	OR	194 J5
TAFT AV	ORA	120 E7
TAFT HWY	KER	78 J4
TAFT ST	TEH	24 B8
TAGE RD	SBD	101 C7
TAGLIO RD	MCO	47 P6
TAHQTZ-MCCLM WY	PMSP	206 K1
TALBERT AV	FTNV	197 G0
TALBERT AV	ORA	98 L2
TALBERT AV	ORA	120 H3
TALBERT LN	SOL	39 L3
TALBOT ST	SDCO	106 L1
TALC CITY RD	INY	70 B7
TALMAGE RD	U	123 L6
TAMALPAIS	MAR	38 Q2
TAMALPAIS DR	CRTM	140 B3
TAMARACK AV	SDCO	107 H3
TAMARACK RD	SHA	13 P4
TAMARACK RD	TEH	19 M4
TAMARACK LK RD	TRI	12 H3
TAMARACK PK RD	SHA	13 H4
TAMPA AV	LA	178 J3
TAMPA AV	LACO	97 B3
TANABE RD	YUB	33 C7
TANATEA ST	RCO	108 A5
TANK FARM RD	KER	78 K1
TANK FARM RD	SLO	76 K2
TANNERY GLCH RD	TRI	11 P7
TAPADERO ST	CAL	41 L0
TAPIA LN	SBD	90 F8
TAPLIN RD	NAPA	29 G5
TAPO RD	VEN	89 P1
TAPO CANYON RD	VEN	89 P0
TARA AV	KER	69 P2
TAR CANYON RD	KIN	66 K9
TARKE RD	SUT	33 F3
TARPON DR	SIS	4 G3
TASSAJARA RD	MON	64 D6
TATE CREEK RD	SIS	13 F1
TAVERN RD	SDCO	108 P2
TAVERNETTI RD	MON	54 P9
TAVERNETTI RD	MON	55 P0
TAVERNOR RD	SAC	40 E2
TAYLOR AV	KER	78 A3
TAYLOR BL	MLBR	144 P5
TAYLOR BLVD	CC	38 P8
TAYLOR LN	SBD	33 K5
TAYLOR RD	CC	39 M5
TAYLOR RD	STA	47 H5
TAYLOR ST	SF	143 E3
TAYLOR ST	SJ	152 F2
TAYLORSVL TRANS	PLU	20 P7
TEAGUE AV	FRCO	57 F6
TEAGUE AV	MON	65 D3
TEALE RD	KER	78 M7
TEALE RD	KER	79 M0
TEAPOT	TUL	68 H4
TECHNOR RD	SIS	5 M2
TECOLOTE RD	SDCO	106 J2
TECOLOTE RD	SDCO	111 A5
TECOPA HOT SPGS	INY	73 M0
TED ELDER RD	SHA	13 H6
TED KIPF RD	IMP	110 G4
TED KIPF RD	IMP	116 M0
TEDOC RD	TEH	17 M6
TEFFT ST	SLO	76 P5
TEGAN RD	SAC	39 E8
TEGNER RD	MCO	47 L7
TEHACHAPI BL	KER	79 M7
TEHACHP-WLW SPG	KER	79 N6
TEHAMA AV	KIN	67 K1
TEHAMA AV	TEH	24 B7
TEHAMA ST	GLE	24 M6
TEJON RD	LACO	90 K5
TELEGRAPH	MPA	49 G2
TELEGRAPH AV	B	156 G2
TELEGRAPH AV	O	156 G2
TELEGRAPH AV	S	160 F0
TELEGRAPH RD	CAL	40 P9
TELEGRAPH RD	CAL	41 P0
TELEGRAPH RD	LACO	89 M0
TELEGRAPH RD	LACO	98 F1
TELEGRAPH RD	LACO	117 M8
TELEGRAPH RD	LACO	118 P1
TELEGRAPH RD	VEN	88 M9
TELEGRPH CYN RD	SDCO	106 N6
TELEGRPH CYN RD	SDCO	111 C6
TELEGRAPH MN RD	SBD	83 G6
TELEPHONE RD	SB	86 C4
TELEPHONE RD	VEN	88 P2
TELESCOPE PK RD	INY	60 L5
TEMESCAL CYN RD	RCO	99 J0
TEMPERANCE AV	FRCO	57 F6
TEMPERANCE AV	FRCO	57 N7
TEMPLE AV	LACO	118 L3
TEMPLE AV	LACO	119 E8
TEMPLE ST	LA	185 B4
TEMPLE ST	LA	186 F2
TEMPLE CITY BL	LACO	118 H1
TEMPLE CREEK	SJCO	40 Q5
TEMPLE CREEK	SJCO	47 A5
TEMPLE HILLS DR	LAG	201 E6
TEMPLETON RD	SLO	76 D1
TENAJA RD	RCO	99 Q3
TENAJA TRUCK TR	RCO	99 Q2
TENMILE RD	MEN	30 K6
TEN MILE CTF RD	MEN	30 K6
TENMILE CUTF RD	MEN	30 K6
TENNANT AV	SCL	54 B6

STREET	CO.	PAGE & GRID
TENNANT RD	SIS	5 L3
TENNANT LAVA BD	MOD	5 M7
TENNANT LAVA BD	SIS	5 N8
TENNANT MT HRBN	SIS	5 M1
TENNESSEE ST E	FRFD	135 J5
TENNESSEE ST	SBD	99 E5
TENNESSEE ST	VAL	134 K4
TENNYSON RD	ALA	45 F8
TEPUSQUET RD	SB	86 C6
TEQUEPIS CYN RD	SB	87 J1
TERCEIRA RD	MCO	55 D8
TERMINAL RD	AVLN	105 N3
TERMINOUS RD	SAC	39 K6
TERMO GRASSHPPR	LAS	14 N8
TERMO GRASSHPPR	LAS	8 P1
TERRA BELLA ST	LACO	117 D1
TERRACE	FRCO	58 H1
TERRACE RD	RCO	100 K7
TERRY MILL RD	SHA	13 Q1
TERWER RIFFL RD	DN	10 A1
TERWILLIGER RD	RCO	108 Q4
TERWILLIGER RD	RCO	108 B4
TESLA RD	ALA	46 F5
TESORO RD	SBD	90 G8
TEST STATION	MNO	43 P5
TEXAS AV	KER	79 P9
TEXAS AV	KER	80 P0
TEXAS RD	STA	47 F4
TEXAS ST	FRFD	135 J1
TEXAS ST	SD	216 B2
TEXAS ST	SDCO	106 K3
TEXAS ST	SDCO	111 B6
TEXAS ST N	SOL	38 H9
TEXAS ST N	FRFD	135 G5
TEXAS HILL	MPA	48 D9
TEXAS HILL RD	YUB	26 Q1
TEXAS SPGS RD	SHA	18 F3
THAMES DR	RED	122 D7
THATCHER RD	SHA	19 E4
THATCHER MLL RD	SHA	19 F4
THATCHER RDG RD	BUT	25 B6
THE BRADSHAW TR	RCO	102 P0
THEDA ST	RCO	99 L4
THE INDIAN RD	MOD	8 G2
THEODORE ST	RCO	99 G6
THEODORIC RD	SBD	84 K4
THING RD	SDCO	112 E4
THIRD ST	C	124 N2
THISSELL RD	SOL	39 D2
THOMAS	SON	37 A8
THOMAS RD	HUM	16 N3
THOMAS RD	KER	90 B4
THOMAS RD	MCO	55 F5
THOMAS RD	SBT	54 H0
THOMAS RD	SHA	18 H2
THOMAS RD	SHA	19 B1
THOMAS ST	KER	80 M1
THOME RD	YUB	33 B6
THOMPSON RD	SUT	33 H4
THOMPSON AV	FRCO	57 G2
THOMPSON AV	FRCO	57 N7
THOMPSON BL	VENT	175 F2
THOMPSON RD	IMP	110 N0
THOMPSON RD	LAS	14 K3
THOMPSON RD	MNO	43 M3
THOMPSON RD	SBD	81 Q5
THOMPSON RD	SLO	76 N4
THOMPSON CYN AV	KER	79 F5
THOMPSON CYN RD	MON	65 E3
THOMSEN RD	SOL	39 E4
THORNBURG ST	SMA	173 J3
THORNE AV	FRE	165 M3
THORNTON AV	ALA	45 H9
THORNTON AV	ALA	46 G1
THOUSND OAKS BL	LACO	105 C9
THOUSND OAKS BL	VEN	105 B7
THOUSND PLMS RD	RCO	100 J9
THOUSAND SPGS	SHA	13 J6
THREE CHOP RD	MEN	22 Q7
THREE FLAGS HWY	KER	80 B6
THREE PINES CYN	KER	80 A3
THREE SLASHS RD	IMP	116 F4
THRIFT RD	MCO	48 P5
THRUSH DR	SIS	5 H3
THUNDER	SDCO	107 G3
THUNDERBIRD BL	KER	80 K5
THUNDERBIRD RD	SBD	91 J5
THUNDER CYN RD	SLO	75 E7
TIBURON BLVD	MAR	140 H8
TICE VALLEY BL	CC	45 A9
TICINO ST	SB	86 C2
TIERNEY RD	HUM	16 H2
TIERRA BUENA	SUT	33 D5
TIERRA DEL SOL	SDCO	112 D9
TIERRA RJADA RD	VEN	88 P8
TIERRA SANTA BL	SDCO	106 H4
TIERRA SANTA BL	SDCO	107 P6
TIFFANY RCH RD	SLO	76 L3
TIGER CREEK RD	SIS	11 E6
TIJ-ENSNADA FWY	BAJA	111 H7
TILTON DR	LACO	89 H8
TIM BELL RD	STA	48 D1
TIMBER COVE RD	SON	37 B1
TIMBER CRATER	SHA	13 H7
TIMBUCTOO RD	YUB	34 C1
TIMM RD	SOL	39 E1
TIMMONS AV	KER	68 P3
TIMMONS RD	SIS	4 P2
TIM MULLEN RD	HUM	16 C2
TIMS RD	SB	86 F9
TIN BARN RD	SON	37 A0
TINDALL RCH RD	MEN	31 E3
TINNEMAHA RD	INY	59 C8
TIOGA PASS RD	MPA	42 Q9
TIOGA PASS RD	MPA	43 Q0
TIOGA PASS RD	MPA	50 A1
TIOGA PASS RD	MPA	63 J6
TIOGA PASS RD	MNO	43 Q0
TIOGA PASS RD	TUO	42 Q9
TIOGA PASS RD	TUO	50 A1
TIOGA PASS RD	TUO	63 L0
TIONESTA RD	MOD	5 N8
TIONESTA RD	MOD	6 N1
TIPPECANOE ST	SBD	99 D4
TIPTOP RD	MPA	49 J4
TISDALE	SUT	33 G3
TITLOW HILL RD	HUM	10 N4
TITSWORTH RD	IMP	110 K4
TIZON RD	RCO	108 A3
TOBACCO	SJCO	40 N4
TOBIN DR	VAL	134 C3
TODAYANA WY	PLA	34 F6
TODD RD	KER	69 P2
TODD RD	SON	37 F8
TODD EYMANN RD	FRCO	58 J6
TODD VALLEY	PLA	34 H7
TOFT DR	RCO	99 M1
TOKAY COLONY	SJCO	40 L4
TOLAND LN	SOL	39 L4
TOLAND RD	VEN	88 M5
TOLAND PARK RD	VEN	88 M5
TOLL GATE WY	BUT	25 E4
TOLL HOUSE RD	FRCO	57 F7
TOLL HOUSE RD	FRCO	58 D0
TOMALES RD	SON	37 H8
TOMALES PETALMA	MAR	37 J7

STREET	CO.	PAGE & GRID
TOM GREEN MN RD	SHA	18 C0
TOMKI RD	MEN	23 N2
TOMPKNS HILL RD	HUM	15 D8
TOM SHAW RD	HUM	16 D2
TOM WELLS RD	LPAZ	104 N0
TONNER CYN RD	ORA	118 P6
TOOBY DR	FRFD	135 G1
TOOME CAMP	TEH	24 D1
TOOMES RD	STA	47 E4
TOPA LN	VEN	88 L4
TOPANGA CYN BL	LA	177 G3
TOPANGA CYN BL	LACO	97 C3
TOPAZ LN	MNO	42 A8
TOPAZ RD	SBD	91 G2
TOPEKA DR	LA	178 L5
TOPO RD	MON	65 B3
TOPO VALLEY RD	SBT	65 A4
TOPOCK DAVIS DM	MOH	95 C8
TOPPEN DORFF LN	HUM	15 E7
TORO CANYON RD	SB	87 L7
TORO CREEK RD	SLO	75 F9
TORO CREEK RD	SLO	76 F0
TORRANCE BLVD	LACO	97 J6
TORRANCE BLVD	LACO	119 D2
TORREY PINES RD	SD	211 E2
TORREY PINES RD	SDCO	106 F1
TORREY PINES RD	SDCO	107 N4
TORREY RD N	VEN	88 M8
TORREY RD S	VEN	88 M8
TOTTEN RD	SHA	13 K9
TOVEY AV	LACO	90 J0
TOWER LINE RD	KER	79 L0
TOWER RD	SLO	76 A2
TOWNE AV	LACO	118 J9
TOWNSEND RD	IMP	110 N4
TOWNSEND RD	SIS	4 K4
TOWNSEND ST	SBD	91 C7
TOWNSEND RD	VEN	89 P0
TOWNSHIP RD	KLAM	5 E2
TOWNSHIP RD	YUB	34 B0
TOWNSHIP RD N	SUT	33 F5
TRABUCO RD	ORA	98 L6
TRABUCO RD	ORA	120 J9
TRACTOR AV	FRCO	66 F6
TRACY AV	KER	78 F1
TRACY BLVD	SBD	100 A7
TRACY BLVD	SJCO	39 Q8
TRAGEDY SPGS RD	AMA	35 P8
TRAIL CANYON RD	INY	72 C0
TRAILS END LN	RCO	108 B4
TRAILS END CAMP	SBD	96 N3
TRAMPA CYN RD	MON	64 B5
TRAMWAY RD	TEH	19 K4
TRANCAS ST	NAP	133 D4
TRANCAS ST	NAPA	133 D7
TRASK AV	GGR	195 F2
TRASK AV	ORA	120 F3
TRAUTWEIN RD	RCO	99 G3
TRAVIS BL	FRFD	135 G2
TRAYNHAM RD	COL	33 G1
TREAT BLVD	CC	38 P9
TREAT BLVD	CC	39 P0
TREDWAY	SJCO	40 L0
TREMONT RD	SOL	39 C4
TREMONT ST	AVLN	105 N2
TRENTHAM RD	IMP	110 P2
TRES CERITOS AV	RCO	99 K7
TRESTLE GLEN	MAR	45 A3
TRESTLE GLEN RD	O	158 G5
TRIANGLE	MPA	49 H3
TRIANGLE RCH RD	MOD	6 M7
TRIANGLE RCH RD	STA	47 F7
TRIMBLE RD	SCL	46 L2
TRIMMER SPGS RD	FRCO	58 H0
TRIMMER SPGS RD	INY	58 F4
TRINITY	TEH	18 N7
TRINITY AV	FRCO	56 H9
TRINITY AV	FRCO	57 M0
TRINITY RD	SON	38 F2
TRINITY ST	FRE	165 K4
TRINITY ALPS RD	TRI	11 P7
TRINITY MTN RD	SHA	12 Q1
TRINITY PINE DR	TRI	17 J2
TRIPP FLATS RD	RIV	100 P2
TRIUNFO CYN RD	LACO	105 C8
TRONA RD	SBD	80 F9
TRONA RD	SBD	81 B0
TRONA AIRPRT RD	INY	71 M3
TRONA WLDRSE RD	INY	71 A5
TROPICANA AV	CLK	74 G7
TROPICANA AV	CLK	210 K4
TROWER	MPA	49 J0
TROWER AV	NAP	133 C0
TROY RD	SBD	92 D4
TRUCKEE AV	TEH	24 B7
TRUCKE ARPRT RD	NEV	27 Q7
TRUCKE-TAHO ARP	NEV	35 B8
TRUESDALE RD	SLO	76 C6
TRUEX RD	BUT	25 H6
TRUMAN RD	KER	89 C7
TRUMAN MDWS RD	MNO	44 P4
TRUMBULL RD	LAS	21 E6
TRUXTUN AV	BKD	166 H3
TSCHIRKY RD	SHA	15 F7
TUBBS RD	SOL	39 D1
TUCACOTA HLS RD	RCO	99 N8
TUCKER RD	LAS	21 P6
TUCKER CYN RD	SLO	76 C6
TUCSON AV	KIN	67 K7
TUDOR RD	SUT	33 H4
TUJUNGA AV	LACO	117 H2
TUJUNGA CYN BL	LACO	117 C4
TUJUNGA CYN RD	LACO	117 A2
TULARE AV	KER	77 D8
TULARE AV	FRCO	57 J5
TULARE AV	TUL	68 C2
TULARE ST	FRE	165 L6
TULAROSA RD	SB	86 G4
TULE LN	CC	39 N5
TULE RD	COL	33 G1
TULE RD	YOL	39 E7
TULE CYN TK TR	RCO	108 B4
TULE CREEK RD	TRI	17 F2
TULEDAD RD	LAS	8 N6
TULE PEAK RD	RCO	108 B3
TULE SPRING RD	INY	72 D0
TULE SPGS TK TR	SDCO	108 M3
TULIP AV	STA	47 K5
TULLY	SJCO	40 M4
TULLY RD	MDO	162 E0
TULLY RD	SCL	46 M3
TULLY RD	STA	47 E5
TULLY CREEK RD	HUM	10 G4
TUMBLEWEED RD	LACO	90 L4
TUNA CANYON RD	LACO	97 D3
TUNGSTEN RD	MNO	51 H7
TUNGSTEN CTY RD	INY	51 L4
TUNITAS CK RD	SMCO	45 L4
TUNNEL RD	B	156 K5
TUOLUMNE AV	FRCO	56 L7
TUOLUMNE BL	MDO	162 M7
TUOLUMNE DR	MLBR	144 Q2
TUOLUMNE RD	STA	47 H5
TUOLUMNE ST	VAL	134 D6
TUPMAN RD	KER	78 J2
TURK ST	SF	142 H1

STREET	CO.	PAGE & GRID
TURK ST	SF	143 P2
TURKEY AV	BUT	25 N8
TURKEY FLAT RD	MON	66 M6
TURKEY HILL RD	KLAM	5 E8
TURLOCK AV	SCL	54 C6
TURLOCK RD	MCO	48 J2
TURLOCK RD	MCO	48 H3
TURNBULL	LACO	98 F2
TURNBULL CYN RD	LACO	118 N2
TURNELL RD	TEH	18 K5
TURNER	SJCO	40 K0
TURNER AV	MCO	47 L7
TURNER AV	SBD	98 E8
TURNER DR	TUL	68 E2
TURNER RD	COL	32 E7
TURNER RD	MCO	47 L6
TURNER RD	STA	47 G6
TURNER ISLND RD	MCO	56 C1
TURQUOISE ST	SD	211 Q0
TURQUOISE ST	SDCO	106 H1
TURQUOISE ST	SDCO	107 Q4
TURRI RD	SLO	75 J9
TURRI RD	SLO	76 J0
TURTLE MTN RD	SBD	95 L4
TURTLE VLY RD	SBD	91 E4
TUSCAN SPGS RD	TEH	18 M7
TUSSING RCH RD	SBD	91 L5
TUSTIN AV	CM	199 H5
TUSTIN AV	NB	199 H5
TUSTIN AV	OR	194 G8
TUSTIN AV	OR	196 E8
TUSTIN AV	ORA	98 K5
TUSTIN AV	ORA	120 D7
TUSTIN AV	ORA	196 K9
TUSTIN AV	ORA	199 H5
TUSTIN AV	SA	196 K9
TUTTLECREEK RD	INY	60 M1
TUTTLETOWN RD	TUO	41 N4
TUXEDO AV N	S	160 G4
TUXFORD ST	LACO	117 D2
TWEEDY BLVD	LACO	117 P7
TWENTIETH ST	C	124 P9
TWENTY-EIGHT MI	STA	47 C8
TWNTY MULE TEAM	INY	72 A1
TWNTY MULE TEAM	KER	80 L4
TWNTYNINE PALMS	SBD	100 C8
TWNTYNINE PALMS	SBD	101 C7
TWENTY-SIX MILE	STA	47 B7
TWIN RD S	MNO	43 J1
TWIN CITIES RD	SAC	39 H8
TWIN LAKES RD	MNO	43 H2
TWIN LAKES RD	TRI	12 J3
TWIN LKS CMPST	ALP	35 N9
TWIN OAKES RD	KER	79 H6
TWIN OAKS VLY	SDCO	107 H5
TWIN PEAKS RD	SDCO	107 L6
TWIN PINES RD	SBD	100 H1
TWIN VALLEY RD	LAK	31 D9
TWIN VALLEY RD	LAK	31 D9
TWIN VIEW BLVD	SHA	18 D4
TWISSELMAN RD	KER	67 P3
TWISSELMAN RD	KER	67 P5
TWIST RD	TUO	41 Q5
TWIST RD	TUO	48 A5
TWITCHLL ISL RD	SAC	39 L5
TWO MILE RD	COL	32 C7
TWO MILE RD	SBD	101 C2
TYLER AV	LACO	118 K2
TYLER AV	AMA	40 C9
TYLER RD	TEH	18 P7
TYLER ST	MONT	167 J9
TYLER ST	RCO	99 G1
TYLER ST	RCO	101 M2
TYLER ST	SAL	171 D3
TYLER ST	SDCO	106 K6
TYLER ST	SDCO	111 B5
TYLER FOOT CRSG	NEV	26 Q3
TYLER GULCH RD	SIS	3 M6
TYLER ISLAND RD	SAC	39 K6
U		
U ST	FRE	165 J9
UBEHEBE RD	INY	60 L8
UKIAH RD	MEN	31 F2
UKIAH BOONVILLE	MEN	31 H0
UKONOM LKOUT RD	SIS	2 Q7
UKONOM LKOUT RD	SIS	10 A7
ULRIC ST	SD	213 G6
ULRIC ST	SDCO	106 J3
ULRIC ST	SDCO	111 A5
UNDERPASS RD	MEN	22 L9
UNDERSTOCK DR	BUT	25 D5
UNDERWOOD RD	MON	54 P4
UNION AV	BKD	166 J8
UNION AV	KER	166 P8
UNION AV	FRFD	135 K4
UNION AV	SB	86 C5
UNION AV	SCL	46 N2
UNION AV	SOL	38 H9
UNION AV	MAN	161 J0
UNION RD	SBT	54 G8
UNION RD	SLO	76 B2
UNION ST	EUR	121 F4
UNION ST	HUM	15 B8
UNION CITY BLVD	ALA	45 G8
UNION HILL RD	TRI	17 D6
UNION RD	KER	78 K3
UNION RIDGE RD	ED	34 N8
UNION SCHOOL RD	SHA	18 C5
UNION SUGAR AV	SB	86 G2
UNITED ST	KER	80 P1
UNIVERSITY AV	PA	147 E2
UNIVERSITY AV	RIV	205 E2
UNIVERSITY AV	RCO	99 F3
UNIVERSITY AV	SAL	171 L0
UNIVERSITY AV	SD	214 Q6
UNIVERSITY AV	SD	215 A7
UNIVERSITY AV	SD	216 A6
UNIVERSITY AV	SDCO	106 K3
UNIVERSITY AV	SDCO	111 B6
UNIVERSITY DR	IRV	200 D5
UNIVERSITY DR	ORA	98 M4
UNIVERSITY DR	ORA	120 K7
UPAS ST	SD	216 C1
UPHAM RD	BUT	25 N9
UPHILL RD	SBD	101 C0
UPJOHN RD W	KER	80 B6
UPLAND RD	VEN	88 Q5
UPPER TER	AVLN	105 P3
UPPER BEAR RIVER	HUM	15 F6
UPPR COUGR FIRE	SIS	4 Q7
UPPR COUGR FIRE	SIS	12 A7
UPPER DIVISN CK	INY	59 D8
UPPER DORRAY RD	CAL	41 F1
UPPER FALL RD	SIS	13 F0
UPPER LK CTY RD	MOD	7 N6
UPR MAD RIV RD	TRI	17 L1
UPPER PALRMO RD	BUT	25 N7
UPPER SHOTGN RD	SHA	12 K4
UPPER S FORK RD	TRI	16 E8
UPPR SUMMRS MDW	MNO	43 J2
UPPER TOBY RCH	HUM	16 Q5
UPPER WILLOW CK	SIS	4 J4
USTON RD	AMA	40 B8
USAL RD	MEN	22 D2
USFS CAMP RD	TRI	17 C1
USONA RD	MPA	49 K4

USTICK RD — STREET INDEX — WINDSOR RIVER RD

STREET	CO.	PAGE & GRID
USTICK RD	STA	47 G5
UTAH AV	SSF	144 C5
UTAH DR	INY	70 C8
UTAH ST	FRFD	135 H2
UTAH TR	SBD	101 C4
UTAH MINE RD	BUT	25 E7
UTICA AV	KIN	67 K1
UTICA AV	KIN	67 K6
UTICA PWRHSE RD	CAL	41 K4
UVAS RD	SCL	54 B4
UXMAL	BAJA	114 D2
V		
V ST	MER	170 K1
VAIL	SJCO	40 G1
VAIL RD	IMP	110 J0
VALENCIA AV	LACO	89 M2
VALENCIA AV	ORA	98 G4
VALENCIA AV	ORA	120 B7
VALENCIA RD	SCR	54 D2
VALENSIN RD	SAC	40 G1
VALENTINE AV	FRCO	57 K4
VALENTINE AV	FRCO	67 A4
VALERIA AV	FRCO	56 D3
VALERIO ST	STB	174 H2
VALK RD	STA	47 D8
VALLECITOS RD	ALA	46 F3
VALLE VISTA AV	VAL	134 H4
VALLE VISTA RD	SBD	101 B3
VALLEY AV	ALA	46 E2
VALLEY BLVD	LACO	97 D9
VALLEY BLVD	LACO	98 E2
VALLEY BLVD	LACO	117 K7
VALLEY BLVD	LACO	118 K1
VALLEY BLVD	SBD	99 D0
VALLEY PKWY	SDCO	107 H7
VALLEY RD	ED	34 P3
VALLEY RD	KER	80 H4
VALLEY RD	MEN	23 P1
VALLEY RD	PLA	34 G1
VALLEY RD	SAC	34 P3
VALLEY RD E	SB	87 L6
VALLEY RD W	MOD	8 G3
VALLEY CTR RD	SBD	92 B2
VLY CENTER RD	SDCO	107 G8
VALLEY CIR BL	LACO	97 B2
VALLEY CTOFF RD	LAS	14 J3
VALLEY FORD RD	SON	37 G7
VALLEY SAGE RD	LACO	89 K7
VALLEY VIEW DR	SBD	102 C4
VALLEY VIEW RD	JKSN	3 A8
VALLEY VIEW RD	SBD	91 B4
VALLEY VIEW ST	ORA	98 J2
VALLEY VIEW ST	ORA	120 E2
VALLEY VW LKOUT	TEH	24 G0
VALLEY VISTA BL	LA	178 N8
VALLEY WELLS RD	INY	71 M3
VALLEY WELLS RD	SBD	81 Q5
VALLEY WEST RD	KER	78 K0
VALLOMBROSA AV	BUT	25 G3
VALLOMBROSA AV	BUT	124 K6
VALLOMBROSA AV	C	124 K6
VALOS RD	KER	78 N8
VALPARAISO AV	SCL	45 K7
VALPREDO AV	KER	78 N6
VAL VERDE	PLA	34 M3
VALYERMO	LACO	90 K4
VAN ALDEN AV	LA	178 M4
VAN ALLEN	SJCO	40 Q5
VAN ALLEN	SJCO	47 C5
VAN ARSDALE RD	MEN	23 P3
VAN BRMMR LKOUT	SIS	5 M3
VAN BUREN BLVD	RCO	99 E0
VAN BUREN ST	MONT	167 K8
VAN BUREN ST	RCO	101 K1
VAN CLIFF	MCO	47 N8
VANDEGRIFT BLVD	SDCO	107 F3
VANDEGRIFT RD	SDCO	107 F2
VANDEN RD	SOL	39 G1
VANDENBERG RD	SB	86 E2
VANDER LINDN RD	IMP	114 B5
VANDER POEL RD	IMP	114 B0
VANDER VEER RD	RCO	101 P5
VAN DOLLEN RD	SLO	66 P2
VAN DUSEN CYN	SBD	92 P0
VAN DUZEN RD	TRI	16 H8
VAN DUZEN RD	TRI	16 K8
VAN DUZEN RD E	TRI	16 J8
VAN GORDN CK RD	SLO	75 C4
VAN LOON CUTOFF	MNO	51 E6
VAN NESS	SFCO	45 C4
VAN NESS AV	FRE	165 J6
VAN NESS AV	LACO	117 P4
VAN NESS AV	SF	143 L1
VAN NESS AV S	SF	142 L5
VAN NESS RD	TRI	12 P0
VAN NUYS BLVD	LACO	89 Q5
VAN NUYS BLVD	LACO	97 B5
VAN NUYS BLVD	LACO	117 C1
VANOWEN ST	BUR	179 E3
VANOWEN ST	LA	177 E1
VANOWEN ST	LA	178 E3
VANOWEN ST	LA	179 E3
VAN SICKLE RD	SOL	39 K0
VARGAS RD	ALA	46 G2
VARNER RD	RCO	100 H7
VARNI RD	SCR	54 E3
VASCO RD	ALA	46 E4
VASCO RD	CC	46 C4
VASQUEZ CYN RD	LACO	89 L4
VASQUEZ CK RD	SBT	55 L7
VASSAR AV	MCO	48 N4
VASSAR ST	RENO	130 L4
VAUGHN RD	RCO	109 B8
VAUGHN RD	SOL	39 D3
VAWTER RD	COL	32 J9
VAWTER RANCH RD	RCO	99 N8
VEDDER RD	SHA	13 N5
VEE BEE ST	RCO	100 H8
VENCILL RD	IMP	114 B4
VENDEL RD	IMP	109 K8
VENICE BLVD	LA	183 P4
VENICE BLVD	LA	184 J4
VENICE BLVD	LA	185 J4
VENICE BLVD	LA	187 F5
VENICE BLVD	LA	188 A1
VENICE BLVD	LACO	97 E5
VENICE BLVD	LACO	117 N0
VENTURA AV	FRCO	57 J6
VENTURA AV	VEN	88 P1
VENTURA AV	VENT	175 D2
VENTURA BLVD	LA	177 L7
VENTURA BLVD	LA	178 L0
VENTURA BLVD	LACO	97 C4
VENTURA FRWY	BUR	179 N5
VENTURA FRWY	LA	177 L6
VENTURA FRWY	LA	178 K3
VENTURA FRWY	LA	179 N5
VENTURA FRWY	LACO	97 C1
VENTURA FRWY	VENT	175 F4
VENTURA FRWY	VEN	88 N0
VENTURA FRWY	VEN	105 A5
VENTURA RD	MCO	48 N2
VENTURA RD	OXN	176 K1
VENTURA RD	VEN	105 B5
VENTURA ST	FRE	165 N6
VENTURA ST	VEN	88 M6
VERA AV	KER	80 B6
VERANO AV	SON	132 H5
VERBENA AV	C	124 F8
VERBENA AV	SBD	91 G5
VERBENA DR	RCO	100 F6
VERDE AV	MCO	47 L7
VERDEMNT RCH RD	SBD	99 B2
VERDE SCHOOL RD	IMP	114 B4
VERDI PEAK RD	SIE	27 M8
VERDUGO AV	BUR	179 M4
VERDUGO AV	LACO	117 G3
VERDUGO BLVD	LACO	117 F6
VERDUGO RD	LACO	117 H6
VERMICULITE MN	SBD	100 D8
VERMONT AV	ANA	193 H5
VERMONT AV	LA	182 P3
VERMONT AV	LA	185 P4
VERMONT AV	LACO	97 H7
VERMONT AV	LACO	119 E4
VERMONT CYN RD	LA	182 F3
VERNON AV	LACO	97 E7
VERNON AV	LACO	117 M4
VERNON AV	LACO	118 G5
VERNON RD	SUT	33 M6
VERSAILLES AV	A	159 D1
VESTA	SDCO	111 C6
VESTA ST	SDCO	106 M4
VESTAL RD	TEH	18 L0
VETERAN AV	LACO	117 K0
VETERANS HALL	TRI	10 P8
VIA CAPRI	SD	211 G1
VIA DE LA VALLE	SDCO	107 L4
VIA DEL REY	MONT	167 K6
VIA DEL REY	MON	53 H8
VIADUCT BLVD	SBDO	207 F2
VIA GAYUBA	MONT	167 M6
VIA PARAISO	MONT	167 L6
VIA RANCHO PKWY	SDCO	107 J7
VIA SECO ST	SBD	92 J1
VIA VERDE	LACO	118 K6
VICHY SPGS RD	MEN	31 E3
VICKREY LN	SOL	38 D9
VICTOR ST	KER	80 C6
VICTORIA AV	RCO	99 G1
VICTORIA AV	RIV	205 K4
VICTORIA CT	KER	79 M4
VICTORIA DR	SDCO	108 P2
VICTORIA ST	LACO	97 H8
VICTORIA ST	LACO	119 C5
VICTORIA ST	ORA	120 K4
VICTORIA ST	SM	199 D0
VICTORIA ST	STB	174 L2
VICTORY AV	STA	47 C7
VICTORY BLVD	BUR	179 F2
VICTORY BLVD	LA	177 F4
VICTORY BLVD	LA	178 G3
VICTORY BLVD	LA	179 F2
VICTORY BLVD	LACO	97 B6
VICTORY BLVD	LACO	117 F0
VICTORY HWY	CC	39 N4
VICTORY PL	BUR	179 E7
VICTORY PL	LACO	117 F4
VICTORY RD	SJCO	40 K2
VICTORY RD	SJCO	47 C6
VIEJAS GRADE	SDCO	108 P3
VIERRA RD	YUB	26 N0
VIEW DR	TUL	58 L3
VIEW LAND RD	LAS	21 J6
VILAS RD	BUT	25 D4
VILLA AV	EC	217 C5
VILLA AV	SR	139 G7
VILLA RD	IMP	110 Q2
VILLA ST	SAL	171 J2
VILLA CREEK RD	SLO	75 E6
VILLAGE RD	SDCO	106 G3
VILLAGE RD	SDCO	107 P5
VLLA L JOLLA DR	SD	211 B4
VLLA MANUCHA RD	STA	47 L5
VILLA PARK RD	ORA	120 E8
VINA RD	TEH	25 D0
VINCENT AV	LACO	118 J5
VINCENT RD	MCO	47 J9
VINCENT RD	MCO	48 J0
VINCENT RD	STA	47 H9
VINCENT RD	STA	48 H0
VINE AV	MCO	48 L2
VINE AV	SJCO	47 C6
VINE ST	LA	181 P7
VINE ST	LACO	117 J3
VINE ST	SDCO	106 G8
VINE ST	SDCO	108 P0
VINE ST	SJ	152 M3
VINE WY	KER	79 C5
VINELAND AV	FRCO	57 K1
VINELAND AV	LACO	97 B6
VINELAND AV	LACO	117 G2
VINELAND RD	KER	78 L8
VINEWOOD AV	MCO	47 K9
VINEWOOD AV	MCO	48 K0
VINEYARD AV	ALA	46 E3
VINEYARD AV	OXN	176 A4
VINEYARD AV	SBD	98 F8
VINEYARD AV	VEN	176 A6
VINEYARD DR	SLO	75 C8
VINEYARD RD	PLA	34 N1
VINEYARD RD	SJCO	40 D1
VINEYARD RD	STA	47 H3
VINEYARD RD	YUB	34 D1
VINEYARD WY	MCO	56 B3
VINEYARD CYN RD	MON	66 M3
VINEYARD CYN RD	MCO	66 M3
VINNUM RD	HUM	16 K2
VINTON GULCH RD	BUT	25 J7
VINTON LOYALTON	PLU	27 G6
VIOLA AV	TEH	24 D7
VIOLA MINERAL	TEH	19 H5
VIRGIL AV	LACO	117 K4
VIRGINIA	SBD	77 P0
VIRGINIA AV	KIN	67 L8
VIRGINIA AV	MDO	162 F2
VIRGINIA AV	SON	38 E2
VIRGINIA RD	LACO	117 H8
VIRGINIA RD	STA	47 F0
VIRGINIA RD	STA	48 F0
VIRGINIA ST	RCO	99 G6
VIRGINIA ST N	RENO	130 D2
VIRGINIA ST S	RENO	130 J3
VIRGINIA LK RD	MNO	43 L3
VIRGINIATOWN RD	PLA	34 J2
VISALIA RD	FRCO	58 K7
VISTA AV	MCO	48 Q6
VISTA AV	RCO	98 H8
VISTA AV	SBD	98 C7
VISTA LN	LAS	21 L3
VISTA RD	SBD	91 E3
VISTA WY	SDCO	107 G3
VISTA CHINO	PMSP	206 E1
VISTA CHINO	RCO	100 H6
VISTA DEL MAR	LACO	97 F5
VISTA DL MAR BL	ELS	189 L0
VISTA DL MAR BL	LACO	117 P1
VISTA DEL VALLE	LA	182 B2
VISTA ENCINA AV	MDO	162 G7
VISTA DE ORO	RCO	101 B5
VISTA GRANDE DR	KER	79 B7
VISTA MINE RD	IMP	116 M0
VIVIAN RD	STA	47 H5
VLASNIK RD	KER	77 E8
VOGEL RD	IMP	113 B9
VOGEL RD	KER	79 N6
VOLCANO CIR	BUT	25 G4
VOLCANO RD	AMA	92 N7
VOLCANO RD	ED	41 E0
VOLCANO PIONEER	AMA	41 D1
VOLCANOVILLE RD	ED	34 H9
VOLLEY RD	PLA	34 G5
VOLTA RD	MCO	55 C6
VOLTAIRE ST	SDCO	106 K1
VOLTAIRE ST	SDCO	111 B4
VON GLAHN	SJCO	47 C5
VOORHESS RD	MCO	48 P6
VORDEN RD	SAC	39 H7
VULCAN MINE RD	SBD	84 Q0
W		
W LN	MCO	48 K2
WAALEW RD	SBD	91 J5
WABASH	SDCO	111 C6
WABASH AV	SBD	99 E6
WABASH BLVD	SD	214 Q5
WABASH BLVD	SD	216 Q4
WABASH BLVD	SDCO	106 L4
WACHTEL WY	SAC	34 P2
WACKERMAN RD	TEH	24 F5
WADDINGTON RD	HUM	15 E8
WADE AV	MCO	48 P8
WADLEIGH RD	COL	32 B6
WAGNER	SJCO	47 C4
WAGNER AV	ANA	194 G0
WAGNER AV	COL	32 H8
WAGON RD	BUT	25 D5
WAGON WHEEL	SBD	101 C1
WAHL RD	IMP	114 B0
WAINWRIGHT	MCO	47 M7
WAKEFIELD	FRCO	58 K1
WALDO RD	YUB	34 E1
WALERGA	PLA	33 N9
WALGROVE AV	LA	187 C4
WALKER DR	SHA	13 K7
WALKER PL	MNO	51 B5
WALKER RD	IMP	109 J9
WALKER RD	MEN	23 Q0
WALKER RD	NAPA	32 P3
WALKER RD	SBD	92 N4
WALKER RD	SIS	3 J5
WALKER RD	SON	37 H8
WALKER ST	GLE	24 G7
WALKER ST	ORA	120 E2
WALKER WY	IMP	116 N2
WALKER BASIN RD	KER	79 G4
WALKER CREEK RD	INY	70 D2
WALKER CREEK RD	SIS	3 J3
WALKER LNDNG RD	SAC	39 J6
WALKER MINE RD	PLU	26 C9
WALKER MINE RD	SHA	18 C3
WALKER PLAINS	BUT	25 F8
WALKUP RD	COL	32 A2
WALL	SJCO	40 M4
WALLACE	SON	38 D0
WALLACE AV	VAL	134 M7
WALLACE RD	KER	78 B4
WALLER ST	SF	141 L8
WALLER ST	SF	142 L0
WALLIS RD	STA	48 G1
WALLY HILL RD	CAL	41 K3
WALMORT RD	SAC	40 F1
WALNUT AV	CC	38 P9
WALNUT AV	FRE	165 Q4
WALNUT AV	FRCO	57 K4
WALNUT AV	KIN	67 G7
WALNUT AV	LACO	117 E4
WALNUT AV	MCO	48 K1
WALNUT AV	ORA	120 H8
WALNUT AV	STA	47 H4
WALNUT AV	STA	47 C7
WALNUT AV	TUL	68 C2
WALNUT AV	U	123 G2
WALNUT AV	YUB	33 D7
WALNUT BLVD	CC	39 Q5
WALNUT DR	COL	32 E6
WALNUT DR	HUM	15 B8
WALNUT DR	NAPA	29 K6
WALNUT DR	SJCO	40 M4
WALNUT LN	GLE	25 M0
WALNUT ST	ANA	193 L2
WALNUT ST	C	124 P1
WALNUT ST	ORA	120 B4
WALNUT ST	PAS	190 J2
WALNUT ST	YOL	134 C5
WALNUT GROVE	SJCO	40 J0
WALNUT GROVE AV	LACO	118 L1
WALSER RD	KER	79 F4
WALTERS RD	LAS	14 H4
WALTERS RD	SOL	39 H1
WALTERS CAMP RD	IMP	116 F4
WALTON AV	SUT	125 P0
WALTON AV S	SUT	33 F5
WALTZ RD	PLA	33 J8
WALTZ RD	SUT	33 J8
WAMBLE RD	STA	47 C9
WAMBLE RD	STA	48 C0
WANGENHEIM RD	STA	47 M5
WARD AV	STA	47 K3
WARD RD	HUM	10 P3
WARD RD	LACO	89 K8
WARD CREEK RD	PLU	26 B8
WARD LAKE RD	LAS	21 H3
WARDLOW RD	LACO	98 J1
WARDLOW RD	LACO	119 D9
WARDLOW RD	LACO	120 D0
WARDS FERRY RD	TUO	41 P6
WARE RD	COL	32 F8
WARE RD	IMP	114 C2
WARING RD	SDCO	106 J4
WARING RD	SDCO	111 A7
WARM SPGS BLVD	ALA	46 J2
WARM SPRINGS RD	INY	51 L7
WARM SPRINGS RD	SON	38 E2
WARNER AV	FTNV	197 D7
WARNER AV	ORA	98 L2
WARNER AV	ORA	120 H4
WARNER AV	ORA	120 J8
WARNER AV	SA	197 D7
WARNER AV	SA	198 C1
WARNER AV	TUS	198 D7
WARNER RD S	LAS	8 H5
WARNER RD W	MOD	8 C5
WARNER ST	C	124 J0
WARNERVILLE RD	STA	47 D8
WARNERVILLE RD	STA	48 D1
WARREGARD RD	CAL	41 G3
WARREN AV	RCO	99 L7
WARREN AV	TEH	18 M5
WARREN FRWY	ALA	45 C7
WARREN FRWY	O	156 P8
WARREN RD	RCO	99 P7
WARREN RD	RCO	99 K7
WARREN VISTA AV	SBD	100 C8
WASCO WY	KER	78 G0
WASCO POND RD	KER	68 P2
WASHBURN WY	KLAM	5 B3
WASHINGTON AV	RCO	99 P4
WASHINGTON AV	SBD	99 D3
WASHINGTON AV	SDCO	106 J1
WASHINGTON AV	SDCO	107 Q8
WASHINGTON AV	SA	195 J7
WASHINGTON AV	SA	196 J0
WASHINGTON BLVD	CUL	183 N6
WASHINGTON BLVD	CUL	187 G5
WASHINGTON BLVD	CUL	188 E1
WASHINGTON BL	DN	1 K7
WASHINGTON BLVD	LA	183 N6
WASHINGTON BLVD	LA	184 K6
WASHINGTON BLVD	LA	185 K2
WASHINGTON BL	LA	186 Q4
WASHINGTON BLVD	LA	187 G1
WASHINGTON BLVD	LACO	97 E8
WASHINGTON BLVD	LACO	98 F1
WASHINGTON BLVD	LACO	117 G8
WASHINGTON BLVD	LACO	118 N0
WASHINGTON BLVD	MCO	47 M9
WASHINGTON BLVD	MCO	48 M0
WASHINGTON BL	PAS	190 D1
WASHINGTON PL	CUL	188 D0
WASHINGTON PL	LA	188 D0
WASHINGTON PL	SD	213 Q4
WASHINGTON RD	MCO	56 B3
WASHINGTON RD	NEV	26 Q8
WASHINGTON RD	SBD	92 J1
WASHINGTON RD	STA	47 J7
WASHINGTON ST	SB	87 B5
WASHINGTON ST	FRCO	66 G6
WASHINGTON ST	LA	187 J3
WASHINGTON ST	MONT	167 K9
WASHINGTON ST	RCO	99 G2
WASHINGTON ST	RCO	100 K9
WASHINGTON ST	RIV	99 N7
WASHINGTON ST	SD	213 Q6
WASHINGTON ST	SD	215 B4
WASHINGTON ST	SDCO	106 K3
WASHINGTON ST	SDCO	111 B5
WASHINGTON ST	SCLR	151 H4
WASHINGTON ST	SNRA	163 F3
WASHINGTON ST	S	160 Q0
WASHINGTON ST	TUO	163 F3
WASHINGTON ST E	SON	38 H1
WASHOE	FRCO	56 K4
WASHOE AV	FRCO	56 G4
WASIOJA RD	SB	77 Q5
WASIOJA RD	SB	87 A3
WATER ST	SC	169 G7
WATER ST	SCR	54 D0
WATER CANYON RD	KER	80 J2
WATER CANYON RD	KER	79 N5
WATERFRONT RD	CC	154 B8
WATERLOO LN	DGL	36 J4
WATERLOO RD	SJCO	40 N2
WATERMAN AV	SBD	99 D4
WATERMAN AV	SBD	207 J8
WATERMAN AV	SBDO	207 J8
WATERMAN BLVD	FRFD	135 E1
WATERMAN RD	SAC	40 E0
WATERS RD	VEN	88 N6
WATERS END RD	SLO	76 K4
WATERS TROUGH RD	SON	37 F7
WATKINS DR	RCO	99 F3
WATKINS RD	TEH	24 F7
WATKINS TR	KER	79 N4
WATSONVILLE RD	SCL	54 B5
WATT AV	SAC	40 B0
WATT LN	BUT	25 P6
WATTENBURG RD	MEN	23 G1
WATTRSN TROUGHS	MNO	51 E2
WATTS DR	KER	79 G5
WATTS VALLEY RD	FRCO	57 H9
WATTS VALLEY RD	FRCO	58 G0
WAUCOBA SALINE	INY	52 Q3
WAUKEENA RD	YOL	39 K1
WAVERLY	SBD	91 C6
WAVERLY	SJCO	40 P6
WAY RD	MCO	55 C9
WAYBUR RD	SUT	33 G4
WEAVER CREEK E	TRI	17 A6
WEAVER CT	KER	79 G7
WEAVER RD	IMP	110 M1
WEAVER HILLS DR	RCO	108 A0
WEAVERVLL SCOTT	TRI	12 F0
WEAVERVLL SCOTT	TRI	11 P6
WEAVERVLL SCOTT	TRI	11 J9
WEBB RD	IMP	110 P5
WEBER AV	FRE	165 E1
WEBER AV	S	160 N5
WEBER RD	SOL	39 E2
WEBSTER AV	RCO	99 J4
WEBSTER RD	SBD	91 B8
WEBSTER ST	A	157 N8
WEBSTER ST	ALA	45 C6
WEBSTER ST	FRFD	135 K3
WEBSTER ST	O	158 H0
WEDEL AV	KER	77 C8
WEED RD	IMP	114 C1
WEED DEETZ RD	SIS	12 C4
WEEDPATCH HWY	KER	78 H8
WEEDS POINT RD	YUB	26 M4
WEEMASOUL RD	TEH	18 N0
WEIMAR CROSS RD	PLA	34 G5
WEINERT RD	IMP	110 P0
WEIR AV	MCO	47 M8
WEIR CANYON RD	ORA	98 H6
WEIS	SUT	33 E2
WEISER RD	KER	77 A5
WEITCHER RD	MOD	14 B8
WELCH CT	CAL	41 N2
WELCOME AV	KER	80 B6
WELDON	FRCO	58 H1
WELLBARN AV	FRCO	57 C8
WELLOCK RD	TRI	17 C7
WELLS AV	RENO	130 H5
WELLS AV N	RENO	130 E5
WELLS DR	LA	178 M5
WELLS RD	COL	32 C6
WELLS RD	RCO	103 M6
WELLS RD	VEN	88 P3
WELLSFORD RD	STA	47 E7
WELLSONA RD	SLO	76 A1
WELTY RD	STA	47 G1
WENDEL RD	LAS	21 J6
WENGLER HILL RD	SHA	19 F1
WENTE ST	ALA	46 E4
WENTWORTH ST	LACO	89 Q6
WENTWORTH ST	LACO	117 C2
WENTWTH SPGS RD	ED	34 J9
WENTWTH SPGS RD	ED	35 J2
WERICK RD	RCO	99 J0
WESCOTT RD	COL	33 E0
WEST AV	FRE	165 C1
WEST AV	FRCO	57 L4
WEST AV	FRCO	67 A4
WEST AV	RCO	116 B4
WEST DR	RCO	100 F6
WEST DR	RCO	100 F6
WEST LN	S	160 A8
WEST LN	SJCO	40 M1
WEST LN	SJCO	160 A8
WEST RD	COL	33 J1
WEST RD	LACO	118 P3
WEST RD	STA	47 L5
WEST ST	ANA	193 K2
WEST ST	EUR	121 B9
WEST ST	O	157 D9
WEST ST	ORA	120 E5
WEST ST	ORA	120 G3
WESTBROOK LN	DN	1 G8
WESTCLIFF DR	NB	199 K5
WEST COAST RD	HUM	16 P4
W END OREGN MTN	TRI	17 B5
WESTERN AV	KER	78 D1
WESTERN AV	LA	182 K0
WESTERN AV	LA	185 N0
WESTERN AV	LACO	97 G7
WESTERN AV	LACO	117 P4
WESTERN AV	LACO	117 G4
WESTERN AV	LACO	119 G4
WESTERN AV	ORA	120 F3
WESTERN CYN RD	LA	182 G1
WESTERN HILL RD	RCO	100 P2
WESTERN MINE	LAK	32 N0
WESTRN MINERALS	KER	78 N1
WESTFALL	MPA	49 H5
WESTFALL W	MPA	49 M1
WESTGATE AV	HUM	9 J8
WESTGATE DR	NAPA	38 F6
WESTHAVEN DR	HUM	9 K9
WESTLAKE BLVD	VEN	105 B8
WEST LAWN AV	FRCO	57 J2
WEST LAWN AV	FRCO	57 P2
WESTMINSTER AV	GGR	195 H2
WESTMINSTER AV	ORA	98 K1
WESTMINSTER AV	ORA	120 F1
WESTMINSTER AV	SA	195 H2
WESTMORELAND RD	IMP	109 Q8
WESTON RD	TEH	24 E2
WEST PORTAL RD	MNO	50 A6
WESTRIDGE RD	TRI	17 H2
WESTSIDE BLVD	MCO	47 L8
WESTSIDE FRWY	FRCO	56 M3
WESTSIDE FRWY	FRCO	66 E8
WEST SIDE FRWY	KER	77 A6
WEST SIDE FRWY	KER	78 M6
WESTSIDE FRWY	KIN	67 L3
WESTSIDE FRWY	MCO	55 C6
WESTSIDE FRWY	STA	47 J3
WEST SIDE HWY	INY	72 C0
WEST SIDE HWY	KER	67 P2
WEST SIDE HWY	KER	78 M0
WESTSIDE RD	IMP	113 B8
WEST SIDE RD	JOS	2 B5
WEST SIDE RD	LAS	8 N0
WESTSIDE RD	MOD	7 H2
WESTSIDE RD	MOD	8 D1
WESTSIDE RD	SHA	18 B3
WESTSIDE RD	SIE	27 H4
WESTSIDE RD	SIE	27 J3
WESTSIDE RD	SON	37 B7
WSIDE POTTR VLY	MEN	31 B3
WESTWOOD BLVD	LA	183 L0
WESTWOOD BLVD	LACO	117 L1
WESTWOOD ST	TUL	68 G6
WET MEADOW RD	MNO	50 A9
WETMORE RD	ALA	46 F4
WEYER RD	STA	47 F8
WEYMOUTH BLUFF	HUM	15 F8
WHEALAN RD	MCO	48 N6
WHEATLAND RD	SUT	33 H8
WHEATLAND RD	YUB	33 H8
WHEDBEE DR	SOL	38 F9
WHEELER RD	IMP	109 N9
WHEELER RD	SBD	91 D4
WHEELER CYN RD	VEN	88 N3
WHEELER NURSERY	SHA	12 N8
WHEELER RDG RD	KER	78 P8
WHEEL GULCH RD	TRI	17 B2
WHISKEY CK RD	COL	32 H8
WHISKEY CK RD	SHA	18 D2
WHSKEY SLIDE RD	CAL	41 H2
WHISLER RD	KER	78 B2
WHITE AV	LACO	98 D6
WHITE AV	LACO	118 J9
WHITE DR	BUT	25 K3
WHITE LN	KER	78 H6
WHITE LN	NAPA	29 G4
WHITE RD	COL	33 H1
WHITE RD	MON	66 L4
WHITE RD	SBD	91 L1
WHITE RD	SCL	46 L3
WHITE COTTGE RD	NAPA	29 D4
WHITE COTTG RD	NAPA	38 B3
WHITE CRANE RD	MCO	47 M9
WHITE CRANE RD	MCO	48 M0
WHITEHORSE RD	MOD	13 E9
WHITEHORSE RD	MOD	14 E0
WHITEHURST RD	SCL	54 D5
WHITE MTN RD	INY	51 K9
WHITE MTN RD	INY	52 J3
WHITE MTN RD	INY	60 N7
WHITE PINE LN	SB	86 F9
WHITE PINE LN	SB	87 F0
WHITEPINE ST	SIS	4 H3
WHITE RIVER RD	KER	69 N1
WHITE ROCK RD	ED	40 A4
WHITE ROCK RD	MPA	49 L1
WHITE ROCK RD	MPA	48 N8
WHITE ROCK RD	MCO	48 P8
WHITE ROCK RD	SHA	17 J5
WHITES BRDGE ST	FRCO	56 J7
WHITES BRIDG ST	FRCO	57 J4
WHITES GULCH RD	SIS	11 E4
WHITES MILL RD	KER	79 A2
WHITEWTR CYN RD	RCO	100 F4
WHITE WOLF RD	TUO	42 Q6
WHITE WOLF RD	TUO	63 J5
WHITLEY AV	KIN	67 G7
WHITLOCK	MPA	49 H2
WHITLOCK RD	IMP	110 N5
WHITLOW RD	HUM	16 L4
WHITMORE AV	STA	47 F6
WHITMORE RD	SHA	18 E8
WHITMORE RD	SHA	19 D0
WHITMRE TUBS RD	MNO	50 E9
WHITMRE TUBS RD	MNO	51 E0
WHITNEY AV	VAL	134 A6
WHITNY PORTL RD	INY	60 L0
WHITSETT AV	LACO	117 G1
WHITTIER AV	RCO	99 L9
WHITTIER BLVD	LA	186 L6
WHITTIER BLVD	LACO	98 E0
WHITTIER BLVD	LACO	117 M8
WHITTIER BLVD	LACO	118 P2
WHITTIER BLVD	ORA	118 P2
WHITTIER AV E	AVLN	105 N2
WHITTLE RD	CAL	41 M3
WHITWELL WY	RCO	108 B4
WHITWORTH RD	MCO	47 P5
WIASMUL RD	SDCO	108 A3
WIBLE RD	KER	166 Q2
WIBLE RD	KER	78 K6
WICKENDEN WY	MOD	8 C0
WICKMAN RD	BUT	25 N3
WICKS ST	SB	86 B5
WIDGEON RD	YOL	39 G6
WIDOW VALLEY RD	MOD	13 G9
WIDOW VALLEY RD	MOD	14 G0
WILBUR	CC	39 N3
WILBUR AV	LA	178 J5
WILBUR SPRGS RD	COL	32 G5
WILCOX RD	SHA	19 B7
WILCOX RD	TEH	18 M6
WILCOX RANCH RD	TUO	41 N4
WILD RD	SBD	91 D3
WILDASS RD	SBT	66 B2
WILDCAT RD	MCO	55 E5
WILDCAT RD	SHA	18 H9
WILDCAT RD	SHA	19 H0
WILDCAT RD	TEH	19 H0
WILD CAT TR	RCO	100 N1
WILDCAT CK RD	SIS	11 E7
WILDCAT CYN RD	CC	45 A6
WILDCAT CYN RD	SDCO	106 F8
WILDCAT CYN RD	SDCO	108 N0
WILD DUCK RD	MCO	55 E9
WILDER RD	HUM	16 F1
WILDER RD	TEH	18 N6
WLDRNSS LDGE RD	MEN	22 H6
WILDER RIDGE RD	HUM	16 N0
WILDHORSE RD	SBD	92 C2
WILDHORSE CY RD	MCO	65 E5
WILDMAN RD	KER	78 L8
WILD PLUM RD	SIE	27 L1
WILDROSE RD	INY	61 P5
WILD WASH RD	SBD	91 F5
WILDWOOD AV	SLT	129 J7
WILDWOOD RD	COL	32 H9
WILDWOOD RD	KER	78 F0
WILDWOOD RD	TRI	17 F4
WILDWOOD RD	TRI	17 J4
WILDWOOD CYN RD	SBD	99 E8
WILEY WELLS RD	RCO	103 Q2
WILFRED CYN RD	MNO	51 E2
WILKINS AV	STA	47 C7
WILKINS RD	IMP	110 F2
WILKINSON RD	IMP	110 H1
WILLARD RD	TEH	18 N5
WILLARD CK RD	LAS	20 J8
WILLIAM RD	BUT	25 J5
WILLIAM ST	SJ	152 L4
WILLIAMS	SJCO	47 C5
WILLIAMS AV	MCO	47 K7
WILLIAMS RD	IMP	110 K3
WILLIAMS RD	KER	79 F4
WILLIAMS RD	KER	80 K6
WILLIAMS RD	LAS	8 M2
WILLIAMS RD	MON	54 K6
WILLIAMS RD	SHA	13 K8
WILLIAMS CK RD	HUM	15 F7
WILLIAMS CK RD	HUM	15 F7
WILLIAMSON RD	KER	79 M7
WILLIAMSON RD	RCO	108 B1
WILLIAMSON RD	TUO	41 P3
WILLIAM TELL TR	KER	79 N4
WILLIAMS VLY RD	PLU	20 N5
WILLIAMS WLL RD	SBD	81 N8
WILLIS RD	MCO	56 C3
WILLMS RD	STA	48 B1
WILLOUGHBY RD	IMP	114 C1
WILLOW AV	FRCO	57 F6
WILLOW AV	GLE	24 M8
WILLOW AV	KER	89 C5
WILLOW AV	CRTM	140 A3
WILLOW DR	KER	78 F1
WILLOW RD	MP	147 D1
WILLOW RD	SBD	91 L4
WILLOW RD	SDCO	106 G8
WILLOW RD	SDCO	108 N0
WILLOW RD	SLO	76 P3
WILLOW RD	SMCO	45 J7
WILLOW ST	LACO	97 J9
WILLOW ST	LACO	119 E7
WILLOW ST	SJ	152 P4
WILLOW WY	LAS	20 E9
WILLOW CREEK RD	INY	52 L6
WILLOW CREEK RD	SBT	55 N4
WILLOW CREEK RD	SLO	75 C9
WILLOW CREEK RD	SLO	76 C0
WILLOW CREEK RD	YUB	26 N4
WILLOW CK AGER	SIS	4 J4
WLLW CK RED RCK	SIS	5 H3
WILLOW GLEN DR	SDCO	106 K8
WILLOW GLEN DR	SDCO	111 B9
WILLOW GLEN RD	YUB	26 P0
WILLOW GLEN RD	YUB	26 N1
WILLOW PASS RD	CC	39 N1
WILLOW POINT RD	YOL	39 E6
WILLOW RCH RD S	MOD	7 H5
WILLOWS RD	SDCO	108 P3
WILLOW SPGS EXT	SIS	13 E0
WILLOW SPGS RD	KER	90 C1
WILLOW SPGS RD	LAS	14 P1
WILLOW SPGS RD	SCL	54 B4
WILLOW VLY RD	NEV	34 B5
WILMINGTON AV	LACO	97 H8
WILMINGTON AV	LACO	119 D6
WILMINGTON BLVD	LA	191 B3
WILMINGTON BLVD	LACO	119 F5
WILSHIRE AV	SBD	101 C4
WILSHIRE BL	BH	183 D2
WILSHIRE BLVD	LA	180 F6
WILSHIRE BLVD	LA	183 D2
WILSHIRE BL	LA	185 E0
WILSHIRE BLVD	LACO	97 D6
WILSHIRE BLVD	LACO	117 K3
WILSHIRE BL	LACO	180 F6
WILSHIRE BLVD	SMON	180 L0
WILSHIRE RD	SBD	92 K0
WILSON AV	COL	32 J8
WILSON AV	MAR	38 L1
WILSON AV	VAL	134 H1
WILSON DR	LA	181 F0
WILSON DR	TUL	68 G9
WILSON RD	COL	32 C6
WILSON RD	MCO	55 B7
WILSON RD	SUT	33 H6
WILSON ST	KER	79 G5
WILSON ST	RIV	100 G0
WILSON WY	PLA	34 H2
WILSON WY	SJCO	40 N2
WILSON BEND RD	COL	33 G2
WILSON CREEK RD	DN	1 N8
WILSON HILL RD	MAR	37 K9
WILSON HILL RD	SHA	19 H2
WILSON LAKE RD	SHA	19 K7
WILSON LANDING	BUT	25 F0
WILSON RANCH RD	SBD	90 K9
WILSON SPGS RD	LAS	14 P1
WILSON SPGS RD	LACO	89 G5
WILSON VLY RD	RCO	108 A1
WILTON PL	LA	181 Q9
WILTON PL	LA	182 P0
WILTON PL	LA	184 G9
WILTON PL	LA	185 G0
WILTON RD	SAC	40 E1
WIMER RD	SJCO	40 L7
WINCHESTER BLVD	SCL	46 P1
WINCHESTER RD	RCO	99 P6
WINCHESTER RD	RCO	99 M7
WINCHUCK RD	CUR	1 F7
WINDING WY	SHA	18 F7
WINDING WY	SR	139 M2
WINDLASS DR	RCO	101 Q5
WINDSONG WY	RCO	108 B2
WINDSOR AV	LACO	117 F8
WINDSOR RD	SON	37 C7
WINDSOR RIV RD	SON	37 C7

SEE PAGE D FOR INSTRUCTIONS

STREET INDEX

STREET	CO.	PAGE & GRID
WINEMAN RD	SLO	76 P5
WINEVILLE AV	SBD	99 D0
WINGATE RD	INY	71 J5
WINGFIELD RD	LAS	21 J1
WINGFIELD RD	LAS	21 K1
WINNETKA AV	LA	178 H0
WINNETKA AV	LACO	97 B3
WINSHIP RD	SOL	39 F4
WINSHIP RD	YUBA	125 M6
WINSLOW RD	IMP	110 E1
WINSOME WY	SHA	18 F3
WINTER GRDNS BL	SDCO	106 H7
WINTER GRDNS BL	SDCO	107 P9
WINTERGREEN RD	SBD	90 L8
WINTERS RD	SBD	100 A8
WINTERS RD	SOL	39 C1
WINTON AV W	ALA	45 F8
WINTON AV W	H	146 K4
WINTON RD	CAL	41 E3
WIRT RD	IMP	110 J3
WISCONSIN AV	COL	32 J9
WISE RD	PLA	33 J9
WISE RD	PLA	34 J1
WISHON AV	FRE	165 D5
WISHON DR	TUL	69 E2
WISTOS LN	LAS	21 J3
WITHERS AV	CC	38 P8
WITHROW RD	SHA	19 F1
WITTER SPG E RD	LAK	31 E5
WIXOM RD	IMP	113 B8
WOHLFORD RD	SDCO	107 H8
WOLF RD	NEV	34 E4
WOLF CREEK RD	ALP	36 Q5
WOLFE RD	CPTO	150 M1
WOLFE RD	SCL	45 M9
WOLFE RD	SCL	46 M0
WOLFE RD	SVL	150 J1
WOLFE RD	VEN	105 B4
WOLFE GRADE	MAR	139 P4
WOLFSEN	MCO	47 Q8
WOLFSEN	MCO	55 A8
WOLFSKILL	SOL	39 C1
WONDER AV	KER	80 M1
WONDERLAND BLVD	SHA	18 C5
WONDERLAND DR	RCO	100 H1
WOO RD	MCO	55 E8
WOOD RD	RCO	99 H3
WOOD RD	SUT	33 E2
WOOD RD	VEN	105 B4
WOOD ST	GLE	24 M6
WOODBINE RD	RCO	100 N5
WOODBRIDGE	SJCO	40 K2
WOODBURY RD	LACO	117 F8
WOODBURY RD	PAS	190 B0
WOOD CANYON RD	INY	71 B6
WOODCUTTERS WY	SHA	19 H2
WOODEN VLY RD	NAPA	38 F7
WOODFORD-TEH RD	KER	79 K4
WOODHILL DR	SHA	13 P1
WOODHOUSE MINE	CAL	41 E2
WOODLAND AV	MCO	48 M5
WOODLAND AV	SR	139 N8
WOODLAND AV	STA	47 E4
WOODLAND AV	TEH	24 E7
WOODLAND WY	SHA	19 G2
WOODLEY RD	SDCO	107 K4
WOOLEY RD E	VEN	105 B3
WOODMAN AV	LACO	97 B5
WOODMAN AV	LACO	117 D0
WOOD RANCH RD	LAS	21 D2
WOODRIDGE RD	SHA	19 G2
WOODROW AV	SC	169 Q4
WOODRUFF AV	LACO	119 C9
WOODRUFF AV	LACO	120 C0
WOODRUFF LN	YUB	33 C6
WOODSIDE AV	SDCO	106 H7
WOODSIDE AV	SDCO	107 P9
WOODSIDE RD	SMCO	45 J6
WOODS LAKE RD	ALP	36 N1
WOODSON AV	TEH	24 E7
WOOD VALLEY RD	SDCO	107 G8
WOODY RD	KER	78 C6
WOODY ST	KER	78 A9
WOODY ST	KER	79 A0
WOODY-GRANIT RD	KER	78 A9
WOODY-GRANIT RD	KER	79 A0
WOOKEY RD	BUT	25 E1
WOOLEY RD	OXN	176 M0
WOOLLOMES AV	KER	68 P1
WOOLLOMES AV	KER	68 P4
WOOLNER AV	FRFD	135 K0
WORDEN AV	MCO	48 N5
WORDEN RD	CAL	41 G2
WORK RD	KER	90 B3
WORKMAN ST	LACO	117 C0
WORKMAN MILL RD	LACO	98 E2
WORKMAN MILL RD	LACO	118 M2
WORMWOOD RD	IMP	113 C9
WORSLEY RD	RCO	100 F5
WORTH AV	TUL	68 H7
WORTH RD	SUT	33 L6
WORTHINGTON RD	IMP	109 P9
WORTHINGTON RD	MCO	47 N5
WORTHINGTON ST	KER	79 A9
WRAGG CANYON RD	NAPA	38 D7
WRAN RD	LAS	21 M4
WREN RD	STA	47 D8
WRIGHT AV	SVL	149 H3
WRIGHT RD	IMP	110 P4
WRIGHTS LAKE RD	ED	35 L6
WRIGLEY RD	HUM	15 C9
WRIGLEY TER RD	AVLN	105 N3
WUNPOST RD	MCO	65 K8
WYANDOTTE AV	BUT	25 M7
WYNDTT MNRS RCH	BUT	25 M8
WYER RD	COL	32 H8
WYLIE DR	MDO	162 C8
WYLIE ST	SB	87 B6
WYMAN CREEK RD	INY	52 J1
WYNCOOP RD	SUT	33 E3
WYNDAM LN	RED	122 L4
WYNDHAVEN DR	TEH	18 M6
WYO AV	GLE	24 G8
WYSE RD	LACO	89 K7
X		
XIMENO AV	LACO	119 F8
Y		
YAJOME ST	NAP	133 F5
YANKEE HILL RD	TUO	41 M5
YAQUI PASS RD	SDCO	108 H8
YARD RD	TEH	18 K6
YELLOW BUTTE RD	SIS	4 P6
YELLOW JACKET	TEH	19 L4
YELLW JACKET RD	MNO	51 C5
YERBA BUENA RD	VEN	105 D6
YERMO RD	SBD	82 P5
YERMO RD	SBD	92 B1
YERMO CUTOFF	SBD	81 Q9
YERMO CUTOFF	SBD	82 Q0
YGNACIO VLY RD	CC	45 A9
YGNACIO VLY RD	CC	39 Q0
YMCA RD	FRCO	58 J7
YOCUM RD	IMP	110 J2
YOKE ST	SHA	18 H5
YOLANDA AV	KER	89 D4
YOLANO RD	SOL	39 E4

STREET	CO.	PAGE & GRID
YOLO AV	FRCO	56 L8
YOLO CO LINE RD	COL	32 J8
YOLO CO LINE RD	COL	33 J1
YORBA LN	SBD	90 G8
YORBA LINDA BL	ORA	98 H5
YORBA LINDA BL	ORA	120 B7
YORK AV	KIN	67 N1
YORK BLVD	LACO	97 C8
YORK BLVD	LACO	117 H7
YORK RD	IMP	116 Q7
YORK RD	SIS	4 J4
YORK ST	NAP	133 H4
YOSEMITE AV	MAN	161 K0
YOSEMITE AV	MCO	48 L5
YOSEMITE AV	SJCO	47 C2
YOSEMITE BL	MDO	162 J8
YOSEMITE BLVD	STA	47 F6
YOSEMITE BLVD	STA	48 E2
YOSEMITE RD	TUO	41 P6
YOSEMITE OAKS	MPA	49 G2
YOU BET RD	NEV	34 D6
YOUD RD	MCO	48 J3
YOUNG AV	COL	32 H8
YOUNG RD	COL	24 P8
YOUNG RD	IMP	110 H3
YOUNG RD	STA	47 G4
YOUNG ST	RCO	99 K8
YOUNG LOVE AV	SC	169 M3
YOUNGS HILL RD	YUB	26 M4
YOUNT ST	NAPA	29 L7
YOUNTVLLE CROSS	NAPA	29 L7
YOUNTVLL CRS RD	NAPA	38 E4
YOWELL RD	MOD	14 G3
YREKA AGER RD	SIS	4 K2
YREKA MONO	SIS	4 K0
YREKA WALKER RD	SIS	3 J7
YTURRIARTE RD	SBT	55 L7
YUBA AV	FRCO	56 H8
YUBA NEVADA RD	YUB	26 Q2
YUBA PASS RD	SIE	27 K3
YUCAIPA BLVD	SBD	99 E7
YUCCA RD	RCO	108 A5
YUCCA RD	SBD	90 J8
YUCCA TR	SBD	100 C8
YUCCA LOMA RD	SBD	91 K6
YUCCA LOMA RD	SBD	91 K6
YUCCA MESA RD	SBD	100 B8
Z		
ZABALA RD	MON	54 L6
ZABRISKIE PT RD	INY	72 A1
ZACA STATION RD	SB	86 F8
ZACHARIAS RD	STA	47 H3
ZACHARY AV	KER	78 B4
ZANES RD	HUM	15 C8
ZAPPONE RD	IMP	116 K0
ZAYANTE RD	SCR	54 B0
ZEDIKER AV	FRCO	57 H9
ZEDIKER AV	FRCO	57 M9
ZEERING RD	STA	47 H5
ZEIGLER PT RD	HUM	10 N7
ZELDA LN	SBD	101 B8
ZENIA RD	MEN	23 F1
ZENIA BLUFF RD	HUM	16 N7
ZENIA LK MTN RD	TRI	16 N8
ZENO RD	LAK	31 E6
ZERKER RD	KER	78 D4
ZERMATT DR	KER	79 N4
ZINC HILL RD	INY	70 C9
ZINC MINE RD	SBD	84 G1
ZINFANDEL LN	NAPA	29 G5
ZINK RD	BUT	25 J9
ZITZMAN RD	SIS	3 P5
ZOGG MINE RD	SHA	18 F2
ZOO DR	LACO	117 H4
ZULU QUEEN MN RD	RCO	102 F0
ZUMWALT	SJCO	47 B4
ZUMWALT RD	COL	32 A7
ZUMWALT RD	COL	32 F7
ZZYZX RD	SBD	83 L2
NUMERIC STREETS		
1ST AV	BARS	208 C3
1ST AV	BUT	25 G2
1ST AV	GLE	24 G9
1ST AV	IMP	115 B6
1ST AV	LPAZ	104 D2
1ST AV	LACO	118 Q3
1ST AV	LACO	120 A3
1ST AV	MCO	47 L8
1ST AV	PLU	20 L1
1ST AV	SD	215 K7
1ST AV	SDCO	106 L3
1ST AV	SDCO	106 N5
1ST AV	SDCO	111 D7
1ST ST	ALA	46 E4
1ST ST	SBD	208 A4
1ST ST	BEN	153 M3
1ST ST	DN	1 G8
1ST ST	DVS	136 J6
1ST ST	FRCO	57 H5
1ST ST	LA	186 E0
1ST ST	LACO	117 K5
1ST ST	NAP	133 K4
1ST ST	ORA	98 K3
1ST ST	ORA	120 G6
1ST ST	RCO	98 G8
1ST ST	SF	143 L7
1ST ST	SJ	151 C9
1ST ST	SJ	152 G2
1ST ST	SA	195 L0
1ST ST	SA	196 L0
1ST ST	SCL	46 K1
1ST ST	SCL	54 D6
1 1/2 AV	KIN	68 C0
2ND AV	COL	33 H3
2ND AV	GLE	24 F8
2ND AV	KIN	68 C0
2ND AV	LPAZ	104 C2
2ND AV	LACO	118 H2
2ND AV	MCO	47 L7
2ND AV	RCO	103 M7
2ND ST	FRFD	135 J1
2ND ST	KER	68 P2
2ND ST	LA	186 F0
2ND ST	LACO	119 F8
2ND ST	MER	170 N1
2ND ST	SDCO	106 J7
2ND ST	SDCO	107 G2
2ND ST	SDCO	107 Q9
2ND ST	SR	139 K5
2ND ST E	BEN	153 L4
2ND ST E	RENO	130 G3
2ND ST E	SOL	38 M7
2ND ST W	RENO	130 G0
2 1/2 AV	KIN	67 D9
3RD AV	FCTY	145 A5
3RD AV	GLE	24 G8
3RD AV	LPAZ	104 C2
3RD AV	MCO	47 M7
3RD AV	NAPA	38 G6
3RD AV	RCO	103 M7
3RD AV	SD	99 B2
3RD AV	SDCO	106 N5
3RD AV	SDCO	111 D7
3RD AV	SMCO	45 G5
3RD ST	BH	183 B5
3RD ST	CC	38 P4

STREET	CO.	PAGE & GRID
3RD ST	COR	215 N3
3RD ST	DVS	136 H7
3RD ST	EUR	121 A4
3RD ST	LB	192 H7
3RD ST	LA	183 B5
3RD ST	LA	184 C2
3RD ST	LA	185 C1
3RD ST	LA	186 G1
3RD ST	LACO	117 K3
3RD ST	NAP	133 L4
3RD ST	RIV	205 F5
3RD ST	SBDO	207 E6
3RD ST	SBD	99 C4
3RD ST	SF	143 M6
3RD ST	SFCO	45 D4
3RD ST	SR	139 K5
3RD ST	YOL	137 F0
4TH AV	CAR	168 H4
4TH AV	GLE	24 G8
4TH AV	KIN	67 A9
4TH AV	MCO	47 M7
4TH AV	MON	168 H4
4TH AV	RCO	103 M6
4TH AV	SD	215 J7
4TH AV	SDCO	106 N4
4TH AV	SDCO	111 D7
4TH ST	BKD	166 L5
4TH ST	COR	215 P5
4TH ST	EC	217 L6
4TH ST	EUR	121 B4
4TH ST	KER	166 L5
4TH ST	LA	186 H1
4TH ST	MAR	38 P2
4TH ST	MOD	8 B2
4TH ST	ONT	203 J7
4TH ST	ONT	204 J2
4TH ST	RCO	99 K4
4TH ST	SBD	99 E7
4TH ST	SDCO	106 L2
4TH ST	SDCO	111 C5
4TH ST	SJ	152 F2
4TH ST	SR	139 J2
4TH ST	SA	196 K3
4TH ST	SCL	54 G8
4TH ST	STR	131 H6
4TH ST E	RENO	130 F3
4TH ST W	RENO	130 F0
5TH AV	CAR	168 H3
5TH AV	GLE	24 G8
5TH AV	GLE	24 J8
5TH AV	KIN	67 B8
5TH AV	LPAZ	104 E1
5TH AV	LACO	118 G2
5TH AV	SBD	92 N7
5TH AV	SBD	99 D6
5TH AV	SDCO	107 J6
5TH AV	SR	139 H2
5TH AV E	SIS	4 K3
5TH ST	DVS	136 H5
5TH ST	EUR	121 B4
5TH ST	HUM	9 Q8
5TH ST	LA	186 H1
5TH ST	RCO	99 G0
5TH ST	SCTO	137 J1
5TH ST	SBD	99 C4
5TH ST	SBD	207 D4
5TH ST	SBDO	207 D4
5TH ST	SF	143 N5
5TH ST	SA	195 K5
5TH ST	TEH	24 B8
5TH ST	VAL	134 P6
5TH ST	VEN	105 B3
5TH ST E	BEN	153 N4
5TH ST E	OXN	176 L7
5TH ST E	VEN	176 L7
5TH ST W	LACO	90 E0
5 1/2 AV	KIN	67 E8
6TH AV	CAR	168 H3
6TH AV	GLE	24 G8
6TH AV	KIN	67 B8
6TH AV	MCO	47 M8
6TH AV	RCO	103 M6
6TH AV	SD	215 J8
6TH AV	SDCO	106 L3
6TH ST	GLE	24 H6
6TH ST	LB	192 G4
6TH ST	LA	184 D4
6TH ST	LA	185 E5
6TH ST	LA	186 H0
6TH ST	ONT	203 H7
6TH ST	RCO	99 G0
6TH ST	YUB	33 F9
6 1/2 AV	KIN	67 E8
7TH	CC	38 P4
7TH AV	CAR	168 J3
7TH AV	KIN	67 B8
7TH AV	LPAZ	104 E1
7TH AV	LACO	118 L3
7TH AV	SF	141 M7
7TH AV	SFCO	45 D3
7TH AV	SCR	54 E0
7TH AV	YUB	33 F6
7TH ST	EUR	121 B5
7TH ST	IMP	110 K0
7TH ST	KER	78 C2
7TH ST	LB	192 G6
7TH ST	LA	185 F5
7TH ST	LA	186 H0
7TH ST	LACO	97 E4
7TH ST	LACO	98 K0
7TH ST	LACO	119 F8
7TH ST	LACO	120 F0
7TH ST	O	157 G5
7TH ST	O	158 K1
7TH ST	RIV	205 E2
7TH ST	RCO	99 F2
7TH ST	RCO	99 K8
7TH ST	SBD	91 M3
7TH ST	SBD	99 E2
7TH ST	SBD	99 E7
7TH ST	SJ	152 G3
7TH ST	SLO	75 H8
7TH ST	STA	47 F7
7TH ST	UPL	203 G8
7TH ST N	MDO	162 J2
7TH ST S	MDO	162 M4
7TH ST S	STA	162 M4
7TH ST W	BEN	153 K2
7TH STANDARD RD	KER	77 F5
7 1/2 AV	KIN	57 Q8
8TH AV	CAR	53 Q6
8TH AV	CAR	168 J3
8TH AV	KIN	67 A7
8TH AV	RCO	103 M7
8TH AV	SD	215 J8
8TH ST	BKD	166 K5
8TH ST	BUT	25 N4
8TH ST	EC	217 G4
8TH ST	IMP	114 B1
8TH ST	LA	185 F1
8TH ST	LA	186 J0
8TH ST	O	157 G5
8TH ST	RCO	99 G8
8TH ST	SBD	98 G8
8TH ST	SDCO	106 M4
8TH ST	SDCO	107 G2

STREET	CO.	PAGE & GRID
8TH ST	SDCO	111 C6
8TH ST	SJCO	40 P2
8TH ST	UPL	203 F8
8TH ST E	DVS	136 G5
8TH ST W	DVS	136 G3
8 1/2 AV	KIN	57 P7
9TH AV	KER	68 N4
9TH AV	KIN	67 A7
9TH AV	LPAZ	104 E1
9TH AV	SD	215 K8
9TH AV	SDCO	107 J6
9TH ST	GGR	195 D1
9TH ST	LB	192 F4
9TH ST	LA	185 G0
9TH ST	LA	186 K0
9TH ST	LA	191 L0
9TH ST	LACO	119 G4
9TH ST	MDO	162 J3
9TH ST	SBD	203 E8
9TH ST	SBDO	207 C5
9TH ST	SF	143 Q3
9TH ST	UPL	203 E8
9TH ST	UPL	204 E2
9TH ST	YUMA	115 C5
9TH ST S	MDO	162 M5
9TH ST S	STA	162 M5
9 1/2 AV	KIN	67 A7
10 MI HOUSE TR	BUT	25 F4
10TH	CC	38 P4
10TH AV	KIN	67 B7
10TH AV	RCO	103 N7
10TH ST	LB	192 F7
10TH ST	RCO	99 J6
10TH ST	SF	142 K6
10TH ST	SJ	152 F3
10TH ST	UPL	203 D8
10TH ST	YUB	33 E6
10TH ST	YUMA	115 C4
10TH ST E	LACO	89 H9
10TH ST W	BEN	153 J0
10TH ST W	LACO	89 H9
10 1/2 AV	KIN	67 F7
11TH AV	KIN	67 B7
11TH AV	LPAZ	104 E1
11TH AV	RCO	103 N6
11TH AV	SD	215 L3
11TH AV	SDCO	106 L3
11TH ST	LAK	31 G6
11TH ST	MDO	162 H2
11TH ST	SBD	91 M3
11TH ST	SJCO	47 D0
11TH ST	YUMA	115 D5
12TH AV	KIN	67 B6
12TH AV	LPAZ	104 E0
12TH AV	SD	215 L9
12TH AV	SDCO	106 L3
12TH ST	MOD	8 A1
12TH ST	O	157 F5
12TH ST	SCTO	137 G4
12TH ST	YUB	33 E6
12TH ST	YUMA	115 D4
12TH ST E	O	159 B5
12TH ST N	SCTO	137 D5
12 3/4 AV	KIN	67 A6
13TH AV	ALA	45 C6
13TH AV	CAR	168 K3
13TH AV	KIN	67 B6
13TH AV	LPAZ	104 E0
13TH AV	O	158 L4
13TH ST	CC	38 P5
13TH ST	SJ	152 E3
13TH ST	YUMA	115 D4
13 1/4 AV	KIN	67 A6
14 MILE HOUSE	BUT	25 E4
14TH AV	KIN	67 B6
14TH AV	LPAZ	104 E0
14TH AV	O	158 K4
14TH AV	RCO	100 G6
14TH AV	RCO	103 N6
14TH AV E	O	158 N7
14TH ST	ALA	146 A3
14TH ST	CC	39 N3
14TH ST	EUR	121 D3
14TH ST	MDO	162 G3
14TH ST	O	157 F5
14TH ST	RIV	99 F8
14TH ST	RIV	205 H4
14TH ST	RCO	99 F3
14TH ST	SBD	99 E6
14TH ST	YUMA	115 D6
14TH ST E	ALA	45 D8
14TH ST E	DVS	136 F4
14TH ST E	O	159 B7
14TH ST W	DVS	136 F4
14 1/2 AV	KIN	67 F6
15TH AV	KIN	67 B6
15TH AV	RCO	103 N5
15TH AV	SDCO	107 J7
15TH ST	KER	80 N1
15TH ST	MDO	162 G3
15TH ST	SCTO	137 K3
15TH ST	YUMA	115 D6
15 1/2 AV	KIN	67 B5
16TH AV	KIN	67 B5
16TH AV	RCO	100 G7
16TH AV	RCO	103 P6
16TH ST	MER	170 H2
16TH ST	SCTO	137 K4
16TH ST	SBD	98 C7
16TH ST	SBD	99 E6
16TH ST	SD	215 M9
16TH ST	SD	216 K0
16TH ST	SDCO	106 L3
17 MILE DR	MON	53 H2
17 MILE DR	MON	167 G1
17 MILE DR	PAC	167 F2
17TH AV	KIN	67 B5
17TH AV	SCR	54 E0
17TH ST	CM	199 H3
17TH ST	MDO	162 G4
17TH ST	ORA	98 K4
17TH ST	ORA	98 M4
17TH ST	ORA	120 G6
17TH ST	ORA	120 J3
17TH ST	ORA	120 L5
17TH ST	SF	141 N9
17TH ST	SF	142 N1
17TH ST	SJ	152 F5
17TH ST	SA	195 H6
17TH ST	SA	196 G1
17TH ST	YUMA	115 E4
18TH AV	KIN	67 B5
18TH AV	RCO	100 G6
18TH AV	RCO	103 P6
18TH ST	BKD	166 H2
18TH ST	LAK	32 J1
18TH ST	SDCO	106 M4
18TH ST	SDCO	111 D6
18TH ST	YUMA	115 E4
18 3/4 AV	KIN	67 B5
19TH AV	KIN	67 B5
19TH AV	SFCO	45 D3
19TH ST	BKD	166 G2
19TH ST	CM	199 F0
19TH ST	KER	80 P1

STREET	CO.	PAGE & GRID
19TH ST	ORA	120 L5
19TH ST	SBD	98 C7
19TH ST	YUMA	115 F4
20TH AV	KIN	67 B4
20TH AV	RCO	100 G6
20TH AV	RCO	103 P5
20TH ST	KER	80 N1
20TH ST	KIN	80 N1
20TH ST	YUMA	115 F4
20TH ST E	LACO	90 G1
20TH ST W	KER	89 C9
20 1/2 AV	KIN	67 F4
21ST AV	KIN	67 H4
21ST ST	BKD	166 G3
21ST ST	MER	170 J7
21ST ST	SCTO	137 M4
21ST ST	SJ	152 E5
21ST ST	YUMA	115 F4
21 1/2 AV	KIN	67 B4
22ND AV	KIN	67 B4
22ND AV	RCO	100 H8
22ND AV	RCO	103 P5
22ND ST	RCO	100 G8
22 1/2 AV	KIN	67 B4
23RD	CC	38 P5
23RD AV	KIN	67 B4
23RD AV	O	158 M5
23RD ST	BKD	166 G5
23RD ST	R	155 H2
23RD ST	SP	155 H2
23RD ST	SMON	187 B3
23RD ST	YUMA	115 G4
23 1/2 AV	KIN	67 C3
24TH AV	KIN	67 B3
24TH AV	RCO	100 H9
24TH AV	RCO	103 Q5
24TH ST	BKD	166 F4
24TH ST	KER	78 G6
24TH ST	SAC	39 C8
24TH ST	SBD	98 C7
24TH ST	SDCO	106 M4
24TH ST	SDCO	111 D6
24TH ST	SJ	152 F6
24 1/2 AV	KIN	67 B3
25TH AV	KIN	67 B3
25TH AV	KIN	67 K3
25TH AV	RCO	103 Q5
25TH AV	SF	141 G5
25TH AV	SM	145 H0
25TH ST	LACO	119 H4
25TH ST	SD	216 L1
25TH ST	SDCO	106 L3
25TH ST E	LACO	90 J1
25TH ST W	KER	89 C9
26TH AV	RCO	101 H0
26TH AV	RCO	103 Q5
26TH ST	SD	216 P2
26 1/4 AV	KIN	67 B3
27TH AV	KIN	67 B3
27TH ST	SDCO	106 Q5
27TH ST	SDCO	111 F7
28TH AV	KIN	67 E2
28TH AV	RCO	101 H0
28TH AV	RCO	116 A6
28TH AV	SM	145 J0
28TH ST	SD	216 K3
28TH ST	SDCO	106 L3
28TH ST	SDCO	111 B6
29TH ST	SCTO	137 K7
30TH AV	KIN	67 H2
30TH AV	RCO	100 J7
30TH AV	RCO	116 A5
30TH AV	SCR	54 E1
30TH ST	BKD	166 E6
30TH ST	KER	80 N2
30TH ST	SD	214 Q3
30TH ST	SD	216 M3
30TH ST	SDCO	106 K4
30TH ST	SDCO	111 B6
30TH ST	SDCO	111 D6
30TH ST E	LACO	90 G1
30TH ST W	KER	89 C8
30TH ST W	LACO	89 F9
31ST AV	SM	145 K0
32ND AV	RCO	101 J1
32ND AV	RCO	116 B5
32ND ST	KER	80 P2
32ND ST	LAK	32 J1
32ND ST	SD	216 M4
32ND ST	SDCO	106 K4
32ND ST	SDCO	111 B6
34TH AV	RCO	100 J7
34TH AV	RCO	116 B5
34TH ST	BKD	166 D5
35TH AV	O	158 P8
35TH AV	RCO	116 B4
36TH AV	KIN	67 K0
36TH AV	RCO	100 K7
36TH AV	RCO	116 B6
36TH ST	LAK	32 J1
37TH ST	KER	80 Q2
38TH AV	RCO	101 K0
38TH AV	RCO	116 C6
38TH ST	SD	216 P6
39TH AV	SM	145 J4
40TH AV	RCO	101 K0
40TH AV	SF	141 H0
40TH AV	SM	145 K3
40TH ST	SBD	99 B3
40TH ST	SD	214 Q7
40TH ST	SDCO	106 L4
40TH ST E	LACO	90 G1
40TH ST W	KER	89 C8
40TH ST W	LACO	89 F8
41ST ST	LACO	117 M5
42ND AV	RCO	100 K9
42ND AV	SM	145 L3
43RD ST	SD	214 Q9
43RD ST	SD	216 B8
44TH AV	RCO	100 L8
47TH AV	RCO	101 L1
47TH AV	SAC	39 C8
47TH ST E	LACO	90 J1
48TH AV	RCO	101 L0
50TH AV	RCO	101 M1
50TH ST E	LACO	90 G1
50TH ST W	KER	89 C8
50TH ST W	LACO	89 F8
51ST ST	LACO	117 M4
52ND AV	RCO	101 M1
54TH AV	RCO	101 M0
54TH ST	RCO	99 F0
54TH ST	SDCO	106 K5
54TH ST	SDCO	111 B7
55TH ST E	LACO	90 G2
57TH ST E	LACO	90 J2
58TH AV	RCO	101 N0
60TH AV	RCO	101 N0
60TH ST	SDCO	106 L5
60TH ST E	LACO	90 F2
60TH ST W	KER	89 D8
60TH ST W	LACO	89 F8
62ND AV	RCO	101 N2
64TH AV	RCO	101 P2
65TH EXPWY	SAC	39 C8
65TH ST E	LACO	90 F2

STREET	CO.	PAGE & GRID
65TH ST W	LACO	89 E8
66TH AV	RCO	101 P2
68TH AV	RCO	101 P2
68TH AV	TEH	18 P8
70TH AV	RCO	101 P2
70TH ST	SDCO	106 K5
70TH ST	SDCO	111 B7
70TH ST E	LACO	90 G2
70TH ST W	LACO	89 D8
72ND AV	RCO	101 Q2
74TH AV	RCO	101 Q2
76TH AV	RCO	101 Q2
76TH ST E	LACO	90 G2
78TH AV	RCO	109 A2
80TH AV	RCO	108 B4
80TH AV	RCO	109 B2
80TH ST E	LACO	90 G2
80TH ST W	KER	89 D7
80TH ST W	LACO	89 G7
81ST AV	RCO	109 B2
82ND AV	RCO	109 B2
84TH AV	RCO	109 B2
85TH ST W	LACO	89 G7
87TH ST E	LACO	90 K3
87TH ST W	LACO	89 H7
90TH ST E	LACO	90 G3
90TH ST W	KER	89 D7
90TH ST W	LACO	89 G7
92ND ST	LACO	117 P5
92ND ST W	LACO	89 H7
95TH ST W	LACO	89 H7
96TH ST E	LACO	90 K3
97TH ST W	LACO	89 H7
98TH AV	ALA	45 D7
98TH AV	O	159 L7
98TH ST W	LACO	89 H7
99-97 CUTOFF	SIS	4 M2
100TH ST E	LACO	90 F3
100TH ST W	KER	89 D7
103RD ST	LACO	117 P5
105TH ST E	LACO	90 H3
106TH ST E	LACO	90 L3
110TH ST E	LACO	90 G3
110TH ST W	KER	79 P7
110TH ST W	LACO	89 D7
115TH ST W	KER	79 P7
120TH ST E	LACO	90 F3
120TH ST W	LACO	89 F6
121ST ST E	LACO	90 L3
130TH ST E	LACO	90 F4
130TH ST W	LACO	89 D6
131ST ST E	LACO	90 L4
135TH ST	LACO	119 A4
137TH ST E	LACO	90 F4
140TH ST E	LACO	90 F4
140TH ST W	KER	89 C6
145TH ST E	LACO	90 H4
147TH ST	KER	89 B5
149TH ST	KER	89 B5
150TH ST E	LACO	90 J4
152ND ST W	KER	89 B5
155TH ST	KER	89 C5
157TH ST W	KER	89 C5
160TH ST W	LACO	89 F5
164TH ST	LACO	119 B3
165TH ST E	LACO	90 H4
170TH ST E	LACO	90 H5
170TH ST W	KER	89 D5
170TH ST W	LACO	89 E5
175TH ST E	LACO	90 H5
180TH ST E	LACO	90 J5
180TH ST W	LACO	89 D5
182ND ST	LACO	119 C4
185TH ST E	LACO	90 H5
185TH ST W	KER	89 C4
190TH ST	LACO	97 H6
190TH ST	LACO	119 C3
190TH ST E	LACO	90 F5
190TH ST W	LACO	89 D4
195TH ST	LACO	119 C9
195TH ST	LACO	120 C0
195TH ST E	LACO	90 E5
195TH ST W	KER	89 C4
200TH ST E	LACO	90 D6
200TH ST E	LACO	90 H5
204TH ST E	LACO	90 L6
210TH ST	KER	89 C4
210TH ST E	LACO	90 G6
215TH ST W	KER	89 C4
220TH ST	LACO	119 D5
220TH ST E	LACO	90 H6
223RD ST	LACO	119 D5
223RD ST E	LACO	90 K6
225TH ST E	LACO	90 E6
228TH ST	LACO	119 D4
230TH ST E	LACO	90 H6
230TH ST W	KER	89 D3
233RD ST E	LACO	90 L6
235TH ST W	KER	89 D3
235TH ST W	LACO	89 E3
240TH ST E	LACO	90 J6
295TH ST W	KER	89 D2
300TH ST W	KER	89 D1
8001	MAD	50 P1
8003	MAD	50 M0
8004	MAD	50 M0
8005	MAD	50 M0
8006	MAD	50 M1
8007	MAD	50 M0
8008	MAD	50 N1
8009	MAD	50 L1
8011	MAD	50 P1
8013	MAD	50 M2
8014	MAD	50 L2
8015	MAD	50 K2
8016	MAD	50 K1
8020	MAD	50 K1
8021	MAD	49 K8
8023	MAD	50 H2
8024	MAD	50 J1
8025	MAD	50 K2
8026	MAD	50 H2
8027	MAD	50 J2
8028	MAD	50 L0
8029	MAD	50 L0
8041	MAD	49 K8
8042	MAD	49 J7
8046	MAD	49 J7
8063	MAD	57 B5
8066	MAD	57 C6
8066	MAD	57 C6
8067	MAD	57 A8
8079	MAD	49 N6
8080	MAD	57 A6
8081	MAD	49 Q6
8082	MAD	49 P7
8083	MAD	49 N7
8084	MAD	49 M5
8086	MAD	49 P4
8087	MAD	57 A4
8088	MAD	57 A5
8089	MAD	49 M6

15566

SEE PAGE D FOR INSTRUCTIONS

CITIES AND COMMUNITIES INDEX

COMMUNITY NAME	CO.	ZIP CODE	PAGE & GRID
ACADEMY	FRCO	93612	57 F8
ACAMPO	SJCO	95226	40 K1
ACTIS	KER	93501	80 Q0
ACTON	LACO	93510	89 L8
ADAMS	LAK	95496	31 L9
ADELAIDA	SLO	93446	75 B8
*ADELANTO	SBD	92301	91 H1
ADIN	MOD	96006	14 G5
AERIAL ACRES	KER	93523	80 N6
AETNA SPRINGS	NAPA	94567	32 P3
AFTON	GLE	95920	25 P1
AFTON	SBD	92309	82 P7
AGATE	RCO	91752	99 F0
AGATE BAY	PLA	95711	35 C8
AGOURA	LACO	91301	97 C1
*AGOURA HILLS	LACO	91301	97 C0
AGUA CALIENTE	SDCO	92086	108 E4
AGUA CALIENTE	SON	95476	38 G2
AGUA CALIENTE HOT SPGS	SDCO	92036	108 M9
AGUA DULCE	LACO	91350	89 K7
AGUANGA	RCO	92302	108 B1
AGUEREBERRY POINT	INY	92328	71 B7
AHWAHNEE	MAD	93601	49 L6
AINSWORTH CORNER	SIS		5 F5
*ALAMEDA	ALA	94501	45 D6
ALAMO	CC	94507	45 B9
ALAMORIO	IMP	92227	110 L2
*ALBANY	ALA	94706	38 Q5
ALBERHILL	RCO	92303	99 L1
ALBION	MEN	95410	30 D3
ALDERCROFT HEIGHTS	SCL	95030	54 A1
ALDERPOINT	HUM	95411	16 N7
ALDER SPRINGS	FRCO	93602	58 B1
ALDER SPRINGS	GLE	95939	23 J9
ALGODONES	BAJA		115 C3
*ALHAMBRA	LACO	91801	118 J0
ALLEGHANY	SIE	95910	26 M7
ALLENDALE	SOL	95688	89 D1
ALLENSWORTH	TUL	93219	68 L1
ALMANOR	PLU	95911	20 M3
ALMONDALE	LACO	93553	90 K3
ALMONTE	MAR	94941	45 A2
ALPAUGH	TUL	93201	67 L9
ALPINE	SDCO	92001	108 P2
ALPINE HEIGHTS	SDCO	92001	108 Q2
ALPINE HIGHLANDS	SDCO	92001	108 P2
ALPINE HILLS	SDCO	92001	108 P1
ALPINE HILLS	SMCO	94025	45 K7
ALPINE MEADOWS	PLA	95730	35 D7
ALPINE PEAKS	PLA	95730	35 D7
ALTA	PLA	95701	34 C8
ALTADENA	LACO	91001	118 F0
ALTA LOMA	SBD	91701	98 C7
ALTAMONT	ALA	94550	46 D5
ALTA SIERRA	KER	93285	69 P4
ALTAVILLE	CAL	95221	41 L2
ALTA VISTA	INY	93514	51 J4
ALTO	MAR	94941	38 P2
ALTON	HUM	95540	15 F8
*ALTURAS	MOD	96101	7 Q1
ALUM ROCK	SCL	95127	46 L3
ALVISO	SCL	95002	46 K1
*AMADOR CITY	AMA	95601	40 E7
AMBLER	TUL	93277	68 C3
AMBOY	SBD	92304	93 J8
AMERICAN HOUSE	PLU	95981	26 J4
*ANAHEIM	ORA	92801	98 H3
ANAHEIM HILLS	ORA	92807	98 H6
*ANDERSON	SHA	96007	18 H4
ANDERSON SPRINGS	LAK	95461	31 M9
ANDRADE	IMP	92283	115 B4
ANGEL ISLAND	MAR	94920	45 B3
*ANGELS CAMP	CAL	95222	41 M2
ANGELUS OAKS	SBD	92305	99 C7
ANGWIN	NAPA	94508	38 B3
ANTELOPE	SAC	95610	34 N0
ANTELOPE ACRES	LACO	93534	89 E7
*ANTIOCH	CC	94509	39 N3
ANZA	RCO	92306	100 P4
APPLEGATE	PLA	95703	34 G5
APPLE VALLEY	SBD	92307	91 K5
APTOS	SCR	95003	54 D2
ARABIA	RCO	92274	101 N3
ARBUCKLE	COL	95912	32 G8
*ARCADIA	LACO	91006	118 G1
*ARCATA	HUM	95521	10 P0
ARCHER	SBD	92319	94 M5
ARCILLA	RCO	91720	99 J1
ARDEN	CLK		74 H6
ARDEN	SAC	95825	40 B0
ARGOS	SBD	92365	93 F0
ARGUS	SBD	93562	71 P2
ARLINGTON	RCO	92503	99 G1
ARMONA	KIN	93202	67 C6
ARNOLD	CAL	95223	41 H5
ARNOLD HEIGHTS	RCO	92508	99 G3
AROMAS	MON	95004	54 F5
ARROWBEAR LAKE	SBD	92308	99 A7
ARROWHEAD SPRINGS	SBD	92404	99 B4
*ARROYO GRANDE	SLO	93420	76 M3
*ARTESIA	LACO	90701	119 B6
ARTOIS	GLE	95913	24 K7
*ARVIN	KER	93203	78 K9
ASHFORD JUNCTION	INY	92328	72 L3
ASH HILL	SBD	92304	93 F4
ASHLAND	JKSN		3 B8
ASPENDELL	INY	93514	51 N3
ASTI	SON	95413	31 N5
ATASCADERO	SLO	93422	76 E0
*ATHERTON	SMCO	94025	45 J7
ATOLIA	SBD	93558	80 H8
*ATWATER	MCO	95301	48 L2
*AUBURN	PLA	95603	34 J4
AUBURNDALE	RCO	91760	98 G8
*AVALON	LACO	90704	105 P9
AVENAL	KIN	93204	66 J9
AVERY	CAL	95224	41 J5
AVILA BEACH	SLO	93424	76 L0
AVON	CC	94523	38 M8
*AZUSA	LACO	91702	118 G5
BABBITT	MIN		44 B2
BADGER	TUL	93603	58 L6
BADWATER	INY	92328	72 D1
BAGDAD	SBD	92304	93 H6
BAKER	SBD	92309	83 J2
*BAKERSFIELD	KER	93301	78 G6
BALBOA	ORA	92661	98 N3
BALCH	SBD	92309	83 P2
BALCH CAMP	FRCO	93657	58 E4
*BALDWIN PARK	LACO	91706	118 J3
BALLARAT	INY	93562	71 H5
BALLARD	SB	93441	86 G8
BALLENA	SDCO	92065	108 K3
BALLICO	MCO	95303	48 J1
BANGOR	BUT	95914	25 P9
BANKHEAD SPRINGS	SDCO	92005	113 D1
BANNER	SDCO	92036	108 K6
*BANNING	RCO	92220	100 G1
BARD	IMP	92222	115 A7
BARDSDALE	VEN	93015	88 N7
BARRETT JUNCTION	SDCO	92017	112 E3
BARSTOW	FRCO	93702	57 H2
*BARSTOW	SBD	92311	91 B8
BARTLETT	INY	93545	60 N2
BARTLETT SPRINGS	LAK	95443	32 D0
BARTON	AMA	92309	41 D2
BASIN	SBD	92309	82 N9
BASSETT	LACO	91746	118 L3
BASSETTS	SIE	96125	27 K1
BASS LAKE	MAD	93604	49 J8
BATAQUES	BAJA		114 F8
BAXTER	PLA	95704	34 C8
BAYSIDE	HUM	95524	10 P0
BAYWOOD PARK	SLO	93401	75 H8
BEAR HARBOR	MEN	95489	22 D2
BEAR VALLEY	ALP	95223	41 D9
BEAR VALLEY	MPA	95338	48 G9
BEAR VALLEY	SDCO	92027	107 H8
BEAR VALLEY SPRINGS	KER	93561	79 L2
BEATTY	NYE		62 F2
BEATTY JUNCTION	INYO	92328	61 M9
*BEAUMONT	RCO	92223	99 G7
BECKWOURTH	PLU	96129	27 E4

COMMUNITY NAME	CO.	ZIP CODE	PAGE & GRID
BEE ROCK	SLO	93928	65 N7
BELDEN	PLU	95915	26 B1
*BELL	LACO	90201	97 E9
BELLA VISTA	KER	93283	79 B8
BELLA VISTA	SHA	96008	18 D6
*BELLFLOWER	LACO	90706	119 B8
*BELL GARDENS	LACO	90201	98 F0
BELLOTA	SJCO	95236	40 M5
BELL SPRINGS	MEN	95440	22 C7
*BELMONT	SMCO	94002	45 H5
*BELVEDERE	MAR	94920	38 Q3
BENBOW	HUM	95440	22 B3
BEND	TEH	96008	18 L6
*BENICIA	SOL	94510	38 M7
BEN LOMOND	SCR	95005	53 B8
BENNETTS WELL	INY	92328	72 F0
BENTON	MNO	93512	51 B5
BERENDA	MAD	93637	56 C9
*BERKELEY	ALA	94701	45 B6
BERRY CREEK	BUT	95916	25 J8
BERRYESSA HIGHLANDS	NAPA	94558	38 C7
BERRYESSA PINES	NAPA	94567	38 B5
BERTELEDA	DN	95531	2 K0
BERTSCH TERRACE	DN	95531	1 L8
BETHANY	SJCO	95376	46 C7
BETTERAVIA	SB	93455	86 B2
*BEVERLY HILLS	LACO	90210	97 D6
BIEBER	LAS	96009	14 J3
BIG BAR	AMA	95704	41 G0
BIG BEAR CITY	SBD	92314	92 P1
*BIG BEAR LAKE	SBD	92315	92 Q0
BIG BEND	SHA	96011	13 L1
BIG BEND	SON	95476	38 H3
BIG CREEK	FRCO	93605	50 P3
*BIGGS	BUT	95917	25 P4
BIG MEADOWS	CAL	95223	41 D8
BIG OAK FLAT	TUO	95305	48 B7
BIG PINE	INY	93513	51 P8
BIG RIVER	SBD	92242	104 C1
BIG SPRINGS	SIS	96064	4 N4
BIG SUR	MON	93920	64 D3
BINGHAMTON	SOL	95625	39 F3
BIOLA	FRCO	93606	57 G2
BIRCH HILL	SDCO	92060	108 E1
BIRCHVILLE	NEV		26 Q3
BIRDS LANDING	SOL	94512	39 L2
*BISHOP	INY	93514	51 L6
BITTERWATER	SBT	93930	65 B5
BLACK POINT	MAR	94947	38 L2
BLACKWELLS CORNER	KER	93249	77 B4
BLAIRSDEN	PLU	96103	27 F1
BLOCKSBURG	HUM	95414	16 L6
BLOOMINGTON	SBD	92316	99 D1
BLOSSOM	TEH	96080	18 N3
BLUE DIAMOND	CLK		74 G3
*BLUE LAKE	HUM	95525	10 N1
BLUE LAKE	LAK	95493	31 E4
*BLYTHE	RCO	92225	103 N7
BOCA	NEV	95737	27 P8
BODEGA	SON	94922	37 G5
BODEGA BAY	SON	94923	37 G4
BODFISH	KER	93205	79 C5
BODIE	MNO	93517	43 H6
BOLINAS	MAR	94924	37 Q9
BOLSA KNOLLS	MON	93906	54 J5
BOMBAY BEACH	IMP	92257	109 D8
*BONANZA	KLAM		5 B8
BONDS CORNER	IMP	92250	114 C4
BONITA	SDCO	92002	106 M5
BONNEFOY	AMA	95642	41 F0
BONSALL	SDCO	92003	107 E4
BOONVILLE	MEN	95415	30 G9
BOOTJACK	MPA	95338	49 J3
BORON	KER	93516	80 P8
BORREGO	SDCO	92004	108 G9
BOSTONIA	SDCO	92021	106 H7
BOULDER OAKS	SDCO	92062	112 B6
BOULEVARD	SDCO	92005	113 C0
BOUSE	LPAZ	92363	104 G6
BOWLES	FRCO	93725	57 L5
BOWMAN	PLA	95707	34 J5
BOX SPRINGS	RCO	92508	99 F3
BOYD	SAC	95670	40 B0
BOYLE HEIGHTS	LACO	90033	117 L6
*BRADBURY	LACO	91010	118 G4
BRADLEY	MON	93426	65 M9
BRANSCOMB	MEN	95417	22 J6
BRANT	SBD	92323	84 H4
*BRAWLEY	IMP	92227	110 M1
*BREA	ORA	92621	118 Q5
BRENDA	LPAZ		104 M7
*BRENTWOOD	CC	94513	39 P4
BRICEBURG	MPA	95345	49 F1
BRICELAND	HUM	95440	16 Q3
BRIDGE HAVEN	SON	95450	37 E4
BRIDGEPORT	MPA	95306	49 K1
BRIDGEPORT	MNO	93517	43 H2
BRIDGEPORT	NEV	95975	34 B3
BRIDGEVIEW	JOS		2 C6
BRIDGEVILLE	HUM	95526	16 H4
*BRISBANE	SMCO	94005	45 E4
BRITE VALLEY	KER	93561	79 M4
BRODERICK	YOL	95605	39 B7
BROOKINGS	CUR		1 E6
BROOKS	YOL	95606	32 N7
BROOKTRAILS VACATN VLG	MEN	95490	22 N9
BROOKTRAIL VACTN VLG W	MEN	95490	22 N8
BROWNS VALLEY	YUB	95918	33 C9
BROWNSVILLE	YUB	95919	26 M1
BRUCEVILLE	SAC	95683	39 G9
BRUSH CREEK	BUT	95916	25 H9
BRYMAN	SBD	92368	91 G3
BRYN MAWR	SBD	92318	99 E4
BRYTE	YOL	95605	39 A6
BUCKEYE	ED	95634	34 J8
BUCKEYE	SHA	96003	18 D3
BUCKHORN LODGE	AMA	95666	41 D2
BUCKHORN SPRINGS	JKSN		4 D2
BUCKMAN SPRINGS	SDCO	92062	108 Q6
BUCK MEADOWS	MPA	95321	49 B1
BUCKS BAR	ED	95684	35 P0
BUCKS LAKE	PLU	95971	26 E2
BUELLTON	SB	93427	86 H7
BUENA	SDCO	92083	107 H4
*BUENA PARK	ORA	90620	98 H3
BUENA VISTA	AMA	95640	40 G6
BUENA VISTA	SON	95476	38 G3
BUHACH	MCO	95340	48 L3
BULLHEAD CITY	MOH		85 L7
BUMMERVILLE	CAL	95257	41 E3
BUNTINGVILLE	LAS	96114	21 L3
*BURBANK	LACO	91501	97 B7
*BURLINGAME	SMCO	94010	45 G5
BURNEY	SHA	96013	13 P5
BURNT RANCH	TRI	95527	10 Q8
BURREL	FRCO	93607	57 P2
BURSON	CAL	95225	40 J7
BURTON	TUL	93257	68 H6
BUTTE CITY	GLE	95920	25 N1
BUTTE MEADOWS	BUT	95921	25 A6
BUTTONWILLOW	KER	93206	78 G0
BYRON	CC	94514	39 Q6
CABAZON	RCO	92230	100 G2
CABBAGE PATCH	CAL	95223	41 E7
CADENASSO	YOL	95607	32 N8
CADIZ	SBD	92319	94 K2
CAIRNS CORNER	TUL	93247	68 E5
CAJON	SBD	92358	91 P1
CAJON PASS	SBD	92397	91 N1
CALABASAS	LACO	91302	97 C2
CALADA	SBD	92309	84 C3
CALAVERITAS	CAL	95249	41 J1
*CALEXICO	IMP	92231	114 D1
CALICO GHOST TOWN	SBD	92398	82 Q0
CALIENTE	KER	93518	79 J3
*CALIFORNIA CITY	KER	93505	80 M3
CALIFORNIA HOT SPRGS	TUL	93207	69 L2
CALIFORNIA VALLEY	SLO	93453	77 H2
CALIMESA	RCO	92320	99 E6
*CALIPATRIA	IMP	92233	110 H2
*CALISTOGA	NAPA	94515	38 B1
CALLAHAN	SIS	96014	11 E8
CALNEVA	LAS	96113	21 N9

COMMUNITY NAME	CO.	ZIP CODE	PAGE & GRID
CALPATRIA	IMP	92233	110 H2
CALPELLA	MEN	95418	31 C2
CALPINE	SIE	96124	27 J3
CALWA	FRCO	93725	57 J5
*CAMARILLO	VEN	93010	88 Q4
CAMBRIA	SLO	93428	75 D4
CAMBRIA PINES	SLO	93428	75 C4
CAMBRIA PINES MANOR	SLO	93428	75 D4
CAMDEN	FRCO	93656	57 Q4
CAMERON CORNERS	SDCO	92006	112 D7
CAMERON PARK	ED	95682	34 P5
*CAMPBELL	SCL	95008	46 M1
CAMP CONIFER	TUL	93271	59 P1
CAMP CONNELL	CAL	95223	41 G6
CAMP KLAMATH	DN	95548	2 Q0
CAMP MEEKER	SON	95419	37 E6
CAMPO	SDCO	92006	112 E7
CAMPO SECO	CAL	95226	40 H7
CAMP SIERRA	FRCO	93634	50 P3
CAMPTONVILLE	YUB	95922	26 N3
CANBY	MOD	96015	14 B6
CANE BRAKE	KER	93255	70 P2
CANOGA PARK	LACO	91303	97 B2
CANTIL	KER	93519	80 H4
CANTUA CREEK	FRCO	93608	56 P6
CANYON CITY	SDCO	92006	112 E6
CANYON CREST HEIGHTS	RCO	92507	99 E3
CANYON DAM	PLU	95923	20 N4
CANYON LAKE	RCO	92380	99 M4
CAPAY	YOL	95607	32 P9
CAPETOWN	HUM	95536	15 H5
CAPISTRANO BEACH	ORA	92624	106 B7
*CAPITOLA	SCR	95010	54 E1
CARBONDALE	AMA	95640	40 E5
CARDIFF-BY-THE-SEA	SDCO	92007	107 L3
CARL INN	TUO	95321	49 B4
CARLOTTA	HUM	95528	16 F1
*CARLSBAD	SDCO	92008	107 H2
*CARMEL	MON	93921	54 N1
CARMEL HIGHLANDS	MON	93921	54 P0
CARMEL VALLEY VILLAGE	MON	93924	54 P4
CARMET	SON	94923	37 F4
CARMICHAEL	SAC	95608	34 Q1
CARNELIAN BAY	PLA	95711	36 C0
CARPENTERVILLE	CUR		1 B5
*CARPINTERIA	SB	93013	87 M8
CARQUINEZ HEIGHTS	SOL	94590	38 M5
*CARSON	LACO	90502	119 C5
CARSON CITY	CRSN		36 D4
CARSON HILL	CAL	95222	41 M3
CARTAGO	INY	93549	70 C3
CARUTHERS	FRCO	93609	57 N4
CASA BLANCA	RCO	92504	99 G2
CASA DE ORO	SDCO	92077	106 K7
CASITAS SPRINGS	VEN	93001	88 N1
CASMALIA	SB	93429	86 C2
CASPER	MEN	95420	30 A2
CASSEL	SHA	96016	13 N6
CASTAIC	LACO	91310	89 K2
CASTELLA	SHA	96017	12 H4
CASTLE CRAG	SHA	96013	12 H4
CASTLE PARK	SDCO	92011	106 N6
CASTRO VALLEY	ALA	94546	46 D0
CASTROVILLE	MON	95012	54 J3
*CATHEDRAL CITY	RCO	92234	100 K6
CATHEYS VALLEY	MPA	95306	49 J1
CAVE JUNCTION	JOS		2 C5
CAYTON	SHA	96013	13 K5
CAYUCOS	SLO	93430	75 F7
CAZADERO	SON	95421	37 C4
CECILVILLE	SIS	96018	11 H3
CEDAR BROOK	FRCO	93641	58 J6
CEDAR CREST	FRCO	93605	50 N4
CEDAR FLAT	PLA	95711	35 C8
CEDAR GLEN	SBD	92321	91 P6
CEDAR GROVE	ED	95709	35 M1
CEDAR GROVE	FRCO	93641	59 H2
CEDARPINES PARK	SBD	92322	91 P2
CEDAR RIDGE	TUO	95370	41 L6
CEDAR VALLEY	MAD	93644	49 K7
CEDARVILLE	MOD	96104	7 Q7
CENTERVILLE	DGL		36 J4
CENTERVILLE	FRCO	93654	57 H8
CENTERVILLE	SHA	96001	18 G3
CENTRAL VALLEY	SHA	96019	18 C4
CENTURY CITY	LACO	90067	117 L2
*CERES	STA	95307	47 G6
*CERRITOS	LACO	90701	98 H1
CHALFANT	MNO	93514	51 G7
CHALLENGE	YUB	95925	26 M2
CHAMBERS LODGE	PLA	95718	35 F8
CHARLESTON PARK	CLK		74 D0
CHASE	SBD	92364	84 L2
CHATSWORTH	LACO	91311	97 A2
CHAWANAKEE	FRCO	93602	50 Q1
CHEMEKETA PARK	SCL	95030	46 Q1
CHEROKEE	BUT	95965	25 J7
CHEROKEE	NEV	93602	26 P4
CHERRY VALLEY	RCO	92223	99 F9
CHESTER	PLU	96020	20 K1
CHICAGO PARK	NEV	95712	34 D5
*CHICO	BUT	95926	25 H3
CHILCOOT	PLU	96105	27 F7
CHINATOWN	SFCO	94108	45 C4
CHINESE CAMP	TUO	95309	41 Q3
*CHINO	SBD	91710	98 E6
CHINQUAPIN	MPA	95389	49 E6
CHIQUITA LAKE	ED	95634	35 H0
CHIRIACO SUMMIT	RCO	92239	101 N8
CHLORIDE CITY	INY	92328	61 K9
CHOLAME	SLO	93431	66 P6
*CHOWCHILLA	MAD	93610	48 Q7
CHROME	GLE	95963	24 H1
CHUALAR	MON	93925	54 M7
CHUBBUCK	SBD	92319	94 N6
*CHULA VISTA	SDCO	92010	106 N5
CIENEGA SPRINGS	LPAZ		104 B3
CIMA	SBD	92323	84 K2
CIRCLE OAKS	NAPA	94599	38 E6
CISCO	PLA	95728	35 A2
CITRUS	SAC	95670	40 A2
CITRUS HEIGHTS	SAC	95610	34 P1
CLAIREMONT	SDCO	92117	106 H2
CLARAVILLE	KER	93283	79 F7
*CLAREMONT	LACO	91711	98 C6
CLARK	STOR		28 L7
CLARKSBURG	YOL	95612	39 E6
CLARKSVILLE	ED	95682	34 Q5
CLAY	SAC	95638	40 G3
*CLAYTON	CC	94517	39 P1
CLEAR CREEK	SIS	96039	2 L8
*CLEARLAKE	LAK	95422	32 J1
CLEARLAKE KEYS	LAK	95423	32 G0
CLEARLAKE OAKS	LAK	95423	32 G0
CLEMENTS	SJCO	95227	40 J4
CLEONE	MEN	95437	22 M4
CLIFF HOUSE	TUO	95321	49 B2
CLINGHOUSE	WSH		28 J8
CLINTON	AMA	95232	41 F1
CLIPPER GAP	PLA	95703	34 H5
CLIPPER MILLS	BUT	95930	26 L2
CLOVERDALE	SHA	96007	18 G2
*CLOVERDALE	SON	95425	31 M4
CLOVER RANGER STATION	MAD	93604	50 H3
*CLOVIS	FRCO	93612	57 G6
CLYDE	CC	94520	38 N9
*COACHELLA	RCO	92236	101 M2
*COALINGA	FRCO	93210	66 G6
COALINGA MINERAL SPGS	FRCO	93210	66 F3
COARSEGOLD	MAD	93614	49 N5
COBB	LAK	95426	31 L9
COCKATOO GROVE	SDCO	92010	106 N7
CODORA	GLE	95970	25 N0
COFFEE CREEK RANCH	TRI	96091	11 J9
COFFING	SAC	95624	40 D0
COHASSET	BUT	95926	25 C4
COLD SPRINGS	TUO	95370	41 L4
COLES STATION	ED	95684	35 Q2
COLEVILLE	MNO	96107	42 B7
*COLFAX	PLA	95713	34 F6
COLLEGE CITY	COL	95931	33 H1
COLLEGEVILLE	SJCO	95206	40 Q3
COLLIERVILLE	SJCO	95220	40 J2

COMMUNITY NAME	CO.	ZIP CODE	PAGE & GRID
COLLINSVILLE	SOL	94585	39 L3
*COLMA	SMCO	94015	45 E3
COLOMA	ED	95613	34 M7
COLONIA LA PUERTA	BAJA		114 K4
COLONIA RECUPERACION	SNRA		115 N1
COLONIA SILVA	BAJA		115 H1
COLONIA ZACATECAS	BAJA		114 N9
*COLTON	SBD	92324	99 D2
COLUMBIA	TUO	95310	41 M4
*COLUSA	COL	95932	33 D0
*COMMERCE	LACO	90040	98 E0
COMPTCHE	MEN	95427	30 C6
*COMPTON	LACO	90220	119 B5
*CONCORD	CC	94520	39 N1
CONFIDENCE	TUO	95370	41 M7
CONSTANTIA	LAS	96019	27 C8
COOKS STATION	AMA	95666	41 B4
COOL	ED	95614	34 K5
COPCO	SIS	96044	4 F4
COPPEROPOLIS	CAL	95228	41 N1
*CORCORAN	KIN	93212	67 G8
CORDELIA	SOL	93063	38 J7
CORNELIAN BAY	PLA	95711	36 C0
*CORNING	TEH	96021	24 D6
*CORONA	RCO	91720	98 G8
CORONA DEL MAR	ORA	92625	98 N3
*CORONADO	SDCO	92118	106 M2
*CORTE MADERA	MAR	94925	38 Q3
COSO JUNCTION	INY	93542	70 H4
*COSTA MESA	ORA	92626	98 M3
COSUMNES	SAC	95683	40 D2
*COTATI	SON	94928	37 G9
COTTAGE SPRINGS	CAL	95223	41 F7
COTTON CENTER	TUL	93257	68 G4
COTTONWOOD	SHA	96022	18 J6
COTTONWOOD SPRING	RCO	92239	101 L7
COULTERVILLE	MPA	95311	48 D7
COURTLAND	SAC	95615	39 G7
COVELO	MEN	95428	23 G1
*COVINA	LACO	91722	118 K5
COVINGTON MILL	TRI	96052	11 N8
COWAN HEIGHTS	ORA	92705	98 K6
COW HOLLOW	SFCO	94123	45 C3
COX	RCO	92255	103 J4
COYOTE	SCL	95013	46 P5
COYOTE WELLS	IMP	92259	113 C5
COZZENS CORNER	SON	95441	31 P5
CRAFTON	SBD	92373	99 D6
CRANMORE	SUT	95645	33 H3
CRANNELL	HUM	95530	10 L0
*CRESCENT CITY	DN	95531	1 L7
CRESCENT MILLS	PLU	95934	20 P5
CRESSEY	MCO	95312	48 K1
CREST	SDCO	92021	112 A1
CRESTLINE	SBD	92325	91 Q4
CRESTMORE	SBD	92316	99 E2
CRESTON	SLO	93432	76 D3
CRESTVIEW	MNO	93514	50 C7
CROCKETT	CC	94525	38 M6
CROMBERG	PLU	96103	27 E0
CROWN POINT	SDCO	92109	106 J1
CROWS LANDING	SIS	95313	47 K4
CRUCERO	SBD	92309	83 P2
*CRYSTAL BAY	DGL		36 C1
*CUDAHY	LACO	90201	97 F8
CUERVOS	BAJA		115 D2
CUESTA BY THE SEA	SLO	93402	75 J8
*CULVER CITY	LACO	90230	97 E6
CUMMINGS	MEN	95477	22 F6
CUMMINGS VALLEY	KER	93561	79 M2
CUNNINGHAM	SON	95472	37 F8
*CUPERTINO	SCL	95014	45 M8
CURRY VILLAGE	MPA	95389	49 D7
CUTLER	TUL	93615	58 N2
CUTTEN	HUM	95534	15 B8
CUYAMA	SB	93214	87 A6
CUYAMACA	SDCO	92036	108 L4
*CYPRESS	ORA	90630	98 J1
DAGGETT	SBD	92327	92 C1
DAIRY	KLAM		5 A7
DAIRYVILLE	TEH	96080	18 P7
DALES	TEH	96080	18 K8
*DALY CITY	SMCO	94014	45 E3
DANA	SHA	96036	13 J6
DANA POINT	ORA	92629	106 B6
DANBY	SBD	92332	94 G5
*DANVILLE	CC	94526	46 B1
DARDANELLE	TUO	95314	42 F3
DARLINGTONIA	DN	95543	2 J1
DARRAH	MPA	95338	49 H4
DARWIN	INY	93522	70 D9
DATE CITY	IMP	92250	114 A4
DAULTON	MAD	93653	57 B2
*DAVIS	YOL	95616	39 B4
DAVIS CREEK	MOD	96108	7 L4
DAVIS DAM	MOH		85 L7
DAWES	SBD	92364	84 N1
DAY	MOD	96056	13 G9
DAYTON	BUT	95926	25 J2
DAYTON	LYON		36 C6
DE BON	SIS	96034	12 C4
DEERHORN FLAT	SDCO	92035	112 C3
DEER PARK	NAPA	94576	38 C3
DEHESA	SDCO	92021	112 A1
*DELANO	KER	93215	68 N3
DEL CERRO	SDCO	92120	106 J5
DEL DIOS	SDCO	92025	107 J6
DELEVAN	COL	95988	24 Q6
DELFT COLONY	TUL	93619	58 N0
DELHI	MCO	95315	47 J9
DELL	SBD	92371	91 N1
DEL LOMA	TRI	96010	11 Q0
*DEL MAR	SDCO	92014	107 M3
DEL PASO HEIGHTS	SAC	95838	33 P8
DEL REY	FRCO	93616	57 K8
*DEL REY OAKS	MON	93940	54 M3
DEL RIO WOODS	SON	95448	31 Q7
DEL ROSA	SBD	92404	99 B4
DELTA	SHA	96051	12 M3
DEMOCRAT HOT SPRINGS	KER	93301	79 D2
DENAIR	STA	95316	47 H8
DENNY	TRI	95538	10 M9
DENVERTON	SOL	94585	39 J1
DERBY ACRES	KER	93268	77 J8
DE SABLA	BUT	95978	25 E5
DESCANSO	SDCO	92016	108 P4
DESCANSO JUNCTION	SDCO	92016	108 P5
DESERT	SBD	92309	84 D4
DESERT BEACH	RCO	92254	101 Q6
DESERT HAVEN	RCO	92240	100 H6
*DESERT HOT SPRINGS	RCO	92240	100 F6
DESERT LAKE	KER	93516	80 P7
DESERT SHORES	IMP	92274	109 C4
DESERT VIEW HIGHLAND	LACO	93550	90 H0
DEVILS DEN	KER	93204	67 P2
DEVORE	SBD	92405	99 A2
DIABLO	CC	94528	46 B1
DIABLO CASA HOT SPGS	MNO	93546	50 E8
DIAMOND BAR	LACO	91765	118 M8
DIAMOND SPRINGS	ED	95619	34 P8
DIAMOND SPRINGS HTS	ED	95619	34 P8
DI GIORGIO	KER	93217	79 J0
DILLON BEACH	MAR	94929	37 H5
DINKEY CREEK	FRCO	93617	58 B4
*DINUBA	TUL	93618	58 N1
DISCOVERY BAY	CC	94514	39 Q6
DIXIELAND	IMP	92251	109 Q7
*DIXON	SOL	95620	39 D3
DOBBINS	YUB	95935	26 P2
DOGTOWN	MPA	95311	48 D9
DOGTOWN	SJCO	95220	40 J4
DORRINGTON	CAL	95223	41 G6
*DORRIS	SIS	96023	5 F1
*DOS PALOS	MCO	93620	56 B1
DOS RIOS	MEN	95429	23 H0
DOUGLAS CITY	TRI	96024	17 D6
*DOWNEY	LACO	90241	98 G0
DOWNIEVILLE	SIE	95936	26 L7
DOYLE	LAS	96019	27 A8
DOYLES CORNER	SHA	96040	13 P6
DOZIER	SOL	94535	39 H3
DRYTOWN	AMA	95699	40 D7
*DUARTE	LACO	91010	118 G3

SEE PAGE D FOR INSTRUCTIONS

CITIES AND COMMUNITIES INDEX

CITIES AND COMMUNITIES INDEX

COMMUNITY NAME	CO.	ZIP CODE	PAGE & GRID
*DUBLIN	ALA	94566	46 E1
DUCOR	TUL	93218	68 L6
DULZURA	SDCO	92017	112 D2
DUNCANS MILLS	SON	95430	37 D4
DUNLAP	FRCO	93621	58 J5
DUNLAP	MEN	95490	30 A6
DUNMOVIN	INY	93542	70 G3
DUNN	SBD	92309	82 P7
DUNNINGAN	YOL	95937	29 K0
*DUNSMUIR	SIS	96025	12 G6
DURHAM	BUT	95938	25 J2
DURMID	RCO	92257	109 B7
DUSTIN ACRES	KER	93268	78 K1
DUTCH FLAT	PLA	95714	33 C7
DYER	ESM		52 D2
EADS	SBD	92347	81 Q4
EAGLE LAKE RESORT	LAS	96130	20 E6
EAGLE MOUNTAIN	RCO	92241	102 H2
EAGLE ROCK	LACO	90041	97 C9
EAGLES NEST	SDCO	92086	108 E5
EAGLEVILLE	MOD	96110	8 E7
EARLIMART	TUL	93219	68 L2
EARP	SBD	92242	104 B2
EAST BAKERSFIELD	KER	93307	78 G7
EAST GUERNEWOOD	SON	95446	37 C4
EAST HIGHLANDS	SBD	92346	99 C5
EAST NICOLAUS	SUT	95622	33 J6
EASTON	FRCO	93706	57 K5
EAST OROSI	TUL	93647	58 N3
EAST QUINCY	PLU	95971	26 C6
EAST SAN DIEGO	SDCO	92105	106 K4
EASTSIDE ACRES	MAD	93622	56 G5
EASTSIDE RANCH	MAD	93622	56 G5
ECHO DELL	SDCO	92016	108 N4
ECHO LAKE	ED	95721	35 L9
EDEN GARDENS	SDCO	92075	107 L3
EDEN HOT SPRINGS	RCO	92353	99 G7
EDGEMONT	RCO	92508	99 G4
EDGEWOOD	SIS	96094	12 B4
EDISON	KER	93220	78 H9
EDNA	SLO	93401	76 L2
EDWARDS AIR FORCE BASE	KER	93523	90 B4
EEL ROCK	HUM	95554	16 L5
EHRENBERG	YUMA		103 N8
EJIDO DURANGO	BAJA		114 M6
EJIDO MARITIMO	BAJA		114 Q6
EL BONITA	SON	95446	37 C5
*EL CAJON	SDCO	92020	106 J7
EL CASCO	RCO	92373	99 F6
*EL CENTRO	IMP	92243	110 Q1
*EL CERRITO	CC	94530	38 Q5
ELDERS CORNERS	PLA	95603	34 H4
ELDERWOOD	TUL	93286	58 P5
EL DESCANSO	BAJA		112 N0
EL DORADO	ED	95623	34 P7
EL DORADO HILLS	ED	95630	34 P4
ELDRIDGE	SON	95431	38 G2
ELECTRA	AMA	95642	41 F1
EL ENCANTO HEIGHTS	SB	93017	87 L2
EL GRANADA	SMCO	94018	45 J3
ELIZABETH LAKE	LACO	93550	89 G6
ELK	MEN	95432	30 E4
ELK CREEK	GLE	95939	24 K1
ELK GROVE	SAC	95624	39 E9
ELK VALLEY	DN	95543	2 F5
ELMIRA	SOL	95625	39 F2
*EL MONTE	LACO	91731	118 K2
ELMORE	IMP	92227	109 J7
ELM VIEW	FRCO	93725	57 M5
EL NIDO	MCO	95317	48 Q3
ELORA	SBD	92364	84 L2
*EL PASO DE ROBLES	SLO	93446	76 B1
EL PORTAL	MPA	95318	49 E4
EL PORVENIR	FRE	93608	56 N5
*EL SEGUNDO	LACO	90245	119 A0
EL SOBRANTE	CC	94803	38 N6
EL TORO	ORA	92630	98 N7
EL VERANO	SON	95433	38 G2
ELVERTA	SAC	95626	33 N8
EMERALD BAY	ED	95733	35 H8
EMERALD BAY	ORA	92651	98 P5
*EMERYVILLE	ALA	94608	45 B5
EMIGRANT GAP	PLA	95715	35 B1
EMPIRE	STA	95319	47 F7
ENCANTO	SDCO	92114	106 L5
ENCINITAS	SDCO	92024	107 K3
ENCINO	LACO	91316	97 C4
ENGINEER SPRINGS	SDCO	92017	112 D2
ENTERPRISE	SHA	96001	18 F5
*ESCALON	SJCO	95320	47 C5
*ESCONDIDO	SDCO	92025	107 J7
ESPARTO	YOL	95627	33 P0
ESSEX	SBD	92332	94 E7
ESTACION	BAJA		114 K6
ESTACION COAHUILA	BAJA		115 N0
ESTRELLA	SLO	93415	76 A3
ETHEDA SPRINGS	FRCO	93633	58 K7
ETIWANDA	SBD	91739	98 C8
*ETNA	SIS	96027	11 B6
ETTERSBURG	HUM	95440	16 P1
EUCALYPTUS HILLS	SDCO	92040	106 G7
*EUREKA	HUM	95501	15 A8
EVELYN	INY	92384	72 F8
*EXETER	TUL	93221	68 C5
*FAIRFAX	MAR	94930	38 P1
*FAIRFIELD	SOL	94533	38 H9
FAIRHAVEN	HUM	95564	15 A7
FAIRMEAD	MAD	93610	56 B8
FAIRMONT	LACO	93534	89 F5
FAIR OAKS	SAC	95628	34 Q1
FAIR PLAY	ED	95684	41 A0
FAIRVIEW	TUL	93238	69 K5
FALES HOT SPRINGS	MNO	93517	43 E0
FALLBROOK	SDCO	92028	107 D4
FALLEN LEAF	ED	95716	35 K9
FALLON	MAR	94932	37 H6
FALL RIVER MILLS	SHA	96028	13 L8
FAMOSO	KER	93250	78 C2
*FARMERSVILLE	TUL	93223	68 C4
FAWNSKIN	SBD	92333	91 P9
FEATHER FALLS	BUT	95940	26 K1
FELLOWS	KER	93224	77 L8
FELIX	CAL	95228	41 M0
FENNER	SBD	92332	94 D8
FERN	SHA	96096	19 C1
FERNBROOK	SDCO	92065	108 M0
*FERNDALE	HUM	95536	15 E6
FERRUM	RCO	92257	109 B6
FIDDLETOWN	AMA	95629	41 C0
FIELD	SBD	92365	82 P5
FIELDBROOK	HUM	95521	10 M1
FIELDS LANDING	HUM	95537	15 C8
*FILLMORE	VEN	93015	88 M7
FINE GOLD	MAD	93643	49 P7
FINLEY	LAK	95435	31 H7
*FIREBAUGH	FRCO	93622	56 G4
FISH CAMP	MPA	93623	49 J6
FISHEL	SBD	92319	94 P5
FISH ROCK	MEN	95445	30 L6
FISH SPRINGS	INY	93513	59 B8
FIVE CORNERS	LAKE		7 B3
FIVE CORNERS	SJCO	95336	47 B3
FIVE POINTS	FRCO	93624	57 Q0
FIVE POINTS	LACO	91732	118 K2
FLEETRIDGE	SDCO	92106	106 L0
FLETCHER HILLS	SDCO	92020	106 H6
FLINN SPRINGS	SDCO	92021	108 P1
FLORIN	SAC	95828	39 C9
FLOURNOY	TEH	96029	24 D3
FLOWING WELLS	RCO	92254	101 P4
FLYNN	SBD	92309	83 Q8
*FOLSOM	SAC	95630	34 N3
*FONTANA	SBD	92335	99 D1
FOOTHILL FARMS	SAC	95841	34 P1
FORBESTOWN	BUT	95963	26 L1
FORD CITY	KER	93268	78 M0
FOREST	SIE	95910	26 M7
FORESTA	MPA	95389	49 D5
FOREST GLEN	TRI	96030	17 J1
FORESTHILL	PLA	95631	34 G7
FOREST HOME	AMA	95640	40 D5
FOREST KNOLLS	MAR	94933	38 N0
FOREST LAKE	LAK	95461	32 L0
FOREST RANCH	BUT	95942	25 D4
FOREST SPRINGS	NEV	95945	34 E4
FORESTVILLE	SON	95436	37 D6
FORKS OF SALMON	SIS	96031	11 F0
FORREST PARK	LACO	91350	89 L5
FORT BIDWELL	MOD	96112	7 H7
*FORT BRAGG	MEN	95437	22 N3
FORT DICK	DN	95538	1 H7
FORT IRWIN	SBD	92311	82 J3
*FORT JONES	SIS	96032	3 N7
FORT ORD VILLAGE	MON	93941	54 L3
FORT ROSS	SON	95450	37 C2
FORT SEWARD	HUM	95438	16 M6
*FORTUNA	HUM	95540	15 E8
FOSTER	SDCO	92040	106 F8
*FOSTER CITY	SMCO	94404	45 G6
FOSTER PARK	VEN	93001	88 N1
FOUNTAIN SPRINGS	TUL	93257	68 L8
*FOUNTAIN VALLEY	ORA	92708	98 L3
FOUR CORNERS	SB	93436	86 G4
FOUR CORNERS	SHA	96016	13 L5
FOUTS SPRINGS	COL	95979	24 Q0
*FOWLER	FRCO	93625	57 L6
FRANKLIN	SAC	95639	39 F8
FRAZIER PARK	KER	93225	88 C6
FREDA	SBD	92280	103 D2
FREDALBA	SBD	92382	99 B6
FREDERICKSBURG	ALP	96120	36 K3
FREDS PLACE	ED	95720	35 L6
FREEDOM	SCR	95019	54 E3
FREEMAN	KER	93527	80 C4
FREEPORT	SAC	95832	39 D8
FREESTONE	SON	95472	37 F6
*FREMONT	ALA	94536	46 H1
FREMONT VALLEY	KER	93519	80 K2
FRENCH CAMP	SJCO	95231	40 Q2
FRENCH CORRAL	NEV	95975	34 A3
FRENCH GULCH	SHA	96033	18 C1
FRESH POND	ED	95725	35 M2
FRESHWATER	HUM	95504	16 B0
*FRESNO	FRCO	93706	57 J4
FRIANT	FRCO	93626	57 D5
FROGTOWN	CAL	95222	41 M2
FRUITVALE	KER	93308	78 G5
FRUTO	GLE	95988	24 K3
FULLER ACRES	KER	93307	78 H8
*FULLERTON	ORA	92631	98 H3
FULTON	SON	95439	37 D8
FURNACE CREEK INN	INY	92328	62 P1
FURNACE CREEK RANCH	INY	92328	62 P0
GADSDEN	YUMA		115 F4
*GALT	SAC	95632	40 H1
GANNS	CAL	95223	41 E7
GARBERVILLE	HUM	95440	16 Q4
*GARDENA	LACO	90247	119 B4
GARDEN FARMS	SLO	93422	76 F3
*GARDEN GROVE	ORA	92640	98 K3
GARDEN PARK	ED	95633	34 L7
GARDEN VALLEY	ED	95633	34 L6
GARDNERVILLE	DGL		36 H4
GAREY	SB	93454	86 B5
GARFIELD	KER	93240	79 C5
GARLOCK	KER	93519	80 F6
GARNET	RCO	92258	100 H5
GASQUET	DN	95543	2 J1
GAVIOTA	SB	93017	86 L7
GAZELLE	SIS	96034	4 Q2
GENESEE	PLU	95983	26 A8
GENOA	DGL		36 G3
GEORGETOWN	ED	95634	34 J8
GERBER	TEH	96035	24 A7
GEYSERVILLE	SON	95441	31 P6
GIANT FOREST	TUL	93271	59 M1
GIBSONVILLE	SIE	95981	26 G6
GILMAN HOT SPRINGS	RCO	92340	99 J8
*GILROY	SCL	95020	54 D6
GISH	SBD	92371	91 N1
GLAMIS	IMP	92248	110 L8
GLASGOW	SBD	92309	83 Q6
GLEN AVON	RCO	92509	99 E1
GLENBROOK BAY	DGL		36 F1
GLENBURN	SHA	96036	13 K7
GLENCOE	CAL	95232	41 F2
*GLENDALE	LACO	91201	97 B7
*GLENDORA	LACO	91740	118 G6
GLEN ELLEN	SON	95442	38 F2
GLENHAVEN	LAK	95443	31 G9
GLENN	GLE	95943	25 M0
GLENNVILLE	KER	93226	69 P1
GLEN OAKS	SDCO	92001	108 P1
GLEN VALLEY	RCO	92370	99 H3
GLENVIEW	LAK	95451	31 K8
GLENVIEW	LACO	90290	97 C3
GLENVIEW	SDCO	92021	106 H8
GOFFS	SBD	92332	84 Q8
GOLDEN SHORES	MOH	92363	96 E0
GOLDEN VALLEY	WSH		28 J3
GOLD HILL	ED	95651	34 M6
GOLD HILL	STOR		36 B6
GOLD RUN	PLA	95717	34 D7
GOLD SPRINGS	TUO	93570	41 L4
GOLD TRAIL PARK	ED	95651	34 M7
GOLETA	SB	93017	87 L3
*GONZALES	MON	93926	54 P8
GONZALEZ ORTEGA	BAJA		114 E4
GOOD HOPE	RCO	92370	99 K3
GOODSPRINGS	CLK		74 M3
GOODYEARS BAR	SIE	95944	26 L6
GORMAN	LACO	93534	88 D8
GOSHEN	TUL	93227	68 B1
GOTTVILLE	SIS	96050	3 H9
GOVERNMENT FLAT	TEH	95939	23 E6
GRAEAGLE	PLU	96103	27 G0
GRANADA HILLS	LACO	91344	89 Q4
*GRAND TERRACE	SBD	92324	99 E3
GRANGEVILLE	KIN	93230	67 C6
GRANITEVILLE	NEV	95959	26 N8
GRANTVILLE	SDCO	92120	106 J4
GRAPEVINE	KER	93301	88 A7
*GRASS VALLEY	NEV	95945	34 C4
GRATON	SON	95444	37 E7
GRAVESBORO	FRCO	93657	58 H1
GRAYSON	STA	95363	47 G2
GREELEY HILL	MPA	95311	48 C9
GREEN ACRES	KER	93308	78 G5
GREEN ACRES	RCO	92343	99 L6
GREENFIELD	KER	93309	78 J7
*GREENFIELD	MON	93927	65 C2
GREEN POINT	MAR	94947	38 L2
GREEN VALLEY FALLS	SDCO	92016	108 N5
GREEN VALLEY LAKE	SBD	92341	99 A6
GREENVIEW	SIS	96037	3 P6
GREENVILLE	PLU	95947	20 P5
GREENWOOD	ED	95635	34 J5
GRENADA	SIS	96038	4 M3
*GRIDLEY	BUT	95948	25 Q4
GRIMES	COL	95950	33 F2
GRIZZLY FLAT	ED	95636	35 Q2
GROMMET	SBD	92280	103 D5
GROSSMONT	SDCO	92041	106 J6
GROVELAND	TUO	95321	48 B8
*GROVER CITY	SLO	93433	76 M1
GROVER HOT SPRINGS	ALP	96120	36 N3
GUADALAJARA	BAJA		115 F2
GUADALUPE	BAJA		112 Q5
*GUADALUPE	SB	93434	76 Q3
GUALALA	MEN	95445	28 M7
GUASTI	SBD	91743	98 D8
GUATAY	SDCO	92031	108 P5
GUINDA	YOL	95637	32 L6
*GUSTINE CITY	MCO	95322	47 N5
HACIENDA	SON	95436	37 C6
HACIENDA HEIGHTS	LACO	91745	118 N4
HAIGHT-ASHBURY	SFCO	94117	45 C3
*HALF MOON BAY	SMCO	94019	45 J2
HALLELUJAH JCT	LAS	96135	28 F0
HAMBURG	SIS	96045	3 K4
HAMILTON BRANCH	PLU	96137	20 L4
HAMILTON CITY	GLE	95951	25 G0
HAMMOND	TUL	93271	58 P8
HAMMONTON	YUB	95901	33 D8
HAM'S STATION	AMA	95666	41 B5
*HANFORD	KIN	93230	67 C7
HAPPY CAMP	SIS	96039	2 K8
HARBIN SPRINGS	LAK	95461	32 M0
HARBISON CANYON	SDCO	92021	108 P1
HARBOR	CUR		1 E6
HARBOR CITY	LACO	90710	119 E4
HARDEN FLAT	TUO	95321	49 B2
HARDWICK	KIN	93230	57 Q5
HARMONY	SLO	93435	75 E5
HARMONY GROVE	SDCO	92025	107 J6
HARRIS	HUM	95447	16 Q6
HARRISBURG	INY	92328	71 B5
HARRISON PARK	SDCO	92036	108 K5
HARTLEY	SOL	95688	39 E1
HARVARD	SBD	92365	82 Q3
HASKELL CREEK	SIE	96124	27 J2
HAT CREEK	SHA	96040	13 Q7
HATFIELD	SIS	96134	5 F7
HAVILAH	KER	93518	79 D5
*HAWAIIAN GARDENS	LACO	90716	98 J1
HAWES	SBD	92347	81 Q2
HAWKINSVILLE	SIS	96097	4 K0
*HAWTHORNE	LACO	90250	119 A3
HAWTHORNE	MIN		44 B2
HAYFORK	TRI	96041	17 F2
*HAYWARD	ALA	94544	45 E9
HAZEL CREEK	SHA	96017	12 K5
*HEALDSBURG	SON	95448	31 Q6
HEBER	IMP	92249	114 B1
HECTOR	SBD	92365	92 D7
HEIGHTS CORNER	KER	93311	78 F4
HELENA	TRI	96042	17 B3
HELENDALE	SBD	92342	91 E3
HELLS GATE	INY	92328	61 J8
HELM	FRCO	93627	57 N1
HENDERSON	CLK		74 G8
HENDERSON VILLAGE	SJCO		40 L1
*HEMET	RCO	92343	99 L8
HENLEY	KLAM		5 C4
HENLEY	SIS	96044	4 G1
HENLEYVILLE	TEH	96021	24 C4
HERALD	SAC	95638	40 G2
*HERCULES	CC	94547	38 N6
HERMIT VALLEY	ALP	95314	42 B2
*HERMOSA BEACH	LACO	90254	119 C0
HERNANDEZ	SBT	95043	65 B9
HERNDON	FRCO	93711	57 G3
HESPERIA	SBD	92345	91 L3
HICKMAN	STA	95323	47 F8
HIDALGO	BAJA		114 H6
HIDDEN GLEN	SDCO	92001	108 Q3
*HIDDEN HILLS	LACO	91302	97 C1
HIDDEN MEADOWS	SDCO	92026	107 G6
HIDDEN VALLEY	LAK	95461	32 M2
HIDDEN VALLEY	PLA	95650	34 M3
HIGGINS CORNER	NEV	95603	34 G3
HIGHLAND	SBD	92346	99 C4
HIGHLAND PARK	LACO	90042	97 C8
HIGHLANDS HARBOR	LAK	95457	32 J1
HIGHTS CORNER	KER	93308	78 E4
HIGHWAY CITY	FRCO	93705	57 H4
HIGHWAY HIGHLANDS	LACO	91214	117 D5
HILLCREST	SHA	96065	13 P2
*HILLSBOROUGH	SMCO	94010	45 G3
HILMAR	MCO	95324	47 K8
HILT	SIS	96043	4 F1
HINDA	RCO	92353	99 F7
HINKLEY	SBD	92347	91 B5
HOAGLIN	TRI	95495	16 P8
HOBART MILLS	NEV	95734	27 P6
HOBERGS	LAK	95496	31 L9
HODGE	SBD	92342	91 D5
HODSON	CAL	95228	41 N0
HOLLAND	JOS		2 C7
*HOLLISTER	SBT	95023	55 G0
HOLLOW TREE	MEN	95455	22 F3
HOLLYWOOD	LACO	90028	97 C6
HOLLYWOOD BEACH	VEN	93043	105 B1
HOLLYWOOD-BY-THE-SEA	VEN	93043	105 B1
HOLMES	HUM	95569	16 H1
HOLT	SJCO	95234	39 P9
*HOLTVILLE	IMP	92250	110 Q3
HOLY CITY	SCL	95026	46 Q1
HOME GARDENS	RCO	91720	99 H0
HOMELAND	RCO	92348	99 K6
HOMER	SBD	92332	95 B2
HONBY	LACO	91351	89 M4
HONCUT	BUT	95965	25 Q7
HONEYDEW	HUM	95545	15 M9
HOOD	SAC	95639	39 F7
HOOPA	HUM	95546	10 K5
HOPE LANDING	SJCO	95686	39 J8
HOPE RANCH PARK	SB	93110	87 L4
HOPETON	MCO	95369	48 H3
HOPE VLY FOREST CAMP	ALP	96120	36 N2
HOPLAND	MEN	95449	31 H3
HORNITOS	MPA	95325	48 H7
HORSE CREEK	SIS	96045	3 J5
HOT SPRINGS	KLAM		5 C1
HOUGH SPRINGS	LAK	95443	32 E1
HOWLAND FLAT	SIE	95981	26 H6
HUASNA	SLO	93420	76 M6
*HUGHSON	STA	95326	47 F8
HULBURD GROVE	SDCO	92016	108 P5
HULLVILLE	LAK	95469	23 P5
HUME	FRCO	93628	58 H8
HUMPHREYS STATION	FRCO	93612	58 D0
*HUNTINGTON BEACH	ORA	92646	98 M1
HUNTINGTON LAKE	FRCO	93634	50 N2
*HUNTINGTON PARK	LACO	90255	97 E8
HURLETON	BUT	95962	25 M9
*HURON	FRCO	93234	67 E1
HYAMPOM	TRI	96046	16 E8
HYDESVILLE	HUM	95547	15 F8
IBIS	SBD	92332	95 B4
IDYLLWILD	RCO	92349	100 L3
IDYLWILD	SCL	95030	46 Q1
IGNACIO	MAR	94947	38 M2
IGO	SHA	96047	18 G2
ILLINOIS VALLEY	JOS		2 D5
*IMPERIAL	IMP	92251	119 A1
*IMPERIAL BEACH	SDCO	92032	106 P3
IMPERIAL GABLES	IMP	92266	116 J1
INCA	RCO	92255	103 K3
INCLINE	MPA	95318	49 E4
INCLINE VILLAGE	WSH		36 B1
INDEPENDENCE	CAL	95245	41 F3
INDEPENDENCE	INY	93526	60 G0
INDIAN FALLS	PLU	95952	26 A5
INDIAN SPRINGS	SDCO	92035	112 B0
*INDIAN WELLS	RCO	92260	100 L8
*INDIO	RCO	92201	101 L1
*INDUSTRY	LACO	91744	118 M5
*INGLEWOOD	LACO	90301	97 F6
INGOT	SHA	96008	18 B8
INSKIP	BUT	95921	25 B6
INVERNESS	MAR	94937	37 L6
INWOOD	SHA	96088	19 F1
INYOKERN	KER	93527	80 A6
*IONE	AMA	95640	40 F6
IOWA HILL	PLA	95713	34 E7
*IRVINE	ORA	92715	98 M5
IRVING'S CREST	SDCO	92065	108 L0
IRWIN	MCO	95380	47 K8
*IRWINDALE	LACO	91706	118 H4
ISLA VISTA	SB	93017	87 M2
*ISLETON	SAC	95641	39 K5
IVANHOE	TUL	93235	68 B3
IVANPAH	SBD	92364	84 G5
*JACKSON	AMA	95642	40 F8
JACKSON GATE	AMA	95642	40 F9
JACUMBA	SDCO	92034	113 D1
JAMACHA	SDCO	92035	106 K8
JAMESBURG	MON	93924	64 B6
JAMESON	RCO	91720	99 K1
JAMESTOWN	TUO	95327	41 N4
JAMUL	SDCO	92035	112 B1
JANESVILLE	LAS	96114	21 K1
JARBO GAP	BUT	95916	25 G7
JENNER-BY-THE-SEA	SON	95450	37 D3
JENNY LIND	CAL	95252	40 L7
JESMOND DENE	SDCO	92026	107 H6
JIMGREY	SBD	93516	81 P1
JIMTOWN	SON	95959	26 N8
JOHANNESBURG	KER	93528	80 G7
JOHNSONDALE	TUL	93236	69 J4
JOHNSON PARK	SHA	96013	13 N5
JOHNSONS	HUM	95546	10 D2
JOHNSTONVILLE	LAS	96130	21 J1
JOHNSTOWN	SDCO	92021	106 H9
JOHNSVILLE	PLU	95921	26 G8
JOLON	MON	93928	65 K3
JONESVILLE	BUT	95921	19 P7
JOSHUA	SBD	92364	84 J3
JOSHUA TREE	SBD	92252	100 C8
JULIAN	SDCO	92036	108 K4
JUNCTION CITY	TRI	96048	17 B4
JUNE LAKE	MNO	93529	50 C6
JUNE LAKE JUNCTION	MNO	93529	50 B6
JUNIPER HILLS	LACO	93543	90 M3
JUNIPER LAKE RESORT	LAS	96020	20 G0
KAGEL CANYON	LACO	91342	117 C3
KANE SPRINGS	IMP	92227	109 J6
KARNAK	SUT	95676	33 M5
KAWEAH	TUL	93237	58 P7
KEARNEY PARK	FRCO	93706	57 J3
KEARSARGE	INY	93526	60 G1
KEDDIE	PLU	95952	26 B5
KEELER	INY	93530	60 N5
KEENE	KER	93531	79 K3
KELLOGG	SON	94515	31 Q9
KELSEYVILLE	LAK	95451	31 H7
KELSO	SBD	92351	83 P8
KENEFICK	SJCO	95220	40 J2
KENO	KLAM		5 C1
KENSINGTON	CC	94708	38 Q6
KENSINGTON	SDCO	92116	106 J4
KENTWOOD IN THE PINES	SDCO	92036	108 K5
KENWOOD	SON	95452	38 E2
KEOUGH HOT SPRINGS	INY	93514	51 N6
KERBY	JOS		2 B5
KERCKOFF POWERHOUSE	FRCO	93602	57 B8
KERENS	SBD	92309	83 Q7
*KERMAN	FRCO	93630	57 J0
KERN CITY	KER	93309	78 H5
KERN RIVER PARK	KER	93306	78 F8
KERNVALE	KER	93240	79 B4
KERNVILLE	KER	93238	69 N5
KESWICK	SHA	96001	18 D3
KETTLEMAN CITY	KIN	93239	67 J3
KEYES	STA	95328	47 G7
KILKARE WOODS	ALA	94586	46 F2
*KING CITY	MON	93930	65 E4
KING COLE	KLAM		4 C6
KINGS BEACH	PLA	95719	36 C0
*KINGSBURG	FRCO	93631	57 N8
KINGSBURY	DGL		36 H2
KINGSTON	SBD	92309	73 N9
KINGSVILLE	ED	95623	34 P7
KINGVALE	NEV	95728	27 Q3
KINSLEY	MPA	95311	49 D2
KIRKVILLE	SUT	95645	33 J3
KIRKWOOD	ALP	95646	36 N0
KIRKWOOD	TEH	96021	24 E7
KIT CARSON	AMA	95644	35 P8
KLAMATH	DN	95548	2 Q0
*KLAMATH FALLS	KLAM		5 A3
KLAMATH GLEN	DN	95548	2 Q1
KLAMATH RIVER	SIS	96050	3 H7
KLAU	SLO	93465	75 C7
KLONDIKE	SBD	92304	93 G4
KNEELAND	HUM	95549	16 C2
KNIGHTSEN	CC	94548	39 P5
KNIGHTS FERRY	STA	95367	48 B1
KNIGHTS LANDING	YOL	95645	33 M4
KNOB	SHA	96076	17 J5
KNOWLES	MAD	93653	49 P3
KNOWLES CORNER	SON	95472	37 F7
KNOXVILLE	NAPA	95637	32 L5
KONO TAYEE	LAK	95458	31 G8
KORBEL	HUM	95550	10 P2
KORBEL	SON	95446	37 C5
KRAMER	SBD	93516	80 P9
KYBURZ	ED	95720	35 M6
LA BARR MEADOWS	NEV	95945	34 D4
*LA CANADA FLINTRIDGE	LACO	91011	97 A8
LA CATORCE	SONR		115 H2
LA CONCHITA	VEN	93001	87 N9
LA COSTA	SDCO	92008	107 J4
LA CRESCENTA	LACO	91214	117 E6
LADERA	SMCO	94025	45 K6
*LAFAYETTE	CC	94549	38 Q8
LA GRANGE	STA	95329	48 E4
*LAGUNA BEACH	ORA	92651	98 P6
LAGUNA HILLS	ORA	92653	98 N6
LAGUNITA	SONR		115 J2
LAGUNITAS	MAR	94938	38 N0
*LA HABRA	ORA	90631	118 P4
*LA HABRA HEIGHTS	LACO	90631	118 P3
LA HONDA	SMCO	94020	41 K2
LAIRDS CORNER	TUL	93257	68 H3
LA JOLLA	SDCO	92037	106 H0
LA JOLLA AMAGO	SDCO	92061	108 F1
LA JOYA	LACO	91350	89 H5
LAKE ALPINE	ALP	95235	42 C0
LAKE ARROWHEAD	SBD	92352	99 A5
LAKE BERRYESSA ESTATES	NAPA	94567	32 P4
LAKE CITY	MOD	96115	7 N6
LAKE CITY	NEV	95959	26 Q6
*LAKE ELSINORE	RCO	92330	99 M3
LAKE FOREST	ORA	92630	98 M6
LAKE FOREST	PLA	95730	35 D9
LAKE HAVASU CITY	MOH		96 L2
LAKEHEAD	SHA	96051	12 N3
LAKE HENSHAW	SDCO	92070	108 G2
LAKE HILLS EST	ED	95630	34 N4
LAKE HUGHES	LACO	93532	89 G4
LAKE ISABELLA	KER	93240	79 B5
LAKE LOS ANGELES	LACO	93550	90 J1
LAKE OF THE WOODS	KER	93225	88 D5
*LAKEPORT	LAK	95453	31 G6
LAKESHORE	FRCO	93634	50 N5
LAKESHORE	SHA	96051	12 P3
LAKESIDE	SDCO	92040	106 G7
LAKESIDE PARK	LACO	91304	97 A1
LAKE TAMARISK	RCO	92239	102 L3
*LAKEVIEW	LAKE		7 B4
LAKEVIEW	RCO	92353	99 H6
LAKEVIEW	SDCO	92040	106 H8
LAKEVIEW HOT SPRINGS	RCO	92370	99 J5
LAKEVIEW TERRACE	LACO	91340	117 C2
LAKEVILLE	SON	95452	38 J2
*LAKEWOOD	LACO	90712	119 D8
LA LOMA	STA	95354	47 E6
*LA MESA	SDCO	92041	106 K5
*LA MIRADA	LACO	90638	118 Q2
LA MISION	BAJA		112 P1
LA MOINE	SHA	96017	12 L4
LAMONT	KER	93241	78 J8
LANARE	FRCO	93656	57 Q1
*LANCASTER	LACO	93534	90 G0
LANDERS	SBD	92284	92 P8
LANGELL VALLEY	KLAM		6 E2
*LA PALMA	ORA	90623	98 H2
LA PLAYA	SDCO	92106	106 L1
LA PORTE	PLU	95981	26 H5
LA PRESA	SDCO	92077	106 L7
*LA PUENTE	LACO	91744	118 M4
*LA QUINTA	RCO	92253	100 M9
*LARKSPUR	MAR	94939	38 P2
LAS CRUCES	SB	93017	86 K7
LA SIERRA	RCO	92505	99 G0
LAS LOMAS	SON	95728	31 P3
LAS VEGAS	CLK	89114	74 E7
LATHROP	SJCO	95330	62 L7
LATON	FRCO	93242	57 Q6
LATROBE	ED	95682	40 B5
LAUGHLIN	CLK		85 K6
*LA VERNE	LACO	91750	118 J8
LAVIC	SBD	92365	92 E8
*LAWNDALE	LACO	90260	119 B3
LAYTONVILLE	MEN	95454	22 J7
LEBEC	KER	93243	88 C7
LEESVILLE	COL	95987	32 D3
LEE VINING	MNO	93541	43 N4
LEGGETT	MEN	95455	22 E5
LE GRAND	MCO	95333	48 N7

SEE PAGE D FOR INSTRUCTIONS

CITIES AND COMMUNITIES INDEX

CITIES AND COMMUNITIES INDEX

COMMUNITY NAME	CO.	ZIP CODE	PAGE & GRID
LELITER	KER	93527	70 P5
LEMONCOVE	TUL	93244	68 A7
*LEMON GROVE	SDCO	92045	106 K5
LEMON VALLEY	WSH		28 H2
*LEMOORE	KIN	93245	67 D5
LENWOOD	SBD	92311	91 B6
LEON	SBD	92392	91 J3
LEONA VALLEY	LACO	93550	89 H7
LEUCADIA	SDCO	92024	107 K3
LEWISTON	TRI	96052	17 C7
LIBERTY FARMS	SOL	95647	39 G4
LIKELY	MOD	96116	8 G2
LINCOLN	JKSN		4 D4
*LINCOLN	PLA	95648	34 J1
LINCOLN ACRES	SDCO	92050	106 M5
LINCOLN VILLAGE	SJCO	95207	40 N1
LINDA	YUB	95961	33 E6
LINDA MAR	SMCO	94044	45 G3
LINDA VISTA	SDCO	92111	106 J2
LINDCOVE	TUL	93221	68 B5
LINDEN	SJCO	95236	40 N4
*LINDSAY	TUL	93247	68 E6
LINGARD	MCO	95340	48 N5
LITCHFIELD	LAS	96117	21 J4
LITTLE BORREGO	SDCO	92004	109 J2
LITTLE LAKE	INY	93542	70 K4
LITTLE RIVER	MEN	95456	30 B4
LITTLEROCK	LACO	93543	90 B3
LITTLE SHASTA	SIS	96064	4 L4
LITTLE VALLEY	LAS	96053	14 N2
LIVE OAK	SAC	95683	40 D4
*LIVE OAK	SUT	95953	33 B5
LIVE OAK PARK	SDCO	92028	107 D5
LIVE OAK SPRINGS	SDCO	92005	112 C9
*LIVERMORE	ALA	94550	46 E3
*LIVINGSTON	MCO	95334	47 L9
LLANADA	SBT	95043	55 M6
LOCH LOMOND	LAK	95426	31 K9
LOCKE	SAC	95649	39 H7
LOCKEFORD	SJCO	95237	40 K3
LOCKWOOD	MON	93932	65 K5
LOCKWOOD VALLEY	VEN	93225	88 E5
LODGE POLE	TUL	93271	59 L2
*LODI	SJCO	95240	40 K1
LODOGA	COL	95979	32 B3
LOGAN HEIGHTS	SDCO	92113	106 M3
LOG CABIN	YUB	95922	26 N4
LOG SPRING	TEH	96074	14 M9
LOLETA	HUM	95551	15 D8
*LOMA LINDA	SBD	92354	99 E4
LOMA MAR	SMCO	94021	45 N5
LOMA PARK	KER	93306	78 G6
LOMA RICA	YUB	95901	25 Q8
*LOMITA	LACO	90717	119 E4
LOMO	BUT	95942	25 A5
*LOMPOC	SB	93436	86 G3
LONDON	TUL	93631	58 P0
LONE PINE	INY	93545	60 L1
LONG BARN	TUO	95335	41 K4
*LONG BEACH	LACO	90801	119 C7
LONGVALE	MEN	95490	22 L9
LONGVIEW	LACO	93553	90 K4
LOOKOUT	MOD	96054	14 G2
LOOMIS	PLA	95650	34 L2
LOOMIS CORNERS	SHA	96003	18 E5
LORAINE	KER	93518	79 H5
LORELLA	KLAM		6 C1
*LOS ALAMITOS	ORA	90720	98 J1
LOS ALAMOS	SB	93440	86 E5
*LOS ALTOS	SCL	94022	45 L8
*LOS ALTOS HILLS	SCL	94022	45 L7
*LOS ANGELES	LACO	90001	118 P7
*LOS BANOS	MCO	93635	55 B8
*LOS GATOS	SCL	95030	46 P0
LOS MOLINOS	TEH	96055	24 B8
LOS OLIVOS	SB	93441	86 G8
LOS OSOS	SLO	93401	75 J8
LOS SERRANOS	SBD	91710	98 F6
LOST HILLS	KER	93249	77 B6
LOTUS	ED	95651	34 L6
LOVELOCK	BUT	95978	25 D6
LOWER LAKE	LAK	95457	32 K1
*LOYALTON	SIE	96118	27 H5
LUCERNE	LAK	95458	31 F7
LUCERNE VALLEY	SBD	92356	91 L8
LUCIA	MON	93920	64 J7
LUDLOW	SBD	92357	93 F2
LUGO	SBD	92345	91 M3
LUNDY	MNO	93541	43 M3
LUNING	MIN		44 C8
*LYNWOOD	LACO	90262	119 A5
LYNWOOD HILLS	SDCO	92010	111 D7
LYONSVILLE	TEH	96075	19 L4
LYTTON	SON	95448	31 P7
MACDOEL	SIS	96058	4 J9
MADELINE	LAS	96119	8 K2
*MADERA	MAD	93637	57 E0
MADISON	YOL	95653	33 P0
MAD RIVER	TRI	95552	16 H8
MADRONE	SCL	95037	46 Q5
MAGALIA	BUT	95954	24 F5
MAGUNDEN	KER	93306	78 G8
MALAGA	FRCO	93725	57 K6
MALIBU BEACH	LACO	90265	97 E2
MALIN	KLAM		5 E8
MAMMOTH LAKES	MNO	93546	50 E7
MANCHESTER	MEN	95459	30 H5
*MANHATTAN BEACH	LACO	90266	119 B0
MANIX	SBD	92365	82 Q5
MANKAS CORNER	SOL	94533	38 G7
*MANTECA	SJCO	95336	47 B2
MANTON	TEH	96059	19 H1
MANZANITA	SDCO	92005	112 C9
MAPLE CREEK	HUM	95550	16 B3
MARCH FIELD	RCO	92508	99 G4
*MARICOPA	KER	93252	78 N0
*MARINA	MON	93933	54 K3
MARINA	SFCO	94123	45 C3
MARINA DEL REY	LACO	90291	97 F4
MARIN CITY	MAR	94965	45 A2
MARINWOOD	MAR	94903	38 M1
MARIPOSA	MPA	95338	49 H2
MARIPOSA PINES	MPA	95338	49 F3
MARKLEEVILLE	ALP	96120	36 N4
MARK WEST SPRINGS	SON	95492	37 B9
MARSHALL STATION	FRCO	93651	57 D8
MARTELL	AMA	95654	40 F8
*MARTINEZ	CC	94553	38 N7
MARTINS FERRY	HUM	95556	10 G4
MAR VISTA	LACO	90066	117 M0
*MARYSVILLE	YUB	95901	33 E6
MASONIC	MNO	93517	43 E4
MATHER	TUO	95339	42 Q3
MAXWELL	COL	95955	32 C6
MAYFAIR	KER	93307	78 H8
*MAYWOOD	LACO	90270	97 F8
MCARTHUR	SHA	96056	13 K8
MCCANN	HUM	95569	16 K3
MCCAULEY	MPA	95318	49 D4
MCCLOUD	SIS	96057	12 F7
*MCFARLAND	KER	93250	78 A3
MCKAYS POINT	TUL	93286	58 Q6
MCKEE BRIDGE	JKSN		3 C4
MCKINLEYVILLE	HUM	95521	10 M0
MCKITTRICK	KER	93251	77 H6
MCMULLIN	FRE	73706	57 K2
MEADOW LAKES	FRCO	93602	58 B1
MEADOW VALLEY	PLU	95956	26 D3
MEADOW VISTA	PLA	95722	34 H4
MECCA	RCO	92254	101 P3
MEEKS BAY	ED	95723	35 G8
MEINERS OAKS	VEN	93023	88 L1
MELOLAND	IMP	92243	114 A2
MENDOCINO	MEN	95460	30 B2
MENDOCINO COAST	MEN	95459	30 G5
*MENDOTA	FRCO	93640	56 J6
*MENLO PARK	SMCO	94025	45 J8
MENTONE	SBD	92359	99 D6
*MERCED	MCO	95340	48 M3
MERCED FALLS	MCO	95369	48 H6
MERCY HOT SPRINGS	FRCO	95043	55 K8
MERIDIAN	SUT	95957	33 E2
*MERRILL	KLAM		5 E6
MESA GRANDE	SDCO	92070	108 H2
MESAVILLE	RCO	92255	103 M5
MESQUITE SPRING	INY	92328	61 D2
METTLER	KER	93301	78 N7
MEXICALI	BAJA		114 D3
MEYERS	ED	95731	36 K1
MICHIGAN BLUFF	PLA	95631	35 G0
MIDDLE RIVER	SJCO	95234	39 P7
MIDDLETOWN	LAK	95461	32 N1
MIDLAND	KLAM		5 C3
MIDLAND	RCO	92255	103 H2
MIDPINES	MPA	95345	49 G2
MIDWAY	ALA	94550	46 D6
MIDWAY	SHA	96088	19 F0
MILFORD	LAS	96121	21 N4
*MILLBRAE	SMCO	94030	45 G4
MILL CREEK	TEH	96061	19 K6
MILL CREEK PARK	SBD	92359	99 C8
MILLIGAN	SBD	92280	94 P7
MILLS	SAC	95670	40 B1
MILLS ORCHARDS	COL	95955	32 C5
*MILL VALLEY	MAR	94942	38 Q2
MILLVILLE	SHA	96062	18 F6
MILO	TUL	93265	68 E9
*MILPITAS	SCL	95035	46 K1
MILTON	CAL	95230	40 M8
MINA	MIN		44 E9
MINDEN	DGL		36 H4
MINERAL	TEH	96063	19 K5
MINERAL KING	TUL	93271	59 P3
MINKLER	FRCO	93657	58 J0
MINNEOLA	SBD	92327	92 C2
MINNESOTA	SHA	96001	18 D3
MINTER VILLAGE	KER	93301	78 E4
MIRABEL PARK	SON	95436	37 D7
MIRACLE HOT SPRINGS	KER	93288	79 C4
MIRA LOMA	RCO	91752	98 E9
MIRAMAR	SDCO	92145	107 N6
MIRAMAR	SMCO	94019	45 J3
MIRA MESA	SDCO	92126	106 F3
MIRA MONTE	VEN	93023	88 L1
MIRAMONTE	FRCO	93641	58 J5
MIRANDA	HUM	95553	16 M4
MIRA VISTA	LAK	95461	31 M9
MISSION BEACH	SDCO	92109	106 J0
MISSION HIGHLANDS	SON	95476	38 G3
MISSION HILLS	SDCO	92103	106 J3
MISSION SAN JOSE	ALA	94538	46 H2
MISSION VIEJO	ORA	92675	98 N7
MISSION VILLAGE	SDCO	92123	107 Q6
MITCHELL MILL	CAL	95255	41 F3
MI-WUK VILLAGE	TUO	95346	41 M8
MOCCASIN	TUO	95347	48 B5
*MODESTO	STA	95350	47 F6
MODJESKA	ORA	92705	98 L8
MOJAVE	KER	93501	80 N0
MOKELUMNE HILL	CAL	95245	40 G9
MONMOUTH	FRCO	93725	57 M5
MONO CAMP	MPA	95338	49 G3
MONO CITY	MNO	93541	43 M4
MONO HOT SPRINGS	FRCO	93642	50 L6
MONO LAKE	MNO	93541	43 N4
MONOLITH	KER	93548	79 M7
MONO VISTA	TUO	95370	41 N6
*MONROVIA	LACO	91016	118 G3
MONSON	TUL	93618	58 P1
*MONTAGUE	SIS	96064	4 L2
MONTALVO	VEN	93003	88 Q3
MONTARA	SMCO	94037	45 H3
*MONTCLAIR	SBD	91763	98 D6
*MONTEBELLO	LACO	90640	118 M0
MONTECITO	SB	93108	87 L6
*MONTEREY	MON	93940	54 M2
MONTEREY HILLS	LACO	90032	117 J7
*MONTEREY PARK	LACO	91754	118 K0
MONTE RIO	SON	95462	37 D5
MONTESANO	SON	95462	37 D4
*MONTE SERENO	SCL	95030	45 P8
MONTEZUMA	SOL	94512	39 K2
MONTGOMERY CREEK	SHA	96065	13 P1
MONTROSE	LACO	91020	117 H5
MOONRIDGE	SBD	92315	92 Q1
MOONSTONE	HUM	95570	9 L9
MOORE	SBD	92364	84 G6
MOORPARK	VEN	93021	88 P7
MOORPARK HOME ACRES	VEN	93021	88 Q7
*MORAGA	CC	94556	45 B8
MORENA	SDCO	92110	112 C6
MORENA	SDCO	92006	112 C6
MORENO	RCO	92360	99 G6
MORENO	SDCO	92040	106 G8
MORETTIS	SDCO	92070	108 G3
*MORGAN HILL	SCL	95037	54 B5
MORMON BAR	MPA	95338	49 J2
MORONGO VALLEY	SBD	92256	100 D4
*MORRO BAY	SLO	93442	75 G8
MOSS BEACH	SMCO	94038	45 H3
MOSS LANDING	MON	95036	54 H2
MOUNTAIN CENTER	RCO	92361	100 L3
MOUNTAIN GATE	SHA	96003	18 C5
MOUNTAIN MESA	KER	93240	79 B6
MOUNTAIN RANCH	CAL	95246	41 H3
MOUNTAIN REST	FRCO	93667	58 C2
MOUNTAIN SPRINGS	CLK		74 J1
MOUNTAIN VIEW	RCO	92509	99 E1
*MOUNTAIN VIEW	SCL	94040	45 K8
MOUNT AUKUM	ED	95656	41 B0
MOUNT BALDY	SBD	91759	90 Q8
MOUNT BULLION	MPA	95338	49 H1
MOUNT HEBRON	SIS	96066	5 K0
MOUNT HELIX	SDCO	92041	106 K6
MOUNT HERMAN	SCR	95041	54 C0
MOUNT LAGUNA	SDCO	92048	108 N8
*MOUNT SHASTA	SIS	96067	12 C5
MOUNT SIGNAL	IMP	92231	114 D0
MT VIEW	JKSN		4 C4
MOUNT WILSON	LACO	91023	118 E1
MUGGINSVILLE	SIS	96032	3 P5
MUIR BEACH	MAR	94965	45 B1
MULFORD GARDENS	ALA	94577	35 J7
MURPHYS	CAL	95247	41 K4
MURPHYS RANCH	CAL	95247	41 K4
MURRIETA	RCO	92362	99 P4
MURRIETA HOT SPRINGS	RCO	92362	99 P5
MUSCOY	SBD	92405	99 B3
MYERS FLAT	HUM	95554	16 M3
MYOMA	RCO	92201	101 L0
NAIRN	MCO	95340	48 L3
NANCEVILLE	TUL	93257	68 G6
*NAPA	NAPA	94558	38 H6
NAPLES	LACO	90803	119 G8
NAPLES	SB	93117	87 L1
NASHVILLE	ED	95675	40 B8
*NATIONAL CITY	SDCO	92050	106 M5
NATOMA	SAC	95630	34 Q3
NAVARRO	MEN	95463	30 E7
NAVELENCIA	FRCO	93654	58 K0
NEED	SAC	95632	40 G1
*NEEDLES	SBD	92363	95 D6
NEENACH	LACO	93534	89 E2
NELSON	BUT	95958	25 L4
NESTOR	SDCO	92154	106 Q4
*NEVADA CITY	NEV	95959	33 B4
NEW ALMADEN	SCL	95042	46 P2
*NEWARK	ALA	94560	45 H9
NEW AUBERRY	FRCO	93602	57 B9
NEWBERRY SPRINGS	SBD	92365	92 D2
NEWBURY PARK	VEN	91320	105 B7
NEWCASTLE	PLA	95658	34 K3
NEW CUYAMA	SB	93214	87 A5
NEW DUNN	SBD	92309	82 N7
NEWELL	MOD	96134	5 H9
NEWHALL	LACO	91321	89 N3
NEWHALL RANCH	LACO	91355	89 L2
NEW IDAHO	LAKE		7 A3
NEW IDRIA	SBT	95027	66 A3
*NEWMAN	STA	95360	47 M5
NEW PINE CREEK	MOD	97635	7 F5
*NEWPORT BEACH	ORA	92660	98 N3
NEWTOWN	ED	95709	35 N0
NEWVILLE	GLE	95963	24 G1
NICASIO	MAR	94946	37 M9
NICE	LAK	95464	31 F7
NICHOLLS WARM SPRINGS	RCO	92225	103 N4
NICOLAUS	SUT	95659	33 K6
NILAND	IMP	92257	110 F1
NIPINNAWASSEE	MAD	93601	49 K5
NIPOMO	SLO	93444	76 P4
NIPTON	SBD	92364	84 E5
NOB HILL	SFCO	94108	45 D4
*NORCO	RCO	91760	98 G8
NORD	BUT	95926	25 G1
NORDEN	NEV	95724	27 Q4
NORMAN	GLE	95988	24 P6
NORTH BEACH	SFCO	94133	45 C3
NORTH BLOOMFIELD	NEV	95959	26 P6
NORTH COLUMBIA	NEV	95959	26 P5
NORTH EDWARDS	KER	93523	80 P6
NORTH FORK	MAD	93643	49 N8
NORTH HIGHLANDS	SAC	95660	34 N0
NORTH HOLLYWOOD	LACO	91601	97 B5
NORTH JAMUL	SDCO	92035	112 B1
NORTH LAS VEGAS	CLK		74 E7
NORTH RICHMOND	CC	94807	38 N4
NORTHRIDGE	LACO	91324	97 A4
NORTH SAN JUAN	NEV	95960	26 P4
NORTH SHORE	RCO	92254	101 Q6
NORTHSTAR	PLA	95732	35 B9
NORTHWOOD	SON	95462	37 D5
NORTON AFB	SBD	92409	99 C4
*NORWALK	LACO	90650	118 Q1
*NOVATO	MAR	94947	38 L2
NOYO	MEN	95437	22 P3
NUBIEBER	LAS	96068	14 J2
NUEVO	RCO	92367	99 J6
NYELAND	VEN	93030	88 Q4
*OAKDALE	STA	95361	47 C7
OAK GLEN	SBD	92399	99 D9
OAK GROVE VALLEY	SDCO	92086	108 C2
OAKGROVE	TUL	93271	59 P1
OAKHURST	MAD	93644	49 L6
*OAKLAND	ALA	94601	45 C5
OAKLEY	CC	94561	39 N5
OAK RUN	SHA	96069	18 C9
OAK VIEW	VEN	93022	88 M1
OAKVILLE	NAPA	94562	38 E3
OASIS	RCO	92274	109 B3
OATMAN	MOH		85 P9
OBRIEN	JOS		2 D4
OBRIEN	SHA	96070	12 Q5
OCCIDENTAL	SON	95465	37 E5
OCEAN BEACH	SDCO	92107	106 K0
OCEANO	SLO	93445	76 N2
*OCEANSIDE	SDCO	92054	107 G1
OCEAN VIEW	SON	95450	37 E4
OCOTILLO	IMP	92259	113 B4
OCOTILLO WELLS	SDCO	92004	109 H2
OGILBY	IMP	92222	115 A3
OILDALE	KER	93308	78 F6
*OJAI	VEN	93023	88 L2
OLANCHA	INY	93549	70 C3
OLD BOULEVARD	SDCO	92005	113 D0
OLD RIVER	KER	93307	78 J5
OLD STATION	SHA	96071	19 C7
OLD TOWN	KER	93561	79 M5
OLD TOWN	LAS	96137	20 K5
OLEMA	MAR	94950	37 M8
OLENE	KLAM		5 B5
OLINDA	ORA	92621	118 Q7
OLINDA	SHA	96007	18 H4
OLINGHOUSE	WSH		28 J8
OLIVEHURST	YUB	95961	33 F7
OLIVENHAIN	SDCO	92024	107 K4
OLIVE VIEW	LACO	91342	117 A0
OMO RANCH	ED	95661	41 B2
O'NEALS	MAD	93645	57 A6
ONO	SHA	96072	18 G1
*ONTARIO	SBD	91761	98 D7
ONYX	KER	93255	79 A8
OPHIR	PLA	95603	34 K3
*ORANGE	ORA	92666	118 P7
*ORANGE COVE	FRCO	93646	58 L2
ORANGEVALE	SAC	95662	34 P2
ORCHARD SHORES	LAK	95423	32 G0
ORDBEND	GLE	95943	25 J0
OREGON HOUSE	YUB	95962	26 Q1
ORICK	HUM	95555	10 F0
ORINDA	CC	94563	38 Q7
ORINDA VILLAGE	CC	94563	38 Q7
*ORLAND	GLE	95963	24 G7
ORLEANS	HUM	95556	10 E6
ORO FINO	SIS	96032	3 P6
ORO GRANDE	SBD	92368	91 H3
ORO LOMA	FRCO	93622	56 E1
OROSI	TUL	93647	58 M3
*OROVILLE	BUT	95965	25 M6
ORR SPRINGS	MEN	95482	31 C0
OTAY	SDCO	92011	106 P5
OUTINGDALE	ED	95684	34 Q9
OWL	RCO	92220	100 G1
*OXNARD	VEN	93030	105 B3
PACHECO	CC	94553	38 N8
PACHUCO	BAJA		115 D2
*PACIFICA	SMCO	94044	45 F2
PACIFIC BEACH	SDCO	92109	106 J0
*PACIFIC GROVE	MON	93950	54 L1
PACIFIC HEIGHTS	SFCO	94115	45 C3
PACIFIC HOUSE	ED	95725	35 M3
PACOIMA	LACO	91331	97 A5
PAHRUMP	NYE		73 E4
PAICINES	SBT	95043	55 J2
PAINTERSVILLE	SAC	95615	39 G7
PAJARO	MON	95076	54 F4
PALA	SDCO	92059	107 D7
PALA MESA VILLAGE	SDCO	92028	107 E6
PALERMO	BUT	95968	25 N6
PALM CITY	SDCO	92154	106 P4
*PALMDALE	LACO	93550	91 J0
PALMDALE EAST	LACO	93550	90 H1
*PALM DESERT	RCO	92260	100 L7
PALMS	LACO	90034	117 M2
*PALM SPRINGS	RCO	92262	100 J6
*PALO ALTO	SCL	94301	45 K7
PALO CEDRO	SHA	96073	18 E6
PALOMA	CAL	95252	40 H9
PALOMAR MOUNTAIN	SDCO	92060	108 E0
*PALOS VERDES ESTATES	LACO	90274	119 E0
PALO VERDE	IMP	92266	116 C5
PALO VERDE	SDCO	92001	108 Q2
PANAMA	KER	93309	78 J5
PANAMINT SPRINGS	INY	93545	71 B1
PANOCHE	SBT	95043	55 M7
PANORAMA CITY	LACO	91402	117 E0
*PARADISE	BUT	95969	25 G5
PARADISE CAY	MAR	94920	38 Q3
PARADISE VALLEY	SCL	95037	54 B4
PARAISO SPRINGS	MON	93960	64 C9
*PARAMOUNT	LACO	90723	119 B8
PARKER DAM	SBD	92267	104 C2
PARKFIELD	MON	93451	66 L5
PARK	CAL	95247	41 L3
PARKER	LPAZ		104 C3
PARK VILLAGE	INY	93328	62 N0
*PARLIER	FRCO	93648	57 L9
*PASADENA	LACO	91101	98 C0
PASKENTA	TEH	96074	24 E2
PASO PICACHO	SDCO	92036	108 M5
*PASO ROBLES	SLO	93446	76 C1
PATRICK CREEK	DN	95543	2 H3
*PATTERSON	STA	95363	47 J3
PATTON	SBD	92346	99 C4
PATTON VILLAGE	LAS	96113	21 N7
PAUMA VALLEY	SDCO	92061	107 E8
PAYNES CREEK	TEH	96075	19 K1
PAYNESVILLE	ALP	96120	36 L3
PEANUT	TRI	96041	17 G3
PEARBLOSSOM	LACO	93553	90 K3
PEARDALE	NEV	95945	34 D3
PEARLAND	LACO	93550	90 J2
PEARSON	INY	93542	70 N4
PEBBLE BEACH	MON	93953	54 M0
PECWAN	HUM	95546	10 D3
PEDLEY	RCO	92509	98 F9
PELICAN CITY	KLAM		5 A3
PENNGROVE	SON	94951	38 G0
PENNINGTON	SUT	95953	33 B3
PENTZ	BUT	95965	25 J6
PEPPERWOOD	HUM	95565	16 H1
PERKINS	SAC	95826	39 C9
*PERRIS	RCO	92370	99 K5
PESCADERO	SMCO	94060	45 N4
*PETALUMA	SON	94952	38 J1
PETER PAM	TUO	95335	41 K9
PETERS	SJCO	95236	40 N5
PETROLIA	HUM	95558	15 K6
PHELAN	SBD	92371	91 L0
PHILLIPS	ED	95735	35 L9
PHILLIPS RANCH	LACO	91766	98 E5
PHILLIPSVILLE	HUM	95558	16 N3
PHILO	MEN	95466	30 G8
PICACHO	IMP	92222	116 L6
*PICO RIVERA	LACO	90660	118 M0
*PIEDMONT	ALA	94611	45 C7
PIERCY	MEN	95467	22 C4
PIKE	SIE	95922	26 N5
PILOT HILL	ED	95664	34 L5
PINE COVE	RCO	92349	100 K2
PINECREST	TUO	95364	42 J1
PINEDALE	FRCO	93650	57 G4
PINE FLAT	TUL	93207	69 L3
PINE GROVE	AMA	95665	41 E1
PINE GROVE	LAK	95426	31 L9
PINE GROVE	MEN	95460	30 A2
PINE GROVE	SHA	96003	18 D5
PINE HILLS	SDCO	92036	108 K4
PINEHURST	FRCO	93641	58 J6
PINEHURST	JKSN		4 C4
PINELAND	PLA	95718	35 E8
PINE MEADOW	RCO	92361	100 N4
PINE MOUNTAIN CLUB	KER	93225	88 C3
PINE RIDGE	FRCO	93602	58 B2
PINE VALLEY	SDCO	92062	108 P6
PINNACLE	SBD	93562	81 B2
PINO GRANDE	ED	95634	35 K1
*PINOLE	CC	94564	38 N5
PINON PINES	KER	93225	88 C5
PINYON PINES	RCO	92361	100 N7
PIONEER	SAC	95666	40 E1
PIONEER	AMA	95666	41 E2
PIONEERTOWN	SBD	92268	100 C6
PIRU	VEN	93040	88 M8
PISGAH	SBD	92365	92 E8
*PISMO BEACH	SLO	93449	76 L2
*PITTSBURG	CC	94565	39 N1
PITTVILLE	SHA	96056	13 K9
PIXLEY	TUL	93256	68 K3
*PLACENTIA	ORA	92670	98 H4
*PLACERVILLE	ED	95667	34 N8
PLAINSBURG	MCO	95333	48 N6
PLAINVIEW	TUL	93267	68 F4
PLANADA	MCO	95365	48 M6
PLASSE	AMA	95666	35 P8
PLASTER CITY	IMP	92269	109 Q6
PLATINA	SHA	96076	17 J6
PLAYA DEL REY	LACO	90291	97 F4
PLEASANT GROVE	SUT	95668	33 L7
*PLEASANT HILL	CC	94523	38 P8
*PLEASANTON	ALA	94566	46 F2
PLEASANT VALLEY	ED	95709	35 P0
*PLYMOUTH	AMA	95669	40 D7
*POINT ARENA	MEN	95468	30 K5
POINT LOMA	SDCO	92106	106 L0
POINT PLEASANT	SAC	95624	39 G8
POINT REYES STATION	MAR	94956	37 M7
POLLARD FLAT	SHA	96017	12 L4
POLLOCK PINES	ED	95726	35 M1
POLVORA	BAJA		114 F7
POMINS	ED	95733	35 F8
POMO	MEN	95469	31 B4
*POMONA	LACO	91766	118 L9
POND	KER	93280	68 P2
PONDEROSA	TUL	93208	69 G4
PONDEROSA BASIN	MPA	95338	49 J5
PONDOSA	SIS	96077	13 G4
POPE VALLEY	NAPA	94567	32 Q4
POPLAR	TUL	93257	68 H5
PORT COSTA	CC	94569	38 M7
*PORTERVILLE	TUL	93257	68 H7
*PORT HUENEME	VEN	93041	105 C3
*PORTOLA	PLU	96122	27 F3
*PORTOLA VALLEY	SMCO	94025	45 L6
POSEY	TUL	93260	69 N2
POSTON	LPAZ		104 F1
POSTON 2	LPAZ		104 G0
POT HOLES	IMP	92222	115 B6
POTRERO	SDCO	92063	112 E5
POTTER VALLEY	MEN	95469	31 B3
*POWAY	SDCO	92064	107 M7
POZO	SLO	93453	76 J4
PRATHER	FRCO	93651	57 C8
PRATTVILLE	PLU	95923	20 M3
PRESIDIO HEIGHTS	SFCO	94118	45 C3
PRESTON	SON	95425	31 L5
PRIEST	TUO	95305	48 B7
PRINCETON	COL	95970	25 P0
PRINCETON BY THE SEA	SMCO	94018	45 J2
PROBERTA	TEH	96078	24 A7
PROGRESO	BAJA		114 E1
PROJECT CITY	SHA	96079	18 C4
PRUNEDALE	MON	93901	54 H5
PUERTA LA CRUZ	SDCO	92086	108 E3
PULGA	BUT	95965	25 F7
PUMPKIN CENTER	KER	93309	78 J6
QUAIL VALLEY	RCO	92380	99 L4
QUAKING ASPEN	TUL	93208	69 G4
QUARTZSITE	LPAZ		104 M2
QUINCY	PLU	95971	26 D5
QUINCY JUNCTION	PLU	95971	26 D5
RACKERBY	YUB	95972	25 N9
RAILROAD FLAT	CAL	95248	41 F2
RAINBOW	SDCO	92028	107 C6
RAISIN CITY	FRCO	93652	57 L2
RAMONA	SDCO	92065	108 K1
RAMSEY	LPAZ		104 M7
RANCHITA	SDCO	92066	108 G6
RANCHO BERNARDO	SDCO	92128	107 L7
RANCHO CALIFORNIA	RCO	92390	99 Q6
RANCHO CORDOVA	SAC	95670	40 B1
*RANCHO CUCAMONGA	SBD	91730	98 C8
*RANCHO MIRAGE	RCO	92270	100 K7
*RANCHO PALOS VERDES	LACO	90274	119 G2
RANCHO PENASQUITOS	SDCO	92129	107 L6
RANCHO SAN DIEGO	SDCO	92077	106 L7
RANCHO SANTA CLARITA	LACO	91350	89 L3
RANCHO SANTA FE	SDCO	92067	107 L5
RANDOLF	SIE	96126	27 K4
RANDSBURG	KER	93554	80 G7
RAVENDALE	LAS	96123	8 Q4
RAYMOND	MAD	93653	49 P2
RED APPLE	CAL	95224	41 J5
RED BANK	TEH	96080	24 A3
*RED BLUFF	TEH	96080	18 H5
REDCREST	HUM	95569	16 J1
*REDDING	SHA	96001	18 F4
*REDLANDS	SBD	92373	99 D4
RED MOUNTAIN	SBD	93558	80 G9
*REDONDO BEACH	LACO	90277	119 D0
REDWAY	HUM	95560	16 P3
*REDWOOD CITY	SMCO	94061	45 J6
REDWOOD ESTATES	SCL	95044	46 Q0
REDWOOD PARK	SMCO	94062	45 K4
REDWOOD VALLEY	MEN	95470	31 C2
*REEDLEY	FRCO	93654	58 L0
RENO	WSH		28 L2
REPRESA	SAC	95671	34 P3
REQUA	DN	95561	1 Q9
RESCUE	ED	95672	34 N5
RESEDA	LACO	91335	97 B4
REWARD	INY	93526	60 H2
*RIALTO	SBD	92376	99 D2
RICARDO	KER	93519	80 G3
RICE	SBD	92280	103 D3
RICHARDSON SPRINGS	BUT	95978	25 F3
RICH BAR	PLU	95915	26 E2
RICHFIELD	TEH	96083	24 C7
RICHGROVE	TUL	93261	68 N5
*RICHMOND	CC	94801	38 P4
RICHMOND	SFCO	94121	45 C4
RICHVALE	BUT	95974	25 M4

CITIES AND COMMUNITIES INDEX

SEE PAGE D FOR INSTRUCTIONS

CITIES AND COMMUNITIES INDEX

COMMUNITY NAME	CO.	ZIP CODE	PAGE & GRID
*RIDGECREST	KER	93555	80 B7
RIITO	SNRA		115 N1
RIMFOREST	SBD	92378	99 A5
RINCON	SDCO	92082	107 E9
RIO BRAVO	KER	93306	78 F9
*RIO DELL	HUM	95562	15 G8
RIO DELL	SON	95486	37 D6
RIO LINDA	SAC	95673	33 P8
RIO NIDO	SON	95471	37 C5
*RIO VISTA	SOL	94571	39 K4
RIPLEY	RCO	92272	103 Q6
*RIPON	SJCO	95366	47 D3
*RIVERBANK	STA	95367	47 D7
RIVERDALE	FRCO	93656	57 Q3
RIVER KERN	KER	93238	69 N6
RIVER PINES	AMA	95675	40 B8
*RIVERSIDE	RCO	92501	99 F2
RIVERTON	ED	95725	35 M3
RIVIERA	MOH		85 M5
RIVIERA HEIGHTS	LAK	95443	31 H7
RIVIERA WEST	LAK	95422	31 H8
ROADS END	TUL	93236	69 K5
ROBBINS	SUT	95676	33 K5
ROBINSONS CORNER	BUT	95948	25 Q5
ROBLA	SAC	95673	33 P8
ROCKAWAY BEACH	SMCO	94044	45 F2
ROCK HAVEN	SDCO	92065	107 L8
*ROCKLIN	PLA	95677	34 M1
ROCKPORT	MEN	95488	22 G3
ROCKVILLE	SOL	94585	38 H8
ROGERS LANDING	MOH		85 M6
*ROHNERT PARK	SON	94928	38 G0
ROHNERVILLE	HUM	95540	15 F9
ROLANDS	SON	95446	37 D5
ROLINDA	FRCO	93705	57 H2
*ROLLING HILLS	LACO	90274	119 G2
*ROLLING HILLS ESTATES	LACO	90274	119 F2
ROMOLAND	RCO	92380	99 L5
ROSAMOND	KER	93560	90 C0
ROSARITO	BAJA		111 L7
ROSEDALE	KER	93308	78 G4
*ROSEMEAD	LACO	91770	118 J0
ROSEMONT	SDCO	92065	107 L9
*ROSEVILLE	PLA	95678	34 M1
ROSEVILLE	SDCO	92106	106 L1
ROSEWOOD	TEH	96022	18 L2
*ROSS	MAR	94957	38 P1
ROUGH AND READY	NEV	95975	34 C3
ROUND MOUNTAIN	SHA	96084	13 Q1
ROVANA	INY	93514	51 J3
ROWLAND HEIGHTS	LACO	91745	118 N5
RUBIDOUX	RCO	92509	99 E1
RUCH	JKSN		3 A4
RUMSEY	YOL	95679	32 K5
RUNNING SPRINGS	SBD	92382	99 B6
RUSSIAN HILL	SFCO	94133	45 C3
RUTH	TRI	95526	17 L1
RUTHERFORD	NAPA	94573	38 D3
RYDE	SAC	95680	39 J6
SABLON	SBD	92280	103 B1
SABRE CITY	PLA	95660	34 P0
*SACRAMENTO	SAC	95813	39 B8
*SAINT HELENA	NAPA	94574	38 D2
SALIDA	STA	95368	47 D4
*SALINAS	MON	93901	54 K4
SALMON CREEK	SON	94923	37 F4
SALT CREEK LODGE	SHA	96051	12 P5
SALTDALE	KER	93519	80 G4
SALTMARSH	SBD	92280	103 A0
SALTON	RCO	92257	109 B6
SALTON CITY	IMP	92274	109 F5
SALTON SEA BEACH	IMP	92274	109 D4
*SALVADOR	NAPA	94558	38 G4
SALTUS	SBD	92304	93 J8
SALYER	TRI	95563	10 N7
SAMOA	HUM	95560	9 Q7
SAN ANDREAS	CAL	95249	41 J1
*SAN ANSELMO	MAR	94960	38 P1
SAN ARDO	MON	93450	65 J7
SAN BENITO	SBT	95023	55 P5
*SAN BERNARDINO	SBD	92402	99 C4
SANBORN	KER	93501	80 P1
*SAN BRUNO	SMCO	94066	45 F4
SAN CARLOS	SDCO	92119	111 A7
*SAN CARLOS	SMCO	94070	45 J6
*SAN CLEMENTE	ORA	92672	106 B7
SANDBERG	LACO	93532	89 F1
*SAND CITY	MON	93955	54 L3
*SAN DIEGO	SDCO	92101	106 K3
SAN DIEGO COUNTRY EST	SDCO	92065	108 L2
*SAN DIMAS	LACO	91773	118 J8
SANDS	SBD	92309	83 P5
SANDY	CLK		74 N0
SAN FELIPE	SDCO	92086	108 G5
*SAN FERNANDO	LACO	91341	117 C1
*SAN FRANCISCO	SFCO	94101	45 C3
*SAN GABRIEL	LACO	91776	118 J0
*SANGER	FRCO	93657	57 J7
SAN GERONIMO	MAR	94963	38 N0
SAN GORGONIO	RCO	92282	100 G3
SAN GREGORIO	SMCO	94074	45 M4
*SAN JACINTO	RCO	92383	99 J9
*SAN JOAQUIN	FRCO	93660	56 M8
*SAN JOSE	SCL	95103	46 M2
*SAN JUAN BAUTISTA	SBT	95045	54 G7
*SAN JUAN CAPISTRNO	ORA	92675	98 Q6
*SAN LEANDRO	ALA	94577	45 D7
SAN LORENZO	ALA	94580	45 E7
SAN LUCAS	MON	93954	65 G6
SAN LUIS	SONR		115 G4
SAN LUIS	YUMA		115 G4
*SAN LUIS OBISPO	SLO	93401	76 H2
SAN LUIS REY	SDCO	92068	107 G3
SAN LUIS REY HEIGHTS	SDCO	92028	107 E4
*SAN MARCOS	SDCO	92069	107 H4
*SAN MARINO	LACO	91108	118 H0
SAN MARTIN	SCL	95046	54 C5
*SAN MATEO	SMCO	94401	45 G5
SAN MIGUEL	SLO	93451	66 P0
SAN ONOFRE	SDCO	92672	106 D9
*SAN PABLO	CC	94806	38 P5
SAN PASQUAL	SDCO	92025	107 J8
SAN PEDRO	LACO	90731	119 H4
SAN QUENTIN	MAR	94964	38 P3
*SAN RAFAEL	MAR	94901	38 N2
SAN RAMON	CC	94583	46 D1
SAN SIMEON	SLO	93452	75 B3
*SANTA ANA	ORA	92701	98 K4
*SANTA BARBARA	SB	93101	87 L5
*SANTA CLARA	SCL	95050	46 L1
*SANTA CRUZ	SCR	95060	53 D8
*SANTA FE SPRINGS	LACO	90670	118 P1
SANTA MARGARITA	SLO	93453	76 G2
*SANTA MARIA	SB	93454	76 Q5
*SANTA MONICA	LACO	90402	97 E4
*SANTA PAULA	VEN	93060	88 N4
SANTA RITA	ALA	94566	46 E2
SANTA RITA	MON	93901	54 J5
SANTA RITA	SB	93436	86 G5
SANTA RITA PARK	MER	93660	56 C2
*SANTA ROSA	SON	95401	37 D9
SANTA SUSANA	VEN	93065	89 Q0
SANTA SUSANA PARK	VEN	93063	97 A1
SANTA VENETIA	MAR	94903	38 N2
SANTA YNEZ	SB	93460	86 H9
SANTA YNEZ RIVER TRACT	SB	93105	87 J3
SANTA YSABEL	SDCO	92070	108 J4
*SANTEE	SDCO	92071	106 H6
SAN YSIDRO	SDCO	92073	106 Q5
*SARATOGA	SCL	95070	46 N0
SATICOY	VEN	93003	88 P3
SATTLEY	SIE	96124	27 K4
SAUGUS	LACO	91350	89 M3
*SAUSALITO	MAR	94965	45 B2
SAWYERS BAR	SIS	96027	11 E3
SCALES	SIE	95981	26 K5
SCHELLVILLE	SON	95476	38 H3
SCISSORS CROSSING	SDCO	92036	108 J7
SCOTIA	HUM	95565	16 G0
SCOTT BAR	SIS	96085	3 L5
SCOTT DAM	LAK	95469	23 P3
SCOTTS CORNER	ALA	94586	46 G3
*SCOTTS VALLEY	SCR	95060	54 C0

COMMUNITY NAME	CO.	ZIP CODE	PAGE & GRID
SCOTTYS CASTLE	INY	92328	61 C3
SCRIPPS MIRAMAR RANCH	SDCO	92131	107 N6
SEACLIFF	SFCO	94121	45 C3
SEACLIFF	VEN	93001	87 N8
*SEAL BEACH	ORA	90740	119 G9
SEARCHLIGHT	CLK		85 E1
SEARCHLIGHT JCT	SBD	92332	85 Q2
SEARS POINT	SON	94952	38 K3
*SEASIDE	MON	93955	54 M3
*SEBASTOPOL	SON	95472	37 E8
SEELEY	IMP	92273	109 A9
SEIAD VALLEY	SIS	96086	3 H2
SEIGLER SPRINGS	LAK	95426	31 K9
*SELMA	FRCO	93662	57 M7
SENECA	PLU	95923	20 P4
SERENA	SB	93013	87 M7
SERENA PARK	SB	93108	87 L7
SERENE LAKES	PLA	95728	35 A5
SERENO DEL MAR	SON	94923	37 F4
SERRA MESA	SDCO	92123	106 J3
SESBANIA	BAJA		114 F5
SEVEN PINES	INY	93526	59 H8
SHADOW HILLS	LAK	95461	32 M0
SHADY DELL	SDCO	92065	107 M9
SHADY GLEN	PLA	95713	34 E6
*SHAFTER	KER	93263	78 E2
SHANDON	SLO	93461	76 B6
SHASTA	SHA	96087	18 E2
SHAVER LAKE HEIGHTS	FRCO	93664	58 B2
SHAVER LAKE POINT	FRCO	93664	50 Q2
SHEEP RANCH	CAL	95250	41 J3
SHELDON	SAC	95624	40 E1
SHELL BEACH	SLO	93449	76 M2
SHELL TRACT	SON		39 N1
SHELTER VALLEY RANCHOS	SDCO	92036	108 K7
SHERIDAN	PLA	95681	34 H0
SHERIDAN	SON	95462	37 D4
SHERMAN OAKS	LACO	91403	97 C5
SHINGLE MILL	SON	95480	31 P0
SHINGLE SPRINGS	ED	95682	34 P6
SHINGLETOWN	SHA	96088	19 G0
SHIVELY	HUM	95565	16 H2
SHORE ACRES	CC	94565	39 M0
SHOSHONE	INY	92384	72 K8
SHUMWAY	LAS	96130	21 C2
SIAM	SBD	92319	94 J3
SIERRA BROOKS	SIE	96135	27 J7
SIERRA CITY	SIE	96125	27 K0
*SIERRA MADRE	LACO	91024	118 G2
SIERRA OAKS VISTA	SAC	95825	29 G8
SIERRAVILLE	SIE	96126	27 K3
*SIGNAL HILL	LACO	90806	119 E7
SILVERADO CANYON	ORA	92676	98 K8
SILVER CITY	LYON		35 B5
SILVER CITY	TUL	93271	59 P3
SILVER FORK	ED	95728	35 M5
SILVER LAKE	LACO	90039	117 J5
SILVERPEAK	ESM		52 C7
SILVER SPRINGS	LYON		26 F8
SILVER STRAND	VEN	93030	105 C2
*SIMI VALLEY	VEN	93065	88 P9
SIMMLER	SLO	93453	77 H2
SISQUOC	SB	93454	86 C5
SITES	COL	95979	32 B5
SKAGGS SPRINGS	SON	95448	31 P4
SKIDOO	INY	92328	61 P6
SKYFOREST	SBD	92385	99 A5
SKY LONDA	SMCO	94062	45 L5
SKY VALLEY	RCO	92240	100 G8
SLEEPY HOLLOW	MAR	94960	38 N1
SLEEPY VALLEY	LACO	91350	89 K6
SLIDE INN	TUO	95335	41 L9
SLOAN	CLK		74 K5
SLOAT	PLU	96127	26 E8
SLOUGHHOUSE	SAC	95683	40 C3
SMARTVILLE	YUB	95977	34 D1
SMITHFLAT	ED	95727	34 N8
SMITH RIVER	DN	95567	1 H7
SMITH STATION	TUO	95321	49 B0
SNELLING	MCO	95369	48 H5
SOBOBA HOT SPRINGS	RCO	92383	99 J9
SODA BAY	LAK	95443	31 H7
SODA SPRINGS	NEV	95728	27 Q4
SODA SPRINGS	SON	95728	31 P1
SOLANA BEACH	SDCO	92075	107 L3
*SOLEDAD	MON	93960	55 Q0
SOLEMINT	LACO	91351	89 M5
SOLVANG	SB	93463	86 H7
SOMERSET	ED	95684	35 Q0
SOMERTON	YUMA		115 E5
SOMES BAR	SIS	95568	10 C8
SOMIS	VEN	93066	88 P5
*SONOMA	SON	95476	38 H2
*SONORA	TUO	95370	41 N5
SONORA JUNCTION	MNO	93517	42 F9
SOQUEL	SCR	95073	54 D1
SOULSBYVILLE	TUO	95372	41 N6
SOUSA CORNERS	SON	95401	37 E7
SOUTH BELRIDGE	KER	93251	77 E5
SOUTH DOS PALOS	MCO	93665	56 E1
*SOUTH EL MONTE	LACO	91733	118 K1
SOUTH FORK	MPA	95318	49 E3
*SOUTH GATE	LACO	90280	97 F8
SOUTH LAKE	KER	93283	79 B7
*SOUTH LAKE TAHOE	ED	95705	36 H1
SOUTH OROVILLE	BUT	95965	25 M7
SOUTH PARK	SON	95404	38 E0
*SOUTH PASADENA	LACO	91030	98 C0
*SOUTH SAN FRANCISCO	SMCO	94080	45 F4
SOUTH SAN GABRIEL	LACO	91770	117 K9
SOUTH TAFT	KER	93268	78 M0
SPANGLER	SBD	93562	81 D1
SPANISH CREEK	PLU	95971	26 B6
SPANISH FLAT WOODLANDS	NAPA	94558	38 C5
SPANISH RANCH	PLU	95956	26 C4
SPARKS	WSH		28 L4
SPAULDING	LAS	96130	21 E5
SPENCEVILLE	NEV	95945	34 E2
SPRECKELS	MON	93962	54 L5
SPRING GARDEN	PLU	95971	26 D8
SPRINGTOWN	ALA	94550	46 D3
SPRING VALLEY	SDCO	92077	106 K6
SPRINGVILLE	TUL	93265	68 F9
SPRINGVILLE	VEN	93010	88 Q3
SQUAW VALLEY	FRCO	93646	58 J3
SQUAW VALLEY	PLA	95730	35 C6
SQUIRREL MTN VALLEY	KER	93240	79 B6
STAFFORD	HUM	95565	16 H0
STAGE COACH	LYON		28 P9
STANDARD	TUO	95373	41 N6
STANDISH	LAS	96128	21 J3
STANFIELD HILL	YUB	95918	26 Q0
STANFORD	SCL	94305	45 K7
STANISLAUS	TUO	95247	41 K5
*STANTON	ORA	90680	98 J3
*STATELINE	WSH		36 H2
STAUFFER	VEN	93225	88 E4
STENT	TUO	95347	41 P4
STEVINSON	MCO	95374	47 M8
STEWART	CRSN		36 E4
STEWART-LENNOX	KLAM		5 B2
STEWARTS POINT	SON	95480	30 P9
STINSON BEACH	MAR	94970	38 Q0
STIRLING CITY	BUT	95978	25 D7
*STOCKTON	SJCO	95201	39 P9
STONYFORD	COL	95979	24 Q2
STOVEPIPE WELLS	INY	92328	61 L6
STRATFORD	KIN	93266	67 E4
STRATHMORE	TUL	93267	68 F5
STRAWBERRY	ED	95735	35 L7
STRAWBERRY	TUO	95375	42 J0
STRAWBERRY VALLEY	YUB	95981	26 L3
STRONGHOLD	MOD	96431	5 G8
STUDIO CITY	LACO	91604	117 H1
STYX	RIV	92255	103 H4
SUGAR LOAF	SBD	92386	92 Q1
SUGARLOAF VILLAGE	TUL	93260	69 M3
SUGAR PINE	MAD	95389	49 J7
SUGARPINE	TUO	95346	41 L7
*SUISUN CITY	SOL	94585	38 J8
SULTANA	TUL	93666	58 N1
SUMMERHOME PARK	SON	95436	37 D6
SUMMERLAND	SB	93067	87 M6

COMMUNITY NAME	CO.	ZIP CODE	PAGE & GRID
SUMMIT CITY	SHA	96089	18 C3
SUN CITY	RCO	92381	99 L5
SUNLAND	LACO	91040	97 A7
SUNNYBROOK	AMA	95640	40 F7
SUNNYMEAD	RCO	92388	99 G4
SUNNYSIDE	SDCO	92002	106 M6
SUNNYSLOPE	RCO	93656	99 E1
*SUNNYVALE	SCL	94086	46 L0
SUNNY VISTA	SDCO	92010	111 D7
SUNOL	ALA	94586	46 G2
SUNSET BEACH	ORA	90742	98 L1
SUNSET ESTATES	PLA	95678	33 L9
SUN VALLEY	LACO	91352	117 E3
SUN VALLEY	WSH		28 K3
SURF	SB	93436	86 G1
*SUSANVILLE	LAS	96130	20 H9
SUTCLIFFE	WSH		28 C5
SUTTER	SUT	95982	33 E4
*SUTTER CREEK	AMA	95685	40 F8
SWANSBORO COUNTRY	ED	95727	34 M9
SWANSEA	INY	93545	60 N4
SWEET BRIER	SHA	96017	12 H4
SWEETLAND	NEV	95959	26 Q3
SWEETWATER	LYON		43 C3
SYCAMORE	COL	95957	33 E0
SYLMAR SQUARE	LACO	91342	117 B1
*TAFT	KER	93268	78 M0
TAFT HEIGHTS	KER	93268	77 M9
TAHOE CITY	PLA	95730	35 D8
TAHOE PINES	PLA	95718	35 E7
TAHOE VILLAGE	DGL	00025	36 H2
TAHOE VISTA	PLA	95732	36 B0
TAHOMA	PLA	95733	35 F8
TAJIGUAS	SB	93017	86 L8
TAKILMA	JOS		2 E6
TALENT	JKSN		3 A7
TALMAGE	MEN	95481	31 F3
TAMARACK	CAL	95223	41 D8
TANCRED	YOL	95606	32 N7
TARZANA	LACO	91356	97 B4
TASSAJARA HOT SPRGS	MON	93924	64 E6
TAYLORSVILLE	PLU	95983	26 A7
TECATE	BAJA		112 F4
TECATE	SDCO	92080	112 E4
TECOLOTE	BAJA		115 E1
TECOPA	INY	92389	73 L0
TECOPA HOT SPRINGS	INY	92389	73 M0
*TEHACHAPI	KER	93561	79 L5
TEHACHAPI EAST	KER	93561	79 M6
*TEHAMA	TEH	96090	24 B7
TELEGRAPH CITY	CAL	95228	40 P9
TELEGRAPH HILL	SFCO	94133	45 C3
TEMECULA	RCO	92390	99 Q5
*TEMPLE CITY	LACO	91780	118 J1
TEMPLETON	SLO	93465	76 D1
TENNANT	SIS	96012	5 P1
TERMINOUS	SJCO	95240	39 L8
TERMO	LAS	96132	8 P3
TERRA BELLA	TUL	93270	68 J6
THE HIGHLANDS	SMCO	94402	45 H4
THE ISTHMUS	LACO	90704	105 N7
THE NARROWS	SDCO	92004	109 H0
THERMAL	RCO	92274	101 N2
THERMALANDS	PLA	95648	34 G2
THE WILLOWS	SDCO	92001	108 P3
THISBE	WSH		28 K8
THOMPSON	LACO	91351	89 M4
THORN	HUM	95489	22 B2
THORNE	MIN		44 A2
THORNTON	SJCO	95686	39 J9
*THOUSAND OAKS	VEN	91360	105 B8
THOUSAND PALMS	RCO	92276	100 J8
THREE ARCH BAY	ORA	92677	98 Q6
THREE POINT	LACO	93532	89 F3
THREE RIVERS	TUL	93271	58 Q8
*TIBURON	MAR	94920	38 Q3
TIERRA DEL SOL	SDCO	92005	112 D9
TIERRASANTA	SDCO	92124	106 H4
TIJUANA	BAJA		111 F7
TIMBER COVE	SON	95450	37 C1
TIMBER LODGE	MPA	95345	49 G2
TIPTON	TUL	93272	68 H2
TISDALE	SUT	95957	33 G3
TOBIN	PLU	95965	26 C1
TOLLHOUSE	FRCO	93667	58 D3
TOMALES	MAR	94971	37 J6
TOOMY	SBD	92365	92 B3
TOPANGA	LACO	90290	97 D3
TOPANGA PARK	LACO	90290	97 C2
TOPAZ	MNO	96133	36 Q7
TOPOCK	MOH		96 F0
*TORRANCE	LACO	90505	119 D3
TOWN & COUNTRY VILLAGE	SAC	95821	39 A9
TOWER HOUSE	SHA	96095	18 D1
TOYON	SHA	96019	18 C4
TRABUCO OAKS	ORA	92678	98 M8
*TRACY	SJCO	95376	46 D8
TRAIL PARK	ED	95651	34 M7
TRANQUILLITY	FRCO	93668	56 L7
TRAVER	TUL	93673	57 P9
TRAVIS AIR FORCE BASE	SOL	94535	39 H1
TRES PINOS	SBT	95075	55 H1
*TRINIDAD	HUM	95570	9 K9
TRINITY CENTER	TRI	96091	11 L8
TRIUNFO	VEN	91362	105 C7
TRONA	SBD	93562	71 N2
TROPICO	KER	93560	89 E0
TROWBRIDGE	SUT	95659	33 J7
TROY	PLA	95728	27 Q3
TRUCKEE	NEV	95734	27 Q6
TUDOR	SUT	95991	33 H5
TUJUNGA	LACO	91042	117 D5
*TULARE	TUL	93274	68 E1
*TULELAKE	SIS	96134	5 G7
TUOLUMNE	TUO	95379	41 N7
TUOLUMNE MEADOWS	TUO	95379	43 Q1
TUPMAN	KER	93276	78 H2
*TURLOCK	STA	95380	47 J8
TURTLE ROCK	ORA	92715	98 M5
*TUSTIN	ORA	92680	98 K5
TUTTLE	MCO	95340	48 M6
TWAIN	PLU	95984	26 B3
TWAIN HARTE	TUO	95383	41 M7
TWAIN HARTE VALLEY	TUO	95383	41 M7
TWENTYNINE PALMS	SBD	92277	101 B3
TWENTY-TWO MILE HOUSE	MAD	93614	57 C5
TWIN BRIDGES	ED	95735	35 L8
TWIN CITIES	SAC	95632	40 G0
TWIN OAKS	SDCO	92083	107 H5
TWIN PEAKS	SBD	92391	91 P4
TYNDALL LANDING	YOL	95698	33 K2
*UKIAH	MEN	95482	31 E2
ULTRA	TUL	93256	68 K6
*UNION CITY	ALA	94587	46 F0
UNIVERSAL CITY	LACO	91608	97 C6
UNIVERSITY CITY	SDCO	92122	106 G0
*UPLAND	SBD	91786	98 D7
UPPER LAKE	LAK	95485	31 E6
VACATION BEACH	SON	95446	37 D4
*VACAVILLE	SOL	95688	39 F1
VALERIE	RCO	92274	101 P1
VALINDA	LACO	91744	118 L4
VALLECITO	CAL	95251	41 L4
VALLECITO	SDCO	92036	108 L9
*VALLEJO	SOL	94590	38 L6
VALLEJO HEIGHTS	SOL	94590	38 L6
VALLEY ACRES	KER	93268	78 K1
VALLEY CENTER	SDCO	92082	107 F8
VALLEY HOME	STA	95384	47 B7
VALLEY OF ENCHANTMENT	SBD	92322	91 Q2
VALLEY SPRINGS	CAL	95252	40 J8
VALLEY WELLS	INY	92366	71 M4
VAL VERDE	RCO	92370	99 H4
VAL VERDE PARK	LACO	91350	89 L1
VAN NUYS	LACO	91408	97 B5
VENICE	LACO	90291	97 F4
VENTUCOPA	SB	93252	87 C8
VEN-TU PARK	VEN	91320	105 B6
*VENTURA	VEN	93001	88 Q2
VERDEMONT	SBD	92407	99 B2
VERDI	WSH		28 L0
VERDI SIERRA PINES	SIE	95737	27 L9
VERDUGO CITY	LACO	91046	117 E4

COMMUNITY NAME	CO.	ZIP CODE	PAGE & GRID
*VERNON	LACO	90058	97 E8
VERONA	SUT	95659	33 M6
VICHY SPRINGS	MEN	95482	31 D3
VICTOR	SJCO	95253	40 L3
VICTORIA	SDCO	92001	108 P3
*VICTORVILLE	SBD	92392	91 J4
VIDAL	SBD	92280	103 C8
VIDAL JUNCTION	SBD	92280	103 B7
VILLA GRANDE	SON	95486	37 D4
*VILLA PARK	ORA	92667	98 J5
VINA	TEH	96092	24 D8
VINCENT	LACO	93550	90 K1
VINEBURG	SON	95487	38 H3
VINTON	PLU	96135	27 F7
VIOLA	SHA	96088	19 F5
VIRGILIA	PLU	95984	26 B3
VIRGINIA CITY	STOR		36 A6
VIRGINIA COLONY	VEN	93021	88 P7
*VISALIA	TUL	93277	68 C2
*VISTA	SDCO	92083	107 G4
VOLCANO	AMA	95689	41 E1
VOLCANOVILLE	ED	95634	34 H7
VOLLMERS	SHA	96051	12 M3
VOLTA	MER	93635	55 B6
VORDEN	SAC	95690	39 H6
WAHTOKE PARK	FRCO	93654	58 K0
WALKER	MNO	96107	42 C9
WALLACE	ED	95254	40 J6
WALMORT	SAC	95683	40 F1
*WALNUT	LACO	91789	118 M6
*WALNUT CREEK	CC	94595	38 Q9
WALNUT GROVE	SAC	95690	39 H7
WALSH LANDING	SON	95450	37 B1
WALSH STATION	SAC	95827	40 C0
WARM SPRING	LACO	91310	89 H3
WARM SPRINGS	ALA	94538	46 J2
WARNER SPRINGS	SDCO	92086	108 F4
*WASCO	KER	93280	77 C2
WASHINGTON	NEV	95986	26 Q8
WASHOE CITY	WSH		28 Q2
*WATERFORD	STA	95386	48 E0
WATERLOO	SJCO	95201	40 M3
*WATSONVILLE	SCR	95076	54 F4
WATTS	LACO	90002	117 P5
WAWONA	MPA	95389	49 G6
WEAVERVILLE	TRI	96093	17 B6
*WEED	SIS	96094	12 C4
WEED PATCH	KER	93307	78 K8
WEIMAR	PLA	95736	34 G6
WEISEL	RCO	91720	99 J0
WEITCHPEC	HUM	95546	10 H5
WELDON	KER	93283	79 A7
WELLINGTON	LYON		36 M9
WELLSONA	SLO	93446	76 A0
WENDEL	LAS	96136	21 J6
WENTWORTH SPRINGS	ED	95725	35 G5
WEOTT	HUM	95571	16 K2
WEST BRANCH	BUT	95941	25 C5
WEST BUTTE	SUT	95953	33 D2
*WEST COVINA	LACO	91790	118 K5
WESTEND	SBD	93562	81 A2
WESTGUERNEWOOD	SON	95462	37 D4
WEST HAVEN FRE	FRE	93234	67 E2
WEST HOLLYWOOD	LACO	90069	117 J2
*WESTLAKE VILLAGE	LACO	91361	105 C8
WESTLEY	STA	95387	47 G2
WEST LOS ANGELES	LACO	90025	117 L1
*WESTMINSTER	ORA	92683	98 K2
*WESTMORLAND	IMP	92281	110 K0
WEST POINT	CAL	95255	41 E2
WESTPORT	MEN	95488	22 K4
WEST SACRAMENTO	YOL	95691	39 B6
WEST SIDE	LAKE		7 C2
WESTVILLE	PLA	95631	35 D1
WESTWOOD	LAS	96137	20 K4
WESTWOOD	LACO	90024	97 D5
WEST YERMO	SBD	92327	92 B1
*WHEATLAND	YUB	95692	33 G8
WHEATON SPRINGS	SBD	92364	84 E3
WHEATVILLE	FRE	93656	57 P1
WHEELER RIDGE	KER	93284	78 P7
WHEELER SPRINGS	VEN	93023	88 K1
WHISKEYTOWN	SHA	96095	18 D1
WHISPERING PINES	LAK	95461	32 M0
WHITE HALL	ED	95725	35 M4
WHITE HORSE	MOD	96054	13 E8
WHITE PINES	CAL	95223	41 G5
WHITE RIVER	TUL	93257	68 N9
WHITETHORN	HUM	95489	22 B1
WHITEWATER	RCO	92282	100 G4
WHITE WOLF	TUO	95389	42 Q6
WHITLEY GARDENS	SLO	93436	76 B4
WHITLOW	HUM	95554	16 K4
WHITMORE	SHA	96096	19 D1
*WHITTIER	LACO	90605	118 N2
WILBUR SPRINGS	COL	95987	32 G4
WILDOMAR	RCO	92395	99 N4
WILDROSE	INY	93562	71 D5
WILLIAMS	COL	95987	32 E7
WILLIAMS	JOS		3 A1
*WILLITS	MEN	95490	23 P0
WILLOW CREEK	HUM	95573	10 M5
WILLOW RANCH	MOD	96138	7 H4
*WILLOWS	GLE	95988	24 M7
WILLOW SPRINGS	KER	93550	89 C7
WILMINGTON	LACO	90744	119 F5
WILSEYVILLE	CAL	95257	41 F3
WILSONIA	TUL	93633	58 J7
WILTON	SAC	95693	40 E2
WINCHESTER	RCO	92396	99 L6
WINCHUCK	CUR		1 F7
WINDSOR	SON	95492	37 C8
WINTER GARDENS	SDCO	92040	106 H7
WINTERHAVEN	IMP	92283	115 B5
*WINTERS	YOL	95694	39 C0
WINTERWARM	SDCO	92028	107 D5
WISHON	MAD	93669	49 M8
WISTER	IMP	92257	110 F1
WITCH CREEK	SDCO	92065	108 J3
WITTER SPRINGS	LAK	95493	31 D6
WOFFORD HEIGHTS	KER	93285	69 P5
WOLF	NEV	95945	34 F3
WONDER VALLEY	FRCO	93657	58 G2
WOODACRE	MAR	94973	38 N1
WOODCREST	RCO	92504	99 H2
WOODFORD	KER	96120	79 K3
WOODFORDS	ALP	96120	36 L3
*WOODLAKE	TUL	93286	58 Q6
*WOODLAND	YOL	95695	33 P3
WOODLAND HILLS	LACO	91364	97 B3
*WOODSIDE	SMCO	94062	45 K5
WOODSIDE VILLAGE	LACO	91792	118 M6
WOODVILLE	TUL	93257	68 G4
WOODY	KER	93287	79 A0
WOOLSEY	SON	95492	37 D8
WORDEN	KLAM		5 E2
WRIGHTS LAKE	ED	95720	35 K6
WRIGHTWOOD	SBD	92397	90 N8
WYANDOTTE	BUT	95965	25 N8
WYNOLA	SDCO	92036	108 J4
YANKEE HILL	BUT	95969	25 H7
YANKEE JIMS	PLA	95631	34 G7
YERMO	SBD	92398	92 B1
YETTEM	TUL	93670	58 N3
YOLO	YOL	95697	33 N3
*YORBA LINDA	ORA	92686	98 H5
YORKVILLE	MEN	95494	31 K2
YOSEMITE FORKS	MAD	93644	49 L6
YOSEMITE VILLAGE	MPA	95389	49 C7
YOUNGSTOWN	SJCO	95220	40 K2
*YOUNTVILLE	NAPA	94599	38 E4
*YREKA	SIS	96097	4 L0
*YUBA CITY	SUT	95991	33 E5
YUCAIPA	SBD	92399	99 E7
YUCCA	MOH		96 C4
YUCCA VALLEY	SBD	92284	100 C8
*YUMA	YUMA		115 B5
ZAMORA	YOL	95698	33 M2
ZENIA	TRI	95495	16 M8
ZEPHYR COVE	DGL		36 G1

2605

SEE PAGE D FOR INSTRUCTIONS

HIGHWAY INDEX

ROUTE NO.	CO.	PAGE & GRID
	FEDERAL	
1	BAJA	111 H8
1D	BAJA	111 H6
2	BAJA	112 G2
2	SONR	115 H7
3	BAJA	112 F4
5	BAJA	114 E3
6	ESM	44 M8
6	MIN	44 N6
6	MNO	51 B5
50	CRSN	36 E3
50	DGL	36 F2
50	ED	35 M2
50	LYON	36 C5
50	SAC	40 B0
51	SAC	39 A8
60	LPAZ	104 M7
66	MOH	96 F1
93	CLK	74 D8
93	MOH	85 B9
95	CLK	74 D6
95	LPAZ	104 N3
95	MIN	44 A1
95	NYE	62 E3
95	RCO	103 F8
95	SBD	85 M3
95	YUMA	115 C8
97	KLAM	5 A3
97	SIS	12 B4
101	CUR	1 C5
101	DN	10 B0
101	HUM	9 H8
101	LACO	97 C2
101	MAR	38 N2
101	MEN	22 D4
101	MON	65 E3
101	SB	86 C4
101	SBT	54 G6
101	SFCO	45 C3
101	SLO	75 C1
101	SMCO	45 F4
101	SCL	54 B6
101	SON	37 C8
101	VEN	88 P0
199	DN	1 J8
199	JOS	2 C5
395	CRSN	36 D4
395	DGL	36 J5
395	INY	59 A8
395	KER	70 P5
395	LAKE	7 A4
395	LAS	8 H2
395	MOD	8 D2
395	MNO	50 C7
395	SBD	91 D1
395	WSH	28 J1
	INTERSTATE	
5	COL	12 F6
5	FRCO	56 M2
5	GLE	24 H6
5	JKSN	4 C1
5	KER	77 D8
5	KIN	67 M4
5	LACO	98 H2
5	MCO	47 Q5
5	ORA	98 H2
5	SAC	39 E8
5	SDCO	106 H1
5	SJCO	39 M9

ROUTE NO.	CO.	PAGE & GRID
5	SHA	18 F5
5	SIS	12 F6
5	STA	47 G1
5	TEH	18 L6
5	YOL	33 L1
8	IMP	113 C3
8	SDCO	106 G9
8	YUMA	115 B6
10	LPAZ	103 N9
10	LACO	98 D1
10	RCO	103 N3
10	SBD	82 P5
15	CLK	74 C8
15	RCO	99 L2
15	SBD	91 E6
15	SDCO	99 B1
15E	RCO	99 H4
15E	SBD	99 A2
40	MOH	96 F2
40	SBD	95 C4
80	CC	38 P5
80	NEV	27 Q5
80	PLA	34 E6
80	SAC	34 P0
80	SFCO	45 C4
80	SOL	38 J8
80	WSH	28 L1
80	YOL	39 B6
205	SJCO	46 D7
210	LACO	98 C2
215	RCO	99 H4
215	SBD	99 B3
280	SCL	45 M8
280	SFCO	45 D3
280	SMCO	45 D3
380	SMCO	45 F4
405	LACO	97 C5
405	ORA	98 L3
480	SFCO	45 C4
505	SOL	39 E1
505	YOL	33 M1
580	ALA	46 E0
580	SJCO	46 E7
605	LACO	98 E2
680	ALA	46 F2
680	CC	38 N8
680	SCL	46 K2
680	SOL	38 L8
780	SOL	38 M6
805	SDCO	106 H3
980	ALA	45 C6
	STATE	
1	HUM	15 E7
1	LACO	97 E3
1	MAR	37 M8
1	MEN	22 F4
1	MON	64 D2
1	ORA	98 N4
1	SFCO	45 C3
1	SLO	75 B3
1	SMCO	45 F3
1	SB	86 D3
1	SCR	53 A5
1	SON	37 D2
1	VEN	105 C4
2	LACO	90 M5
2	SBD	90 N7
3	SIS	11 C7
3	TRI	11 M8
4	ALP	36 Q4

ROUTE NO.	CO.	PAGE & GRID
4	CAL	41 F7
4	CC	38 N6
4	SJCO	39 Q8
4	STA	40 P8
6	MNO	51 B5
7	LACO	98 F0
9	SCL	45 N8
9	SCR	53 A7
12	CAL	41 J0
12	NAPA	38 H5
12	SAC	39 K5
12	SJCO	39 L9
12	SOL	39 J1
12	SON	38 E1
13	ALA	45 B7
14	KER	80 B5
14	LACO	89 B0
16	AMA	40 D5
16	COL	32 J5
16	SAC	39 C9
16	YOL	32 M7
17	ALA	45 E7
17	MAR	38 P3
17	SCL	46 K2
17	SCR	54 B1
18	LACO	90 K7
18	SBD	91 K1
19	LACO	98 D1
20	COL	32 D8
20	LAK	31 G8
20	MEN	22 Q6
20	NEV	34 B5
20	SUT	33 E4
20	YUB	33 C8
22	ORA	98 K2
23	LACO	105 D8
23	VEN	88 Q6
24	ALA	45 B6
24	CC	38 Q8
25	MON	65 E7
25	SBT	65 C6
26	CAL	41 F2
26	SJCO	40 M6
27	LACO	97 A3
28	CRSN	36 E2
28	PLA	35 C9
28	WSH	36 B1
29	LAK	31 F6
29	NAPA	38 C2
29	SOL	38 L6
30	LACO	98 C6
30	SBD	99 B3
31	RCO	98 F9
32	BUT	25 G1
32	GLE	24 G7
32	TEH	19 L8
33	FRCO	56 F3
33	KER	67 P2
33	KIN	67 L1
33	MCO	47 P5
33	SJCO	47 E1
33	SLO	87 B8
33	SB	87 B8
33	STA	47 G2
33	VEN	88 F0
34	VEN	88 Q5
35	SFCO	45 D3
35	SMCO	45 J4
35	SCL	46 P0
36	SHA	17 L9
36	HUM	16 G4
36	LAS	20 H9

ROUTE NO.	CO.	PAGE & GRID
36	PLU	20 L1
36	TEH	18 M5
36	TRI	17 J0
37	SOL	38 K6
37	SON	38 K4
38	SBD	91 P9
39	KLAM	5 B4
39	LACO	98 C4
39	ORA	98 L2
41	FRCO	57 H5
41	KER	66 P9
41	KIN	67 E4
41	MAD	57 D5
41	MPA	63 N4
41	SLO	76 F1
42	LACO	97 F8
43	FRCO	57 N7
43	KER	68 N2
43	KIN	67 F8
43	TUL	68 J0
44	LAS	20 D1
44	SHA	18 E5
45	COL	32 B9
45	GLE	24 H9
45	YOL	33 L4
46	KER	77 B1
46	JOS	2 B7
46	SLO	75 D8
47	LACO	97 K8
48	LACO	89 E1
49	AMA	40 C7
49	CAL	41 G0
49	ED	34 L6
49	MAD	49 L6
49	MPA	49 G0
49	NEV	34 B4
49	PLA	34 J4
49	PLU	27 G6
49	SIE	26 M5
49	TUO	41 N4
49	YUBA	26 M5
50	ED	34 P5
50	SAC	39 B9
52	SDCO	106 H2
53	LAK	32 H1
54	SDCO	106 K7
55	ORA	98 K5
56	SDCO	107 M7
57	LACO	98 E5
57	ORA	98 J4
58	KER	77 G8
58	SBD	91 B4
58	SLO	76 G3
59	MCO	48 K4
60	LACO	98 E2
60	RCO	99 E2
61	ALA	45 D6
62	RCO	100 F5
62	SBD	103 D2
63	FRCO	58 K2
63	TUL	58 N3
65	KER	68 Q6
65	PLA	34 J1
65	TUL	68 D5
65	YUB	33 G7
66	JKSN	4 B1
66	KLAM	4 C7
66	SBD	98 C7
67	SDCO	106 H7
68	MOH	85 K7
68	MON	54 M2
70	BUT	25 J6

ROUTE NO.	CO.	PAGE & GRID
70	KLAM	5 A7
70	LAS	27 F8
70	PLU	26 C1
70	SUT	33 K7
70	YUB	33 C6
71	LACO	98 E6
71	RCO	98 F7
71	SBD	98 F7
72	LPAZ	104 F3
72	LACO	98 F1
72	ORA	98 G3
73	ORA	98 M4
74	ORA	98 Q8
74	RCO	100 L1
75	SDCO	106 M3
76	SDCO	107 D7
78	IMP	109 J5
78	RCO	103 Q6
78	SDCO	107 G4
79	RCO	99 G8
79	SDCO	108 C2
82	SCL	46 L0
82	SMCO	45 F4
83	SBD	98 E7
84	ALA	46 G2
84	SMCO	45 K6
84	YOL	39 C6
85	SCL	46 L0
86	IMP	109 D4
86	RCO	101 M2
87	SCL	46 M2
88	ALP	36 K4
88	AMA	35 Q7
88	DGL	36 H4
88	SJCO	40 H5
89	ALP	36 M3
89	ED	36 L1
89	MNO	36 P7
89	NEV	27 N7
89	PLA	35 B7
89	PLU	20 L1
89	SHA	13 J5
89	SIE	27 L5
89	SIS	12 F8
89	TEH	19 J7
90	ORA	98 G5
91	LACO	97 F5
91	ORA	98 H4
91	RCO	99 G0
92	ALA	45 G6
92	SMCO	45 G6
94	SDCO	106 K5
95	LPAZ	103 N9
95	MOH	85 N6
95	NYE	62 E3
96	HUM	10 G5
96	SIS	10 C8
98	IMP	113 B4
99	BUT	25 H3
99	FRCO	57 G3
99	JKSN	3 B9
99	KER	78 E5
99	MAD	57 F2
99	MCO	48 M3
99	SAC	39 E9
99	SJCO	47 C3
99	STA	47 G6
99	SUT	33 G5
99	TEH	18 P7
99	TUL	68 F2
100	CRSN	36 E4
104	AMA	41 E2

ROUTE NO.	CO.	PAGE & GRID
104	SAC	40 F5
107	LACO	97 H6
108	MNO	42 F8
108	STA	47 C7
108	TUO	41 M7
110	LACO	97 D8
111	IMP	109 C7
111	RCO	100 H4
112	ALA	45 D7
113	SOL	39 E3
113	SUT	33 J5
113	YOL	33 Q4
115	IMP	110 J2
116	SON	37 D6
117	SDCO	106 Q6
118	LACO	97 A7
118	VEN	88 P4
119	KER	78 J3
120	MNO	51 B3
120	SJCO	47 C2
120	STA	48 B1
120	TUO	41 Q4
121	NAPA	38 E7
121	SON	38 J3
124	AMA	40 E7
125	SDCO	106 F6
126	LACO	89 M1
126	VEN	88 M6
127	INY	72 D7
127	SBD	72 Q8
128	MEN	30 E5
128	NAPA	38 D3
128	SON	38 A0
128	YOL	39 C1
129	SCR	54 F6
130	SCL	46 L4
131	MAR	38 Q3
132	MPA	48 D7
132	SJCO	47 F0
132	STA	47 F3
133	ORA	98 P6
134	LACO	97 C7
135	SB	86 B4
136	INY	60 M3
137	TUL	68 E3
138	LACO	90 H1
138	SBD	91 N0
139	LAS	14 H5
139	MOD	14 B6
140	KLAM	5 B5
140	LAKE	7 B0
140	MCO	47 N6
140	MPA	49 E4
142	ORA	120 A8
144	SB	87 L5
145	FRCO	57 L1
145	MAD	57 D2
146	CLK	74 H8
146	MON	55 Q2
146	SBT	55 P4
147	CLK	74 E8
147	PLU	20 L4
149	BUT	25 K5
150	SB	87 M8
150	VEN	88 L3
151	SHA	18 C4
152	MAD	56 B5
152	MCO	56 C3
152	SCL	54 D7
152	SCR	54 E4
154	SB	87 H0
155	KER	68 N3

ROUTE NO.	CO.	PAGE & GRID
156	MON	54 H4
156	SBT	54 E9
157	CLK	73 D9
159	CLK	74 F5
160	CLK	73 H8
160	NYE	73 C4
160	SAC	39 A8
161	CLK	74 N4
161	SIS	5 F3
162	BUT	25 N2
162	GLE	24 K2
162	MEN	22 L9
163	CLK	85 L4
163	SDCO	106 H3
164	CLK	84 D8
164	LACO	98 E1
165	MCO	47 P8
166	KER	77 N1
166	SB	86 A2
166	SLO	76 P6
167	MNO	43 K8
168	FRCO	57 E9
168	INY	51 P8
168	MNO	52 H5
169	HUM	10 G4
170	LACO	97 B6
172	TEH	19 K6
173	SBD	91 P4
174	NEV	34 D6
175	LAK	31 J8
175	MEN	31 H5
176	SB	86 B4
177	RCO	102 F6
178	INY	72 K7
178	KER	70 Q0
178	SBD	81 B1
180	FRCO	56 J8
182	MNO	43 E3
183	MON	54 J4
184	KER	78 G8
185	ALA	45 D7
188	SDCO	112 E4
189	SBD	91 Q4
190	INY	61 L5
190	TUL	68 H3
191	BUT	25 H5
192	SB	87 L5
193	ED	34 K7
193	PLA	34 K3
195	RCO	101 P3
198	FRCO	66 D9
198	KIN	67 D5
198	MON	65 F7
198	TUL	58 P9
200	HUM	9 N9
201	TUL	58 P3
202	KER	79 M5
204	KER	78 G6
206	DGL	36 G3
206	SBD	99 B3
207	DGL	36 H2
208	DGL	36 M8
208	MEN	22 F3
209	DGL	36 G4
209	SDCO	106 L1
213	LACO	97 H7
216	TUL	68 A4
217	SB	87 L3
218	MON	54 M2
219	STA	47 D5
220	SOL	39 H6
223	KER	78 K6

ROUTE NO.	CO.	PAGE & GRID
224	SB	87 M8
225	SB	87 M4
227	SLO	76 K2
229	SLO	76 E3
232	VEN	88 Q3
233	MAD	56 B7
236	SCR	53 A7
237	SCL	46 K2
238	ALA	46 F0
243	RCO	100 H1
245	TUL	58 M5
246	SB	86 G4
247	SBD	91 F8
249	FRCO	58 K6
250	ORA	98 J4
253	MEN	31 G1
254	HUM	16 L3
255	HUM	9 P9
259	SBD	99 C3
263	SIS	4 K1
264	ESM	52 C1
265	ESM	52 B8
266	MNO	52 H4
267	ESM	61 B4
267	PLA	35 B9
269	FRCO	67 B0
270	MNO	43 J3
271	MEN	22 C4
273	SHA	18 E4
274	SDCO	106 H2
281	LAK	31 J9
282	SDCO	106 L2
284	PLU	27 E7
299	HUM	10 M3
299	LAS	14 J1
299	MOD	14 C6
299	SHA	13 P2
299	TRI	17 B6
330	SBD	99 B5
338	LYON	43 C3
341	LYON	36 C6
341	WSH	28 P4
359	MIN	44 A2
360	MIN	44 H8
371	RCO	100 P3
372	NYE	73 E3
373	NYE	62 N7
374	NYE	62 G1
428	WSH	36 B4
429	WSH	36 B3
430	WSH	28 J2
431	WSH	28 P3
435	WSH	28 M3
445	WSH	28 C6
446	WSH	28 E8
447	WSH	28 D9
512	CRSN	36 D4
513	CRSN	36 D4
604	CLK	74 E8
647	WSH	28 L2
649	WSH	28 M2
650	WSH	28 L4
651	WSH	28 L2
655	WSH	28 M3
666	WSH	28 K3
667	WSH	28 K3

568

SEE PAGE E FOR INSTRUCTIONS

POINTS OF INTEREST INDEX

COPYRIGHT, © 1983 BY Thomas Bros Maps

NAME & ADDRESS	PAGE & GRID
AIRPORTS	
ALTURAS MUNICIPAL AIRPORT, 1 mi W of Alturas	8 B1
ARCATA AIRPORT, off Hwy 101 at Airport Rd	9 M9
AUBURN AIRPORT, 4 mi N of Auburn	34 H4
BAKERSFIELD AIRPARK, Watts Dr & Union Av	78 H7
BENTON AIRPORT, Gold St, Redding	122 G0
BISHOP AIRPORT, 2 mi E of Bishop	51 K6
BURBANK-GLENDALE-PASADENA, 2627 N Hollywood Wy	179 A2
CANNON INTERNATIONAL AIRPORT, 2 of Reno	28 M4
CARSON AIRPORT, Carson City, Nevada	36 C5
CATALINA AIR & SEA TERMINAL, Harbor Blvd	191 G0
CHICO MUNICIPAL AIRPORT, 5 mi NW of Chico	25 F2
DOUGLAS COUNTY AIRPORT, Minden, Nevada	36 G4
FRESNO-CHANDLER DOWNTOWN AIRPORT, Amador & Thorne	165 L2
JOHN MCNAMARA FIELD, nr Crescent City	1 K7
JOHN WAYNE AIRPORT, MacArthur Blvd	198 N3
LAKE COUNTY AIRPORT, SW of Clear Lake off Hwy 175	31 H6
LAKEVIEW MUNICIPAL AIRPORT, near jct of 140 & 395	7 B3
LIVERMORE AIRPORT, Stanley Blvd, Livermore	46 E3
LONE PINE AIRPORT, 1 mile south of Lone Pine	60 L3
LONG BEACH MUNICIPAL, 4100 Donald Douglas Dr	119 D8
LOS ANGELES INTERNATIONAL, 1 World Wy	189 E4
MADERA AIRPORT, Hwy 99 & Av 17	56 D9
McCARRAN INTERNATIONAL, 5 miles S of Las Vegas	210 N5
MEADOWS FIELD, Skyway & Airport Drs	78 F6
MERCED MUNICIPAL AIRPORT, 2 mi SW of Merced	170 Q0
NORTH LAS VEGAS AIR TERMINAL, 3.5 miles NW of L V	74 D6
OAKLAND INTERNATIONAL, Doolittle & Airport Wy	159 M3
ONTARIO INTERNATIONAL AIRPORT, 2 mi E of Ontario	204 P8
OROVILLE AIRPORT, 3 mi SW of Oroville	25 M5
PALMDALE AIRPORT, Sierra Hwy	90 G1
PALM SPRINGS MUNICIPAL, 2 mi E of Palm Springs	206 J9
PLACERVILLE AIRPORT, S of Hwy 50 near Smithflat	35 N0

NAME & ADDRESS	PAGE & GRID
REDDING MUNICIPAL AIRPORT, 7 miles SE of Redding	18 F5
SACRAMENTO CO METRO ARPRT, 12 mi NW of Sacramento	33 P6
SAN DIEGO INTERNATIONAL AIRPORT, Lindbergh Field	215 D3
SAN FRANCISCO INTL, Airport Wy off Bayshore Fwy	144 G6
SAN JOSE MUNICIPAL AIRPORT, 1661 Airport Bl	151 B5
SANTA BARBARA AIRPORT, James Fowler Rd	87 L2
SANTA MONICA MUNICIPAL AIRPORT	187 A4
SHAFTER KERN COUNTY AIRFIELD, Lerdo Hwy	78 D3
SISKIYOU COUNTY AIRPORT, Montague	4 K3
SUSANVILLE AIRPORT, 5 mi SE of Susanville	21 J2
SUTTER COUNTY AIRPORT, off Samuel Dr	125 M9
TEHACHAPI-KERN CO AIRPORT, Green & J Sts	79 M6
TRUCKEE AIRPORT, 4 miles E of Truckee	35 A8
UKIAH AIRPORT, State St	123 P7
VENTURA COUNTY AIRPORT, Oxnard	176 K0
AMUSEMENT PARKS	
DISNEYLAND, Habor Bl, Anaheim Amusement park-7 theme sections, rides, shops.	193 K3
KNOTTS BERRY FARM, 8039 Beach Bl, Buena Park Ride 'Corkscrew' & 'Log Ride'; shops, rstrnts.	120 D3
LION COUNTRY SAFARI, N of Laguna Beach off I-5 Drive through wild animal park.	120 L8
MARINELAND, 6600 Palos Verdes Dr Ocean zoo with whales, seals & porpoises.	119 G1
MARINE WORLD/AFRICA USA, off US 101, Redwood City Oceanarium & African game collection; shows.	145 L7
MARRIOTTS GREAT AMERICA, 1 Great America Pkwy Family amusement park, American history theme.	46 K1
SEA WORLD, 1720 S Shores Rd, Mission Bay Park Marine life amusement pk, shows; Japanese Vlg.	212 E5
SIX FLAGS MAGIC MOUNTAIN, I-5 at Valencia Av Family amusement park; thrill rides and shops.	89 M2

NAME & ADDRESS	PAGE & GRID
UNIVERSAL STUDIOS & AMPHITHEATER, Univ City Plaza Features tours of movie and TV sets; shows.	181 B2
BEACHES	
ARROYO BURRO BEACH COUNTY PARK, 2981 Cliff Dr Swimming, picnicking, surf fishing.	87 M4
AVILA STATE BEACH, Front St Fishing, fire rings, swimming.	76 L1
BAKER BEACH, NW shore Presidio, San Francisco Fishing, hiking nearby, no swimming.	141 F2
BOLSA CHICA BEACH STATE PARK, N of Huntington Bch Sandy beach, body surfing, picnicking.	120 J1
CABRILLO BEACH, E of Pacific Av, San Pedro Public boat ramp, surf fishing, barbeque pits.	119 H5
CAPISTRANO BEACH, San Juan Capistrano Sandy beach, body surfing, picnicking.	202 P6
CAPITOLA BEACH STATE PARK, off Hwy 1 near Aptos Sandy beach, tide pools.	54 E1
CARLSBAD STATE BEACH, 3 mi S of Carlsbad Bl Fish, swim, surf, camp, store, concessions.	107 H1
CARMEL RIVER BEACH STATE PARK, Scenic Rd Skin diving, fishing, bird watching sites.	168 N2
CARPINTERIA BEACH STATE PARK, Linden Av Camping, picnicking, fishing pier, boat ramp.	87 M7
CAYUCOS STATE BEACH, on Ocean Front Rd Fishing pier, barbeque & picnic facilities.	75 F6
CORONA DEL MAR STATE BEACH, Corona Del Mar Sandy beach, tidepools, body surfng, picnckng.	120 M6
DOHENY BEACH STATE PARK, Puerto & Del Obispo St Surfing, camping, fire rings & picnic areas.	202 M3
EAST BEACH, E Cabrillo Bl BBQ & picnic facilities, volleyball courts.	174 L9

SEE PAGE E FOR INSTRUCTIONS

POINTS OF INTEREST INDEX

POINTS OF INTEREST INDEX

*Information acquired from the AAA listing.   **SEE PAGE E FOR INSTRUCTIONS**

POINTS OF INTEREST INDEX

NAME & ADDRESS	PAGE & GRID
*HACIENDA, 3950 Las Vegas Bl, Las Vegas Casino, restaurants, entertainment, shops.	210 L2
*HARRAH'S RENO, 3131 S Virginia St Name entertainment & recreational facilities.	130 F3
*HARRAH'S, on US 50, Stateline, Nevada Casino, cafe, theater, restraunts, sauna.	129 C8
*HARVEY'S, on US 50, Stateline, Nevada Casino, pool, cafes, restaurants.	129 B7
*HERITAGE INN, 204 Harding Blvd, Roseville 75 large rooms, spacious grounds; restaurant.	34 M1
*HILL HOUSE INN, Mendocino 21 rooms, Victorian decor, near ocean.	30 B3
*HILTON HOTEL, E of San Francisco Int Airport Restaurant, entertainment, swimming pool.	144 L6
*HILTON HOTEL & TOWER, Mason & O'Farrell Sts Shops, sundeck & pool; air, RR & bus transprt.	143 M4
*HILTON INN RESORT-MONTEREY, 1000 Aguajito Rd 203 units; pool, sauna, putting green, tennis.	168 D5
*HOLIDAY INN, 3475 Las Vegas Bl, Las Vegas Casino, entertainment, shops.	210 E3
*HOLIDAY INN-UNION SQUARE, Powell & Sutter Sts 400 units; restaurant & coffee shop.	143 L5
HOTEL CONTINENTAL, Flamingo & Paradise Rds, L V 400 units; pool, restaurant, slot casino.	210 F7
*HOTEL DEL CORONADO, on Coronado Peninsula Elegant beachfront hotel built in the 1880's.	111 C5
*HYATT DEL MONTE, 1 Old Golf Course Rd, Monterey 408 rooms, pools & whirlpool, golf, tennis.	54 L2
*HYATT LAKE TAHOE RESORT HOTEL, Country Club Dr 460 rooms, pool, beach, sauna, tennis.	36 C2
*HYATT LOS ANGELES INTERNATIONAL, 6225 W Century Opposite airport, offers airport transportatn.	189 C4
*HYATT REGENCY LOS ANGELES, Hope & 7th Sts 487 units; at Broadway Plaza; LAX transport.	186 J0
*HYATT REGENCY, 5 Embarcadero Ctr, San Francisco Striking arch, glss elvatr, revolvng rftp bar.	143 J8
*HYATT SAN JOSE, 1740 N 1st St 475 rooms, putting green; dining room.	46 L2
*HYATT ON UNION SQUARE, 345 Stockton St, SF 693 units; 3 restaurants, entertainment.	143 L5
*THE INN AT RANCHO SANTA FE, Linea del Cielo 75 rooms and cottages on tree-shaded grounds.	107 L5
*JADE TREE INN, Junipero St near 5th, Carmel 55 units; ocean view, fireplace, pool, lanais.	168 H4
*LA COSTA HOTEL & SPA, Costa Del Mar Rd, Carlsbad 350 rooms & houses, golf, tennis, health spa.	107 J4
LANDMARK HOTEL, Paradise Rd, Las Vegas Lovely rooms; restaurant, showrooms & casino.	209 P5
*LA QUINTA HOTEL, Eisenhower Dr, La Quinta 150 rooms, lovely grounds, pool, tennis, golf.	100 M8
*LAS VEGAS HILTON, 3000 Paradise Rd Casino, restaurants, star entertainment.	209 N8
*L'ERMITAGE, 9291 Burton Wy, Beverly Hills Elegant suites in the European tradition.	183 C5
*LOS ANGELES HILTON HOTEL, Wilshire at Figueroa 1200 units; pool, shopping-public facilities.	185 H9
*MADONNA INN, US 101 at Madonna Rd, Sn Luis Obspo 109 units; unusually decorated rooms; restrnt.	172 M0
*MARINA HOTEL, 3805 Las Vegas Blvd 870 units; pool, 2 restaurants, casino.	210 K3
*MARINA INTERNATIONAL HOTEL, 4200 Admiralty Wy 136 units; patios/balconies, pool; LAX trans.	187 J4
*MARINERS INN, 6180 Moonstone Beach Dr, Cambria 26 rooms, whirlpool, across from the beach.	75 D3
*MARK HOPKINS HOTEL, 1 Nob Hill, San Francisco Elegnt lndmrk htl, panrmic view 'Top of Mark'.	143 K4
*MARRIOTT HOTEL, 5855 W Century Bl, Los Angeles Very large hotel, transport to airport.	189 C7
*MARRIOTT INN, 200 Marina Blvd, Berkeley 242 rooms, indoor pool, sauna; restaurant.	45 B5
*MARRIOTT'S RANCHO LAS PALMAS, Bob Hope Dr 348 rooms, pools, golf, tennis, bicycles.	100 K5
*MARRIOTTS SANTA BARBARA BILTMORE, 1260 Channel 169 rooms, overlooks ocean, pool, restaurant.	87 M6
*MAXIM, 160 E Flamingo, Las Vegas Casino, restaurant, entertainment, shops.	210 G2
*MGM GRAND, 3645 Las Vegas Bl, Las Vegas Casino, restaurants, entertainment.	210 F3
*MGM GRAND HOTEL-RENO, 2500 E 2nd St, Reno Casino, restaurants, theatres, shows, shops.	26 B0
*MINT, 100 E Fremont St, Las Vegas Casino, restaurant, entertainment, arcade.	209 D5
MISSION INN, 7th St & Orange, Riverside Historic inn, open during restoration.	205 F3
*MOONSTONE INN, 5860 Moonstone Beach Dr, Cambria 7 rooms with an ocean view from each.	75 D3
MURPHY'S HOTEL, off Hwy 4 in Murphys Historical monument still in full operation.	31 Q1
*NAPA VALLEY LODGE BEST WESTERN, Yountville 55 rooms, lovely view, pool & whirlpool.	38 E5
*PACIFIC PLAZA, 501 Post St, San Francisco 140 units; restaurant, pay valet garage.	143 M3
*PALM SPRINGS SPA HOTEL, Indian Av N & Tahquitz-M 230 units; pool, 2 hot minerl pools, steam rm.	206 J2
*PEPPER TREE MOTOR INN, 3850 State St, Sta Barbra 150 rooms, patios, 2 pools & sauna; restaurnt.	87 L4
*PICADILLY INN AIRPORT, 5115 E McKinley, Fresno 185 rooms, pool, whirlpool; restaurant.	57 H6
*PICADILLY INN-SHAW, 2305 W Shaw Av, Fresno 203 rooms, pool, airport trans; restaurant.	57 G4
*QUAIL LODGE, 8205 Valley Greens Dr, Carmel Vly 100 rooms, scenic grounds, golf, tennis.	54 N2
*QUEEN MARY, Pier J, Long Beach British liner now serves as hotel & restrnt.	192 M8
*QUEENSWAY BAY HILTON, 700 Queensway Dr, Long Bch Located on the waterfront next to Queen Mary.	192 L7
*RAMADA INN, 114 E Highway 246, Buellton 98 rooms, pool, convention & conference facil.	86 H7
*RANCHO BERNARDO INN, 17550 Bernardo Oaks Dr 151 rooms, 2 pools, golf, bicycling, tennis.	107 K7
*RED LION MOTOR INN, 1830 Hilltop Dr, Redding 194 rooms, pool, putting green; dining room.	18 E5

NAME & ADDRESS	PAGE & GRID
*RED LION MOTOR INN, 2001 Point West Wy, Sacto 448 rooms, pools, airport trans; dining room.	39 A9
*REGISTRY HOTEL, 18800 MacArthur Blvd Across from John Wayne Airport.	198 N4
*RENO HILTON, 255 N Sierra Lovely hotel with pool, casino & restaurants.	130 G2
*RIO BRAVE RESORT, 11200 Lake Ming Rd 112 rooms, tennis, golf, pools; airstrip.	78 F9
*RIVIERA, 2901 Las Vegas Bl, Las Vegas Casino, restaurants, entertainment, shops.	209 N4
ROYAL AMERICANA, Convention Center Dr, Las Vegas Convenient location near LV Convention Center.	209 Q6
*SACRAMENTO INN, 1401 Arden Wy 387 rooms, 3 pools, putting green;dining room.	39 A9
*SAHARA (DEL WEBB'S), 2535 Las Vegas Bl, Ls Vegas Casino, restaurants, entertainment, shops.	209 L5
*SAHARA-RENO (DEL WEBB'S), 255 N Sierra St Casino, restaurant, entertainment, shops.	129 B7
*SAN DIEGO HILTON, 1775 E Mission Bay Dr 356 units; pool, beach; rental boats & bikes.	212 H8
*SANDS, 3355 Las Vegas Bl, Las Vegas Casino, restaurants, star entertainment.	210 D3
*SANDS HOTEL & CASINO, RENO, Arlington & 3rd Gambling, cafe, shops.	130 F1
*SAN LUIS BAY INN, Box 188, Avila Beach 76 rooms, ocean view, golf, swim; dining room.	76 L1
*SANTA BARBARA INN, 435 Milpas St S 71 units; across from the beach, pool.	174 H7
*SANTA CLARA MARRIOTT, Great America Parkway 502 rooms; near Great America Theme Park.	46 E3
*THE SHASTA INN, 2180 Hilltop Dr, Redding 148 rooms, pool & whirlpool; restaurant.	18 D4
SHENANDOAH HOTEL, 120 E Flamingo Rd, Las Vegas Casino, shows and restaurant.	210 G2
*SHERATON AT FISHERMAN'S WHARF, 2500 Mason St, SF 525 units; pool, restaurant and coffee shop.	143 E3
*SHERATON INN, 45 John Glenn Dr, Concord 168 rooms, pool; dining room, entertainment.	39 N0
*SHERATON NEWPORT BEACH, 4545 MacArthur Blvd Beautiful facilities, entertainment.	198 P3
*SHERATON PLAZA, 6101 W Century Blvd Beautiful facilities, easy access to LAX.	189 C5
*SHERATON PLAZA-PALM SPRINGS, 400 E Tahquitz-McC 263 units; pool, saunas, whirlpools, diningrm.	206 K2
*SHERATON SANTA BARBARA HOTEL, 1111 E Cabrillo 150 rooms, ocean view, pool; dining room.	87 L6
*SHERATON SUNNYVALE INN, 1100 N Mathilda Av 174 rooms, pool; restaurant, cocktail lounge.	46 K0
*SHORE CLIFF LODGE, 2555 Price St, Pismo Beach 99 rooms, ocean view, heated pool; restaurant.	76 L2
*SILVERADO COUNTRY CLUB RESORT, 1600 Atlas Peak 260 rooms, 7 pools, golf, tennis, bicycles.	54 N2
SILVER SLIPPER, on the Strip, Las Vegas Casino, restaurant and shows.	209 P3
*SMUGGLERS INN, 3737 N Blackstone Av, Fresno 210 rooms, beautiful landscape, pool; restrnt.	57 H4
*SOUTH COAST PLAZA HOTEL, 666 Anton Bl, Costa Msa 400 units; pool, putting green, tennis.	198 J0
*STANFORD COURT, 905 California St, Nob Hill Gracious 1900s decor in Old Stanford House.	143 K4
STARDUST HOTEL, 3000 Las Vegas Blvd S Casino, restaurant, entertainment, pool.	209 P3
*STOCKTON HILTON, 2323 Grand Canal 202 rooms, 3 pools; dining room & coffee shop.	40 N1
SUNDANCE HOTEL & CASINO, 3rd & Fremont, Las Vegas 650 units; restaurant, buffet and casino.	209 D5
*SUNNYVALE HILTON INN, 1250 Lakeside Dr 299 rooms, pool, airport trans, restaurant.	46 K0
*TICKLE PINK MOTOR INN, 155 Highland Dr, Carmel 29 rooms, beautiful view and lovely location.	54 P1
*THE TREE HOUSE BEST WESTERN, off I-5, Mt Shasta 69 rooms, indoor pool, bicycles; dining room.	12 D5
*TROPICANA, 3801 Las Vegas Bl, Las Vegas Casino, cafe, entertainment, theater, shops.	210 K3
*UNION PLAZA HOTEL, 1 Main St, Las Vegas Casino, restaurant, entertainment.	209 C5
*UNIVERSITY HILTON, 3540 E Figueroa St, LA 241 units; next to USC campus; pool.	185 Q5
*VACATION VILLAGE, Mission Bay Pk, San Diego 449 bungalows, rooms & suites; 5 pools.	212 J2
WAWONA HOTEL, S entrance to Yosemite Valley A grand mountain resort built in the 1800's.	49 G7
*WEST BEACH MOTOR LODGE, Cabrillo Bl & Bath St 45 units; across from yacht harbor & beach.	174 M5
*THE WESTGATE, 2nd Av at C St, San Diego 223 units; elegant decor; restaurant.	215 H7
*WESTIN BONAVENTURE, 6th & Flower, Los Angeles Rooftop restaurnt & revolvng cocktl lounge.	186 G0
*WESTIN ST FRANCIS, Union Square, San Francisco Fashionable shops, skyline view from elevator.	143 M4
*WESTWOOD MARQUIS, Hilgard Av near Wilshire Bl,LA 250 elegant suites; pool, sauna, whirlpool.	180 E7
MISSIONS	
MSN BASILICA SAN DIEGO DE ALCALA, 10818 SD Msn Rd 1769, 1st missn estblshd along El Camino Real.	214 G8
MISSION LA PURIMISA CONCEPCION, 15 mi W of US 101 1787, 11th missn, rebuilt by original methods.	86 F3
MISSION NUESTRA SENORA DE LA SOLEDAD, off US 101 1791, 13th missn, stood in ruins for 100 yrs.	65 A0
MISSION SAN ANTONIO DE PADUA, off U S 101 1771, 3rd msn, one of largest restored missns.	107 D7
MISSION SAN ANTONIO DE PALA, off Hwy 76 Built in 1816 to help the Sn Luis Rey Mission.	65 J2
MISSION SAN BUENAVENTURA, Main & Figueroa Sts 1782, 9th missn, last founded by Father Serra.	175 E2
MISSION SAN CARLOS BORROMEO, Lasuen Dr, Carmel 1770, 2nd missn, burial place of Father Serra.	168 M3
MSN SAN FERNANDO REY DE ESPANA, 15151 SF Msn Bl 1797, 17th msn, destroyed by '71 quake; rstrd.	117 C0

NAME & ADDRESS	PAGE & GRID
MISSION SAN FRANCISCO DE ASIS, Dolores & 16th Sts 1776, 6th missn, chapel unchanged for 175 yrs.	142 M4
MISSION SAN FRANCISCO SOLANO, Spain & 1st Sts 1823, 21st missn, northernmost & last of msns.	132 J7
MISSION SAN GABRIEL ARCANGEL, 1120 Old Mill Rd 1771, 4th missn, at crossroads in early Calif.	117 J9
MISSION SAN JOSE, 43300 Mission Blvd 1777, 14th missn, noted for outstanding music.	46 H2
MISSION SAN JUAN BAUTISTA, off US 101 1797, 15th msn, near othr buildngs of msn era.	98 Q7
MISSION SAN JUAN CAPISTRANO, off I-5 at Ortega 1776, 7th mission, swallows return annually.	202 C8
MISSION SAN LUIS OBISPO, Chorro & Monterey Sts 1772, 5th missn, first msn to use tile roofs.	172 H4
MISSION SAN LUIS REY DE FRANCIA, on Hwy 76 1798, 18th missn, most successful of all msns.	107 G3
MISSION SAN MIGUEL ARCANGEL, 801 Mission St 1797, 16th missn, last msn secularized - 1834.	65 P9
MISSION SAN RAFAEL ARCANGEL, A St & 5th Av 1817, 20th missn, founded to aid sick Indians.	139 J6
MISSION SANTA BARBARA, Laguna & Los Olivos Sts 1786, 10th missn, famed as most beautiful msn.	174 E2
MISSION SANTA CLARA DE ASIS, Grant & Franklin St 1777, 8th missn, bell dated 1798 still clangs.	151 F3
MISSION SANTA CRUZ, School & Emmet Sts 1791, 12th msn, destroyed, replica built 1931.	53 D8
MISSION SANTA INES, 1760 Mission Dr 1804, 19th mission, favorite mission of many.	86 H8
PARKS, STATE & FEDERAL, & NATIONAL FORESTS	
ALAMEDA PARK, Micheltorea & Anacapa Sts Displays 280 species of plants and shrubs.	174 H4
AMERICAN RIVER PARKWAY, from Nimbus Dam 23 mi long greenbelt along banks of Sacto Riv.	137 A3
ANCIENT BRISTLECONE PINE FOREST, White Mountn Rd 4600 yr old pine forest, nature trails.	52 J0
ANDREW MOLERA STATE PARK, W of Hwy 1, Big Sur 50 campsites, sandy beach, hiking, meadows.	64 D3
ANGELES NATIONAL FOREST, N of Los Angeles In rugged mtns of LA, hiking & winter sports.	117 A7
ANGEL ISLAND STATE PARK, E San Francisco Bay Isl pk has hiking, bike rentl, picnc, day use.	45 B4
ANNADEL STATE PARK, Channel Dr Riding & hiking.	37 F9
ANZA BORREGO DESERT STATE PARK, San Diego County Beautiful wildflowers in spring; camp, hike.	109 K1
ARCATA STATE AZALEA RESERVE, Arcata Beautiful azaleas bloom late May - early June.	10 P1
ARMSTRONG REDWOODS STATE PARK, E of Ft Ross Giant redwoods, picnicking, hiking trails.	37 C5
AUSTIN CREEK STATE RECREATION AREA, E of Ft Ross Camp, horseback ride, meadows, vllys, forests.	37 B4
BIDWELL MUNICIPAL PARK, E 4th St, Chico Swimming pool, picnic, golf, nature trails.	124 L3
BIG BASIN REDWOODS STATE PARK, on Hwy 236 First state park to preserve redwoods.	45 Q6
BLISS MEMORIAL STATE PARK, north of Emerald Bay Dense forest, trails, camping, beach area.	35 H9
BOTHE-NAPA VALLEY STATE PARK, on Hwy 29 Hiking, picnic & camping areas, swimming pool.	38 C1
BROOKSIDE PARK, Rosemont Av, Pasadena Site of Rosebowl; swimming, hiking, golfing.	190 H1
BURBANK MEMORIAL GARDENS, Santa Rosa Av A living memorial dedicated to the naturalist.	131 K6
BUTANO STATE PARK, E of Hwy 1 at Gazos Creek Rd Camping, recreational facilities.	45 P5
CALAVERAS BIG TREES STATE PARK, E of Arnold 2 giant Redwood groves - self-guided tours.	41 H7
CASTLE CRAG STATE PARK, S of Dunsmuir Pinnacles, crags, cliffs, green pines, rec.	12 H6
CASWELL MEMORIAL STATE PARK, Hwy 99 S of Manteca Camp, fish, swim, hike, picnic.	47 D3
CHABOT REGIONAL PARK, Lake Chabot 5000 acre park; fish, picnic, moto-X, boat.	45 D9
CHANNEL ISLANDS NATIONAL PARK, off Santa Barbara Consists of 5 islands, 20 to 60 mi offshore.	87 P4
CLEAR LAKE STATE PARK, near Lakeport Camp, boat, wtrski, hike, fish, swim, picnic.	31 G7
CLEVELAND NATL FOREST, San Diego & Orange Co's Hiking, boating, riding, fishing, camping.	108 L3
COWELL REDWOODS STATE PARK, 5 miles N on Hwy 9 Equestrn trails, hiking, fishing, picnic grds.	53 C8
CUYAMACA RANCHO STATE PARK, on Hwy 79, Julian In old Indian territory; camp, hike; horses.	108 M9
DEL NORTE COAST REDWOODS ST PK, S of Crescent Cty Dense forests, giant redwoods, good camping.	1 M8
DEVIL'S POSTPILE NATL MONUMNT, Mammoth Lakes Area Spectacular mass of hexagonal basalt columns.	50 F5
DONNER MEMORIAL STATE PARK, 2 mi W of Truckee Rec at Donner Lake, Donner Prty memorial, mus.	35 A6
DRY LAGOON BEACH STATE PARK, south of Orick Coast sand dunes; camp, boat at Stone Lagoon.	9 H8
EL DORADO NATIONAL FOREST, north of Hwy 88 Rugged mtns, dense foliage, scattered lakes.	129 M6
EMERALD BAY STATE PARK, Emerald Bay Scenic; camping, swimming, picnicking.	35 H9
FREMONT NATIONAL FOREST, SE Oregon Good fishing, camping & rock climbing.	7 D5
GOLDEN GATE PARK, between Lincoln Wy & Fulton St Vast city park, walk, equestrn trails, skate.	141 L3
GRIZZLY CREEK REDWOODS STATE PARK, E of Fortuna Scenic; camp, fish, nature trails, creeks.	16 G3
GROVERS HOT SPRINGS STATE PARK, W of Markleeville Camping, swim at hot springs, fish in creeks.	36 N3
HENRY COE STATE PARK, 14 mi NE of Morgan Hill Picturesque; camp & picnic grnds, day use fee.	46 P7
HUMBOLDT REDWOODS STATE PARK, Redwood Hwy Tallest redwoods, camp, fish, picnic, hike.	16 K1
INYO NATIONAL FOREST, near Calif-Nevada border Winter sports, boat facilities, camping.	51 N6

SEE PAGE E FOR INSTRUCTIONS

*Information acquired from the AAA listing.

SEE PAGE E FOR INSTRUCTIONS

POINTS OF INTEREST

SEE PAGE E FOR INSTRUCTIONS

POINTS OF INTEREST INDEX

POINTS OF INTEREST INDEX

POINTS OF INTEREST INDEX

NAME & ADDRESS	PAGE & GRID
UNDERSEA GARDENS, Anchor Wy, Crescent City View sea plants & animals, scuba diving show.	1 L7
UNION SQUARE, Geary, Powell, Post & Stockton Sts Fashionable shopping center; park, fountain.	143 M5
UNION STATION, 800 N Alameda St, Los Angeles One of the landmarks of Los Angeles.	186 F4
VIKINGSHOLM, at Emerald Bay Large Scandanavian castle with furnishings.	35 H9
VISITOR CENTER YOSEMITE VILLAGE, Yosemite Lodge Displays, photos of Yosemite, films.	63 C5
WATTS TOWER, 1765 E 107th St Unusual tower studded with glass & shell.	117 P5
WAYFARER'S CHAPEL, 5755 Palos Verde Dr Striking glass church sits atop hill by sea.	119 G3
WESTSIDE & CHERRY VALLEY RR, 8 mi E of Sonora Activities - rides on train & antique autos.	41 N6
WHISKEYTOWN-SHASTA-TRINITY REC, NW of Redding Camp, backpack, picnic, boat, water sports.	18 B0
WHITNEY PORTAL, W from Lone Pine Starting point for Mt Whitney trail.	59 M9
WILLIAM S HART PARK, Newhall Av at Sn Fernando Rd Tour the silent screen actor's beautiful home.	89 N3
WINCHESTER MYSTERY HOUSE, Winchester Bl, San Jose Fascinating house and museum.	151 P2
WOODMINSTER AMPHITHEATER, S of Orinda Centerpiece of pk, sumr concerts, light opera.	45 B7
WRIGLEY MEMORIAL & BOTANICAL GDN, Avalon Cyn Rd Beautiful cactus, flowers & trees at monument.	105 P1
YOSEMITE FALLS, Yosemite National Park Two beautiful waterfalls fall over 2,400 feet.	63 B6
YOSEMITE VALLEY, Mariposa County Picturesque, campng, domes, wtrflls, meadow.	63 A1
ZABRISKIE POINT, off Hwy 190 near Death Valley Overlooks Death Vly from badland of Black Mtn.	72 A1

RECREATION LAKES, RIVERS & MARINAS

NAME & ADDRESS	PAGE & GRID
ALPINE LAKE, 51 mi NE of Angels Camp 100+ dev sites - boat, backpack, fish, swim.	42 C1
ANTELOPE LAKE, 45 miles NE of Quincy 200+ dev sites - boat, waterski, fish, hike.	18 M1
AQUATIC PARK, foot of Polk St, San Francisco Curved fishing pier creates cold swim lagoon.	45 B5
BALBOA MARINA, 2751 W Pacific Coast Hwy One of the largest marinas on the west coast.	199 M2
BARNHILL MARINA, Inner Harbor, Alameda Pleasure boat marina in the Inner Harbor.	157 L9
BASS LAKE, E of Oakhurst 220+ dev sites - boat, waterski, fish, hike.	49 M8
BENICIA MARINA, end of E 3rd St Pleasure boat marina south of Benicia Point.	153 P3
BERKELEY AQUATIC PARK, Foot of Bancroft Av Saltwatr lake, watr sports, model boat racing.	45 B5
BERKELEY MARINA, foot of University Av Base for poplr sport fshng fleet, fshng pier.	45 A5
BIG BEAR LAKE, off Hwy 18 Resort area has many winter & summer sports.	91 Q9
BIG SAGE RESERVOIR, NW of Alturas Boating, fishing, no camping facilities.	7 N0
BLACK BUTTE LAKE, 9 miles west of Orland 90+ dev sites - boat, waterski, fish, hike.	24 G4
BLUE LAKE, 42 mi SE of Alturas 40+ dev sites - boat, waterski, fish, hike.	8 H5
BOCA RESERVOIR, NE of Truckee 90+ dev sites - boat, waterski, fish, hike.	27 P8
BOWMAN LAKE, 40 mi NE of Nevada City Primitive sites-fish, backpack, swim, picnic.	27 N1
BRIDGEPORT RESERVOIR, just north of Bridgeport 60+ dev sites - boat, fish, swim, backpack.	43 G3
BUCKS LAKE, southwest of Quincy 70+ dev sites - boat, waterski, fish, hike.	26 D2
BULLARDS BAR RESERVOIR, E of Camptonville 90+ dev sites - boat, watrski, fish, picnic.	26 N3
BUTTE LAKE, Lassen Volcanic National Park 90+ dev sites - sail, fish, swim, backpack.	20 F1
CAMANCHE RESERVOIR, W OF San Andreas 1150+ dev sites - boat, fish, hike, swim.	40 J5
CAMP FAR WEST RESERVOIR, 29 mi NW of Auburn 30+ dev sites - boat, waterski, fish, swim.	34 G1
CAPLES LAKE, near Kirkwood on Hwy 88 30+ dev sites - boat, fish, hike, horses.	36 N1
CATALINA YACHT HARBOR, Avalon Bay, Catalina Islnd Yacht moorings, glass bottom boat tours.	105 M3
CHANNEL ISLANDS HARBOR, Oxnard Small marina, Channel Islands Museum.	105 C1
CHERRY LAKE, 31 mi E of Tuolumne 40+ dev sites - boat, waterski, fish, horses.	42 M2
CLEAR LAKE, near Lakeport 140+ dev sites - boat, waterski, fish, hike.	31 G7
COLORADO RIVER, on the California-Arizona border Camp, hike along the river; boat, swim.	116 J5
COLUSA-SACRAMENTO RIVER RECREATION AREA, Colusa Undev camps, boat, fish, picnic, waterski.	32 C8
CONVICT LAKE, 37 miles north of Bishop 90+ dev sites - boat, fish, backpack, horses.	51 F0
COYOTE RESERVOIR, N of Gilroy 70+ dev sites - boat, waterski, fish, hike.	54 B7
CROWLEY LAKE, 35 miles north of Bishop Dev campsites - boat, waterski, fish, picnic.	51 F1
CUYAMACA RESERVOIR, off Hwy 79 south of Julian Camping, fishing, duck hunting; no swimming.	108 L5
DANA POINT MARINA, S of Del Obispo St Shopping, restaurants, boating facilities.	202 N2
DON PEDRO RESERVOIR, W of Coulterville 500+ dev sites - hseboat, watrski, fish, hike.	48 D5
DORRIS RESERVOIR, east of Alturas Good fishing & swimming; day use only.	8 B3
DOWNTOWN LONG BEACH MARINA, off Shoreline Dr New marina will open Fall 1982.	192 K9
EAGLE LAKE, 20 mi N of Susanville 300+ dev sites - boat, waterski, fish, hike.	20 D8

NAME & ADDRESS	PAGE & GRID
EL CAPITAN RES, El Monte Rd E CA 67 N I-8 Fish, boat, camp nrby Lk Jennings Co Pk.	108 N1
ELLERY LAKE, 10 miles west of Lee Vining 10+ dev sites - boat, fish, rock climb, hike.	43 P3
FALLEN LEAF LAKE, southwest of South Lake Tahoe 200+ dev sites - boat, fish, swim, horses.	35 J9
FOLSOM LAKE STATE PARK, 1 mi N of Folsom Dev camps - boat, fish, waterski, horses.	34 N3
FRENCHMAN RES STATE REC AREA, 35 mi N of Chilcoot 140+ dev sites - boat, waterski, fish, hike.	27 C7
FRENCH MEADOWS RESERVOIR, NE of Michigan Bluff 100+ dev sites - boat, fish, swim, hike.	35 E4
GOLDEN GATE NATL REC AREA, Sn Frncsco & Marin Cos Gardens, historic sites, rec facilities.	142 A2
GOLDEN GATE YACHT CLUB, off Marina Bl, SF Private yacht club at SF yacht harbor.	142 B0
GOOSE LAKE, north of Alturas Camping, fishing, waterfowl hunting.	7 H3
HELL HOLE RESERVOIR, NE of Michigan Bluff 50+ dev sites - boat, waterski, fish, hike.	35 F4
HOGAN RESERVOIR, 3 mi W of San Andreas Dev & undev sites - boat, fish, hike, swim.	40 K8
HUNTINGTON HARBOUR, Huntington Beach Waterfront homes & marina facilities.	120 H0
HUNTINGTON LAKE, north of Camp Sierra 300+ dev sites - boat, waterski, fish, horses.	50 N3
ICE HOUSE RESERVOIR, 12 mi N of Riverton 80+ dev sites - boat, fish, swim, hike.	35 L5
INDIAN CREEK RESERVOIR, east of Markleeville 20+ dev sites - boat, fish, backpack, picnic.	36 M4
IRON GATE RESERVOIR & LAKE COPCO, NE of Henley Camp, picnic, fish, swim, raft, hike, hunt.	4 F4
JACK LONDON MARINA, Embarcadero, Oakland Pleasure boat marina in the Inner Harbor.	157 K8
JACKSON MEADOW RESERVOIR, SE of Sierra City 120+ dev sites - boat, waterski, fish, hike.	27 M2
JENKINSON LAKE, 18 mi E of Placerville 290+ dev sites - boat, fish, swim, hike.	35 M2
JUNE LAKE LOOP, 18 miles north of Mammoth Lakes 280+ dev sites - boat, fish, backpack, horses.	40 F2
JUNIPER LAKE, Lassen Volcanic National Park Sail, swim, backpack, hike, picnic, horses.	20 G1
LAKE ALMANOR, southwest of Susanville 170+ dev sites - boat, waterski, fish, hike.	20 L2
LAKE AMADOR, 7 mi S of Ione Dev camps - boat, fish, waterslide, hike.	40 G7
LAKE ARROWHEAD, Hwy 173 Charming resort area; fishing, winter sports.	91 P4
LAKE BERRYESSA, on Hwy 128, Napa County Camping, fishing, waterskiing, resorts.	32 Q6
LAKE BRITTON, 13 mi N of Burney 120+ dev sites - boat, waterski, fish, horses.	13 K4
LAKE CACHUMA RECREATION AREA, 11 mi S of Solvang Fishing, boating, camping; no swimming.	87 H0
LAKE CASITAS RECREATION AREA, 11311 Santa Ana Rd Fishing, boating, camping.	88 M0
LAKE DAVIS, north of Portola 110+ dev sites - boat, fish, hike, picnic.	27 D2
LAKE HENSHAW, off CA 76, Santa Ysabel 400+ dev sites - fish, boat, hike.	108 F3
LAKE HODGES, off S6 on Lake Dr, Escondido Owned by SD City for day use only; fish, boat.	107 K6
LAKE ISABELLA, 48 mi NE of Bakersfield One of the most complete rec lakes in Calif.	79 A6
LAKE JENNINGS, Jennings Pk Rd N off I-8 RV & tent camping; boat, limited fishing.	108 P1
LAKE KAWEAH, 17 mi E of Visalia via Hwy 198 Campsites, boating, fishing, swimming.	68 A7
LAKE McCLOUD, 12 mi S of McCloud Undev campsites - boat, fish, picnic, hike.	12 H8
LAKE McCLURE, S of Coulterville 550+ dev sites - housebt, fish, swim, picnic.	48 F7
LAKE MEAD NATL RECREATION AREA, Hwy 93 & Lakeshre One of largest artificial lakes in the world.	85 A4
LAKE MENDOCINO, N of Ukiah 300+ dev sites - boat, waterski, fish, hike.	31 D3
LAKE MERRITT, downtown Oakland Large natural salt water lake.	158 H2
LAKE MOHAVE, E of Searchlight, Nevada Boat, fish, swim, camp, beaches, marinas.	85 F5
LAKE NACIMIENTO, 40 mi NW of Paso Robles 350+ dev sites - waterski, boat, swim, hike.	65 P6
LAKE OROVILLE STATE REC AREA, NE of Oroville 200+ dev sites - boat, waterski, fish, horses.	25 L7
LAKE PERRIS, off Ramona Expressway Bike trails, boat rentals, camping.	99 H5
LAKE PILLSBURY, near Scott Dam 100+ dev sites - boat, waterski, fish, hike.	23 P6
LAKE SABRINA, 18 mi SW of Bishop Dev sites - boat, fish, backpack, picnic.	51 N3
LAKE SAN ANTONIO RECREATION AREA, W of Bradley 650+ dev sites-boat, fish, swim, hike, horses.	65 M7
LAKE SHASTA, off I-5 north of Redding 400+ sites - houseboating, fishing, wtrskiing.	18 B4
LAKE SHASTINA, 7 mi N of Weed 70+ dev sites - boat, waterski, fish, hike.	4 Q4
LAKE SISKIYOU, 3 mi W of Mt Shasta 280+ dev sites - boat, fish, windsurf.	12 F5
LAKE SPAULDING, N of Emigrant Gap 20+ dev sites - boat, waterski, hike, fish.	35 A2
LAKE SUCCESS, 20 mi E of Tipton via Hwy 190 100+ dev sites - boat, fish, swim, hike.	68 G7
LAKE TAHOE, California-Nevada border Dev camps, boat, wtrski, fish, swim, horses.	35 E9
LAKE VALLEY RESERVOIR, E of Emigrant Gap Camp, boat, fish, swim, hike, picnic.	35 B2
LEWISTON LAKE, 35 mi NW of Redding 90+ dev sites - sail, canoe, fish, hunt.	17 A8
LITTLE GRASS VALLEY RESERVOIR, W of Gibsonville 240+ dev sites - boat, waterski, fish, hike.	26 G5
LONG BEACH MARINA & MARINE STADIUM, Long Beach One of the largest marinas on the west coast.	120 H0

NAME & ADDRESS	PAGE & GRID
LOON LAKE, NW of Emerald Bay 50+ dev sites - boat, fish, hike, picnic.	35 H6
LOPEZ LAKE, 23 mi N of Santa Maria 300+ sites - boat, waterski, fish, picnic.	76 K4
LOWER NEWPORT BAY, Newport Beach Leads to vast estuary in Upper Newport Bay.	199 N5
LUNDY LAKE, 12 miles north of Lee Vining 30+ dev sites - boat, fish, picnic, backpack.	43 M3
MADERA LAKE PARK & REC AREA, NE of Madera Good bass fishing, camping, boating.	57 C1
MAMMOTH POOL RESERVOIR, east of Bass Lake 60+ dev sites - boat, waterski, fish, hike.	50 L2
MANZANITA LAKE, Lassen Volcanic National Park 170+ dev sites - sail, fish, hike, horses.	19 F6
MARINA DEL REY, Via Marina Berths more than 10,000 yachts.	187 K5
MARTINEZ YACHT HARBOR, Martinez Small pleasure craft marina.	154 A2
MARTIS CREEK RESERVOIR, SE of Truckee 20+ dev sites - sail, fish, swim, hike.	35 A9
MEDICINE LAKE, 48 miles NE of McCloud 70+ dev sites - boat, waterski, fish, horses.	5 P6
MILLERTON LAKE REC AREA, 22 miles east of Madera 130+ dev sites - boat, waterski, fish, horses.	57 D6
MISSION BAY, Mission Bay Park, W of I-5 Separate courses for diverse water sports.	212 F6
MONTEREY MARINA, Ocean View Blvd Small craft harbor near Fisherman's Wharf.	167 H9
MORENA LAKE, Oak Rd & Buckmn Spgs Rd, W I-8 Campsites, fishing, boating, hiking, horses.	112 C6
NOYO HARBOR, south of Fort Bragg Small, scenic eastern-like fishing village.	22 P3
OCEANSIDE HARBOR, 1540 Harbor Dr N Deep sea & sport fishing; pier fishng; sailng.	107 G1
OTAY RESERVOIR, Wueste Rd, E Chula Vista S D City lk, co campgrd; fish, boat, no swim.	111 D9
PARDEE RESERVOIR, 3.5 mi E of Buena Vista 180+ dev sites & pool - boat, fish, bicycle.	40 H8
PINE FLAT RESERVOIR REC AREA, 20 mi N of Fresno Dev camps - houseboat, waterski, fish, hike.	58 F3
PROSSER CREEK RESERVOIR, N of Truckee Dev & undev sites - boat, fish, swim, picnic.	27 P6
PYRAMID LAKE RECREATION AREA, off I-5 25+ dev sites-boat, waterski, fish, swim.	88 G9
ROCK CREEK LAKE, SW of Toms Place 220+ dev sites - boat, fish, backpack, picnic.	51 J2
ROLLINS RESERVOIR, N of Colfax 240+ dev sites - boat, waterski, fish, hike.	34 D6
RUTH LAKE, N of Ruth 60+ dev sites - boat, waterski, fish, horses.	16 K9
SADDLEBAG LAKE, 12.5 miles north of Lee Vining 20+ dev sites - boat, fish, mtn climb, hike.	43 N2
ST FRANCIS YACHT CLUB, off Marina Bl, Sn Francsco Long established yacht club in the Bay Area.	142 B0
SALT SPRINGS RESERVOIR, 20.5 mi SE of Hams Sta 20+ dev sites - boat, fish, swim, hike.	41 C7
SAN LUIS RESERVOIR, 16 mi W of Los Banos 70+ dev sittes - boat, waterski, fish, hike.	55 C4
SANTA BARBARA YACHT HARBOR, W Cabrillo Bl Boat rentals, hoist & ramp, sport fishing.	174 M7
SANTA MARGARITA LAKE, 19 mi from San Luis Obispo 80+ dev sites - boat, fish, swim, hike, picnc.	76 H4
SAN VICENTE RESERVOIR, Moreno Av, off CA 67 S D City lake, day use; boat, fish, no swim.	108 N0
SCOTTS FLAT RESERVOIR, E of Nevada City 180+ dev sites - boat, waterski, goldpn, fish.	34 B6
SHAVER LAKE, south of Camp Sierra 60+ dev sites - boat, waterski, fish, hike.	50 Q3
SILVER LAKE, 50 mi NE of Jackson 90+ dev sites - boat, fish, horseback ride.	35 P9
SILVERWOOD LAKE STATE RECREATION AREA, Hwy 138 Swimming, fishing, boating, camping.	91 P3
SOUTH LAKE, 22 mi SW of Bishop Dev sites - boat, fish, backpack, picnic.	51 P4
SOUTH LAKE TAHOE-EL DORADO STATE REC AREA, Hwy 50 Boating, fishing, swimming, picnicking.	129 H1
STAMPEDE RESERVOIR, 15 mi N of Truckee 250+ dev sites - boat, waterski, fish, hike.	27 M7
STATE UNDERSEA PARK, Hwy 1 & Temple Hills Good divng area, fish, shells, rock formtions.	202 J3
STONY GORGE RESERVOIR, 20 miles west of Willows 140+ dev sites - boat, waterski, fish, swim.	24 L2
STOW LAKE, Stow Lake Dr in Golden Gate Park Largest manmade lake in park, boating.	141 L4
SUTHERLAND RES, Sutherland Dam Dr off CA 78 Fish, boat, camp nrby Black Cyn, El Loro Rnch	108 J2
TIOGA LAKE, 12 miles west of Lee Vining 10+ dev sites - boat, fish, picnic, hike.	43 P3
TOPAZ LAKE, east of Markleeville 200+ dev sites - boat, waterski, fish, swim.	36 N8
TRINITY LAKE, 44 mi NW of Redding 400+ sites - sail, wtrski, fish, horsbck ride.	12 M0
TULLOCH RESERVOIR, SE of Copperopolis 60+ dev sites - boat, fish, swim, picnic.	41 P1
TURLOCK RESERVOIR, southwest of La Grange 60+ dev sites - boat, waterski, fish, hike.	48 F3
TWIN LAKES, 13 miles southwest of Bridgeport 180+ dev sites - boat, fish, backpack, horses.	50 F6
UNION VALLEY RESERVOIR, 17 mi N of Riverton 270+ dev sites - boat, fish, swim, hike.	35 K4
VALLEJO MARINA, off Mare Island Causeway Recreational marina near Mare Islnd Naval Res.	134 K1
VENTURA HARBOR, 1603 Anchors Way Dr Includes 2 marinas, boat rentals, launch ramp.	175 N7
VIRGINIA LAKES, 18.5 miles north of Lee Vining 40+ dev sites - boat, fish, backpack, horses.	43 M2
WEST VALLEY RESERVOIR, 22 miles SE of Alturas Camp, boat, waterski, fish, swim, hike, hunt.	8 G3
WHISKEYTOWN LAKE, S of Hwy 299, W of Redding 150+ sites - sail, fish, waterski, hike, swim.	18 D1
YOSEMITE LAKE & PARK, N of Merced off Lake Rd Boat, sail, waterski, fish, hike, picnic.	48 K5

SEE PAGE E FOR INSTRUCTIONS

POINTS OF INTEREST INDEX

NAME & ADDRESS	PAGE & GRID
SKI AREAS	
ALPINE MEADOWS, Hwy 89 South of Tahoe City	35 D6
BADGER PASS, Hwy 41 in Yosemite National Park	49 E7
BOREAL RIDGE, Hwy 80 near Boreal Ridge	35 B5
CHINA PEAK, north of Hwy 168 at Huntington Lake	50 N3
COPPERVALE SKI HILL, Hwy 36 E of Westwood	20 J4
COTTAGE SPRINGS PEAK, Hwy 4 W of JCT with Hwy 207	41 F8
DONNER SUMMIT, Hwy 80 near Donner Pass	35 B5
ECHO SUMMIT, Hwy 50 W of Vade	35 L8
GRANLIBAKKEN, Hwy 89 SW of jct with Hwy 28	35 C7
HAPPY HILL, Hwy 18 near Big Bear Lake	100 B3
HEAVENLY VALLEY, Hwy 50 South of Stateline	36 K2
HOLIDAY HILL, Hwy 2 N of Wrightwood	90 N7
HOMEWOOD SKI AREA, Hwy 89 North of Tahoe Pines	35 F4
HORSE MTN SKI AREA, Hwy 299 E of Blue Lake	10 M2
INCLINE, Hwy 27 near Incline Vlg	36 B2
JUNE MOUNTAIN, Hwy 158 off 395 at June Lake	50 C5
KIRKWOOD SKI RESORT, Hwy 88 near Carson Pass	36 N1
KRATKA RIDGE, Jct of Hwy 2 and Hwy 39	90 M5
LASSEN NATL PARK SKI AREA, Hwy 89 E of Hwy 36	19 J5
MAMMOTH MOUNTAIN, Hwy 203 W of Hwy 395 at Mam Lk	164 G0
MOUNTAIN HIGH, Hwy 2 N of Wrightwood	90 N6
MT ABEL, Hwy 33 S of Ventucopa	87 D9
MT BALDY, N of Hwy 83 on Mt Baldy Rd	90 P8
MT REBA WINTER SKI AREA, N of Bear Valley	42 CO
MT ROSE BOWL, Hwy 27 N of Carson City	28 N3
NORTHSTAR-AT-TAHOE, Hwy 267 N of JCT with Hwy 28	27 Q8
PAPOOSE SKI AREA, Hwy 89 near Olympic Valley	35 C7
PLA VADA SKI HILL, Hwy 80 N of Donner Pass	27 M4
PLUMAS-EUREKA SKI BOWL, Hwy 70 N of Hwy 89	26 G7
POWDER BOWL, Hwy 89 North of Lake Forest	35 D7
RENO SKI BOWL, Hwy 27 East of Incline Village	28 M2
SHIRLEY MDWS SKI AREA, Hwy 155 W of Alta Sierra	79 B4
SIERRA SKI RANCH, Hwy 50 east of Kyburz	35 M7
SIGNAL HILL, Hwy 80 SW of Donner	35 A7
SILVER BASIN, Hwy 88 north of Kit Carson	35 N8
SKI SUNDOWN, Hwy 88 W of Silver Lake	35 Q7
SKI SUNRISE, Hwy 2 N of Wrightwood	90 M7
SNOW VALLEY, Hwy 330 W of Big Bear Lake	99 A8
SODA SPRINGS, Hwy 80 near Soda Springs	35 C6
SQUAW VALLEY, Off Hwy 89 at Squaw Valley	35 D6
STOVER MOUNTAIN SKI AREA, SW of Jct Hwys 36 & 89	20 M1
SUGAR BOWL, Hwy 80 South of Norden	35 B6
TAHOE-DONNER, Hwy 80 near jct with Hwy 89	27 Q8
TAHOE SKI BOWL, Hwy 89 South of Tahoe Pines	35 F6
YUBA PASS, E of Hwy 49 btwn Sierra City & Bassets	27 K1
THEATER	
AHMANSON THEATER, 135 N Grand Av	186 F1
Part of the Music Center; dramatic productns.	
DOROTHY CHANDLER PAVILION, 135 N GRAND AV	186 F1
Part of the Music Center; musical performnces.	
GEARY THEATER, 415 Geary St at Mason St	143 M4
The Amer Conservatory Theatr performs nightly.	
GREEK THEATER, 2700 N Vermont Av, Los Angeles	182 G3
Natural amphitheatre in Griffith Park.	
HOLLYWOOD BOWL, 2301 N Highland Av	157 L6
Natural amphitheater, seats 20,000.	
HUNTINGTON HARTFORD THEATRE, 1615 N Vine St	181 L7
More serious drama of well known stars.	
IRVINE MEADOWS AMPHITHEATER, 8800 Irvine Ctr Dr	120 L8
Concerts under the stars.	
JOHN ANSON FORD THEATER, 2580 Cahuenga Blvd	157 K7
Features occasional outdoor jazz concerts.	
L A STAGE WEST, Canon Dr, Beverly Hills	183 D5
Features off-Broadway plays.	
MANN'S CHINESE THEATRE, 6925 Hollywood Bl	181 K4
Famed forecourt with footprints of stars.	
MARK TAPER FORUM, 135 N Grand Av	186 F1
Part of the Music Center; experimental drama.	
THE MUSIC CENTER, 135 N Grand Av, Los Angeles	186 F1
3 theatre complex for drama, music & opera.	
PANTAGES THEATER, 6233 Hollywood Blvd	181 L7
Features many Broadway productions.	
PARAMOUNT THEATER, 2025 Broadway	158 F0
30's movie hse is now ctr for performing arts.	
SHRINE AUDITORIUM, Jefferson & Figueroa, L A	185 P6
A variety of musical programs & exhibits.	
SHUBERT THEATRE, 2020 Avenue of the Stars	183 F1
The stage for many broadway plays.	
TERRACE THEATER, Ocean Blvd, Long Beach	192 J8
Features drama, opera, dance & symphony.	
WILSHIRE THEATER, Wilshire & La Cienega	183 E8
Classic theater - features plays & musicals.	
WINERIES	
AHLGREN VINEYARD, Boulder Creek	45 P8
Family-owned winery; tours by appointment.	
ALMADEN VINEYARD, 1530 Blossom Hill Rd, San Jose	46 N3
Historic museum, sparkling wine cellar; tour.	
ALTA VINEYARD CELLAR, Schramsberg Rd, Calistoga	29 E1
Tasting and retail sales by appointment.	
AMADOR WINERY, Hwy 49, Amador City	40 E8
Tasting room open daily.	
BEAULIEU VINEYARD, 1960 St Helena Hwy, Rutherford	29 H5
Open daily for tasting and guided tours.	
BERINGER, 2000 Main St, St Helena	29 G3
Tours of Rhine House, Beringer caves; tasting.	
BOEGER WINERY, 1709 Carson, Placerville	35 MO
Wine tasting.	
BROOKSIDE WINERY, off Hwy 85	148 P1
Wine tasting, sales.	
DAVID BRUCE, 21439 Bear Creek Rd, Los Gatos	45 Q8
Tasting room and tours available.	

NAME & ADDRESS	PAGE & GRID
BUENA VISTA WINERY, Old Winery Rd, Sonoma	38 H4
Historcl landmark of state's 1st wine cellars.	
BURGESS CELLARS, Deer Park Rd, St Helena	29 D4
Guided tours by appointment; sales daily.	
CAKEBREAD CELLARS, Hwy 29 btwn Oakville & Ruthrfd	29 J6
Tours by appointment only.	
CAREY CELLARS, 1711 Alamo Pintado Rd, Solvang	86 H8
Open for tours and tasting.	
CAREY WINERY, 1695 Martinez St, San Leandro	45 E7
Tasting room open daily.	
CAYMUS VINEYARDS, 8700 Conn Creek Rd, Rutherford	29 J7
Guided tours and tasting by appointment.	
CHARLES KRUG WINERY, off Hwy 29, St Helena	29 F4
Guided tours and wine tasting daily.	
CHATEAU CHEVALIER, 3101 Spring Mtn Rd, St Helena	29 F2
Tours by appointment; store open daily.	
CHATEAU MONTELENA, 1429 Tubbs Ln, Calistoga	29 BO
Tours by appointment; store open daily.	
CHATEAU ST JEAN, 8555 Sonoma Hwy, Kenwood	38 E2
Tours by appointment, self-guided tours.	
CHRISTIAN BROTHERS, 4411 Redwood Rd, Napa	29 F3
Open daily for tasting and tours.	
CHRISTIAN BROTHERS, 2555 Main St, St Helena	29 P6
Tours for champagne tasting & tours.	
CLOS DU VAL, 5330 Silverado Tr, Napa	29 L9
Tours by appointment only; retail sales.	
CONN CREEK WINERY, Silverado Tr, St Helena	29 H6
Tours and tasting by appointmnt; retail sales.	
CRESTA BLANCA WINERY, 2399 N State St, Ukiah	31 D2
Tours, wine tasting.	
CUVAISON WINERY, 4550 Silverado Tr, Calistoga	29 C1
Tasting; no tours.	
DOMAINE CHANDON, California Dr, Yountville	29 L7
Tours, salon museum and restaurant.	
DRY CREEK, 3770 Lambert Bridge Rd, Healdsburg	31 Q6
Tasting room open daily.	
DURNEY VINEYARD, Carmel Valley	64 A5
Tours by appointment only.	
EDMEADES VINEYARDS, 5500 State Hwy 128, Philo	30 F6
Tasting room open daily; tours by appointment.	
EL DORADO VINEYARDS, 3551 Carson Rd, Camino	35 N1
Wine tasting.	
ESTRELLA RIVER WINERY, Hwy 176, Paso Robles	76 B3
Tours and tasting available.	
FETZER VINEYARDS, 1150 Bel Arbes Rd, Redwood Vly	31 H2
Tasting room; tours by appointment only.	
FIRESTONE WINERY, Hwy 176, Los Olivos	86 E8
Wine tasting, tours & sales.	
FOPPIANO, 12707 Old Redwood Hwy, Healdsburg	37 B7
Tasting room open daily; tours by appointment.	
FRANCISCAN VINEYARDS, 1178 Galleron Rd, Rutherfrd	29 H5
Tasting and self-guided tours daily.	
FREEMARK ABBEY WINERY, Hwy 29, St Helena	29 E3
Guided tours and retail sales daily.	
GEYSER PEAK WINERY, Canyon Rd, Geyserville	31 P6
Wine tasting daily; tours by appointment.	
GRAND CRU, 1 Vintage Ln, Glen Ellen	38 F2
Open weekends for tasting; tours by appointmt.	
GRAND PACIFIC, 134 Paul Dr £9, San Rafael	38 N2
Tasting room: 341 San Anselmo Av, San Anselmo.	
GRGICH HILLS CELLAR, Hwy 29 north of Rutherford	29 H5
Informal tours and sales daily.	
GUNDLACH-BUNDSCHU, 3775 Thornberry Rd, Sonoma	38 H3
Open daily for tasting and tours.	
HACIENDA, 1000 Vineyard Ln, Sonoma	38 H4
Open daily for tasting; tours by appointment.	
HANNS KORNELL CHAMPAGNE CELLARS, Larkmead Ln	29 D2
Guided tours and tasting daily.	
HEITZ CELLARS, 436 St Helena Hwy	29 G5
Tours by appointment only.	
HOFFMAN MOUNTAIN RANCH, Adelaida Rd, Paso Robles	76 CO
Tasting room open; tours by appointment only.	
HUSCH VINEYARDS, 4900 Hwy 128, Philo	30 F6
Winery tours, tasting room open daily.	
INGLENOOK VINEYARD, 1991 St Helena Hwy S, Ruthrfd	29 J5
Wine tasting, museum & gift shop; tours.	
ITALIAN SWISS COLONY, River Rd, Asti	31 M6
Tours and tasting available daily.	
JOHNSON'S ALEXANDER VLY, 8333 Hwy 128, Healdsburg	31 Q7
Open daily for tasting and tours.	
ROBERT KEENAN WINERY, Spring Mountain Rd, St Hlna	29 F2
Tours and retail sales by appointment only.	
KENWOOD, 9592 Sonoma Hwy, Kenwood	38 E2
Open daily for tasting; tours by appointment.	
KIRIGIN CELLARS, 11550 Watsonville Rd, Gilroy	54 C5
Tasting room open daily; tours by appointment.	
KONOCTI CELLARS, Hwy 29 at Thomas Dr, Kelseyville	31 G6
Tasting room, group tours by appointment.	
KORBELL & BROS, 13260 Old River Rd, Guerneville	37 C5
Champagne tasting room; tours.	
LANDMARK VINEYARDS, 9150 Los Amigos Rd, Windsor	37 B8
Open Sat & Sun, or by appointment; tours.	
LA PURISIMA WINERY, 725 Sunnyvale-Saratoga Rd	149 C7
Tours & tasting on Sat; daily by appointment.	
LAWRENCE WINERY, Corbett Cyn Rd, San Luis Obispo	76 K2
Tasting room open daily.	
LE BAY CELLARS, 28900 Dutcher Ck Rd, Cloverdale	31 N4
Tasting room, tours by appointment.	
LOS ALAMOS WINERY, off Hwy 101, Los Alamos	86 E5
Wide selection of wines.	
LOUIS M MARTINI, 254 St Helena Hwy	29 G4
Guided tours and wine tasting room open daily.	
MARKHAM WINERY, Hwy 29 at Deer Park Rd	29 F3
Guided tours by appointment.	
MARTINI & PRATI, 2191 Laguna Rd, Santa Rosa	37 D7
Open weekdays for tasting; no tours available.	
MAYACAMAS VINEYARDS, off Mt Veeder Rd, Napa	29 N5
Tours by appointment only.	
MIRASSOU VINEYARDS, 3000 Aborn Rd, San Jose	46 N4
Tasting room and tours available.	
MONDAVI WINERY, 7801 St Helena Hwy, Oakville	29 J5
Tasting & tours; musical events & art exhibit.	

NAME & ADDRESS	PAGE & GRID
MONTEREY VINEYARDS, 800 S Alta St, Gonzales	54 P8
Tours and tasting available.	
NAPA CREEK WINERY, Silverado Tr, St Helena	29 G5
Retail sales.	
NAPA WINE CELLARS, 7481 St Helena Hwy	29 K6
Informal tours and tasting daily.	
NAVARRO WINERY, 5801 Hwy 128, Philo	30 E7
Tasting room open daily; tours by appointment.	
NERVO WINERY, 19550 Geyserville Av, Geyserville	31 P6
Open daily for tasting; no tours.	
NICHELINI, 2349 Lower Chiles Valley Rd, St Helena	38 E7
Tasting & tours Saturday and Sunday.	
OBESTER, 12341 San Mateo Rd, Half Moon Bay	45 J4
Weekend tours & tasting; rural coastal valley.	
OZEKI SAN BENITO, 249 Hillcrest Rd, Hollister	55 G1
Tasting room, Pier 39, San Francisco.	
P & M STAIGER, Hopkins Gulch Rd, Boulder Creek	45 Q9
Small, family-owned winery.	
PARDUCCI WINE CELLARS, 501 Parducci Rd, Ukiah	31 D1
Tasting room, tours hourly.	
PASTORI, 23189 Geyserville Av, Cloverdale	31 N6
Open daily for tasting; no tours.	
PAUL MASSON, 13159 Saratoga Av, Saratoga	46 N1
Self-guided tour, tasting.	
PEDRIZZETTI WINERY, 1845 San Pedro Av, Morgan Hll	54 B6
Tasting room on Hwy 101, Morgan Hill.	
PEDRONCELLI, 1220 Canyon Rd, Geyserville	31 P5
Open all week for tasting; tours by appointmt.	
JOSEPH PHELPS VINEYARDS, 200 Taplin Rd, St Helena	29 G6
Guided tours by appointment; sales Mon-Sat.	
POPE VALLEY WINERY, Pope Valley Rd, Pope Valley	29 A4
Tours by appointment; retail sales.	
RAYMOND VINEYARD & CELLAR, 849 Zinfandel Ln	29 G5
Tours by appointment only.	
RIDGE VINEYARDS, 17100 Monte Bello Rd, Cupertino	45 M8
Tasting and occasional tours.	
ROSS-KELLER WINERY, 900 McMurray Rd, Buellton	86 G6
Tours and tasting available.	
ROUND HILL CELLARS, Lodi Ln, St Helena	29 E3
Tours by appointment; retail sales.	
RUTHERFORD HILL WINERY, End of Rutherford Hill Rd	29 G6
Tours daily; tasting 2nd Saturday each month.	
RUTHERFORD VINTNERS, 1673 St Helena Hwy S	29 H4
Tasting room; group tours by appointment.	
SAN MARTIN WINERY, 13000 Depot Av, San Martin	54 C5
Tasting room open year around.	
SANTA BARBARA, 202 Anacapa St, Santa Barbara	86 G5
Santa Barbara tasting room open.	
SANTA YNEZ VALLEY, 365 N Refugio Rd, Santa Ynez	86 H9
Tours and tasting on Saturday; M-F by appoint.	
SCHRAMSBERG VINEYARDS, Peterson Dr, Calistoga	29 D1
Tours by appointment.	
SEBASTIANI VINEYARDS & WINERY, 389 4th St E	132 K9
1st vineyard in Sonoma Vly; tours and tasting.	
SHOWN & SONS VINEYARDS, Silverado Tr, Rutherford	29 H6
Tours and tasting by appointmnt; retail sales.	
SIERRA VISTA WINERY, 4560 Cabernet, Pleasant Vly	35 PO
Wine tasting.	
SIMI WINERY, 16275 Healdsburg Av, Healdsburg	31 Q7
Wine tasting, guided tours.	
SMITH-MADRONE VINEYARDS, 4022 Spring Mtn Rd	29 E1
Tours by appointment; lovely view of Napa Vly.	
SODA ROCK, 8015 Hwy 128, Healdsburg	31 Q7
Wine tasting; historic stone winery building.	
SONOMA VINEYARDS, 11455 Old Redwood Hwy, Windsor	37 B6
Guided tours and tasting room.	
SOUVERAIN, Independence Ln & Hwy 101, Geyserville	31 P6
Open daily for tasting and tours; restaurant.	
SPRING MOUNTAIN VINEYARDS, 2805 Spring Mtn Rd	29 G2
Tours by appointment only.	
STAG'S LEAP WINE CELLARS, 5766 Silverado Tr	29 L8
Tours by appointment only.	
STERLING VINEYARDS, 1111 Dunaweal Ln, Calistoga	29 D2
Tasting & tours; aerial tramway to htltp wnry.	
STONEGATE WINERY, 1183 Dunaweal Ln, Calistoga	29 D1
Tours by appointment; retail sales most days.	
SUNRISE WINERY, Empire Grade Rd, Santa Cruz	45 Q6
Housed in the Vincent Locatelli Winery.	
SUTTER HOME, 227 St Helena Hwy S, St Helena	29 G4
Tasting room and gift shop.	
TOPOLOS AT RUSSIAN RIVER, 5700 Gravenstein Hwy	37 D5
Tasting room; tours by appointment.	
TREFETHEN VINEYARDS, Oak Knoll Av, Napa	29 N8
Tours, tasting and retail sales by appointmnt.	
TRENTADUE, 19170 Redwood Hwy, Geyserville	31 P7
Open all week for tasting.	
TURGEON & LOHR, 1000 Lenzen Av, San Jose	151 L9
Tasting, sales & guided tours.	
VEGA VINEYARDS, 9495 Santa Rosa Rd, Buellton	86 H6
Tours and tasting available.	
VENTANA VINEYARDS, Los Coches Rd W of Greenfield	65 B2
New Monterey district winery.	
VILLA MT EDEN, Oakville Cross Rd, Oakville	29 J7
Tours weekdays by appointment.	
V SATTUI WINERY, White Ln at Hwy 29 S, St Helena	29 G5
Tasting room, tours, gift shop; founded 1885.	
WEIBEL CHAMPAGNE, Stanford Av, Mission San Jose	46 H2
Champagne tasting room.	
WEIBEL WINERY, 7051 N State St, Redwood Valley	31 C2
Tasting room and gift shop; no tours.	
WENTE BROS, 5555 Tesla Rd, Livermore	46 F5
4th generation winery; excellent tour/tasting.	
WHITEHALL LANE WINERY, St Helena Hwy S	29 H4
Retail sales.	
WOODBURY WINERY, 32 Woodland Av, San Rafael	139 M8
By appointment only.	
YORK MOUNTAIN WINERY, Hwy 46, Templeton	75 D7
Tasting room; tours by appointment only.	
YVERDON VINEYARDS, 3787 Spring Mtn Rd, St Helena	29 F1
Tours by appointment; sales daily.	
ZACA MESA WINERY, Foxen Cyn Rd, Los Olivos	86 E8
Tour provides a good overview of winemaking.	

2457

CAN YOU HELP US?

If you run across a worthwhile point of interest your California Road Atlas does not show, please tell us. Your discoveries can help us increase the usefulness of the Atlas for everyone.

I RECOMMEND: _____

NAME OF POINT OF INTEREST

Located at: _____

EXACT ADDRESS   CROSS STREETS

CITY	COUNTY		PAGE	GRID

Comments: _____
_____
_____
_____
_____
_____

NAME & ADDRESS:
_____
_____
_____
_____

I purchased my California Road Atlas from:
☐ BOOKSTORE   ☐ PERSONAL MAP DISTRIBUTOR   ☐ MARKET
☐ STATIONERY   ☐ DISCOUNT STORE   ☐ OTHER

I would like to see more of the following in the next issue
☐ MORE STREETS   ☐ POINTS OF INTEREST   ☐ OTHER _____

I would like to see other states in this format:
☐ YES   ☐ NO _____
Suggested other states

Please send me a price list.

TEAR FROM RINGS, 3 FOLD, STAPLE OR TAPE TOGETHER

- -

No Postage
Necessary
If Mailed
In The
United States

BUSINESS REPLY MAIL
First Class Permit No. 7480   Irvine, CA

POSTAGE WILL BE PAID BY ADDRESSEE

Thomas Bros. Maps

17731 Cowan
Irvine, CA 92714

Thomas Guides and Directories

California, Oregon, Washington and Arizona **STREET GUIDES** ● California **FLOOD and EARTHQUAKE ZONES**
California **ROCK PRODUCTS** ● California, Oregon, Washington and Arizona **CENSUS TRACTS** ● California, Oregon and
Washington **ZIP CODES** ● California, Oregon, Washington and Arizona **WALL MAPS** ● California **FOLDING POCKET MAPS**

With a new look and a new name, the 1983 Thomas Guides are everything you could want in a street atlas:
- Beautifully printed in color
- Easy to read, and simple to use
- Handy 8" x 9" format
- Alphabetical street name index
- Cities and communities statistical information

- Zip codes
- Hospital and emergency phone numbers for each county
- Points of interest (with addresses and phone numbers)
- Heavy-gauge cover for extra durability
- Wear resistant, rounded corners
- Double Wire ring bound for easy use — opens flat

1983 Thomas Guides
For over 65 years people have depended on our "Popular Street Atlases" for their accuracy and superb craftsmanship. And now, we've made them even better.

— COUNTIES COVERED BY THE THOMAS GUIDES —

ITEM	NAME
SOUTHERN CALIFORNIA COUNTIES	
3050	Kern County
3054	Los Angeles County
4054	Los Angeles - Orange Counties Combination
3055	Orange County
4055	Orange-Los Angeles Counties Combination
3056	Riverside County
3051	San Bernardino County
4051	San Bernardino-Riverside Counties Combination
3057	San Diego County
4057	San Diego-Orange Counties Combination
3052	Santa Barbara County
4052	Santa Barbara-Ventura Counties Combination
3053	Ventura County
4053	Ventura-Los Angeles Counties Combination
ARIZONA COUNTIES	
3072	Phoenix (Maricopa County)
WASHINGTON COUNTIES	
3090	King County
4090	King-Pierce Counties Combination
4091	King-Pierce-Snohomish Counties Combination
4092	King-Snohomish Counties Combination
3091	Pierce County
3092	Snohomish County

ITEM	NAME
NORTHERN CALIFORNIA COUNTIES	
3028	Alameda County (with Cross Street Index)
4028	Alameda-Contra Costa Counties Combination
4037	Alameda-Santa Clara Counties Combination
3027	Contra Costa County
3044	Fresno County
4025	Golden Gate Counties (Marin-San Francisco-San Mateo-Santa Clara)
3025	Marin County
3042	Monterey County
3021	Napa-Solano-Yolo-Colusa-Lake Counties
4021	Napa-Solano-Yolo-Sonoma Counties Combination
3023	Sacramento County
4023	Sacramento-Napa-Solano-Yolo Counties Combination
3035	San Francisco County (with Cross Street Index)
3036	San Mateo County
3037	Santa Clara County
4036	Santa Clara-San Mateo Counties Combination
3020	Sonoma County
4020	Sonoma-Marin Counties Combination
OREGON COUNTIES	
3099	Portland Metropolitan Area (Multnomah, Washington, Clackamas-OR, Vancouver-WA)